ESSENTIAL READINGS IN
COMPARATIVE
POLITICS SECOND EDITION

ESSENTIAL READINGS IN COMPARATIVE POLITICS

SECOND EDITION

EDITED BY

PATRICK H. O'NEIL AND RONALD ROGOWSKI

W. W. NORTON & COMPANY

New York • London

W. W. Norton & Company has been independent since its founding in 1923, when William Warder Norton and Mary D. Herter Norton first published lectures delivered at the People's Institute, the adult education division of New York City's Cooper Union. The Nortons soon expanded their program beyond the Institute, publishing books by celebrated academics from America and abroad. By mid-century, the two major pillars of Norton's publishing program—trade books and college texts—were firmly established. In the 1950s, the Norton family transferred control of the company to its employees, and today—with a staff of four hundred and a comparable number of trade, college, and professional titles published each year—W. W. Norton & Company stands as the largest and oldest publishing house owned wholly by its employees.

Manufacturing by Courier Westford
Composition by PennSet, Inc.

Library of Congress Cataloging-in-Publication Data

Essential readings in comparative politics / edited by Patrick H. O'Neil and Ronald Rogowski.— 2nd ed.
    p. cm.
    Includes bibliographical references.

    ISBN-13: 978-0-393-92950-8 (pbk.)
    ISBN-10: 0-393-92950-7 (pbk.)

    1. Comparative government. I. O'Neil, Patrick H., 1966– II. Rogowski, Ronald.

JF51.E77 2006
320.3—dc22

2006047324

W. W. Norton & Company, Inc., 500 Fifth Avenue, New York, N.Y. 10110
www.wwnorton.com
W. W. Norton & Company Ltd., Castle House,
75/76 Wells Street, London W1T 3QT

3 4 5 6 7 8 9 0

CONTENTS

PREFACE

Notoriously, the field of comparative politics lacks an agreed-upon core. More even than in other subfields of political science, one scholar's meat is another's poison—or, at best, a bland and uninteresting dish. Thus to bring together the "essentials" of comparative politics in a volume of manageable dimensions presented us with a serious challenge but also, in our view, an irresistible opportunity. Where textbooks inevitably only summarize the original literature, if they discuss it at all, we have long thought it crucial—not least in our own teaching—to expose our students to the key works and original ideas and to show how they fit together into a larger and more generous understanding of comparative politics. Thus when Ann Shin and Roby Harrington suggested, on behalf of W. W. Norton, that we collaborate on a set of original readings to complement *Essentials of Comparative Politics*, we quickly overcame our initial trepidation and took up the challenge.

The readings have been chosen and organized to serve a number of purposes. On most topics, we have combined one or more "classic" pieces—widely recognized as having shaped the present field—with more recent influential contributions. Other works provide valuable surveys of changes in the field over time. Where possible, we have juxtaposed contending views on a topic, giving readers the opportunity to weigh the merits of competing arguments. Finally, we have sought to include a number of shorter and contemporary pieces that help link theory to current political events and developments. The headnotes to each chapter explain more fully our rationale for including the readings we did. The chapters of this volume parallel those of *Essentials of Comparative Politics*, often tying to concepts directly addressed in that textbook. They are also meant to flesh out ideas and developments addressed in the *Cases for Comparative Politics*.

While this collection is addressed primarily to undergraduates who are deepening their knowledge of comparative politics, we intend it also as a contribution—and in our view a highly necessary one—to *intra*disciplinary professional dialogue. Far too many graduate students and practicing scholars, in our view, are forgetting or ignoring the impressive breadth and depth of comparative politics. We thus intend this volume as both an introduction and a remedy. Now in its second edition, we have refined and improved our selections, seeking to strike a balance between complexity and accessibility.

We owe deep and extensive thanks to the various individuals who contributed to this work. Our Norton editor Ann Shin played a critical role in initiating this project and reviewing our choices. Project editor Sarah Mann helped maintain order in the face of constant changes, updates, and second thoughts. Our thanks, too, to those external reviewers who considered our selections and provided important suggestions on how the breadth and depth of the reader might be improved. Allison Benter and Pam Lawson have caught more errors and omissions in the "final" text than we care to count; our deep gratitude also to them. Finally, thanks to all those students with whom we have shared these readings in past. Their responses, tacit and explicit, greatly influenced our selections and rationale. We hope that these readings can serve comparative politics courses across a range of levels, and that students and faculty alike will find them both wide-ranging and compelling.

Patrick H. O'Neil
Ronald Rogowski
December, 2005

ESSENTIAL READINGS IN COMPARATIVE
COMPARATIVE
POLITICS SECOND EDITION

1 WHAT IS COMPARATIVE POLITICS?

The ancestry of comparative politics can be traced back to ancient Greece and Aristotle and to the classic social theorists of the Renaissance and Enlightenment. From its modern revival in the late nineteenth century until the mid-1950s, it was a predominantly legalistic, normative, and descriptive enterprise: it focused on legal texts; it argued about how institutions should be, rather than analyzing their actual characteristics; and it described—often in numbing detail—how countries' institutions worked. However, there was almost no explicit comparison of countries' institutions, and political scientists demonstrated little interest in what we would now call the comparative method.

All of this changed with stunning rapidity in the late 1950s and 1960s, as leading comparativists rediscovered the "grand tradition" in social theory (particularly in the work of Karl Marx and Max Weber). Through such works as Anthony Downs's An Economic Theory of Democracy, *political scientists also discovered the possibilities of game-theoretic and economic approaches.*

In a work that has already become a modern classic, Mark Lichbach and Alan Zuckerman give a brilliant capsule history of these developments and focus our attention on what they and many others regard as the three major theories that have emerged within the field of comparative politics: the cultural, the structural, and the rational-choice approaches. Lichbach and Zuckerman trace the intellectual antecedents of these approaches, examine the reasons for their ascendance, and address the research questions that each theory pushes to the fore.

Lichbach and Zuckerman also note that despite their disagreements, today's comparativists agree on the need for comparison and explanation. Most would also agree with the great sociologist Max Weber (1864–1920) that social-scientific explanation is best achieved by what we now call a model—or, as Weber put it, a conjecture or hypothesis about people's behavior that (a) "makes sense" in terms of what we already know about how people think, (b) is "fertile," meaning that it logically implies predictions about behavior

1

that we are not immediately studying, and (c) is "testable," particularly in a comparative setting.

In their highly influential text, An Introduction to Models in the Social Sciences, *first published in 1975, James March and Charles Lave explained to beginning undergraduates what the "modeling enterprise," and comparison and explanation in the social sciences generally, was all about. Their homespun (and often politically incorrect) illustrations provide profound insight into how modern students of comparative politics reason, argue, and research. The excerpt presented here includes chapters one and two of the original book.*

MARK I. LICHBACH AND ALAN S. ZUCKERMAN

RESEARCH TRADITIONS AND THEORY IN COMPARATIVE POLITICS: AN INTRODUCTION

The Common Heritage of Comparative Politics

Comparativists inherit their dream of theorizing about politics from the founders of social theory. Their intellectual forebears represent the pantheon of Western thought. In the classic survey of the field's intellectual origins, Harry Eckstein (1963) highlights the past masters.

> Comparative politics . . . has a particular right to claim Aristotle as an ancestor because of the primacy that he assigned to politics among the sciences and because the problems he raised and the methods he used are similar to those still current in political studies (Eckstein 1963: 3).

Machiavelli and Montesquieu, Hobbes and Smith are the progenitors who lived during the

From *Comparative Politics: Rationality, Culture, and Structure* (New York: Cambridge University Press, 1997), pp. 3–8.

Renaissance and the Enlightenment. The classic theorists of social science—Karl Marx, Max Weber, Emile Durkheim, Vilfredo Pareto, Gaetano Mosca, and Roberto Michels—established the field's research agenda, mode of analysis, and contrasting theoretical visions. Several seminal theorists of contemporary political science—Harry Eckstein, David Apter, Robert Dahl, Seymour Lipset, Karl Deutsch, Gabriel Almond, and Sidney Verba—drew on this heritage to rebuild and reinvigorate the field of comparative politics. A shared, grand intellectual vision motivates comparativists.

Comparativists want to understand the critical events of the day, a position that ensures that dreams of theory address the political world as it exists, not formal abstractions or utopias. Just as Marx and Weber responded to the fundamental transformations associated with the rise of capitalism, just as Marx developed a general strategy for a socialist revolution and Weber grappled with the theoretical and normative demands of the bureaucratic state, and just as Mosca, Pareto, and Michels strove to understand the possibilities and limits of democratic rule, students of comparative politics examine pressing questions in the context of their immediate political agenda. The contemporary study of comparative politics therefore blossomed in response to the political problems that followed World War II. New forms of conflict emerged: Communist threats; peasant rebellions and revolutions; social movements, urban riots, student upheavals, military coups, and national liberation struggles swept the world. Government decisions replaced markets as foci for economic development. New states followed the disintegration of colonial empires, and the worldwide movement toward democratic rule seemed to resume after the fascist tragedies. The challenges of the current era—domestic conflict, state-building, the political bases of economic growth, and democratization, to note but a few—stand at the center of today's research, indicating that the need to respond to contemporary issues guides the field.

Comparative politics therefore asserts an ambitious scope of inquiry. No political phenomenon is foreign to it; no level of analysis is irrelevant, and no time period beyond its reach. Civil war in Afghanistan; voting decisions in Britain; ethnic conflict in Quebec, Bosnia, and Burundi; policy interactions among the bureaucracies of the European Union in Brussels, government agencies in Rome, regional offices in Basilicata, and local powers in Potenza; the religious bases of political action in Iran, Israel, and the United States; the formation of democracies in Eastern Europe and the collapse of regimes in Africa; and global economic patterns are part of the array of contemporary issues that stand before the field. Questions about the origins of capitalism; the formation of European states; the rise of fascism and the collapse of interwar democracies; and the transition to independence after colonial rule are some of the themes of past eras that still command our attention.

Second, comparativists assert an ambitious intellectual vision in that they approach these substantive concerns with general questions in mind. Anyone who studies the politics of a particular country—whether Germany or Ghana, the United Arab Emirates or the United States of America—so as to address abstract issues, does comparative politics. Anyone who is interested in who comes to power, how, and why—the names, places, and dates of politics in any one place or other—in order to say something about the politics of succession or the determinants of vote choice, is a comparativist. In other words, students of comparative politics examine a case to reveal what it tells us about a larger set of political phenomena, or they relate the particulars of politics to more general theoretical ideas about politics.

Comparativists therefore insist that analysis requires explicit comparisons. Because events of global historical significance affect so many countries in so short a period of time, studies of single countries and abstract theorizing are woefully inadequate to capture epoch-shaping developments. More than three decades ago, when the founders of the contemporary field of comparative politics initiated the most recent effort to merge theory and data in the study of politics, they therefore established another of the field's guiding principles: The proper study of politics requires systematic comparisons.[1]

Finally, comparativists assert a grand intellectual vision in that their generalizations are situated in the context of the Big Questions of social thought: Who rules? How are interests represented? Who wins and who loses? How is authority challenged? Why are some nations "developed"? These questions have produced much contemporary theorizing about the connections among social order, the state, civil society, and social change, especially in democracies. Comparativists engage the basic issues that inform social and political thought.

In sum, comparative politics follows the lead of the grand masters in their approach to substantive issues, to the scope of inquiry, to the nature of theory-building, and to the enduring problems of social thought. As comparativists address politically significant matters, explore a range of political phenomena, propose general explanatory propositions based on systematic evidence from multiple cases, and address Big Questions, they move along a path first marked by the founders of social science.

The Competing Traditions in Comparative Politics

In spite of this shared dream, long-standing disagreements separated the field's forebears and contrasting research schools characterize current efforts to build theories in comparative politics. When many of today's senior scholars were graduate students, their training included courses that compared psychological and culturalist approaches, institutional studies of political organizations, structural-functional and systems analyses, cybernetics and modes of information theory, pluralist, elitist, and Marxist analyses, modernization theory and its alternatives of dependency and world-systems theories, and rational choice theory, to name the most obvious. Most of these perspectives have disappeared and some have formed new combinations. Today, rational choice theories, culturalist approaches, and structural analyses stand as the principal competing theoretical schools in comparative politics. Rational choice theorists follow a path laid out by Hobbes, Smith, and Pareto; culturalists continue work begun by Montesquieu and developed by Weber and Mosca; and structuralists build on Marx's foundations and add to Weber's edifice. The themes and debates of contemporary comparative politics are therefore rooted in the enduring questions of social thought. They continue to lie at the center of work in all the social sciences.

Rationalists begin with assumptions about actors who act deliberately to maximize their advantage. This research school uses the power of mathematical reasoning to elaborate explanations with impressive scope. Analysis begins at the level of the individual and culminates in questions about collective actions, choices, and institutions. Following the path first charted by Downs (1957), Olson (1968), and Riker (1962), rational choice theory has spread to address diverse problems: from electoral choice to revolutionary movements, from coalitions to political economy, and from institution formation to state-building. Here, the clarity of mathematical reasoning takes pride of place; powerful abstract logics facilitate a shared understanding among the members of the research school.

As comparativists engage in fieldwork in diverse societies, they grapple with the need to understand varied ways of life, systems of meaning, and values. As students who cut their teeth on the abstractions of modernization and dependency theory encounter the realities of particular villages, political parties, and legislatures, they seek to ground their observations in the politics that is being analyzed. Following the lead of social and cultural anthropologists, many comparativists adhere to Geertz's (1973) admonition to provide "thick descriptions." Culturalists therefore provide nuanced and detailed readings of particular cases, frequently drawn from fieldwork, as they seek to understand the phenomena being studied. This stance usually joins strong doubts about both the ability to generalize to abstract categories and the ability to provide explanations that apply to more than the case at hand.

Structuralists draw together long-standing interests in political and social institutions. Many emphasize the formal organizations of governments; some retain Marx's concern with class relations; some study political parties and interest groups; some combine these into analyses of how states and societies interact; and some emphasize the themes of political economy. Although these scholars display diverse patterns of reasoning, from mathematical models to verbal arguments, and many modes of organizing empirical evidence, they continue to follow Marx's and Weber's contention that theory and data guide social analysis.

* * * These research traditions take strong

positions on the methodological issues that divide comparativists.[2] Rational choice theorists seek to maximize the ability to provide universal laws that may be used in nomothetic explanations. They consider problems of reliability—the concern with the evidence required to support generalizations from the particular to sets of cases—as a challenge to research design. Cultural interpreters maximize the importance of reliability as they describe the constellations of particular cases and minimize the value of generalist research expectations. They interpret particular events, decisions, and patterns, eschewing any need to tie explanations to general principles. Structural analysts who follow Marx offer universal theories that include causal accounts. At the same time, they struggle to tie reliable descriptions into powerful generalizations; they grapple self-consciously with the requirements of case selection and how best to move from the particular analysis to the set of cases about which they seek to theorize. Comparativists' long-standing debates over method thus reappear in the three research traditions.

However, * * * the dispute among the schools goes beyond the ideographic-nomothetic divide. The traditions differ with respect to ontology: Rationalists study how actors employ reason to satisfy their interests, culturalists study rules that constitute individual and group identities, and structuralists explore relations among actors in an institutional context. Reasons, rules, and relations are the various starting points of inquiry. The traditions also differ with respect to explanatory strategy: Rationalists perform comparative static experiments, culturalists produce interpretive understandings, and structuralists study the historical dynamics of real social types. Positivism, interpretivism, and realism are the possible philosophies of social science.

Moreover, * * * no school displays a rigid and uniform orthodoxy. Rationalists debate the utility of relaxing the core assumption that defines individuals as maximizers of their self-interest. They differ as well over the proper form of explanation, some seeking covering laws and

others proposing causal accounts, as they debate the necessity of transforming formal models into accounts of events. Continuing the debate initiated by Marx and Weber, structuralists differ over the ontological status of their concepts: Are social class, ethnicity, state, and other concepts that characterize this research school natural types? Are political processes best seen as determined and closed ended or probabilistic and open-ended processes? Structuralists differ as well over the utility of nomothetic and causal explanations. Culturalists disagree over the theoretical importance of generalizations drawn from their fieldwork. May one derive or test general propositions from the analysis of a particular village? Do public opinion surveys provide an adequate picture of people's goals, values, and identities? They differ over the nature of explanation in comparative politics as well. Some culturalists reject any form of covering law or causal accounts, offering only interpretations of political life in particular places; others move toward the mainstream of comparative politics, incorporating values and systems of meaning into theories that adhere to the standard forms of explanation. In short, as Lichbach makes clear in his essay, ideal-type rationalists, culturalists, and structuralists need to be identified so that we may recognize how practicing comparativists employ a battery of ideal-type strategies in their concrete empirical work.

Comparative politics is dominated today by rationalist, culturalist, and structuralist approaches. What explains the imperialist expansion of these schools and the disappearance of earlier approaches? [For one thing,] These schools share an ontological and epistemological symmetry. They offer—indeed force—choices along the same dimensions. Furthermore, at a more fundamental level, the themes of the research schools rest at the heart of the human sciences. Reason, rules, and relations are unique to social theory. Focusing on these themes sets research in the social sciences apart from the physical sciences, providing a fundamental basis on which to theorize about political phenomena. Rationalist, culturalist, and structuralist theories are thus embedded in strong research communities, scholarly traditions, and analytical languages.

NOTES

1. Classic works that appeared to herald the emergence of comparative politics as a subdiscipline of political science include Almond and Coleman (1960). Almond and Verba (1963), Beer and Ulam (1958), Dahl (1966; 1971), Eckstein and Apter (1963), Holt and Turner (1970), Huntington (1968), La Palombara and Weiner (1966), Lipset and Rokkan (1967), Moore (1966), Przeworski and Teune (1970); Pye and Verba (1965), Riker (1962), and Sartori (1970). At the same time, two journals, *Comparative Politics* and *Comparative Political Studies*, appeared, helping to institutionalize the subfield.

2. There is also a long-standing debate in comparative politics about methodology. As comparativists propose explanations that cover sets of cases, perhaps based on causal accounts, they grapple with questions that relate to theory-building, concept formation, and case selection: How do concepts carry across cases? What is the value of treating concepts as variables that are measured by indicators? What is the proper use of case-specific information in theories that cover many cases? How does the choice of cases affect the general propositions offered? Are there requirements that define the number of cases that need to be included in an analysis? What is the relevance of single case studies to

the development of theory? How can single case studies be used to speak to general sets of phenomena? Is it possible or desirable to include all relevant instances in the analysis? Is it possible to devise an adequate methodology that permits powerful generalizations based on the observation of a small number of cases? These questions raise problems of external validity, the ability to generalize beyond the case being observed.

Nearly thirty years ago, Sartori (1970) drew attention to fundamental questions of concept formation. At that same time, Lijphart (1971) and Przeworski and Teune (1970) initiated a controversy about the proper methodology of comparative research, in which Eckstein (1975), Ragin (1987), Ragin and Becker (1992), and Skocpol and Somers (1980) have offered significant alternative positions (see Collier 1993 for a review of this literature). Most recently, Collier and Mahon (1993), Collier (1993), and Sartori (1994) illustrate further developments concerning the proper formation of concepts, and King, Keohane, and Verba (1994; 1995) initiated a productive debate over issues of research design in comparative politics. On the latter, see especially Bartels (1995), Brady (1995), Caporaso (1995), Collier (1995), Laitin (1995), Mohr (1996), Rogowski (1995), and Tarrow (1995). There is a natural affinity between studies of research design and comparative method that is frequently overlooked. King, Keohane, and Verba (1994; 1995) argue that there is only one scientific method. Hence, their strictures resemble those proposed by Cook and Campbell (1979).

CHARLES A. LAVE AND JAMES G. MARCH

OBSERVATION, SPECULATION, AND MODELING

This [essay] is about the social sciences. It is not, however, a grand tour of what the social sciences are. It is a first excursion into a few domains of social science imagination. It does not claim the scholarly virtues of comprehensiveness and balance. It is a brief introduction to the pleasures of thinking about human behavior.

To speak of pleasures is probably dangerous and certainly pretentious. Few people rely solely on any social science for their pleasures, and attaining a suitable level of ecstasy involves work. We regret the latter problem. It is a nuisance, but God has chosen to give the easy problems to the physicists. We do not regret the former problem. We have no intention of suggesting that poetry and sex be abandoned. Rather, we invite you, in the moments left between Byron and bed, to join us in speculating about ordinary human existence.

Speculation presumes observation. We rely on the difficult and creative drudgery required to retrieve the record of social events. The data are lost in the files of bureaucracies, diaries of servants, accounts of businesses, and memories of participants. They are discovered through the paraphernalia of research and manipulated by the technology of inference. Precise and imaginative empirical observation distinguishes fine work in anthropology, business administration, demography, economics, education, geography, history, journalism, law, linguistics, political science, psychology and sociology.

Many smart and patient people have accumulated knowledge from observations of individuals, groups, and institutions in society. Others have articulated the methodology of the social sciences. We are in debt to both traditions, but our approach is different. Our theme is more a way of thinking about observations than an inventory of them; it is more concerned with the invention of conjectures than with the formal rules for talking about them.

We propose a practical guide to speculation. We explore the arts of developing, elaborating, contemplating, testing, and revising models of human behavior. The point of view is that of a person trying to comprehend the behavior around him. The primary emphasis is on using a few simple concepts and a little imagination to understand and enjoy individual and collective human behavior.

Speculation is the soul of the social sciences. We cherish attempts to discover possible interpretations of behavior. The effort is complicated and subtle; it has a distinguished history. Aristotle, Smith, Toynbee, Marx, Malinowski, Camus, James, Weber, Dostoevsky, Freud, Durkheim, Cervantes and a host of other figures have added to our understanding of human behavior.

Despite such an impressive ancestry our ambitions are not heroic. We think that playing with ideas is fun. We think there are some interesting ideas in the social sciences. We think that an increase in the quality of speculation both in the social sciences and in everyday life would be good. We would like to contribute to an understanding of models in the social sciences and to enjoyment of their pleasure.

What is a model? How do you invent one? What are some common models in the social sciences? How do you apply them to new situations? What makes a good model? This book attempts to answer such questions by engaging the reader in the process of invention. By the end of the book we will have presented enough

From Charles A. Lave and James G. March, *An Introduction to Models in the Social Sciences* (New York: HarperCollins, 1975).

examples of models to make a definition super-
fluous. At the outset however, we begin with an
inelegant characterization: A model is a simplified picture of a part of the real world. It has
some of the characteristics of the real world, but
not all of them. It is a set of interrelated guesses
about the world. Like all pictures, a model is
simpler than the phenomena it is supposed to
represent or explain.

Consider a scale model of a train. We call it a
"model" train because it has some of the characteristics of a train. It is similar in appearance to a
real train, has similar parts, and possibly moves
in a similar manner. It does not have all of the
characteristics of a real train, however. By examining a scale model of a train, we can learn something about a real train's general size and design
but we can not tell much about its horsepower,
speed, capacity, or mechanical dependability.

Since a model has only some of the characteristics of reality it is natural to have several different models of the same thing each of which
considers a different aspect. A diagram of the energy flow in the train's power plant would also be
a model of the train. It would be useful for answering some questions that the scale model
does not. Neither of these models, however,
could tell us whether the train would be an economic success. To determine that we need a performance table (model) showing the relations
among tonnage hauled, speed, and fuel consumption. There are many other possible models of a
train, each representing some but not all of the
train's attributes. Each could be used to say
something, but not everything, about a real train.

Whether we are talking of modeling trains,
societies, groups, or individuals, the modeling
process is the same. We construct models in order to explain and appreciate the world. Sometimes we call our simplifications theories,
paradigms, hypotheses, or simply ideas. In a
more formal treatise we might make distinctions
among some of the labels; but we will not do so
here. We will talk simply of models as a generic
term for any systematic set of conjectures about
real world observations.

Speculative models are central to science,
history, and literature. They are also a part of
normal existence. We are constantly forming
partial interpretations of the world in order to
live in it. Because we do not always label our
daily guesses about the world as "models," we
sometimes overlook the extent to which we are
all theorists of human behavior. The activity is
not mysterious.

We will treat models of human behavior as a
form of art, and their development as a kind of
studio exercise. Like all art, model building requires a combination of discipline and playfulness. It is an art that is learnable. It has explicit
techniques, and practice leads to improvement.
We can identify a few of the necessary skills:

1. An ability to *abstract* from reality to a model.
   Problems in social science are complex and
   frequently personal. It is necessary, but not
   easy, to form abstract representations of a
   delicately intricate reality.
2. A facility at *derivation* within an abstract
   model. Models become rich through their
   implications. It is necessary to devise models that yield significant derivations and
   to develop skill at producing meaningful
   implications.
3. A competence at *evaluating* a model. Not all
   models are good ones. Some are unattractive
   because their derivations are inaccurate;
   some because their consequences are immoral; some because they are unaesthetic. It
   is necessary to know how to reject inadequate models.
4. A *familiarity with some common models*. The
   number of models in the social sciences is
   large; but a few are common enough to
   make familiarity with them essential. It is
   necessary to have command of a few standard models and to know how to apply them
   to a wide variety of situations.

It is possible to identify a set of common
models in the social sciences that are relatively
simple, easily modified to extend their scope,
and suggestive of the varieties of formal reason-

ing that might be used. And though they do not immediately require more than high school mathematics, they do involve abstraction, derivation, and evaluation.

* * * Four such models [dominate the modern social sciences:]

1. *Individual Choice.* The processes by which individuals choose among alternatives, make decisions, and solve problems. For example, investment behavior, gambling, voting, occupational choice, consumer behavior, the selection of mates. The basic model is a model of rational choice under risk. We examine the fundamentals of decision trees, expected value calculations, and alternative criteria for rational choice. The rational model is applied to a variety of choice situations found throughout the study of human behavior.

2. *Exchange.* Exchange as a special case of individual and collective choice. We introduce the basic ideas of indifference curves and the ways in which mutually acceptable trades are made in the market, the cold war, small groups, marriage, and politics. Some effort is made to apply the basic model (drawn largely from economics) to a variety of "noneconomic" situations.

3. *Adaptation.* Modification of behavior by individuals and collectivities in response to experience. The basic model is a probability learning model taken from psychology. The ideas are applied to learning, personality development, socialization, organizational change, attitude change, and cultural change. Special attention is given to superstitious learning and mutual adaptation.

4. *Diffusion.* The spread of behaviors, attitudes, knowledge, and information through a society. The basic models are borrowed from epidemiology and sociology and include both simple versions of contact, transmission, and contagion and more complicated models of the spread of a "disease" in a social structure. The models are applied to the spread of fads, innovations, rumors, political allegiances, emotions, and ideas.

* * * A reader who [is familiar with these models] should be able to make a first approach to asking theoretically interesting questions about almost any situation involving human behavior.

Models of choice, exchange, adaptation, and diffusion are not the only kinds of models we might have considered. Indeed, the variations are considerable and limited mostly by our ability to invent interesting metaphors. The social sciences include ideas about *transition*: how people change from one job to another, from one social class to another over time. The social sciences include ideas about *demography*: how entry (birth) rates, exit (death) rates, and the movement of people (migration) change the age distribution and other features of a population of a society or a part of society. The social sciences include ideas about *structure*: how attitudes, memory, social positions, classes, associations, and language are organized.

Each of these, as well as the four models with which we will deal, is an exhibit in modern social science art. Each has its admirers and its critics; each has its geniuses and its hacks. We hope that the identification of model building as a form of art is not empty, although it may be optimistic. It is intended to communicate the frustrations, aesthetic charm, and unanticipated discovery to be found in the analysis of human behavior.

The major pleasures of the social sciences stem from an elementary property of human beings: Man is capable of producing more complex behavior than he is capable of understanding. The behavior of an infant baffles a psychologist, and vice versa. As a result, models of human behavior are knowledge, ideology, and art. They are metaphors by which we seek to ensure that our understanding of behavior, the complexity of behavior, and the number of questions about behavior all increase over time. Our excitements are those of participating in this spiral.

We invite you to join the game. Participation requires effort, but it does not (in the beginning) require extensive knowledge about the literature of the social sciences. We have used these materials in formal courses and in casual reading, in graduate seminars and in freshman required courses, in professional schools and in high schools, in the United States and abroad. Prior exposure to the social sciences sometimes helps, but a willingness to play with ideas, to construct images, and to solve puzzles seems much more important.

*   *   *

* * * We hope that you will experience some of the enjoyment that we do in the activity. We hope you will discover a general style of approaching the social sciences that encourages a playful exercise of disciplined thought, allows the invention of new ways for thinking about familiar things, and treats human behavior as mystery and social scientists as detectives or artists.

*   *   *

Introduction

The best way to learn about model building is to do it. We invite you to speculate about human behavior. The procedure we have adopted is a familiar one. It is used by novelists in developing characters or events, by historians in interpreting history, by children in training their parents, and by astronomers in creating theories of the universe.

Despite such testimonials, our procedure is not the only procedure for examining human behavior. Intelligent people differ on how to give meaning to observable phenomena. They differ even more on a variety of special issues that we will happily ignore. If we had some unique vision of the only way to approach social science, we would be delighted to present it. If we knew of some major new solutions to the ancient

complications of the search for interesting meanings, we would hurry to announce them. Our intentions are incomparably more modest. We have found one common approach to interpreting human behavior both fruitful and enjoyable. We hope you may find it similarly rewarding.

We ask you to practice your skill at imagining speculations. In each section we start with an observation and then speculate about processes that might have produced the observed fact. The examples are all taken from the world of ordinary experience: government, college life, friendship, and population control. They even include one example drawn from the physical world simply to demonstrate that the process of speculation is fun there too.

Contact and Friendship

Suppose we were interested in the patterns of friendship among college students. Why are some people friends and not others? We might begin by asking all of the residents of single rooms along a particular dormitory corridor to give us a list of their friends. These lists of friends are our initial data, the result we wish to understand.

If we stare at the lists for a while to see what they mean, we eventually notice a pattern in them: Friends tend to live close to each other; they tend to have adjacent dormitory rooms. What does this mean? What process could have produced this pattern of friendship?

One feature of this book is that we will often ask you to stop and do some thinking. We are serious.

STOP AND THINK. Devote a moment's time to thinking of a possible process that might produce this observed result.

One *possible* process that might have led to this result is the following:

Each spring the director of campus housing allows students to indicate their dormitory room preference for the following year; groups of friends take advantage of this and ask to have each other as roommates or to be put in adjacent rooms.

This process is a speculation about a prior world. *If* the real world had once been like our model world, then the observed facts would have been a logical consequence. That is, this speculative prior world would have produced our observed result, namely, that friends tend to have adjacent rooms. Thus we have found a model, a process, that accounts for the facts. We do not stop here, however. We next ask: What other consequences does this model have? What else does it imply? It also implies that the students in each dormitory friendship group must have known each other previously; hence they must have attended the university during the previous year; hence there will be fewer friendship clusters among freshmen.

Is this further implication of our speculative prior world correct? To test it we first examine the friendship patterns in a dormitory of juniors and seniors, and, as expected, we discover groups of friends living next to each other.

We also examine a dormitory that has only freshmen and discover that there are as many groups of friends clustered there too, which is not an expected result (according to the model). This result would not have been predicted by our model unless the freshmen knew each other prior to college. Perhaps the freshman friendship clusters consist of students who knew each other in high school and who asked for adjacent rooms. We look at information on the backgrounds of freshmen to see whether this is true; but we discover that almost all of the students come from different high schools.

So our speculative model world does not do a very good job of explaining what we have observed. Some process other than mutual selection by prior friends must be involved. We think about it some more and try to imagine another process that could have led to these results. Our new speculation (which is probably the one you yourself thought of when the question was first posed) is as follows:

College students come from similar backgrounds. As a result, they have enough experiences, problems, and values in common that they are capable of becoming friends with each other. Pairs of college students who live near each other will have frequent opportunities for interaction and hence are likely to discover these common characteristics.

Thus students who live close to one another will become friends. This new speculation explains the presence of friendship clusters in freshmen dorms as well as in junior-senior dorms. Does it have any other implication?

***STOP AGAIN*. Think about it. Hint: what about changes in these friendship clusters over time?**

Since the chance of contact increases over time, the friendship clusters should grow in size as the school year progresses. You would expect the average friendship cluster to be relatively small in October, bigger in December, and still bigger by May. To test this prediction, you would have to run questionnaires at two or three separate dates. If you did so and discovered that the prediction was correct, the model would seem somewhat more impressive.

In summary: We made an observation (friendship clusters around adjacent rooms); we speculated about a model world (mutual selection by preexisting friends) to explain this result; we looked at other implications of the model world (no friendship clusters in freshmen dorms) to see if they were true. Since they were not true, we created a new model, with a new process inherent in it (similarity of values and opportunity to meet cause friendship), we then examined the implications of the new model world (cluster size increases over time) and found that they were true.

So far we have formulated a model of college students discovering similarities. We would now like to make our model more general, to find some new model that includes this model as an implication. Can you think of such a more general model?

***STOP AND THINK*. Remember you still want to include the predictions we made earlier and**

yet find a more general model that predicts new behaviors as well, perhaps beyond the campus scene. Hint: Look at the parts of the existing model that restrict its area of applicability.

One possible approach to reformulation proceeds as follows: College students are people. Perhaps our speculation about college students is true about all people. Now our theory becomes:

Most people have enough experiences, problems, and values in common that they are capable of being friends. Pairs of people are likely to discover these common characteristics when they live close to one another.

The model is a broad, powerful statement about the world. If it is true, does it have any nonuniversity implications? Racial integration is a potential area for its application. The model predicts more friendships between blacks and whites who live in integrated neighborhoods than would be found between blacks and whites who do not live near each other; it also predicts that opinions of blacks and whites toward each other will be more positive and favorable in integrated neighborhoods.

A group of social scientists decided to test some of these predictions.[1] They chose two housing areas—one segregated and the other integrated—to see whether there were differences in friendships and attitudes. Both areas were public housing projects; and both were carefully compared to assure that other variables that might also influence interracial attitudes would be similar in both projects.

The social scientists questioned white residents of the two housing projects about their relations with their neighbors and about their attitudes toward blacks. They found that whites living in the integrated project reported far more neighborly relations with blacks than was true of whites living in the segregated project. They also found that integration produced large changes in white attitudes toward blacks. Among those whites who had originally held unfavorable attitudes toward blacks before moving into the housing project, 92% of those in the segregated project

still had unfavorable attitudes, while more than half of those in the integrated project now held favorable attitudes toward blacks. Thus the predictions of the model were confirmed.

With the extension of our speculation from college students to people and from dormitories into neighborhoods, we have not yet exhausted the possibilities for developing the model.

STOP AND THINK. Reread the model, and then try to think of ways in which you might reformulate the ideas to make them even more general. *Hint:* Think about the process by which friendships are formed.

Perhaps you thought of something like this. The reason people in neighborhoods discover each other's values is because they have contact through communication. Now our model becomes:

Most people have enough experiences, problems, and values in common that they are capable of being friends. Pairs of people are likely to discover these common characteristics when they communicate with each other.

Thus people who communicate with each other will become friends. Now we can use our model not only to predict some features of college life and some features of residential neighborhood life but also some consequences of communication through visiting, writing, telephoning, or television.

STOP AND THINK. Speculate about the implications of the changing communication patterns in our society; for example, grandparents no longer live in the same household as their grandchildren, and children now leave home earlier and live farther away. Use the new extended model to predict the change in friendship patterns which might result from the change in communication patterns. Some of your speculations may seem false, but this is simply a sign that you are doing the job well and being imaginative. At this stage it is more important to be creative than to be critical. (You are on your own on this question—no answer will be given below.)

But now suppose, finally, that a friend of yours proposes the following:

> Most people have enough differences in experiences, problems, and values that they are capable of being enemies. Pairs of people are likely to discover these differences when they communicate with each other.

Thus people who communicate with each other will become enemies.

In reviewing our original dormitory data, we see that this new model predicts that the size of enemy groups will increase over the course of the school year. That is, the number of people disliked by any one person will increase over the year. It is possible, therefore, to revise the model to take account of both effects (friend production and enemy production) by changing it to something like the following:

> Most people have enough experiences, problems, and values in common that they are capable of being friends. At the same time, most people have enough experience, problems, and values that differ that they are capable of being enemies. Pairs of people discover their common and differing characteristics through communication.[2]

At this point we have a broad, provocative speculation. We cannot stop here, however, for we now have to deal with a major problem implicit in this model: What determines the initial pattern of communication? How do two people happen to begin by discussing shared characteristics rather than conflicting characteristics? To what extent do expectations about others become self-fulfilling? That is, do friends confine their communication to things they agree on, whereas enemies discuss each other's differences?

The fact that initially prejudiced whites changed their feelings toward blacks after moving into an integrated housing project is grounds for optimism. Perhaps communications about shared values are more powerful than communications about differences. Perhaps closeness creates strong incentives to discover shared values. Or perhaps the experience of solving joint problems (for example, dirty streets, landlord problems, school issues) creates the incentive to discover shared values.

Since our current model places primary emphasis on the pattern of communication, you might wish to add some speculations of the following kinds:

1. Friends tend to communicate about common values; enemies communicate about differing values. As a result, two people who start out being friends (either through chance or positive expectations) will become better friends; two people who start out being enemies will become worse enemies.

2. Situations in which there is general social agreement about appropriate behavior and appropriate interpretations of behavior will more likely produce communication about shared values than will situations in which there is less general agreement. Thus two persons who initially meet in a well-defined, normatively regulated situation will be more likely to become friends than if they had met in normatively unregulated situations. (Could this be a possible reason why stable societies impose relatively elaborate politeness rules for first encounters among people?)

3. Strangers would rather be friends than enemies (because enemies are more "expensive.") Thus two people initially try to communicate about shared values. "Mistakes" occur when a person guesses wrong about which values are shared, or when he is forced to communicate to an audience of several different people. Thus two persons from similar cultures are more likely to become friends than two persons from different cultures. On the average, the smaller the group within which a first encounter between two persons occurs, the more likely they are to become friends. On the average, the larger the group of strangers, the more inane the conversation. This is one reason why, counter to intuition, large parties of strangers are duller than small parties of strangers, per gallon of liquid served.

STOP. **If you have taken the time to exercise your imagination at each step of these examples, you should now have a sense of the basic nature of the model-building procedure that we are presenting and its pleasures. You may find it useful at this point to retrace the process and devote some time to your own speculations rather than ours.**

Not all speculation concerns human behavior. We can play the same game with observations made about the physical world. Figure 2.1, for

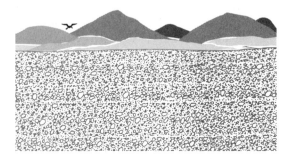

Figure 2.1: Gravel pit wall with stratified layers of rock. There are mountains in the background. Adapted from Geology Illustrated *by John S. Shelton, W. H. Freeman and Company. Copyright © 1966. Reproduced with permission.*

example, shows an excavation in Southern California. Other excavations near this particular area all show the same structure: parallel layers of rocks with smaller rocks and sand between them. Why does the excavation look like this? What kind of geological process might have produced this end result? How did the rocks get there? Why are they layered the way they are?

STOP AND THINK. **Try to think of some geological process that might have produced this result.**

A possible process might be:

This area is actually the bed of an ancient ocean; the layers are the result of successive deposits of rock and sand washed there by the ocean; then the land was pushed up out of the ocean by some kind of geological upheaval.

This imagined process is a speculation about a prior world. *If* the real world had once been like our model world, then the observed facts would have been a logical consequence. Thus we have found a model, a process, that accounts for the facts.

If our speculation about the prior world is true, are there any other facts that we should also observe?

STOP AND THINK. **Think of some other consequences that follow from the model. What are its other observable geological implications? Try to think of at least one other implication before you continue reading.**

If this were an ancient ocean bed, there should also be marine debris as well as rocks, for example, fossils of some kind. A careful examination of the excavations, however, shows no fossils or other marine debris. This causes us to doubt the ocean-bed model. A further cause of doubt is that the surface of the ground is exactly parallel to the rock layers exposed by the excavation. It is unlikely that the land would have been raised exactly straight up out of the ocean or that subsequent erosion of the surface could have worn it exactly parallel to the former floor.

So our speculation, or model, about the origin of this area is in trouble. The model correctly explains the layers of rocks, but, unfortunately, it also predicts two things that are not true. Thus it is unlikely that our model is correct. Let us try to think of some other model that might have generated the observed result.

STOP. **Can you think of an alternative?**

An alternative possible model is:

The area in the picture was formed by rocks washed down from the mountains in the background; torrential rains and flooding carried the rocks from the mountains; successive layers represent successive floods.

Could this alternative version of the prior world have created the known results? It does explain the layers of rocks; it predicts the lack of marine fossils; and it also predicts that the surface should be exactly parallel to the rock layers, since the process is presumably still going on in a slow fashion. But is there anything else that this new version of the prior world would predict? If the process we have imagined were true, would it have led to any other results?

STOP AND THINK about this for a moment.

If the model were true, we might also expect that the type of rocks in the excavation will be the same as the type of rocks found in the mountains. We might also expect that excavations closer to the mountains will show larger rocks than the ones in the drawing, since the large rocks could not have been washed so far. And, finally, we might also expect to find a very slight upslope from this area toward the mountains. All three of these predictions were confirmed by field work. The last model then appears to be a reasonable speculation.

A Model of the Model-Building Process

You should now have some notion of what a model is and how models are created. A model is a simplified representation of the real world. Models are created by speculating about processes that could have produced the observed facts. Models are evaluated in terms of their ability to predict correctly other new facts.

Models are simplified representations of the world because it is impossible to represent the full complexity of the world (notice that the geological model did not specify the dates of the floods, the amount of water in each, the types of rocks washed down, the names and ages of any trees that might have been uprooted, and so on) and also because minute details are unnecessary. Our simple model has only enough detail to make it applicable to other situations.

If you think back over the procedure we used to build the model, it works as follows (though usually not nearly so neatly):

Step 1
Observe some facts.

Step 2
Look at the facts *as though they were the end result of some unknown process* (*model*). Then *speculate about processes that might have produced such a result.*

Step 3
Then *deduce other results* (implications/consequences/predictions) *from the model.*

Step 4
Then ask yourself *whether these other implications are true and produce new models if necessary.*

First we started with some facts (the rock formations exposed by the excavation) that we wanted to explain. Next we constructed an imaginary model world (the ocean bed) that could have produced these observed facts. We then asked if there were other consequences or predictions implied by the imagined model world. We found two such predictions (presence of fossils and surface irregularity) but discovered that neither prediction was confirmed in the real world. So we rejected our initial guess about the prior world and imagined an alternative prior world (floods from the mountains). This alternative model not only accounted for all of the known facts, but from it we also predicted three new results, which were all confirmed. Thus we now feel confident that the process we imagined is what actually produced the result that we wanted to explain. Therefore, we have a good model because it explains why the rocks in the excavation look the way they do.

The explanatory procedure should now be relatively clear: It involves a constant interplay between the real world and the model world. The main difference between this explanatory procedure and the kind of thinking we usually do is that this procedure is more systematic and more creative. In ordinary thinking when we have a result to explain, we are usually content to think of some simple explanation and then stop. This is incomplete thinking; it stops before the process is fully carried out. The real fun is to continue thinking and see what other ideas the explanation can generate, to ask ourselves: *If this explanation is correct, what else would it imply*? Once you learn to do it easily, you will find genuine creative enjoyment associated with this interplay between explanation and prediction.

Responsibility Corrupts

Governments frequently appoint task forces or commissions to study serious, complex issues such as crime, unemployment, education, narcotics, or student unrest. Sometimes such commissions are appointed because the sheer complexity of a problem makes concentrated, impartial study a necessity. Sometimes they are appointed for political reasons in an effort to bury a currently controversial, but probably short-lived, issue. And sometimes they are appointed to rubber stamp and legitimize a program that an administrator has already decided he wants to implement. The make-up of these commissions is usually very diverse: One often finds conservative businessmen, lawyers, professors, civil servants, and liberal labor union leaders all mixed together. In spite of the complexity of the issues being investigated, in spite of the variety of motivation for appointing the commissions, and in spite of the diversity of their memberships, there is a common pattern in the final reports of task forces or commissions. They often end up criticizing the policies of the government that appointed them; they usually make recommendations that can be characterized as moderate; and the members usually agree unanimously or nearly unanimously. That is, the diversity of opinions on the commission is usually resolved in a moderate, action-oriented direction, apparently by changing the opinions of the participants, particularly those of the more doctrinaire members.

For example, the report of President Nixon's Commission on Campus Unrest was published in 1970. Among the commission members were a police chief, a governor, a newspaper editor, an attorney, a law school dean, a retired Air Force general, a university president, a professor, and a graduate student. The commission did not issue the kind of report that might have been expected, given the probable initial biases of its members. The report expressed a good deal of criticism not only toward students but also toward the government and universities. It said:

> Most student protestors are neither violent nor extremist. . . . The roots of student activism lie in unresolved conflicts in our national life, but the many defects of the universities have also fueled campus unrest. . . . The university's own house must be placed in order. . . . Actions—and inactions—of government at all levels have contributed to campus unrest. The words of some political leaders have helped to inflame it. Law enforcement officers have too often reacted ineptly or overreacted. At times, their response has degenerated into uncontrolled violence. . . . We recommend that the President seek to convince public officials and protestors alike that divisive and insulting rhetoric is dangerous.

In the next few pages we will show the kind of thought processes carried out by one of the authors as he tried to understand why commissions behave the way they do. Some of the steps that follow took longer to formulate than others, and some are slightly expanded to make the thinking more explicit.

> ***STOP.*** **Think about the observation. Why would commissions be moderate (and critical) in their reports? See if you can form some speculations of your own.**

The reading of the newspaper story about the commission on student unrest and the observation that moderation and a tendency to criticize the government were common to such commissions was the observed *result* I wanted to explain. I asked myself *how* such a result could occur; what *process* could have led to this result? Thus my first try at an explanatory process was:

> People on commissions who hold diverse opinions ultimately decide to compromise a little bit. They do so in a kind of trading process in which each gains a little and each gives up a little. Thus the final report represents a middle ground among the diverse views.

I next tried to broaden the model, to make it more general and abstract. The first step was to look at all of the verbs and nouns in the model to see if they could be made less specific. "Commission" and "final report" were broadened first, since it seems possible that the compromise process is true of all group behavior. My second try was:

> People who hold diverse opinions will tend to compromise their differences and end up supporting some opinion in the middle, in order to obtain common agreement.

Notice that "commissions" was dropped altogether and that "final report" was broadened to become "opinions." This model is broader than the first try, though it is limited to opinions. Could any other verbs or nouns be broadened? It seemed possible that behavior might be changed as well. So the language was broadened to include actions as well as opinions. The third try was:

> People with conflicting goals and opinions will tend to compromise their differences in order to obtain common agreement.

The third try was substantially broader than the first, and I now had a model with applications in the whole area of human decision making. Does the model work? Are its predictions correct?

The simplest prediction is that we should observe evidence of compromise in the final reports of task forces. There was such evidence of compromise—the reports always seemed to endorse some position in the middle of the spectrum of original opinions held by the participants. But something else was also apparent. There were rarely any strong dissenting "minority reports." Nor were there many instances of commission members "repudiating" a report upon their return to private life. Perhaps most of the participants had actually *changed* their opinions rather than simply compromised them for the sake of the report. If this were true, it was not a result that would be predicted by the model. Some other process must be involved,

therefore, and the model must be modified to take account of it or else be discarded in favor of a different model.

***STOP AND THINK.* How would you modify the model? What sort of process might lead to an actual change in personal opinions?**

Why would the opinions of the people on the commission be changed as a result of their participation in the activities of the commission? My first try at a new model was something like this:

> It is easier to hold extreme views if you are not confronted with their consequences and if you are not exposed to alternative views. People on commissions do have the strong possibility of having their reports implemented and hence are forced to think about the actual consequences of their decisions. It is hard to cling to extreme ideas when faced with the possibility of human misery resulting from them.[3]

This seemed to be an interesting beginning, and I next tried to broaden it. The model should apply to all decision-making situations, not only to commissions, and it should apply to actions as well as opinions. A second try was:

> People in positions of responsibility tend to moderate their beliefs and actions as a result of confrontation with actual consequences and exposure to alternative ideas.

The model now suggests a reason why idealists, of either the right or the left, tend to modify their ideological purity and become more moderate once they are given real world responsibilities. What about other possible predictions from the model? It predicts the same moderating effect on successful candidates for public office, and there is at least some casual evidence of this if we look at campaign utterances and compare them with subsequent actions while in office. It also predicts that leaders of radical movements (of either left or right) will tend to disappoint their fellows if they achieve office in a larger sphere. They will probably be viewed as "sellouts" to the establishment.

For other predictions I tried to think of examples of offices with differing amounts of responsibility and power. The model says that it is easier to maintain extremist views in relatively powerless offices. Thus the president of a local chapter of a minor political social group can easily maintain right-wing views in spite of being president. Likewise, an antibusiness member of Congress may have his views only slightly moderated by his being a congressman, for he is only one vote out of 435. But the model does say that a congressman will exercise the greatest moderation of his views in those areas in which he has committee assignments (since committees are more powerful and carry greater responsibility); and similarly the model predicts that on those occasions when Congress overrules a committee, the congressional action will be more extreme (in either direction) than the committee recommendation. Finally, the model predicts that really powerful and responsible positions such as Chief Justice of the U.S. Supreme Court or President of the United States will have the most effect upon the men or women who hold them.

STOP. **Review the argument and the derivations. Are there other speculations that might explain our original observation? Are the others better or worse than this set of ideas?**

The Case of the Dumb Question

Suppose you are sitting in class when the person next to you asks a really dumb question. This is your observed fact. Can you imagine a process that might produce such an observed event? Let us suppose that you also know that the person next to you is a football player. Then you might begin with a simple model, particularly if you are not a football player:

Football players are dumb.

Using this as a base, can we generalize it into a more interesting idea? You might want to begin by broadening "football player" to "athlete," producing the following new statement:

Athletes are dumb.

The change has made your model more general (but not necessarily more correct), but the model still has no sense of process. Why might athletes appear dumb? Is appearing dumb an inherent characteristic of people who are good at sports? Is it due to something that happens after people take up sports in a serious way? Or is there some other explanation?

STOP AND THINK. **Is there some possible process that would make athletes appear dumb?**

One possible model for our observations might be:

Being a good athlete requires large amounts of practice time; being smart in class requires large amounts of study time. The amount of free time is so limited that you cannot both study and practice well.

This is a much more general explanation. It makes a variety of interesting predictions. Not only does it explain why athletes appear dumb in class, but it also predicts that any time-consuming activity will produce the same effect. Thus people who spend large amounts of time on student government or the school paper will also appear dumb in class. Of course, this is not the only possible model. An alternative might be:

Everyone wants to feel successful. Achieving recognition in any one area is enough to make most people content.

According to this model, athletes will not work hard to achieve recognition in academic work because they already have recognition as athletes. Thus they will appear dumb in class. It also predicts that other individuals who are successful in school in important activities (for instance, student politics, social events) will appear dumb in class.

Or you might have imagined a quite different process:

We tend to be jealous of success in others. When we are jealous of someone, we attempt subconsciously to lower his apparent success in class by interpreting his questions as "dumb."

According to this model, athletes (who are correctly identified as athletes) will ask questions that appear simplistic to other persons (who are relatively unsuccessful in athletics). Other individuals who are successful in other nonacademic pursuits will also ask what appear to be dumb questions.

STOP. Now we have three different models explaining the dumb football player, and undoubtedly you have thought of others. Which of the models is best? We will consider this question in the next chapter, but you might think a little about it now.

The Case of the Smart Women

The data collected to test the various ideas of this partially true story were often casual and nonrigorous. A social scientist noticed that women having a particular religious background tended to do better academic work at his university than women having other religious backgrounds. Religion Z maintains a private educational system that many of its members attend instead of public schools. The Z schools have a certain amount of religious content, are often relatively strict, and are usually segregated by sex.

STOP. Why do Z women do better academic work than non-Z women? What kind of process could produce this result?

The social scientist who made the initial observation immediately thought of two possible explanations:

Model 1. Z women are inherently smarter than non-Z women.

Model 2. There is something special about Z high schools that prepares students better for college work.

Model 1 is not a good model because it has no sense of process to it. Nonetheless, there is a possible test to check it out. We might simply give IQ tests to random samples of Z and non-Z girls in order to test the assumptions of the model. As a general rule, however, we will discourage assumption testing as a way of validating models. A little bit of imagination devoted to looking for testable predictions will generally be more profitable. In this case we suspect, from general biological knowledge, that if there were a systematic genetic-linked difference between the intelligence of Z women and that of non-Z women, there would be a similar systematic difference between Z men and non-Z men. Now we can avoid the tedious task of administering intelligence tests to everyone. Instead, we simply (and cleverly) check to see if Z men have better grade records than non-Z men. We do so and discover that there is no difference between the two groups of men. This leads us to doubt Model 1.

Model 2 asserts that there is something superior about the Z schools. But if this were true, then again we would expect Z men to be outstanding compared to non-Z men. Perhaps it is only the Z women's schools that are special, however. Casual conversation with Z men and women did not reveal any plausible differences between the Z schools that they attended. Thus Model 2 does not seem valid either, although we might want to keep it in mind. The differences between schools might be subtle. Are there any alternative models?

STOP AND THINK. What other explanations might there be for the social scientist's observation?

If you have read any modern discussions on educated women, you might have thought of the following model, which was also suggested by one of the Z women:

Model 3. Men seem to confuse masculinity and intelligence; a smart woman is threatening to them. So when a woman shows her intelligence, she gets criticized or ignored. After a while, women who want male approval learn to act dumb so as not to offend men. Since the Z schools are segregated by sex, their women graduates haven't been conditioned to be quiet in class and play dumb. With only other women around they get more chance to develop their intellectual potential.

Is this a good model? The process is certainly clear, and it does account for the original observation of disproportionately smart Z women and average Z men. Can we now make some interesting predictions? The essential variables in the model seem to be the degree of contact with men and the values of the men contacted. This in turn suggests some possible natural experiments:

1. Z women should gradually, over time, become conditioned by their new college environment. So the difference between Z women and non-Z women should be much smaller in senior classes than in freshmen classes.
2. There are many noncoeducational colleges. Graduates of women's colleges should do better in graduate school than women graduates of coeducational colleges.
3. Some women are largely indifferent to additional male approval, perhaps because they are strongly career oriented, perhaps because they are certain of their standing (either high or low) among men. Women in career-oriented programs will do better than women in liberal arts programs; women who are married will do better than women who are not; women who are distinctively unattractive to men will do better than others.

STOP. **Is Model 3 a good one? Or are there other models? Perhaps professors like the way in which Z women deal with teachers. Maybe you can think of some other explanation. See what predictions you can derive from your own model.**

On Becoming a Social Scientist

Recruitment into college majors is not a random process; rather, there are systematic biases in the motivations, attitudes, and abilities of stu-

dents who select certain majors. Students make choices that at least in a modest way match their expectations about a field with their own aspirations and their own views of their personal abilities. Counseling from parents, friends, and teachers guides a student into a commitment that is relatively consistent with his talents. As a result, students with greater interest and aptitude in art are disproportionately represented among art majors, and students with greater interest and aptitude in mathematics are disproportionately represented among mathematics majors. In a reasonably efficient "market" these simple mechanisms serve to attract students to interests and careers that are generally consistent with their abilities; but, as we know well from an examination of the ways in which sex biases permeates such a system, the market is far from perfect.

STOP. **Think about how you might form a model of the process by which people become committed to a field of study.** *Hint:* **Maybe they learn to like what they are good at.**

Consider the following simple model of the process:

1. There exists a set of alternative fields (for example, political science, history, mathematics).
2. There is a set of basic ability dimensions (for example, verbal fluency, problem solving, imagery). Success in the various fields depends upon the possession of some combination of these talents; the talents leading to success in the various fields overlap considerably, though they are not identical. There is also a random component (error) in success within each field. The magnitude of the random component varies from field to field.
3. Each child is characterized by a value (score) on each basic ability dimension. Although the correlation among these values is strongly positive, it is not perfect.
4. Initially, a child has no preferences among these fields; children develop preferences on

the basis of experience, tending to prefer those in which they are successful; they modify subsequent experiences (insofar as possible) to increase the time spent in fields that are preferred.

Within the model the process by which preferences are developed is simple. A child is presented with a series of opportunities to choose an academic interest; a choice is made on the basis of initial preferences; some level of success or failure is experienced, depending on the relation among the child's abilities, the abilities necessary for success in the field, and some random component; preferences among the various alternative interests are modified on the basis of success.

Such a model is hardly adequate to explain all features of the choice of major; it does, however, capture (or at least is consistent with) the major features of currently received doctrine about (1) individual abilities, (2) the relation between talent and performance in a field, and (3) individual learning of preferences.

STOP AND THINK. **What does the model leave out? Are there important factors omitted by this simplification?**

You may have noted two conspicuous factors that have been ignored by our gradual commitment model.

1. *Market Value.* A strict adaptation model ignores anticipations of future economic and social successes associated with various occupations and thus with various fields. At least some of the enthusiasm for medicine as a career stems from expectations on the part of students (and their parents) of the economic and social position that such a career confers.

2. *Social Norms.* The appropriateness of certain fields (and certain talents) for certain people is regulated by social rules as well as by adaptation to intrinsic talent. Most conspicuous among rules are the regulations related to ethnic group status and sex. Moreover, expectations with respect to the match between ethnic group or sex on the one hand and performance on the other form a major filter for the interpretation of success.

This description of an individual adaptation model subject to the outside press of the market and social norms is reasonable. It is also prima facie efficient and neutral; the process will tend to match up abilities and interests.

The model also predicts some other things. For example, it predicts that the speed of commitment by an individual to a field will depend on the variance of abilities in the individual (that is, those whose abilities are relatively specialized will become committed earlier than those whose ability levels are relatively equal for a wide range of fields); on the relative specialization of the field (that is, fields requiring abilities that are not required by other fields will tend to secure commitment relatively early); on the general level of ability of the individual (that is, those with relatively high ability will tend to become committed before those with relatively low ability); and on the magnitude of the random component in determining success in a field (that is, fields with a high random component will tend to secure later commitment and to attract relatively less able individuals).

According to this model, the social and behavioral sciences for example, will tend to recruit those students with high abilities in relevant areas, although it will lose some students having high social science ability to other fields when those students also had high abilities relevant to the other fields (particularly to fields with heavy overlap in the abilities required for success). Subject to "errors" in allocation due to chance elements in rewards, time limitations on experience, variations in market values, and social norms, the process allocates students to the places in which their abilities lie.

The errors of allocation, however, are important. If we are interested in understanding some features of how one becomes a social science major, we may be particularly interested in discovering features in the process that might produce systematic errors in the choice of social science.

STOP. Review the process we have specified. Can you see any way in which the selection of a social science major might be systematically biased?

If our model is correct, development of interest in behavioral and social science is subject to several sources of error:

1. Virtually nothing of the behavioral and social sciences is taught in the first 12 years of American schools. The exceptions are small and somewhat misleading: Geography (that is, maps, place names, and the distribution of natural and human resources), civics (that is, constitutional and legal forms), and modern history comprise the normal fare (perhaps supplemented with an exposure to sex and family living). In some schools there is an effort to introduce a bit of economics, psychology, cultural anthropology, or sociology; but these efforts touch an insignificant number of students rather late in their precollegiate days. "Social studies" in the American school is frequently history with an hour's discussion of current events on Friday.

2. The skills required in the social and behavioral sciences are far from unique to those fields. If we assume that the skills required for a modern social or behavioral scientist include the skills of analysis, model building, hypothesis forming, speculation, data interpreting, and problem solving, it is clear that social science deals in widely demanded skills. In particular, it seems obvious that such skills are highly correlated with the skills involved in mathematics, natural sciences, history, and creative writing.

3. Social norms leading students toward social science tend to be antianalytical. The behav-

ioral sciences are associated (quite appropriately) with human beings and social problems. As a result, they are associated (quite inappropriately) with a rejection of things, quantities, abstractions, and special skills. The norms tend often to be relatively "antiprofessional."

4. The social sciences appear to have a relatively high random component in their evaluation procedures. The reliability of grading appears to be less than in some other fields. As a result, students of relatively low ability do, on the average, better in social science than in other fields—even if the average performance and average ability levels are held constant.

When we superimpose these facts on the basic model, we obtain a series of predictions about possible errors in the choice of social science as a field of interest:

1. Since the abilities appropriate to the social and behavioral sciences are similar to, or correlated with, the abilities appropriate to fields more commonly offered at the precollegiate level (for example, mathematics, natural science, history, English), many students with high potential for work in social science will have learned to prefer (and have a commitment to) another field by the time they come to college.

2. A disproportionate share of those students who say they want to be social scientists on entering college will be "residual students," students who have not as yet found a field for commitment. In effect, this means that many will be students who are not particularly good at mathematics, physics, chemistry, English, history, or biology.

3. Insofar as a student has learned to prefer social science in his precollegiate training, he will have learned to prefer social science in terms of some combination of current events, social and human problems, and institutional description, or (disproportion-

ately) because of error in the earlier evaluation scheme.

The fundamental conclusion can be stated in a grossly simple way: If our model is correct, many social science students will be either inept at necessary skills or persuaded that those skills are irrelevant; many students with the skills necessary for social science will be strongly committed to competitive fields long before college or graduate school. This will be true in general, but it will be less true of individuals (for instance, women, blacks) who are channeled into social science by social norms than of other groups; it will be less true of fields that provide good economic prospects (for instance, economics, law) than other fields.

We have pondered the implications of such a model for the teaching of social science. As teachers, we have sometimes feared that some of our students might be expecting the wrong things from social science; that some students who would be good social scientists never took the right courses; and that some of the enthusiasm and intelligence of our students was buried beneath learned instincts for pedantry. This book, in fact, is a partial response to these concerns.

We have also pondered the implications of the model for understanding why we became social scientists. Was it really because we were not very good at anything else? We do not think so, and we have taken solace in the observation that good models of human behavior are rarely precise interpretations of individual actions.

For example, suppose one of our models generates the following prediction: Wealthy people tend to be more politically conservative than poor people. This is a good prediction about human behavior. But it does not necessarily describe an individual. Former Mayor Lindsay of New York is both wealthy and liberal. So are many other people. We do not expect such a model to predict individual human behavior; we only expect it to predict appreciably better than chance. If we questioned wealthy people about their political views and discovered that 60% were conservative, while only 20% of poor people were conservative, we would say that the model did a reasonably good job of predicting aggregate human behavior.

The prediction that wealthy individuals will tend to be politically conservative is still useful and interesting even if you know some wealthy individuals who are not. Thus if you were soliciting votes for a liberal cause, you would know that your chances of obtaining support from wealthy people would be relatively low. You might concentrate your efforts on other segments of the population and advertise in *Newsweek* rather than in the *Wall Street Journal*.

Thus although our model of how errors are made in the discovery of an interest in social science suggests that there will be more mistakes in social science than in some other fields, it does not necessarily apply to us, or to you. On the other hand, even if it does apply and we are here for all kinds of "erroneous" reasons, we have nevertheless rather grown to like it; and you might also.

The Politics of Population

Human societies sometimes face a population problem. A population problem exists when it is generally agreed within the society that the natural processes of birth and death are creating economic or social difficulties and should be modified. Historically, different societies have reacted to this situation in different ways. For example, some societies have increased the average life expectancy of their citizens through improved health-care systems. Some societies have increased the death rate selectively with respect to age, sex, and social class through wars, infanticide, or inefficient health care. Some societies have decreased, or increased, the birth rate through modifying social norms with respect to homosexuality or marriage, through encouraging women to work outside the home or to stay home, through contraceptives, or through moral persuasion.

STOP. Since this kind of question is profoundly important ethically, we might wish to speculate about the process by which societies arrive at different solutions to the population problem. Under what circumstances will societies engage in infanticide, birth control, medical research, women's liberation, or war? What is the process involved?

A possible way of looking at the problem follows. Since any population is limited by some kinds of scarce resources, a society decides who will share in those resources. One aspect of that decision is the question of who will live and who will not. Any combination of policies with respect to health care, birth control, work, war, and social norms is a decision about whose life will be relatively favored in the society and whose will be relatively unfavored. In this sense every society discriminates in favor of some people and against others.

Suppose we think of society as consisting of various age groups (for example, old people, young adults, children, unborn). Various possible population control procedures clearly have different consequences for the different age groups. A society that invests money in research on cancer and heart disease, for example, discriminates in favor of middle- and old-age people. A society that practices infanticide discriminates against babies. A society that practices birth control discriminates against the unborn.

If we look at the problem this way, our task becomes that of identifying a process by which a society might come to discriminate in one way or the other.

STOP AND THINK. Can you form any hypotheses about the decision process within a society?

You might have said something like this:

Individuals and groups within a society pursue their own self-interests. It is in the interest of every individual to promote discrimination in favor of his own age group and other age groups to which he expects to belong. Each group of individuals within the society has a certain amount of power. The greater the relative power of a group, the greater the discrimination in its favor.

A moment's reflection on the power structure within societies immediately suggests two predictions:

1. All societies will tend to discriminate against the unborn. That is, faced with an overpopulation problem, they will tend to prefer birth control to increasing the death rate.
2. The broader the sharing of power within the living society (for example, the more democratic it is), the greater the discrimination against the unborn.

The first of these predictions sounds interesting and provocative, but it is not easy to evaluate. The second, however, can be examined. A social scientist who did not have this specific problem in mind has invented a measure of the democracy of a political system and has applied it to some modern political systems. His results are presented in Table 2.1 along with crude birth and death rates.

Our model says that relatively democratic countries will discriminate more against the unborn than will relatively undemocratic countries. This means that we would expect to find that relatively democratic countries had relatively low birth rates and relatively long life expectancies. Is this the case?

STOP. Think about how you would decide whether these data support the model.

One procedure that might have occurred to you is to plot pairs of observations as we have done in Figures 2.2 and 2.3. In Figure 2.2 each country is a point. Each country is located on the figure according to the democratic index for that country and the crude birth rate for that country.

STOP AGAIN. What does the model predict about such a figure?

According to our model more democratic countries will discriminate *more* against the un-

Table 2.1 Democracy, Birth Rates, and Death Rates

Country	Democratic Index	Crude Birth Rate	Death Rate 60–64-Yr.-Old (Males)
Great Britain	236.3	18.3	27.6
France	231.4	17.7	26.1
Finland	229.2	16.9	34.6
Sweden	225.8	15.9	18.6
Netherlands	220.9	19.9	33.1
Belgium	214.9	16.4	29.1
Japan	212.7	18.6	—
Luxembourg	210.1	16.0	24.7
Norway	209.7	17.5	16.5
New Zealand	209.4	22.8	26.3
Denmark	205.7	18.0	19.3
Israel	203.2	25.8	26.8
W. Germany	199.4	17.9	—
Italy	198.6	19.2	21.8
Canada	196.8	21.4	23.5
United States	190.9	19.4	29.2
Venezuela	188.3	—	—
Austria	186.9	17.9	—
Chile	184.6	32.8	—
Ireland	181.4	22.1	27.0
India	172.7	—	—
Switzerland	169.3	18.8	25.6
Mexico	121.9	44.2	41.8

Source: Deane E. Neubauer, "Some Conditions of Democracy," *American Political Science Review* 61 (1967) 1002–1009. Reprinted with permission.

born. Thus a high democratic index should lead to a low birth rate. This appears to be generally true. One quick and inelegant way of checking is to draw a vertical line through the middle (*median*) value with respect to birth rate. These are the dashed lines in Figure 2.2. These lines divide the space into four rectangular areas. If our model is correct, we should find that the points are concentrated in the upper left and lower right areas. If you check, you will find that there are fourteen points in these two areas and only four points in the other two.

In Figure 2.3 each country is again a point. Here the points are located according to the democratic index for that country and the crude death date for 60–64-year-old males in that country. We have drawn the equivalent dashed lines.

STOP. What does the model predict?

Our model predicts that the more democratic countries will discriminate *less* against 60–64-year-olds. Thus we predict that a high democratic index will be associated with low death rate. This does not appear to be true. Our data arrange themselves so that there are exactly four points in each of three of the quadrants and five points in the fourth.

STOP. Can you generate any other predictions that might be wrong? So far we have

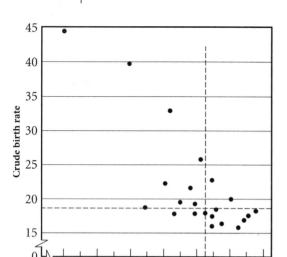

Figure 2.2: Democracy and birth rates.

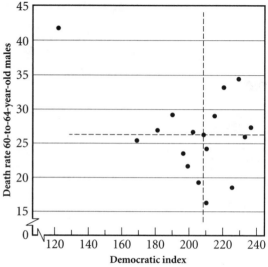

Figure 2.3: Democracy and death rates.

talked mostly about good predictions, but much of the art of model building lies in finding bad predictions.

At least one other problematic prediction occurs to us. We have talked entirely about age groups and the relatively weak political position of the unborn. In effect, we have developed the implications of a pure political model in which the powerful discriminate against the less powerful. There are other political groups that are relatively weak. Consider blacks in the United States, who have, by almost any plausible measure, less political power on the average than whites. Thus, according to the model, you would expect that age-specific death rates would be higher and age-specific birth rates lower among blacks than among whites. In fact, the first proposition is true, but the second is not.

One possible explanation is that this is something unique to the problems of blacks in America. However, this thought can be quickly dispelled. Spanish-speaking Americans also have less political power on the average than do Anglos. Yet birth rates and death rates are both high among Spanish-speaking Americans. Such a situation appears to have been true historically for many minority groups within the United

States. American society seems systematically to discriminate against living members of ethnic minority groups and against unborn children of dominant social groups.

Thus it is possible that our model is simply wrong. One of the important realities of model building is that not all predictions are correct. Indeed, as we will suggest in more detail in the next chapter, although we enjoy being right, most theoretical development comes from being wrong.

Three Rules of Thumb for Model Building

Model building as you have done it in this chapter is not a novel activity. It is something we all do all the time. We speculate about things that happen to us or that we see happening to others. It is not mysterious, but it probably can be improved by a little attention to some elementary rules. In Chapter Three we will suggest some more detailed rules of thumb. Here we will simply note three general rules that we have been using repeatedly in making the speculations in this chapter. They are probably sensible much of the time, though they are not absolute truths.

Rule 1: Think "Process." *A good model is almost always a statement about a process, and many bad models fail because they have no sense of process. When you build a model, look at it for a moment and see if it has some statement of process in it.*

EXAMPLE

Your chemistry professor shows up in class but has forgotten to bring along last week's homework papers. He apologizes, and you turn to the person next to you and say, "What can you expect from absent-minded professors?" This is your explanatory model for the professor's behavior. This is a common, ordinary, but poor model. Look at it for a moment. Where is the process? One way to put a process into the model is to ask *why* professors are absent-minded. If you think about it for a moment, you will be able to think of a number of processes that might produce absent-minded professors.

Model 1. Busy people try to devote their limited time to the things they consider most important. The professor does not consider teaching important, and so he did not bother to go by his office and find the homework papers.

Model 2. You become a professor by learning to be a good problem solver. Good problem solving involves almost single-minded concentration. So the professor occasionally forgets to do one thing because he is concentrating on another.

The models are different from each other, but each involves a sense of process, or relationship. One way to be certain that your models involve a sense of process is to see if you can derive general relational statements from them, that is: The greater X is, the greater Y will be. Thus Model 1 contains the following general relational statement: The busier someone is, the more likely he is to concentrate on important things. And Model 2 contains this general relational statement: The tougher the problem and the harder someone is concentrating on it, the more likely he is to forget other things.

Rule 2: Develop Interesting Implications. *Much of the fun in model building lies in finding interesting implications in your models. In the problems associated with this course you will repeatedly be asked to develop interesting implications from some model. Whether something is considered interesting obviously involves a judgment, but there is a good strategy for producing interesting predictions: Look for natural experiments.*

EXAMPLE

An uninteresting prediction from Model 1 would be: Make the professor value his students more, and he will then become less absent-minded. Or from Model 2: Get the professor to work on easier problems, and he will become less absent-minded. These are relatively uninteresting because they ask us to run an experiment in a situation in which we probably cannot.

The way to find more interesting predictions is to think about the process involved in each model and then look for natural instances in which the key variables in the process vary. In Model 2, for example, it is not simple to vary the difficulty of the professor's problems, but you can easily find instances of similar situations and hence can predict that people (business executives; architects, football coaches) in other occupations that demand concentrated, abstract thought will occasionally forget things, too. Or you can predict that the professor will be just as absent-minded when engaged in his laboratory research as when he is engaged in teaching.

Or, for Model 1, you cannot easily make the professor value some given class of students more, but you can search for natural occurrences of this event. For example, if you believe that he values the students in his graduate research seminar more than the students in his freshman introductory class, you would predict less absent-minded behavior with respect to the graduate students. Suppose you did make such observations and discovered that he was equally forgetful in his graduate classes; and furthermore that his freshmen lectures are well prepared, that he seems to have great quantities of careful notes, and that he often spends so much time answering questions after the freshman class that he is late for his next class. You would then be highly skeptical of the truth of Model 1.

> **Rule 3: Look for Generality.** *Ordinarily, the more situations a model applies to, the better it is and the greater the variety of possible implications. Finding generality involves the ordinary process of generalizing nouns and verbs.*

EXAMPLE

Expand "college professors" to "busy people"; expand "forgetting homework papers" to "forgetting anything"; expand "bringing papers" to "one kind of work." Finding generality also involves asking repeatedly why the process we have postulated is true. We ask: Is there another model that, if true, would include our model as an implication? That is, we look for a more general model that predicts our model and other things as well. Model 2, for instance, can be generalized to a large family of learning models that can be formulated to predict what would happen if people learned to be good social scientists or executives.

From such simple heuristics, a little experience, some playfulness, and a bit of luck come good models, and some bad ones. Indeed, it is the creativity with which we specify bad models that leads us to good ones.

REFERENCES

Robert Henri, *The Art Spirit* (Philadelphia: Lippincott, 1960; first published in 1923).

Leo Rosten, *The Joys of Yiddish* (New York: McGraw-Hill, 1968).

Richard S. Rudner, *Philosophy of Social Science* (Englewood Cliffs, N.J.: Prentice-Hall, 1966).

Herbert A. Simon, *Models of Man* (New York: Wiley, 1957).

Arthur L. Stinchcombe, *Constructing Social Theories* (New York: Harcourt Brace Jovanovich, 1968).

Josephine Tey, *The Daughter of Time* (London: Macmillan, 1951).

NOTES

1. Martin Deutsch and Mary Evan Collins, "Interracial Housing," in William Peterson, ed., *American Social Patterns*, (Garden City, N.Y.: Doubleday, 1956).

2. Actually, the process implicit in this model should be clarified somewhat. We are *not* saying that out of every 100 people there are 70 who are inherently like us and who could become our friends and 30 people who are inherently different from us who could become our enemies; and communication allows us to identify the two different groups. Rather, the model says that almost anyone is capable of becoming either a friend or enemy, depending on whether you communicate about your similarities or your differences.

3. Note an alternative theory: People on commissions want to have their reports implemented. They believe (from experience?) that extreme reports rarely are implemented.

2 THE STATE

At the center of most discussions of comparative politics lies the state, the organization that wields power over people and territory. In this section we will consider the ways in which we think about and measure the state, and how these have changed over time. A theoretical discussion of the state is complemented by more concrete discussions of the challenges that states confront in the current international system.

Max Weber is often cited as one of the forefathers of modern social science. In addition to political science, the fields of sociology and economics also owe a debt to Weber. Indeed, at the time of his writing, in the late nineteenth and early twentieth century, these fields were not clearly distinguished from one another. Politics as a Vocation (1918) was a speech originally presented at Munich University, in which he sought to lay out some of the most basic ways in which he understood political power. Weber provides the modern definition of the state (a monopoly of force over territory) and from there outlines what he believes to be the central forms of political authority (traditional, charismatic, rational-legal). For Weber, the development of the modern state occurs alongside the growing domination of the bureaucracy and rational legal authority—politics as a profession, rather than a calling or an inherited role. Thus, charismatic or traditional leaders gave way to the modern professional state. In spite of the profound influence of Weber's work, by the mid-twentieth century, state-focused analysis began to lose favor, particularly in the United States. Swept up in the so-called behavioral revolution, political scientists began to concentrate more on societal factors, downplaying the degree to which the state itself was an important source of politics.

However, over the past two decades, political scientists have returned their attention to the idea of state power and how the state's autonomy and capacity can shape such things as the emergence of democracy or economic progress (topics that we discuss in Chapters 4 and 6). Comparative politics has again become a much more state-focused field of study.

A wide range of contemporary scholars has refocused on the state as an important variable in comparative politics. Jeffery Herbst's "War and the State in Africa" (1990) draws on historical studies of state formation in Europe to consider whether we can expect a similar outcome in other parts of the world, such as Africa. In Europe, the author notes, interstate war was a critical component in the development of the modern state, helping to improve taxation, administration, and the development of symbols to establish national identity, a process that occurred over many centuries. In Africa, however, states have not formed out of a long process of warfare, but rather are the remnants of empires that once dominated the continent. These states are ill-equipped to carry out most administrative tasks and lack the kind of national unity that can help build state legitimacy. There is a terrible irony, then: the absence of interstate war across Africa has left the continent with an array of weak states that cannot secure either prosperity or security. Indeed, one could go so far as to argue that the lack of war between states has resulted in horrific wars within them, such as the civil conflicts of Liberia or the genocide of Rwanda. Herbst is skeptical that peaceful state-building policies could serve as an alternative to war, and though he does not suggest that war between countries should be welcomed in Africa in order to build stronger states, it is hard not to draw such an uncomfortable conclusion. In the foreseeable future, the author anticipates an Africa of "permanently weak states."

In the years since Herbst's work was written, Africa and other parts of the world have seen the rise of something much worse than the weak states Herbst discusses. This is what is known as the "failed state." From the former Soviet Union to Latin America, Asia, and Africa, various countries have teetered on the edge or plunged into the abyss of state failure, where the most basic functions of the state—including the monopoly of force—have broken down, leading to civil conflict and anarchy. These have become a tremendous concern not only because of the suffering that such state failures have caused, but also because of the fear that failed states often provide the perfect breeding ground for terrorism. Robert Rotberg considers this in "The New Nature of Nation-State Failure" (2002). Where states fail, we see greater civil conflict, weak infrastructure, inequality, corruption, and economic decline. As we learned from Herbst, it is very difficult to build a strong state, and for a failed state, this task is even more difficult. Policymakers, Rotberg argues, should take more care to identify and strengthen states in danger of collapse before they are beyond assistance and become an international threat.

Scholars are concerned about not only the power of the state, but also the state's future direction. In "The New Religious State" (1995), Mark Juergensmeyer addresses what he considers to be the most important challenge to modern states in the coming decades, specifically religious fundamentalism, which he refers to as "religious nationalism." Juergensmeyer notes that the rise of the modern state was driven in part by the rise of national identity and ideology, which served to make the state the sovereign authority and to push religion out of public life. However, across the world, religion has reemerged as an ideology in its own right, and some fundamentalists assert that the state and faith should be merged into a single authority that recognizes only the sovereignty of God. What are the implications of this development for domestic and international politics? Would religious states inherently be hostile to democracies and other nonreligious states? These questions are largely academic now, but they may become critical as religion and politics continue to clash in future.

MAX WEBER

POLITICS AS A VOCATION

This lecture, which I give at your request, will necessarily disappoint you in a number of ways. You will naturally expect me to take a position on actual problems of the day. But that will be the case only in a purely formal way and toward the end, when I shall raise certain questions concerning the significance of political action in the whole way of life. In today's lecture, all questions that refer to what policy and what content one should give one's political activity must be eliminated. For such questions have nothing to do with the general question of what politics as a vocation means and what it can mean. Now to our subject matter.

What do we understand by politics? The concept is extremely broad and comprises any kind of *independent* leadership in action. One speaks of the currency policy of the banks, of the discounting policy of the Reichsbank, of the strike policy of a trade union; one may speak of the educational policy of a municipality or a township, of the policy of the president of a voluntary association, and, finally, even of the policy of a prudent wife who seeks to guide her husband. Tonight, our reflections are, of course, not based upon such a broad concept. We wish to under-

stand by politics only the leadership, or the influencing of the leadership, of a *political* association, hence today, of a *state*.

But what is a "political" association from the sociological point of view? What is a "state"? Sociologically, the state cannot be defined in terms of its ends. There is scarcely any task that some political association has not taken in hand, and there is no task that one could say has always been exclusive and peculiar to those associations which are designated as political ones: today the state, or historically, those associations which have been the predecessors of the modern state. Ultimately, one can define the modern state sociologically only in terms of the specific means peculiar to it, as to every political association, namely, the use of physical force.

"Every state is founded on force," said Trotsky at Brest-Litovsk. That is indeed right. If no social institutions existed which knew the use of violence, then the concept of "state" would be eliminated, and a condition would emerge that could be designated as "anarchy," in the specific sense of this word. Of course, force is certainly not the normal or the only means of the state—nobody says that—but force is a means specific to the state. Today the relation between the state and violence is an especially intimate one. In the past, the most varied institutions—beginning with the sib—have known the use of physical

From H. H. Gerth and C. Wright Mills, eds., trans. *From Max Weber: Essays in Sociology* (New York: Galaxy, 1958), pp. 77–87.

force as quite normal. Today, however, we have to say that a state is a human community that (successfully) claims the *monopoly of the legitimate use of physical force* within a given territory. Note that "territory" is one of the characteristics of the state. Specifically, at the present time, the right to use physical force is ascribed to other institutions or to individuals only to the extent to which the state permits it. The state is considered the sole source of the "right" to use violence. Hence, "politics" for us means striving to share power or striving to influence the distribution of power, either among states or among groups within a state.

This corresponds essentially to ordinary usage. When a question is said to be a "political" question, when a cabinet minister or an official is said to be a "political" official, or when a decision is said to be "politically" determined, what is always meant is that interests in the distribution, maintenance, or transfer of power are decisive for answering the questions and determining the decision or the official's sphere of activity. He who is active in politics strives for power either as a means in serving other aims, ideal or egoistic, or as "power for power's sake," that is, in order to enjoy the prestige-feeling that power gives.

Like the political institutions historically preceding it, the state is a relation of men dominating men, a relation supported by means of legitimate (i.e. considered to be legitimate) violence. If the state is to exist, the dominated must obey the authority claimed by the powers that be. When and why do men obey? Upon what inner justifications and upon what external means does this domination rest?

To begin with, in principle, there are three inner justifications, hence basic *legitimations* of domination.

First, the authority of the "eternal yesterday," i.e. of the mores sanctified through the unimaginably ancient recognition and habitual orientation to conform. This is "traditional" domination exercised by the patriarch and the patrimonial prince of yore.

There is the authority of the extraordinary and personal *gift of grace* (charisma), the absolutely personal devotion and personal confidence in revelation, heroism, or other qualities of individual leadership. This is "charismatic" domination, as exercised by the prophet or—in the field of politics—by the elected war lord, the plebiscitarian ruler, the great demagogue, or the political party leader.

Finally, there is a domination by virtue of "legality," by virtue of the belief in the validity of legal statute and functional "competence" based on rationally created *rules*. In this case, obedience is expected in discharging statutory obligations. This is domination as exercised by the modern "servant of the state" and by all those bearers of power who in this respect resemble him.

It is understood that, in reality, obedience is determined by highly robust motives of fear and hope—fear of the vengeance of magical powers or of the power-holder, hope for reward in this world or in the beyond—and besides all this, by interests of the most varied sort. Of this we shall speak presently. However, in asking for the "legitimations" of this obedience, one meets with these three "pure" types: "traditional," "charismatic," and "legal."

These conceptions of legitimacy and their inner justifications are of very great significance for the structure of domination. To be sure, the pure types are rarely found in reality. But today we cannot deal with the highly complex variants, transitions, and combinations of these pure types, which problems belong to "political science." Here we are interested above all in the second of these types: domination by virtue of the devotion of those who obey the purely personal "charisma" of the "leader." For this is the root of the idea of a *calling* in its highest expression.

Devotion to the charisma of the prophet, or the leader in war, or to the great demagogue in the *ecclesia* or in parliament, means that the leader is personally recognized as the innerly "called" leader of men. Men do not obey him by virtue of tradition or statute, but because they believe in him. If he is more than a narrow and vain upstart of the moment, the leader lives for his cause and "strives for his work." The devotion of his disciples, his followers, his personal party friends is oriented to his person and to its qualities.

Charismatic leadership has emerged in all places and in all historical epochs. Most importantly in the past, it has emerged in the two figures of the magician and the prophet on the one hand, and in the elected war lord, the gang leader and *condotierre* on the other hand. *Political* leadership in the form of the free "demagogue" who grew from the soil of the city state is of greater concern to us; like the city state, the demagogue is peculiar to the Occident and especially to Mediterranean culture. Furthermore, political leadership in the form of the parliamentary "party leader" has grown on the soil of the constitutional state, which is also indigenous only to the Occident.

These politicians by virtue of a "calling," in the most genuine sense of the word, are of course nowhere the only decisive figures in the crosscurrents of the political struggle for power. The sort of auxiliary means that are at their disposal is also highly decisive. How do the politically dominant powers manage to maintain their domination? The question pertains to any kind of domination, hence also to political domination in all its forms, traditional as well as legal and charismatic.

Organized domination, which calls for continuous administration, requires that human conduct be conditioned to obedience towards those masters who claim to be the bearers of legitimate power. On the other hand, by virtue of this obedience, organized domination requires the control of those material goods which in a given case are necessary for the use of physical violence. Thus, organized domination requires control of the personal executive staff and the material implements of administration.

The administrative staff, which externally represents the organization of political domination, is, of course, like any other organization, bound by obedience to the power-holder and not alone by the concept of legitimacy, of which we have just spoken. There are two other means, both of which appeal to personal interests: material reward and social honor. The fiefs of vassals, the prebends of patrimonial officials, the salaries of modern civil servants, the honor of knights, the privileges of estates, and the honor of the civil servant comprise their respective wages. The fear of losing them is the final and decisive basis for solidarity between the executive staff and the power-holder. There is honor and booty for the followers in war; for the demagogue's following, there are "spoils"—that is, exploitation of the dominated through the monopolization of office—and there are politically determined profits and premiums of vanity. All of these rewards are also derived from the domination exercised by a charismatic leader.

To maintain a dominion by force, certain material goods are required, just as with an economic organization. All states may be classified according to whether they rest on the principle that the staff of men themselves own the administrative means, or whether the staff is "separated" from these means of administration. This distinction holds in the same sense in which today we say that the salaried employee and the proletarian in the capitalistic enterprise are "separated" from the material means of production. The power-holder must be able to count on the obedience of the staff members, officials, or whoever else they may be. The administrative means may consist of money, building, war material, vehicles, horses, or whatnot. The question is whether or not the power-holder himself directs and organizes the administration while delegating executive power to personal servants, hired officials, or personal favorites and confidants, who are non-owners, i.e. who do not use the material means of administration in their own right but are directed by the lord. The distinction runs through all administrative organizations of the past.

These political associations in which the material means of administration are autonomously controlled, wholly or partly, by the dependent administrative staff may be called associations organized in "*estates*." The vassal in the feudal association, for instance, paid out of his own pocket for the administration and judicature of the district enfeoffed to him. He supplied his own equipment and provisions for war, and his subvassals did likewise. Of course, this had consequences for the lord's position of power, which only rested upon a relation of personal faith and upon the fact that the legitimacy of his possession of the fief and the social honor of the vassal were derived from the overlord.

However, everywhere, reaching back to the earliest political formations, we also find the lord himself directing the administration. He seeks to take the administration into his own hands by having men personally dependent upon him: slaves, household officials, attendants, personal "favorites," and prebendaries enfeoffed in kind or in money from his magazines. He seeks to defray the expenses from his own pocket, from the revenues of his patrimonium; and he seeks to create an army which is dependent upon him personally because it is equipped and provisioned out of his granaries, magazines, and armories. In the association of "estates," the lord rules with the aid of an autonomous "aristocracy" and hence shares his domination with it; the lord who personally administers is supported either by members of his household or by plebeians. These are propertyless strata having no social honor of their own; materially, they are completely chained to him and are not backed up by any competing power of their own. All forms of patriarchal and patrimonial domination, Sultanist despotism, and bureaucratic states belong to this latter type. The bureaucratic state order is especially important; in its most rational development, it is precisely characteristic of the modern state.

Everywhere the development of the modern state is initiated through the action of the prince. He paves the way for the expropriation of the autonomous and "private" bearers of executive power who stand beside him, of those who in their own right possess the means of administration, warfare, and financial organization, as well as politically usable goods of all sorts. The whole process is a complete parallel to the development of the capitalist enterprise through gradual expropriation of the independent producers. In the end, the modern state controls the total means of political organization, which actually come together under a single head. No single official personally owns the money he pays out, or the buildings, stores, tools, and war machines he controls. In the contemporary "state"—and this is essential for the concept of state—the "separation" of the administrative staff, of the administrative officials, and of the workers from the material means of administrative organization is completed. Here the most modern development begins, and we see with our own eyes the attempt to inaugurate the expropriation of this expropriator of the political means, and therewith of political power.

The revolution [of Germany, 1918] has accomplished, at least in so far as leaders have taken the place of the statutory authorities, this much: the leaders, through usurpation or election, have attained control over the political staff and the apparatus of material goods; and they deduce their legitimacy—no matter with what right—from the will of the governed. Whether the leaders, on the basis of this at least apparent success, can rightfully entertain the hope of also carrying through the expropriation within the capitalist enterprises is a different question. The direction of capitalist enterprises, despite far-reaching analogies, follows quite different laws than those of political administration.

Today we do not take a stand on this question. I state only the purely *conceptual* aspect for our consideration: the modern state is a compulsory association which organizes domination. It has been successful in seeking to monopolize the legitimate use of physical force as a means of domination within a territory. To this end the state has combined the material means of organization in the hands of its leaders, and it has expropriated all autonomous functionaries of estates who formerly controlled these means in their own right. The state has taken their positions and now stands in the top place.

During this process of political expropriation, which has occurred with varying success in all countries on earth, "professional politicians" in another sense have emerged. They arose first in the service of a prince. They have been men who, unlike the charismatic leader, have not wished to be lords themselves, but who have entered the *service* of political lords. In the struggle of expropriation, they placed themselves at the princes' disposal and by managing the princes' politics they earned, on the one hand, a living and, on the other hand, an ideal content of life. Again, it is *only* in the Occident that we find this kind of professional politician in the service of powers other than the princes. In the past, they have been the most important power instrument of the prince and his instrument of political expropriation.

Before discussing "professional politicians" in detail, let us clarify in all its aspects the state of affairs their existence presents. Politics, just as economic pursuits, may be a man's avocation or his vocation. One may engage in politics, and hence seek to influence the distribution of power within and between political structures, as an "occasional" politician. We are all "occasional" politicians when we cast our ballot or consummate a similar expression of intention, such as applauding or protesting in a "political" meeting, or delivering a "political" speech, etc. The whole relation of many people to politics is restricted to this. Politics as an avocation is today practiced by all those party agents and heads of voluntary political associations who, as a rule, are politically active only in case of need and for whom politics is, neither materially nor ideally, "their life" in the first place. The same holds for those members of state counsels and similar deliberative bodies that function only when summoned. It also holds for rather broad strata of our members of parliament who are politically active only during sessions. In the past, such strata were found especially among the estates. Proprietors of military implements in their own right, or proprietors of goods important for the administration, or proprietors of personal prerogatives may be called "estates." A large portion of them were far from giving their lives wholly, or merely preferentially, or more than occasionally, to the service of politics. Rather, they exploited their prerogatives in the interest of gaining rent or even profits; and they became active in the service of political associations only when the overlord of their status-equals especially demanded it. It was not different in the case of some of the auxiliary forces which the prince drew into the struggle for the creation of a political organization to be exclusively at his disposal. This was the nature of the *Rate von Haus aus* [councilors] and, still further back, of a considerable part of the councilors assembling in the "Curia" and other deliberating bodies of the princes. But these merely occasional auxiliary forces engaging in politics on the side were naturally not sufficient for the prince. Of necessity, the prince sought to create a staff of helpers dedicated wholly and exclusively to serving him, hence making this their major vocation. The structure of the emerging dynastic political organization, and not only this but the whole articulation of the culture, depended to a considerable degree upon the question of where the prince recruited agents.

A staff was also necessary for those political associations whose members constituted themselves politically as (so-called) "free" communes under the complete abolition or the far-going restriction of princely power.

They were "free" not in the sense of freedom from domination by force, but in the sense that princely power legitimized by tradition (mostly religously sanctified) as the exclusive source of all authority was absent. These communities have their historical home in the Occident. Their nucleus was the city as a body politic, the form in which the city first emerged in the Mediterranean culture area. In all these cases, what did the politicians who made politics their major vocation look like?

There are two ways of making politics one's vocation: Either one lives "for" politics or one lives "off" politics. By no means is this contrast an exclusive one. The rule is, rather, that man does both, at least in thought, and certainly he also does both in practice. He who lives "for" politics makes politics his life, in an internal sense. Either he enjoys the naked possession of the power he exerts, or he nourishes his inner balance and self-feeling by the consciousness that his life has *meaning* in the service of a "cause." In this internal sense, every sincere man who lives for a cause also lives off this cause. The distinction hence refers to a much more substantial aspect of the matter, namely, to the economic. He who strives to make politics a permanent *source of income* lives "off" politics as a vocation, whereas he who does not do this lives "for" politics. Under the dominance of the private property order, some—if you wish—very trivial preconditions must exist in order for a person to be able to live "for" politics in this economic sense. Under normal conditions, the politician must be economically independent of the income politics can bring him. This means, quite simply, that the politician must be wealthy or must have a personal position in life which yields a sufficient income.

This is the case, at least in normal circumstances. The war lord's following is just as little concerned about the conditions of a normal economy as is the street crowd following of the revolutionary hero. Both live off booty, plunder, confiscations, contributions, and the imposition of worthless and compulsory means of tender, which in essence amounts to the same thing. But necessarily, these are extraordinary phenomena. In everyday economic life, only some wealth serves the purpose of making a man economically independent. Yet this alone does not suffice. The professional politician must also be economically "dispensable," that is, his income must not depend upon the fact that he constantly and personally places his ability and thinking entirely, or at least by far predominantly, in the service of economic acquisition. In the most unconditional way, the rentier is dispensable in this sense. Hence, he is a man who receives completely unearned income. He may

be the territorial lord of the past or the large landowner and aristocrat of the present who receives ground rent. In Antiquity and the Middle Ages they who received slave or serf rents or in modern times rents from shares or bonds or similar sources—these are rentiers.

Neither the worker nor—and this has to be noted well—the entrepreneur, especially the modern, large-scale entrepreneur, is economically dispensable in this sense. For it is precisely the entrepreneur who is tied to his enterprise and is therefore *not* dispensable. This holds for the entrepreneur in industry far more than for the entrepreneur in agriculture, considering the seasonal character of agriculture. In the main, it is very difficult for the entrepreneur to be represented in his enterprise by someone else, even temporarily. He is as little dispensable as is the medical doctor, and the more eminent and busy he is the less dispensable he is. For purely organizational reasons, it is easier for the lawyer to be dispensable; and therefore the lawyer has played an incomparably greater, and often even a dominant, role as a professional politician. We shall not continue in this classification; rather let us clarify some of its ramifications.

The leadership of a state or of a party by men who (in the economic sense of the word) live exclusively for politics and not off politics means necessarily a "plutocratic" recruitment of the leading political strata. To be sure, this does not mean that such plutocratic leadership signifies at the same time that the politically dominant strata will not also seek to live "off" politics, and hence that the dominant stratum will not usually exploit their political domination in their own economic interest. All that is unquestionable, of course. There has never been such a stratum that has not somehow lived "off" politics. Only this is meant: that the professional politician need not seek remuneration directly for his political work, whereas every politician without means must absolutely claim this. On the other hand, we do not mean to say that the propertyless politician will pursue private economic advantages through politics, exclusively, or even predominantly. Nor do we mean that he will not think, in the first place, of "the subject matter." Nothing would be more incorrect. According to all experience, a care for the economic "security" of his existence is consciously or unconsciously a cardinal point in the whole life orientation of the wealthy man. A quite reckless and unreserved political idealism is found if not exclusively at least predominantly among those strata who by virtue of their propertylessness stand entirely outside of the strata who are interested in maintaining the economic order of a given society. This holds especially for extraordinary and hence revolutionary epochs. A non-plutocratic recruitment of interested politicians, of leadership and following, is geared to the self-understood precondition that regular and reliable income will accrue to those who manage politics.

Either politics can be conducted "honorifically" and then, as one usually says, by "independent," that is, by wealthy, men, and especially by rentiers. Or, political leadership is made accessible to propertyless men who must then be rewarded. The professional politician who lives "off" politics may be a pure "prebendary" or a salaried "official." Then the politician receives either income from fees and perquisites for specific services—tips and bribes are only an irregular and formally illegal variant of this category of income—or a fixed income in kind, a money salary, or both. He may assume the character of an "entrepreneur," like the *condottiere* or the holder of a farmed-out or purchased office, or like the American boss who considers his costs a capital investment which he brings to fruition through exploitation of his influence. Again, he may receive a fixed wage, like a journalist, a party secretary, a modern cabinet minister, or a political official. Feudal fiefs, land grants, and prebends of all sorts have been typical, in the past. With the development of the money economy, perquisites and prebends especially are the typical rewards for the following of princes, victorious conquerors, or successful party chiefs. For loyal services today, party leaders give offices of all sorts—in parties, newspapers, co-operative societies, health insurance, municipalities, as well as in the state. *All* party struggles are struggles for the patronage of office, as well as struggles for objective goals.

MARK JUERGENSMEYER

THE NEW RELIGIOUS STATE

One of the most interesting—some would say disturbing—features of the post–Cold War era is the resurgence of religious politics. It appears as a dark cloud over what many regard as the near-global victory of liberal democracy following the collapse of the Soviet Empire.[1] It fuels regional disputes in North Africa, the Middle East, and South Asia and may be leading toward what Samuel Huntington has apocalyptically called "the clash of civilizations."[2] It has led to some impressive gains: radical religious parties are now firmly established not only in Iran but in Algeria, Sudan, Egypt, India, Afghanistan, Pakistan, the incipient Palestine, and elsewhere in what was once called the Third World. Although it is tempting to dismiss

From Mark Juergensmeyer, *Comparative Politics* (July 1995), pp. 379–91. Some of the author's notes have been omitted.

the religious activists involved in these uprisings as "fundamentalists," their goals and their motivations are as political as they are religious. For this reason I prefer to call them "religious nationalists," implying that they are political actors striving for new forms of national order based on religious values.[3]

The question I will pursue in this essay is how religious nationalists conceive this relationship between religion and politics. In the past several years, I have examined various movements of religious nationalism, including Hindu and Sikh partisans in India, militant Buddhists in Sri Lanka and Mongolia, Christian activists in eastern Europe and Latin America, right-wing Jewish politicians in Israel, and Islamic activists in the Middle East and Central Asia. I have described some of these movements in other essays and in a recent book.[4] Therefore, I will not discuss these cases in depth here, but rather will explore an issue that I believe is central to virtually all of these movements: their assumption that religion can replace liberal democracy in providing the ideological glue that holds a nation together and that it can provide the justification for a modern religious state.

In this essay I will first describe how traditional religion can play the same ideological role that secular nationalist theories play in providing a theoretical basis for a nation-state. Because of this ideological role, I will then show, religion and liberal democratic ideas are seen as competitive in both the West and the Third World. Finally, I will explore a kind of resolution of this competition: the rise of a potent new synthesis between the nation-state and religion.

The Confrontation of Two Ideologies of Order

One of the most striking features of religious nationalists' rhetoric is the way that it juxtaposes religion with western notions of national ideology. Secular nationalism is "a kind of religion," one of the leaders of the Iranian revolution pro-

claimed.[5] He and other religious nationalists regard secularism not only as a religion, but as one peculiar to the West.[6] They assume that secular nationalism responds to the same sorts of needs for collective identity, ultimate loyalty, and moral authority to which religion has traditionally responded. Some go further and state that the western form of secular nationalism is simply a cover for Christianity. For evidence, they offer the fact that the word "Christian" is used in the title of some political parties in Europe. But whether or not secular nationalism in the West is overtly labeled Christian, most religious activists see it as occupying the same place in human experience as Islam in Muslin societies, Buddhism in Theravada Buddhist societies, and Hinduism and Sikhism in Indian society. To these Muslims, Buddhists, Hindus, and Sikhs it is perfectly obvious; the West's secular nationalism competes in every way with religion as they know it.

Behind this charge is a certain vision of social reality, one that involves a series of concentric circles. The smallest are families and clans; then come ethnic groups and nations; the largest, and implicitly most important, are global civilizations. Among these civilizations are to be found Islam, Buddhism, and what some who hold this view call "Christendom" and others call "western civilization." Particular nations such as Germany, France, and the United States, in this conceptualization, stand as subsets of Christendom/western civilization; similarly, Egypt, Iran, Pakistan, and other nations are subsets of Islamic civilization.

Are they correct in this assessment, that the social functions of traditional religion and secular nationalism are so similar they both can be regarded as two aspects of a similar phenomenon? Huntington's recent essay seems to agree.[7] Earlier, Benedict Anderson suggested that religion and secular nationalism are both "imagined communities;" Ninian Smart regarded them both as "world-views."[8] In an interesting way, these scholars concur with religious nationalists' understanding of the social character of religion: like secular nationalism, religion has the ability to command communal loyalty and to legitimize authority. To this extent I agree with Anderson and Smart—and with many religious nationalists—that religion and secular nationalism are species of the same genus. I prefer to call this genus "ideologies of order."

My use of the word "ideology" should not be misconstrued as an effort to revive the meanings attached to it by Karl Marx or Karl Mannheim or by those identified with the "end of ideology" debate some years ago.[9] Rather, I use it in the original, late-eighteenth-century sense. At that time a group of French *idéologues*, as they called themselves, were attempting to build a science of ideas based on the theories of Francis Bacon, Thomas Hobbes, John Locke, and René Descartes that would be sufficiently comprehensive to replace religion. According to one of the *idéologues*, Destutt de Tracy, whose book *Elements of Ideology* introduced the term to the world, "logic" was to be the sole basis of "the moral and political sciences."[10] In proposing their own "science of ideas" as a replacement for religion, the *idéologues* were in fact putting what they called ideology and what we call religion on an equal plane. Perhaps Clifford Geertz, among modern users of the term, has come closest to its original meaning by speaking of ideology as a "cultural system."[11]

To make clear that I am referring to the original meaning of the term and not to "political ideology" in a narrow sense or to a Marxian or Mannheimian notion of ideology, I will refer to what I have in mind as "ideologies of order." Both religious and secular nationalistic frameworks of thought are ideologies of order in the following ways: they both conceive of the world around them as a coherent, manageable system; they both suggest that there are levels of meaning beneath the day-to-day world that explain things unseen; they both provide identity for and evoke loyalty from secular communities; and they both provide the authority that gives social and political order a reason for being. In doing so they define how an individual should properly act in the world, and they relate persons to the social whole.

I have defined both nationalism and religion in terms of order as well as ideology. For this definition there is ample precedent. Regarding nationalism, Karl Deutsch has pointed out the importance of orderly systems of communication in fostering a sense of nationalism. Ernest Gellner argues that the political and economic network of a nation-state requires a spirit of nationalism that draws upon a homogeneous culture, a unified pattern of communication, and a common system of education. Other social scientists have stressed the psychological aspect of national identity: the sense of historical location that is engendered when individuals feel they are a part of a larger, national history. But behind these notions of community are also images of order, for nationalism always involves the loyalty to an authority who, as Max Weber observed, holds a monopoly over the "legitimate use of physical force" in a given society.[12] Anthony Giddens describes nationalism as the "cultural sensibility of sovereignty," implying that the awareness of being subject to such an authority—an authority invested with the power of life and death—is what gives nationalism its potency.[13] It is not only an attachment to a spirit of social order but also an act of submission to an ordering agent.

Religion has also been defined in terms of order, albeit in a conceptual more than a political or social sense. Clifford Geertz, for example, sees religion as the effort to integrate messy everyday reality into a pattern of coherence that takes shape at a deeper level.[14] Robert Bellah also thinks of religion as an attempt to reach beyond ordinary phenomena in a "risk of faith" that allows people to act "in the face of uncertainty and unpredictability" on the basis of a higher order of reality.[15] Peter Berger specifies that such faith is an affirmation of the sacred, which acts as a doorway to a more certain kind of truth.[16] Louis Dupré prefers to avoid the term "sacred" but integrates elements of both Berger's and Bellah's definitions in his description of religion as "a commitment to the transcendent as to *another* reality."[17] In all of these cases there is a tension between this imperfect, disorderly world and a perfected, orderly one to be found at a higher, transcendent state or in a cumulative moment in time. As Durkheim, whose thought is fundamental to each of these thinkers, was adamant in observing, religion has a more encompassing force than can be suggested by any dichotomization of the sacred and the profane. To Durkheim, the religious point of view includes both the notion that there is such a dichotomy and the belief that the sacred side will always, ultimately, reign supreme.[18]

From this perspective, both religion and secular nationalism are about order. They are therefore potential rivals. Either could claim to be the guarantor of orderliness within a society; either could claim to be the ultimate authority for social order. Such claims carry with them an extraordinary degree of power, for contained within them is the right to give moral sanction for life and death decisions, including the right to kill. When either nationalism or religion assumes this role by itself, it reduces the other to a peripheral social role.

The rivalry has historical roots. Earlier in history it was often religion that denied moral authority to secular politicians, but in recent centuries, especially in the West, it has been the other way around. Political authorities now attempt to monopolize the authority to sanction violence. They asserted this authority long before the advent of the nation-state, but usually in collusion with religious authority, not in defiance of it. What is unusual about the modern period is how victorious the secular state has been in denying the right of religious authorities to be ultimate moral arbiters. In the modern state, the state alone is given the moral power to kill (albeit for limited purposes, military defense, police protection, and capital punishment). Yet all of the rest of the state's power to persuade and to shape the social order is derived from these fundamental powers. In Max Weber's view, the monopoly over legitimate violence in a society is the very definition of a state. But the secular state did not always enjoy a monopoly over this right,

and in challenging its authority, today's religious activists, wherever they assert themselves around the world, reclaim the traditional right of religious authorities to say when violence is moral and when it is not.

Religious conflict is one indication of the power of religion to sanction killing. The parties in such an encounter may command a greater degree of loyalty than contestants in a purely political war. Their interests can subsume national interests. In some cases a religious battle may preface the attempt to establish a new religious state. It is interesting to note, in this regard, that the best known incidents of religious violence throughout the contemporary world have occurred in places where it is difficult to define or accept the idea of a nation-state. Palestine, the Punjab, and Sri Lanka are the most obvious examples, but the revolutions in Iran, Nicaragua, Afghanistan, Tajikistan, and the countries of eastern Europe also concern themselves with what the state should be like and what elements of society should lead it. In these instances, religion provides the basis for a new national consensus and a new kind of leadership.

Modern religious activists are thereby reasserting the role of religion in most traditional societies where religion, as Donald E. Smith puts it, "answers the question of political legitimacy."[19] In the modern West, this legitimacy is provided by nationalism, a secular nationalism. But even here, religion continues to wait in the wings, a potential challenge to the nationalism based on secular assumptions. Perhaps nothing indicates the continuing challenge of religion more than the persistence of religious politics in American society, including most recently the rise of politically active religious fundamentalists in the 1980s and the potency of the Christian right in the 1992 and 1994 national elections. Religion is ready to demonstrate that, like secular nationalism, it can provide a faith in the unitary nature of a society that will authenticate both political rebellion and political rule.

Competition between Religion and Secular Nationalism in the West

Putting aside the recent electoral victories of America's religious right, secular nationalism has largely been the victor in the competition between religion and secular nationalism that has been going on in the West for several centuries now. At one time, the medieval church possessed "many aspects of a state," as one historian put it, and it had commanded more political power "than most of its secular rivals."[20] Perhaps more important, religion provided the legitimacy on which the power of monarchy and civil order was based. By the mid-nineteenth century, however, the Christian church had ceased to have much influence on European or American politics. The church—the great medieval monument of Christendom with all its social and political panoply—had been replaced by churches, various denominations of Protestantism and a largely depoliticized version of Roman Catholicism. These churches functioned like religious clubs, voluntary associations for the spiritual edification of individuals in their leisure time, rarely cognizant of the social and political world around them.

Secular nationalism began to replace religion several centuries ago as the ideological agent of political legitimacy. But the form in which we know it today—as the ideological ally of the nation-state—did not appear in England and American until the eighteenth century. Only by then had the nation-state taken root deeply enough to nurture an ideological loyalty of its own, unassisted by religious or ethnic identifications, and only by then had the political and military apparatus of the nation-state expanded sufficiently to encompass a large geographic region. Prior to that time, as Giddens explains, "the administrative reach" of the political center was so limited that rulers did not govern in "the modern sense."[21] Until the advent of the nation-state, the authority of a political center did not systematically and equally cover an entire population, so that what appeared to be a single homogeneous polity was in fact a congeries of fiefdoms. The further one got from the center of power, the weaker was the grip of centralized political influence, until at the periphery whole sections of a country might exist as a political no man's land. Therefore, one should speak of countries prior to the modern nation-state as having frontiers rather than boundaries.

The changes of the late eighteenth and nineteenth centuries included the development of the technical ability to knit a country together through roads, rivers, and other means of transportation and communication, the economic ability to do so through an increasingly integrated market structure, an emerging world economic system which was based on the building blocks of nation-states, the development of mass education which socialized each generation of youth into a homogeneous society, and the emergence of parliamentary democracy as a system of representation and an expression of the will of people. The glue that held all these changes together was secular nationalism: the notion that individuals naturally associate with the people and place of their ancestral birth in an economic and political system identified with a nation-state. Secular nationalism was thought to be not only natural, but also universally applicable and morally right. Although it was regarded almost as a natural law, secular nationalism was ultimately viewed as an expression of neither god nor nature but of the will of a nation's citizens. The ideas of John Locke about the origins of a civil community and the "social contract" theories of Jean-Jacques Rousseau required very little commitment to religious belief. Although they allowed for a divine order that made the rights of humans possible, their ideas did not directly buttress the power of the church and its priestly administrators, and they had the effect of taking religion—at least church religion—out of public life.

At the same time religion was becoming less political, secular nationalism was becoming more religious. It became clothed in romantic and xenophobic images that would have startled its Enlightenment forbears. The French Revolution, the model for much of the nationalist fervor that developed in the nineteenth century, infused a religious zeal into revolutionary democracy, which took on the trappings of church religion in the priestly power meted out to its demagogic leaders and in the slavish devotion to what it called "the temple of reason." According to Alexis de Tocqueville, the French Revolution "assumed many of the aspects of a religious revolution."[22] The American Revolution also had a religious side: many of its leaders had been influenced by eighteenth-century Deism, a religion of science and natural law which was "devoted to exposing [church] religion to the light of knowledge."[23] As in France, American nationalism developed its own religious characteristics, blending the ideals of secular nationalism and the symbols of Christianity into a "civil religion."

The nineteenth century fulfilled de Tocqueville's prophecy that the "strange religion" of secular nationalism would, "like Islam, overrun the whole world with its apostles, militants, and martyrs."[24] It was spread throughout the world with an almost missionary zeal and was shipped to the newly colonized areas of Asia, Africa, and Latin America as part of the ideological freight of colonialism. It became the ideological partner of what came to be known as "nation-building." As the colonial governments provided their colonies with the political and economic infrastructures to turn territories into nation-states, the ideology of secular nationalism emerged as a by-product of the colonial nation-building experience. As it had in the West in previous centuries, secular nationalism in the colonized countries in the nineteenth and twentieth centuries came to represent one side of a great encounter between two vastly different ways of perceiving the sociopolitical order and the relationship of the individual to the state: one informed by religion, the other by a notion of a secular compact.

In the mid-twentieth century, when the colonial powers retreated, they left behind the geographical boundaries they had drawn and the political institutions they had fashioned. Created as administrative units of the Ottoman, Hapsburg, French, and British empires, the borders of most Third World nations continued after independence, even if they failed to follow the natural divisions among ethnic and linguistic communities. By the second half of the twentieth century, it seemed as if the cultural goals of the colonial era had been reached: although the political ties were severed, the new nations retained all the accoutrements of westernized countries. The only substantial empire to remain virtually intact until 1990 was the Soviet Union. It was based on a different vision of political order, of course, in which international socialism was supposed to replace a network of capitalist nations. Yet the perception of many members of the Soviet states was that their nations were not so much integral units in a new internationalism as they were colonies in a secular Russian version of imperialism. This perception became dramatically clear after the breakup of the Soviet Union and its sphere of influence in the early 1990s, when old ethnic and national loyalties sprang to the fore.

Competition between Religion and Secular Nationalism in the Third World

The new nations that emerged as the "Third World" in the middle of the twentieth century had to confront the same competition between religion and nationalism as the West has had to confront, but in a very short period of time, and they simultaneously had to contend with the political by-products of colonial rule. If accommodating religion was difficult for the West, efforts to bridle religion in the new nations were a thousand times more problematic. There, the political competition of religion was much more obvious. Given religious histories that were part of national heritages, religious institutions that were sometimes the nations' most effective systems of communication, and religious leaders who were often more devoted, efficient, and intelligent than government officials, religion could not be ignored. The attempts to accommodate it, however, have not always been successful * * *

*   *   *

A New Synthesis: The Religious Nation-State

Religious activists are well aware that, if a nation starts with the premise of secular nationalism, religion is often made marginal to the political order. This marginality is especially onerous from many revolutionary religious perspectives, * * * because they regard the two ideologies as unequal: the religious one is far superior. Rather than to start with secular nationalism, they prefer to begin with religion.

The implication of this way of speaking is not that religion is antithetical to nationalism, but that religious rather than secular nationalism is the appropriate premise on which to build a nation, even a modern nation-state. In fact, virtually every reference to nationhood used by religious nationalists assumes that the modern nation-state is the only way in which a nation can be construed.

Although the link between religion and nationalism has historical precedents, the present attempt to forge an alliance between religion and the modern democratic nation-state is a new development in the history of nationalism, and it immediately raises the question whether it is possible: whether what we in the West think of as a modern nation—a unified, democratically controlled system of economic and political administration—can in fact be accommodated within religion. Many western observers would automatically answer no. Even as acute an interpreter of modern society as Giddens regarded most religious cultures as at best a syncreticism

between "tribal cultures, on the one hand, and modern societies, on the other."[25]

Yet by Giddens' own definition of a modern nation-state, postrevolutionary Iran would qualify: the Islamic revolution in Iran has solidified not just a central power but a systematic control over the population that is more conducive to nationhood than the monarchical political order of the shah. A new national entity came into being that was quite different from both the polity under the old Muslim rulers and the nation the shah ineptly attempted to build. The shah dreamed of creating Ataturk's Turkey in Iran and bringing to his country what he perceived as the instant modernity brought to Turkey by Ataturk. Ironically, Khomeini—along with his integrative religious ideology and his grass-roots network of mullahs—ultimately accomplished the unity and national organization that the shah had sought.

A similar claim is made in India, where Hindu nationalists are emphatic on the point that "Hindutva," as they call Hindu national culture, is the defining characteristic of Indian nationalism. In Sri Lanka, according to one Sinhalese writer, "it is clear that the unifying, healing, progressive principle" that held together the entity known as Ceylon throughout the years has always been "the Buddhist faith."[26] The writer goes on to say that religion in Sri Lanka continues to provide the basis for a "liberating nationalism" and that Sinhalese Buddhism is "the only patriotism worthy of the name, worth fighting for or dying for."[27] Similar sentiments are echoed in movements of religious nationalism in Egypt, Israel, and elsewhere in the world.

In these efforts to accommodate modern politics, has religion compromised its purity? Some religious leaders think that it has. In favoring the nation-state over a particular religious congregation as its major community of reference, religion loses the exclusivity held by smaller, subnational religious communities, and the leaders of those communities lose some of their autonomy. Many religious leaders are therefore suspicious of religious nationalism. Among them are religious utopians who would rather build their own isolated political societies than to deal with the problems of a whole nation, religious liberals who are satisfied with the secular nation-state the way it is, and religious conservatives who would rather ignore politics altogether. Some Muslims have accused Khomeini of making Islam into a political ideology and reducing it to the terms of modern politics. Moreover, as Bernard Lewis claims, most Islamic rebellions are aimed in the opposite direction: to shed Islam of the alien idea of the nation-state.[28] Yet, even if that is their aim, one of the curious consequences of their way of thinking is the appropriation of many of the most salient elements of modern nationhood into an Islamic frame of reference. Rather than ridding Islam of the nation-state, they too have created a new synthesis.

Modern movements of religious nationalism, therefore, are subjects of controversy within both religious and secular circles. The marriage between religious faith and the nation-state is an interesting turn in modern history, frought with dangers, for even if it is possible, the radical accommodation of religion to nationalism may not necessarily be a good thing. A merger of the absolutism of nationalism with the absolutism of religion might create a rule so vaunted and potent that it might destroy itself and its neighbors as well. The actions of religious terrorists in the 1980s and early 1990s in South Asia and the Middle East warrant some of those fears. When a society's secular state and its religious community are both strong and respected, the power of life and death that is commanded by any single absolute authority—be it secular or religious—may be held tenuously in check. Without that balance, an absolute power of the worst sort could claim its most evil deeds to be legitimate moral duties. The revolutionary religious movements that have emerged in many parts of the world in the 1980s and 1990s exhibit some of those dangers—as well as many of the more hopeful aspects—of the religious nationalists' synthesis between the two great ideologies of order.

*   *   *

NOTES

1. For the optimistic point of view that liberal democracy has triumphed, see Francis Fukuyama. "The End of History," *The National Interest*, 16 (Summer 1989). 3–18: and *The End of History and the Last Man* (New York: The Free Press, 1992), pp. xi–xxiii.

2. Samuel P. Huntington, "The Clash of Civilizations?," *Foreign Affairs*, 72 (Summer 1993), 2–11: and "If Not Civilizations, What? Paradigms of the Post-Cold War World," *Foreign Affairs*, 72 (November—December 1993). 186–94.

3. See Mark Juergensmeyer. "Why Religious Nationalists Are Not Fundamentalists." *Religion*, 23 (Spring 1993).

4. See Mark Juergensmeyer. "The Logic of Religious Violence," in David C. Rapoport, ed., *Inside Terrorist Organizations* (London: Frank Cass. 1988), pp. 172–93: "What the Bhikkhu Said: Reflections on the Rise of Militant Religious Nationalism." *Religion*, 20 (1990), 53–75: and *The New Cold War? Religious Nationalism Confronts the Secular State* (Berkeley: University of California Press, 1993). Some of the book's arguments and revised segments from it have been incorporated into this essay.

5. Abolhassan Banisadr, *The Fundamental Principles and Precepts of Islamic Government* (Lexington: Mazda Publishers, 1981), p. 40.

6. Interview with Dr. Essem el Arian. Member of the National Assembly, Cairo, January 11, 1989; Sheik Ahmed Yassin, Gaza, January 14, 1989; and Bhikkhu Udawawala Chandrananda, Kandy, Sri Lanka, January 5, 1991.

7. Huntington, "Clash of Civilizations?"

8. Benedict Anderson, *Imagined Communities: Reflections on the Origin and Spread of Nationalism* (London: Verso, 1983); and Ninian Smart, *Worldviews: Crosscultural Explorations of Human Beliefs* (New York: Scribner's, 1983).

9. Karl Marx and Friedrich Engels, *The German Ideology* (New York: International Publishers, 1939); Karl Mannheim, *Ideology and Utopia* (New York: Harcourt, Brace and World, 1936); David Apter, ed., *Ideology and Discontent* (New York: The Free Press, 1964); and Chaim I. Waxman, ed., *The End of Ideology Debate* (New York: Simon and Schuster, 1964).

10. Destutt de Tracy, *Elements of Ideology*, in Richard H. Cox. *Ideology, Politics, and Political Theory* (Belmont: Wadsworth Publishing Company, 1969), p. 17.

11. Clifford Geertz, "Ideology as a Cultural System," in Apter, ed.

12. Max Weber, "Politics as a Vocation," in Hans H. Gerth and C. Wright Mills, eds., *From Max Weber: Essays in Sociology* (New York: Oxford University Press, 1946), p. 78. Regarding the state's monopoly on violence, see John Breuilly, *Nationalism and the State* (Manchester: Manchester University Press, 1982); and Anthony D. Smith, *Theories of Nationalism* (London: Duckworth, 1971).

13. Anthony Giddens, *A Contemporary Critique of Historical Materialism, Volume Two: The Nation-State and Violence* (Berkeley: University of California Press, 1985), p. 219.

14. Clifford Geertz, "Religion as a Cultural System," reprinted in William A. Lessa and Evon Z. Vogt, eds., *Reader in Comparative Religion: An Anthropological Approach*, 3rd ed. (New York: Harper and Row, 1972), p. 168.

15. Robert Bellah, "Transcendence in Contemporary Piety," in Donald R. Cutler, *The Religious Situation: 1969* (Boston: Beacon Press, 1969), p. 907.

16. Peter Berger, *The Heretical Imperative* (New York: Doubleday, 1980), p. 38. See also Peter Berger, *Sacred Canopy: Elements of a Sociological Theory of Religion* (Garden City: Doubleday, 1967).

17. Louis Dupré, *Transcendent Selfhood: The Loss and Rediscovery of the Inner Life* (New York: Seabury Press, 1976), p. 26. For a discussion of Berger's and Dupré's definitions, see Mary Douglas, "The Effects of Modernization on Religious Change," *Daedalus*, 111 (Winter 1982), 1–19.

18. Émile Durkheim, *The Elementary Forms of the Religious Life* (London: George Allen and Unwin, 1976), pp. 38–39.

19. Donald E. Smith, ed., *Religion, Politics, and Social Change in the Third World: A Sourcebook* (New York: The Free Press, 1971), p. 11.

20. Joseph Strayer, *Medieval Statecraft and the Perspectives of History* (Princeton: Princeton University Press, 1971), p. 323.

21. Giddens, *Nation-State*, p. 4.

22. Alexis de Tocqueville, *The Old Regime and the French Revolution* (New York: Doubleday Anchor Books, 1955), p. 11. See also John McManners, *The French Revolution and the Church* (Westport: Greenwood Press, 1969).

23. Ernst Cassirer, *The Philosophy of the Enlightenment* (Boston: Beacon Press, 1955), p. 171. Among the devotees of Deism were Thomas Jefferson, Benjamin Franklin, and other founding fathers of America.

24. De Tocqueville, *The Old Regime*, p. 13.

25. Giddens, *The Nation-State*, p. 71.

26. D. C. Vejayavardhana, *The Revolt in the Temple: Composed to Commemorate 2,500 Years of the Land, the Race, and the Faith* (Colombo: Sinha Publications, 1953), reprinted in Smith, ed., *Religion, Politics and Social Change*, p. 105.

27. Vejayavardhana, *The Revolt in the Temple*, p. 105.

28. Bernard Lewis, *The Political Language of Islam* (Chicago: University of Chicago Press, 1988).

JEFFREY HERBST

WAR AND THE STATE IN AFRICA

Most analyses assume that in Africa, as elsewhere, states will eventually become strong. But this may not be true in Africa, where states are developing in a fundamentally new environment. Lessons drawn from the case of Europe show that war is an important cause of state formation that is missing in Africa today. The crucial role that war has played in the formation of European states has long been noted. Samuel P. Huntington argued that "war was the great stimulus to state building," and Charles Tilly went so far as to claim that "war made the state, and the state made war."[1] Similarly, two of the most successful states in the Third World today, South Korea and Taiwan, are largely "warfare" states that have been molded, in part, by the near constant threat of external aggression. However, studies of political development and state consolidation in Africa and many other parts of the Third World have all but ignored the important role that war can play in political development.

The role of war has not been examined because the vast majority of states in Africa and elsewhere in the world gained independence without having to resort to combat and have not faced a security threat since independence.[2] Those scholars who have analyzed the military in the developing world have studied the armed forces' role in economic and political processes but have not examined the changes that war could potentially effect on a state.[3] Studying the military and studying warfare are not the same, especially in the area of state consolidation, because warfare has independent effects on economic policies, administrative structures, and the citizenry's relationship with the state that

have very little to do with the military.[4] Finally, beyond the usual problem of trying to study the impact of a factor that is missing, there is a less excusable normative bias which has sometimes prevented students of politics from examining the effects of war. The question of whether it is only possible to create a nation out of "blood and iron" is apparently one that many analysts find too disturbing to examine.[5]

Comparison of the European case with that of Africa is therefore crucial to understanding whether the analogy holds. War in Europe played an important role in the consolidation of many now-developed states: war caused the state to become more efficient in revenue collection; it forced leaders to dramatically improve administrative capabilities; and it created a climate and important symbols around which a disparate population could unify. While there is little reason to believe that war would have exactly the same domestic effects in Africa today as it did in Europe several centuries ago, it is important to ask if developing countries can accomplish in times of peace what war enabled European countries to do. I conclude that they probably cannot because fundamental changes in economic structures and societal beliefs are difficult, if not impossible, to bring about when countries are not being disrupted or under severe external threat.

The next section of this article outlines how war affected state formation in Europe, with particular attention to two crucial developments: the creation of centralized and efficient structures to collect taxes, and the development of nationalism. I then compare the European experience of state-building through warfare to the relative peace that Africa has experienced since the 1960s. While African states have benefited from peace, their development has been stunted by the very problems that war helped European countries to solve. I

From *International Security* 14, no. 4. (Spring 1990), pp. 117–39.

then evaluate the possibilities that African states might develop strategies to solve these fundamental problems in times of peace. I conclude that some states will probably be unsuccessful in finding ways of building the state in times of peace and will therefore remain permanently weak. Accordingly, the international community will have to develop non-traditional policies for helping a new brand of states: those that will continue to exist but that will not develop. Other states, perceiving that peace locks them into a permanently weak position, may be tempted to use war as a means of resolving their otherwise intractable problems of state consolidation.

Effects of War on State Consolidation: The European Case

It is instructive to look at war's impact on European societies because, as will be noted below, war in Europe helped alleviate some of the problems that affect African countries today. At the most basic level, war in Europe acted as a filter whereby weak states were eliminated and political arrangements that were not viable either were reformed or disappeared. Weak states do exist in Europe today—Belgium is one example—but the near-constant threat of war did prompt most states to become stronger to survive. The contrast between this evolutionary development and the current situation in the Third World, where even states that are largely dependent on foreign aid will continue to exist for the foreseeable future, is dramatic. It is, of course, important not to generalize too much because war had many different effects over time, and even in the same period states reacted in a variety of ways to external threats. However, war did affect the ability of European states to increase taxation and contributed to the forging of national identities in many countries. It is therefore important to examine the potential impact of external threat to better understand state consolidation in the Third World.

Taxes

Perhaps the most noticeable effect of war in European history was to cause the state to increase its ability to collect significantly more revenue with greater efficiency and less public resistance. Given the freedom of European states to attack each other, those states that could raise money quickly could successfully threaten their neighbors with a war that might lead to significant damage or even complete destruction. Richard Bean writes, "Once the power to tax had been successfully appropriated by any one sovereign, once he had used that power to bribe or coerce his nobility into acquiescence, that state could face all neighboring states with the choice of being conquered or of centralizing authority and raising taxes."[6] While success in war depends on many factors including technology, tactics, and morale of the troops, raising sufficient revenue was a necessary condition to prevent defeat. States that did not raise sufficient revenue for war perished. As Michael Mann notes, "A state that wished to survive had to increase its extractive capacity to pay for professional armies and/or navies. Those that did not would be crushed on the battlefield and absorbed into others—the fate of Poland, of Saxony, of Bavaria in [the seventeenth and eighteenth centuries]. No European states were continuously at peace. It is impossible to escape the conclusion that a peaceful state would have ceased to exist even more speedily than the militarily inefficient actually did."[7]

War affects state finances for two reasons. First, it puts tremendous strains on leaders to find new and more regular sources of income. While rulers may recognize that their tax system is inadequate, a war may be the only thing that forces them to expend the necessary political capital and undertake the coercion required to gain more revenue. For instance, in Mann's study of taxation in England between 1688 and 1815, he finds that there were six major jumps in state revenue and that each corresponds with the beginning of a war.[8] The association between the need to fight and the need to collect revenue is perhaps clearest in Prussia, where the main tax collection agency was called the General War Commissariat.[9]

Second, citizens are much more likely to acquiesce to increased taxation when the nation is at war, because a threat to their survival will overwhelm other concerns they might have about increased taxation. In fact, taxation for a war can be thought of as a "lumpy" collective good: not only must the population pay to get the good, but it must also pay a considerable amount more than the current level of taxation, because a small increase in revenue is often not enough to meet the new security threat facing the state.[10] In this way, taxation for a war is like taxation for building a bridge: everyone must pay to build the bridge and a small increase in revenue will not be enough, because half a bridge, like fighting half a war, is useless.

Thus, war often causes a "ratchet effect" whereby revenue increases sharply when a nation is fighting but does not decline to the *ante bellum* level when hostilities have ceased.[11] Once governments have invested the sunken costs in expanding tax collection systems and routinized the collection of new sources of revenue, the marginal costs of continuing those structures are quite low and the resources they collect can be used for projects that will enhance the ruling group's support.

While it is not a universal rule, war in other societies at other times often played the same kind of role that war did in Europe. For instance, Joseph Smaldone writes in his study of the Sokoto Caliphate (in what is now Nigeria) between 1500 and 1800:

> War was the principal instrument for the establishment and extension of political authority over subject people and foreign territory, and for the organization, maintenance, and reinforcement of that authority. The demands of perennial war evoked institutions to subordinate the sectors of society crucial to the interests of these militarized polities. The permanent requirement to mobilize human and material resources for military pur-

> poses [i.e., taxation] intensified tendencies toward the monopolization of power and the elaboration of auxiliary institutions of social control.[12]

Similarly, the South Korean and Taiwanese states have been able to extract so many resources from their societies in part because the demands to be constantly vigilant provoked the state into developing efficient mechanisms for collecting resources and controlling dissident groups.[13] A highly extractive state also could cloak demands for greater resources in appeals for national unity in the face of a determined enemy.

Nationalism

War also had a major impact on the development of nationalism of Europe. Indeed, the presence of a palpable external threat may be the strongest way to generate a common association between the state and the population. External threats have such a powerful effect on nationalism because people realize in a profound manner that they are under threat because of who they are as a nation; they are forced to recognize that it is only as a nation that they can successfully defeat the threat. Anthony Giddens recounts the effects of World War I: "The War canalized the development of states' sovereignty, tying this to citizenship and to nationalism in such a profound way that any other scenario [of how the international system would be ordered] came to appear as little more than idle fantasy."[14] Similarly, Michael Howard notes the visceral impact of wars on the development of nationalism throughout Europe:

> Self-identification as a Nation implies almost by definition alienation from other communities, and the most memorable incidents in the group-memory consisted in conflict with and triumph over other communities. France *was* Marengo, Austerlitz and Jena: military triumph set the seal on the new-found national consciousness. Britain *was* Trafalgar—but it had been a nation for four hundred years, since those earlier battles Crecy and Agincourt. Russia *was* the triumph of 1812. Germany *was* Gravelotte and Sedan.[15]

In Europe there was an almost symbiotic relationship between the state's extractive capacity and nationalism: war increased both as the population was convinced by external threat that they should pay more to the state, and as, at the same time, the population united around common symbols and memories that were important components of nationalism. Fighting wars may be the only way whereby it is possible to have people pay more taxes and at the same time feel more closely associated with the state.

The Absence of Interstate War in the Modern Era

While trying to study the chaos caused by administrative disintegration, the forceful crushing of ethnic challenges, and large-scale human rights abuses, many scholars have generally assumed that poor countries today face even more external challenges than European states did in their formative periods.[16] In fact, since the end of the Second World War, very few Third World states have fought interstate wars of the type that affected the evolution of European states. The few Third World interstate wars that have occurred (e.g., India-Pakistan, Iran-Iraq, China-Vietnam) have obscured the fact that the vast majority of Third World states most of the time do not face significant external threats. States like Israel, South Korea, or Taiwan, where national survival has been a real consideration in national politics, are exceptional and even these countries have survived intact.

Even in Africa, the continent seemingly destined for war given the colonially-imposed boundaries and weak political authorities, there has not been one involuntary boundary change since the dawn of the independence era in the late 1950s, and very few countries face even the prospect of a conflict with their neighbors. Most of the conflicts in Africa that have occurred were not, as in Europe, wars of conquest that threatened the existence of other states, but conflicts over lesser issues that were resolved without threatening the existence of another state. For instance, Tanzania invaded Uganda in 1979 to overthrow Idi Amin, not to conquer Uganda. Similarly, the war in the Western Sahara is a colonial question, not a conflict between independent states. Even South Africa's destabilization efforts against its neighbors are primarily attempts to influence the policies of the majority-ruled countries, not to change the borders of the region. Lesotho or Swaziland would not exist today if South Africa had any real territorial ambitions. In the few conflicts that did have the potential to threaten fundamentally the existence of states—Somalia's attempt to invade Ethiopia in the 1970s and Libya's war against Chad in the 1970s and 1980s—the aggressor did not succeed.[17]

African states have seldom fought interstate wars and the continent has not witnessed significant boundary changes, because independent leaders have continued the system of boundary maintenance that the colonial powers first developed to regulate the scramble for Africa in the late 1800s.[18] African leaders recognized in the early 1960s that a potentially large number of groups would want to secede from the states they are presently in, to join others or create entirely new ones. In order to prevent the continent from being thrown into the chaos of large-scale boundary changes in which the stability and integrity of any state could be threatened, they created a system of explicit norms, propounded by the Organization of African Unity in 1963, which declared any change in the inherited colonial boundaries to be illegitimate. Most of the continent has, accordingly, refused to recognize boundary changes (e.g., Biafra, Eritrea) even where the principle of self-determination might have led them to do so. This system has been successful in preserving African national boundaries and has so far deterred almost all countries from initiating the kind of conquest wars that were so common in European history. The system that maintained the inherited borders as inviolate was strengthened somewhat inadvertently, because two of the largest states on the continent (Nigeria and Zaire), which could conceivably have threatened their much smaller neighbors, faced significant secessionist threats (from the Ibo and Kataganese respectively) and therefore worked resolutely to strengthen the norm that the borders should not be changed.

The stability of new states, especially in Africa, is a remarkable development given that the vast majority of the over one hundred countries in the Third World that have gained their independence since 1945 are poor, have weak administrative structures, and consist of populations that are splintered along regional or ethnic lines. In other words, they are precisely the kind of states that before 1945 were routinely invaded and taken over by stronger states in their region or by external powers. Yet, very few states in the Third World, despite their evident military and political weaknesses, face any significant external threat.

In contrast, Tilly estimates, the "enormous majority" of states in Europe failed. Peace was the exception and long periods with no major fighting were almost unknown, as for centuries weak states were routinely defeated and populations regularly absorbed by foreign rulers.[19] The psychology of Europe in its formative centuries, where state survival was a very real issue of constant concern to leaders, is so different from the outlook facing Third World leaders today as to suggest that there has been a fundamental change in the survival prospects of weak states and that control of territory is no longer correlated with military power.[20]

Problems of State Consolidation in Africa

African states face numerous problems in their efforts to consolidate power. They are poor, short of trained manpower, and confront societies that are often fragmented and have little orientation to the state as a whole. Many other Third World nations face these same problems although they are often most extreme in Africa, given the poverty of the continent and the fragility of the states. Elites can come to power but, given the precariousness of control in countries where rules governing leadership and succession have not been institutionalized, they may be displaced. Once they lose power, or are prevented from gaining it, ambitious politicians have no other opportunity to accumulate wealth or power because the state controls the badges of status and many of the free-floating resources in the economy, such as they are.[21] Even when they do control the apex of the state, elites may feel that because of their country's vulnerability to exogenous shocks (e.g., sudden sharp drops in the price of their raw material exports) and the presence of sophisticated multinational enterprises and well-connected minority groups (e.g., Lebanese in West Africa, Indians in East Africa), they are not really in control of their own destiny and therefore are vulnerable. As a result of their gross insecurities, these "lame Leviathans"[22] try desperately to control ever-greater parts of society through outright ownership or regulation. However, since they are weak, their efforts are almost inevitably clumsy, heavy-handed, and authoritarian.

Therefore, although the average state in Africa compared to other states is small (as measured by government spending as a percentage of gross domestic product [GDP],[23] it appears to be too large because its clumsy extractive efforts cause so much damage compared to the benefits that it delivers. Thus arises the image of so many African states as "overdeveloped" or "swollen."[24] The problems confronted by states in Africa can be illustrated by comparing their experience with European states in two areas where war had a significant impact: the state's ability to extract resources through taxes, and the degree of nationalism in the countries south of the Sahara.

A classic example of how weak state power causes the state to institute desperate and self-defeating economic policies is in the area of government revenue. Government revenue poses a major problem for all African states and many others in the Third World. These states are desperately short of revenue to fund even minimal state services (e.g., pay nurses' salaries, buy books for schools, supply transport for agricultural extension services) that their populations have long been promised. In addition to these recurrent costs, Third World countries are in need of more extensive and more efficient tax systems because the process of development requires large expenditures on infrastructure to promote economic activity throughout the country and to handle the ramifications of development, especially the large expenses incurred by urbanizing countries.[25] W. Arthur Lewis estimates that the public sector in Third World countries should be spending on the order of 20 percent of GDP on services, exclusive of defense and debt repayment.[26] However, when defense (2.5 percent of GDP) and debt repayments (3.4 percent of GDP) are subtracted, the average African country spends only 15.7 percent of its GDP on all government functions.[27] While these figures are only rough estimates given the problems associated with African economic statistics, they do illustrate the extent of the fiscal crisis facing African states.

Due to the weakness of administrative and statistical structures in Africa, many governments rely on taxation of foreign trade, because imports and exports must physically pass through a relatively small number of border posts that can be easily manned. Thus, the average African state depends on revenue from tariffs for 20.5 percent of total revenue, compared to all developing countries which, on average, gain 12.9 percent of their revenue from tariffs, and industrialized countries where tariffs account for only 1.3 percent of total revenue.[28]

Unfortunately, funding the state through indirect taxes on foreign trade damages national economies because leaders are compelled to erect ever-greater administrative controls on imports. These tariffs promote corruption, smuggling and, most importantly, over-valued exchange rates, because governments grow to rely on administrative controls rather than the market to regulate imports. Overvalued exchange rates in turn lead to wide-spread damage within poorer economies as exporters are universally hurt, the population is encouraged to become dependent on imported food, and black markets quickly develop to take advantage of distorted prices.[29] Beyond the immediate damage caused by a tax system dependent on imports and exports, this *type* of tax system is particularly inappropriate for Third World countries. These countries need guarantees of slow and steady increases in government revenue above the rate of economic growth in order to accomplish the tasks crucial to development: build transport and communications systems, establish utilities, and create educational systems.[30]

Another major problem facing leaders in Africa is the absence of a strong popular identity with the state. The lack of a popular consensus over national purpose both aggravates the state's clumsy efforts to extract resources and is itself exacerbated by an insecure, authoritarian elite. Indeed, the picture of African societies widely accepted today is of populations trying desperately to escape the clutches of the state, rather than becoming more involved in it, and certainly not willing to pay more taxes to it.[31] Twenty-five years after "the nationalist period," there are few signs of nationalism in most African countries despite the now *pro forma* exhortations from propaganda organs to engage in state-building. Indeed, the majority of states still have difficulty creating viable symbols to attract the loyalties of their citizens.

Not surprisingly, therefore, there are today very few attempts in African countries to forge a national consensus on major issues, much less a national identity. For instance, most formulas to decrease inter-ethnic tension concentrate only on ameliorating the negative aspects of ethnic conflict by accomodating it through decentralized government structures and preferential policies.[32] However, formulas such as federalism often are inappropriate in countries where national institutions are not strong. Federalist solutions broke down in Sudan and Uganda, among other places, because the incentives for leaders to attempt to gain total control were much greater than the barriers posed by recently adopted institutional arrangements.[33] Moreover, no matter how well accommodationist formulas of intra-societal conflict work, almost everyone in Africa and elsewhere in the Third World would agree that a more basic national loyalty by all societal groups would still be desirable. However, the means by which to induce a disparate society to identify more with the nation-state are unknown in Africa and few in the current era are even attempting to speculate on how to develop a national consensus.

Difficulties of State Consolidation without War

War in Europe played such an important role in the evolution of the state mechanism and society's relationship with the state because it is extraordinarily difficult, outside times of crisis, to reform elemental parts of the governmental system, such as the means of taxation, or to effect a real change in national identity. For instance, since taxes are so consequential to every business decision, the tax system over time reflects a large number of political bargains made by the state with different interest groups. Often governments find it too politically difficult to provide direct subsidies to those they want to favor, so the tax system is a convenient backdoor to aid politically important groups without incurring opprobrium. The political bargains that constitute the tax system develop a momentum of their own because individuals and businesses base their future economic decisions on the incentives and disincentives in the existing tax code. Indeed, Joseph Schumpeter called the fiscal system "a collection of hard, naked facts" and claimed that "the spirit of a people, its cultural level, its social structure, the deeds its policy may prepare—all this and more is written in its fiscal history, stripped of all phrases."[34]

Therefore, even minor changes such as alterations in the level of taxation or shifts in the tax burden, as the United States and most Western European countries have made in the last few years, engender tremendous political battles. Not only the previously favored political groups but all those that simply followed the signals sent out by government will forcefully oppose fiscal reform. Greater changes in the nature of the tax system are even more difficult. Edward Ames' and Richard Rapp's conclusion that tax systems "last until the end of the government that instituted them" and that tax systems in some European countries survived "almost intact" from the thirteenth and fourteenth centuries until the late eighteenth century may be an exaggeration, but their conclusions suggest just how much inertia a particular system for collecting government revenue can develop over time.[35] Other than war, no type of crisis demands that the state increase taxes with such forcefulness, and few other situations would impel citizens to accept those demands, or at least not resist them as strongly as they otherwise might have. It is therefore hard to counter Tilly's argument that "the formation of standing armies provided the largest single incentive to extraction and the largest single means of state coercion over the long run of European state-making."[36]

Domestic security threats, of the type African countries face so often, may force the state to increase revenue; however, these crises are almost never as grave as the type of external threat the European states had to confront, because they do not threaten the very existence of the state. In addition, domestic conflicts result in fragmentation and considerable hostility among different segments of the population. As a result, the state does not necessarily achieve the greater revenue efficiency gains engendered by an external crisis. Indeed, in a civil war—as in Nigeria in the late 1960s—parts of the state are fighting against each other, which hardly promotes efficiency in tax collection. Public acceptance of tax increases, a crucial factor in allowing European states to extract greater resources in times of war, will be a much more complicated issue in civil disputes. As Mann notes, "the growth of the modern state, as measured by finances, is explained primarily not in domestic terms but in terms of geopolitical relations of violence."[37]

The obstacles posed by large peasant populations, significant nonmonetarized sectors, and widespread poverty are, of course, important contributors to the revenue crisis of the African state. However, these problems do not fully explain why poor states do not extract greater resources from society in a manner that is less economically harmful. Factors such as political will, administrative ability, and the population's willingness to be taxed—issues that can be affected by the decisions of political leaders—are also crucial in understanding why states are unable to achieve their potential level of taxation in a benign manner.[38] For instance, Margaret Levi successfully shows that in such diverse cases as republican Rome, France and England in the Middle Ages, eighteenth-century Britain, and twentieth-century Australia, levels of taxation were affected primarily by political constraints faced by rulers, despite the fact that most of these economies also posed significant barriers to increased tax collection.[39]

Nor has there been any success in developing means to cause the population to identify more with the state, other than fighting a war. Nationalism, which was never nearly as strong or widespread (especially outside the major cities) in Africa as many had thought, was palpable in the late colonial period because there was a "relevant other"—the colonialists—who could be easily identified as oppressors and around which a nominal national identity could be built.[40] However, since independence in most African countries, there has been no "relevant other" to oppose, so it has been extremely difficult to create nation-wide symbols of identity. There has therefore been no way of generating a national identity in Africa such as wars forged in Europe. Anthony Smith writes, "the central difficulty of 'nation-building' in much of Africa and Asia is

the lack of any shared historical mythology and memory on which state elites can set about 'building' the nation. The 'nation' [is built up] from the central fund of culture and symbolism and mythology provided by shared historical experiences."[41] The result is the anomie in most African countries today.

It could be argued that the lack of nationalism simply reflects the fact that African countries are artificial groupings of disparate peoples and therefore are not really nation-states. However, no "natural" nation-states are mature at birth with populations that have readily agreed to a central identity. Rather, the goal of those who want to create the nation-state is to convince different groups that they do, in fact, share a common identity. This is why even in Europe, which today seems to have nation-states that are more "natural" than Africa's, war had such a crucial role to play in the forging of common identities.

Indeed, the symbiotic relationship that war fostered in Europe between tax collection and nationalism is absent in Africa, precisely because there is no external threat to encourage people to acquiesce in the state's demands, and no challenge that causes them to respond as a nation. Instead, the African state's clumsy efforts at greater extraction are met by popular withdrawal rather than by a populace united around a common identity.

Of course, not all wars led to the strengthening of administrative institutions and greater nationalism. For example, Joseph Strayer notes that the Hundred Years War "was so exhausting for both sides that it discouraged the normal development of the apparatus of the state. There was a tendency to postpone structural reforms, to solve problems on an ad hoc basis rather than [to create] new agencies of government, to sacrifice efficiency for immediate results."[42] However, the Hundred Years War was exceptional because of its length and it therefore did not allow rulers to consolidate the gains usually achieved after facing a short period of external danger. Yet overall, the historical record suggests that war was highly efficient in promoting state consolidation in Europe, and that it would be much more difficult for states to accomplish the same tasks in peacetime.

Are There Peaceful Routes to State Consolidation?

Since African and other Third World countries need to transform important parts of their governmental systems, including their fiscal arrangements, and to promote nationalism, but do not have the traditional avenue of war to aid them, the immediate question is whether they can follow a path other than that adopted by Europe to consolidate state power and to develop new national identities to reduce the divisions between society and the state.

Once again it is interesting to focus on government revenue because the issue is so decisive in its own right and because tax systems are such a good reflection of the basic bargains in society. In an age with reduced levels of interstate war, African countries are faced with the problem of trying to increase the capacity of the state without being able to use wars to "ratchet up" the state's extractive ability. Given the evidence of European fiscal inertia, it is clear that it will be even more difficult to institute major reforms when states are operating in normal circumstances. The one clear chance African countries did have to institute major reforms was at independence, because at that moment political arrangements were in such flux that significant new initiatives could be undertaken. Indeed, some African countries (e.g., Mozambique, Angola) did make massive changes in their political economy (e.g., nationalization, collectivization); unfortunately, these particular reforms were economically ruinous because their socialist policies distorted economies even more than in most African countries. Once independence becomes the normal situation, as it has in African countries, it becomes extraordinarily difficult for leaders to make basic reforms of political arrangements, such as fiscal systems, which might hurt powerful groups. As Peter Bachrach and Morton Baratz noted in the context of American politics, dominant values, myths, rituals, and institutions quickly ossify so that crucial issues, such as fiscal reform, are not even on the agenda.[43] There appears to be no impetus from inside African countries to disrupt the current fiscal arrangements significantly. Indeed, much of the argument that there is currently a significant economic crisis in Africa, and that this crisis was caused by malfunctioning government policies, came from outside the continent.[44]

However, it could be argued that structural adjustment, pressed on African countries by the International Monetary Fund (IMF), the World Bank, and bilateral donors, could serve many state-making functions. As external actors dedicated to fundamental reforms of the economy and of the way the state operates, the IMF and other donors are not subject to the same rigidities that paralyze domestic reformers. The IMF and other actors who insist on fundamental reform could pressure African states for significant changes in their tax system. Demands from an external actor are similar to war, in that a leader can legitimately argue to its population that it has no choice in asking them to make very difficult sacrifices because it is under too much external pressure.

It would be a major mistake, however, to take too far the analogy between pressure from actors such as the IMF and the effects of war. For instance, war produced such spectacular gains in governmental efficiency because the state itself felt threatened. The IMF, or any other actor, cannot produce that feeling; indeed, structural adjustment has been least successful when it has tried to address the issues of how the state itself operates in areas such as public enterprises or fiscal arrangements.[45] The cost to the state itself in failing to adopt a structural adjustment program can be severe, but falls far short of what war would threaten. The IMF will never cause a state to disappear. At worst, a state can simply opt for the high cost of breaking off relations with the IMF.

Nor does external pressure of the type the Fund exerts produce any change in national identity. While leaders can occasionally rally people against the external threat posed by "imperialists," these sentiments usually are not long-lasting because the population may be unable to distinguish between international actors supposedly draining away the nation's funds during a structural adjustment exercise, and those national leaders who led their country into such a spectacular economic debacle. While Europe's leaders in previous centuries hardly treated their populations well by modern standards, it was usually unambiguous that people would be better off if they won the war than if they lost.

The prospects of structural adjustment fostering some kind of nationalism based on resisting foreigners is also limited because the IMF is not really a "relevant other" to a largely peasant population, and cannot induce changes in national consciousness of the type that wars in Europe produced. Unlike a war where the entire population was threatened because of its national identity, structural adjustment will help certain groups unambiguously (e.g., peasants who grow export crops), clearly hurt some (e.g., the urban population dependent on imported food), and have ambiguous effects on many others. Further, the intensity in shared experience that a war generates simply cannot be replicated by, say, protracted negotiations over the IMF's Extended Fund Facility.

The Likelihood of War in Africa

If internal reform seems improbable and there is no other external threat that can perform quite the same role as war, the question becomes whether at some point in the future African leaders will begin to see war as a potential avenue for state-making. Some leaders may look to war simply because they are truly concerned about the fate of the nation and see no other option. Others may not be concerned particularly with nation-building, but may find that their countries have suffered economic decline for so long that the possibilities for their own personal enrichment have become severely limited, and therefore will seek to seize the assets of other countries. So far, the system that has preserved the continent's boundaries has not been significantly tested because most leaders considered it obvious that they were better off with their inherited boundaries than they would be in a chaotic war situation where sovereignty or considerable territory might be lost. However, especially in the context of decades of economic decline, it is possible that some African leaders may recalculate the benefits of a peace that locks them into perpetual weakness. Instead, they may try to increase their state's extractive ability and divert their citizens from inter-ethnic squabbles by seizing upon the multitude of provocations, always present, to provoke a fight with neighboring states. Paul Colinvaux presents the extreme case for the prospects of interstate war in Africa:

> Africa holds the greatest possibilities for the aspiring general. . . . That there will be battles between African nations as they build their African continent in a new image is as certain as anything in history. For each country there must come times when wealth, hopes, ambitions, and numbers all rise together. It then needs only access to high-quality weapons for an aggression to be an attractive undertaking.[46]

If significant interstate wars break out when provocations are small but elites realize what war could do for the state and the nation, it would not be a strikingly new development. Rather, increased interstate warfare in Africa would simply be a return to the European norm. Whether war in Africa today would actually bring about the same kind of changes that it did in Europe centuries ago is unclear, but the possibility that leaders might become so desperate that they try in some fundamental way to alter the political rules under which their nations function should not be ignored.

Many are the possible provocations that could bring about significant interstate war in Africa. Certainly, there are plenty of border disputes and fragments of ethnic groups that need to be rescued from "foreign domination" to provide enough rationalization for hostile action against other African countries. Conflicts between language blocs (e.g., English versus French),[47] disputes over control of crucial rivers and railroads (especially given the number of land-locked countries), or the simple need to have more land for populations that double every twenty years provide many other potential reasons for war in Africa. More than a few African leaders might someday agree with Bismarck, a brilliant consolidator of a "new nation," on the only real way to unite a fragmented people:

> Prussia . . ., as a glance at the map will show, could no longer wear unaided on its long narrow figure the panoply which Germany required for its security; it must be equally distributed over all German peoples. We should get no nearer the goal by speeches, associations, decisions of majorities; we should be unable to avoid a serious contest, a contest which could only be settled by blood and iron.[48]

Although African countries had more or less equal defense capabilities at independence, the growing differential in force projection capabilities have led some to suggest that Africa will experience much greater resort to force in the future. Inventories of tanks and other armored vehicles as well as artillery, jet fighters, and naval craft have increased considerably throughout the continent. For instance, just in the period between 1966 and 1981, the number of countries in sub-Saharan Africa with tanks increased from two to eighteen, the number with field artillery went from seven to thirty-six, the number with light armor went from thirteen to thirty-six, and the number possessing jet aircraft went from six to twenty-one.[49] Countries such as Nigeria and Zaire have developed military capabilities that are far greater than their neighbors'. So far, the assurance of stability that is the central advantage of the current African state system has almost always been more attractive than whatever reasons African leaders may have had

to begin conflict with their neighbors. However, as President Nyerere of Tanzania showed when he invaded Uganda to depose Idi Amin, even strong proponents of African norms can be driven to interstate conflict if they believe that the costs of not acting are high enough. In the future, African leaders may find that, despite all their efforts, economic reform cannot progress and they cannot get their citizenry to unite around national symbols; it is conceivable that then the deterrent value of the norms of sovereignty may seem much less powerful than they do now. If these norms no longer provided protection to a large number of states, they would lose all meaning throughout the African continent. While the timing of these wars is not predictable, it should be obvious that the incentives that African leaders have to incite wars for the purposes of state-making are significant and may become much stronger in the future when the futility of domestic reform during times of business as usual, that is, peace, becomes clear.

The Permanently Weak State: A New Development

Much of this discussion has focused on the potential opportunities for African states that, in a European-type state system, might have engaged in battle, won (or at least not lost too badly), and thereby used war in order to further state building. However, it should be recognized that another class of states in Africa is directly affected by the current absence of war: those states that would have lost badly and would have been absorbed by the winners. These states range from those that are just geographic anachronisms left by colonialism (e.g., The Gambia, Djibouti), and very small states in the shadow of giants (e.g., Benin and Togo, close to Nigeria, or Rwanda and Burundi bordering Zaire), to those that simply lack significant resources for development or defense (e.g., Mali, Mauritania). In Europe during the formative centuries, disintegration of weak states like these was a regular occurrence.

Weak states that were defeated then became the poorer regions of richer countries, but at least they had a chance to share in the revenue and resources of a viable state. Yet the absence of a truly competitive state system that penalizes military weakness means that even those states that have no other prospects than long-term dependence on international aid will survive in their crippled form for the foreseeable future. Perhaps the only task of state consolidation that these otherwise weak states can accomplish is to physically capture their populations within the stable boundaries of the African state system.[50]

The presence of permanently weak states that will not be eliminated is a new development in international relations and one that poses novel development challenges. All theoretical work on development so far, no matter what the ideological predisposition of the authors, has implicitly assumed that somehow the nation-states as they currently exist are viable arrangements for development, if only they follow the proper strategies and receive enough help from the international community. This assumption was appropriate for the European context where centuries of war had eliminated states that simply were not viable. However, for Africa, whose states have not been tested by an international system that severely punishes political weakness, there is little reason to believe that many of them will be able to have a favorable enough geographic position, control adequate natural resources, gain the support of a significant portion of their populations, and construct strong administrative structures to ever develop. In the long term, these states may disappear if interstate wars finally do break out in Africa.

In the meantime, what is to be done with states that exist but cannot develop? It is far too early to write off any state's prospects. We have been wrong about the development prospects of many states both in Africa (where scholars were too optimistic) and elsewhere in the world, such as East Asia.[51] It would also be morally unacceptable simply to allow these countries to gradually slide from the world's view into a twilight of perpetual poverty because nature and history have been unkind to them. However, thought must be given to nontraditional alternatives for aid to states that in previous times would simply have been defeated and absorbed by stronger neighbors in a war. For instance, the international community might consider rewarding those countries in the Third World that have taken in economic migrants from non-viable states.[52] The West could consider providing additional aid to those countries willing to engage in some kind of regional integration to mitigate the problems of unchanging boundaries, much as countries that have adopted more rational economic policies have attracted greater aid from donors. The world may simply have to recognize that a certain number of countries are locked into non-viable positions, and develop a long-term approach to their welfare rather than acting surprised every time the inevitable famine or ecological disaster occurs.

Conclusion

It is important not to glorify war. The wars that Europe went through caused immense suffering for generations and wholesale destruction of some societies. Yet it is undeniable that out of this destruction emerged stronger political arrangements and more unified populations. No one would advocate war as a solution to Africa's political and economic problems, where the costs of interstate war could be even higher than in Europe. It is doubtful that, if African countries do start fighting wars, they will undergo exactly the same processes of state consolidation that war engendered in Europe. However, it should be recognized that there is very little evidence that African countries, or many others in the Third World, will be able to find peaceful ways to strengthen the state and develop national identities. In particular, the prospects for states that will not disappear, but simply cannot develop, must be examined. At the same time, we must recognize the possibility that some

African leaders in the future may come to believe that the costs of peace—limits on reform possibilities and a fragmented population—are so high that war may not seem like such an undesirable alternative. If African leaders do indeed make this calculation, the suffering that Africa has seen in the last twenty-five years may only be a prelude to much more dangerous developments.

NOTES

1. Samuel P. Huntington, *Political Order in Changing Societies* (New Haven: Yale University Press, 1968), p. 123; and Charles Tilly, "Reflections on the History of European State-Making," in Charles Tilly, ed., *The Formation of National States in Western Europe* (Princeton: Princeton University Press, 1975), p. 42. An important recent addition to this literature is Brian M. Downing, "Constitutionalism, Warfare and Political Change in Early Modern Europe," *Theory and Society*, Vol. 17, No. 1 (January 1988), pp. 7–56. The general literature on warfare's effect on society is voluminous. An early work which concentrates on some of the themes examined here is Hans Delbrück, *History of the Art of War within the Framework of Political History*, Vol. III, trans. Walter J. Renfroe, Jr. (Westport, Conn.: Greenwood Press, 1982).

2. For instance, in Morris Janowitz's classic study of the military in the developing world, the political, social, and economic functions of the military are studied extensively but the potential effects of war, or of peace, are not analyzed. Morris Janowitz, *The Military in the Political Development of New Nations: An Essay in Comparative Analysis* (Chicago: University of Chicago Press, 1964), p. 12.

3. The literature is reviewed by Henry Bienen, "Armed Forces and National Modernization: Continuing the Debate," *Comparative Politics*, Vol. 16, No. 1 (October 1983), pp. 1–16.

4. Gabriel Ardent, "Financial Policy and Economic Infrastructure of Modern States and Nations," in Tilly, *The Formation of National States*, p. 89.

5. A useful corrective to the conventional view is provided by John A. Hall, "War and the Rise of the West," in Colin Creighton and Martin Shaw, eds., *The Sociology of War and Peace* (London: Macmillan, 1987).

6. Richard Bean, "War and the Birth of the Nation State," *Journal of Economic History*, Vol. 33, No. 1 (March 1973), p. 220.

7. Michael Mann, "State and Society, 1130–1815: An Analysis of English State Finances," in Mann, *States, War and Capitalism: Studies in Political Sociology* (Oxford: Basil Blackwell, 1988), p. 109.

8. Michael Mann, *The Sources of Social Power* (Cambridge: Cambridge University Press, 1986), p. 486.

9. Michael Duffy, "The Military Revolution and the State, 1500–1800," in Michael Duffy, ed., *The Military Revolution and the State, 1500–1800*, Exeter Studies in History No. 1 (Exeter, U.K.: University of Exeter, 1980), p. 5.

10. "Lumpy" goods are products which are not useful if only part is purchased. Margaret Levi, *Of Rule and Revenue* (Berkeley: University of California Press, 1988), pp. 56–57.

11. Mann, *Sources of Social Power*, pp. 483–490.

12. Joseph P. Smaldone, *Warfare in the Sokoto Caliphate: Historical and Sociological Perspectives* (Cambridge: Cambridge University Press, 1977), p. 139. The same point is made by Richard L. Roberts in his *Warriors, Merchants, and Slaves: The State and the Economy in the Middle Niger Valley, 1700–1914* (Palo Alto: Stanford University Press, 1987), p. 20.

13. Joel S. Migdal, *Strong Societies and Weak States: State-Society Relations and State Capabilities in the Third World* (Princeton: Princeton University Press, 1988), p. 274.

14. Anthony Giddens, *The Nation-State and Violence*, vol. II of *A Contemporary Critique of Historical Materialism* (Berkeley: University of California Press, 1985), p. 235.

15. Michael Howard, *War and the Nation State* (Oxford: Clarendon Press, 1978), p. 9. Emphasis in the original.

16. See, for instance, Joseph LaPalombara, "Penetration: A Crisis of Governmental Capacity," in Leonard Binder, et al., *Crises and Sequences in Political Development* (Princeton: Princeton University Press, 1971), p. 222.

17. In 1977 Somalia, as part of its irredentist project to create "Greater Somalia," invaded Ethiopia in the hope of annexing the Ogaden; the Ethiopians, with significant help from the Soviet Union and Cuba, defeated Somalia in 1978. David D. Laitin and Said S. Samatar, *Somalia: Nation in Search of a State* (Boulder, Colo.: Westview, 1987), pp. 140–143. In 1973 Libyan forces invaded Chad by moving forces into the disputed Aozou strip. The Libyan military presence gradually expanded until a dramatic series of conflicts with the Chadian government (heavily supported by France and the United States) in 1987 forced the Libyans to agree to an end to hostilities. John Wright, *Libya, Chad and the Central Sahara* (London: Hurst, 1989), pp. 126–146.

18. This argument is developed in Jeffrey Herbst, "The Creation and Maintenance of National Boundaries in Africa," *International Organization*, Vol. 43, No. 4 (Fall 1989), pp. 673–692.

19. Tilly, "Reflections on the History of European State-Making," p. 38.

20. Ibid., p. 81.

21. Richard Hodder-Williams, *An Introduction to the Politics of Tropical Africa* (London: Allen and Unwin, 1984), p. 95.

22. Thomas M. Callaghy, "The State and the Development of Capitalism in Africa: Theoretical, Historical, and Comparative Reflections," in Donald Rothchild and Naomi Chazan, eds., *The Precarious Balance: State and Society in Africa* (Boulder, Colo.: Westview, 1988), p. 82.

23. The share of total gross domestic product of sub-Saharan African states is smaller, at 21.6 percent, than the developing country average of 25.5 percent. (Both figures are from 1984.) International Monetary Fund (IMF), *Government Finance Statistics Yearbook 1988* (Washington, D.C.: IMF, 1988), p. 94.

24. See, for instance, Larry Diamond, "Class Formation in the Swollen African State," *The Journal of Modern African Studies*, Vol. 25, No. 4 (December 1987), pp. 592–596; and Nzongola-Ntalaja, "The Crisis of the State in Post-Colonial Africa," in Nzongola-Ntalaja, *Revolution and Counter-Revolution in Africa* (London: Zed Books, 1987), p. 85.

25. W. Arthur Lewis, *The Evolution of the International Economic Order* (Princeton: Princeton University Press, 1978), p. 39.

26. W. Arthur Lewis, *Development Planning: The Essentials of Economic Policy* (New York: Harper and Row, 1966), p. 115.

27. Calculated from IMF, *Government Finance Statistics Yearbook 1988*, pp. 58, 74, and 94.

28. Calculated from ibid., p. 54.

29. See World Bank, *Accelerated Development in Sub-Saharan Africa: An Agenda for Action* (Washington, D.C.: World Bank, 1981), pp. 24–30.

30. Alex Radian, *Resource Mobilization in Poor Countries: Implementing Tax Policies* (New Brunswick, NJ: Transaction Books, 1980), pp. 13–17.

31. See Rothchild and Chazan, *The Precarious Balance*.

32. See, for instance, Donald L. Horowitz, *Ethnic Groups in Conflict* (Berkeley: University of California Press, 1985), pp. 563–680.

33. Buganda had a degree of autonomy when Uganda gained independence and the Kabaka, the traditional ruler of the Buganda people, was the country's first president.

However, this arrangement fell apart in 1966 when then Prime Minister Milton Obote overthrew the Kabaka and invaded Buganda. Crawford Young, *The Politics of Cultural Pluralism* (Madison: University of Wisconsin Press, 1976), pp. 149–156. In 1983, President Gaafar Mohamed Nimeiri of the Sudan effectively abrogated the Addis Ababa agreement which had given autonomy to Southern Sudan. The Sudan has been embroiled in a civil war ever since. Mansour Khalid, *Nimeiri and the Revolution of Dis-May* (London: KPI, 1985), pp. 234–240.

34. Joseph A. Schumpeter, "The Crisis of the Tax State," in Alan T. Peacock, et al., eds., *International Economic Papers*, No. 4 (London: Macmillan, 1954), pp. 6–7.

35. Edward Ames and Richard T. Rapp, "The Birth and Death of Taxes: A Hypothesis," *Journal of Economic History*, Vol. 37, No. 1 (March 1977), p. 177.

36. Tilly, "Reflections on the History of European State-Making," p. 73.

37. Mann, *Sources of Social Power*, p. 490.

38. Raja J. Chelliah, "Trends in Taxation in Developing Countries," *International Monetary Fund Staff Papers*, Vol. 18, No. 2 (July 1971), p. 312. On the possibility of changing fiscal arrangements in Africa, see Dennis Anderson, *The Public Revenue and Economic Policy in African Countries*, World Bank Discussion Paper No. 19 (Washington, D.C.: World Bank, 1987), pp. 14–15.

39. For instance, see Levi, *Of Rule and Revenue*, p. 105.

40. The importance of the "relevant other" concept in developing group cohesion is explored by Young, *The Politics of Cultural Pluralism*, p. 42.

41. Anthony D. Smith, "State-Making and Nation-Building," in John A. Hall, ed., *States in History* (Oxford: Basil Blackwell, 1986), p. 258.

42. Joseph R. Strayer, *On the Medieval Origins of the Modern State* (Princeton: Princeton University Press, 1970), p. 60.

43. Peter Bachrach and Morton S. Baratz, "Two Faces of Power," *American Political Science Review*, Vol. 56, No. 4 (December 1962), p. 950.

44. For instance, the World Bank's report, *Accelerated Development in Sub-Saharan Africa*, was crucial in noting the dimensions of Africa's economic crisis; it set the agenda for reform of African economies.

45. Jeffrey Herbst, "Political Impediments to Economic Rationality: Why Zimbabwe Cannot Reform its Public Sector," *The Journal of Modern African Studies*, Vol. 27, No. 1 (March 1989), pp. 67–85.

46. Paul Colinvaux, *The Fates of Nations: A Biological Theory of History* (London: Penguin, 1980), pp. 219–220.

47. Ibid., p. 219.

48. Otto, Prince von Bismarck, *Bismarck, the Man and the Statesman: Being the Reflections and Reminiscences of Otto, Prince von Bismarck, Written and Dictated by Himself after his Retirement from Office*, translated under the supervision of A.J. Butler, Vol. I (New York: Harper and Brothers, 1899), p. 313.

49. William G. Thom, "Sub-Saharan Africa's Changing Military Capabilities," in Bruce E. Arlinghaus and Pauline H. Baker, eds., *African Armies: Evolution and Capabilities* (Boulder, Colo.: Westview, 1986), p. 101. See also Walter L. Barrows, "Changing Military Capabilities in Black Africa," in William Foltz and Henry Bienen, eds., *Arms and the African: Military Influence and Africa's International Relations* (New Haven: Yale University Press, 1985), p. 99 and p. 120; and Henry Bienen, "African Militaries as Foreign Policy Actors," *International Security*, Vol. 5, No. 2 (Fall 1980), p. 176.

50. See Jeffrey Herbst, "Migration, the Politics of Protest, and State Consolidation in Africa," *African Affairs*, Vol. 89, No. 355 (April 1990), pp. 183–203.

51. In the 1950s American administrations debated whether South Korea could achieve any increase in living standards and if Amer-

ican aid should be devoted to simply preventing the country from getting poorer.
Clive Crook, "Trial and Error," *The Economist*, September 23, 1989, p. 4.

52. See Jeffrey Herbst, "Migration Helps Poorest
of Poor," *Wall Street Journal*, June 15, 1988,
p. 12.

ROBERT I. ROTBERG

THE NEW NATURE OF NATION-STATE FAILURE

Nation-states fail because they can no longer
deliver positive political goods to their
people. Their governments lose legitimacy
and, in the eyes and hearts of a growing plurality
of its citizens, the nation-state itself becomes
illegitimate.

Only a handful of the world's 191 nation-
states can now be categorized as failed, or collapsed, which is the end stage of failure. Several
dozen more, however, are weak and serious candidates for failure. Because failed states are hospitable to and harbor nonstate actors—warlords
and terrorists—understanding the dynamics of
nation-state failure is central to the war against
terrorism. Strengthening weak nation-states in
the developing world has consequently assumed
new urgency.

Defining State Failure

Failed states are tense, deeply conflicted, dangerous, and bitterly contested by warring factions.
In most failed states, government troops battle
armed revolts led by one or more rivals. Official
authorities in a failed state sometimes face two
or more insurgencies, varieties of civil unrest,
differing degrees of communal discontent, and a
plethora of dissent directed at the state and at
groups within the state.

From *The Washington Quarterly* 25, no. 3, (Summer
2002), pp. 85–96.

The absolute intensity of violence does not
define a failed state. Rather, it is the enduring
character of that violence (as in Angola, Burundi, and Sudan), the direction of such violence
against the existing government or regime, and
the vigorous character of the political or geographical demands for shared power or autonomy that rationalize or justify that violence that
identifies the failed state. Failure for a nation-
state looms when violence cascades into all-out
internal war, when standards of living massively
deteriorate, when the infrastructure of ordinary
life decays, and when the greed of rulers overwhelms their responsibilities to better their people and their surroundings.

The civil wars that characterize failed states
usually stem from or have roots in ethnic, religious, linguistic, or other intercommunal enmity. The fear of "the other" that drives so much
ethnic conflict may stimulate and fuel hostilities
between ruling entities and subordinate and
less-favored groups. Avarice also propels antagonism, especially when discoveries of new, frequently contested sources of resource wealth,
such as petroleum deposits or diamond fields,
encourage that greed.

There is no failed state without disharmonies
between communities. Yet, the simple fact that
many weak nation-states include haves and
have-nots, and that some of the newer states
contain a heterogeneous collection of ethnic, religious, and linguistic interests, is more a con-
tributor to than a root cause of nation-state

failure. In other words, state failure cannot be ascribed primarily to the inability to build nations from a congeries of ethnic groups. Nor should it be ascribed baldly to the oppression of minorities by a majority, although such brutalities are often a major ingredient of the impulse toward failure.

In contrast to strong states, failed states cannot control their borders. They lose authority over chunks of territory. Often, the expression of official power is limited to a capital city and one or more ethnically specific zones. Indeed, one measure of the extent of a state's failure is how much of the state's geographical expanse a government genuinely controls. How nominal is the central government's sway over rural towns, roads, and waterways? Who really rules up-country, or in particular distant districts?

In most cases, driven by ethnic or other intercommunal hostility or by regime insecurity, failed states prey on their own citizens. As in Mobutu Sese Seko's Zaire or the Taliban's Afghanistan, ruling cadres increasingly oppress, extort, and harass the majority of their own compatriots while favoring a narrowly based elite. As in Zaire, Angola, Siaka Stevens's Sierra Leone, or Hassan al-Turabi's pre-2001 Sudan, patrimonial rule depends on a patronage-based system of extraction from ordinary citizens. The typical weak-state plunges toward failure when this kind of ruler-led oppression provokes a countervailing reaction on the part of resentful groups or newly emerged rebels.

Another indicator of state failure is the growth of criminal violence. As state authority weakens and fails, and as the state becomes criminal in its oppression of its citizens, so general lawlessness becomes more apparent. Gangs and criminal syndicates assume control over the streets of the cities. Arms and drug trafficking become more common. Ordinary police forces become paralyzed. Anarchy becomes more and more the norm. For protection, citizens naturally turn to warlords and other strong figures who express ethnic or clan solidarity, thus pro-

jecting strength at a time when all else, including the state itself, is crumbling.

Fewer and Fewer Political Goods

Nation-states exist to deliver political goods—security, education, health services, economic opportunity, environmental surveillance, a legal framework of order and a judicial system to administer it, and fundamental infrastructural requirements such as roads and communications facilities—to their citizens. Failed states honor these obligations in the breach. They increasingly forfeit their function as providers of political goods to warlords and other nonstate actors. In other words, a failed state is no longer able or willing to perform the job of a nation-state in the modern world.

Failed states are unable to provide security—the most central and foremost political good—across the whole of their domains. Citizens depend on states and central governments to secure their persons and free them from fear. Because a failing state is unable to establish an atmosphere of security nationwide and is often barely able to assert any kind of state power beyond a capital city, the failure of the state becomes obvious even before rebel groups and other contenders threaten the residents of central cities and overwhelm demoralized government contingents, as in contemporary Liberia and recent Sierra Leone.

Failed states contain weak or flawed institutions—that is, only the executive institution functions. If legislatures exist at all, they are rubber-stamp machines. Democratic debate is noticeably absent. The judiciary is derivative of the executive rather than being independent, and citizens know that they cannot rely on the court system for significant redress or remedy, especially against the state. The bureaucracy has long ago lost its sense of professional responsibility and exists solely to carry out the orders of the executive and, in petty ways, to oppress citizens. The military is possibly the only institution with any remaining integrity, but the armed forces of failed states are often highly politicized, without the esprit that they once exhibited.

Deteriorating or destroyed infrastructures typify failed states. Metaphorically, the more potholes (or main roads turned to rutted tracks), the more likely a state will exemplify failure. As rulers siphon funds from the state, so fewer capital resources are available for road crews, and maintaining road or rail access to distant provinces becomes less and less of a priority. Even refurbishing basic navigational aids along arterial waterways, as in the Democratic Republic of the Congo (DRC), succumbs to neglect. Where the state still controls the landline telephone system, that form of political and economic good also betrays a lack of renewal, upkeep, investment, and bureaucratic interest. Less a metaphor than a daily reality is the index of failed connections, repeated required dialing, and interminable waits for repair or service. If state monopolies have permitted private entrepreneurs to erect cell telephone towers and offer mobile telephone service, cell telephones may already have rendered the government's landline monopoly obsolete. In a state without a government, such as Somalia, the overlapping system of privately provided cell telephone systems is effective.

In failed states, the effective educational and health systems have either been privatized (with a resulting hodgepodge of shady schools and medical clinics in the cities) or have slowly slumped to increasingly desperate levels of decrepitude. Teachers, physicians, nurses, and orderlies are paid late or not at all, and absenteeism rises. Textbooks and essential medicines become scarce. X-ray machines cannot be repaired. Reports to the relevant ministries go unanswered; and parents, students, and patients—especially rural ones—slowly realize that the state has abandoned them to the forces of nature and to their own devices. Sometimes, where a failed state is effectively split (Sudan), essential services are still provided to the favored

half (northern Sudan) but not to the half engulfed by war. Most of the time, however, the weakened nation-state completely fails to perform. Literacy falls, infant mortality rises, the AIDS epidemic overwhelms any health infrastructure that exists, life expectancies plummet, and an already poor and neglected citizenry becomes even poorer and more immiserated.

Failed states provide unparalleled economic opportunity, but only for a privileged few. Those close to the ruler or the ruling oligarchy grow richer while their less-fortunate brethren starve. Immense profits can be made from currency speculation, arbitrage, and knowledge of regulatory advantages. But the privilege of making real money when everything else is deteriorating is confined to clients of the ruling elite or to especially favored external entrepreneurs. The responsibility of a nation-state to maximize the well-being and personal prosperity of all of its citizens is conspicuously absent, if it ever existed.

Corruption flourishes in failed states, often on an unusually destructive scale. Petty or lubricating corruption is widespread. Levels of venal corruption escalate, especially kickbacks on anything that can be put out to bid, including medical supplies, textbooks, bridges; unnecessarily wasteful construction projects solely for the rents they will generate; licenses for existing and nonexisting activities; the appropriating by the ruling class of all kinds of private entrepreneurial endeavors; and generalized extortion. Corrupt ruling elites invest their gains overseas, not at home. A few build numerous palaces or lavish residences with state funds. Military officers always benefit from these corrupt regimes and feed ravenously from the same illicit troughs as their civilian counterparts.

An indicator, but not a cause, of failure is declining real national and per capita levels of gross domestic product (GDP). The statistical foundations of most states in the developing world are shaky, most certainly, but failed states—even, or particularly, failed states with abundant natural resources—show overall worsening GDP figures, slim year-to-year growth rates, and greater disparities of income between the wealthiest and poorest fifths of the population. High official deficits (Zimbabwe's reached 30 percent of GDP in 2001) support lavish security spending and the siphoning of cash by elites. Inflation usually soars because the ruling elite raids the central bank and prints money. From the resulting economic insecurity, often engineered by rulers to maximize their own fortunes and their own political as well as economic power, entrepreneurs favored by the prevailing regime can reap great amounts of money. Smuggling becomes rife. When state failure becomes complete, the local currency falls out of favor, and some or several international currencies take its place. Money changers are everywhere, legal or not, and arbitrage becomes an everyday national pursuit.

Sometimes, especially if climatic disasters intervene, the economic chaos and generalized neglect that is endemic to failed states can lead to regular food scarcities and widespread hunger—even to episodes of starvation and resulting international humanitarian relief efforts. Natural calamities can overwhelm the resources even of nonfailed but weak states in the developing world. But when unscrupulous rulers and ruling elites have consciously sucked state competencies dry, unforeseen natural disasters or manmade wars can drive ignored populations over the edge of endurance into starvation. Once such populations have lost their subsistence plots or sources of income, they lose their homes, forfeit already weak support networks, and are forced into an endless cycle of migration and displacement. Failed states offer no safety nets, and the homeless and destitute become fodder for anyone who can provide food and a cause.

A nation-state also fails when it loses a basic legitimacy—when its nominal borders become irrelevant and when one or more groups seek autonomous control within one or more parts of the national territory or, sometimes, even across its borders. Once the state's capacity deteriorates and what little capacity still remains is devoted largely to the fortunes of a few or to a favored ethnicity or community, then there is every reason to expect less and less loyalty to the state on the part of the excluded and the disenfranchised. When the rulers are seen to be working for themselves and their kin, and not for the state, their legitimacy, and the state's legitimacy, plummets. The state increasingly is perceived as owned by an exclusive class or group, with all others pushed aside.

Citizens naturally become more and more conscious of the kinds of sectional or community loyalties that are their main recourse and their only source of security and economic opportunity. They transfer their allegiances to clan and group leaders, some of whom become warlords. These warlords or other local strongmen derive support from external and local supporters. In the wilder, more marginalized corners of failed states, terror can breed along with the prevailing anarchy that emerges from state breakdown and failure.

A collapsed state is an extreme version of a failed state. It has a total vacuum of authority. A collapsed state is a mere geographical expression, a black hole into which a failed polity has fallen. Dark energy exists, but the forces of entropy have overwhelmed the radiance that hitherto provided some semblance of order and other vital political goods to the inhabitants embraced by language affinities or borders. When a state such as Somalia collapses (or Lebanon and Afghanistan a decade ago and Sierra Leone in the late 1990s), substate actors take over. They control regions and subregions, build their own local security apparatuses, sanction markets or other trading arrangements, and even establish an attenuated form of international relations. By definition, they are illegitimate and unrecognized, but some may assume the trappings of a quasi-state, such as Somaliland in northern Somalia. Yet, within the collapsed state prevail disorder, anomic behavior, and the kinds of anarchic mentality and entrepreneurial pursuits—especially gun and drug running—that are compatible with networks of terror.

Contemporary State Failure

This decade's failed states are Afghanistan, Angola, Burundi, the DRC, Liberia, Sierra Leone, and Sudan. These seven states exemplify the criteria of state failure. Beyond those states is one collapsed state: Somalia. Each of these countries has typified state failure continuously since at least 1990, if not before. Lebanon was once a failed state. So were Bosnia, Tajikistan, and Nigeria. Many other modern states approach the brink of failure, some much more ominously than others. Others drift disastrously downward from weak to failing to failed.

Of particular interest is why and how states slip from endemic weakness (Haiti) toward failure, or not. The list of weak states is long, but only a few of those weak and badly governed states necessarily edge into failure. Why? Even the categorization of a state as failing—Colombia and Indonesia, among others—need not doom it unquestionably to full failure. Another critical question is, what does it take to drive a failing state into collapse? Why did Somalia not stop at failure rather than collapsing?

Not each of the classical failed and collapsed states fully fills all of the cells on the matrix of failure. To be termed a failure, however, a state certainly needs to demonstrate that it has met most of the explicit criteria. "Failure" is meant to describe a specific set of conditions and to exclude states that only meet a few of the criteria. In other words, how truly minimal are the roads, the schools, the hospitals, and the clinics? How far has GDP fallen and infant mortality risen? How far does the ambit of the central government reach? How little legitimacy remains? Most importantly, because civil conflict is decisive for state failure, can the state still provide security to its citizens and to what extent? Continuously? Only on good days and nights? Has the state lost control of large swaths of territory or only some provinces and regions?

Several test cases are interesting. Sri Lanka has been embroiled in a bitter and destructive civil war for 19 years. The rebel Liberation Tigers of Tamil Eelam (LTTE), a Tamil separatist insurgency, has at times in the last decade controlled as much as 15 percent of Sri Lanka's total land mass. Additionally, with relative impunity, the LTTE has been able to assassinate prime ministers, bomb presidents, kill off rival Tamils, and last year even wreak destruction at the nation's civil aviation terminal and main air force base. But, as unable as the Sinhala-dominated governments of Sri Lanka have been to put down the LTTE rebellion, so the nation-state has remained merely weak, never close to failure. For 80 percent of Sri Lankans, the government performs reasonably well. Since the early 1990s, too, Sri Lanka has exhibited robust levels of economic performance. The authority of successive governments, even before the recent ceasefire, extended securely to the Sinhala-speaking 80 percent of the country, and the regime recaptured some of the contested Tamil areas. Before the truce, road maintenance, educational and medical services, and the other necessary political goods continued to be delivered despite the civil war, to some limited degree even into the war-torn parts of the country. For all of these reasons, despite a consuming internal conflict founded on majority-minority discrimination and deprivation and on ethnic and religious differences, Sri Lanka has successfully escaped failure.

Indonesia is another example of weakness avoiding failure despite widespread insecurity. As the world's largest Muslim nation, its farflung archipelago harbors the separatist wars of Aceh in the west and Papua (Irian Jaya) in the east, plus Muslim-Christian conflict in Ambon and the Mulukus, Muslim-Christian hostility in Sulawesi, and ethnic xenophobic outbursts in West Kalimantan. Given all of these conflictual situations, none of which have become less bitter since the end of Suharto's dictatorship, suggesting that Indonesia is approaching failure is easy. Yet, as one argument goes, only the insurgents in Aceh and Papua want to secede from the state; and, even in Aceh, official troops have the upper hand. Elsewhere, hostilities are intercommunal and not directed against the government or the state. Unlike the low-level war in Aceh, they do not threaten the integrity and resources of the state. Overall, most of Indonesia is still secure and is "glued" together well by an abiding sense of nationalism. The government still projects power and authority. Despite dangerous economic and other vicissitudes in the post-Suharto era, the state provides most of the other necessary political goods and remains legitimate. Indonesia need not be classified as anything other than a weak state, but the government's performance and provision of security should be monitored closely.

What about Colombia? An otherwise well-endowed, prosperous, and stable state has the second-highest murder rate per capita in the world, its politicians and businessmen wear flak jackets and travel with armed guards, and three private armies control relatively large chunks of its territory with impunity. The official defense and political establishment has effectively ceded authority in those zones to the insurgencies and to drug traffickers. Again, why should Colombia not be ranked as a failed state? Although it could deteriorate into further failure, at present the Colombian government still performs for the 70 percent of the nation that remains under official authority. It provides political goods, even some improving security, for the large part of the state under official authority. When and if the government of Colombia can reassert itself into the disputed zones and further reduce drug trafficking, the power of the state will grow and a weak, endangered state such as Colombia can move away from possible failure toward the stronger side of the equation.

Zimbabwe is an example of a once unquestionably strong African state—indeed, one of the strongest—that has fallen rapidly through weakness to the very edge of failure. All that Zimbabwe lacks in order to join the ranks of failed states is a widespread internal insurgent movement directed at the government, which could still emerge. Meanwhile, per capita GDP has re-

ceded by 10 percent annually for two years. During the same period, inflammation has galloped from 30 percent to 116 percent. The local currency has fallen against the U.S. dollar from 38:1 to 400:1. Foreign and domestic investment have largely ceased. Health and educational services are almost nonexistent and shrinking further. Road maintenance and telephone service are obviously suffering. Judicial independence survives, but barely, and not in critical political cases. The state has also been preying on its own citizens for at least two years. Corruption is blatant and very much dominated by the avaricious ruling elite. Zimbabwe is an example of a state that, like Sierra Leone and the DRC at earlier moments in history, has been driven into failure by human agency.

Indonesia, Colombia, Sri Lanka, and Zimbabwe are but four among a large number of nation-states (two dozen by a recent count) that contain serious elements of failure but will probably avoid failure, especially if they receive sufficient outside assistance. They belong to a category of state that is designated weak but that encompasses and spreads into the category of failing—the precursor to true failure. Haiti, Chad, and Kyrgyzstan, from three continents, are representative examples of perpetual weakness. Argentina has recently joined an analogous rank; Russia was once a candidate. Fiji, the Solomon Islands, Tajikistan, Lebanon, Nigeria, Niger, and Burkina Faso remain vulnerable to further deterioration. Even Kenya is a weak state with some potential for definitive failure if ethnic disparities and ambitions provoke civil strife.

The list of states in weakness is longer and hardly static. Some of the potentially stronger states move in and out of weakness and nearer or farther from failure. Others are foreordained weak. Particular decisions by ruling groups would be needed to destabilize members of this second group further and drive them into failure.

The Hand of Man

State failure is man-made, not merely accidental nor—fundamentally—caused geographically, environmentally, or externally. Leadership decisions and leadership failures have destroyed states and continue to weaken the fragile polities that operate on the cusp of failure. Mobutu's kleptocratic rule extracted the marrow of Zaire/DRC and left nothing for his national dependents. Much of the resource wealth of that vast country ended up in Mobutu's or his cronies' pockets. During four decades, hardly any money was devoted to uplifting the Congolese people, improving their welfare, building infrastructures, or even providing more than rudimentary security. Mobutu's government performed only for Mobutu, not for Zaire/DRC.

Likewise, oil-rich Angola continues to fail because of three decades of war, but also because President Eduardo dos Santos and his associates have refused to let the Angolan government deliver more than basic services within the large zone that they control. Stevens (1967–1985) decapitated the Sierra Leonean state in order to strengthen his own power amid growing chaos. Sierra Leone has not yet recovered from Stevens's depredations. Nor has Liberia been resuscitated in the aftermath of the slashing neglect and unabashed greed of Samuel Doe, Prince Johnson, and Charles Taylor. In Somalia, Mohammed Siad Barre arrogated more and more power and privilege to himself and his clan. Finally, nothing was left for the other pretenders to power. The Somali state was gutted, the abilities of the Somali government to provide political goods endlessly compromised, and the descent into failure and then full collapse followed.

President Robert Gabriel Mugabe has personally led Zimbabwe from strength to the precipice of failure. His high-handed and seriously corrupt rule bled the resources of the state into his own pocket, squandered foreign exchange, discouraged domestic and international investment, subverted the courts, and this year drove his country to the very brink of starvation. In Sri Lanka, Solomon and Sirimavo Bandaranaike, one after the other, drove the LTTE into reactive combat by abrogating minority rights and vitiating the social contract on which the country called Ceylon had been created. In Afghanistan, Gulbuddin Hakmatyar and Burrhan ul-Din Rabani tried to prevent Afghans other than their fellow Pushtun and Tajik nationals from sharing the perquisites of governance; their narrowly focused, self-enriching decisions enabled the Taliban to triumph and Afghanistan to become a safe harbor for terrorists.

Preventing State Failure

Strengthening weak states against failure is far easier than reviving them after they have definitively failed or collapsed. As the problem of contemporary Afghanistan shows, reconstruction is very long, very expensive, and hardly a smooth process. Creating security and a security force from scratch, amid bitter memories, is the immediate need. Then comes the re-creation of an administrative structure—primarily re-creating a bureaucracy and finding the funds with which to pay the erstwhile bureaucrats and policemen. A judicial method is required, which means the establishment or reestablishment of a legitimate legal code and system; the training of judges, prosecutors, and defenders (as attempted recently in East Timor); and the opening of courtrooms and offices. Restarting the schools, employing teachers, refurbishing and re-equipping hospitals, building roads, and even gathering statistics—all of these fundamental chores take time, large sums of money (especially in war-shattered Afghanistan), and meticulous oversight in postconflict nations with overstretched human resources. Elections need not be an early priority, but constitutions must be written eventually and elections held in order to encourage participatory democracy.

Strengthening states prone to failure before

they fail is prudent policy and contributes significantly to world order and to minimizing combat, casualties, refugees, and displaced persons. Doing so is far less expensive than reconstructing states after failure. Strengthening weak states also has the potential to eliminate the authority and power vacuums within which terror thrives.

From a policy perspective, however, these are obvious nostrums. The mechanisms for amelioration are also more obvious than obscure. In order to encourage responsible leadership and good governance, financial assistance from international lending agencies and bilateral donors must be designed to reinforce positive leadership only. Outside support should be conditional on monetary and fiscal streamlining, renewed attention to good governance, reforms of land tenure systems, and strict adherence to the rule of law. External assistance to create in-country jobs by reducing external tariff barriers (e.g., on textiles) and by supporting vital foreign direct investment is critical. So is support for innovations that can reduce importation and exportation transport expenditures for the weak nations, improve telephone and power systems through privatization, open predominantly closed economies in general, create new incentives for agricultural productivity, and bolster existing security forces through training and equipment.

All these ingredients of a successful strengthening process are necessary. The developed world can apply tough love and assist the developing and more vulnerable world to help itself in many more similarly targeted ways. In addition to the significant amounts of cash (grants are preferred over loans) that must be transferred to help the poorer nations help themselves, however, the critical ingredient is sustained interest and sustained assistance over the very long run. Nothing enduring can be accomplished instantaneously. If the world order wants to dry up the reservoirs of terror, as well as do good more broadly, it must commit itself and its powers to a campaign of decades, not months. The refurbishment and revitalization of Afghanistan will take much more than the $4.7 billion pledged and the many years that Secretary of State Colin L. Powell has warned the U.S. people will be necessary to make Afghanistan a self-sufficient state. Strengthening Indonesia, for example, would take a concerted effort for decades. So would strengthening any of the dangerous and needy candidates in Africa or in Central Asia.

Preventing state failure is imperative, difficult, and costly. Yet, doing so is profoundly in the interest not only of the inhabitants of the most deprived and ill-governed states of the world, but also of world peace.

Satisfying such lofty goals, however—making the world much safer by strengthening weak states against failure—is dependent on the political will of the wealthy big-power arbiters of world security. Perhaps the newly aroused awareness of the dangers of terror will embolden political will in the United States, Europe, and Japan. Otherwise, the common ingredients of zero-sum leadership; ethnic, linguistic, and religious antagonisms and fears; chauvinistic ambition; economic insufficiency; and inherited fragility will continue to propel nation-states from weakness toward failure. In turn, that failure will be costly in terms of humanitarian relief and postconflict reconstruction. Ethnic cleansing episodes will recur, as will famines, and in the thin and hospitable soils of newly failed and collapsed states, terrorist groups will take root.

3 NATIONS AND SOCIETY

The readings presented in this chapter address three basic issues: **nationalism, ethnic conflict**, and **"civilizational" conflict.**

Eric Hobsbawm's discussion of the rise of modern **nationalism** in his 1962 book, The Age of Revolution: 1789–1848, continues to offer insights into present-day ethnic conflicts around the globe. His crucial insight, that nationalism is always linked to the rapid rise of an indigenous middle class and to the spread of literacy in the native language, remains valid today and has been stressed in analyses of (among other cases) Québecois, Basque, Eritrean, and Kurdish nationalism. It is also important to remember, as Hobsbawm notes, that many (although of course not all) of the "national" languages claimed by such groups—such as Croatian, Romanian, Gaelic, Norwegian, and Czech— were as much invented (i.e., constructed out of a welter of dialects) as revived.[1]

Ethnic conflict obviously takes a heavy toll on societies both poor (e.g., Rwanda) and rich (e.g., Northern Ireland), but in a 1997 article in Quarterly Journal of Economics. William Easterly and Ross Levine went as far as to suggest that ethnic fragmentation, particularly in sub-Saharan African countries, accounted for both bad policies and low rates of economic growth.

Political scientists and economists quickly took exception to Easterly and Ross's methods and conclusions, and in 1998 and 2000, Paul Collier and others at the World Bank advanced a radical counterargument: most "ethnic" conflicts and seemingly ethnic civil wars were based not on "grievance" but on "greed." Civil wars, they showed, erupted and persisted precisely in those countries, mostly poor, with huge and marketable reserves of valuable natural resources—oil, diamonds, copper ore, and mahogany. Collier's arguments were summarized in the 2003 article from The Economist that is reproduced here. In the meantime, Collier refined his theory in an article in the British journal Economic Policy, presented here in slightly abridged form, showing that ethnic fragmentation per se had no negative impact on countries' growth, particularly in democracies.

The leading comparativist and eminent development specialist Samuel P. Huntington argued, in a 1993 article (presented here in slightly abridged *form) and a 1996 book, that the twenty-first century would be characterized by a **"conflict of civilizations"** rather than (as considered heretofore) by conflicts of nations, of ideologies, or even of ethnicities. Huntington viewed "civilization" as a far more encompassing category, and he focused particularly on what he saw as the likely conflict between Islam and the West. Initially, his dire prognosis was widely dismissed as an exaggeration, but it gained immense currency after the events of September 11, 2001, the wars with Afghanistan and Iraq, the terrorist attacks on Madrid and London, and the growing tensions between immigrant and native populations within Europe (epitomized in the French urban riots).*

Yet the Nobel-Prize-winning economist and philosopher Amartya Sen exposes, in the 2002 New Republic article reproduced here, the contradictions and oversimplifications in Huntington's argument. Sen warns that the "conflict of civilizations" approach may exacerbate, and even be used to justify, the conflict it ostensibly seeks to analyze. As Sen states, "Complicated theory can sometimes bolster uncomplicated bigotry and can make the world a much more flammable place than it needs to be."

ERIC HOBSBAWM

NATIONALISM

Every people has its special mission, which will cooperate towards the fulfilment of the general mission of humanity. That mission constitutes its nationality. Nationality is sacred.

> Act of Brotherhood of Young Europe, 1834

The day will come . . . when sublime Germania shall stand on the bronze pedestal of liberty and justice, bearing in one hand the torch of enlightenment, which shall throw the beam of civilization into the remotest corners of the earth, and in the other the arbiter's balance. The people will beg her to settle their disputes; those very people who now show us that might is right, and kick us with the jackboot of scornful contempt.

> From Siebenpfeiffer's speech at the Hambach Festival, 1832

From Eric Hobsbawm, *The Age of Revolution* (London: Weidenfeld & Nicholson, 1962), pp. 132–45. Some of the author's notes have been omitted.

After 1830, as we have seen, the general movement in favour of revolution split. One product of this split deserves special attention: the self-consciously nationalist movements.

The movements which best symbolize this development are the 'Youth' movements founded or inspired by Giuseppe Mazzini shortly after the 1830 revolution: Young Italy, Young Poland, Young Switzerland, Young Germany, and Young France (1831–6) and the analogous Young Ireland of the 1840s, the ancestor of the only lasting and successful revolutionary organization on the model of the early nineteenth-century conspiratory brotherhoods, the Fenians or Irish Republican Brotherhood, better known through its executive arm of the Irish Republican Army. In themselves these movements were of no great importance; the mere presence of Mazzini would have been enough to ensure their total ineffectiveness. Symbolically they are of extreme importance, as is indicated by the adoption in subsequent nationalist movements of such labels as "Young Czechs" or "Young Turks." They mark the distintegration of the European revolutionary movement into national segments. Doubtless each of these segments had much the same political programme strategy, and tactics as the others, and even much the same flag—almost invariably a tricolour of some kind. Its members saw no contradiction between their own demands and those of other nations, and indeed envisaged a brotherhood of all, simultaneously liberating themselves. On the other hand each now tended to justify its primary concern with its own nation by adopting the role of a Messiah for all. Through Italy (according to Mazzini), through Poland (according to Mickiewicz), the suffering peoples of the world were to be led to freedom; an attitude readily adaptable to conservative or indeed imperialist policies, as witness the Russian Slavophils with their championship of Holy Russia, the Third Rome, and the Germans who were subsequently to tell the world at some length that it would be healed by the German spirit. Admittedly this ambiguity of nationalism went back to the French Revolution. But in those days there had been only *one* great and revolutionary nation and it made sense (as indeed it still did) to regard it as the headquarters of all revolutions, and the necessary prime mover in the liberation of the world. To look to Paris was rational; to look to a vague "Italy," "Poland," or "Germany" (represented in practice by a handful of conspirators and emigrés) made sense only for Italians, Poles, and Germans.

If the new nationalism had been confined only to the membership of the national-revolutionary brotherhoods, it would not be worth much more attention. However, it also reflected much more powerful forces, which were emerging into political consciousness in the 1830s as the result of the double revolution. The most immediately powerful of these were the discontent of the lesser landowners or gentry and the emergence of a national middle and even lower-middle class in numerous countries, the spokesmen for both being largely professional intellectuals.

The revolutionary role of the lesser gentry is perhaps best illustrated in Poland and Hungary. There, on the whole, the large landed magnates had long found it possible and desirable to make terms with absolutism and foreign rule. The Hungarian magnates were in general Catholic and had long been accepted as pillars of Viennese court society; very few of them were to join the revolution of 1848. The memory of the old *Rzeczpospolita* made even Polish magnates nationally minded, but the most influential of their quasi-national parties, the Czartoryski connection, now operating from the luxurious emigration of the Hotel Lambert in Paris, had always favoured the alliance with Russia and continued to prefer diplomacy to revolt. Economically they were wealthy enough to afford what they needed, short of really titanic dissipation, and even to invest enough in the improvement of their estates to benefit from the economic expansion of the age, if they chose to. Count Széchenyi, one of the few moderate liberals from this class and a champion of economic improvement, gave a year's income for the new Hungarian Academy of Sciences—some 60,000 florins. There is no evidence that his standard of life suffered from such disinterested generosity. On the other hand the numerous gentlemen who had little but their birth to distinguish them from other impoverished farmers—one in eight of the Hungarian population claimed gentlemanly status—had neither the money to make their holdings profitable nor the inclination to compete with Germans and Jews for middle-class wealth. If they could not live decently on their rents, and a degenerate age deprived them of a soldier's chances, then they might, if not too ignorant, consider the law, administration, or some intellectual position, but no bourgeois activity. Such gentlemen had long been the stronghold of opposition to absolutism, foreigners, and magnate rule in their respective countries, sheltering (as in Hungary) behind the dual buttress of

Calvinism and county organization. It was natural that their opposition, discontent, and aspiration for more jobs for local gentlemen should now fuse with nationalism.

The national business classes which emerged in this period were, paradoxically, a rather less nationalist element. Admittedly in disunited Germany and Italy the advantages of a large unified national market made sense. The author of *Deutschland über Alles* apostrophized

> Ham and scissors, boots and garters,
> Wool and soap and yarn and beer,

because they had achieved, what the spirit of nationality had been unable to, a genuine sense of national unity through customs union. However, there is little evidence that, say, the shippers of Genoa (who were later to provide much of the financial backing for Garibaldi) preferred the possibilities of a national Italian market to the larger prosperity of trading all over the Mediterranean. And in the large multinational empires the industrial or trading nuclei which grew up in particular provinces might grumble about discrimination, but at bottom clearly preferred the great markets open to them now to the little ones of future national independence. The Polish industrialists, with all Russia at their feet, took little part as yet in Polish nationalism. When Palacky claimed on behalf of the Czechs that "if Austria did not exist, it would have to be invented," he was not merely calling on the monarchy's support against the Germans, but also expressing the sound economic reasoning of the economically most advanced sector of a large and otherwise backward empire. Business interests were sometimes at the head of nationalism, as in Belgium, where a strong pioneer industrial community regarded itself, with doubtful reason, as disadvantaged under the rule of the powerful Dutch merchant community, to which it had been hitched in 1815. But this was an exceptional case.

The great proponents of middle-class nationalism at this stage were the lower and middle professional, administrative and intellectual strata, in other words the *educated* classes. (These are not, of course, distinct from the business classes, especially in backward countries where estate administrators, notaries, lawyers, and the like are among the key accumulators of rural wealth.) To be precise, the advance guard of middle-class nationalism fought its battle along the line which marked the educational progress of large numbers of "new men" into areas hitherto occupied by a small elite. The progress of schools and universities measures that of nationalism, just as schools and especially universities became its most conscious champions: the conflict of Germany and Denmark over Schleswig-Holstein in 1848 and again in 1864 was anticipated by the conflict of the universities of Kiel and Copenhagen on this issue in the middle 1840s.

The progress was striking, though the total number of the "educated" remained small. The number of pupils in the French state *lycées* doubled between 1809 and 1842, and increased with particular rapidity under the July monarchy, but even so in 1842 it was only just under 19,000. (The total of all children receiving secondary education then was about 70,000.) Russia, around 1850, had some 20,000 secondary pupils out of a total population of sixty-eight million. The number of university students was naturally even smaller, though it was rising. It is difficult to realize that the Prussian academic youth which was so stirred by the idea of liberation after 1806 consisted in 1805 of not much more than 1,500 young men all told; that the *Polytechnique*, the bane of the post-1815 Bourbons, trained a total of 1,581 young men in the entire period from 1815 to 1830, i.e., an annual intake of about one hundred. The revolutionary prominence of the students in the 1848 period makes us forget that in the whole continent of Europe, including the unrevolutionary British Isles, there were probably not more than 40,000 university students in all. Still their numbers rose. In Russia it rose from 1,700 in 1825 to 4,600 in 1848. And even if they did not, the transformation of society and the universities (cf. chapter 15) gave them a new consciousness of themselves as a social group. Nobody remembers that in 1789 there were something like 6,000 students in the University of Paris, because they played no independent part in the Revolution. But by 1830 nobody could possibly overlook such a number of young academics.

Small elites can operate in foreign languages; once the cadre of the educated becomes large enough, the national language imposes itself (as witness the struggle for linguistic recognition in the Indian states since the 1940s). Hence the moment when textbooks or newspapers in the national language are first written, or when that language is first used for some official purpose, measures a crucial step in national evolution. The 1830s saw this step taken over large areas of Europe. Thus the first major Czech works on astronomy, chemistry, anthropology, mineralogy, and botany were written or completed in this decade; and so, in Rumania, were the first school textbooks substituting Rumanian for the previously current Greek. Hungarian was adopted instead of Latin as the official language of the Hungarian Diet in 1840, though Budapest University, controlled from Vienna, did not abandon Latin lectures until 1844. (However, the struggle for the use of Hungarian as an official language had gone on intermittently since 1790.) In Zagreb, Gai published his *Croatian Gazette* (later: *Illyrian National Gazette*) from 1835 in the first literary version of what had hitherto been merely a complex of dialects. In countries which had long possessed an official national language, the change cannot be so easily measured, though it is interesting that after 1830 the number of German books published in Germany (as against Latin and French titles) for the first time consistently exceeded 90 per cent; the number of French ones after 1820 fell below 4 per cent.[1] More generally the expansion of publishing gives us a comparable indication. Thus in Germany the number of books published remained much the same in 1821 as in 1800—about 4,000 titles a year, but by 1841 it had risen to 12,000 titles.

Of course the great mass of Europeans, and of non-Europeans, remained uneducated. Indeed, with the exception of the Germans, the Dutch, Scandinavians, Swiss, and the citizens of the USA, no people can in 1840 be described as literate. Several can be described as totally illiterate, like the Southern Slavs, who had less than one-half per cent literacy in 1827 (even much later only one per cent of Dalmatian recruits to the Austrian army could read and write), or the Russians, who had two per cent (1840), and a great many as almost illiterate, like the Spaniards, the Portuguese (who appear to have had barely 8,000 children in all *at school* after the Peninsular War) and, except for the Lombards and Piedmontese, the Italians. Even Britain, France, and Belgium were 40 to 50 per cent illiterate in the 1840s. Illiteracy is no bar to political consciousness, but there is, in fact, no evidence that nationalism of the modern kind was a powerful mass force except in countries already transformed by the dual revolution: in France, in Britain, in the USA and—because it was an economic and political dependency of Britain—in Ireland.

To equate nationalism with the literate class is not to claim that the mass of, say, Russians, did not consider themselves "Russian" when confronted with somebody or something that was not. However, for the masses in general the test of nationality was still religion: the Spaniard was defined by being Catholic, the Russian by being Orthodox. However, though such confrontations were becoming rather more frequent, they were still rare, and certain kinds of national feeling, such as the Italian, were as yet wholly alien to the great mass of the people, which did not even speak the national literary language but mutually almost incomprehensible *patois*. Even in Germany patriotic mythology has greatly exaggerated the degree of national feeling against Napoleon. France was extremely popular in Western Germany, especially among soldiers, whom it employed freely. Populations attached to the Pope or the Emperor might express resentment against their enemies, who happened to be the French, but this hardly implied any feelings of national consciousness, let alone any desire for a national state. Moreover, the very fact that nationalism was represented by middle class and gentry was enough to make the poor man suspicious. The Polish radical-democratic revolutionaries tried earnestly—as did the more advanced of the South Italian Carbonari and other conspirators—to mobilize the peasantry even to the point of offering agrarian reform. Their failure was almost total. The Galician peasants in 1846 opposed the Polish revolutionaries even though these actually proclaimed the abolition of serfdom, preferring to massacre gentlemen and trust to the Emperor's officials.

The uprooting of peoples, which is perhaps the most important single phenomenon of the nineteenth century, was to break down this deep, age-old and localized traditionalism. Yet over most of the world up to the 1820s hardly anybody as yet migrated or emigrated, except under the compulsion of armies and hunger, or in the traditionally migratory groups such as the peasants from Central France who did seasonal building jobs in the north, or the travelling German artisans. Uprooting still meant, not the mild form of homesickness which was to become the characteristic psychological disease of the nineteenth century (reflected in innumerable sentimental popular songs), but the acute, killing *mal de pays* or *mal de cœur* which had first been clinically described by doctors among the old Swiss mercenaries in foreign lands. The conscription of the revolutionary wars revealed it, notably among the Bretons. The pull of the remote northern forests was so strong that it could lead an Estonian servant-girl to leave her excellent employers the Kügelgens in Saxony, where she was free, and return home to serfdom. Migration and emigration, of which the migration to the USA is the most convenient index, increased notably from the 1820s, though it did not reach anything like major proportions until the 1840s, when one and three-quarter millions crossed the North Atlantic (a little less than three times the figure for the 1830s). Even so, the only major migratory nation

outside the British Isles was as yet the German, long used to sending its sons as peasant settlers to Eastern Europe and America, as travelling artisans across the continent and as mercenaries everywhere.

We can in fact speak of only one Western national movement organized in a coherent form before 1848 which was genuinely based on the masses, and even this enjoyed the immense advantage of identification with the strongest carrier of tradition, the Church. This was the Irish Repeal movement under Daniel O'Connell (1785–1847), a golden-voiced lawyer–demagogue of peasant stock, the first—and up to 1848 the only one—of those charismatic popular leaders who mark the awakening of political consciousness in hitherto backward masses. (The only comparable figures before 1848 were Feargus O'Connor (1794–1855), another Irishman, who symbolized Chartism in Britain, and perhaps Louis Kossuth (1802–1894), who may have acquired something of his subsequent mass prestige before the 1848 revolution, though in fact his reputation in the 1840s was made as a champion of the gentry, and his later canonization by nationalist historians makes it difficult to see his early career at all clearly.) O'Connell's Catholic Association, which won its mass support and the not wholly justified confidence of the clergy in the successful struggle for Catholic Emancipation (1829), was in no sense tied to the gentry, who were in any case Protestant and Anglo-Irish. It was a movement of peasants, and such elements of a native Irish lower-middle class as existed in that pauperized island. 'The Liberator' was borne into leadership by successive waves of a mass movement of agrarian revolt, the chief motive force of Irish politics throughout that appalling century. This was organized in secret terrorist societies which themselves helped to break down the parochialism of Irish life. However, his aim was neither revolution nor national independence, but a moderate middle-class Irish autonomy by agreement or negotiation with the British Whigs. He was, in fact, not a nationalist and still less a peasant revolutionary but a moderate middle-class autonomist. Indeed, the chief criticism which has been not unjustifiably raised against him by later Irish nationalists (much as the more radical Indian nationalists have criticized Gandhi, who occupied an analogous position in his country's history) was that he could have raised all Ireland against the British, and deliberately refused to do so. But this does not alter the fact that the movement he led was genuinely supported by the mass of the Irish nation.

II

Outside the zone of the modern bourgeois world there were, however, movements of popular revolt against alien rule (i.e., normally understood as meaning rule by a different religion rather than a different nationality) which sometimes appear to anticipate later national movements. Such were the rebellions against the Turkish Empire, against the Russians in the Caucasus, and the fight against the encroaching British raj in and on the confines of India. It is unwise to read too much modern nationalism into these, though in backward areas populated by armed and combative peasants and herdsmen, organized in clan groups and inspired by tribal chieftains, bandit-heroes, and prophets, resistance to the foreign (or better, the unbelieving) ruler could take the form of veritable people's wars quite unlike the elite nationalist movements in less Homeric countries. In fact, however, the resistance of Mahrattas (a feudal-military Hindu group) and Sikhs (a militant religious sect) to the British in 1803–18 and 1845–49 respectively have little connection with subsequent Indian nationalism and produced none of their own.[2] The Caucasian tribes, savage, heroic, and feud-ridden, found in the puritan Islamic sect of Muridism a temporary bond of unity against the invading Russians and in Shamyl (1797–1871) a leader of major stature; but there is not to this day a Caucasian nation, but merely a congeries of small mountain peoples in small Soviet republics. (The Georgians and Armenians, who have formed nations in the modern sense, were not involved in the Shamyl movement.) The

Bedouin, swept by puritan religious sects like the Wahhabi in Arabia and the Senussi in what is today Libya, fought for the simple faith of Allah and the simple life of the herdsman and raider against the corruption of taxes, pashas, and cities; but what we know as Arab nationalism—a product of the twentieth century—has come out of the cities, not the nomadic encampments.

Even the rebellions against the Turks in the Balkans, especially among the rarely subdued mountain peoples of the south and west, should not be too readily interpreted in modern nationalist terms though the bards and braves of several—the two were often the same, as among the poet-warrior bishops of Montenegro—recalled the glories of quasi-national heroes like the Albanian Skanderbeg and the tragedies like the Serbian defeat at Kossovo in the remote battles against the Turks. Nothing was more natural than to revolt, where necessary or desirable, against a local administration of a weakening Turkish Empire. However, little but a common economic backwardness united what we now know as the Yugoslavs, even those in the Turkish Empire, and the very concept of Yugoslavia was the product of intellectuals in Austro-Hungary rather than of those who actually fought for liberty.[3] The Orthodox Montenegrins, never subdued, fought the Turks, but with equal zest they fought the unbelieving Catholic Albanians and the unbelieving, but solidly Slav, Moslem Bosnians. The Bosnians revolted against the Turks, whose religion many of them shared, with as much readiness as the Orthodox Serbs of the wooded Danube plain, and with more zest than the Orthodox "old Serbs" of the Albanian frontier-area. The first of the Balkan peoples to rise in the nineteenth century were the Serbs under a heroic pig-dealer and brigand Black George (1760–1817), but the initial phase of his rising (1804–7) did not even claim to be against Turkish rule, but on the contrary for the Sultan against the abuses of the local rulers. There is little in the early history of mountain rebellion in the Western Balkans to suggest that the local

Serbs, Albanians, Greeks, and others would not in the early nineteenth century have been satisfied with the sort of non-national autonomous principality which a powerful satrap, Ali Pasha "the Lion of Jannina" (1741–1822), for a time set up in Epirus.

In one and only one case did the perennial fight of the shepherding clansmen and bandit-heroes against *any* real government fuse with the ideas of middle-class nationalism and the French Revolution: in the Greek struggle for independence (1821–30). Not unnaturally Greece therefore became the myth and inspiration of nationalists and liberals everywhere. For in Greece alone did an entire people rise against the oppressor in a manner which could be plausibly identified with the cause of the European left; and in turn the support of the European left, headed by the poet Byron who died there, was of very considerable help in the winning of Greek independence.

Most Greeks were much like the other forgotten warrior-peasantries and clans of the Balkan peninsula. A part, however, formed an international merchant and administrative class also settled in colonies or minority communities throughout the Turkish Empire and beyond, and the language and higher ranks of the entire Orthodox Church, to which most Balkan peoples belonged, were Greek, headed by the Greek Patriarch of Constantinople. Greek civil servants, transmuted into vassal princes, governed the Danubian principalities (the present Rumania). In a sense the entire educated and mercantile classes of the Balkans, the Black Sea area, and the Levant, whatever their national origins, were hellenized by the very nature of their activities. During the eighteenth century this hellenization proceeded more powerfully than before, largely because of the marked economic expansion which also extended the range and contacts of the Greek diaspora. The new and thriving Black Sea grain trade took it into Italian, French, and British business centres and strengthened its links with Russia; the expansion of Balkan trade brought Greek or Grecized merchants into Cen-

tral Europe. The first Greek language newspapers were published in Vienna (1784–1812). Periodic emigration and resettlement of peasant rebels further reinforced the exile communities. It was among this cosmopolitan diaspora that the ideas of the French Revolution—liberalism, nationalism, and the methods of political organization by masonic secret societies—took root. Rhigas (1760–98), the leader of an early obscure and possibly pan-Balkanist revolutionary movement, spoke French and adapted the *Marseillaise* to Hellenic conditions. The *Philiké Hetairía*, the secret patriotic society mainly responsible for the revolt of 1821, was founded in the great new Russian grain port of Odessa in 1814.

Their nationalism was to some extent comparable to the elite movements of the West. Nothing else explains the project of raising a rebellion for Greek independence in the Danube principalities under the leadership of local Greek magnates; for the only people who could be described as Greeks in these miserable serf-lands were lords, bishops, merchants, and intellectuals. Naturally enough that rising failed miserably (1821). Fortunately, however, the Hetairía had also set out to enrol the anarchy of local brigand-heroes, outlaws, and clan chieftains in the Greek mountains (especially in the Peloponnese), and with considerably greater success—at any rate after 1818—than the South Italian gentlemen Carbonari, who attempted a similar proselytization of their local banditti. It is doubtful whether anything like modern nationalism meant much to these "klephts," though many of them had their "clerks"—a respect for and interest in book-learning was a surviving relic of ancient Hellenism—who composed manifestoes in the Jacobin terminology. If they stood for anything it was for the age-old ethos of a peninsula in which the role of man was to become a hero, and the outlaw who took to the mountains to resist any government and to right the peasant's wrongs was the universal political ideal. To the rebellions of men like Kolokotrones, brigand and cattle-dealer, the nationalists of the Western type gave leadership and a pan-hellenic rather than a purely local scale. In turn they got from them that unique and awe-inspiring thing, the mass rising of an armed people.

The new Greek nationalism was enough to win independence, though the combination of middle-class leadership, klephtic disorganization, and great power intervention produced one of those petty caricatures of the Western liberal ideal which were to become so familiar in areas like Latin America. But it also had the paradoxical result of narrowing Hellenism to Hellas, and thus creating or intensifying the latent nationalism of the other Balkan peoples. While being Greek had been little more than the professional requirement of the literate Orthodox Balkan Christian, hellenization had made progress. Once it meant the political support for Hellas, it receded, even among the assimilated Balkan literate classes. In this sense Greek independence was the essential preliminary condition for the evolution of the other Balkan nationalisms.

Outside Europe it is difficult to speak of nationalism at all. The numerous Latin American republics which replaced the token Spanish and Portuguese Empires (to be accurate, Brazil became and remained an independent monarchy from 1816 to 1889), their frontiers often reflecting little more than the distribution of the estates of the grandees who had backed one rather than another of the local rebellions, began to acquire vested political interests and territorial aspirations. The original pan-American ideal of Simón Bolívar (1783–1830) of Venezuela and San Martín (1788–1850) of the Argentine was impossible to realize, though it has persisted as a powerful revolutionary current throughout all the areas united by the Spanish language, just as pan-Balkanism, the heir of Orthodox unity against Islam, persisted and may still persist today. The vast extent and variety of the continent, the existence of independent foci of rebellion in Mexico (which determined Central America), Venezuela, and Buenos Aires, and the special problem of the centre of Spanish colonialism in Peru, which was liberated from without, imposed automatic fragmentation. But the Latin American revolutions were the work of small groups of patricians, soldiers and gallicized *évolués*, leaving the mass of the Catholic poor-white population passive and the Indians indifferent or hostile. Only in Mexico was independence won by the initiative of a popular agrarian, i.e., Indian, movement marching under the banner of the Virgin of Guadalupe, and Mexico has consequently ever since followed a different and politically more advanced road from the remainder of continental Latin America. However, even among the tiny layer of the politically decisive Latin Americans it would be anachronistic in our period to speak of anything more than the embryo of Colombian, Venezuelan, Ecuadorian, etc. "national consciousness."

Something like a proto-nationalism, however, existed in various countries of Eastern Europe, but paradoxically it took the direction of conservatism rather than national rebellion. The Slavs were oppressed everywhere, except in Russia and in a few wild Balkan strongholds, but in their immediate perspective the oppressors were, as we have seen, not the absolute monarchs, but the German or Magyar landlords and urban exploiters. Nor did the nationalism of these allow any place for Slav national existence: even so radical a programme as that of the German United States proposed by the republicans and democrats of Baden (in South-west Germany) envisaged the inclusion of an Illyrian (i.e., Croat and Slovene) republic with its capital in Italian Trieste, a Moravian one with its capital in Olomouc, and a Bohemian one led by Prague. Hence the immediate hope of the Slav nationalists lay in the emperors of Austria and Russia. Various versions of Slav solidarity expressed the Russian orientation, and attracted Slav rebels—even the anti-Russian Poles—especially in times of defeat and hopelessness as after the failure of the risings in 1846. "Illyrianism" in Croatia and a moderate Czech nationalism expressed the Austrian trend, and both received deliberate support from the Habsburg rulers, two of whose leading ministers—Kolowrat and the chief of the police system, Sedlnitzky—were themselves Czechs.

Croatian cultural aspirations were protected in the 1830s, and by 1840 Kolowrat actually proposed what was later to prove so useful in the 1848 revolution, the appointment of a Croat military *ban* as chief of Croatia, and with control over the military frontier with Hungary, as a counterweight to the obstreperous Magyars. To be a revolutionary in 1848 therefore came to be virtually identical with opposition to Slav national aspirations; and the tacit conflict between the "progressive" and the "reactionary" nations did much to doom the revolutions of 1848 to failure.

Nothing like nationalism is discoverable elsewhere, for the social conditions for it did not exist. In fact, if anything, the forces which were later to produce nationalism were at this stage opposed to the alliance of tradition, religion, and mass poverty which produced the most powerful resistance to the encroachment of Western conquerors and exploiters. The elements of a local bourgeoisie which grew up in Asian countries did so in the shelter of the foreign exploiters whose agents, intermediaries and dependants they largely were. The Parsee community of Bombay is an example. Even if the educated and "enlightened" Asian was not a *compradore* or a lesser official of some foreign ruler or firm (a situation not dissimilar to that of the Greek diaspora in Turkey), his first political task was to Westernize—i.e., to introduce the ideas of the French Revolution and of scientific and technical modernization among his people, against the united resistance of traditional rulers and traditional ruled (a situation not dissimilar to that of the gentlemen-Jacobins of Southern Italy). He was therefore doubly cut off from his people. Nationalist mythology has often obscured this divorce, partly by suppressing the link between colonialism and the early native middle classes, partly lending to earlier anti-foreign resistance the colours of a later nationalist movement. But in Asia, in the Islamic countries, and even more in Africa, the junction between the *évolués* and nationalism, and between both and the masses, was not made until the twentieth century.

Nationalism in the East was thus the eventual product of Western influence and Western conquest. This link is perhaps most evident in the one plainly Oriental country in which the foundations of what was to become the first modern colonial nationalist movement[4] were laid: in Egypt. Napoleon's conquest introduced Western ideas, methods, and techniques, whose value an able and ambitious local soldier, Mohammed Ali (Mehemet Ali), soon recognized. Having seized power and virtual independence from Turkey in the confused period which followed the withdrawal of the French, and with French support, Mohammed Ali set out to establish an efficient and Westernizing despotism with foreign (mainly French) technical aid. European left-wingers in the 1820s and 30s hailed this enlightened autocrat, and put their services at his disposal, when reaction in their own countries looked too dispiriting. The extraordinary sect of the Saint-Simonians, equally suspended between the advocacy of socialism and of industrial development by investment bankers and engineers, temporarily gave him their collective aid and prepared his plans of economic development. * * * They thus also laid the foundation for the Suez Canal (built by the Saint-Simonian de Lesseps) and the fatal dependence of Egyptian rulers on vast loans negotiated by competing groups of European swindlers, which turned Egypt into a centre of imperialist rivalry and anti-imperialist rebellion later on. But Mohammed Ali was no more a nationalist than any other Oriental despot. His Westernization, not his or his people's aspirations, laid the foundations for later nationalism. If Egypt acquired the first nationalist movement in the Islamic world and Morocco one of the last, it was because Mohammed Ali (for perfectly comprehensible geopolitical reasons) was in the main paths of Westernization and the isolated self-sealed Sherifian Empire of the Moslem far west was not, and made no attempts to be. Nationalism, like so many other characteristics of the modern world, is the child of the dual revolution.

NOTES

1. In the early eighteenth century only about 60 per cent of all titles published in Germany were in the German language; since then the proportion had risen fairly steadily.

2. The Sikh movement has remained largely *sui-generis* to this day. The tradition of combative Hindu resistance in Maharashtra made that area an early centre of the Indian nationalism, and provided some of its earliest—and highly traditionalist—leaders, notably B. G. Tilak; but this was at best a regional, and far from dominant strain in the movement. Something like Mahratta nationalism may exist today, but its social basis is the resistance of large Mahratta

working class and underprivileged lower-middle class to the economically and until recently linguistically dominant Gujeratis.

3. It is significant that the present Yugoslav regime has broken up what used to be classed as the Serb nation into the much more realistic sub-national republics and units of Serbia, Bosnia, Montenegro, Macedonia, and Kossovo-Metohidja. By the linguistic standards of nineteenth-century nationalism most of these belonged to a single "Serb" people, except the Macedonians, who are closer to the Bulgarians, and the Albanian minority in Kosmet. But in fact they have never developed a single Serb nationalism.

4. Other than the Irish.

THE ECONOMIST

THE GLOBAL MENACE OF LOCAL STRIFE

In a confetti of medicines, pens and second-hand shirts, armed looters rage through Bunia's main market-place. Startled, the local dogs stop feeding on the rotting human corpses scattered among the empty fruit and vegetable stalls. The mob, which is also looking for food, finds none, and moves on. The pack resumes feeding in quick, delicate bites.

Once a prosperous gold town, ringed by fertile green hills, Bunia, in eastern Congo, was ransacked and deserted last week. Where one gold-trader had his shop, only a gold-paint picture of a pair of scales remains. Every other stall has been gutted, too; boy warriors with AK-47s clamber in and out of jagged holes in once smoothly plastered walls.

The cyclone struck after the Ugandan army,

a plunderous occupying force, withdrew. The two largest local tribes, the Hema and the Lendus, then began to fight for control. First, Lendu militiamen poured into town, killing Hemas and burning their houses. Days later, Hema warriors counter-attacked and chased the Lendus away. No one can say how many died, but the fighting seems to have put at least 250,000 people to flight.

The death toll since Congo's war began in 1998 is higher, at between 3.1m and 4.7m, than in any other ongoing war. But otherwise the conflict is typical of today's wars. The combatants are mostly irregular militias, their victims mostly unarmed, and the fighting has gone on for nearly five years. A century ago most conflicts were between nations, and 90% of casualties were soldiers; today almost all wars are civil, and 90% of the victims are civillians.

From *The Economist* (May 22, 2003).

Civil wars are much more common than they were 40 years ago. This is mainly because, back then, most of the countries currently fighting were colonies, so powerful outside forces imposed stability. Counting only wars with more than 1,000 violent deaths, about one country in eight is embroiled in one. This proportion peaked around 1990, after the superpowers stopped bankrolling rebels who attacked each other's allies. But post–cold war peacemaking seems to have fizzled, and civil wars are getting longer. An average conflict lasts eight years, more than twice the norm before 1980.

Why is this happening? Some blame tribalism: a pleasingly simple thesis that both seems to fit the facts, and gives outsiders an excuse for indifference and inaction. But the reality is more complex. Tribes often quarrel, but ethnic passions on their own are rarely enough to stoke a full-blown war. The Hema and the Lendus, for example, have been trying to wipe each other out only since Uganda started arming rival tribal militias in 1999, in the hope of controlling the mineral-rich region around Bunia. If tribalism is the problem, ethnically homogenous countries should be peaceful—but look at Somalia.

Or at Sudan, whose civil war is often seen as a simple conflict between Arab Muslims and black non-Muslims. The view from the battlefield is cloudier, however. Last year, your correspondent met David Matwok, a young militiaman in the pay of Sudan's Arab government, who was lying on his back on the savannah with both legs broken by bullets. Mr. Matwok was a member of the Nuer tribe; so were the rebels who shot him, during a pitched battle. The battlefield had seen Nuer fight Nuer before: among the still-bleeding corpses were scattered human vertebrae and clean-picked skulls, like golf balls on a vast green fairway. Every bone had once belonged to a Nuer.

And why were they fighting? According to the rebel commander, "Even where you are sitting, there is oil." Money trumps kinship. Mr. Matwok begged for water, but his fellow tribesmen told him they hoped wild animals would eat him.

All wars are different, of course. Each arises from a unique combination of causes, and each requires a different sort of solution. Nonetheless, by looking at what the most conflict-prone places have in common, it is possible to identify likely risk factors. This, in turn, might help to prevent wars in the future.

What Causes Wars?

A new study by Paul Collier of the World Bank and others, which examines the world's civil wars since 1960, concludes that although tribalism is often a factor, it is rarely the main one. Surprisingly, the authors found that societies composed of several different ethnic and religious groups were actually less likely to experience civil war than homogenous societies.

However, in multi-ethnic societies where one group forms an absolute majority, the risk of war is 50% higher than in societies where this is not the case. This is perhaps because minorities fear that even if the country is democratic, they will be permanently excluded from power.

The most striking common factor among war-prone countries is their poverty. Rich countries almost never suffer civil war, and middle-income countries rarely. But the poorest one-sixth of humanity endures four-fifths of the world's civil wars.

The best predictors of conflict are low average incomes, low growth, and a high dependence on exports of primary products such as oil or diamonds. The World Bank found that when income per person doubles, the risk of civil war halves, and that for each percentage point by which the growth rate rises, the risk of conflict falls by a point. An otherwise typical country whose exports of primary commodities account for 10% of GDP has an 11% chance of being at war. At 30% of GDP, the risk peaks at about one in three.

Why are poor, stagnant countries so vulnerable? Partly because it is easy to give a poor man a cause. But also, almost certainly, because poverty and low or negative growth are often symptoms of corrupt, incompetent government, which can provoke rebellion. They are also common in immature societies, whose people have not yet figured out how to live together.

Natural resources tend to aggravate these problems. When a state has oil, its leaders can grow rich without bothering to nurture other kinds of economic activity. Corrupt leaders often cement their support base by sharing the loot with their own ethnic group, which tends to anger all the other groups.

Most countries have what Mr. Collier calls "ethnic romantics who dream of creating an ethnically 'pure' political entity." If oil is found beneath their home region, their calls for secession suddenly start to sound attractive to those who live there, and abhorrent to everyone else. Oil was one reason why Biafra tried to secede from Nigeria, and why the Nigerian government fought so hard to prevent it.

Secessionist leaders in Aceh, an oil-endowed part of Indonesia, told potential supporters that secession would make them as rich as the people of Brunei. This ten-fold exaggeration raised expectations that were impossible to meet, which may explain why the rebels went back to war despite a peace deal in December promising Aceh autonomy and 70% of the cash from its oil and gas.

Guns Cost Money

Laurent Kabila, the rebel who overthrew the dictator Mobutu Sese Seko, once boasted that all he needed to mount a revolution was $10,000 and a satellite telephone. He was exaggerating. Recruiting soldiers in Congo (which was then called Zaire) is cheap, because the country is so poor, but it is not that cheap. Guns have grown less costly since old Soviet armouries emptied on to the black market, but they are not free. In fact, Kabila had a budget in the millions, partly because he enjoyed the backing of a foreign power, Rwanda, and partly because he used his sat-

phone to sell mineral rights he did not yet control to unscrupulous foreign firms.

Rebellions almost always start for political reasons. But since sustaining even the crudest guerrilla war requires cash, rebel leaders have to find ways of raising the stuff. Many, including most in Africa, receive money from neighbouring governments hostile to the one they are fighting. Some rebel groups are supported by an ethnic diaspora whose members, since they live abroad, do not have to endure the consequences of the wars they help fund.

In countries with abundant natural resources, however, rebels have less need to beg. Alluvial diamonds, the sort that can be plucked from riverbeds without sophisticated mining equipment, have financed rebel groups in Angola and Sierra Leone. Illegal logging, another low-tech business, fuels fighting in Liberia and Cambodia. In Congo, half a dozen national armies and countless rebel groups have fought over some of the world's richest deposits of gold, cobalt, diamonds and coltan.

In countries with high tariffs, rebels can make money by seizing a stretch of border and charging smugglers less than the government would. Afghan fighters, for example, have prospered from the protectionism of Afghanistan's neighbours. Rebel areas are also ideal for growing drugs. An estimated 95% of the world's opium comes from war-torn nations, and Colombia's rebels thrive on coca.

Rebels rarely pump oil. It requires capital, skills and technology, and the firms that have these things prefer to deal with legitimate governments. But rebels can still profit from oil, by extorting money from oil firms. One technique, popular in Colombia and Nigeria, is to kidnap their employees and demand ransoms. Another is to threaten to blow up pipelines. Firms usually pay up. During the 1990s, European companies handed over an estimated $1.2 billion to rebel extortionists, a sum far greater than official European aid to the governments of the countries in question. Ransom insurance, now available, has the effect of raising ransom demands, and so increases the profits to be made from violence.

From Comrades-in-Arms to Cosa Nostra

Rebellions rarely begin as criminal business ventures, but they often mutate into them. Their leaders can grow fabulously rich. By one estimate, Jonas Savimbi, the late Angolan guerrilla chief, amassed $4 billion from selling diamonds, ivory and anything else his men could steal. Besides paying for bullets, such profits give rebel commanders a powerful incentive to keep fighting. Says Mr. Collier: "Asking a rebel leader to accept peace may be a little like asking a champion swimmer to empty the pool." Savimbi only laid down his weapons for good when he was shot dead.

War creates a vicious circle. When rebel groups start to make money, they attract greedy leaders. At the same time, war makes it harder for peaceful people to earn a living. No one wants to build factories in war zones. People with portable skills flee, and those with money stash it offshore. Peasants find it hard to farm when rebels keep plundering their villages.

Poverty fosters war, and war impoverishes. In Congo, a combination of violence and official neglect has all but destroyed the country's roads, telephones and organs of government. Whole regions are cut off from the centre. Rubaruba Zabuloni, for example, has been fighting for nearly 40 years. A dwarfish 69-year-old with a crew-cut and a black fur hat, he leads a 7,000-man militia in the hills above Lake Tanganyika. In the 1960s, he fought with Che Guevara; in later years, the Soviet Union continued to send arms. He is unaware of the demise of either.

The big foreign armies involved in Congo's war have more or less made peace, and a new central government is gradually forming. But dozens of smaller, local conflicts continue to blaze. They are fought with low-tech weapons: machetes, bows and a few guns. An endless cycle of atrocities creates an endless cycle of grudges, which fuel more micro-wars. "When we kill a Rwandan," said Mr. Zabuloni's personal witch-doctor, "we fry up his penis and eat it. It makes you fearless. Would you like to try it?"

Being a rebel footsoldier is no way to make a fortune, but it may be better than the alternative, particularly if the alternative is to be a rebel footsoldier's victim. One of the gun-waving boys in Bunia put it pithily. Asked why he chose to take up arms, Singoma Mapisa fiddled shyly with his new Seiko watch—a happy acquisition on a Congolese soldier's pay of nothing—and replied: "The Lendus murdered my parents. How else could I survive?" He was later seen pilfering two Mickey Mouse satchels, which could prove useful if he ever goes to school.

A typical civil war leaves a country 15% poorer than it would otherwise have been, and with perhaps 30% more people living in absolute poverty. The damage persists long afterwards. Skills and capital continue to flee, because people do not trust the peace: half of newly peaceful countries revert to war within a decade.

Infant mortality also remains high, not least because war nurtures disease. Refugees carry malaria from areas where the population is immune to a particular strain to areas where it is not. One study found that for each 1,000 refugees who flee from one tropical country to another, the host country suffers an extra 1,406 cases of malaria.

Rampaging armies are also efficient vectors for AIDS. Soldiers are more likely than civilians to be infected, and too often inclined to spread the virus forcibly. One study found that halving military manpower correlates with a one-quarter reduction in HIV among low-risk adults. Some researchers even blame war for the first spread of the AIDS pandemic, conjecturing that a small localised infection was carried far and wide through mass rape during the Ugandan civil war of the 1970s.

Besides scattering refugees and spreading disease, civil wars often disrupt trade across whole regions. Congo's war blocked the river along which the Central African Republic's trade used to flow, aggravating the CAR's economic malaise and perhaps contributing to a recent succession of coup attempts by unpaid soldiers. In all, having a neighbour at war reduces economic growth by about 0.5% each year.

Give Peace a Chance

Since countries prone to civil war are poor, stagnant places, anything that promotes growth ought to help. Governments in poor countries should strive to keep corruption, inflation and trade barriers low, while attempting to build better health, education and legal systems.

To guard against future insurgency, governments of newly peaceful countries often keep lavishing cash on the army. Military spending averages 4.5% of GDP in the first decade of peace, down from 5% during the war, but up from 2.8% before it. Such spending actually increases the risk of another war, because it wastes resources that could improve people's lives, and signals to rebels and people alike that the gov-

ernment is preparing for another war.

Spending on health and education, by contrast, seems to provide an immediate boost to the economy of a newly peaceful nation. This is surprising. The benefits of social spending usually take years to show up in the growth figures. But in countries emerging from war, a new school or clinic shows that the government is serious about peace, which buoys confidence and may encourage private investment.

Once war gathers pace, the vicious circle is hard to break. Intervention by proper armies with orders to shoot to kill can work: British troops helped save Sierra Leone, and the French legionnaires in Côte d'Ivoire have reduced the carnage there. The UN, whose peacekeepers are often ill-prepared for actual fighting, has a less impressive record. In Bunia last week, 700 Uruguayan peacekeepers were unable to prevent a massacre outside their barracks because their mandate was too feeble. The UN managed to broker a ceasefire on May 16th, but the only reason the fighting has stopped in Bunia is that one side has won. Out in the hills, the killing continues.

PAUL COLLIER

ETHNIC DIVERSITY: AN ECONOMIC ANALYSIS

1. Introduction

Nation-building has been seen as the decline of ethnic or local loyalties and their replacement by allegiance to a nation. The new states of the developing world have often yet to go through this process: people identify more strongly with their kin group, ethnic group, or religious group, than

From *Economic Policy* 32 (April 2001), pp. 127–66.

with the nation. The power of such sub-national identities is commonly regarded as a curse. Societies divided by ethnicity are seen as less likely to reach co-operative solutions, and more likely to victimize minorities.

The most serious charge levelled against ethnic differentiation is that it is the prime cause of violent civil conflict. The evidence seems to bear this out. The developing countries are more ethnically diverse than the OECD societies, and they suffer a much higher incidence of civil war.

Among developing countries, Africa is more ethnically diverse than other regions and it has the highest incidence of civil war, a phenomenon often interpreted as the post-colonial re-emergence of ancestral ethnic hatreds. Ethnic conflicts in developing countries have become a major policy concern to OECD governments, triggering both humanitarian and military interventions. In addition to the massive military and financial interventions in the former Yugoslavia, during the 1990s Belgium, Britain, France and the USA all dispatched troops to African conflicts. Such policy interventions were partly motivated by the manifestly debilitating consequences of civil war for the society in which it occurs. However, there was probably also an element of self-interest. Civil wars have social repercussions far beyond the boundaries of the affected state. Refugees create waves of migration, and the diasporas are often drawn into the conflict. Indeed, many civil wars have a penumbra of illegal migration and drug trafficking which directly affect OECD societies.

Ethnic differentiation has also come to be seen as detrimental to economic management. Easterly and Levine (1997) report that ethnic diversity reduces the rate of economic growth. They explain this in terms of a hypothesized effect of diversity upon political choices. Diverse societies are alleged to find it more difficult to reach cooperative solutions, and to be more likely to waste resources in distributional struggles. The economic consequences of this allegedly dysfunctional politics are claimed to be huge. Easterly and Levine attribute Africa's present poverty predominantly to its unusually high ethnic diversity. The title of their article, "Africa's Growth Tragedy: Policies and Ethnic Divisions," aptly summarizes the proposition: ethnic divisions are responsible for economic policies which are so impoverishing as to be tragic. As with civil war, impoverishment casts a long shadow: OECD governments attempt to remedy it through aid programs, motivated both by compassion and by fear of the social and political consequences of bordering on regions of extreme poverty.

These two detrimental effects of ethnic differentiation can be nested. Civil war can be viewed as the extreme manifestation of the more general phenomenon of dysfunctional politics. The underlying propositions are that ethnic divisions make cooperation more difficult and victimization more likely.

If strong sub-national ethnic identification is indeed dysfunctional, then there appears to be two solutions. Governments could engage in the sort of virulent nationalism which Europe used in its own building of national identities. The obvious danger in this process is that it risks international conflict, as happened in Europe. Alternatively, governments could accede to the demand for ethnic self-determination, creating many new states. This solution gained momentum during the 1990s although it has some evident limitations. In this paper I argue that neither of these solutions is necessary because the premises on which they are based are false. With a few specific exceptions, ethnic diversity neither increases the risk of civil war, nor reduces economic growth. Multi-ethnic societies can usually be socially and economically fully viable.

In Section 2 I set out the current state of knowledge: what is meant by ethnic identity, and why is it thought to be dysfunctional? In Sections 3 and 4 I venture beyond the literature. In Section 3 I investigate how ethnic politics might affect economic performance, deriving predictions from theories of political choice and testing them on global data. In Section 4 I turn to the causes of large scale violence. I investigate how ethnic differentiation might effect civil conflict. Building on new theories of conflict which stress the importance of the budget constraint faced by the rebel organization, I test three predictions on global data. In Section 5 I draw out some implications for policy. Ethnic diversity is not "guilty as charged." It does not, usually, cause slower growth, and it does not, usually, cause civil war. The international community may need to rethink its current tolerant approach to secession.

2. What Do We Know and What are the Gaps?

How does ethnicity sometimes come to be the basis for social and political identity?

Ethnicity as a basis for identity is a social rather than a physiological phenomenon. As a *cultural* phenomenon ethnicity is nevertheless, highly persistent: people chose to pass on their culture by marrying within their own group (Bisin and Verdier, 2000). However, as a *political* phenomenon, ethnic identity is considerably more fluid. This is indeed implied by "national building"—in Europe perceptions of identity changed during the eighteenth and nineteenth century from being (say) Scottish or Breton to being British or French. The process is recounted for eighteenth-century Britain in *Britons: Forging the Nation* (Colley, 1992), and for nineteenth-century France in *Peasants into Frenchmen* (Weber, 1975). Currently, in much of the developing world the most powerful levels of social identity are neither the nation nor the region, but the kin group and the tribe. One of the developments in New Institutional Economics has been to reinterpret kin groups not as primitive emotional bonds but as efficient responses to problems of information and contract enforcement in traditional economies. Posner (1980) brilliantly shows why kinship was (and remains) such an efficient basis for collective action. Basing group membership upon kinship provides clear rules of lifetime membership, thereby overcoming the standard problems of adverse selection. Kinship also provides high observability of behaviour: the involvement and gossip of relatives ensures that the group is well informed about anti-social behaviour, and this discourages moral hazard. Kin groups are thus well placed both to enforce bilateral contracts among members, and to provide group-level insurance or defence, anchored on a robust web of reciprocal obligations. The value of kin groups applies in a variety of contexts: Posner's original application was to high-risk agriculture, but Greif (1992) shows their value in medieval long distance trade, and Biggs *et al.* (1996) show their value in manufacturing. On this view, kin groups are efficient responses to the information and contract enforcement problems of market economies. An implication is that a society composed of multiple kin groups is more efficient than a homogenous, but atomized, society. Kin groups do not divide a pre-existing whole, but rather aggregate an atomized society into groups large enough to reap the gains from collective action.

While the basis of social identity in developing countries may usually be the kin group, effective political groupings are too large to be based upon social interaction, and so must be based upon an *imagined* shared identity (Anderson, 1983). Where collective action is already based upon ties of blood as in kin groups, it is easy to conjure up imagined larger blood-related political groupings. For example, in Africa the advent of colonialism created opportunities for large political groupings to secure economic advantages. Kin groups "invented tradition" as they amalgamated into large tribes, although in practice language seems to have been the main basis for tribal agglomeration. The three main tribal groupings in Nigeria (Yoruba, Ibo and Hausa-Fulani) appear to date from the nineteenth century, while the currently dominant Kenyan tribe, the Kalenjin, dates back only to the 1940s. This process of amalgamation is continuing. Daniel Posner (1999) shows how African tribes have formed durable political alliances, so that societies are considerably less fractionalized politically than implied by tribal identity. Modern ethnic political loyalties thus start from reciprocal economic obligations within a kin-group, extend to an imagined community of shared interest within a tribe, and often extend to alliances with other tribes to form a political party.

Given that in many societies ethnicity, real or imagined, is the basis for social and political identity, what are its consequences?

To research these issues empirically, social

scientists need a quantitative measure of how societies differ with respect to the extent of ethnic differentiation. The most widely used measure is the "index of ethno-linguistic fractionalization" (ELF). Homogenous societies are scored zero, and the theoretical maximum of 100 would be reached if each person belonged to a distinct group. The observed range is from zero to 93. This measure has some serious problems. Daniel Posner (1999) describes some substantial inaccuracies. Further, representation by a single number can lose critical information. We might expect that victimization arises in societies in which one or more minorities face a majority, while an inability to co-operate arises in societies in which there are many groups, none with a majority, yet the ELF index cannot distinguish between them. I term these two circumstances *dominance* and *fragmentation* and I will show below that they have significantly different consequences. Examples of societies with ethnic politics in which there is a majority ethnic group and one or more ethnic minorities are Malaysia, Belgium, Northern Ireland, Canada, South Africa and Rwanda. In these societies the fear of ethnic politics is that it will lead to the permanent exclusion of other groups and discrimination against them. However, most societies are characterized neither by ethnic dominance nor by homogeneity, but by fragmentation.

A recent literature suggests that kin groups may also create substantial problems of co-operation between members of different groups. I consider four studies in ascending order of size and complexity of organization. Miguel (1999) studies school boards in different areas of Kenya. He shows that to function effectively, the boards need to be able to enforce obligations within the community—for example, the duty to make financial contributions to the school. He finds that those boards which are ethnically diverse are less able to do this, since board members are less willing to criticize someone from their own ethnic group in front of members from other groups. Alesina *et al.* (1999) investigate a larger type of community and a more general decision, namely city government in the USA. They find that the more ethnically diverse is the electorate, the worse is the productivity of public expenditure. They suggest that diversity increases the problems of collective action because more of the benefits are external to the group. Together with Ashish Garg, I analysed the effect of ethnic diversity in the Ghanaian labour market (Collier and Garg, 1999). We also found that ethnic diversity had consequences which must have been highly problematic. Controlling for other characteristics, workers from whichever tribe was locally the largest were commanding a substantial wage premium. We explained this in terms of the power of kin group patronage in promotions, with larger groups having disproportionate power. The highest level of organization and generality of decision is that analysed by Easterly and Levine (1997). Here the adverse consequence is on the national growth rate, and the inferred mechanism is poor national economic policy. Easterly and Levine infer that ethnic diversity makes political cooperation more difficult. Thus, at various sizes of organization, ethnic diversity appears to make co-operation more difficult.

However, there is also counter-evidence. Although Miguel convincingly establishes why ethnic diversity is dysfunctional within a Kenyan school board, the explanation cannot account for the other examples of the costs of diversity. In the school boards diversity nullifies the co-operation which can otherwise be achieved by kin groups. Diversity only takes the society back to the non co-operative outcome of atomistic homogeneity. Obviously this cannot be the explanation for Easterly and Levine's result that ethnically diverse societies grow less rapidly than ethnically homogenous societies. It turns out that the ethnical diversity of cities analysed by Alesina *et al.* is characterized by dominance, not fragmentation. Thus, the costs of diversity which they find might only occur in conditions of dominance. If so, this would be an important qualification since, unlike US cities, most ethnically diverse countries are characterized by fragmentation rather than dominance. My own study with Garg distinguished between the public sector and the private sector. We found that in the public sector the patronage-induced wage premium for the locally largest tribe was 25% whereas in the private sector it was zero. We interpreted this as suggesting that in the private sector competition forced firms to curb the patronage power of kin groups, so that ethnic diversity was only a problem for public sector organizations. Recall that both the Miguel and Alesina et al. studies were of public sector organizations. Easterly and Levine simply use the ELF score as a measure of ethnic diversity and do not distinguish between dominance and fragmentation so that again, potentially, all the costs of diversity could be due to dominance. Further, as argued by Arcand et al. (2000), if the adverse effect of ethnic diversity works through poor policy choice, then once policy choices are added to the Easterly and Levine growth regression, the negative coefficient upon ethnic diversity should diminish. They add a range of macroeconomic policies to the regression and show that the coefficient on ethnic diversity does not diminish. Thus, rather than amounting to a unified critique of ethnic diversity, the literature may simply show that it can have negative effects in particular circumstances. Perhaps ethnic diversity is damaging if it takes the form of dominance; perhaps it is damaging in the public sector. A more nuanced analysis seems to be required.

Another literature considers an altogether darker supposed consequence of ethnic diversity, not as an impediment to co-operation, but as an incitement to victimization and civil war. Horowitz (1985) shows that ethnic identity is often accompanied by hostility to other groups. The problem of victimization of minorities, such as Jews in Europe and the Tutsi in Rwanda, has been extensively analysed, most notably through the "Minorities at Risk" project (Gurr, 1993). Emminghaus et al. (1998: p. 140) conclude that "the formation of cultural identities about primordial sentiments without the parallel or subsequent development of civil identities has led to primordial violence in today's world." However, both political science and economics has countervailing theories which argue that ethnic hatred does not provide a good explanation for large-scale violent conflict. Two distinguished political scientists, Fearon and Laitin (1999), analyse the Minorities at Risk data and roundly reject both cultural differences and the degree of cultural and economic discrimination against minorities as explanations for episodes of major violence. Similarly, Bates (1999) finds that while political protest is more common in ethnically diverse societies, political violence is less common. He concludes, "it is diversity, not homogeneity that lowers the risk of conflict" (p. 31). Economists have also developed a countervailing theory of civil war. Starting with the pioneering work of Grossman (1991), they have focused upon the budget constraint for rebellion: trying to identify the circumstances in which rebellion is financially profitable. In Grossman's work the very rationale for rebellion is financial: rebels are indistinguishable from criminal bandits. More recently, in my own work (Collier, 2000a, b), the motivation for rebellion is allowed to be more general, but financial and military viability are treated as important constraints. The core of the analysis is the differential ability of rebel organizations to raise finance, depending upon the opportunities for predation of primary commodity exports and for the taxation of diasporas. The predicted effects of ethnic diversity depend upon whether it takes the form of dominance or fragmentation. Dominance (one ethnic group in a permanent majority) may well produce victimization and so increase the risk of rebellion. Fragmentation, however, is predicted to make rebellion more difficult because to be militarily viable a rebel organization must maintain cohesion. If diversity reduces organizational cohesion, rebel recruitment is more problematic in diverse societies. Thus, in diverse societies, even if people hate each other more than in homogenous societies, they are less able to translate hatred into large-scale organized violence. Here, the "ethnic hatred" and economic theories of the causes of conflict radically diverge in a testable way. My empirical work with Anke Hoeffler (Collier and Hoeffler, 1998, 2000), attempts to test these rival theories on a comprehensive data set of civil wars between 1960–99. We find that whereas ethnic dominance indeed doubles the risk of civil war, fragmentation significantly *reduces* the risk. Thus, as with the literature on ethnic diversity and co-operation, the case against diversity is less robust and less general than might appear at first sight.

3. Does Ethnic Diversity Cause Dysfunctional Politics?

If democratic politics is dysfunctional in ethnically diverse societies, then an implication might be that ethnically diverse societies need a strong leader "above" politics to avoid these pressures. This argument is beloved of third-world dictators: their ethnically diverse societies need them.

I now compare the effect of ethnic politics in democracy and dictatorship. This requires a counterfactual, how political choices are made in the absence of ethnic loyalties. Unsurprisingly, modern theories of political choice seldom yield unambiguous predictions. Even something as basic as the relative efficacy of dictatorship and democracy turns out to be *a priori* ambiguous, a result which is consistent with the empirical literature. My argument will be that usually the introduction of party loyalties based on ethnicity does not substantially change outcomes, but that in two specific circumstances it is likely to have significant negative effects.

3.1. Ethnic Diversity in Democracies

I begin with the effect of ethnic parties in democracies. To analyse the democratic political process, it is useful to contrast two commonly used approaches to legislative decision-taking. One is the process originally analysed by Downs (1957), in which voter preferences are distributed only over a single issue, such as the rate of taxation, so that these preferences can be arrayed along a left-right spectrum. In the second, voters have preferences over multiple issues. Potentially, ethnic politics can take place within either of these systems.

3.1.1. SINGLE-ISSUE POLITICS.

Single-issue politics is a good point of embarkation. I will assume that the government is constrained so that all electors must benefit equally from the provision of a public good financed out of taxation: so that the single issue is to choose the rate of taxation. Electors have different preferences because they differ by income: high-income voters will prefer a low income tax rate, and low-income voters will prefer a high income tax rate.

In the absence of identity politics, Down's model produces a clear result. Parties compete to form a minimum winning coalition, and the winner is the party which attracts the support of the median voter. Thus, the tax rate will be set at that rate preferred by someone with median income (although this need not be socially optimal). Now introduce ethnic politics: each ethnic group has its own political party, supported by all members of the group. What happens depends upon whether income differences are related to ethnic differences. First, suppose that the two are unrelated: the distribution of income is the same for each ethnic group. In this case, ethnic politics does not change the median voter outcome, although the process by which democracy reaches the tax rate decision is different. With ethnic politics the important democratic process is that which is internal to each party. Regardless of which ethnic party is in power, with internal democracy each party will represent the median voter within its ethnic group. By assumption, all of these median voters have the same interests. Hence, ethnic politics makes no difference to political decisions regardless of whether diversity takes the form of fragmentation or dominance.

Now consider the other extreme, where incomes differ so much between ethnic groups that all the members of the richest group are richer than all the members of the next group, and so on (income is "lexicographic" in ethnicity). That ethnic party which contains the voter with the median economic interest now becomes the pivotal party, able to determine the government. However, this pivotal ethnic party need not maximize the well-being of the voter with the median economic interest. This voter is already locked into supporting the party by virtue of his or her ethnic identity. Hence, if the party is internally democratic, it will be driven to maximizing the well-being of the voter who is at the median of the party rather than at the median of the electorate as a whole. Whether this difference is important depends upon the nature of ethnic diversity. If there is fragmentation then the median voter within the pivotal party is likely to have interests very close to those of the median elector. If, however, there is ethnic dominance then the divergence may be greater. Consider, for example, a stylized version of South African politics in which the black party holds 65% of the vote, with whites and Asians having higher incomes than blacks. Now, ethnic politics delivers policies which maximize the well-being of the 33rd percentile as opposed to the 50th percentile with ethnicity-free politics. However, paradoxically, as ethnic dominance increases, the divergence diminishes. If the dominant ethnic group has 90% of the electorate, then its party maximizes the interest of around the 46th percentile.

To summarize, in single-issue politics ethnic politics is scarcely alarming. If ethnic identities are unrelated to economic interests ethnic politics has no effect. Even when ethnic identity is strongly correlated with economic interest, ethnic politics makes surprisingly little difference. When diversity takes the form of fragmentation ethnic politics will normally have only a negligible effect. When it takes the form of ethnic dominance, it will only have a substantial effect if the dominant group has a small plurality, and if, at the same time, there is a large difference between the income of this group and other groups.

3.1.2. MULTI-ISSUE POLITICS.

Single-issue politics is not, however, a very illuminating window on the political process. Now consider an extreme form of multi-issue politics, namely, the distribution of expenditure. Instead of the good financed out of taxation being a public good which benefits all electors equally, suppose that it benefits only the electors of the constituency in which it is located. Further, suppose that the taxation needed to finance it has disincentive effects and so reduces the growth rate of the economy. The higher is public expenditure, the lower is growth. The political process must now decide on the pattern of public expenditure bearing in mind the resulting taxation. In the absence of identity politics, political parties (if they exist at all), will be weak. Legislators depend for their survival on their ability to deliver expenditure to local voters, rather than on party loyalties. In general, games such as this have no "core": there is no equilibrium and the likely outcome is therefore instability (Inman and Rubenstein, 1997). The political system continues to try to build a minimum winning coalition which captures all the benefits of public expenditure for its own members. However, no such coalition can persist. Any group which assembles 51% support can always be supplanted by some other alliance. Hence, majorities keep forming and breaking up. As Drazen (2000, pp. 71–72) notes: "Indeterminacy in general . . . is seen as perhaps the major defect of majority voting as a choice mechanism." However, whichever group is temporarily in power has an incentive to sacrifice overall growth for redistribution to its own supporters. It consequently chooses a high tax rate in order to benefit from the resulting expenditure. Each group only benefits temporarily from the expenditure, but since the tax rate is sustained, there is a continuous sacrifice of growth. * * *

Now introduce identity politics. First consider

the consequences of exogenous party loyalties in the case of fragmentation: no ethnic group constitutes a majority. Since unstable minimum winning coalitions inflict costs on most or all groups in society, there are mutual gains from co-operation if only a bargain can be negotiated and enforced. Since the game is played repeatedly, if there were only two players (the leaders of two political parties), there would be no dilemma: in a two-person repeated game both players come to deploy a tit-for-tat strategy, and this enforces cooperation. A reasonable presumption is that the more players are in the game, the less likely it is that legislators can escape from the dilemma (Hardin, 1997), although Drazen (2000) shows that this need not be the case in sufficiently complex models of political bargaining. If legislators are grouped into strong parties which can discipline their behaviour and so enforce agreements, the number of players is reduced and so co-operation may become easier. This suggests that in a parliamentary system, the presence of exogenously given party identity, on whatever basis, is useful. If the alternative to ethnic politics is parties which are too weak to control legislators, ethnic identity might be an improvement. However, comparing among societies all of which have ethnic politics, the more ethnically fractionalized is the society, and hence the greater the number of political parties, the more difficult it might be to arrive at the co-operative solution. Thus, differentiation into, say, three equal parties may be an improvement on homogeneity, but differentiation into thirty parties would be worse than into three.

Now consider identity politics in the circumstances of ethnic dominance. Suppose, as before, that there is ethnic politics in "South Africa" with one ethnic group holding a majority of 65%. If the group holds together it can now capture 100% of the expenditure and so does very well. Ethnic identity may be sufficiently strong to enforce cohesion on the dominant ethnic group, producing a stable winning coalition, although the group would be inefficiently large. If it could do so without losing cohesion, the party

of the dominant ethnic group would slim down to representing just 51% of the electorate, conferring larger benefits on its remaining members. Assuming that an ethnic party is only able to keep a stable political majority by including its entire ethnic group, then an interesting paradox follows. A dominant ethnic group will do more damage to growth the smaller is its majority. * * * While ethnic politics in the context of ethnic dominance is liable to produce discrimination against the minority, this is obviously not specific to ethnicity as a basis for political identity. Any system in which electoral allegiance is based on identity will have the same tendency if one party has a permanent majority.

To summarize, inserting ethnic parties into democratic systems generates the following propositions. In the (probably unusual) circumstances of single issue politics, ethnic fragmentation will not have large effects. Ethnic dominance may have moderately large effects, but there will be no systematic effect on growth. In the (more usual) circumstances of multi-issue politics, without identity politics the expectation is of instability due to the lack of an equilibrium. Ethnic dominance confers durable power on a winning coalition which then has an incentive to sacrifice growth for redistribution, although the incentive is weaker than for a *minimum* winning coalition. Limited ethnic fragmentation facilitates co-operative outcomes which avoid or reduce the costs of unstable minimum winning coalitions. However, the greater the extent of ethnic fragmentation, the more difficult it is to reach a co-operative solution.

3.1.3. DIFFERENCES IN THE ROLE OF IDENTITY POLITICS.

Before turning to econometric testing of these propositions it is useful to "ground truth" them against the differing role of identity politics in the democracies of America, Europe and Africa. American political allegiance, at least at the national level, is not strongly related to identity: many voters are willing to switch between parties based on current interests. In Europe political allegiance is more influenced by identity, with the basis for identity being class, religion, language or history rather than ethnicity. Because European electors tend to have these exogenous loyalties to parties, and the party leaders control candidate nominations, parties are much stronger than in America, with party leaderships controlling how legislators vote. In Africa party identification is normally ethnic except where such identification is deliberately suppressed.

The above analysis of multi-issue politics would predict that in America the weakness of parties due to the absence of identity politics would produce unstable minimum winning coalitions. This is not borne out in American experience. Instead of congressional voting being characterized by minimum winning coalitions of changing composition, most spending votes are supported by large majorities, the phenomenon being known as "pork barrel politics." A large body of theory has developed to explain this behaviour (see for example, Weingast, 1979). The argument is that changing minimum winning coalitions would be highly disadvantageous for the legislators. Periodically, they would be unable to provide any benefits to their local electors and so would risk being defeated. Legislators have therefore evolved a pattern of behaviour in which each legislator is given equal powers over the agenda. Specifically, each has the power of proposing an expenditure which benefits his locality. Legislators may devise benefits which are complex non-monetary transfers, thereby making it more difficult for voters to understand the true costs and beneficiaries (Coate and Morris, 1995). Proposals are log-rolled, an implicit norm of deference among legislators amounting to "I'll scratch your back if you'll scratch mine." While this is good for legislators, it is not good for the economy. The projects must be paid for and so, as with minimum winning coalitions, the outcome is that expenditure is too high. The problem is that there is no process for internalizing the externalities of the taxes needed to pay for

the expenditures, analogous to the "restaurant bill problem" in which if a group of people agree to share the bill, they all have an incentive to over-eat. Hence, pork-barrel log-rolling results in inefficient reductions in growth. To counter this, the American constitution gives veto powers to the President.

Evidently, the practical problem in democratic politics appears to be pork-barrel log-rolling rather than unstable minimum winning coalitions. Potentially, however, exogenous strong parties can again reduce the problem. Party leaders internalize the negative fiscal externalities of pork-barrel politics. Empowered by stable voter allegiance they can co-operate to rein in log-rolling and so improve economic performance.

The European parliamentary system, being more characterized by identity politics, is therefore predicted to have less of a problem with log-rolling. Further, the huge variation within European politics in the number of parties provides a test of the proposition that fragmentation will reduce the durability of inter-party co-operation. Both of these propositions find empirical support. Schofield (1997) shows that within Europe variation in the number of parties (associated with whether or not there is proportional representation) is associated with a shorter life of governing coalitions. However, he argues that the effect is too weak to constitute a substantial problem.

Recent democratizations in Africa provide an unusual opportunity to see what happens when ethnic politics is suppressed. There are currently two experiments in which a party contest previously based on ethnicity was purged of ethnic identity. In the 1960s both Ugandan and Nigerian political parties were ethnically based with legislator voting following these party lines. After a period of dictatorship democracy has been re-established, but with constitutional changes which suppress the old parties. In Uganda legislators are elected to parliament, but are not allowed to campaign except as individuals: there are no parties. In Nigeria, two new political parties were imposed by the departing military government, each with requirements to be multi-ethnic. The result to date has been a dramatic confirmation of Weingast's theory that weak parties produce legislative log-rolling. As in America, both legislatures have had a strong, universalist, pro-expenditure bias.

3.2. Dictatorship

I now turn from democracy to dictatorship. With or without ethnic parties, democracy is unlikely to reach the hypothetical social-planning optimum. An all-powerful, all-knowing dictator could *be* the social planner, for example, overcoming the restaurant bill problem. However, even the benevolent social-planning dictator is in practice not all-knowing. Indeed, he will lack much information revealed through democratic processes and so miss opportunities for mutually beneficial political deals. Hence, *a priori*, it is ambiguous whether benevolent dictatorships are more or less efficient than democracy. More fundamentally, there is no particular reason why a dictator should have this objective. Olsen (1991) argues that in the absence of democratic checks, rulers will tend to abrogate property rights. Indeed, because they lack the power to bind themselves, even benevolent dictators face a classic time-consistency problem in which potential investors cannot infer from current benevolence that future policy will not become predatory. Empirical studies of the effect of dictatorship on economic performance have generally failed to find a clear effect (Benabou, 1996), suggesting that the scope for a social planner to outperform democracy roughly offsets the scope for dictators to be more predatory than elected politicians.

The theoretical literature on dictatorship has not previously analysed the effect of ethnic diversity. A useful starting place is to consider the power-base of the dictator. A benevolent dictator who succeeds in realizing the gains of social planning may be sufficiently popular not to need military support: was Lee Kwan Yew a dictator of Singapore or an astonishingly successful politician? In what follows I will treat benevolent

dictators as random "acts of God," distributed without relation to ethnic diversity. Instead, I focus on those dictators who do not take the social planning route to the maintenance of power. They must rely upon an army. In Section 2 I suggested that rebel military organizations need cohesion and so must avoid the impediments to co-operation introduced by recruiting across ethnic boundaries. Self-serving dictatorships are analogous to rebel organizations and face the same constraint. Further, in ethnically diverse societies, kinship or tribal loyalties are likely to be useful in maintaining military cohesion. Currently, the most spectacular example of the use of kinship by a dictator is surely Saddam Hussein's control over the Iraqi military, with key positions dominated by his own Tikriti clan. The pattern is widespread: either dictators shape the army around their own ethnic identity (as with Saddam Hussein), or perhaps more commonly, an army which is already ethnically distinctive produces a coup leader from its ranks (as with Idi Amin in Uganda). This relationship between ethnic cohesion and the power base of dictatorship has the important implication that *the more ethnically fractionalized is the society, the narrower is the maximum military support base of the dictatorship.* In turn, unless this is offset by other differences, this lower maximum will imply that on average predatory dictatorships will have narrower support bases the more ethnically fractionalized is the society. Note that the relationship only holds on average. One exception is that even in an ethnically homogenous society a dictatorship may choose to build a support base which is socially very narrow, as in Duvalier's Haiti. A second is that a society which is highly fractionalized may happen to have a dictatorship based on its largest ethnic group, whereas a relatively unfractionalized society may have a dictatorship based on its smallest ethnic group, the latter being smaller than the former.

The size of the military support base is important because in practice dictators are not individually all-powerful. A dictator who failed to satisfy the material aspirations of his military support base would be replaced by an internal coup. For example, the Nigerian military replaced its dictator on several occasions while maintaining the same ethnic power base. An approximation to this state of affairs is to characterize the dictator as the elected leader but on a franchise confined to his own ethnic group. The military power of the ethnic group confers on it the power to determine policy. The outcome which would be expected then follows from the above analysis of ethnic dominance in the context of multi-issue politics. As in that case, the government is free to redistribute in favour of the ruling ethnic group. The key difference is that now the "winning coalition" need not constitute a majority of the population. Far from trying to make such discrimination discreet, as Coate and Morris suggest happens in democracies, the dictator needs to demonstrate his favouritism as visibly as possible. The threat he faces is not national voter anger at the costs of patronage but an internal coup from within the group he needs to favour. He must locate infrastructure in the locality of his ethnic group, and he must skew public employment to those members of his group who come to the capital for jobs. For example, during the time of President Kenyatta, a Kikuyu, the main Kikuyu city grew very rapidly at the expense of non-Kikuyu cities such as Kisumu and Mombasa. When President Moi took over, he built a new international airport in the small town which was the heartland of his own minor tribe, the Kalenjin. Over the years, employment in the post office, the part of the public sector most intensive in unskilled labour, has become dominated by the Kalenjin.

Recall from the previous analysis that the costs of ethnic dominance are predicted to be *decreasing* in the size of the dominant group. The smaller is the group, the stronger is the incentive for it to choose redistribution to itself at the expense of growth to the economy as a whole. In the context of democracy, this rising cost as the size of the group diminishes was checked by the barrier of 50%: below this level the group is not in power. However, in dictatorship, there is no such barrier. Remarkably small ethnic groups have always been able to retain military power. In eleventh-century England and Southern Italy the Norman ethnic group seized and maintained power to their own advantage despite constituting only some 2% of the population. In twentieth-century Burundi and South Africa ethnic minorities of less than 20% of the population did likewise.

Such narrow winning coalitions would have a much stronger incentive to sacrifice growth than the larger winning coalitions in democracies and this leads to a clear prediction: *dictatorship will tend to be more detrimental to growth the more ethnically fractionalized is the society.*

3.3. Testable Hypotheses

I now bring together the testable propositions on the effects of ethnic differentiation in democracy and dictatorship, and see whether they are supported by econometric evidence. The likely effects of ethnic diversity in different political systems are summarized in Table 1. The presumption that ethnic politics is damaging regardless of the political system is not supported by the theories discussed above. Rather, ethnic diversity is predicted to be damaging in particular circumstances, namely dominance and dictatorship. Other than in these circumstances theory does not provide a clear prediction. Ethnic politics may facilitate the internalization of externalities lacking when party leaders cannot control legislators. However, ethnicity may simply substitute for some other basis for stable voter allegiance, as with the class identity politics common in Europe, or other features of the constitution may compensate for the effects of weak parties.

In societies characterized by ethnic dominance the government has both the power and the incentive to trade off redistribution at the expense of growth. Whether the system is democratic or dictatorial will make no difference if the same group is in power, but the dictatorship will be radically worse if it permits a minority to maintain power. In democracy, the problem

Table 1. Ethnicity and the political process: a summary

	Ethnic fragmentation	**Ethnic dominance**	**Homogeneity**
Single-issue democracy	Similar to the median voter outcome	Fairly similar to the median voter outcome	Two parties: Median voter outcome. Multiple parties: close to median voter outcome
Multi-issue democracy	Ethnic parties may reduce the economic costs of instability or log-rolling (like PR)	Stable winning coalition uses its power to choose redistribution at the expense of growth	Instability or log-rolling: both result in choice of redistribution at the expense of growth
Benevolent dictatorship	Better or worse than democracy	Better or worse than democracy	Better or worse than democracy
Predatory dictatorship	Strong preference for redistribution at the expense of growth	Moderate preference for redistribution at the expense of growth, identical to multi-issue democracy if the same group is in power	Mild preference for redistribution at the expense of growth

diminishes the larger is the ethnic majority, and if there is single-issue politics.

In ethnically fragmented societies predatory dictatorships will be highly damaging, with narrow groups exploiting their power at the expense of overall growth. In ethnically homogenous societies predatory dictatorships may be just as narrowly based and hence just as damaging, but they will tend to be less narrowly based. Outside the context of dictatorship, ethnic fragmentation does not appear likely to produce markedly worse politics than ethnic homogeneity, and indeed the political system might work better.

3.4. Empirically Testing the Hypotheses

These analytic predictions are empirically testable. I use the conventional Barro–Lee data set which includes all countries for which sufficient data are available. I arrange the data so that the dependent variable is the growth rate for a country over the period 1960–90. I introduce explanatory variables which help to control for non-policy influences on growth, such as whether a country is landlocked, but exclude policies as explanatory variables because these are the result of the political process.

First, I test for the effects of ethnic diversity. Recall that the Easterly and Levine proposition is that ethnic diversity is directly detrimental because it produces bad political decisions. Above, I have argued that this is not sufficiently nuanced: in democracies the effects of ethnic politics are likely to be small and ambiguously signed, whereas in dictatorships ethnic loyalties are liable to intensify predatory behaviour. I test this more nuanced proposition against that of Easterly and Levine. I do this by interacting the measure of ethnic diversity (ELF) with a measure of political rights. The core results are shown in Table 2: this interaction term is highly significant and large.[1] Ethnic diversity has no adverse effects on growth in fully democratic societies, but reduces growth by up to three percentage points in dictatorships.

In the last two columns of Table 2, I test for

Table 2. Growth, ethnic composition and political rights.
(Dependent variable: per capita GDP growth, average 1960–90)

Variable	Baseline		New sample			
	Coeff.	t-stat.	Coeff.	t-stat.	Coeff.	t-stat.
ELF*political rights	−0.005	−3.26	−0.005	−3.72	−0.005	−3.37
Dominance	—	—	—	—	−0.55	−1.33
Ln GDP	−0.81	−2.67	−0.88	−3.37	−0.87	−3.35
Ln Population growth	−0.83	−2.57	−0.98	−3.57	−0.97	−3.56
Landlocked	−0.93	−1.80	−0.90	−1.95	−0.93	−2.02
Constant	8.99	3.59	9.62	4.46	9.60	4.46
F	6.27		8.47		7.18	
Adjusted R^2	0.18		0.23		0.23	
n	94		102		102	

Notes: ELF*political rights = the product of ethno-linguistic fractionalization (indexed 0–100) and the Gastil index of political rights (1–7, higher values being less democratic, rescaled onto the range 0–6).
Dominance = a dummy taking the value 1 when the largest ethnic group constitutes between 45% and 60% of the population.
Ln GDP = ln of per capita GDP.
Ln Population growth = ln of the rate of population growth.
Landlocked = a dummy taking the value 1 of the country is landlocked.

the effects of ethnic dominance. Recall that unlike in the case of ethnic fragmentation, I predict that ethnic dominance will reduce growth regardless of the political system. The magnitude of this negative effect is predicted to diminish with the size of the dominant group. I approximate this effect by introducing a dummy variable which takes the value of unity over a particular size range of the largest ethnic group. I experiment with different ranges. For example, it may be that a group is able to control national policy even if its share of the population is slightly less than 50%. Conversely, a group with 95% of the population may find that the benefits of exploiting the minority are outweighed by the costs. I find that for all possible values the sign of the ethnic dominance dummy is negative, but the effect is at its maximum and the significance level highest for the range 45–60%. This regression provides some weak support for the hypothesis that ethnic dominance is detrimental to the growth process. Societies with such a dominant ethnic group on average lose over half a percentage point of the growth rate. The effect is only statistically significant at 18%, far below conven-

tional levels. However, the results are still of some interest. The significance level measures how often we would get this result by chance were we drawing a sample of 102 countries randomly from a much larger population of countries. In fact, 102 countries is quite close to being the entire population. Thus, we should conclude that on average countries with ethnic dominance had quite substantially slower per capita growth, but that there was considerable variation around this average. The inclusion of ethnic dominance does not alter the coefficient on the interaction of ethnic diversity and the political system, or its level of significance.

To conclude, there are both theoretical reasons and empirical evidence to support three propositions on the effect of ethnic differentiation on political outcomes. The most important proposition is the negative one that in democracies, except in circumstances of dominance, ethnic diversity does not significantly adversely affect economic performance. Contrary to the apparent implications of Easterly and Levine and Alesina et al., ethnic diversity is not, therefore, in general problematic for economic policy.

The second proposition is that ethnically diverse societies are peculiarly ill-suited to dictatorship. This is precisely contrary to the self-justifying arguments of third world dictators. The third proposition is that ethnic dominance is likely to worsen economic performance, regardless of the political system. The empirical evidence for this proposition is weaker. Further, most ethnically diverse societies are not characterized by dominance. Taken together, these propositions evidently do not amount to a condemnation of ethnic diversity.

Recall that the microeconomics literature on ethnicity in organization has found some quite substantial negative effects. At least within the public sector, there was disturbing evidence that ethnic diversity is detrimental to performance. Evidently, this does not "scale up" to worse overall national economic performance. Perhaps this is because the effects on public sector performance are too small to show up in aggregate performance. Alternatively, it may be because worse performance in the public sector is offset by enhanced performance in the private sector. The New Institutional Economics perspective is after all that kin groups enhance the economic performance of the group. Possibly, in the public sector the benefit for the group is the capture of rents (as in Ghana), whereas in the private sector it is enhanced productivity.

*   *   *

Before considering the implications further, I turn to the effect of diversity on the risk of civil conflict. Even if diversity is normally unproblematic for the economy, it might sometimes be disastrous for the society.

4. Does Ethnic Diversity Cause Civil War?

While popular discussion of the cause of civil conflict focuses upon the motivations of the rebels, I have found it more revealing to focus on how rebellion is organized and financed. In ef-

fect, I am emphasizing the budget constraint rather than preferences as an explanation for variation in behaviour. I first explain the basic theoretical idea. I then discuss the econometric evidence which supports this model over rival accounts which emphasize rebel grievances. Taking the theoretical results as a baseline I then investigate how ethnicity affects the risk of conflict through three routes.

4.1. The Financing of Rebellion

The basic theoretical analysis treats the motivation for rebellion as exogenous. In effect, I assume that in all societies there are some groups keen to further their objectives through organized large scale violence, and what determines whether this happens is the feasibility of maintaining a military organization opposed to the government but on its territory.

A rebel organization must be able to defend itself from government forces. This military survival constraint depends partly upon geography and partly upon the ability of the government to finance defence expenditure. The constraint determines the minimum size of rebellion which is viable, and in turn, this affects the cost of rebellion. The larger a rebel organization must be to survive militarily, the more demanding are the financing requirements. The other component of the cost of rebellion is the ease or difficulty of recruitment of rebel labour. While the size of the government army can be assumed to be in steady state, the rebel organization is wholly dependent upon current recruitment and so is disproportionately sensitive to the current tightness of the labour market. Hence, the costs of rebel recruitment are assumed to be increasing both in per capita income, and in the rate of growth. The ability to rebel then depends upon the available sources of finance. In the basic model the source of rebel finance is predation of primary commodity exports. These activities are assumed to be particularly vulnerable in view of their location-specific rents and their long transport routes to ports. Hence, the basic predictions of the analysis (for a formal analysis see Collier, 2000b) are that the risk of rebellion will be increasing in primary commodity dependence and decreasing in per capita income and the rate of growth.[2]

Although this abstracts from the motivation for rebellion, the conditions under which a rebellion is financially viable are also those under which it is financially attractive. Hence, a more cynical interpretation of this, and the supporting econometric evidence discussed below, is to see finance as *motivating* rather than merely *enabling* rebellion. The econometric evidence cannot discriminate between the two interpretations, but case study evidence sometimes points strongly to finance as a motivation. For example, during the civil war in Sierra Leone, the predation of the diamond fields by the RUF rebel organization could be interpreted as either enabling or motivating. However, during the peace negotiations, the rebel leader rejected the offer of the Vice-Presidency, insisting additionally upon being Chairman of the Council of Mineral Resources. Such behaviour is hard to interpret as other than revealing motivation. Those rebellions which appear least related to financial motivation are ethnic liberation secession movements. However, even here the underlying motivation may often be the capture of primary commodity rents.

The financial rationale for secession on the part of rich districts was first modelled analytically by Buchanan and Faith (1987). Their insight can usefully be linked to Anderson's notion that political communities must be "imagined." The population of a district which initially "imagines" itself as belonging to the larger nation can reimagine itself as a distinct political community once natural resources are discovered. Since ethnic groups, like natural resources, are also geographically concentrated, the resulting political community may be broadly coincident with some ethnic group. Thus, the creation of a political community for the control of a region's natural resources may also create a political community for the ethnic group.

I will give five examples, three of which are related to oil discoveries and price shocks. In Zaire, copper and diamonds are concentrated in the south-east. The secessionist Katanga movement was formed in this region shortly after independence. In Nigeria, the oil discoveries of the 1960s were also concentrated in the south-east. The secessionist Biafra movement was formed in this region in 1967. In the UK the oil discoveries were concentrated off the shores of Scotland. The secessionist Scottish National Party, after years with negligible electoral support, suddenly broke through in 1974, months after oil became valuable due to the hike in the oil price. In Indonesia, the oil discoveries were concentrated on the outer islands, notably Aceh with a per capita GDP triple the national average. The secessionist Merdeka Aceh movement was formed in 1979 by a local businessman. In Ethiopia, the richest region was the coastal belt which had been industrialized by the Italians, Eritrea, with a per capita GDP double the national average. In 1951 the Eritrean population voted for federation with Ethiopia (suggesting that at that stage it was not an imagined nation), but a decade later the Ethiopian government dissolved the Federation, and hence drastically reduced fiscal autonomy. The Eritrean Liberation Front was formed shortly after this dissolution. Four of these five new political communities went on to mount secessionist civil wars. In such situations, although the conflict takes on the appearance of a demand for ethnic liberation, ethnicity is secondary to geography. For example, the Eritrean secession aggregated nine different ethno-linguistic groups into a common political community, while splitting the Tigrini ethno-linguistic group between Eritrea and Ethiopia. Hence, what appears to be a demand for ethnic liberation based on a primordial sense of identity, may more reasonably be interpreted as, at root, an attempt to control lucrative primary commodities which has created the ethnic identity as a by-product.

4.2. Quantitative Empirical Evidence

Together with Anke Hoeffler, I have tested this model against alternative explanations of conflict based on the intensity of objective grievance (Collier and Hoeffler, 1998, 2000). The data set covers 161 countries over the period 1960–99, arranged into five-year sub-periods, giving a total of 1288 potential observations. In 73 of these observations a civil war broke out. Here a civil war is defined as is conventional in the conflict literature as a conflict between a government and an identifiable non-government organization which takes place on the territory of the government and causes at least 1000 combat-related deaths. We then try to explain why conflict erupted in these 73 instances but not in the other 1215 instances. Our methodology is that of logit regressions, with the risk being explained by the characteristics in the preceding five-year period. We then use non-nested tests to compare the model with alternatives in which both ethnicity and various measures of grievance are included. The basic model performs surprisingly well, with around 30% of the variance explained and all variables significant with the expected signs and survives a battery of robustness tests.

The effects of primary commodity dependence are very powerful: comparing two societies with otherwise mean characteristics, the risk of conflict is less than 1% if the society has no primary commodity exports, whereas it is 23% if such exports constitute a quarter of GDP. Nor is this simply a cross-section association. When the regression is run as a fixed effects panel, so that the only variation in primary commodity export dependence is over time, the relationship remains the same: an increase in primary commodity dependence increases the risk of conflict.

The importance of primary commodities in conflict has recently been recognized outside the research community. The NGO Global Witness has conducted a campaign against "conflict diamonds," highlighting their role in the conflicts of Angola and Sierra Leone. De Beers, the world's largest diamond company, has ceased to purchase diamonds on the open market and has proposed a plan to tighten regulation of the market. With Antwerp as the world's major trading

centre for diamonds, Europe is critical for the effective implementation of this plan. The objective is to create a substantial discount in the price rebel movements receive for diamonds, thereby squeezing them financially. A second primary commodity which is now recognized as central to rebellion is cocaine. For example, this generates around $500m annually for the FARC rebel movement in Colombia. Because OECD governments have persuaded developing country governments to make production illegal, they have created a demand for territory which is not under government control. Rebels supply such territory to drug growers in exchange for a rent (Brito and Intriligator, 1992).

Whereas primary commodity exports are thus important risk factors, some grievances widely assumed to fuel conflict appear to be unimportant. Neither the degree of income inequality, nor the degree of political rights are significant, and their inclusion in the model is rejected by non-nested tests. There is some evidence from Europe that income inequality increases voter support for "revolutionary" propositions (MacCulloch, 1999), but evidently, such support does not translate into large scale organized killing. The unimportance of grievance variables strengthens the argument that large scale organized killing is dependent upon the unusual circumstances which produce organizational feasibility more than upon motivation. Indeed, the only variables which non-nested tests show must be added to the basic model are three measures of ethnic and religious diversity. I now focus in detail on these effects.

Ethnicity enters the model in three ways. First, ethnic dominance might be a sufficiently compelling grievance factor that it affects the risk of conflict. In the previous section I discussed why with dominance there is both the ability and the incentive for the majority to exploit the minority. The structural permanence of this condition, and the inability of democracy to resolve it, may make organized violence more likely. In the simple theory of Section 3, dominance abruptly becomes a problem once the group exceeds 50% of the electorate. This is also the point of maximum incentive to exploit. Thereafter, exploitation diminishes as the share of the majority group increases. In testing the effect of dominance on conflict risk Hoeffler and I follow the same procedure as for its effects on economic performance, introducing a dummy variable which takes the value unity if the largest ethnic group is in a particular size range, the range being determined by experiment. We also test this specification against a variable which simply measures the share of the population constituted by the largest ethnic group. * * * This specification is also preferred to that in which the population share of the largest ethnic group is included. So defined, societies with ethnic dominance have around double the risk of civil war of other societies. This is consistent with the theory that in this range majorities have both the ability and the incentive to exploit minorities. Evidently, given this structural problem, it is arbitrary whether the rebel group is drawn from the minority, as in Sri Lanka, or whether the minority pre-emptively controls the government, but faces rebellion from within the majority, as in Burundi. While the model thus finds evidence that ethnic dominance is problematic, the scale of the effect should be kept in perspective. The effect of ethnic dominance can, according to the model, be fully offset for the mean country by reducing dependence upon primary commodities from 16% of GDP to 11%.

The second way by which ethnic diversity enters the model is through fragmentation. Recall that the rebel organization is assumed to need cohesion and for this must avoid recruiting across boundaries of identity. Societies which are fragmented by ethnicity or indeed by other types of identity thus pose greater problems for rebel organizations. A possible example of this is Irian Jaya in Indonesia. This province is dependent upon primary commodity exports and over the past 30 years many small groups have attempted to mount armed opposition to rule from Indonesia. However, none of these groups succeeded in building a viable rebel organization of any scale. A likely reason for this is that Irian Jaya is so astonishingly ethnically fragmented, with some 450 distinct language groups: the groups simply cannot cohere into a military organization. In principle, the same effect would be generated by religious fractionalization as by ethnic fractionalization. Societies divided by both ethnicity and religion would potentially be even more protected from rebellion if the religious divisions were cross-cutting over the ethnic divisions. A society equally divided into e ethnic groups and r religious groups, with religion cross-cutting ethnicity, would be divided into $e \cdot r$ distinct cells. There is good data on the composition of societies according to religion, but unfortunately, this cannot be related to ethnic divisions. At one extreme, ethnic and religious divisions might be coincident, and at the other they may be perfectly cross-cutting, and so the empirical testing must allow for these possibilities. To incorporate the effects of religious fractionalization Hoeffler and I built a measure of religious fractionalization, RF, precisely corresponding to the index of ethno-linguistic fractionalisation (for details see Collier and Hoeffler, 2000).

One possibility is that both ethnic diversity and religious diversity matter but that there is no interaction effect. We test for this by introducing both measures into the logit regression. At the other extreme, only the interaction effect might matter. We measure the interaction effect by constructing an index of "social fractionalization" which proxies the concept $e \cdot r$. The interaction term is approximately the product of the two measures of diversity, ELF · RF. However, if there is religious homogeneity but ethnic diversity, the measure of social fractionalization should collapse to the measure of ethnic diversity rather than to zero (and conversely if there is religious diversity but ethnic homogeneity). To allow for this we measure the index of social fractionalization as the interaction term ELF · RF plus whichever is the maximum of ELF and RF. In practice, this is a very minor modification and the measure of social fractionalization performs virtually identically whether it is defined in this way or more simply as ELF · RF. * * * In each case we control for ethnic dominance which non-nested tests show to have a distinct effect which should be included in the model. The interaction effect "social fractionalization" dominates the direct effects of religious and ethnic diversity. Indeed, once "social fractionalization" is included, neither direct effect is significant. Thus, ethnic and religious divisions are apparently usually cross-cutting. Not only does social fractionalization dominate the direct effects, it is highly significant with a *negative* sign, and is a large effect. Hence, the risk of civil war is *lower* in societies which are fractionalized by ethnicity and religion. Such societies might well have higher levels of hatred, but this does not usually translate into large-scale organized killing.

This effect of ethnic and religious diversity also accounts for why so many civil wars *appear* to be caused by ethnic or religious hatreds. Most societies are to some degree diverse. Where rebellions occur in such societies, the organizational constraint of cohesion will tend to confine recruitment to a single cell of the ethno-religious matrix. Rebellion will be *patterned* by ethnicity and religion even if it is not *caused* by ethnic and religious differences. A good example of this process is the recent violent attempted *coup d'état* in Fiji (Frank, 2000). The demands of the coup leader, George Speight, were ostensibly entirely related to ethnic power: he claimed to want a transfer of power from the Indian part of the population to the aboriginal group. However, beneath this apparent instance of ethnically motivated political violence was a quite different story. Fiji has the world's largest plantations of mahogany. Indeed, it is forecast to supply two-thirds of the entire world market, constituting the single most important asset in Fiji. In 1998 the government began the process of putting out to tender the management contract for the mahogany plantations. Two companies were shortlisted: the Commonwealth Development Corporation (CDC) and a private American company. The American company hired a local businessman as its representative, none other than George Speight. Eventually, the government awarded the contract to the CDC. Shortly after losing the contract, Mr. Speight launched his coup. The loss of the contract by an American company to the Commonwealth Development Corporation evidently did not provide a very robust basis for a popular political uprising against a democratic government. Mr. Speight indeed loudly denied that the motivation was the loss of the mahogany contract. Instead, as noted above, he chose ethnicity as his rallying cry: the government happened to be drawn from a predominantly Indian party, whereas Mr. Speight was not Indian. In short, the conflict was ethnically *patterned*, but not ethnically *caused*.

Taken together, the effect of ethnic dominance and cross-cutting fractionalization produce a broadly non-monotonic relationship between the number of ethnic groups and the risk of conflict. Moving from one to two groups almost inevitably switches the society into ethnic dominance. Usually, this is not fully offset by the benign effect of the increased fractionalization, so the society overall becomes more at risk. Moving from two to many groups almost inevitably switches the society back out of ethnic dominance and gradually increases fragmentation, making the society safer than were it homogenous.

The third way by which ethnic diversity enters the model is through diasporas living in Europe and America. Although the basic model considers only primary commodity predation as a source of rebel finance, an obvious extension is to consider financial contributions from diasporas living in high-income countries. Angoustures and Pascal (1996) provide a chilling series of case studies showing how such diasporas are currently organized by rebel movements to finance conflict. This role of diasporas has a long history. For example, Irish-Americans assisted the secession of Eire from the UK, Jewish-Americans assisted the secession of Israel, Eritreans in Europe and America were the main source of finance for the secession of Eritrea from Ethiopia, and currently Tamils in Canada are financing the attempt of the Tamil Tigers to secede from Sri Lanka. Hoeffler and I investigated the effect of diasporas more formally, using data on diasporas in America. The size of the diaspora for, say Somalia, was measured as the number of people born in Somalia but resident in the USA, relative to the resident population of Somalia. Since civil war increases emigration, a large diaspora might simply proxy previous conflict. In order to control for this, we estimated a migration model, based upon income differences and time lags, and in all cases where there had been a civil war, replaced the actual diaspora population in America subsequent to the outbreak of the conflict, with a predicted population based on the counterfactual of continued peace. Both with and without this correction we found that the larger was the diaspora the greater was the risk of conflict. The risk applied, however, only in post-conflict situations. Post-conflict, countries temporarily have a very high risk of further conflict. We show that this is not spuriously due to an omitted variable: a dummy variable for whether a country has had a previous conflict is insignificant. Rather, conflict generates risks which gradually fade again. The effect of diasporas is significantly and substantially to slow down the rate at which these risks fade. Large diasporas appear to keep conflicts alive. This is consistent both with the case study evidence and with theory. Diasporas in OECD economies have the income to finance rebel organizations, often have romantic attachments to their ethnic identity to counter the anomie they experience in their host societies, and do not suffer the consequences of the violence which they finance. They are consequently often more extreme than the populations which they purport to defend.

In order to tap the potential that a diaspora offers, a rebel organization needs to sell ethnic vengeance. Hence, rebellions need to generate a discourse of ethnic hatred. Thus, in most societies rebellions will not only be organized along ethnic lines, they will be justified in terms of ethnic grievance, and supported by ethnic diasporas. It is unsurprising that in these circumstances ethnic diversity will appear to cause violent conflict. Nevertheless, these appearances are entirely consistent with the big brute fact that ethnic diversity usually makes a society safer. Whether societies suffer an outbreak of civil war is determined more by the financial and military opportunities for rebellion rather than by ethnic hatreds or other objective grievances.

5. Policy Implications

I started with two charges which are widely made against societies in which ethnicity is the basis for social identity. Ethnically differentiated societies would find co-operation difficult and victimization of minorities easy. The inability to co-operate would manifest itself in dysfunctional politics and consequently worse economic performance. The tendency to victimization of minorities would manifest itself as dysfunctional societies beset by violent civil conflict. Such sweeping charges are not justified either theoretically or empirically. As a first approximation, ethnically diverse democracies do not have worse economic performance and are actually safer than homogenous societies.

The fallacious popular orthodoxy that ethnically diverse societies are unviable is directly reflected in current policy towards multi-ethnic societies. Despair has encouraged radical social and political engineering, involving population movements and intricate border redesign and secession, in order to achieve ethnically less diverse, and hence supposedly more viable, states. The trend to secession since the end of the Cold War, much of it violent, has been remarkable: Eritrea, Slovakia, Slovenia, Croatia, Macedonia, Bosnia, Chechnya, Quebec, Belgium, Kosovo, Montenegro, the Western Sahara, East Timor, Somaliland, Aceh and the Niger Delta are all recent examples of completed, incipient or potential creation of small ethnic states. I have argued that such secessions are often at root economic rather than ethnic. The patina of legitimacy associated with ethnic historicism and political grievance should disguise neither the tendency of secessionist violence to be concentrated in regions well endowed with primary commodities, nor the absence of a statistical relationship with inequality and political oppression. Secessionist states would probably be *more*, rather than less prone to conflict. It is self-evident that as the number of countries increases, so does the risk of *international* war. For example, the secession of Eritrea from Ethiopia has not brought peace but rather reclassified a conflict from a civil war to an international war, bringing with it a severe cost escalation as both parties are now able to field an airforce. However, the more telling point is that such states are also liable to be more prone to *civil* conflict. First, if endowments of primary commodities tend to be the basis for secession, the resulting states would be more dependent upon primary commodities than if they were part of larger political entities. As an approximation, each extra percentage point of dependence upon primary commodities raises the risk of conflict by one percentage point. Secondly, secessionist states would have less ethnic heterogeneity. Recall that contrary to popular perception, this would increase the risk of conflict. Thirdly, as secessions occur from ethnically fragmented states, the residual state is liable to switch from ethnic fragmentation to ethnic dominance. The secessionist state is also more likely to be characterized by ethnic dominance than by ethnic homogeneity. On average, this doubles the risk of conflict. Such a process occurred in the former Yugoslavia: the secession of Slovenia (with international support), created the precedent for the secession of Croatia, which in turn converted the Yugoslav state from being ethnically fragmented, to a Serb majority. The Serb government thereby acquired the power to discriminate in favour of its own supporters. Thus, the main policy implication is perhaps that the international community has a stronger interest than is currently recognized in the preservation of large, multi-ethnic societies such as Russia, Indonesia and Nigeria.

Since primary commodity dependence increases the risk of conflict, which in ethnically diverse societies then becomes organized on ethnic lines, a further implication is the desirability of export diversification. In Africa dependence on primary commodities has actually increased over the past 30 years and this may have contributed to the region's rising incidence of conflict. By contrast, over the same period other developing regions have on average sharply reduced primary commodity dependence and some of this difference is presumably attributable to economic policy.

While popular opinion has greatly exaggerated the difficulties faced by ethnically diverse societies, I have argued that diversity does create some problems.

At the level of the individual organization ethnic identity sometimes enhances co-operation and sometimes impedes it. Ethnic group identity is interpreted by institutional economics as an endogenous response to the need for co-operation and evidence from both households and businesses illustrates that ethnicity can be useful in enforcing reciprocity. However, in the public sector there is evidence that ethnically differentiated organizations encounter problems. Thus, a third policy issue is how best to respond to the problem of public sector performance in ethnically diverse societies. I suggest two approaches which are not exclusive. Ethnic employment patronage in the public sector can be countered by greater transparency in hiring and promotion, perhaps reinforced by targets and quota protection for minorities. In developed countries most large organizations now have such explicit policies to safeguard minorities. Thus, there are established procedures which are known to be effective and which could be implemented in the public sectors of ethnically diverse societies. An additional approach is to accept that the public sector may be relatively less effective in diverse societies than in homogenous societies, so that the boundary between public and private activity should be drawn somewhat differently.

At the level of aggregate economic performance there is an important exception to the general proposition that ethnic diversity is not a problem. Dictatorships are on average substantially more damaging in ethnically diverse societies than in homogenous societies. Hence, a fourth policy implication is the need for democratization in those ethnically diverse societies which are currently dictatorships. Encouraging democratization is partly simply a matter of the climate of opinion. If the claim by dictators that they are the alternative to chaos is called into question, then their hold on power is weakened. However, it is also a policy choice for OECD governments: for many years Western governments actively propped up dictators.

A fifth policy implication concerns societies characterized by ethnic dominance. There is a theoretical argument and some weak supporting evidence that such countries have worse economic performance. By itself this would not constitute a sufficient basis for policy intervention. However, there is stronger evidence that ethnic dominance increases the risk of violent civil conflict. Taken together, this suggests that there is a need for better protection of minority rights in societies with ethnic majorities. In developing countries, the struggle for democracy has generally taken the form of empowering the majority against an elite, whether colonial or domestic military. Rights to equal treatment, individual or group, now need to be incorporated into the popular conception of democracy. The recent European Union concern to include protection of minorities as a condition for the continued inclusion of the Austrian government is a powerful practical instance of this redefinition.

A final policy issue, particularly pertinent for European governments, is the role of ethnic diasporas living in Europe and America in promoting violent conflict and separatist movements in their countries of origin. Individual OECD governments are somewhat reluctant to police the external activities of diaspora organizations: often these organizations have some influence in host country political parties. Because of the collective nature of the benefits, contrasted with the individual incidence of the costs, OECD governments need to co-ordinate their policy towards diasporas. Inter-national policy co-ordination is usually difficult and is only worthwhile if the benefits are substantial. It would, however, be ironic if the peaceful, prosperous and increasingly multi-ethnic societies of the OECD inadvertently financed the break up of developing countries into violent and impoverished ethnic theme parks.

NOTES

1. The baseline result in Table 2 is from Collier (2000a), which discusses the sources of variables and shows that the result is robust to a range of alternative specifications and dominates any direct effects of political rights and ethnic diversity. The new sample adds eight countries for which data was not previously available. Further results available from the author show that no other size of group comes as close to being significant, and that the addition of an interaction term between this dummy variable and political rights is completely insignificant.
2. Empirically, Collier and Hoeffler (2000) find that the risk of conflict increases strongly in the share of primary commodity exports until the latter are around 26% of GDP, beyond which risk diminishes.

REFERENCES

Alesina, A., R. Baqir and W. Easterly (1999). "Public goods and ethnic divisions," *Quarterly Journal of Economics*.

Anderson, B. (1983). *Imagined Communities*, Verso, London.

Angoustures, A. and V. Pascal (1996). "Diasporas et Financement des Conflicts," in F. Jean and

J-C. Rufin (eds.), *Economie des Guerres Civiles*, Hachette, Paris.

Arcand, J-L., P. Guillaumont and S. Guillaumont (2000). "How to make a tragedy: on the alleged effect of ethnicity on growth," *Journal of International Development*, 12.

Bates, R. (1999). Ethnicity, capital formation and conflict, Social Capital Initiative Working Paper 12, World Bank, Washington D.C.

Benabou, R. (1996). "Inequality and growth," in B. Bernanke and J. Rotemberg (eds.) *NBER Macroeconomics Annual*, MIT Press, Cambridge, MA.

Biggs, T., M. Raturi and P. Srivastava (1996). Enforcement of contracts in an African credit market, RPED Discussion Paper, World Bank, Washington D.C.

Bisin, A. and T. Verdier (2000). "Beyond the melting pot: cultural transmission, marriage and the evolution of ethnic and religious traits," *Quarterly Journal of Economics*.

Brito, D. L. and M. D. Intriligator (1992). "Narco-traffic and guerrilla warfare: a new symbiosis," *Defence Economics*.

Buchanan, J. M. and R. L. Faith (1987). "Secession and the limits of taxation: towards a theory of internal exit," *American Economic Review*.

Coate, S. and S. Morris (1995). "On the form of transfers to special interests," *Journal of Political Economy*.

Colley, L. (1992). *Britons: Forging the Nation*, Yale University Press, New Haven.

Collier, P. (1999). "The political economy of ethnicity," in B. Pleskovic and J.E. Stiglitz (eds.) *Annual Bank Conference on Development Economics, 1998*, World Bank, Washington D.C.

Collier, P. (2000a). "Ethnicity, politics and economic performance," *Economics and Politics*.

Collier, P. (2000b). "Rebellion as a quasi-criminal activity," *Journal of Conflict Resolution*.

Collier, P. and A. Garg (1999). "On kin groups and wages in the Ghanaian labour market," *Oxford Bulletin of Economics and Statistics*.

Collier, P. and A. Hoeffler (1998). "On the economic causes of civil war," *Oxford Economic Papers*.

Collier, P. and A. Hoeffler (2000). Greed and grievance in civil war, Policy Research Working Paper 2355, World Bank, Washington D.C.

Collier, P., A. Hoeffler and C. Pattillo (2001). "Flight capital as a portfolio choice," *World Bank Economic Review*.

Downs, A. (1957). *An Economic Theory of Democracy*, Harper & Row, New York.

Drazen, A. (2000). *Political Economy in Macroeconomics*, Princeton University Press, Princeton.

Easterly, W. and R. Levine (1997). "Africa's growth tragedy: policies and ethnic divisions," *Quarterly Journal of Economics*.

Emminghaus, W., P. Kimmel and E. Stewart (1998). "Primal violence illuminating culture's dark side," in E. Weiner (ed.), *The Handbook of Inter-Ethnic Coexistence*, The Continuum Publishing Company, New York.

Esteban, J. and D. Ray (1994). "On the measurement of polarization," *Econometrica*.

Fearon, J. D. and D. D. Laitin (1999). "Weak states, rough terrain, and large-scale ethnic violence since 1945," mimco, Dept. of Political Science, Stanford University.

Frank, R. (2000). "Fiji mahogany fuels latest resource battle in troubled region," *Wall Street Journal*, 13 September, Al.

Greif, A. (1992). "Institutions and international trade: lessons from the commercial revolution," *American Economic Review*.

Grossman, H. I. (1991). "General equilibrium model of insurrections," *American Economic Review*.

Gurr, T. R. (1993). *Minorities at Risk: A Global View of Ethnopolitical Conflicts*, United States Institute of Peace, Washington D.C.

Hardin, R. (1997). "Economic theories of the state," in Mueller (ed.) (1997).

Hoeffler, A. (1998). "Econometric studies of growth, convergence and conflicts," D.Phil. thesis, University of Oxford.

Horowitz, D. (1985). *Ethnic Groups in Conflict*, University of California Press, Berkeley.

Inman, R. P. and D. R. Rubinfeld (1997). "The political economy of federalism," in Mueller (ed.) (1997).

Lipset, S.M. (1960). *Political Man*, Anchors Books, New York.

MacCulloch, R. (1999). "What makes a revolution," Working paper B24, Center for European Integration Studies, Bonn.

Mehlum, H. and K. Moene (2000). "Contested power and political instability," Discussion paper, Department of Economics, University of Oslo.

Meltzer, A. and S. Richards (1981). "A rational theory of the size of government," *Journal of Political Economy*.

Miguel, T. (1999). "Ethnic diversity and school funding in Kenya," mimeo, Department of Economics, Harvard University.

Mueller, D. (ed.) (1997). *Perspectives on Public Choice*, Cambridge University Press, Cambridge.

Ognedal, T. (1999). "Comments on T. Eggertsson, 'Limits to institutional reforms,'" *Scandinavian Journal of Economics*.

Olson, M. (1991). "Autocracy, democracy and prosperity," in R. Zeckhauser (ed.) *Strategy and Choice*, MIT Press, Cambridge, MA.

Posner, D. N. (1999). "Ethnic fractionalization in Africa," mimeo, Department of Political Science, UCLA, Los Angeles.

Posner, R. A. (1980). "A theory of primitive society with special reference to law," *Journal of Law and Economics*.

Schofield, N. (1997). "Multiparty electoral politics," in Mueller (ed.), (1997).

Shubik, M. (1982). *Game Theory in the Social Sciences, Concepts and Solutions*, MIT Press, Cambridge, MA.

Singer, J. D. and M. Small (1994). *Correlates of War Project: International and Civil War Data, 1816–1992*, Inter-University Consortium for Political and Social Research, Ann Arbor, MI.

Stigler, G. J. (1964). "A theory of oligopoly," *Journal of Political Economy*.

Tocqueville, A. de (1959). *Democracy in America*. Vintage Books, New York.

Weber, E. (1975). *Peasants into Frenchmen*, Stanford University Press, Stanford.

Weingast, B. (1979). "A rational choice perspective on congressional norms," *American Journal of Political Science*.

SAMUEL P. HUNTINGTON

THE CLASH OF CIVILIZATIONS?

The Next Pattern of Conflict

World politics is entering a new phase, and intellectuals have not hesitated to proliferate visions of what it will be—the end of history, the return of traditional rivalries between nation states,

From *Foreign Affairs* 72, no. 3 (Summer 1993), pp. 22–49.

and the decline of the nation state from the conflicting pulls of tribalism and globalism, among others. Each of these visions catches aspects of the emerging reality. Yet they all miss a crucial, indeed a central, aspect of what global politics is likely to be in the coming years.

It is my hypothesis that the fundamental source of conflict in this new world will not be primarily ideological or primarily economic. The great divisions among humankind and the dominating source of conflict will be cultural. Nation states will remain the most powerful actors in world affairs, but the principal conflicts of global politics will occur between nations and groups of different civilizations. The clash of civilizations will dominate global politics. The fault lines between civilizations will be the battle lines of the future.

Conflict between civilizations will be the latest phase in the evolution of conflict in the modern world. For a century and a half after the emergence of the modern international system with the Peace of Westphalia, the conflicts of the Western world were largely among princes—emperors, absolute monarchs and constitutional monarchs attempting to expand their bureaucracies, their armies, their mercantilist economic strength and, most important, the territory they ruled. In the process they created nation states, and beginning with the French Revolution the principal lines of conflict were between nations rather than princes. In 1793, as R. R. Palmer put it, "The wars of kings were over; the wars of peoples had begun." This nineteenth-century pattern lasted until the end of World War I. Then, as a result of the Russian Revolution and the reaction against it, the conflict of nations yielded to the conflict of ideologies, first among communism, fascism-Nazism and liberal democracy, and then between communism and liberal democracy. During the Cold War, this latter conflict became embodied in the struggle between the two superpowers, neither of which was a nation state in the classical European sense and each of which defined its identity in terms of its ideology.

These conflicts between princes, nation states and ideologies were primarily conflicts within Western civilization, "Western civil wars," as William Lind has labeled them. This was as true of the Cold War as it was of the world wars and the earlier wars of the seventeenth, eighteenth and nineteenth centuries. With the end of the Cold War, international politics moves out of its Western phase, and its center-piece becomes the interaction between the West and non-Western civilizations and among non-Western civilizations. In the politics of civilizations, the peoples and governments of non-Western civilizations no longer remain the objects of history as targets of Western colonialism but join the West as movers and shapers of history.

The Nature of Civilizations

During the Cold War the world was divided into the First, Second and Third Worlds. Those divisions are no longer relevant. It is far more meaningful now to group countries not in terms of their political or economic systems or in terms of their level of economic development but rather in terms of their culture and civilization.

What do we mean when we talk of a civilization? A civilization is a cultural entity. Villages, regions, ethnic groups, nationalities, religious groups, all have distinct cultures at different levels of cultural heterogeneity. The culture of a village in southern Italy may be different from that of a village in northern Italy, but both will share in a common Italian culture that distinguishes them from German villages. European communities, in turn, will share cultural features that distinguish them from Arab or Chinese communities. Arabs, Chinese and Westerners, however, are not part of any broader cultural entity. They constitute civilizations. A civilization is thus the highest cultural grouping of people and the broadest level of cultural identity people have short of that which distinguishes humans from other species. It is defined both by common objective elements, such as language, history, religion, customs, institutions, and by the subjective self-identification of people. People have levels of identity: a resident of Rome may define himself with varying degrees of intensity as a Roman, an Italian, a Catholic, a Christian, a European, a Westerner. The civilization to which he belongs is the broadest level of identification with which he intensely identifies. People can and do redefine their identities and, as a result, the composition and boundaries of civilizations change.

Civilizations may involve a large number of people, as with China ("a civilization pretending to be a state," as Lucian Pye put it), or a very small number of people, such as the Anglophone Caribbean. A civilization may include several nation states, as is the case with Western, Latin American and Arab civilizations, or only one, as is the case with Japanese civilization. Civilizations obviously blend and overlap, and may include subcivilizations. Western civilization has two major variants, European and North American, and Islam has its Arab, Turkic and Malay subdivisions. Civilizations are nonetheless meaningful entities, and while the lines between them are seldom sharp, they are real. Civilizations are dynamic; they rise and fall; they divide and merge. And, as any student of history knows, civilizations disappear and are buried in the sands of time.

Westerners tend to think of nation states as the principal actors in global affairs. They have been that, however, for only a few centuries. The broader reaches of human history have been the history of civilizations. In *A Study of History*, Arnold Toynbee identified 21 major civilizations; only six of them exist in the contemporary world.

Why Civilizations Will Clash

Civilization identity will be increasingly important in the future, and the world will be shaped in large measure by the interactions among seven or eight major civilizations. These include Western, Confucian, Japanese, Islamic, Hindu, Slavic-Orthodox, Latin American and possibly African civilization. The most important conflicts of the future will occur along the cultural fault lines separating these civilizations from one another.

Why will this be the case?

First, differences among civilizations are not only real; they are basic. Civilizations are differentiated from each other by history, language, culture, tradition and, most important, religion. The people of different civilizations have different views on the relations between God and man, the individual and the group, the citizen and the state, parents and children, husband and wife, as well as differing views of the relative importance of rights and responsibilities, liberty and authority, equality and hierarchy. These differences are the product of centuries. They will not soon disappear. They are far more fundamental than differences among political ideologies and political regimes. Differences do not necessarily mean conflict, and conflict does not necessarily, mean violence. Over the centuries, however, differences among civilizations have generated the most prolonged and the most violent conflicts.

Second, the world is becoming a smaller place. The interactions between peoples of different civilizations are increasing; these increasing interactions intensify civilization consciousness and awareness of differences between civilizations and commonalities within civilizations. North African immigration to France generates hostility among Frenchmen and at the same time increased receptivity to immigration by "good" European Catholic Poles. Americans react far more negatively to Japanese investment than to larger investments from Canada and European countries. Similarly, as Donald Horowitz has pointed out, "An Ibo may be . . . an Owerri Ibo or an Onitsha Ibo in what was the Eastern region of Nigeria. In Lagos, he is simply an Ibo. In London, he is a Nigerian. In New York, he is an African." The interactions among peoples of different civilizations enhance the civilization-consciousness of people that, in turn, invigorates differences and animosities stretching or thought to stretch back deep into history.

Third, the processes of economic modernization and social change throughout the world are separating people from longstanding local identities. They also weaken the nation state as a source of identity. In much of the world religion has moved in to fill this gap, often in the form of movements that are labeled "fundamentalist." Such movements are found in Western Christianity, Judaism, Buddhism and Hinduism, as well as in Islam. In most countries and most religions the people active in fundamentalist movements are young, college-educated, middle-class technicians, professionals and business persons. The "unsecularization of the world," George Weigel has remarked, "is one of the dominant social facts of life in the late twentieth century." The revival of religion, "la revanche de Dieu," as Gilles Kepel labeled it, provides a basis for identity and commitment that transcends national boundaries and unites civilizations.

Fourth, the growth of civilization-consciousness is enhanced by the dual role of the West. On the one hand, the West is at a peak of power. At the same time, however, and perhaps as a result, a return to the roots phenomenon is occurring among non-Western civilizations. Increasingly one hears references to trends toward a turning inward and "Asianization" in Japan, the end of the Nehru legacy and the "Hinduization" of India, the failure of Western ideas of socialism and nationalism and hence "re-Islamization" of the Middle East, and now a debate over Westernization versus Russianization in Boris Yeltsin's country. A West at the peak of its power confronts non-Wests that increasingly have the desire, the will and the resources to shape the world in non-Western ways.

In the past, the elites of non-Western societies were usually the people who were most involved with the West, had been educated at Oxford, the Sorbonne or Sandhurst, and had absorbed Western attitudes and values. At the same time, the populace in non-Western countries often remained deeply imbued with the indigenous culture. Now, however, these relationships are being reversed. A de-Westernization and indigenization of elites is occurring in many non-Western countries at the same time that Western, usually American, cultures, styles and habits become more popular among the mass of the people.

Fifth, cultural characteristics and differences are less mutable and hence less easily compromised and resolved than political and economic ones. In the former Soviet Union, communists can become democrats, the rich can become poor and the poor rich, but Russians cannot become Estonians and Azeris cannot become Armenians. In class and ideological conflicts, the key question was "Which side are you on?" and people could and did choose sides and change sides. In conflicts between civilizations, the question is "What are you?" That is a given that cannot be changed. And as we know, from Bosnia to the Caucasus to the Sudan, the wrong answer to that question can mean a bullet in the head. Even more than ethnicity, religion discriminates sharply and exclusively among people. A person can be half-French and half-Arab and simultaneously even a citizen of two countries. It is more difficult to be half-Catholic and half-Muslim.

Finally, economic regionalism is increasing. The proportions of total trade that were intraregional rose between 1980 and 1989 from 51 percent to 59 percent in Europe, 33 percent to 37 percent in East Asia, and 32 percent to 36 percent in North America. The importance of regional economic blocs is likely to continue to increase in the future. On the one hand, successful economic regionalism will reinforce civilization-consciousness. On the other hand, economic regionalism may succeed only when it is rooted in a common civilization. The European Community rests on the shared foundation of European culture and Western Christianity. The success of the North American Free Trade Area depends on the convergence now underway of Mexican, Canadian and American cultures. Japan, in contrast, faces difficulties in creating a comparable economic entity in East Asia because Japan is a society and civilization unique to itself. However strong the trade and investment links Japan may develop with other East Asian countries, its cultural differences with those countries inhibit and perhaps preclude its promoting regional economic integration like that in Europe and North America.

Common culture, in contrast, is clearly

facilitating the rapid expansion of the economic relations between the People's Republic of China and Hong Kong, Taiwan, Singapore and the overseas Chinese communities in other Asian countries. With the Cold War over, cultural commonalities increasingly overcome ideological differences, and mainland China and Taiwan move closer together. If cultural commonality is a prerequisite for economic integration, the principal East Asian economic bloc of the future is likely to be centered on China. This bloc is, in fact, already coming into existence. As Murray Weidenbaum has observed.

> Despite the current Japanese dominance of the region, the Chinese-based economy of Asia is rapidly emerging as a new epicenter for industry, commerce and finance. This strategic area contains substantial amounts of technology and manufacturing capability (Taiwan), outstanding entrepreneurial, marketing and services acumen (Hong Kong), a fine communications network (Singapore), a tremendous pool of financial capital (all three), and very large endowments of land, resources and labor (mainland China) . . . From Guangzhou to Singapore, from Kuala Lumpur to Manila, this influential network—often based on extensions of the traditional clans—has been described as the backbone of the East Asian economy.[1]

Culture and religion also form the basis of the Economic Cooperation Organization, which brings together ten non-Arab Muslim countries: Iran, Pakistan, Turkey, Azerbaijan, Kazakhstan, Kyrgyzstan, Turkmenistan, Tadjikistan, Uzbekistan and Afghanistan. One impetus to the revival and expansion of this organization, founded originally in the 1960 by Turkey, Pakistan and Iran, is the realization by the leaders of several of these countries that they had no chance of admission to the European Community. Similarly, Caricom, the Central American Common Market and Mercosur rest on common cultural foundations. Efforts to build a broader Caribbean-Central American economic entity bridging the Anglo-Latin divide, however, have to date failed.

As people define their identity in ethnic and religious terms, they are likely to see an "us" versus "them" relation existing between themselves and people of different ethnicity or religion. The end of ideologically defined states in Eastern Europe and the former Soviet Union permits traditional ethnic identities and animosities to come to the fore. Differences in culture and religion create differences over policy issues, ranging from human rights to immigration to trade and commerce to the environment. Geographical propinquity gives rise to conflicting territorial claims from Bosnia to Mindanao. Most important, the efforts of the West to promote its values of democracy and liberalism as universal values, to maintain its military predominance and to advance its economic interests engender countering responses from other civilizations. Decreasingly able to mobilize support and form coalitions on the basis of ideology, governments and groups will increasingly attempt to mobilize support by appealing to common religion and civilization identity.

The clash of civilizations thus occurs at two levels. At the micro-level, adjacent groups along the fault lines between civilizations struggle, often violently, over the control of territory and each other. At the macro-level, states from different civilizations compete for relative military and economic power, struggle over the control of international institutions and third parties, and competitively promote their particular political and religious values.

The Fault Lines between Civilizations

The fault lines between civilizations are replacing the political and ideological boundaries of the Cold War as the flash points for crisis and bloodshed. The Cold War began when the Iron Curtain divided Europe politically and ideologically. The Cold War ended with the end of the Iron Curtain. As the ideological division of Europe has disappeared, the cultural division of

Europe between Western Christianity, on the one hand, and Orthodox Christianity and Islam, on the other, has reemerged. The most significant dividing line in Europe, as William Wallace has suggested, may well be the eastern boundary of Western Christianity in the year 1500. This line runs along what are now the boundaries between Finland and Russia and between the Baltic states and Russia, cuts through Belarus and Ukraine separating the more Catholic western Ukraine from Orthodox eastern Ukraine, swings westward separating Transylvania from the rest of Romania, and then goes through Yugoslavia almost exactly along the line now separating Croatia and Slovenia from the rest of Yugoslavia. In the Balkans this line, of course, coincides with the historic boundary between the Hapsburg and Ottoman empires. The peoples to the north and west of this line are Protestant or Catholic; they shared the common experiences of European history—feudalism, the Renaissance, the Reformation, the Enlightenment, the French Revolution, the Industrial Revolution; they are generally economically better off than the peoples to the east; and they may now look forward to increasing involvement in a common European economy and to the consolidation of democratic political systems. The peoples to the east and south of this line are Orthodox or Muslim; they historically belonged to the Ottoman or Tsarist empires and were only lightly touched by the shaping events in the rest of Europe; they are generally less advanced economically; they seem much less likely to develop stable democratic political systems. The Velvet Curtain of culture has replaced the Iron Curtain of ideology as the most significant dividing line in Europe. As the events in Yugoslavia show, it is not only a line of difference; it is also at times a line of bloody conflict.

Conflict along the fault line between Western and Islamic civilizations has been going on for 1,300 years. After the founding of Islam, the Arab and Moorish surge west and north only ended at Tours in 732. From the eleventh to the thirteenth century the Crusaders attempted with

temporary success to bring Christianity and Christian rule to the Holy Land. From the fourteenth to the seventeenth century, the Ottoman Turks reversed the balance, extended their sway over the Middle East and the Balkans, captured Constantinople, and twice laid siege to Vienna. In the nineteenth and early twentieth centuries as Ottoman power declined Britain, France, and Italy established Western control over most of North Africa and the Middle East.

After World War II, the West, in turn, began to retreat; the colonial empires disappeared; first Arab nationalism and then Islamic fundamentalism manifested themselves; the West became heavily dependent on the Persian Gulf countries for its energy; the oil-rich Muslim countries became money-rich and, when they wished to, weapons-rich. Several wars occurred between Arabs and Israel (created by the West). France fought a bloody and ruthless war in Algeria for most of the 1950s; British and French forces invaded Egypt in 1956; American forces went into Lebanon in 1958; subsequently American forces returned to Lebanon, attacked Libya, and engaged in various military encounters with Iran; Arab and Islamic terrorists, supported by at least three Middle Eastern governments, employed the weapon of the weak and bombed Western planes and installations and seized Western hostages. This warfare between Arabs and the West culminated in 1990, when the United States sent a massive army to the Persian Gulf to defend some Arab countries against aggression by another. In its aftermath NATO planning is increasingly directed to potential threats and instability along its "southern tier."

This centuries-old military interaction between the West and Islam is unlikely to decline. It could become more virulent. The Gulf War left some Arabs feeling proud that Saddam Hussein had attacked Israel and stood up to the West. It also left many feeling humiliated and resentful of the West's military presence in the Persian Gulf, the West's overwhelming military dominance, and their apparent inability to shape their own destiny. Many Arab countries, in addition to the oil exporters, are reaching levels of economic and social development where autocratic forms of government become inappropriate and efforts to introduce democracy become stronger. Some openings in Arab political systems have already occurred. The principal beneficiaries of these openings have been Islamist movements. In the Arab world, in short, Western democracy strengthens anti-Western political forces. This may be a passing phenomenon, but it surely complicates relations between Islamic countries and the West.

Those relations are also complicated by demography. The spectacular population growth in Arab countries, particularly in North Africa, has led to increased migration to Western Europe. The movement within Western Europe toward minimizing internal boundaries has sharpened political sensitivities with respect to this development. In Italy, France and Germany, racism is increasingly open, and political reactions and violence against Arab and Turkish migrants have become more intense and more widespread since 1990.

On both sides the interaction between Islam and the West is seen as a clash of civilizations. The West's "next confrontation," observes M. J. Akbar, an Indian Muslim author, "is definitely going to come from the Muslim world. It is in the sweep of the Islamic nations from the Maghreb to Pakistan that the struggle for a new world order will begin." Bernard Lewis comes to a similar conclusion:

> We are facing a mood and a movement far transcending the level of issues and policies and the governments that pursue them. This is no less than a clash of civilizations—the perhaps irrational but surely historic reaction of an ancient rival against our Judeo-Christian heritage, our secular present, and the worldwide expansion of both.[2]

Historically, the other great antagonistic interaction of Arab Islamic civilization has been with the pagan, animist, and now increasingly Christian black peoples to the south. In the past, this antagonism was epitomized in the image of Arab slave dealers and black slaves. It has been reflected in the ongoing civil war in the Sudan between Arabs and blacks, the fighting in Chad between Libyan-supported insurgents and the government, the tensions between Orthodox Christians and Muslims in the Horn of Africa, and the political conflicts, recurring riots and communal violence between Muslims and Christians in Nigeria. The modernization of Africa and the spread of Christianity are likely to enhance the probability of violence along this fault line. Symptomatic of the intensification of this conflict was Pope John Paul II's speech in Khartoum in February 1993 attacking the actions of the Sudan's Islamist government against the Christian minority there.

On the northern border of Islam, conflict has increasingly erupted between Orthodox and Muslim peoples, including the carnage of Bosnia and Sarajevo, the simmering violence between Serbs and Albanians, the tenuous relations between Bulgarians and their Turkish minority, the violence between Ossetians and Ingush, the unremitting slaughter of each other by Armenians and Azeris, the tense relations between Russians and Muslims in Central Asia, and the deployment of Russian troops to protect Russian interests in the Caucasus and Central Asia. Religion reinforces the revitalization of ethnic identities and restimulates Russian fears about the security of their southern borders. This concern is well captured by Archie Roosevelt:

> Much of Russian history concerns the struggle between the Slavs and the Turkic peoples on their borders, which dates back to the foundation of the Russian state more than a thousand years ago. In the Slavs' millennium-long confrontation with their eastern neighbors lies the key to an understanding not only of Russian history, but Russian character. To understand Russian realities today one has to have a concept of the great Turkic ethnic group that has preoccupied Russians through the centuries.[3]

The conflict of civilizations is deeply rooted elsewhere in Asia. The historic clash between Muslim and Hindu in the subcontinent manifests itself now not only in the rivalry between Pakistan and India but also in intensifying religious strife within India between increasingly militant Hindu groups and India's substantial Muslim minority. The destruction of the Ayodhya mosque in December 1992 brought to the fore the issue of whether India will remain a secular democratic state or become a Hindu one. In East Asia, China has outstanding territorial disputes with most of its neighbors. It has pursued a ruthless policy toward the Buddhist people of Tibet, and it is pursuing an increasingly ruthless policy toward its Turkic-Muslim minority. With the Cold War over, the underlying differences between China and the United States have reasserted themselves in areas such as human rights, trade and weapons proliferation. These differences are unlikely to moderate. A "new cold war," Deng Xaioping reportedly asserted in 1991, is under way between China and America.

The same phrase has been applied to the increasingly difficult relations between Japan and the United States. Here cultural difference exacerbates economic conflict. People on each side allege racism on the other, but at least on the American side the antipathies are not racial but cultural. The basic values, attitudes, behavioral patterns of the two societies could hardly be more different. The economic issues between the United States and Europe are no less serious than those between the United States and Japan, but they do not have the same political salience and emotional intensity because the differences between American culture and European culture are so much less than those between American civilization and Japanese civilization.

The interactions between civilizations vary greatly in the extent to which they are likely to be characterized by violence. Economic competition clearly predominates between the American and European subcivilizations of the West and between both of them and Japan. On the Eurasian continent, however, the proliferation of ethnic conflict, epitomized at the extreme in "ethnic cleansing," has not been totally random.

It has been most frequent and most violent between groups belonging to different civilizations. In Eurasia the great historic fault lines between civilizations are once more aflame. This is particularly true along the boundaries of the crescent-shaped Islamic bloc of nations from the bulge of Africa to central Asia. Violence also occurs between Muslims, on the one hand, and Orthodox Serbs in the Balkans, Jews in Israel, Hindus in India, Buddhists in Burma and Catholics in the Philippines. Islam has bloody borders.

Civilization Rallying: The Kin-Country Syndrome

Groups or states belonging to one civilization that become involved in war with people from a different civilization naturally try to rally support from other members of their own civilization. As the post–Cold War world evolves, civilization commonality, what H. D. S. Greenway has termed the "kin-country" syndrome, is replacing political ideology and traditional balance-of-power considerations as the principal basis for cooperation and coalitions.

*   *   *

Civilization rallying to date has been limited, but it has been growing, and it clearly has the potential to spread much further. As the conflicts in the Persian Gulf, the Caucasus and Bosnia continued, the positions of nations and the cleavages between them increasingly were along civilizational lines. Populist politicians, religious leaders and the media have found it a potent means of arousing mass support and of pressuring hesitant governments. In the coming years, the local conflicts most likely to escalate into major wars will be those, as in Bosnia and the Caucasus, along the fault lines between civilizations. The next world war, if there is one, will be a war between civilizations.

The West Versus the Rest

The west is now at an extraordinary peak of power in relation to other civilizations. Its super-power opponent has disappeared from the map. Military conflict among Western states is unthinkable, and Western military power is unrivaled. Apart from Japan, the West faces no economic challenge. It dominates international political and security institutions and with Japan international economic institutions. Global political and security issues are effectively settled by a directorate of the United States, Britain and France, world economic issues by a directorate of the United States, Germany and Japan, all of which maintain extraordinarily close relations with each other to the exclusion of lesser and largely non-Western countries. Decisions made at the U.N. Security Council or in the International Monetary Fund that reflect the interests of the West are presented to the world as reflecting the desires of the world community. The very phrase "the world community" has become the euphemistic collective noun (replacing "the Free World") to give global legitimacy to actions reflecting the interest of the United States and other Western powers.[4] Through the IMF and other international economic institutions, the West promotes its economic interests and imposes on other nations the economic policies it thinks appropriate. In any poll of non-Western peoples, the IMF undoubtedly would win the support of finance ministers and a few others, but get an overwhelmingly unfavorable rating from just about everyone else, who would agree with Georgy Arbatov's characterization of IMF officials as "neo-Bolsheviks who love expropriating other people's money, imposing undemocratic and alien rules of economic and political conduct and stifling economic freedom."

Western domination of the U.N. Security Council and its decisions, tempered only by occasional abstention by China, produced U.N. legitimation of the West's use of force to drive Iraq out of Kuwait and its elimination of Iraq's sophisticated weapons and capacity to produce such weapons. It also produced the quite unprecedented action by the United States, Britain and France in getting the Security Council to demand that Libya hand over the Pan Am 103 bombing suspects and then to impose sanctions when Libya refused. After defeating the largest Arab army, the West did not hesitate to throw its weight around in the Arab world. The West in effect is using international institutions, military power and economic resources to run the world in ways that will maintain Western predominance, protect Western interests and promote Western political and economic values.

That at least is the way in which non-Westerners see the new world, and there is a significant element of truth in their view. Differences in power and struggles for military, economic and institutional power are thus one source of conflict between the West and other civilizations. Differences in culture, that is basic values and beliefs, are a second source of conflict. V. S. Naipaul has argued that Western civilization is the "universal civilization" that "fits all men." At a superficial level much of Western culture has indeed permeated the rest of the world. At a more basic level, however, Western concepts differ fundamentally from those prevalent in other civilizations. Western ideas of individualism, liberalism, constitutionalism, human rights, equality, liberty, the rule of law, democracy, free markets, the separation of church and state, often have little resonance in Islamic, Confucian, Japanese, Hindu, Buddhist or Orthodox cultures. Western efforts to propagate such ideas produce instead a reaction against "human rights imperialism" and a reaffirmation of indigenous values, as can be seen in the support for religious fundamentalism by the younger generation in non-Western cultures. The very notion that there could be a "universal civilization" is a Western idea, directly at odds with the particularism of most Asian societies and their emphasis on what distinguishes one people from another. Indeed, the author of a review of 100 comparative studies of values in different societies concluded that "the values that are most important in the West are least important worldwide."[5] In the political realm, of course, these differences are most manifest in the efforts of the United States and other Western powers to induce other peoples to adopt Western ideas concerning democracy and human rights. Modern democratic government originated in the West. When it has developed in non-Western societies it has usually been the product of Western colonialism or imposition.

The central axis of world politics in the future is likely to be, in Kishore Mahbubani's phrase, the conflict between "the West and the Rest" and the responses of non-Western civilizations to Western power and values.[6] Those responses generally take one or a combination of three forms. At one extreme, non-Western states can, like Burma and North Korea, attempt to pursue a course of isolation, to insulate their societies from penetration or "corruption" by the West, and, in effect, to opt out of participation in the Western-dominated global community. The costs of this course, however, are high, and few states have pursued it exclusively. A second alternative, the equivalent of "band-wagoning" in international relations theory, is to attempt to join the West and accept its values and institutions. The third alternative is to attempt to "balance" the West by developing economic and military power and cooperating with other non-Western societies against the West, while preserving indigenous values and institutions; in short, to modernize but not to Westernize.

The Torn Countries

In the future, as people differentiate themselves by civilization, countries with large numbers of peoples of different civilizations, such as the Soviet Union and Yugoslavia, are candidates for dismemberment. Some other countries have a fair degree of cultural homogeneity but are divided over whether their society belongs to one civilization or another. These are torn countries. Their leaders typically wish to pursue a band-wagoning strategy and to make their countries members of the West, but the history, culture and traditions of their countries are non-Western. The most obvious and prototypical torn country is Turkey. The late twentieth-century leaders of Turkey have followed in the Attaturk tradition and defined Turkey as a modern, secular, Western nation state. They allied Turkey with the West in NATO and in the Gulf War; they applied for membership in the European Community. At the same time, however, elements in Turkish society have supported an Islamic revival and have argued that Turkey is basically a Middle Eastern Muslim society. In addition, while the elite of Turkey has defined Turkey as a Western society, the elite of the West refuses to accept Turkey as such. Turkey will not become a member of the European Community, and the real reason, as President Ozal said, "is that we are Muslim and they are Christian and they don't say that." Having rejected Mecca, and then being rejected by Brussels, where does Turkey look? Tashkent may be the answer. The end of the Soviet Union gives Turkey the opportunity to become the leader of a revived Turkic civilization involving seven countries from the borders of Greece to those of China. Encouraged by the West, Turkey is making strenuous efforts to carve out this new identity for itself.

During the past decade Mexico has assumed a position somewhat similar to that of Turkey. Just as Turkey abandoned its historic opposition to Europe and attempted to join Europe, Mexico has stopped defining itself by its opposition to the United States and is instead attempting to imitate the United States and to join it in the North American Free Trade Area. Mexican leaders are engaged in the great task of redefining Mexican identity and have introduced fundamental economic reforms that eventually will lead to fundamental political change. In 1991 a top adviser to President Carlos Salinas de Gortari described at length to me all the changes the

Salinas government was making. When he finished, I remarked: "That's most impressive. It seems to me that basically you want to change Mexico from a Latin American country into a North American country." He looked at me with surprise and exclaimed: "Exactly! That's precisely what we are trying to do, but of course we could never say so publicly." As his remark indicates, in Mexico as in Turkey, significant elements in society resist the redefinition of their country's identity. In Turkey, European-oriented leaders have to make gestures to Islam (Ozal's pilgrimage to Mecca); so also Mexico's North American-oriented leaders have to make gestures to those who hold Mexico to be a Latin American country (Salinas' Ibero-American Guadalajara summit).

Historically Turkey has been the most profoundly torn country. For the United States, Mexico is the most immediate torn country. Globally the most important torn country is Russia. The question of whether Russia is part of the West or the leader of a distinct Slavic-Orthodox civilization has been a recurring one in Russian history. That issue was obscured by the communist victory in Russia, which imported a Western ideology, adapted it to Russian conditions and then challenged the West in the name of that ideology. The dominance of communism shut off the historic debate over Westernization versus Russification. With communism discredited Russians once again face that question.

*   *   *

To redefine its civilization identity, a torn country must meet three requirements. First, its political and economic elite has to be generally supportive of and enthusiastic about this move. Second, its public has to be willing to acquiesce in the redefinition. Third, the dominant groups in the recipient civilization have to be willing to embrace the convert. All three requirements in large part exist with respect to Mexico. The first two in large part exist with respect to Turkey. It is not clear that any of them exist with respect to Russia's joining the West. The conflict between liberal democracy and Marxism-Leninism was between ideologies which, despite their major differences, ostensibly shared ultimate goals of freedom, equality and prosperity. A traditional, authoritarian, nationalist Russia could have quite different goals. A Western democrat could carry on an intellectual debate with a Soviet Marxist. It would be virtually impossible for him to do that with a Russian traditionalist. If, as the Russians stop behaving like Marxists, they reject liberal democracy and begin behaving like Russians but not like Westerners, the relations between Russia and the West could again become distant and conflictual.[7]

The Confucian-Islamic Connection

The obstacles to non-Western countries joining the West vary considerably. They are least for Latin American and East European countries. They are greater for the Orthodox countries of the former Soviet Union. They are still greater for Muslim, Confucian, Hindu and Buddhist societies. Japan has established a unique position for itself as an associate member of the West: it is in the West in some respects but clearly not of the West in important dimensions. Those countries that for reason of culture and power do not wish to, or cannot, join the West compete with the West by developing their own economic, military and political power. They do this by promoting their internal development and by cooperating with other non-Western countries. The most prominent form of this cooperation is the Confucian-Islamic connection that has emerged to challenge Western interests, values and power.

Almost without exception, Western countries are reducing their military power; * * * so also is Russia. China, North Korea and several Middle Eastern states, however, are significantly expanding their military capabilities. They are doing this by the import of arms from Western and non-Western sources and by the development of indigenous arms industries. * * *

The non-Western nations * * * also have absorbed, to the full, the truth of the response of the Indian defense minister when asked what lesson he learned from the Gulf War: "Don't fight the United States unless you have nuclear weapons." Nuclear weapons, chemical weapons and missiles are viewed, probably erroneously, as the potential equalizer of superior Western conventional power. China, of course, already has nuclear weapons; Pakistan and India have the capability to deploy them. North Korea, Iran, Iraq, Libya and Algeria appear to be attempting to acquire them. A top Iranian official has declared that all Muslim states should acquire nuclear weapons, and in 1988 the president of Iran reportedly issued a directive calling for development of "offensive and defensive chemical, biological and radiological weapons."

Centrally important to the development of counter-West military capabilities is the sustained expansion of China's military power and its means to create military power. Buoyed by spectacular economic development, China is rapidly increasing its military spending and vigorously moving forward with the modernization of its armed forces. It is purchasing weapons from the former Soviet states; it is developing long-range missiles.

*   *   *

A Confucian-Islamic military connection has thus come into being, designed to promote acquisition by its members of the weapons and weapons technologies needed to counter the military power of the West. It may or may not last. At present, however, it is, as Dave McCurdy has said, "a renegades' mutual support pact, run by the proliferators and their backers." A new form of arms competition is thus occuring between Islamic-Confucian states and the West. In an old-fashioned arms race, each side developed its own arms to balance or to achieve superiority against the other side. In this new form of arms competition, one side is developing its arms and the other side is attempting not to balance but to limit and prevent that arms build-up while at the same time reducing its own military capabilities.

Implications for the West

This article does not argue that civilization identities will replace all other identities, that nation states will disappear, that each civilization will become a single coherent political entity, that groups within a civilization will not conflict with and even fight each other. This paper does set forth the hypotheses that differences between civilizations are real and important; civilization-consciousness is increasing; conflict between civilizations will supplant ideological and other forms of conflict as the dominant global form of conflict; international relations, historically a game played out within Western civilization, will increasingly be de-Westernized and become a game in which non-Western civilizations are actors and not simply objects; successful political, security and economic international institutions are more likely to develop within civilizations than across civilizations; conflicts between groups in different civilizations will be more frequent, more sustained and more violent than conflicts between groups in the same civilization; violent conflicts between groups in different civilizations are the most likely and most dangerous source of escalation that could lead to global wars; the paramount axis of world politics will be the relations between "the West and the Rest"; the elites in some torn non-Western countries will try to make their countries part of the West, but in most cases face major obstacles to accomplishing this; a central focus of conflict for the immediate future will be between the West and several Islamic-Confucian states.

This is not to advocate the desirability of conflicts between civilizations. It is to set forth descriptive hypotheses as to what the future may be like. If these are plausible hypotheses, however, it is necessary to consider their implications for Western policy. These implications should be divided between short-term advantage and long-term accommodation. In the short term it is clearly in the interest of the West to promote greater cooperation and unity within its own civilization, particularly between its European and North American components; to incorporate into the West societies in Eastern Europe and Latin America whose cultures are close to those of the West; to promote and maintain cooperative relations with Russia and Japan; to prevent escalation of local inter-civilization conflicts into major inter-civilization wars; to limit the expansion of the military strength of Confucian and Islamic states; to moderate the reduction of Western military capabilities and maintain military superiority in East and Southwest Asia; to exploit differences and conflicts among Confucian and Islamic states; to support in other civilizations groups sympathetic to Western values and interests; to strengthen international institutions that reflect and legitimate Western interests and values and to promote the involvement of non-Western states in those institutions.

In the longer term other measures would be called for. Western civilization is both Western and modern. Non-Western civilizations have attempted to become modern without becoming Western. To date only Japan has fully succeeded in this quest. Non-Western civilizations will continue to attempt to acquire the wealth, technology, skills, machines and weapons that are part of being modern. They will also attempt to reconcile this modernity with their traditional culture and values. Their economic and military strength relative to the West will increase. Hence the West will increasingly have to accommodate these non-Western modern civilizations whose power approaches that of the West but whose values and interests differ significantly from those of the West. This will require the West to maintain the economic and military power necessary to protect its interests in relation to these civilizations. It will also, however, require the West to develop a more profound understanding of the basic religious and philosophical assumptions underlying other civilizations and the ways in which people in those civilizations see their interests. It will require an effort to identify elements of commonality between Western and other civilizations. For the relevant future, there will be no universal civilization, but instead a world of different civilizations, each of which will have to learn to coexist with the others.

NOTES

1. Murray Weidenbaum, *Greater China: The Next Economic Superpower?*, St. Louis: Washington University Center for the Study of American Business, Contemporary Issues, Series 57, February 1993, pp. 2–3.

2. Bernard Lewis, "The Roots of Muslim Rage," *The Atlantic Monthly*, vol. 266, September 1990, p. 60; *Time*, June 15, 1992, pp. 24–28.

3. Archie Roosevelt, For Lust of Knowing, Boston: Little, Brown, 1988, pp. 332–333.

4. Almost invariably Western leaders claim they are acting on behalf of "the world community." One minor lapse occurred during the run-up to the Gulf War. In an interview on "Good Morning America," Dec. 21, 1990, British Prime Minister John Major referred to the actions "the West" was taking against Saddam Hussein. He quickly corrected himself and subsequently referred to "the world community." He was, however, right when he erred.

5. Harry C. Triandis, *The New York Times*, Dec. 25, 1990, p. 41, and "Cross-Cultural Studies of Individualism and Collectivism," *Nebraska Symposium on Motivation*, vol. 37, 1989, pp. 41–133.

6. Kishore Mahbubani, "The West and the Rest," *The National Interest*, Summer 1992, pp. 3–13.

7. Owen Harries has pointed out that Australia is trying (unwisely in his view) to become a torn country in reverse. Although it has been a full member not only of the West but also of the ABCA military and intelligence core of the West, its current leaders are in effect proposing that it defect from the West, redefine itself as an Asian country and cultivate

close ties with its neighbors. Australia's future, they argue, is with the dynamic economies of East Asia. But, as I have suggested, close economic cooperation normally requires a common cultural base. In addition, none of the three conditions necessary for a torn country to join another civilization is likely to exist in Australia's case.

AMARTYA SEN

CIVILIZATIONAL IMPRISONMENTS: HOW TO MISUNDERSTAND EVERYBODY IN THE WORLD

I

Conflict between civilizations has been a popular topic for a long time—well before the dreadful events of September 11 ushered in a period of open confrontation and pervasive distrust in the world. Yet these terrible happenings have had the effect of magnifying the ongoing interest in the so-called "clash of civilizations," of which the classic statement can be found in Samuel Huntington's famous and ambitiously impressive book *The Clash of Civilizations and the Remaking of World Order*, which appeared five years before the World Trade Center was targeted. Indeed, many leading commentators have tended to see a firm connection between global conflicts and civilization confrontations—most notably, between "Western" and "Islamic" civilizations. The intellectual basis of that thesis and related ideas requires a close examination, both for its obvious epistemic interest and—more immediately—for its far-reaching relevance to practical politics in the contemporary world. The need for that critical scrutiny is now greater than it has ever been.

The thesis of a civilizational clash can be ideologically linked with a more general idea that provides the methodological foundation of the "clash thesis." This concerns the program of cat-

From *The New Republic* (June 10, 2002), pp. 28–33.

egorizing people of the world according to some single—and allegedly commanding—system of classification. To see any person wholly, or even primarily, as a member of a so-called civilization (in Huntington's categorization, as a member of "the Western world," "the Islamic world," "the Hindu world," or "the Buddhist world") is already to reduce people into this one dimension. The deficiency of the clash thesis, I would argue, begins well before we get to the point of asking whether the disparate civilizations (among which the population of the world is forcefully partitioned out) must necessarily—or even typically—clash. No matter what answer we give to this question, by even pursuing the question in this restrictive form we implicitly give credibility to the allegedly unique importance of one categorization over all the other ways in which people of the world may be classified.

Opponents of the "clash theory" can actually contribute to its intellectual foundation if they accept the same singular classification of the world population. The same impoverished vision of the world—divided into boxes of civilizations—is shared by those who preach amity among discrete and disjunctive civilizations and those who see them as clashing. In disputing the obtuse and gross generalization that members of the Islamic civilization have an essentially belligerent culture, for example, it is common enough to argue that they actually share a culture of peace. But this simply replaces one stereotype with another; and it involves accepting an implicit presumption that people who happen to be Muslim by religion would be much the same in other ways as well.

Aside from all the difficulties in defining civilizational categories as disparate units (on which more presently), the arguments on both sides suffer from a shared faith in the presumption that seeing people exclusively, or primarily, in terms of religion-based civilizations to which they are assumed to belong is a good way of understanding human beings. Civilizational partitioning is a pervasively intrusive phenomenon in social analysis (stifling other ways of seeing people) even without its being supplemented by the incendiary belief in the particular thesis of a civilizational clash.

If "the clash of civilizations" is the grand thesis about the divisions of the contemporary world, there are lesser but still influential claims that relate contrasts of cultures and identities to the conflicts—and the profusion of atrocities— that we see in different parts of the world today. Instead of one majestically momentous partition, as in Huntington's world, that splits the world's population into contending civilizations, the lesser variants of the approach view local populations as being respectively split into clashing groups, with divergent cultures and disparate histories that tend, in an almost "natural" way, to breed enmity toward each other. Conflicts involving Hutus and Tutsis in Rwanda, and Serbs and Albanians in the former Yugoslavia, and Hindus and Muslims in the subcontinent, and so on, are then re-interpreted in lofty historical terms, reading into them much more than contemporary politics. Modern conflicts that call for analysis in terms of contemporary events and machinations are then interpreted as ancient feuds—real or imagined—that place today's players in pre-ordained roles in an allegedly ancestral play. The "civilizational" approach to contemporary conflicts (in grander or lesser versions) serves as a major obstacle to focusing

more fully on the actual prevailing politics and the dynamics of contemporary events.

It is not hard to understand why the civilizational approach is so appealing to so many people. It invokes the richness of history, and it seems to call upon the depth and the gravity of cultural analysis, seeking profundity of understanding in a way that an immediate political analysis of the "here and now" would seem to lack. If I am disputing the civilizational approach, it is not because I do not see its attractions and intellectual temptations. Indeed, I am reminded of an event nearly fifty years ago, shortly after I first arrived in England from India as a student at Cambridge. A kindly fellow student took me to see the recently released film *Rear Window*, in which I encountered James Stewart looking at some very suspicious events in the house opposite his own. Like the James Stewart character, I too, in my naïve way, became convinced that a gruesome murder had been committed in the apartment across the courtyard; but my intellectual friend went on explaining to me (amid whispered requests from neighbors urging him to shut up) that he was quite certain that there was no murder at all, no basis in reality for James Stewart's (and my own) suspicion, and that the whole film was really an indictment of McCarthyism in America, which encouraged everyone to watch the activities of other people with great suspicion. "This film is a critique," my friend informed the novice from the Third World, "of the growing Western culture of snooping." Such a film, I had to agree, would have been in many ways a much more penetrating and solemn work, but I kept wondering whether it was, in fact, the film that we were watching. What must be similarly asked is whether what we are watching in the world in which we live is actually a clash of civilizations, or something much more mundane that merely looks like a civilizational clash to determined seekers of profundity.

The depth that civilizational analysis seeks is not exclusive, though, to the high road of intellectual analysis. In some ways, civilizational analysis mirrors and magnifies common beliefs that flourish in not particularly intellectual circles. The invoking of, say, "Western" values against "non-Western" values is rather commonplace in public discussions, and it makes regular headlines in tabloids as well as figuring in political rhetoric and anti-immigrant oratory (from the United States and Canada to Germany, France, and the Netherlands). In the aftermath of September 11, the stereotyping of Muslims came often enough from people who are no great specialists in civilizational categories (to say the least). But theories of civilizational clash have often provided allegedly dispassionate and sophisticated foundations for coarse popular beliefs. Complicated theory can sometimes bolster uncomplicated bigotry and can make the world a much more flammable place than it needs to be.

II

What, then, are the difficulties of civilizational analysis? I shall begin by discussing a little more the problem that I claimed was its most basic weakness: the presumption that a person can be regarded pre-eminently not as an individual with many affiliations, nor as a member of many different groups, but as a member merely of one particular group, which gives her a uniquely important identity. The implicit belief in the overarching power of a singular classification is not only gross, it is also grossly confrontational in form and in implication. Such a divisive view goes not only against the old-fashioned belief (which tends to be ridiculed these days as much too soft-headed) that "we are all basically just human beings," but also against the important understanding that we are *diversely* different. Indeed, I would argue that the main hope of harmony in the contemporary world lies in the plurality of our identities, which cut across each other and work against sharp divisions around one single hardened line of impenetrable identity. Our shared humanity gets savagely challenged when the confrontation is unified into a

solitary—and allegedly dominant—system of classification; this is much more divisive than the universe of plural and diverse categorizations that shape the world in which we actually live.

The realization that we each have multiple identities may sound like a much grander idea than it is. Indeed, it is a very elementary recognition. In our normal lives, we see ourselves as members of a variety of groups: we belong to all of them. The same person can be an American citizen of Malaysian origin with Chinese racial characteristics, a Christian, a libertarian, a political activist, a woman, a poet, a vegetarian, an asthmatic, a historian, a schoolteacher, a birdwatcher, a baseball fan, a lover of jazz, a heterosexual, a supporter of gay and lesbian rights, and a person deeply committed to the view that creatures from outer space regularly visit Earth in colorful vehicles and sing tantalizing songs. Each of these collectivities, to all of which this individual belongs, gives her a particular identity, which—depending on the context—can be quite important; but none of them has a unique and pre-ordained role in defining this person.

The relative importance of the different groups to which any person belongs can vary, depending on the context and the person's priorities. Being a teetotaler, for example, can be a more important identity when one is invited to a wine-tasting party than the same person's identity as, say, a poet or an American or a Protestant. It need not cause any problem for action choice, either, especially when the demands associated with different identities do not, in fact, conflict. In many contexts, however, the different components of one's identity may well compete in one's decision regarding what to do. One may have to choose the relative importance to attach to one's activism as a citizen over one's love of baseball if a citizens' meeting clashes with a promising game. One has to decide how to deal with alternative claims on one's attention and loyalties that compete with one another.

Identity, then, cannot be only a matter of "discovery" (as communitarian philosophers often claim); it is a matter of choice as well. It is possible that the often-repeated belief that identity is a matter of "discovery" is encouraged by the fact that the choices we can make are constrained by feasibility, and sometimes the constraints are very exacting. The feasibilities will certainly depend on particular circumstances. The constraints may be especially strict in defining the extent to which we can persuade others to take us to be different from what they take us to be. A Jewish person in Nazi Germany could not easily choose a different identity from the one with which others marked him or her. The freedom in choosing the importance to attach to our different identities is always constrained, and in some cases very sharply so.

This point is not in dispute. The fact that we always choose within particular constraints is a standard feature of every choice. As any theorist of choice knows, choices of all kinds are always made within particular feasibility restrictions. As students of elementary economics all have to learn, the theory of consumer choice does not deny the existence of a budget that restrains the consumer's purchasing ability. The presence of the budget constraint does not imply that there is no choice to be made, but only that the choice has to be made within that constraint. What is true in elementary economics is also true in complex political and social decisions. While the Jewish person in Nazi Germany may have had difficulty in paying attention to her other identities, there are many other contexts that give more room for effective choice, in which the competing claims of other affiliations (varying from nationality, language, and literature to profession and political belief) will demand serious attention and require a reflective resolution.

There is also the ethical issue regarding the status of identity-based claims of any kind vis-à-vis arguments that do not turn on any identity whatsoever. Our duty to other human beings may not necessarily be linked only to the fact that we share a common human identity, but rather to our sense of concern for them irrespective of any sharing of identity. Moreover, the reach of our concern may apply to other species as well, despite the lack of a shared human identity and the non-invoking of any other identity that would try to translate a general ethical argument into a specialized identity-centered morality. (I have discussed these distinctions in these pages in "Other People," December 18, 2000.)

While religious categories have received much airing in recent years, they cannot be presumed to obliterate other distinctions and other concerns, and even less be taken to be the only relevant system of classifying people across the globe. It is the plurality of our identities, and our right to choose how we see ourselves (with what emphases and what priorities), that the civilizational classifications tend to overlook, in a largely implicit—rather than transparent—way.

The civilizational classifications have often closely followed religious divisions. Huntington contrasts "Western civilization" with "Islamic civilization," "Hindu civilization," "Buddhist civilization," and so on; and while hybrid categories are accommodated (such as "Sinic civilization" or "Japanese civilization"), the alleged battlefronts of religious differences are incorporated into a carpentered vision of one dominant and hardened divisiveness. By categorizing all people into those belonging to "the Islamic world," "the Christian world," "the Hindu world," "the Buddhist world," and so on, the divisive power of classificatory priority is implicitly used to place people firmly inside a unique set of rigid boxes. Other divisions (say, between the rich and the poor, between members of different classes and occupations, between people of different politics, between distinct nationalities and residential locations, between language groups, and so on) are all submerged by this allegedly preeminent way of seeing the differences between people.

The belief in a unique categorization is both a serious descriptive mistake and an ethical and political hazard. People do see themselves in very many different ways. A Bangladeshi Muslim is not only a Muslim but also a Bengali and a

Bangladeshi, possibly quite proud of Bengali literature. The separation of Bangladesh from Pakistan was driven not by religion, but by language, literature, and politics. A Nepalese Hindu is not only a Hindu, but also has political and ethnic characteristics that have their own relevance, and that allow Nepal to be, unlike India, an officially Hindu state (indeed, the only one in the world). Poverty, too, can be a great source of solidarity across other boundaries. The kind of division highlighted by the so-called "anti-globalization" protesters (one of the most globalized movements in the world) tries to unite the underdogs of the world economy, cutting across religious or national or civilizational lines of division. The multiplicity of categories works against rigid separation and its ignitable implications.

III

Aside from being morally and politically destructive, the epistemic content of the classification according to so-called civilizations is highly dubious. It could not but be so, since in focusing on one exclusive way of dividing the people of the world, the approach has to cut many corners. In describing India as a "Hindu civilization," for example. Huntington's exposition of the alleged "clash of civilizations" has to downplay the fact that India has more Muslims than any other country in the world, with the exception of Indonesia and marginally Pakistan. India may or may not be placed within the arbitrary definition of "the Muslim world," but it is still the case that India (with its 125 million Muslims—more than the entire populations of Britain and France put together) has a great many more Muslims than nearly every country in the so-called "Muslim world."

It is impossible to think of "Indian civilization" without taking note of the major role of Muslims in the history of India. Indeed, it is futile to try to have an understanding of the nature and the range of Indian art, literature, music, or food without seeing the extensive interactions that were not deterred by barriers of religious communities. And Muslims are not, of course, the only non-Hindu group that helps to constitute India. The Sikhs are a major presence, as are the Jains. Not only is India the country of origin of Buddhism, but Buddhism was the dominant religion of India for more than a millennium. Atheistic schools of thought—the Charvaka and the Lokayata—have also flourished in the country from at least the sixth century B.C.E. to the present day. There have been Christian communities in India from the fourth century C.E.—two hundred years before there were Christian communities in Britain. Jews came to India shortly after the fall of Jerusalem; Parsees started coming in the eighth century.

Given all this, Huntington's description of India as a "Hindu civilization" is an epistemic and historical absurdity. It is also politically combustible. It tends to add a superficial and highly deceptive credibility to the extraordinary neglect of history—and of present realities—that some Hindu fundamentalists have tried to champion, most recently in an exceptionally barbaric way in Gujarat. Even though these political groups seem to be trying their best to overturn Indian secularism, the secular constitution of India as well as the large majority of Indians who are committed to secularism would make it hard to achieve this. The fact that the poison of sectarian violence so far has not spread beyond the limits of one state—Gujarat, with a ruling government that is at best grossly incompetent but most likely a great deal worse—is perhaps ground for some cautious optimism about the future of India. But the human costs of violent extremism have been truly monumental.

The portrayal of India as a Hindu civilization may be a simple-minded mistake, but crudity of one kind or another is present in the characterizations of other civilizations as well. Consider what is called "Western civilization." Indeed, the champions of "the clash of civilizations," in line with their belief in the profundity of this singular line of division, tend to see tolerance as a special and perennial feature of Western civilization, extending way back into history. Huntington insists that the "West was West long before it was modern," and cites (among other allegedly special features such as "social pluralism") "a sense of individualism and a tradition of individual rights and liberties unique among civilized societies." This, too, is at best a gross oversimplification.

Tolerance and liberty are certainly among the important achievements of modern Europe (leaving out aberrations such as Nazi Germany or the intolerant governance of British or French or Portuguese empires in Asia and Africa). But to see a unique line of historical division there—going back over the millennia—is quite fanciful. The championing of political liberty and religious tolerance, in its full contemporary form, is not an old historical feature in any country or any civilization in the world. Plato and Aquinas were not less authoritarian in their thinking than was Confucius. This is not to deny that there were champions of tolerance in classical European thought, but if this is taken to give credit to the whole Western world (from the ancient Greeks to the Ostrogoths and the Visigoths), there are similar examples in other cultures.

The Indian emperor Ashoka's dedicated championing of religious and other kinds of tolerance in the third century B.C.E. (arguing that "the sects of other people all deserve reverence for one reason or another") is certainly among the earliest political defenses of tolerance anywhere. The recent Bollywood movie *Ashoka* (made, as it happens, by a Muslim director) may or may not be accurate in all its details, but it rightly emphasizes the importance of secularism in Ashoka's thinking two and a half millennia ago and indicates its continuing relevance in contemporary India. While a later Indian emperor, Akbar, the Great Mughal, was making similar pronouncements on religious tolerance in Agra at the end of the sixteenth century ("No one should be interfered with on account of religion, and anyone is to be allowed to go over to a religion that pleases him"), the Inquisitions were active in Europe and Giordano Bruno was being burned in the Campo dei Fiori in Rome.

Similarly, what is often called "Western science" draws on a world heritage. There is a chain of intellectual relations that links Western mathematics and science to a collection of distinctly non-Western practitioners. Even today, when a modern mathematician at, say, Princeton invokes an "algorithm" to solve a difficult computational problem, she helps to commemorate the contributions of the ninth-century Arab mathematician Al-Khwarizmi, from whose name the term "algorithm" is derived. (The term "algebra" comes from his book *Al-Jabr wa-al-Muqabilah*.) The decimal system, which evolved in India in the early centuries of the first millennium, arrived in Europe at the end of that millennium, transmitted by the Arabs. A large group of contributors from different non-Western societies —Chinese, Arab, Iranian, Indian, and others— influenced the science, the mathematics, and the philosophy that played a major part in the European Renaissance and, later, in the European Enlightenment.

In his *Critical and Miscellaneous Essays*, Thomas Carlyle claimed that "the three great elements of modern civilization" are "Gunpowder, Printing, and the Protestant Religion." While the Chinese cannot be held responsible for Protestantism, their contribution to Carlyle's list of civilizational ingredients is not insignificant, though it is less total than it is in the case of Francis Bacon's earlier list, in *Novum Organum*, of "printing, gunpowder, and the magnet." The West must get full credit for the remarkable achievements that occurred in Europe during the Renaissance, the Enlightenment, and the Industrial Revolution, but the idea of an immaculate Western conception would require a genuinely miraculous devotion to parochialism.

Not only is the flowering of global science and technology not an exclusively West-led phenomenon, there were major global advances in the world that took the form of international encounters far away from Europe. Consider printing, which features in Carlyle's list, and which Bacon put among the developments that "have changed the whole face and state of things throughout the world." The technology of printing was a great Chinese achievement, but the use to which the Chinese put this new method was not confined merely to local or parochial pursuits. Indeed, the first printed book was a Sanskrit treatise in Buddhist philosophy, *Vajracchedika-prajnaparamita Sutra* (sometimes referred to as the "Diamond Sutra"), translated into Chinese from Sanskrit in the early fifth century and printed four centuries later in 868 C.E. The translator of the Diamond Sutra, Kumarajiva, was half Indian and half Turkish. He lived in a part of eastern Turkistan called Kucha, traveled extensively in India, and later moved to China, where he headed the newly established institute of foreign languages in Xi'an in the early fifth century: The West figured not at all in the first stirring of what came to be a mainstay of Western civilization.

IV

The narrowness of the civilizational mode of thinking has many far-reaching effects. It fuels alienation among people from different parts of the world, and it encourages a distanced and possibly confrontational view of others. Even the resistance to so-called "Westernization" by non-Western activists frequently takes the form of shunning "Western" (or what some Western spokesmen have claimed to be exclusively "Western") objects, even though they are among the historical products of diverse global interactions.

Indeed, in a West-dominated world, many non-Western people tend to think of themselves quintessentially as "the other," in contradistinction to the West. (This phenomenon has been beautifully analyzed by Akeel Bilgrami in an essay called "What Is a Muslim?" in *Identities*, edited by Kwame Anthony Appiah and Henry Louis Gates Jr.) The political force of this phenomenon makes the effects of Western expropriation of a global heritage even more disastrous. It plays a regressive role in the self-identification of the colonial and postcolonial world, and in parts of the "anti-globalization" movement. It takes a heavy toll by inciting parochial tendencies and needless confrontations; it tends to undermine the possibility of objectivity in science and knowledge; and it deflects attention from the real issues to be faced in contemporary globalization (including the ways and means of reducing massive inequality of opportunities without losing the technological and economic rewards of global interaction).

To focus just on the grand religious classification, in its civilizational garb, is not only to miss many significant concerns and ideas that can move people. Such a focus also has the effect of lessening the importance of other priorities by artificially magnifying the voice of religious authority. The clerics are then treated as the *ex officio* spokesmen for the so-called "Islamic world," even though a great many Muslims have profound differences with what is proposed by one mullah or another. The same would apply to other religious leaders' being seen as the spokespeople for their "flocks." The singular classification not only makes one distinction among many into a uniquely inflexible barrier, it also gives a commanding voice to the "establishment" figures in the respective religious and sectarian hierarchy, while other voices are muffled.

A person's religious or civilizational identity may well be very important for her, but it is one membership among many. The question we have to ask is not, say, whether Islam (or Hinduism or Christianity) is a peace-loving religion or a combative one, but how a religious Muslim (or Hindu or Christian) may combine his or her religious beliefs or practices with other commitments and values, with other features of personal identity. To see one's religious—or civilizational—affiliation as an all-engulfing identity would be a deeply problematic diagnosis. There have been fierce warriors as well as great champions of peace among devoted members of each religion; and rather than asking which one is the "true believer" and which one a "mere imposter," we should accept that our religious faith does not in itself resolve all the decisions that we must make in our lives, including those concerning our political and social priorities and the corresponding issues of conduct and action. Both the proponents of peace and tolerance and the patrons of war and intolerance can belong to the same religion (and may be, in their own ways, true believers) without this being seen as a contradiction. The domain of one's religious identity does not vanquish all other aspects of one's understanding and affiliation.

The increasing use of a religion-based singular civilization classification also makes the Western response to global terrorism and conflict oddly counterproductive. Respect for other civilizations is shown by praising the religious books of "other people," rather than by taking note of the many-sided involvements and achievements of different peoples in a globally interactive world. As Britain goes down the slippery slope of intensifying faith-based schools (Islamic and Sikh schools are already established, and Hindu ones may come soon), the focus is on what divides people rather than what unites them. The cultivation of analytical and critical reasoning, which Western chauvinists usurp as being quintessentially Western, has to take a back seat to religious education, in which the children of new immigrants are expected to find their "own culture." The sad effect of narrowing the intellectual horizon of young children is further compounded by the gross confusion of civilization with religion.

There is no historical reason, for example, why the championing of the Arab or Muslim heritage has to concentrate only on religion and not also on science and mathematics, to which Arab and Muslim scholars have contributed so much in the past. But crude civilizational classifications have tended to put the latter in the basket of "Western science," leaving other civilizations to mine their pride only in religious depths. The

non-Western activists, then, focus on those issues that divide them from the West (religious beliefs, local customs, and cultural specificities) rather than on those things that reflect global interactions (science, mathematics, literature, and so on). The dialectics of the "negation of negation" then extracts a heavy price in fomenting more confrontations in the world.

Moreover, the chosen method of giving each "community" its "own culture" makes the respective religious and theological authorities much more powerful in the schooling of immigrants to Britain, when they are sent to the "faith-based" schools. Religion-based divisions are intensified not only by the efforts of anti-Western religious fundamentalists, but also by the West's own arrangements related to seeing "other people" simply in terms of religion, ignoring the many-sided civilizations from which the immigrants come.

V

The reliance on civilizational partitioning fails badly, then, for a number of distinct reasons. First, the classifications are often based on an extraordinary epistemic crudeness and an extreme historical innocence. The diversity of traditions *within* distinct civilizations is effectively ignored, and major global interactions in science, technology, mathematics, and literature over millennia are made to disappear so as to construct a parochial view of the uniqueness of Western civilization.

Second, there is a basic methodological problem involved in the implicit presumption that a civilizational partitioning is the uniquely relevant distinction, and must swamp other ways of identifying people. It is bad enough that those who foment global confrontations or local sectarian violence try to impose a pre-chosen unitary and divisive identity on people who are to be recruited as the "foot soldiers" of political brutality, but that task gets indirectly yet significantly aided by the implicit support that the warriors get from theories of singular categorization of the people of the world.

Third, there is a remarkable neglect of the role of choice and reasoning in decisions regarding what importance to attach to the membership of any particular group, or to any particular identity (among many others). By adopting a unique and allegedly predominant way of categorizing people, civilizational partitioning can materially contribute to the conflicts in the world. To deny choice when it does exist is not only an epistemic failure (a misunderstanding of what the world is like); it is also an ethical delinquency and a political dereliction of responsibility. There is a critical need to recognize the plurality of our identities, and also to acknowledge the fact that, as responsible human beings, we have to choose (rather than inertly "discover") what priorities to give to our diverse associations and affiliations. In contrast, the theorists of inescapable "clashes" try to deny strenuously—or to ignore implicitly—the multiplicity of classifications that compete with each other, and the related need for us all to take decisional responsibilities about our priorities. People are seen as belonging to rigid prisons of allegedly decisive identities.

In a well-known interview, Peter Sellers once remarked: "There used to be a 'me,' but I had it surgically removed." In their respective attempts to impose a single and unique identity on us, the surgical removal of the actual "me" is done by others—the religious fundamentalist, the nationalist extremist, the Western chauvinist, the sectarian provocateur. We have to resist such an imprisonment. We must insist upon the liberty to see ourselves as we would choose to see ourselves, deciding on the relative importance that we would like to attach to our membership in the different groups to which we belong. The central issue, in sum, is freedom. To make our identity into a prison is not social wisdom. It is intellectual surrender.

4 POLITICAL ECONOMY

The field of political economy, the concept of laissez-faire *economic liberalism, and the modern discipline of economics are all generally considered to have originated with Adam Smith's* The Wealth of Nations, *published in 1776. Many of Smith's most important ideas, particularly the division and specialization of labor, were already familiar to literate Europeans from earlier works, including Bernard Mandeville's witty and enduring poem* Fable of the Bees, *first published in 1705, and the French* Encyclopédie *of the 1750s. But it was Smith who, through plain examples and seemingly irrefutable logic, convinced three generations of European and American elites that free markets and minimal government would maximize economic growth. The excerpts from* The Wealth of Nations *included here encapsulate Smith's arguments on the division of labor, the self-regulating nature of capitalism (the "**invisible hand**"), the advantages of free trade, and the importance of limited but effective government.*

*Perhaps the most fundamental, and certainly the most counterintuitive, argument in political economy is that **free international trade** benefits all countries, and perhaps particularly poorer countries.[1] Virtually every serious student of political economy today, as well as political theorists and practitioners of almost all ideological persuasions—liberals, conservatives, social democrats, most Marxists[2]— from poor and rich countries alike, believe in free trade and expanding world markets. (Mercantilists of course do not accept free trade, but the current stagnation of the Japanese economy has cast mercantilism into almost as much disrepute as Communism.)*

Why is the intellectual case for free trade so strong? Smith's argument had seemed to depend on differences between countries in absolute *advantage (i.e., that a product could be produced in one country with fewer hours of labor than in another.) But what if a country were at absolute disadvantage in every product? The great early economist David Ricardo argued, with what most still consider to be airtight logic, that free trade would benefit all countries so long as there were differences in* relative *advantage. In the brief excerpt from Ricardo's* Principles of Political Economy *(1817) presented here,*

Ricardo argues that even if one country (in his example, England) is at absolute disadvantage in producing both wine and cloth (i.e., more hours of labor are required to produce each product in England than in Portugal), it still has comparative advantage in one, and will benefit from trading freely with an absolutely advantaged country (in this case, Portugal). Ricardo's insights have been clarified and amplified by more recent research, and The Economist *article ("Trade Winds") included here is an excellent distillation of all that current economic theory has to say about the issue of international trade. It begins with a recapitulation of Ricardo's theory. These two readings encapsulate the core of the "classical" political economy of international trade.*

The other important question of classical political economy is what role the government does, or should, play in the economy. Smith, and economic liberals generally, advocated a minimalist state, and The Economist *article on "The Hidden Cost of Taxes" makes the classical case for this, explaining that taxes impose "deadweight loss" on the economy. But political economists, particularly in light of the post-Communist experiences, have begun to see that more than Smith's minimalist state is needed. In his 1991 survey, presented here in slightly abridged form, the Nobel-winning economic historian Douglass North shows through logic and historical example how important governments—or, more generally, institutions—have been for economic progress.*

Government then, must be involved in the economy, but how much? Social democratic and Christian democratic governments throughout Europe have erected what Americans would regard as lavishly expensive welfare states, yet their economies seem—at least until recently—not to have suffered, and perhaps to have benefited. In their pioneering and important essay (considerably abridged here), Alberto Alesina, Edward Glaeser, and Bruce Sacerdote try to explain the enduring differences in government spending and intervention between Europe and the United States, and to say whether it matters for social inequality and economic growth. (For more on the modern welfare state, see Chapter 7.)

NOTES

1. This is not the same thing as saying that every *person* benefits in every country. When the United States trades with China, skilled U.S. workers gain but unskilled U.S. workers lose; while in China unskilled workers benefit but skilled workers lose. Yet the gains of skilled U.S. workers far outweigh our unskilled workers' loss, just as the gains of unskilled Chinese workers far exceed the losses to skilled Chinese workers.

2. Karl Marx was as avid a supporter of free trade as Adam Smith had been, and every early Marxist party in Europe was free-trading. Social Democrats today, in all developed countries, are among the strongest supporters of trade expansion. Communist regimes of course walled themselves off from world markets; but in this, as in almost all else, they were diametrically opposed to original Marxism.

ADAM SMITH

AN INQUIRY INTO THE NATURE AND CAUSES OF THE WEALTH OF NATIONS

Of the Division of Labour[1]

The greatest improvement[2] in the productive powers of labour, and the greater part of the skill, dexterity, and judgment with which it is any where directed, or applied, seem to have been the effects of the division of labour.

The effects of the division of labour, in the general business of society, will be more easily understood, by considering in what manner it operates in some particular manufactures.

*   *   *

To take an example, therefore,[3] from a very trifling manufacture; but one in which the division of labour has been very often taken notice of, the trade of the pin-maker; a workman not educated to this business (which the division of labour has rendered a distinct trade),[4] nor acquainted with the use of the machinery employed in it (to the invention of which the same division of labour has probably given occasion), could scarce, perhaps, with his utmost industry, make one pin in a day, and certainly could not make twenty. But in the way in which this business is now carried on, not only the whole work is a peculiar trade, but it is divided into a number of branches, of which the greater part are likewise peculiar trades. One man draws out the wire, another straights it, a third cuts it, a fourth points it, a fifth grinds it at the top for receiving

From Edwin Cannan, ed., Adam Smith, *An Inquiry into the Nature and Causes of the Wealth of Nations* (Chicago: The University of Chicago Press, 1976. Originally published in 1776.) Book I, pp. 7–19, Book IV, pp. 474–81, 208–9. Some notes have been omitted; those that follow are Cannan's.

the head; to make the head requires two or three distinct operations; to put it on, is a peculiar business, to whiten the pins is another; it is even a trade by itself to put them into the paper; and the important business of making a pin is, in this manner, divided into about eighteen distinct operations, which, in some manufactories, are all performed by distinct hands, though in others the same man will sometimes perform two or three of them.[5] I have seen a small manufactory of this kind where ten men only were employed, and where some of them consequently performed two or three distinct operations. But though they were very poor, and therefore but indifferently accomodated with the necessary machinery, they could, when they exerted themselves, make among them about twelve pounds of pins in a day. There are in a pound upwards of four thousand pins of a middling size. Those ten persons, therefore, could make among them upwards of forty-eight thousand pins in a day. Each person, therefore, making a tenth part of forty-eight thousand pins, might be considered as making four thousand eight hundred pins in a day. But if they had all wrought separately and independently, and without any of them having been educated to this peculiar business, they certainly could not each of them have made twenty, perhaps not one pin in a day; that is, certainly, not the two hundred and fortieth, perhaps not the four thousand eight hundredth part of what they are at present capable of performing, in consequence of a proper division and combination of their different operations.

In every other art and manufacture, the effects of the division of labour are similar to what they are in this very trifling one; though, in many of them, the labour can neither be so much subdivided, nor reduced to so great a simplicity of operation. The division of labour, however, so far as it can be introduced, occasions, in every art, a proportionable increase of the productive powers of labour. The separation of different trades and employments from one another, seems to have taken place, in consequence of this advantage. This separation too is generally carried furthest in those countries which enjoy the highest degree of industry and improvement; what is the work of one man in a rude state of society, being generally that of several in an improved one.

*   *   *

This great increase of the quantity of work which, in consequence of the division of labour, the same number of people are capable of performing,[6] is owing to three different circumstances; first to the increase of dexterity in every particular workman; secondly, to the saving of the time which is commonly lost in passing from one species of work to another; and lastly, to the invention of a great number of machines which facilitate and abridge labour, and enable one man to do the work of many.[7]

*   *   *

It is the great multiplication of the productions of all the different arts, in consequence of the division of labour, which occasions, in a well-governed society, that universal opulence which extends itself to the lowest ranks of the people. Every workman has a great quantity of his own work to dispose of beyond what he himself has occasion for; and every other workman being exactly in the same situation, he is enabled to exchange a great quantity of his own goods for a great quantity, or, what comes to the same thing, for the price of a great quantity of theirs. He supplies them abundantly with what they have occasion for, and they accommodate him as amply with what he has occasion for, and a general plenty diffuses itself through all the different ranks of the society.

*   *   *

Of the Principle which gives Occasion to the Division of Labour

This division of labour, from which so many advantages are derived, is not originally the effect of any human wisdom, which foresees and intends that general opulence to which it gives occasion.[8] It is the necessary, though very slow and gradual, consequence of a certain propensity in human nature which has in view no such extensive utility; the propensity to truck, barter, and exchange one thing for another.

* * * [T]his propensity * * * is common to all men, and to be found in no other race of animals, which seem to know neither this nor any other species of contracts. * * *

Nobody ever saw a dog make a fair and deliberate exchange of one bone for another with another dog.[9] Nobody ever saw one animal by its gestures and natural cries signify to another, this is mine, that yours; I am willing to give this for that.

*   *   *

But man has almost constant occasion for the help of his brethren, and it is in vain for him to expect it from their benevolence only. He will be more likely to prevail if he can interest their self-love in his favour, and show them that it is for their own advantage to do for him what he requires of them. Whoever offers to another a bargain of any kind, proposes to do this. Give me that which I want, and you shall have this which you want, is the meaning of every such offer; and it is in this manner that we obtain from one another the far greater part of those good offices which we stand in need of. It is not from the benevolence of the butcher, the brewer, or the baker, that we expect our dinner, but from their regard to their own interest. We address ourselves, not to their humanity but to their self-love, and never talk to them of our own necessities but of their advantages. Nobody but a beggar chuses to depend chiefly upon the benevolence of his fellow-citizens.

*   *   *

As it is by treaty, by barter, and by purchase, that we obtain from one another the greater part of those mutual good offices which we stand in need of, so it is this same trucking disposition which originally gives occasion to the division of labour. In a tribe of hunters or shepherds a particular person makes bows and arrows, for example, with more readiness and dexterity than any other. He frequently exchanges them for cattle or for venison with his companions; and he finds at last that he can in this manner get more cattle and venison, than if he himself went to the field to catch them. From a regard to his own interest, therefore, the making of bows and arrows grows to be his chief business, and he becomes a sort of armourer. Another excels in making the frames and covers of their little huts or moveable houses. He is accustomed to be of use in this way to his neighbours, who reward him in the same manner with cattle and with venison, till at last he finds it his interest to dedicate himself entirely to this employment, and to become a sort of house-carpenter. In the same manner a third becomes a smith or a brazier; a fourth a tanner or dresser of hides or skins, the principal part of the clothing of savages. And thus the certainty of being able to exchange all that surplus part of the produce of his own labour, which is over and above his own consumption, for such parts of the produce of other men's labour as he may have occasion for, encourages every man to apply himself to a particular occupation, and to cultivate and bring to perfection whatever talent or genius he may possess for that particular species of business.[10]

*   *   *

Of Restraints upon the Importation from Foreign Countries of such Goods as can be Produced at Home

*   *   *

No regulation of commerce can increase the quantity of industry in any society beyond what its capital can maintain. It can only divert a part of it into a direction into which it might not otherwise have gone; and it is by no means certain that this artificial direction is likely to be more advantageous to the society than that into which it would have gone of its own accord.

Every individual is continually exerting himself to find out the most advantageous employment for whatever capital he can command. It is his own advantage, indeed, and not that of the society which he has in view. But the study of his own advantage naturally, or rather necessarily leads him to prefer that employment which is most advantageous to the society.

*   *   *

. . . [E]very individual . . . necessarily endeavours so to direct that industry, that its produce may be of the greatest possible value.

The produce of industry is what it adds to the subject or materials upon which it is employed. In proportion as the value of this produce is great or small, so will likewise be the profits of the employer. But it is only for the sake of profit that any man employs a capital in the support of industry; and he will always, therefore, endeavour to employ it in the support of that industry of which the produce is likely to be of the greatest value, or to exchange for the greatest quantity either of money or of other goods.

But the annual revenue of every society is always precisely equal to the exchangeable value of the whole annual produce of its industry, or rather is precisely the same thing with that exchangeable value. As every individual, therefore, endeavours as much as he can both to employ his capital in the support of domestic industry, and so to direct that industry that its produce may be of the greatest value; every individual necessarily labours to render the annual revenue of the society as great as he can. He generally, indeed, neither intends to promote the public interest, nor knows how much he is promoting it. By preferring the support of domestic to that of foreign industry, he intends only his own security; and by directing that industry in such a manner as its produce may be of the greatest value, he intends only his own gain, and he is in this, as in many other cases, led by an invisible hand to promote an end which was no part of his intention. Nor is it always the worse for the society that it was no part of it. By pursuing his own interest he frequently promotes that of the society more effectually than when he really intends to promote it. I have never known much good done by those who affected to trade for the public good. It is an affectation, indeed, not very common among merchants, and very few words need be employed in dissuading them from it.

What is the species of domestic industry which his capital can employ, and of which the produce is likely to be of the greatest value, every individual, it is evident, can, in his local situation, judge much better than any statesman or lawgiver can do for him. The statesman, who should attempt to direct private people in what manner they ought to employ their capitals, would not only load himself with a most unnecessary attention, but assume an authority which could safely be trusted, not only to no single person, but to no council or senate whatever, and which would no-where be so dangerous as in the hands of a man who had folly and presumption enough to fancy himself fit to exercise it.

To give the monopoly of the home-market to the produce of domestic industry, in any particular art or manufacture, is in some measure to direct private people in what manner they ought to employ their capitals, and must, in almost all cases, be either a useless or a hurtful regulation. If the produce of domestic can be brought there as cheap as that of foreign industry, the regulation is evidently useless. If it cannot, it must generally be hurtful. It is the maxim of every prudent master of a family, never to attempt to make at home what it will cost him more to make than to buy. The taylor does not attempt to make his own shoes, but buys them of the shoemaker. The shoemaker does not attempt to make his own clothes, but employs a taylor. The farmer attempts to make neither the one nor the other, but employs those different artificers. All of them find it for their interest to employ their whole industry in a way in which they have some advantage over their neighbours, and to purchase with a part of its produce, or what is the same thing, with the price of a part of it, whatever else they have occasion for.

What is prudence in the conduct of every private family, can scarce be folly in that of a great kingdom. If a foreign country can supply us with a commodity cheaper than we ourselves can make it, better buy it of them with some part of the produce of our own industry, employed in a way in which we have some advantage. The general industry of the country, being always in proportion to the capital which employs it, will not thereby be diminished, no more than that of the above-mentioned artificers; but only left to find out the way in which it can be employed with the greatest advantage. It is certainly not employed to the greatest advantage, when it is thus directed towards an object which it can buy cheaper than it can make. The value of its annual produce is certainly more or less diminished, when it is thus turned away from producing commodities evidently of more value than the commodity which it is directed to produce. According to the supposition, that commodity could be purchased from foreign countries cheaper than it can be made at home. It could, therefore, have been purchased with a part only of the commodities, or what is the same thing, with a part only of the price of the commodities, which the industry employed by an equal capital would have produced at home, had it been left to follow its natural course. The industry of the country, therefore, is thus turned away from a more, to a less advantageous employment, and the exchangeable value of its annual produce, instead of being increased, according to the intention of the lawgiver, must necessarily be diminished by every such regulation.

*   *   *

The natural advantages which one country has over another in producing particular commodities are sometimes so great, that it is acknowledged by all the world to be in vain to struggle with them. By means of glasses, hotbeds, and hotwalls, very good grapes can be raised in Scotland, and very good wine too can be made of them at about thirty times the expence for which at least equally good can be brought from foreign countries. Would it be a reasonable law to prohibit the importation of all foreign wines, merely to encourage the making of claret and burgundy in Scotland? But if there would be a manifest absurdity in turning towards any employment, thirty times more of the capital and industry of the country, than would be necessary to purchase from foreign countries an equal quantity of the commodities wanted, there must be an absurdity, though not altogether so glaring, yet exactly of the same kind, in turning towards any such employment a thirtieth, or even a three hundredth part more of either. Whether the advantages which one country has over another, be natural or acquired, is in this respect of no consequence. As long as the one country has those advantages, and the other wants them, it will always be more advantageous for the latter, rather to buy of the former than to make. It is an acquired advantage only, which one artificer has over his neighbour, who exercises another trade; and yet they both find it more advantageous to buy of one another, than to make what does not belong to their particular trades.

*   *   *

All systems either of preference or of restraint, therefore, being thus completely taken away, the obvious and simple system of natural liberty establishes itself of its own accord. Every man, as long as he does not violate the laws of justice, is left perfectly free to pursue his own interest his own way, and to bring both his industry and capital into competition with those of any other man, or order of men. The sovereign is completely discharged from a duty, in the attempting to perform which he must always be exposed to innumerable delusions, and for the proper performance of which no human wisdom or knowledge could ever be sufficient; the duty of superintending the industry of private people, and of directing it towards the employments most suitable to the interest of the society. According to the system of natural liberty, the sovereign has only three duties to attend to; three duties of great importance, indeed, but plain and intelligible to common understandings: first, the duty of protecting the society from the violence and invasion of other independent societies; secondly, the duty of protecting, as far as possible, every member of the society from the injustice or oppression of every other member of it, or the duty of establishing an exact administration of justice; and, thirdly, the duty of erecting and maintaining certain public works and certain public institutions, which it can never be for the interest of any individual, or small number of individuals, to erect and maintain; because the profit could never repay the expence to any individual or small number of individuals, though it may frequently do much more than repay it to a great society.

The proper performance of those several duties of the sovereign necessarily supposes a certain expence; and this expence again necessarily requires a certain revenue to support it.

*   *   *

NOTES

1. This phrase, if used at all before this time, was not a familiar one. Its presence here is probably due to a passage in Mandeville, *Fable of the Bees*, pt. ii. (1729), dial. vi., p. 335: 'CLEO. . . . When once men come to be governed by written laws, all the rest comes on apace . . . No number of men, when once they enjoy quiet, and no man needs to fear his neighbour, will be long without learning to divide and subdivide their labour. HOR. I don't understand you. CLEO. Man, as I have hinted before, naturally loves to imitate what he sees others do, which is the reason that savage people all do the same thing: this hinders them from meliorating their condition, though they are always wishing for it: but if one will wholly apply himself to the making of bows and arrows, whilst another provides food, a third builds huts, a fourth makes garments, and a fifth utensils, they not only become useful to one another, but the callings and employments themselves will, in the same number of years, receive much greater improvements, than if all had been promiscuously followed by every one of the five. HOR. I believe you are perfectly right there; and the truth of what you say is in nothing so conspicuous as it is in watch-making, which is come to a higher degree of perfection than it would have been arrived at yet, if the whole had always remained the employment of one person; and I am persuaded that even the plenty we have of clocks and watches, as well as the exactness and beauty they may be made of, are chiefly owing to the division that has been made of that art into many branches.' The index contains, 'Labour, The usefulness of dividing and subdividing it'. Joseph Harris, *Essay upon Money and Coins*, 1757, pt. i., § 12, treats of the 'usefulness of distinct trades,' or 'the advantages accruing to mankind from their betaking themselves severally to different occupations,' but does not use the phrase 'division of labour'.

2. Ed. 1 reads 'improvements'.

3. Another and perhaps more important reason for taking an example like that which follows is the possibility of exhibiting the advantage, of division of labour in statistical form.

4. This parenthesis would alone be sufficient to show that those are wrong who believe Smith did not include the separation of employments in 'division of labour'.

5. In Adam Smith's *Lectures*, p. 164, the business is, as here, divided into eighteen operations. This number is doubtless taken from the *Encyclopédie*, tom. v. (published in 1755), *s.v.* Épingle. The article is ascribed to M. Delaire, 'qui décrivait la fabrication de l'épingle dans les ateliers même des ouvriers,' p. 807. In some factories the division was carried further. E. Chambers, *Cyclopædia*, vol. ii., 2nd ed., 1738, and 4th ed., 1741, *s.v.* Pin, makes the number of separate operations twenty-five.

6. Ed. 1 places 'in consequence of the division of labour' here instead of in the line above.

7. 'Pour la célérite du travail et la perfection de l'ouvrage, elles dépendent entièrement de la multitude des ouvriers rassemblés. Lorsqu'une manufacture est nombreuse, chaque opération occupe un homme différent. Tel ouvrier ne fait et ne fera de sa vie qu'une seule et unique chose; tel autre une autre chose: d'où il arrive que chacune s'exécute bien et promptement, et que l'ouvrage le mieux fait est encore celui qu'on a à meilleur marché. D'ailleurs le goût et la façon se perfectionment nécessairement entre un grand nombre d'ouvriers, parce qu'il est difficile qu'il ne s'en rencontre quelques-uns capables de réfléchir, de combiner, et de trouver enfin le seul moyen qui puisse les mettre audessus de leurs semblables; le moyen ou d'épargner la matière, ou d'allonger le temps, ou de surfaire l'industrie, soit par une machine nouvelle, soit par une manœuvre plus commode.'—*Encyclopédie*,

tom i. (1751), p. 717, *s.v.* Art. All three advantages mentioned in the text above are included here.

8. *I.e.*, it is not the effect of any conscious regulation by the state or society, like the 'law of Sesostris,' that every man should follow the employment of his father, referred to in the corresponding passage in *Lectures*, p. 168. The denial that it is the effect of individual wisdom recognising the advantage of exercising special natural talents comes lower down, p. 19.

9. It is by no means clear what object there could be in exchanging one bone for another.

10. This is apparently directed against Harris, *Money and Coins*, pt. i., § II, and is in accordance with the view of Hume, who asks readers to 'consider how nearly equal all men are in their bodily force, and even in their mental powers and faculties, ere cultivated by education'.—'Of the Original Contract,' in *Essays, Moral and Political*, 1748, p. 291.

DAVID RICARDO

ON FOREIGN TRADE

Under a system of perfectly free commerce, each country naturally devotes its capital and labour to such employments as are most beneficial to each. This pursuit of individual advantage is admirably connected with the universal good of the whole. By stimulating industry, by regarding ingenuity, and by using most efficaciously the peculiar powers bestowed by nature, it distributes labour most effectively and most economically: while, by increasing the general mass of productions, it diffuses general benefit, and binds together by one common tie of interest and intercourse, the universal society of nations throughout the civilized world. It is this principle which determines that wine shall be made in France and Portugal, that corn shall be grown in America and Poland, and that hardware and other goods shall be manufactured in England.

In one and the same country, profits are, generally speaking, always on the same level; or differ only as the employment of capital may be more or less secure and agreeable. It is not so between different countries. If the profits of capital employed in Yorkshire, should exceed those of capital employed in London, capital would speedily move from London to Yorkshire, and an equality of profits would be effected; but if in consequence of the diminished rate of production in the lands of England, from the increase of capital and population, wages should rise, and profits fall, it would not follow that capital and population would necessarily move from England to Holland, or Spain, or Russia, where profits might be higher.

If Portugal had no commercial connexion with other countries, instead of employing a great part of her capital and industry in the production of wines, with which she purchases for her own use the cloth and hardware of other countries, she would be obliged to devote a part of that capital to the manufacture of those commodities, which she would thus obtain probably inferior in quality as well as quantity.

From David Ricardo, *Principles of Political Economy and Taxation* (London: J. Murray, 1817).

The quantity of wine which she shall give in exchange for the cloth of England, is not determined by the respective quantities of labour devoted to the production of each, as it would be, if both commodities were manufactured in England, or both in Portugal.

England may be so circumstanced, that to produce the cloth may require the labour of 100 men for one year; and if she attempted to make the wine, it might require the labour of 120 men for the same time. England would therefore find it her interest to import wine, and to purchase it by the exportation of cloth.

To produce the wine in Portugal, might require only the labour of 80 men for one year, and to produce the cloth in the same country, might require the labour of 90 men for the same time. It would therefore be advantageous for her to export wine in exchange for cloth. This exchange might even take place, notwithstanding that the commodity imported by Portugal could be produced there with less labour than in England. Though she could make the cloth with the labour

of 90 men, she would import it from a country where it required the labour of 100 men to produce it, because it would be advantageous to her rather to employ her capital in the production of wine, for which she would obtain more cloth from England, than she could produce by diverting a portion of her capital from the cultivation of vines to the manufacture of cloth.

Thus England would give the produce of the labour of 100 men, for the produce of the labour of 80. Such an exchange could not take place between the individuals of the same country. The labour of 100 Englishmen cannot be given for that of 80 Englishmen, but the produce of the labour of 100 Englishmen may be given for the produce of the labour of 80 Portuguese, 60 Russians, or 120 East Indians. The difference in this respect, between a single country and many, is easily accounted for, by considering the difficulty with which capital moves from one country to another, to seek a more profitable employment, and the activity with which it invariably passes from one province to another in the same country.

THE ECONOMIST

TRADE WINDS

Time was when trade flows were of interest mainly to economic experts and executives of big corporations. But over the past few years, the movement of goods and services across national boundaries has become the subject of intense public attention all over the world. To the public at large, trade is the most obvious manifestation of a globalising world economy.

From *The Economist* (November 6, 1997).

Measured by the volume of imports and exports, the world economy has become increasingly integrated in the years since the second world war. A fall in barriers to trade has helped stimulate this growth. The volume of world merchandise trade is now about 16 times what it was in 1950, while the world's total output is only five-and-a-half times as big (see chart 1). The ratio of world exports to GDP has climbed from 7% to 15% (chart 2).

Virtually all economists, and most politicians,

Chart 1
Opening
Volume, 1950=100

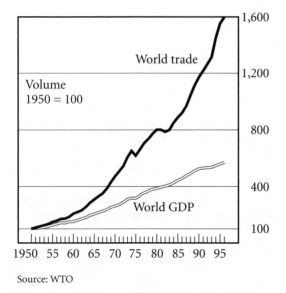

Source: WTO

Chart 2
Spot the pattern
Merchandise exports
as % of GDP, 1990 prices

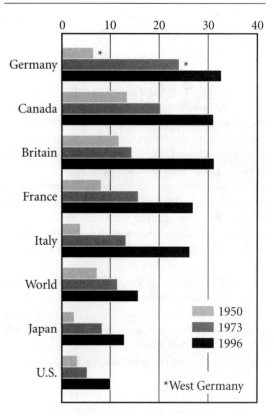

Source: A. Maddison (unpublished paper)

would agree that freer trade has been a blessing. However, the economists and politicians would probably give quite different reasons for thinking so.

Politicians, by and large, praise greater trade because it means more exports. This, in turn, purportedly means more jobs—and, if the exports involve sophisticated products such as cars or jet engines, more "good" jobs. The American government, zealous to promote exports, has even produced estimates that try to show how many new jobs are created by each $1 billion of American sales abroad.

This is misleading. A big export order may well cause an individual company to add workers, but it will have no effect on a country's total employment, which is determined mainly by how fast the economy can expand without risking inflation and by microeconomic obstacles, such as taxes that deter employers from hiring or workers from seeking jobs. America, where exports are a relatively small fraction of GDP, has fuller employment than Germany, where exports loom larger.

Gains from Trade

To economists, the real benefits of trade lie in importing rather than in exporting. Politicians frequently urge consumers to favour domestically made goods, and portray a widening trade deficit as a Bad Thing. But economists know that the only reason for exporting is to earn the wherewithal to import. As James Mill, one of the first trade theorists, explained in 1821:

> The benefit which is derived from exchanging one commodity for another, arises, in all cases, from the commodity [taken], not the commodity given.

Table 1. Gains from trade

	Output and consumption under autarky		Output after specialisation		Consumption after trade	
	Bicycles	*Computers*	*Bicycles*	*Computers*	*Bicycles*	*Computers*
East	125	5	250	0	130	10
West	250	50	150	70	270	60

This benefit arises even if one country can make everything more cheaply than all others. The basic theory that explains this, the principle of comparative advantage, has existed since Mill's day. His contemporary, David Ricardo, usually gets the credit for expounding it.

To see how this theory works, think about why two countries—call them East and West— might gain from trading with one another. Suppose, for simplicity, that each has 1,000 workers, and each makes two goods: computers and bicycles.

West's economy is far more productive than East's. To make a bicycle, West needs the labour of two workers; East needs four. To make a computer, West uses ten workers while East uses 100. Suppose that there is no trade, and that in each country half the workers are in each industry. West produces 250 bicycles and 50 computers. East makes 125 bikes and five computers.

Now suppose that the two countries specialise. Although West makes both bikes and computers more efficiently than East, it has a bigger edge in computer-making. It now devotes most of its resources to that industry, employing 700 workers to make computers and only 300 to make bikes. This raises computer output to 70 and cuts bike production to 150 (see table 1). East switches entirely to bicycles, turning out 250. World output of both goods has risen. Both countries can consume more of both if they trade.

At what price? Neither will want to import what it could make more cheaply at home. So West will want at least five bikes per computer; and East will not give up more than 25 bikes per computer. Suppose the terms of trade are fixed

at 12 bicycles per computer and that 120 bikes are exchanged for ten computers. Then West ends up with 270 bikes and 60 computers, and East with 130 bicycles and ten computers. Both are better off than they would be if they did not trade.

This is true even though West has an "absolute advantage" in making both computers and bikes. The reason is that each country has a different "comparative advantage." West's edge is greater in computers than in bicycles. East, although a costlier producer in both industries, is a relatively less-expensive maker of bikes. So long as each country specialises in products in which it has a comparative advantage, both will gain from trade.

Fair Deal

Some critics of trade say that this theory misses the point. They argue that trade with developing countries, where wages tend to be lower and work hours longer than in Europe and North America, is "unfair," and will wipe out jobs in high-wage countries.

It is generally accepted that trade with poor countries has been one of the factors reducing the wages of unskilled workers, relative to skilled ones, in the United States. That said, the threat to rich-country workers from developing-country competition is often overstated.

For a start, it is important not to confuse absolute and comparative advantage. Even if developing countries were cheaper producers of everything under the sun, they could not have a comparative advantage in everything. There would still be work for people in high-wage countries to do.

Moreover, it is not true that countries with cheap labour always have lower costs. Wage differences generally reflect differences in productivity; companies in low-wage countries often need far more labour to produce a given amount of output, and must deal with less efficient communications and transportation systems. In most cases hourly wages are not decisive in determining where a product is made.

Suppose that the "fair traders" succeed in eradicating international differences in production costs, so that a given product costs precisely the same to make in different countries. In that case, no country would have a comparative advantage, and hence there would be no trade. Rich-country workers, who are also consumers, would lose.

At first blush, real-world trade patterns would seem to challenge the theory of comparative advantage. Most trade occurs between countries which do not have huge cost differences. America's biggest trading partner, for instance, is Canada. Well over half the exports from France, Germany and Italy go to other European Union countries. Moreover, these countries sell similar things to each other: cars made in France are exported to Germany, while German cars go to France, dependent largely upon consumers' differing tastes rather than differences in costs.

The importance of geography and the role of similar but different products appealing to diverse tastes expand our understanding of why trade occurs. But they do not overturn the fundamental insight of the theory of comparative advantage. The agricultural exports of Australia, say, or Saudi Arabia's reliance on oil, clearly stem from their natural resources. Poorer countries tend to have relatively more unskilled labour, so they tend to export simple manufactures, such as clothing. So long as relative production costs differ between countries, there are gains to be had from trade.

Enter the State

What is confusing, perhaps, is that comparative advantage is often the product of history and chance, not of differences in natural resources or workers' skills. A stark example is America's civil-aircraft industry. There is no God-given reason why the production costs of jumbo jets, relative to other goods and services, should be lower in America than in Japan. But they are: America's early embrace of airmail, its large purchases of military aircraft and the great public demand for air travel in a large country all helped American plane makers get big early on, allowing them to achieve per-plane costs lower than those of foreign competitors.

A logical question follows: if comparative advantage can be created, why should governments not help create it? The idea is that through subsidies, such as those given by several European nations to finance the European-made Airbus passenger jets, governments can promote their own national champions and hobble foreign rivals. Since the late 1970s, a stream of theoretical research has shown that governments can use such "strategic trade policy," in principle, to make their own citizens better off.

The theoretical work, however, has shed little light on how, in practice, governments can select which industries to subsidise—and which to tax in order to finance the subsidy—so that, in the end, the country's welfare is improved. And then there is the matter of politics: once the government has agreed to support "strategic" industries, every industry will assert its strategic importance in order to share in the pie. Under real-world political pressures, the allure of strategic trade policy fades quickly.

Governments' intervention in trade is not limited to fine calculations of strategy. There is plenty of aid to politically sensitive industries, such as agriculture. And governments often rush to obstruct "unfair" competition from abroad.

Anti-dumping duties are a case in point. In theory, these are intended to keep foreign producers from "dumping" goods abroad at less

Table 2. Anti-trade

Summary of anti-dumping actions, 1996

	New actions	*Measures in force**
South Africa	30	31
Argentina	23	30
EU	23	153
United States	21	311
India	20	15
Australia	17	47
Brazil	17	24
Korea	13	14
Indonesia	8	na
Israel	6	na
Canada	5	96
Peru	5	4
New Zealand	4	27
Chile	3	0
Mexico	3	95
Venezuela	3	3
Malaysia	2	na
Colombia	1	7
Guatemala	1	na
Thailand	1	1
Japan	0	3
Singapore	0	2
Turkey	0	37
Total	206	900

Source: WTO   *31 December 1996

than their cost of production, by subjecting the goods to extra import duties. In practice, they are a politically neat method of protecting a particular industry. Once the favoured weapon of rich-world governments, anti-dumping duties have been been taken up eagerly by developing countries (table 2).

Despite such machinations, world trade flows more freely than it used to. This is due mainly to international agreements under which governments agree to forswear trade barriers— most notably, the General Agreement on Tariffs and Trade (GATT). All told, there have been eight rounds of GATT talks since 1947, in which

countries have cut their import tariffs. Tariffs on manufactured goods are now down to around 4% in industrial countries.

The most recent GATT round, the Uruguay round, ended in 1993. The Uruguay round did much more than cut tariffs on goods. It heralded a big institutional change, creating the World Trade Organization (WTO), which now boasts 132 members, as a successor to GATT. It also made three big changes to the rules of world trade. First, it began the process of opening up the most heavily protected industries, agriculture and textiles.

Second, the Uruguay round vastly extended the scope of international trade rules. The rules were extended to cover services, as well as goods. New issues, such as the use of spurious technical barriers to keep out imports and the protection of foreigners' "intellectual property," such as patents and copyrights, were addressed for the first time.

Of these new agreements, the one in services is especially interesting. A lot of trade no longer involves putting things into a crate and sending them abroad on ships. Many services can be traded internationally: a British construction firm can build an airport in Japan, and an American insurance company can sell its products in Germany.

Lots to Talk About

The WTO estimates that commercial-service trade was worth $1.2 trillion in 1996, around one-quarter of the value of trade in goods. The services agreement, plus a recent deal on telecommunications trade, should ease the barriers that limit such trade.

The third change wrought by the Uruguay round was the creation of a new system for settling disputes. In the past, countries could (and sometimes did) break GATT rules with impunity. Under the new system, decisions can be blocked only by a consensus of WTO members. Once found guilty of breaking the rules (and after appeal) countries are supposed to mend their ways. This system so far seems to be working better than the old one, and is helping to build up the new institution's credibility.

Despite these recent advances, there are plenty of difficulties ahead. Some countries, such as America and France, would like to see the WTO address itself to the relationships between trade, labour standards and the environment. Others, notably India and Malaysia, are opposed. In 1996 the WTO's members agreed to study the issues, but there is no agreement about whether the WTO should go further.

THE ECONOMIST

THE HIDDEN COST OF TAXES

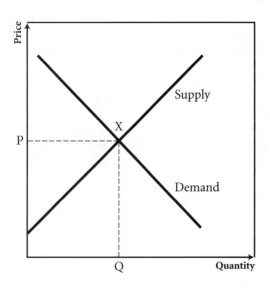

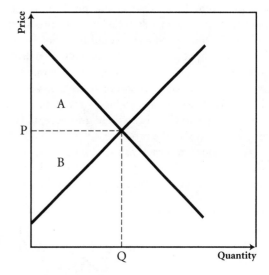

The first diagram shows a demand curve and a supply curve for some hypothetical good. Usually, as the price of a good comes down, the quantity demanded increases; the demand curve therefore slopes downwards from left to right. Usually, as the price of a good goes up, the supply of it rises too; so the supply curve slopes upwards. With buyers and sellers free to trade, a balance of supply and demand will be established at the point where the two curves cross—point X, where the price is P and where the same quantity, Q, is both demanded and supplied. That point of equilibrium gives the market's answer to how much of the good will be traded and at what price.

Turning to the second diagram, the shaded area between the demand and supply curves, to the left of the point where they cross, has a special significance, because it represents the net addition to social welfare that is created when

From *The Economist* (September 18, 1997).

the good is bought and sold at the market price.

If you divide the area into two, the upper part, A, represents the so-called consumer surplus. Every unit of the good sold when supply equals demand—the whole of the quantity Q in the diagram—is sold at the market price, P. But smaller quantities of the good could have been sold for more than P. Only for the last (or marginal) unit sold is P the top price the consumer would be willing to pay. In effect, therefore, all but that last unit have been sold for less than they are worth to the consumer. The area A adds up all these surpluses, unit by unit, showing the value of all the transactions to consumers over and above the price they paid.

By the same logic, the lower part of the area between the demand and supply curves in the second diagram, B, represents the producers' surplus. Only the last unit supplied costs its producer exactly P. Other producers would have been willing to supply at a lower price, enough to deliver some smaller quantity of goods to the market. When these not-on-the-margin units are sold at the market price, their producers are paid more than they would have been willing to accept. The area B adds up all the producer surpluses.

The third diagram shows what happens when a tax is imposed, raising the price paid by consumers from P to Pc, and lowering the price received by suppliers to Ps. At these new prices, Qt is demanded and supplied. The amount of the tax (the difference between Pc and Ps) multiplied by the number of units sold (Qt) gives the revenue raised for the government (area C in the diagram). Both the consumer surplus, A, and the producer surplus, B, are accordingly smaller than before.

That was to be expected. The point is, though, that the two surpluses, added together, have shrunk by more than the amount taken away in tax. Now that the quantity of goods supplied has fallen to Qt, the triangle D has disappeared: it is not part of the government's tax yield, and it is no longer part of the economic surplus; it has simply vanished. This part of the reduction in the surplus is a pure loss to the economy, known in the jargon as the deadweight cost of the tax. The implication is that if the government raised the area C in taxes and then handed the money straight back as lump sums to consumers and producers, the economy would still be poorer than before because the area D would still be missing.

In the last diagram the tax is twice as big as before. The price to consumers has increased once more, and the quantity supplied has fallen further. The consumer and producer surpluses are also smaller. The government's tax revenue,

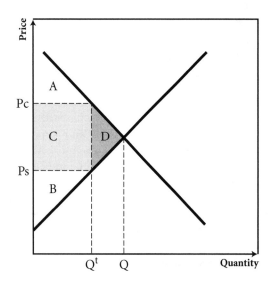

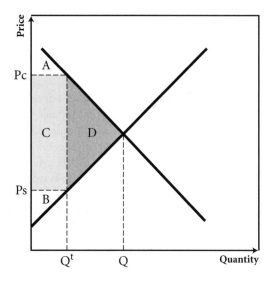

C, may quite possibly be smaller too, despite the higher tax rate, because of the smaller quantity traded. The deadweight cost, however, has increased fourfold.

If the demand and supply curves were indeed curves rather than straight lines, the relationship between tax rise and pure economic loss would not be quite so simple. But the basic point would be the same: in general, the deadweight cost of a tax rises exponentially as the tax goes up.

DOUGLASS C. NORTH

INSTITUTIONS

Institutions are the humanly devised constraints that structure political, economic and social interaction. They consist of both informal constraints (sanctions, taboos, customs, traditions, and codes of conduct), and formal rules (constitutions, laws, property rights). Throughout history, institutions have been devised by human beings to create order and reduce uncertainty in exchange. Together with the standard constraints of economics they define the choice set and therefore determine transaction and production costs and hence the profitability and feasibility of engaging in economic activity. They evolve incrementally, connecting the past with the present and the future; history in consequence is largely a story of institutional evolution in which the historical performance of economies can only be understood as a part of a sequential story. Institutions provide the incentive structure of an economy; as that structure evolves, it shapes the direction of economic change towards growth, stagnation, or decline. In this essay I intend to elaborate on the role of institutions in the performance of economies and illustrate my analysis from economic history.

What makes it necessary to constrain human interaction with institutions? The issue can be most succinctly summarized in a game theoretic context. Wealth-maximizing individuals will usually find it worthwhile to cooperate with other players when the play is repeated, when they possess complete information about the other player's past performance, and when there are small numbers of players. But turn the game upside down. Cooperation is difficult to sustain when the game is not repeated (or there is an endgame), when information on the other players is lacking, and when there are large numbers of players.

These polar extremes reflect contrasting economic settings in real life. There are many examples of simple exchange institutions that permit low cost transacting under the former conditions. But institutions that permit low cost transacting and producing in a world of specialization and division of labor require solving the problems of human cooperation under the latter conditions.

It takes resources to define and enforce exchange agreements. Even if everyone had the same objective function (like maximizing the firm's profits), transacting would take substantial resources; but in the context of individual wealth-maximizing behavior and asymmetric information about the valuable attributes of what is being exchanged (or the performance of agents), transaction costs are a critical determinant of economic performance. Institutions and

From *Journal of Economic Perspectives* 5, no. 1 (Winter 1991), pp. 97–112.

the effectiveness of enforcement (together with the technology employed) determine the cost of transacting. Effective institutions raise the benefits of cooperative solutions or the costs of defection, to use game theoretic terms. In transaction cost terms, institutions reduce transaction and production costs per exchange so that the potential gains from trade are realizeable. Both political and economic institutions are essential parts of an effective institutional matrix.

The major focus of the literature on institutions and transaction costs has been on institutions as efficient solutions to problems of organization in a competitive framework (Williamson, 1975; 1985). Thus market exchange, franchising, or vertical integration are conceived in this literature as efficient solutions to the complex problems confronting entrepreneurs under various competitive conditions. Valuable as this work has been, such an approach assumes away the central concern of this essay: to explain the varied performance of economies both over time and in the current world.

How does an economy achieve the efficient, competitive markets assumed in the foregoing approach? The formal economic constraints or property rights are specified and enforced by political institutions, and the literature simply takes those as a given. But economic history is overwhelmingly a story of economies that failed to produce a set of economic rules of the game (with enforcement) that induce sustained economic growth. The central issue of economic history and of economic development is to account for the evolution of political and economic institutions that create an economic environment that induces increasing productivity.

Institutions to Capture the Gains from Trade

Many readers will be at least somewhat familiar with the idea of economic history over time as a series of staged stories. The earliest economies are thought of as local exchange within a village

(or even within a simple hunting and gathering society). Gradually, trade expands beyond the village: first to the region, perhaps as a bazaar-like economy; then to longer distances, through particular caravan or shipping routes; and eventually to much of the world. At each stage, the economy involves increasing specialization and division of labor and continuously more productive technology. This story of gradual evolution from local autarky to specialization and division of labor was derived from the German historical school. However, there is no implication in this paper that the real historical evolution of economies necessarily paralleled the sequence of stages of exchange described here.[1]

I begin with local exchange within the village or even the simple exchange of hunting and gathering societies (in which women gathered and men hunted). Specialization in this world is rudimentary and self-sufficiency characterizes most individual households. Small-scale village trade exists within a "dense" social network of informal constraints that facilitates local exchange, and the costs of transacting in this context are low. (Although the basic societal costs of tribal and village organization may be high, they will not be reflected in additional costs in the process of transacting.) People have an intimate understanding of each other, and the threat of violence is a continuous force for preserving order because of its implications for other members of society.[2]

As trade expands beyond a single village, however, the possibilities for conflict over the exchange grow. The size of the market grows and transaction costs increase sharply because the dense social network is replaced; hence, more resources must be devoted to measurement and enforcement. In the absence of a state that enforced contracts, religious precepts usually imposed standards of conduct on the players. Needless to say, their effectiveness in lowering the costs of transacting varied widely, depending on the degree to which these precepts were held to be binding.

The development of long-distance trade,

perhaps through caravans or lengthy ship voyages, requires a sharp break in the characteristics of an economic structure. It entails substantial specialization in exchange by individuals whose livelihood is confined to trading and the development of trading centers, which may be temporary gathering places (as were the early fairs in Europe) or more permanent towns or cities. Some economies of scale—for example, in plantation agriculture—are characteristic of this world. Geographic specialization begins to emerge as a major characteristic and some occupational specialization is occurring as well.

The growth of long distance trade poses two distinct transaction cost problems. One is a classical problem of agency, which historically was met by use of kin in long-distance trade. That is, a sedentary merchant would send a relative with the cargo to negotiate sale and to obtain a return cargo. The costliness of measuring performance, the strength of kinship ties, and the price of "defection" all determined the outcome of such agreements. As the size and volume of trade grew, agency problems became an increasingly major dilemma.[3] A second problem consisted of contract negotiation and enforcement in alien parts of the world, where there is no easily available way to achieve agreement and enforce contracts. Enforcement means not only such enforcement of agreements but also protection of the goods and services en route from pirates, brigands, and so on.

The problems of enforcement en route were met by armed forces protecting the ship or caravan or by the payment of tolls or protection money to local coercive groups. Negotiation and enforcement in alien parts of the world entailed typically the development of standardized weights and measures, units of account, a medium of exchange, notaries, consuls, merchant law courts, and enclaves of foreign merchants protected by foreign princes in return for revenue. By lowering information costs and providing incentives for contract fulfillment this complex of institutions, organizations, and instruments made possible transacting and en-

gaging in long-distance trade. A mixture of voluntary and semi-coercive bodies, or at least bodies that effectively could cause ostracism of merchants that didn't live up to agreements, enabled long-distance trade to occur.[4]

This expansion of the market entails more specialized producers. Economies of scale result in the beginnings of hierarchical producing organizations, with full-time workers working either in a central place or in a sequential production process. Towns and some central cities are emerging, and occupational distribution of the population now shows, in addition, a substantial increase in the proportion of the labor force engaged in manufacturing and in services, although the traditional preponderance in agriculture continues. These evolving stages also reflect a significant shift towards urbanization of the society.

Such societies need effective, impersonal contract enforcement, because personal ties, voluntaristic constraints, and ostracism are no longer effective as more complex and impersonal forms of exchange emerge. It is not that these personal and social alternatives are unimportant; they are still significant even in today's interdependent world. But in the absence of effective impersonal contracting, the gains from "defection" are great enough to forestall the development of complex exchange. Two illustrations deal with the creation of a capital market and with the interplay between institutions and the technology employed.

A capital market entails security of property rights over time and will simply not evolve where political rulers can arbitrarily seize assets or radically alter their value. Establishing a credible commitment to secure property rights over time requires either a ruler who exercises forebearance and restraint in using coercive force, or the shackling of the ruler's power to prevent arbitrary seizure of assets. The first alternative was seldom successful for very long in the face of the ubiquitous fiscal crises of rulers (largely as a consequence of repeated warfare). The latter entailed a fundamental restructuring of the polity such as occurred in England as a result of the Glorious Revolution of 1688, which resulted in parliamentary supremacy over the crown.[5]

The technology associated with the growth of manufacturing entailed increased fixed capital in plant and equipment, uninterrupted production, a disciplined labor force, and a developed transport network; in short, it required effective factor and product markets. Undergirding such markets are secure property rights, which entail a polity and judicial system to permit low costs contracting, flexible laws permitting a wide latitude of organizational structures, and the creation of complex governance structures to limit the problems of agency in hierarchical organizations.[6]

In the last stage, the one we observe in modern western societies, specialization has increased, agriculture requires a small percentage of the labor force, and markets have become nationwide and worldwide. Economies of scale imply large-scale organization, not only in manufacturing but also in agriculture. Everyone lives by undertaking a specialized function and relying on the vast network of interconnected parts to provide the multitude of goods and services necessary to them. The occupational distribution of the labor force shifts gradually from dominance by manufacturing to dominance, eventually, by what are characterized as services. Society is overwhelmingly urban.

In this final stage, specialization requires increasing percentages of the resources of the society to be engaged in transacting, so that the transaction sector rises to be a large percentage of gross national product. This is so because specialization in trade, finance, banking, insurance, as well as the simple coordination of economic activity, involves an increasing proportion of the labor force.[7] Of necessity, therefore, highly specialized forms of transaction organizations emerge. International specialization and division of labor requires institutions and organizations to safeguard property rights across international boundaries so that capital markets (as well as other kinds of exchange) can take place with

credible commitment on the part of the players.

These very schematic stages appear to merge one into another in a smooth story of evolving cooperation. But do they? Does any necessary connection move the players from less complicated to more complicated forms of exchange? At stake in this evolution is not only whether information costs and economies of scale together with the development of improved enforcement of contracts will permit and indeed encourage more complicated forms of exchange, but also whether organizations have the incentive to acquire knowledge and information that will induce them to evolve in more socially productive directions.

In fact, throughout history, there is no necessary reason for this development to occur. Indeed, most of the early forms of organization that I have mentioned in these sections still exist today in parts of the world. There still exist primitive tribal societies; the Suq (bazaar economies engaged in regional trade) still flourishes in many parts of the world; and while the caravan trade has disappeared, its demise (as well as the gradual undermining of the other two forms of "primitive" exchange) has reflected external forces rather than internal evolution. In contrast, the development of European long-distance trade initiated a sequential development of more complex forms of organization.

The remainder of this paper will examine first some seemingly primitive forms of exchange that failed to evolve and then the institutional evolution that occurred in early modern Europe. The concluding section of the paper will attempt to enunciate why some societies and exchange institutions evolve and others do not, and to apply that framework in the context of economic development in the western hemisphere during the 18th and 19th centuries.

When Institutions Do Not Evolve

In every system of exchange, economic actors have an incentive to invest their time, resources, and energy in knowledge and skills that will improve their material status. But in some primitive institutional settings, the kind of knowledge and skills that will pay off will not result in institutional evolution towards more productive economies. To illustrate this argument, I consider three primitive types of exchange—tribal society, a regional economy with bazaar trading, and the long-distance caravan trade—that are unlikely to evolve from within.

As noted earlier, exchange in a tribal society relies on a dense social network. Elizabeth Colson (1974, p. 59) describes the network this way:

> The communities in which all these people live were governed by a delicate balance of power, always endangered and never to be taken for granted: each person was constantly involved in securing his own position in situations where he had to show his good intentions. Usages and customs appear to be flexible and fluid given that judgement on whether or not someone has done rightly varies from case to case. . . . But this is because it is the individual who is being judged and not the crime. Under these conditions, a flouting of generally accepted standards is tantamount to a claim to illegitimate power and becomes part of the evidence against one.

The implication of Colson's analysis as well as that of Richard Posner in his account of primitive institutions (1980) is that deviance and innovation are viewed as threats to group survival.

A second form of exchange that has existed for thousands of years, and still exists today in North Africa and the Middle East is that of the Suq, where widespread and relatively impersonal exchange and relatively high costs of transacting exist.[8] The basic characteristics are a multiplicity of small-scale enterprises with as much as 40 to 50 percent of the town's labor force engaged in this exchange process; low fixed costs in terms of rent and machinery; a very finely drawn division of labor; an enormous number of small transactions, each more or less independent of the next; face to face contacts; and goods and services that are not homogeneous.

There are no institutions devoted to assembling and distributing market information; that is, no price quotations, production reports, employment agencies, consumer guides, and so on. Systems of weights and measures are intricate and incompletely standardized. Exchange skills are very elaborately developed, and are the primary determinant of who prospers in the bazaar and who does not. Haggling over terms with respect to any aspect or condition of exchange is pervasive, strenuous, and unremitting. Buying and selling are virtually undifferentiated, essentially a single activity; trading involves a continual search for specific partners, not the mere offers of goods to the general public. Regulation of disputes involves testimony by reliable witnesses to factual matters, not the weighting of competing, juridical principles. Governmental controls over marketplace activity are marginal, decentralized, and mostly rhetorical.

To summarize, the central features of the Suq are (1) high measurement costs; (2) continuous effort at clientization (the development of repeat-exchange relationships with other partners, however imperfect); and (3) intensive bargaining at every margin. In essence, the name of the game is to raise the costs of transacting to the other party to exchange. One makes money by having better information than one's adversary.

It is easy to understand why innovation would be seen to threaten survival in a tribal society but harder to understand why these "inefficient" forms of bargaining would continue in the Suq. One would anticipate, in the societies with which we are familiar, that voluntary organizations would evolve to insure against the hazards and uncertainties of such information asymmetries. But that is precisely the issue. What is missing in the Suq are the fundamental underpinnings of institutions that would make such voluntary organizations viable and profitable. These include an effective legal structure and court system to enforce contracts which in turn depend on the development of political institutions that will create such a framework. In their absence there is no incentive to alter the system.

The third form of exchange, caravan trade, illustrates the informal constraints that made trade possible in a world where protection was essential and no organized state existed. Clifford Geertz (1979, p. 137) provides a description of the caravan trades in Morocco at the turn of the century:

> In the narrow sense, a zettata (from the Berber TAZETTAT, 'a small piece of cloth') is a passage toll, a sum paid to a local power . . . for protection when crossing localities where he is such a power. But in fact it is, or more properly was, rather more than a mere payment. It was part of a whole complex of moral rituals, customs with the force of law and the weight of sanctity—centering around the guest-host, client-patron, petitioner-petitioned, exile-protector, suppliant-divinity relations—all of which are somehow of a package in rural Morocco. Entering the tribal world physically, the outreaching trader (or at least his agents) had also to enter it culturally.
>
> Despite the vast variety of particular forms through which they manifest themselves, the characteristics of protection in the Berber societies of the High and Middle Atlas are clear and constant. Protection is personal, unqualified, explicit, and conceived of as the dressing of one man in the reputation of another. The reputation may be political, moral, spiritual, or even idiosyncratic, or, often enough, all four at once. But the essential transaction is that a man who counts 'stands up and says' (*quam wa qal*, as the classical tag has it) to those to whom he counts: 'this man is mine; harm him and you insult me; insult me and you will answer for it.' Benediction (the famous *baraka*), hospitality, sanctuary, and safe passage are alike in this: they rest on the perhaps somewhat paradoxical notion that though personal identity is radically individual in both its roots and its expressions, it is not incapable of being stamped onto the self of someone else.

While tribal chieftains found it profitable to protect merchant caravans they had neither the military muscle nor the political structure to extend, develop, and enforce more permanent property rights.

Institutional Evolution in Early Modern Europe

In contrast to many primitive systems of exchange, long distance trade in early modern Europe from the 11th to the 16th centuries was a story of sequentially more complex organization that eventually led to the rise of the western world. Let me first briefly describe the innovations and then explore some of their underlying sources.[9]

Innovations that lowered transaction costs consisted of organizational changes, instruments, and specific techniques and enforcement characteristics that lowered the costs of engaging in exchange over long distances. These innovations occurred at three cost margins: (1) those that increased the mobility of capital, (2) those that lowered information costs, and (3) those that spread risk. Obviously, the categories are overlapping, but they provide a useful way to distinguish cost-reducing features of transacting. All of these innovations had their origins in earlier times; most of them were borrowed from medieval Italian city states or Islam or Byzantium and then elaborated upon.

Among the innovations that enhanced the mobility of capital were the techniques and methods evolved to evade usury laws. The variety of ingenious ways by which interest was disguised in loan contracts ranged from "penalties for late payment," to exchange rate manipulation (Lopez and Raymond, 1955, p. 163), to the early form of the mortgage; but all increased the costs of contracting. The costliness of usury laws was not only that they made the writing of contracts to disguise interests complex and cumbersome, but also that enforceability of such contracts became more problematic. As the demand for capital increased and evasion became more general, usury laws gradually broke down and rates of interest were permitted. In consequence, the costs of writing contracts and the costs of enforcing them declined.

A second innovation that improved the mobility of capital, and the one that has received the most attention, was the evolution of the bill of exchange (a dated order to pay, say 120 days after issuance, conventionally drawn by a seller against a purchaser of goods delivered) and particularly the development of techniques and instruments that allowed for its negotiability as well as for the development of discounting methods. Negotiability and discounting in turn depended on the creation of institutions that would permit their use and the development of centers where such events could occur: first in fairs, such as the Champagne fairs that played such a prominent part in economic exchange in 12th and 13th century Europe; then through banks; and finally through financial houses that could specialize in discounting. These developments were a function not only of specific institutions but also of the scale of economic activity. Increasing volume obviously made such institutional developments possible. In addition to the economies of scale necessary for the development of the bills of exchange, improved enforceability of contracts was critical, and the interrelationship between the development of accounting and auditing methods and their use as evidence in the collection of debts and in the enforcement of contracts was an important part of this process (Yamey, 1949; Watts and Zimmerman, 1983).

Still a third innovation affecting the mobility of capital arose from the problems associated with maintaining control of agents involved in long distance trade. The traditional resolution of this problem in medieval and early modern times was the use of kinship and family ties to bind agents to principals. However, as the size and scope of merchant trading empires grew, the extension of discretionary behavior to others than kin of the principal required the development of more elaborate accounting procedures for monitoring the behavior of agents.

The major developments in the area of information costs were the printing of prices of various commodities, as well as the printing of manuals that provided information on weights, measures, customs, brokerage fees, postal systems, and, particularly, the complex exchange rates between monies in Europe and the trading world. Obviously these developments were primarily a function of the volume of international trade and therefore a consequence of economies of scale.

The final innovation was the transformation of uncertainty into risk. By uncertainty, I mean here a condition wherein one cannot ascertain the probability of an event and therefore cannot arrive at a way of insuring against such an occurrence. Risk, on the other hand, implies the ability to make an actuarial determination of the likelihood of an event and hence insure against such an outcome. In the modern world, insurance and portfolio diversification are methods for converting uncertainty into risks and thereby reducing, through the provision of a hedge against variability, the costs of transacting. In the medieval and early modern world, precisely the same conversion occurred. For example, marine insurance evolved from sporadic individual contracts covering partial payments for losses to contracts issued by specialized firms. As De Roover (1945, p. 198) described:

> By the fifteenth century marine insurance was established on a secure basis. The wording of the policies had already become stereotyped and changed very little during the next three or four hundred years. . . . In the sixteenth century it was already current practice to use printed forms provided with a few blank spaces for the name of the ship, the name of the master, the amount of the insurance, the premium, and a few other items that were apt to change from one contract to another.

Another example of the development of actuarial, ascertainable risk was the business organization that spread risk through either portfolio diversification or institutions that permitted a large number of investors to engage in risky activities. For example, the commenda was a contract employed in long distance trade between a sedentary partner and an active partner who accompanied the goods. It evolved from its Jewish, Byzantine, and Muslim origins (Udovitch, 1962) through its use at the hands of Italians to the

English Regulated Company and finally the Joint Stock Company, thus providing an evolutionary story of the institutionalization of risk.

These specific innovations and particular institutional instruments evolved from interplay between two fundamental economic forces: the economies of scale associated with a growing volume of trade, and the development of improved mechanisms to enforce contracts at lower costs. The causation ran both ways. That is, the increasing volume of long distance trade raised the rate of return to merchants of devising effective mechanisms for enforcing contracts. In turn, the development of such mechanisms lowered the costs of contracting and made trade more profitable, thereby increasing its volume.

The process of developing new enforcement mechanisms was a long one. While a variety of courts handled commercial disputes, it is the development of enforcement mechanisms by merchants themselves that is significant. Enforceability appears to have had its beginnings in the development of internal codes of conduct in fraternal orders of guild merchants; those who did not live up to them were threatened with ostracism. A further step was the evolution of mercantile law. Merchants carried with them in long distance trade mercantile codes of conduct, so that Pisan laws passed into the sea codes of Marseilles; Oleron and Lubeck gave laws to the north of Europe, Barcelona to the south of Europe; and from Italy came the legal principle of insurance and bills of exchange (Mitchell, 1969, p. 156).

The development of more sophisticated accounting methods and of notarial records provided evidence for ascertaining facts in disputes. The gradual blending of the voluntaristic structure of enforcement of contracts via internal merchant organizations with enforcement by the state is an important part of the story of increasing the enforceability of contracts. The long evolution of merchant law from its voluntary beginnings and the differences in resolutions that it had with both the common and Roman law are a part of the story.

The state was a major player in this whole process, and there was continuous interplay between the state's fiscal needs and its credibility in its relationships with merchants and the citizenry in general. In particular, the evolution of capital markets was critically influenced by the policies of the state, since to the extent the state was bound by commitments that it would not confiscate assets or use its coercive power to increase uncertainty in exchange, it made possible the evolution of financial institutions and the creation of more efficient capital markets. The shackling of arbitrary behavior of rulers and the development of impersonal rules that successfully bound both the state and voluntary organizations were a key part of this whole process. The development of an institutional process by which government debt could be circulated, become a part of a regular capital market, and be funded by regular sources of taxation was also a key part (Tracy, 1985; North and Weingast, 1989).

It was in the Netherlands, Amsterdam specifically, that these diverse innovations and institutions were combined to create the predecessor of the efficient modern set of markets that make possible the growth of exchange and commerce. An open immigration policy attracted businessmen. Efficient methods of financing long distance trade were developed, as were capital markets and discounting methods in financial houses that lowered the costs of underwriting this trade. The development of techniques for spreading risk and transforming uncertainty into actuarial, ascertainable risks as well as the creation of large scale markets that allowed for lowering the costs of information, and the development of negotiable government indebtedness all were a part of this story (Barbour, 1949).

Contrasting Stories of Stability and Change

These contrasting stories of stability and change go to the heart of the puzzle of accounting for changes in the human economic condition. In the former cases, maximizing activity by the actors will not induce increments to knowledge and skills which will modify the institutional framework to induce greater productivity; in the latter case, evolution is a consistent story of incremental change induced by the private gains to be realized by productivity-raising organizational institutional changes.

What distinguished the institutional context of western Europe from the other illustrations? The traditional answer of economic historians has been competition among the fragmented European political units accentuated by changing military technology which forced rulers to seek more revenue (by making bargains with constituents) in order to survive (North and Thomas, 1973; Jones, 1981; Rosenberg and Birdzell, 1986). That is surely part of the answer; political competition for survival in early modern Europe was certainly more acute than in other parts of the world. But it is only a partial answer. Why the contrasting results within western Europe? Why did Spain, the great power of 16th century Europe, decline while the Netherlands and England developed?

To begin to get an answer (and it is only a beginning), we need to dig deeper into two key (and related) parts of the puzzle: the relationship between the basic institutional framework, the consequent organizational structure, and institutional change; and the path dependent nature of economic change that is a consequence of the increasing returns characteristic of an institutional framework.

In the institutional accounts given earlier, the direction and form of economic activity by individuals and organizations reflected the opportunities thrown up by the basic institutional framework of customs, religious precepts, and formal rules (and the effectiveness of enforcement). Whether we examine the organization of trade in the Suq or that in the Champagne Fairs, in each case the trader was constrained by the institutional framework, as well as the traditional constraints common to economic theory.

In each case the trader would invest in acquiring knowledge and skills to increase his wealth. But in the former case, improved knowledge and skills meant getting better information on opportunities and having greater bargaining skills than other traders, since profitable opportunities came from being better informed and being a more skilled bargainer than other traders. Neither activity induced alteration in the basic institutional framework. On the other hand, while a merchant at a medieval European fair would certainly gain from acquiring such information and skills, he would gain also from devising ways to bond fellow merchants, to establish merchant courts, to induce princes to protect goods from brigandage in return for revenue, to devise ways to discount bills of exchange. His investment in knowledge and skills would gradually and incrementally alter the basic institutional framework.

Note that the institutional evolution entailed not only voluntary organizations that expanded trade and made exchange more productive, but also the development of the state to take over protection and enforcement of property rights as impersonal exchange made contract enforcement increasingly costly for voluntary organizations which lacked effective coercive power. Another essential part of the institutional evolution entails a shackling of the arbitrary behavior of the state over economic activity.

Path dependence is more than the incremental process of institutional evolution in which yesterday's institutional framework provides the opportunity set for today's organizations and individual entrepreneurs (political or economic). The institutional matrix consists of an interdependent web of institutions and consequent political and economic organizations that are characterized by massive increasing returns.[10] That is, the organizations owe their existence to the opportunities provided by the institutional framework. Network externalities arise because of the initial setup costs (like the de novo creation of the U.S. Constitution in 1787), the learning effects described above, coordination effects via contracts with other organizations, and adaptive expectations arising from the prevalence of contracting based on the existing institutions.

When economies do evolve, therefore, nothing about that process assures economic growth. It has commonly been the case that the incentive structure provided by the basic institutional framework creates opportunities for the consequent organizations to evolve, but the direction of their development has not been to promote productivity-raising activities. Rather, private profitability has been enhanced by creating monopolies, by restricting entry and factor mobility, and by political organizations that established property rights that redistributed rather than increased income.

The contrasting histories of the Netherlands and England on the one hand and Spain on the other hand reflected the differing opportunity sets of the actors in each case. To appreciate the pervasive influence of path dependence, let us extend the historical account of Spain and England to the economic history of the New World and the striking contrast in the history of the areas north and south of the Rio Grande River.

In the case of North America, the English colonies were formed in the century when the struggle between Parliament and the Crown was coming to a head. Religious and political diversity in the mother country was paralleled in the colonies. The general development in the direction of local political control and the growth of assemblies was unambiguous. Similarly, the colonist carried over free and common socage tenure of land (fee simple ownership rights) and secure property rights in other factor and product markets.

The French and Indian War from 1755–63 is a familiar breaking point in American history. British efforts to impose a very modest tax on colonial subjects, as well as curb westward migration, produced a violent reaction that led via a series of steps, by individuals and organizations, to the Revolution, the Declaration of Independence, the Articles of Confederation, the Northwest Ordinance, and the Constitution, a sequence of institutional expressions that formed a consistent evolutionary pattern despite the precariousness of the process. While the American Revolution created the United States, post-revolutionary history is only intelligible in terms of the continuity of informal and formal institutional constraints carried over from before the Revolution and incrementally modified (Hughes, 1989).

Now turn to the Spanish (and Portuguese) case in Latin America. In the case of the Spanish Indies, conquest came at the precise time that the influence of the Castilian Cortes (parliament) was declining and the monarchy of Castile, which was the seat of power of Spain, was firmly establishing centralized bureaucratic control over Spain and the Spanish Indies.[11] The conquerors imposed a uniform religion and a uniform bureaucratic administration on an already existing agricultural society. The bureaucracy detailed every aspect of political and economic policy. There were recurrent crises over the problem of agency. Wealth-maximizing behavior by organizations and entrepreneurs (political and economic) entailed getting control of, or influence over, the bureaucratic machinery. While the nineteenth century Wars of Independence in Latin America turned out to be a struggle for control of the bureaucracy and consequent policy as between local colonial control and imperial control, nevertheless the struggle was imbued with the ideological overtones that stemmed from the American and French revolutions. Independence brought U.S.-inspired constitutions, but the results were radically different. In contrast to those of the United States, Latin American federal schemes and efforts at decentralization had one thing in common after the Revolutions. None worked. The gradual country-by-country reversion to centralized bureaucratic control characterized Latin America in the 19th century.[12]

The divergent paths established by England and Spain in the New World have not converged despite the mediating factors of common ideological influences. In the former, an institutional framework has evolved that permits complex impersonal exchange necessary to political stability as well as to capture the potential economic benefits of modern technology. In the latter, "personalistic" relationships are still the key to much of the political and economic exchange. They are the consequence of an evolving institutional framework that has produced erratic economic growth in Latin America, but neither political nor economic stability, nor realization of the potential of modern technology.

The foregoing comparative sketch probably raises more questions than it answers about institutions and the role that they play in the performance of economies. Under what conditions does a path get reversed, like the revival of Spain in modern times? What is it about informal constraints that gives them such a pervasive influence upon the long-run character of economies? What is the relationship between formal and informal constraints? How does an economy develop the informal constraints that make individuals constrain their behavior so that they make political and judicial systems effective forces for third party enforcement? Clearly we have a long way to go for complete answers, but the modern study of institutions offers the promise of dramatic new understanding of economic performance and economic change.

NOTES

1. In an article written many years ago (North, 1955), I pointed out that many regional economies evolved from the very beginning as export economies and built their development around the export sector. This is in comparison and in contrast to the old stage theory of history derived from the German historical school, in which the evolution was always from local autarky to gradual evolution of specialization and division of labor. It is this last pattern that is described here, even though it may not characterize the particular evolution that in fact has occurred.

2. For an excellent summary of the anthropological literature dealing with trade in tribal societies, see Elizabeth Colson (1974).

3. Jewish traders in the Mediterranean in the 11th century "solved" the agency problem as a result of close community relationships amongst themselves that lowered information costs and enabled them to act as a group to ostracize and retaliate against agents who violated their commercial code. See Avner Greif (1989).

4. Philip Curtin's *Cross Cultural Trade in World History* (1984) summarizes a good deal of the literature, but is short on analysis and examination of the mechanisms essential to the structure of such trade. The Cambridge Economic History, Volume III (1966), has more useful details on the organization of such trade.

5. North and Weingast (1989) provide a history and analysis of the political institutions of 17th century England leading up to the Revolution of 1688 and of the consequences for the development of the English capital market.

6. See North (1981), particularly chapter 13, and Chandler (1977). Joseph Stiglitz's (1989) essay, "Markets, Market Failures, and Development," details some of the theoretical issues.

7. The transaction sector (that proportion of transaction costs going through the market and therefore measureable) of the U.S. economy was 25 percent of GNP in 1870 and 45 percent of GNP in 1970 (Wallis and North, 1986).

8. There is an extensive literature on the Suq. A sophisticated analysis (on which I have relied) focused on the Suq in Sefrou, Morocco is contained in Geertz, Geertz, and Rosen (1979).

9. For a much more detailed description and analysis of the evolution of European trade see Tracy (forthcoming), particularly Volume II. For a game theoretic analysis of one

aspect of this trade revival see Milgrom, North and Weingast (1990).

10. The concept of path dependence was developed by Brian Arthur (1988, 1989) and Paul David (1985) to explore the path of technological change. I believe the concept has equal explanatory power in helping us understand institutional change. In both cases increasing returns are the key to path dependence, but in the case of institutional change the process is more complex because of the key role of political organizations in the process.

11. The subsequent history of Spanish rise and decline is summarized in North and Thomas (1973).

12. For a summary account of the Latin American experience, see Veliz (1980) or Glade (1969).

REFERENCES

Arthur, W. Brian, "Self-Reinforcing Mechanisms in Economics." In Anderson, Phillip W., Kenneth J. Arrow, and David Pines, eds., *The Economy as an Evolving Complex System*. Reading, MA: Addison-Wesley, 1988.

Arthur, W. Brian, "Competing Technologies, Increasing Returns, and Lock-In by Historical Events," *Economic Journal*, 1989, *99*, 116–31.

Barbour, Violet, "Capitalism in Amsterdam in the Seventeenth Century," *Johns Hopkins University Studies in Historical and Political Science*, Volume LXVIII. Baltimore: The Johns Hopkins University Press, 1949.

The Cambridge Economic History. Cambridge: Cambridge University Press, 1966.

Chandler, Alfred, *The Visible Hand*. Cambridge: The Belknap Press, 1977.

Colson, Elizabeth, *Tradition and Contract: The Problem of Order*. Chicago: Adeline Publishing, 1974.

Curtin, Philip D., *Cross-Cultural Trade in World History*. Cambridge: Cambridge University Press, 1984.

David, Paul, "Clio and the Economics of QWERTY," *American Economic Review*. 1985, *75*, 332–37.

De Roover, F. E., "Early Examples of Marine Insurance," *Journal of Economic History*, November 1945, *5*, 172–200.

Geertz, C., H. Geertz, and L. Rosen, *Meaning and Order in Moroccan Society*. Cambridge: Cambridge University Press, 1979.

Glade, W. P., *The Latin American Economies: A Study of Their Institutional Evolution*. New York: American Book, 1969.

Greif, Avner, "Reputation and Economic Institutions in Medieval Trade: Evidences from the Geniza Documents," *Journal of Economic History*, 1989.

Hughes, J. R. T., "A World Elsewhere: The Importance of Starting English." In Thompson, F. M. L., ed., *Essays in Honor of H. J. Ha-bakkuk*. Oxford: Oxford University Press, 1989.

Jones, E. L., *The European Miracle: Environments, Economies, and Geopolitics in the History of Europe and Asia*. Cambridge: Cambridge University Press, 1981.

Kalt, J. P. and M. A. Zupan, "Capture and Ideology in the Economic Theory of Politics," *American Economic Review*, 1984, *74*, 279–300.

Lopez, Robert S., and Irving W. Raymond, *Medieval Trade in the Mediterranean World*. New York: Columbia University Press, 1955.

Milgrom, P. R., D. C. North, and B. R. Weingast, "The Role of Institutions in the Revival of Trade: The Medieval Law Merchant," *Economics and Politics*, March 1990, *II*.

Mitchell, William, *An Essay on the Early History of the Law Merchant*. New York: Burt Franklin Press, 1969.

Nelson, Douglas, and Eugene Silberberg, "Ideology and Legislator Shirking," *Economic Inquiry*, January 1987, *25*, 15–25.

North, Douglass C., "Location Theory and Regional Economic Growth," *Journal of Political Economy*, June 1955, *LXIII*, 243–258.

North, Douglass C., *Structure and Change in Economic History*. New York: Norton, 1981.

North, Douglass C., and Robert Thomas, *The Rise of the Western World: A New Economic History*. Cambridge: Cambridge University Press, 1973.

North, Douglass C., and Barry R. Weingast, "The Evolution of Institutions Governing Public Choice in 17th Century England," *Journal of Economic History*, November 1989, *5*, 172–200.

Posner, Richard, "A Theory of Primitive Society, with Special Reference to the Law," *Journal of Law and Economics*, April 1980, *XXIII*, 1–54.

Rosenberg, Nathan, and L. E. Bridzell, *How the West Grew Rich: The Economic Transformation of the Industrial World*. New York: Basic Books, 1986.

Stiglitz, Joseph, "Markets, Market Failures, and Development," *American Economic Review*, 1989, *79*, 197–203.

Tracy, James, *A Financial Revolution in the Hapsburg Netherlands: Renters and Rentiers in the Country of Holland, 1515–1565*. Berkeley: University of California Press, 1985.

Tracy, James, *The Rise of Merchant Empires*. Cambridge: Cambridge University Press, forthcoming.

Udovitch, Abraham, "At the Origins of the Western Commenda: Islam, Israel, Byzanteum?" *Speculum*, April 1962, *XXXVII*, 198–207.

Veliz, C., *The Centralist Tradition of Latin America*. Princeton: Princeton University Press, 1980.

Wallis, John J., and Douglass C. North, "Measuring the Transaction Sector in the American Economy, 1870–1970." In Engermann, Stanley, and Robert Gallman, eds., *Income and Wealth: Long-Term Factors in American Economic Growth*. Chicago: University of Chicago Press, 1986.

Watts, R., and J. Zimmerman, "Agency Problems, Auditing, and the Theory of the Firm: Some Evidence," *Journal of Law and Economics*, October 1983, *XXVI*, 613–633.

Williamson, Oliver E., *Markets and Hierarchies: Analysis and Antitrust Implications*. New York: Free Press, 1975.

Williamson, Oliver E., *The Economic Institutions of Capitalism*. New York: Free Press, 1985.

Yaney, B. S., "Scientific Bookkeeping and the Rise of Capitalism," *Economic History Review*, Second Series, 1949, *II*, 99–113.

ALBERTO ALESINA, EDWARD GLAESER, AND BRUCE SACERDOTE

WHY DOESN'T THE UNITED STATES HAVE A EUROPEAN-STYLE WELFARE STATE?

European governments redistribute income among their citizens on a much larger scale than does the U.S. government. European social programs are more generous and reach a larger share of citizens. European tax systems are more progressive. European regulations designed to protect the poor are more intrusive. In this paper we try to understand why.

The literature on the size of government is rich and varied. However, here we do not focus

From *Brookings Papers on Economic Activity* 2 (2001), pp. 1–69. Some of the authors' notes have been omitted.

on the size of government as such, but rather on the redistributive side of government policies. Thus our goal is in one sense narrower than answering the question, "What explains the size of government?" since we focus on a single, but increasingly important, role of fiscal policy. Yet in another sense our focus is broader, because redistributive policies go beyond the government budget—think, for instance, of labor market policies.

We consider economic, political, and behavioral explanations for these differences between the United States and Europe. Economic explanations focus on the variance of income and the skewness of the income distribution before taxes and transfers, the social costs of taxation, the volatility of income, and expected changes in income for the median voter. We conclude that most of these theories cannot explain the observed differences. Before-tax income in the United States has both higher variance and a more skewed distribution. There is no evidence that the deadweight losses from taxation are lower in Europe. And the volatility of income appears to be lower in Europe than in the United States. However, there is some possibility that middle-class households in the United States have a greater chance of moving up in the income distribution, which would make the median voter more averse to redistribution.

Political explanations for the observed level of redistribution focus on institutions that prevent minorities from gaining political power or that strictly protect individuals' private property. Cross-country comparisons indicate the importance of these institutions in limiting redistribution. For instance, at the federal level, the United States do not have proportional representation, which played an important role in facilitating the growth of socialist parties in many European countries. America has strong courts that have routinely rejected popular attempts at redistribution, such as the income tax or labor regulation. The European equivalents of these courts were swept away as democracy replaced monarchy and aristocracy. The federal structure of the

United States may have also contributed to constraining the role of the central government in redistribution.

These political institutions result from particular features of U.S. history and geography. The formation of the United States as a federation of independent territories led to a structure that often creates obstacles to centralized redistributive policies. The relative political stability of the United States over more than two centuries means that it is still governed by an eighteenth-century constitution designed to protect property. As world war and revolution uprooted the old European monarchies, the twentieth-century constitutions that replaced them were more oriented toward majority rule, and less toward protection of private property. Moreover, the spatial organization of the United States—in particular, its low population density—meant that the U.S. government was much less threatened by socialist revolution. In contrast, many of Europe's institutions were either established by revolutionary groups directly or by elites in response to the threat of violence.

Finally, we discuss reciprocal altruism as a possible behavioral explanation for redistribution. Reciprocal altruism implies that voters will dislike giving money to the poor if, as in the United States, the poor are perceived as lazy. In contrast, Europeans overwhelmingly believe that the poor are poor because they have been unfortunate. This difference in views is part of what is sometimes referred to as "American exceptionalism."[1]

Racial discord plays a critical role in determining beliefs about the poor. Since racial minorities are highly overrepresented among the poorest Americans, any income-based redistribution measures will redistribute disproportionately to these minorities. Opponents of redistribution in the United States have regularly used race-based rhetoric to resist left-wing policies. Across countries, racial fragmentation is a powerful predictor of redistribution. Within the United States, race is the single most important predictor of support for welfare. America's troubled race relations are clearly a major reason for the absence of an American welfare state.

The Size and Structure of Redistributive Policies in the United States and Europe

In this section we review the basic facts about the level of redistribution to the poor in the United States and Europe.

Government Spending

Table 1 summarizes the magnitude and composition of government spending in Europe and in the United States, using data from the Organization for Economic Cooperation and Development (OECD). In addition to reporting averages for the countries in the European Union, we provide separate data on the United Kingdom (the one EU country with a relatively small government), Germany (the largest EU country), and Sweden (as the prototype of a country with an especially large welfare state), and France.

General government spending in the countries in the European Union averages 48 percent of GDP; it is 38 percent in the United Kingdom and 60 percent in Sweden. General government spending in the United States is smaller than any of these, at 36 percent of GDP. The composition of spending is also instructive. The largest differences between the United States and Europe are in transfers to households (including social security) and subsidies. In fact, the sum of these two categories of spending is almost twice as large, as a share of GDP, in Europe as in the United States (20 percent versus 11 percent). The difference in transfers and subsidies accounts for 8 percentage points of the 12-percentage-point difference in total spending. Consumption of goods and services and government wages are also higher in Europe, but the difference relative to the United States is much smaller than that for transfers. Public investment is actually higher in the United States than in the average EU country. Of course, military spending is higher in the United States than in Europe (data not shown), even today when U.S. defense spending is low by post–World War II standards. Western Europe since World War II has been a free rider on defense provided by the United States. If the United States had not spent more

Table 1. Composition of General Government Expenditure, 1999[a]

Percent of GDP

Country	Total	Consumption		Subsidies	Transfers and other social benefits[b]	Gross investment
		Goods and services	Wages and salaries			
United States[c]	35.5	5.2	9.2	0.2	11.0	3.1
European Union[d]	47.9	8.4	12.0	1.5	18.1	2.8
France	51.0	10.0	13.7	1.3	20.1	3.0
Germany	47.4	10.7	8.3	1.7	20.5	1.8
Sweden	60.2	10.3	16.7	2.0	21.1	2.5
United Kingdom	38.3	11.0	7.4	0.6	15.7	1.0

Source: *OECD Economic Outlook*, no. 68, 2000.
a. Details may not sum to totals because of excluded categories.
b. Includes social security.
c. Data are for 1998.
d. Simple average for fourteen EU countries (excludes Luxembourg).

Table 2. Government Expenditure on Social Programs, 1995

Percent of GDP

Country	Total	Old age disability, and survivors' benefits	Family benefits	Unemployment and labor market programs	Health benefits [a]	Other [b]
United States	15.8	7.3	0.6	0.6	6.3	1.0
European Union [c]	25.4	12.4	2.1	3.2	5.9	1.8
France	30.1	14.1	2.6	3.1	8.0	2.3
Germany	28.0	12.5	2.0	3.7	8.1	1.6
Sweden	33.0	14.8	3.9	4.7	5.9	3.8
United Kingdom	22.5	10.6	2.4	1.3	5.7	2.5

Source: OECD, *OECD Social Expenditure Database 1980–1996*, 1999.
a. Also includes inpatient care, ambulatory medical services, and pharmaceutical goods.
b. Includes expenditure on occupational injury and disease benefits, sickness benefits, housing benefits, and benefits to low-income households.
c. Simple average for the fifteen EU countries.

to defend Western Europe and itself from the Soviet threat, the difference in the overall size of government would be even larger.

The OECD offers a different breakdown of government social spending; these data are presented in table 2 for 1995, the latest year for which they are available. In all categories except health, the United States spends a smaller proportion of GDP than the European average. The differences are particularly large in family allowances and unemployment compensation and other labor market programs. By this accounting, social spending in the United States was about 16 percent of GDP in 1995, whereas the European average was about 25 percent.[2]

Consider the other non-European OECD countries (not shown in the tables). The size of government in Canada (52 percent of GDP) is similar to that in France and slightly above the European average. Japan and Australia have governments that are smaller than Canada's (36 and 38 percent of GDP) but still slightly larger than the U.S. government, whereas New Zealand's government, at 41 percent of GDP, is roughly midway between those of the United States and Europe. The average for the non-European, non-U.S. OECD countries falls some-

where in between the United States and Europe. Thus, in comparing the United States and Europe, we are comparing two extremes in the OECD group.

Differences in the overall size of government or even in the size of transfer programs are only indirectly related to the extent of redistribution from the rich to the poor. For instance, the social security system involves flows from the young to the old as well as from the rich to the poor. Nevertheless, it is uncontroversial that a predominant share of public goods, and especially transfers, favors the poor disproportionately.

The Structure of Taxation

Table 3 summarizes the composition of government revenue in Europe and the United States. The most striking differences are in social security contributions and taxes on goods and services. However, there are important differences in the structure of taxation even within Europe.[3] Our concern here is with the tax burden of the rich relative to that of the poor. To calculate a precise measure of the progressivity of the tax system across all these countries would require an entire paper (at least) devoted to unraveling

Table 3. Composition of General Government Revenue, 1999

Percent of GDP

			Tax revenue					
			Direct taxes		Social security	Property	Goods and	Nontax
Country	Total	Total	Households	Businesses	contributions[a]	income	services	revenue[b]
United States	31.0	15.1	12.4	2.8	7.1	1.0	7.7	7.2
European Union[c]	45.4	15.3	11.8	3.4	13.6	2.0	14.4	5.7
France	50.4	12.2	9.5	2.7	19.3	2.8	16.0	4.9
Germany	44.5	12.0	10.3	1.5	19.6	0.7	12.2	9.9
Sweden	57.9	22.4	19.0	3.3	14.7	3.8	17.0	8.1
United Kingdom	40.4	16.3	12.5	3.8	8.0	2.1	14.0	4.0

Source: *OECD Economic Outlook 2001*, no. 68, 2000; and OECD, Revenue Statistics 1965–1999, 2000.
a. Includes other current transfers.
b. Data are for 1997.
c. Simple average for fourteen EU countries (excludes Luxembourg).

the intricacies of the different tax codes. Although such a task is beyond the scope of this paper, a simple attempt is made in figure 1. We assembled data on the different income tax brackets of the European countries and took a cross-country average. We then subtracted this average from the corresponding federal income tax brackets in the United States; figure 1 plots that difference. Thus, for a given level of income, a positive value in the figure implies that the marginal tax rate in the United States exceeds the European average, and a negative value indicates the opposite. The figure shows that marginal tax rates in the United States are higher than in Europe for low levels of income (up to about 50 percent of the average worker's wage) and lower for higher levels of income. Also, the difference between the United States and Europe becomes larger in absolute value as income rises. In short, the income tax system is much more progressive in Europe than in the United States.[4]

Historical Trends in the Size of Government

Understanding the reasons for these striking differences between the United States and Europe requires that we know something of the history

of redistribution in both regions. In particular, we want to know *when* the size of government, and especially the size of the welfare state in Eu-

Figure 1. Difference between U.S. and EU Marginal Income Tax Rates, 1999–2000.[a]

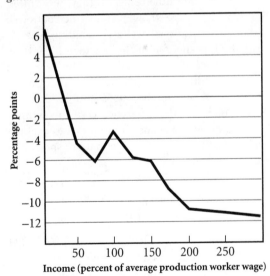

Income (percent of average production worker wage)

Source: Authors' calculations based on data from OECD, Taxing Wages, 1999–2000, 2001.
a. Years are fiscal years, U.S. marginal income tax rate minus a simple average of rates for fourteen EU countries (excludes Denmark) for each income level.

Table 4. Government Expenditure on Subsidies and Transfers, 1870–1998[a]

Percent of GDP

Country	1870	1937	1960	1970	1980	1998
United States	0.3	2.1	5.0	7.5	10.4	11.0
European Union[b]	0.8	6.8	11.5	13.1	19.0	21.0
France	1.1	7.2	14.1	14.8	18.2	21.6
Germany	0.5	7.0	7.0	15.4	20.4	22.0
Sweden	0.7	. . .	8.6	12.4	21.6	23.4
United Kingdom	. . .	10.3	9.2	. . .	. . .	16.6
Memorandum:						
EU–U.S.	0.5	4.7	6.5	5.6	8.7	9.9

Source: Authors' calculations based on data from Tanzi and Schuknecht (2000), and *OECD Economic Outlook*, no. 68, 2000.
a. Or the closest year for which data are available.
b. Simple average of Austria, Belgium, France, Germany, Greece, Ireland, Italy, the Netherlands, Spain, and the United Kingdom.

rope, diverged from that in the United States. Did the two share a similar size of government for a while and then diverge, or has the difference always been present?

Table 4 provides a clear answer: from the very beginning of the expansion of the public sector in the late nineteenth century, the United States and Europe show very distinct patterns. Although the ratio of welfare spending was already high at the end of the nineteenth century, the absolute difference grew as the welfare state expanded both in Europe and in the United States, especially in the 1960s and 1970s. This observation that the difference is of long standing is important, because it allows us to exclude explanations of the difference that are specific to a certain period or event.

Income Support Policies and Safety Nets

In addition to the aggregate data provided above, it is useful to compare specific programs for income support and safety nets. We consider Germany, Sweden, and the United States, and we focus on a representative household. We will determine the extent to which existing programs and their provisions can be beneficial to such a household when it experiences increased hard-

ship. We examine the costs of raising a child, of sickness, of disability, and of extreme poverty. We discuss unemployment policies in the context of more general labor market regulations in the next subsection.

Our representative household is composed of two adults and two children. The adults, both aged thirty-five, are average production workers with fifteen years of work experience. The two children are aged eight and twelve, to take a benchmark often used by social security administrations. The monthly before-tax earnings of an average production worker in the three countries, in 1999 dollars adjusted for purchasing power parity (PPP), are $2,498 in the United States, $2,561 in Germany, and $1,880 in Sweden.

FAMILY BENEFITS

Child benefits are available in Germany and Sweden for every parent, without regard to income, until the child reaches eighteen (in Germany) or sixteen (in Sweden), but those limits can be extended if the child pursues higher education. By contrast, family allowances do not exist in the United States.[5] However, special allowances for children of low-income families are allocated under the Temporary Assistance for Needy Families program (TANF, which replaced the Aid to Families with Dependent Children, or AFDC, program in the mid-1990s), as discussed below. To summarize, each child entitles the representative household to monthly benefits (again in 1999 PPP-adjusted dollars) of $136 in Germany, $87 in Sweden, and zero in the United States.

HEALTH CARE

The public health care systems of Germany and Sweden also differ significantly from that of the United States. Both Germany and Sweden provide universal coverage, with unlimited benefits including payments of doctors' fees, hospitalization, and the cost of pharmaceutical products. The United States, on the other hand, relies on two programs, Medicare and Medicaid, which target mainly the elderly and low-income households, respectively. If one of the members of our representative U.S. family became sick and had to visit a doctor or stay in a hospital, he or she would not be eligible for public funds or services (although a large fraction of employers offer health insurance as part of their compensation package). In contrast, the representative German or Swedish household would have most of these expenses covered by the public health care program. A small part of the cost is borne by the household in the form of a deductible. In Germany the household pays a deductible of $9 for each day of hospitalization; in Sweden the hospitalization deductible is $8, and in addition there is a deductible of $10 to $14 for medical treatment, again in 1999 PPP dollars.

SICKNESS AND ACCIDENTAL INJURY BENEFITS

Sickness benefits are intended to replace the loss of earnings due to sickness of a household's income earners. Once again, the coverage and the extent of benefits differ radically between the United States and the two European countries examined here. Indeed, only five states in the United States offer any kind of sickness benefit (there is no federal benefit), whereas German and Swedish legislation guarantees benefits for all persons in paid employment; these benefits replace up to 70 percent and 80 percent of gross earnings, respectively. If the head of our representative U.S. household fell sick (and was fortunate enough to live in one of the five states that offer sickness benefits), he or she would receive (in 1999 PPP dollars) between $452 and $1,576 a month (between 18 and 63 percent of the average wage); the representative household head in Germany would receive $1,793 a month, and his or her Swedish counterpart would receive $1,504 a month. The U.S. household's benefits would last for a maximum of fifty-two weeks, whereas those of the German household would expire only after seventy-eight weeks, and those of the Swedish household could continue indefinitely.

Accidental injuries occurring in the enterprise or in connection with the working situation of the employee are covered in all three countries, including every state in the United States, and these benefits are quite comparable. German and Swedish workers who suffer on-the-job injuries see their income replaced according to the amounts allocated by sickness benefits, whereas American workers receive the equivalent of two-thirds of their average weekly earnings, up to a maximum of $270 to $714 a week, depending on the state.

DISABILITY BENEFITS

All three countries also have provisions to replace income lost due to inability to engage in any gainful activity. Participation is compulsory in all three systems, and coverage is based on work history. The United States and Germany require at least five years of employment before a worker can receive benefits; in Sweden the requirement is three years. But the extent of coverage differs dramatically across the three countries. Whereas in the United States the disability pension is based on the worker's average monthly earnings, the Swedish scheme provides a basic minimum pension, augmented by an income-based supplementary pension, care allowances, and handicap allowances; German pensions are computed using the level of income and the number of years of contribution. For the representative production worker, disability benefits amount to $1,063 in the United States and $1,496 in Sweden (again in 1999 PPP dollars). These correspond to 43 percent and 80 percent of the average wage, respectively.

POVERTY RELIEF

In all three countries, certain government programs are directed at persons who are unable to support themselves but are not covered under the schemes described above. These persons may fail to meet eligibility criteria because of insufficient past contributions, or their incomes may be too low to allow them to take part in insurance schemes. The programs that provide these pure cash transfers differ in structure across the three countries. Germany and Sweden rely on unlimited and unconditional plans (called Sozialhilfe and Socialbidrag, respectively), which are meant primarily to alleviate poverty. Additional plans covering the costs of housing and heating are also available for German residents. The United States, on the other hand, offers an array of plans targeting different groups in the population. Supplemental Security Income (SSI) targets aged, blind, and disabled persons with annual income below $5,808; the federal payment can be augmented by a state supplement. The TANF program, mentioned above, is limited to two years of assistance; recipients who are able to work must find employment at the end of that period. Other plans, such as those for food and nutrition assistance and those for housing assistance, also provide relief to low-income households.

A representative U.S. household that has zero income and has exhausted all other claims to regular benefits could be eligible for $1,306 in monthly benefits under these programs ($726 from SSI, or 29 percent of the average monthly wage, and $580 from TANF, or 23 percent of the average wage).[6] Its German counterpart would be eligible to receive $1,008 a month, and its Swedish counterpart $888 a month (39 percent and 47 percent of the average wage, respectively, again in 1999 PPP-adjusted dollars). These amounts do not include benefits available under additional programs such as housing allowances.

Labor Market Policies

Not all redistributive policies involve government expenditure. Legislation in several other areas also determines the degree of government involvement in redistributing income. An obvious case is that of labor market policies. Labor regulations such as those that set a minimum wage may keep real wages higher than they would be otherwise.[7] * * * The available data on minimum wages in Europe and the United States * * * are from several different sources, but all tell a very similar story. In the European Union the minimum wage is 53 percent of the average wage, against 39 percent in the United States. In France the minimum wage is around 65 percent of the average manufacturing wage, compared with 36 percent in the United States.

* * * Other measures of labor market regulation, using data assembled by Stephen Nickell and Richard Layard[8] [buttress our point.] Although a fair amount of variation is observed within Europe, on all measures the United States scores lower (often much lower) than the European average.

Scores on these measures for a group of non-European, non-U.S. OECD countries (Australia, Canada, Japan, and New Zealand) lie somewhere in between those of the United States and continental Europe. On some measures these countries may be closer to the United States, and on others closer to Europe. Overall, however, the United States and Europe appear to be polar extremes.

Has It Worked?

The consequences of the greater expansion of the welfare state in Europe than in the United States are important, but well beyond the already broad scope of this paper. We want to explain the *causes* of this difference, not its consequences. Nevertheless, it is worth pausing to briefly characterize the conventional wisdom (if there is any) on this issue. Needless to say, the question of the impact of a large welfare state is difficult to answer and loaded with ideological biases. We think that a fair and relatively uncontroversial assessment of the effect of these different levels of redistributive policies in the broadest possible terms is as follows.

As Vito Tanzi and Ludger Schuknecht forcefully argue in a recent study of the growth of government, averages of several key social indicators such as health measures, life expectancy, and educational achievement are not that different between countries with a large government like those in continental Europe and countries with a small government like that in the United States.[9] On the other hand, a large body of research has shown that after-tax income inequality is lower in countries with larger governments and, in particular, in countries with higher social spending.[10] As is well known, comparing inequality and poverty rates across countries is a minefield. However, it is quite clear that after-tax income inequality is relatively low in the Nordic countries, intermediate in central and southern Europe, higher in the United Kingdom, and higher still in the United States.[11]

When one compares the distribution of disposable income across population deciles in the United States and Europe, a striking and interesting difference is the much lower proportion of income accruing to the lowest decile in the United States. That is, the greater inequality in the United States does not stem from the top decile being particularly wealthy relative to the median, so much as from the bottom decile being particularly poor. For instance, in the 1980s the average income among the lowest decile was about a third of the median in the United States, compared with more than 55 percent in many European countries, including France, and more than 60 percent in several Nordic countries.[12] Another way of looking at this is to compute the fraction of the population with incomes below 50 percent of the median. (Many European countries use this as a definition of the poverty line.) Depending on the criteria used, this fraction was around 17 to 18 percent in the United States in the 1980s, against values of 5 to 8 percent in Sweden and Germany.[13]

In the 1990s income inequality increased sharply in the United Kingdom and somewhat less sharply in the United States. In the continental European countries, changes in income inequality in the last decade were smaller. It would appear that, because of a smaller emphasis on policies that redistribute toward the poor, the bottom decile of the income ladder in the United States is less well off than the bottom decile in European countries. That is, the U.S. poor are really poor.[14]

How much the reduction in inequality achieved by a more redistributive government "costs" in terms of slower growth because of higher taxation, more intrusive regulation, and so forth is a large and difficult question that we cannot even begin to answer here. Assar Lindbeck provides an excellent and exhaustive discussion of this issue for Sweden.[15] His conclusion is that in the long run the trade-off between redistribution and growth is rather steep. In 1970, before the explosion of its welfare state, Sweden had an income per capita equivalent to 115 percent of that in the average OECD country—the fourth-highest of all. By 1995, however, Sweden's income per capita was only 95 percent of the OECD average, and Sweden had fallen to sixteenth place. One may wonder whether the trade-off is so steep at levels of social protection less extreme than Sweden's. Other countries with extended welfare states have not done as poorly as Sweden. Also, certain aspects of redistributive policies, such as a well-functioning public education system, may foster human capital accumulation. A related issue is the cost in terms of employment formation and growth of labor protection, but this is another immense topic that would require not one but several papers to do it justice.

Charity and the Private Provision of Welfare

The preceding evidence makes it clear that European countries provide more public welfare than the United States. But Americans engage in more private provision of welfare (that is, charity) than do Europeans. As private citizens, Americans appear to give more of their time and their money to the poor than do Europeans.

We use the World Values Survey to calculate the share of adults in each of several European countries who are members of charitable organizations. The World Values Survey is a collection of surveys where the same questions are asked in different countries in different years. Between 600 and 2,000 people are interviewed in each country; appendix B provides details on the countries and survey years. Although membership in charitable organizations is an imperfect measure of the time contribution to charity (it does not measure the intensity of involvement), it is one of the best measures available. In the United States, 11 percent of respondents say that they participated in a charitable group over the last year; the average for the European countries in the survey is 4 percent. The European country with the highest proportion of membership in private charities is the Netherlands, with almost 9 percent of respondents saying that they participate. At the other end of the spectrum is Denmark, where 2 percent of individuals claim to have participated in these activities.

This work corroborates the large literature on private charity in the United States. For example, the U.K. National Council for Volunteer Organizations and the not-for-profit group United for a Fair Economy document that charitable contributions in the United States totaled $190 billion in 2000, or $691 a person. This compares with reported contributions per capita of $141 in the United Kingdom and $57 for Europe as a whole. Notably, a large fraction of American donors make charitable contributions even though they take only the standard deduction on their income taxes. This means that, for many Americans, contributions are not being driven by the tax deductibility of charitable donations. Theda Skocpol, Marshall Ganz, and Ziad Munson document the national coverage of the many U.S. volunteer groups who provide a rich variety of forms of assistance.[16]

These results suggest, but hardly prove, two implications. First, public provision of welfare in part crowds out private charity. As argued by Glaeser and Andrei Shleifer, if government transfers to particular individuals fall as private donations rise, these transfers will reduce the incentive for private charity.[17] These results also suggest that Europe's more generous provision of welfare does not stem from a greater innate endowment of altruism in Europe.

*   *   *

Conclusion

Why is redistribution so much greater in Europe than in the United States? We have examined three sets of explanations, which we labeled economic, political, and behavioral. The economic explanations do not explain much of the puzzle. Before-tax income inequality is higher, and the income distribution appears to be more skewed, in the United States than in Europe. There does not appear to be more income uncertainty in Europe, nor is there evidence that the European tax system is more efficient. There may be more chance for upward mobility among politically powerful groups in the United States. Overall, we think that standard economic models of income redistribution do a poor job of explaining the differences between the United States and Europe.

On the other hand, political variables,

including the electoral system (in particular, proportionality and, in the United States, the two-party system) and the role of the courts, are important. The two-party system and the lack of proportional representation in the United States created obstacles that blocked the formation of a strong and lasting socialist party. In contrast, the upheaval in continental Europe over the last century has meant that no durable institutions remained to protect property against popular demand for redistribution. Monumental differences in the history and geography of the two regions, such as the Civil War and the open frontier in the United States during the nineteenth century, contributed to create a different climate and different attitudes toward the relationship between the individual and the state.

The behavioral explanations also seem very important. Racial fragmentation in the United States and the disproportionate representation of ethnic minorities among the poor clearly played a major role in limiting redistribution, and indeed, racial cleavages seem to serve as a barrier to redistribution throughout the world. This history of American redistribution makes it quite clear that hostility to welfare derives in part from the fact that welfare spending in the United States goes disproportionately to minorities. Another important difference is that Americans dislike redistribution because they tend to feel that people on welfare are lazy, whereas Europeans tend to feel that people on welfare are unfortunate. Apart from the fact that, in the United States, there is indeed a stronger connection between effort and earnings than in Europe, we do not know what explains these differences in beliefs.

Our bottom line is that Americans redistribute less than Europeans for three reasons: because the majority of Americans believe that redistribution favors racial minorities, because Americans believe that they live in an open and fair society and that if someone is poor it is his or her own fault, and because the political system is geared toward preventing redistribution. In fact, the political system is likely to be endogenous to these basic American beliefs.

*　　*　　*

NOTES

1. Lipset (1996).
2. Total social spending in table 2 is not meant to coincide with the item "Transfers and other social benefits" in table 1. Apart from the fact that the two tables refer to different years, the definitions of the two items differ. For instance, health expenditure in table 2 includes the wages of government workers in the health sector, which would be included under "Wages and salaries" in table 1.
3. In fact, a hotly debated issue within the European Union is precisely the harmonization of tax structures across members.
4. In other countries with federal systems, such as Germany, the structure of taxation also entails automatic redistribution from richer to poorer regions. This is not so, or at least not to the same extent, across U.S. states. Some geographical redistribution does, however, occur within school districts in the United States. See Oates (1999) and the references cited therein.
5. The United States does have a fixed child tax credit ($600 per child in 2001), and the amount of the earned income tax credit increases with the number of children in the family (but is available only to low-income workers).
6. This value refers to the state of Massachusetts, which pays the highest TANF benefits among states in the program.
7. One may argue, correctly, that in many cases labor regulations end up redistributing in favor of the unionized or otherwise "protected" segment of the labor force, at the expense of other workers.
8. Nickell and Layard (1999); Nickell (1997).
9. Tanzi and Schuknecht (2000).
10. See, for instance, Atkinson (1995).
11. This picture emerges, for instance, from the detailed studies by Atkinson (1995).
12. Atkinson (1995, pp. 49–51).

13. Atkinson (1995, p. 90).

14. It should be clear, however, that this inverse relationship between inequality and the size of government is not monotonic. That is, certain countries are much more successful than others in reducing inequality for a given amount of social spending: the welfare state in different countries has had different degrees of success in reaching the truly needy. One problem is that, in certain countries (Italy being a perfect example), welfare spending is too biased in favor of pensions. See Boeri (2000).

15. Lindbeck (1997).

16. Skocpol, Ganz, and Munson (2000). Although Putnam (1999) argues that civic voluntarism has declined in the United States, we do not address this decline here. Rather we focus on the differences over space, not over time.

17. Glaeser and Shleifer (2001b).

REFERENCES

Atkinson, A. B. 1995. *Incomes and the Welfare State: Essays on Britain and Europe*. Cambridge University Press.

Boeri, Tito. 2000. *Structural Change, Welfare Systems and Labour Reallocation: Lessons from the Transition of Formerly Planned Economies*. Oxford University Press.

Glaeser, Edward L., and Andrei Shleifer. 2001. "Not-for-Profit Entrepreneurs." *Journal of Public Economics* 81(1): 99–115.

Lindbeck, Assar. 1997. "The Swedish Experiment." *Journal of Economic Literature* 35(3): 1273–1319.

Lipset, Seymour Martin. 1996. *American Exceptionalism: A Double-Edged Sword*. Norton.

Nickell, Stephen. 1997. "Unemployment and Labor Market Rigidities: Europe versus North America." *Journal of Economic Perspectives* 11(3): 55–74.

Nickell, Stephen, and Richard Layard. 1999. "Labor Market Institutions and Economic Performance." In *Handbook of Labor Economics*, Volume 3C, edited by Orley Ashenfelter and David Card. Amsterdam: North Holland.

Oates, W. 1999. "An Essay on Fiscal Federalism." *Journal of Economic Literature* 37(3): 1120–49.

Skocpol, Theda, Marshall Ganz, and Ziad Munson. 2000. "A Nation of Organizers: The Institutional Origins of Civic Voluntarism in the United States." *American Political Science Review* 94(3): 527–46.

Tanzi, Vito, and Ludger Schuknecht. 2000. "Public Spending in the Twentieth Century: A Global Perspective." Cambridge University Press.

5 AUTHORITARIANISM AND TOTALITARIANISM

When we think about different kinds of regimes around the world, we tend to think only in terms of democracy or authoritarianism. In democratic societies, authoritarianism is often viewed almost as a temporary aberration until a subject people are able to throw off their fetters and join the free world. As such, it might seem less important to understand the complexities of authoritarianism than concentrate on how countries make the transition from there to democracy. But authoritarianism is a much more diverse and entrenched form of politics. Remember that it is democracy that is the newcomer to political life, having been established relatively recently in human history, and that less than half of the world's population currently lives in fully free countries.

Juan Linz and Alfred Stepan's chapter on nondemocratic regimes (1996) is in many ways a culmination of research these two scholars have been conducting since the 1960s. For them, to understand how countries become democratic, it is important to understand their nondemocratic form. Linz and Stepan lay out a comprehensive analysis of the difference between totalitarianism and authoritarianism, and how each has an impact on the most basic facets of nondemocratic rule. Why does this matter? Put simply, Linz and Stepan argue that the type of authoritarian or totalitarian regime strongly affects how and if democracy will take its place. The institutions of nondemocratic rule will shape the path open to democracy in the future. This kind of analysis, sometimes called "path dependent," has grown in recent years in the study of comparative politics and is consistent with a greater focus on institutions as actors in their own right.

Larry Diamond, another prominent scholar of authoritarianism and democracy, takes up this question of how authoritarianism and democracy interact with his 2002 piece on what he calls "hybrid regimes," or what is commonly referred to as "illiberal regimes". Over the past two decades we have seen an impressive advance of democracy around the world, as nondemocratic regimes have given way in Latin America, the former Soviet Union and Eastern Europe, Asia, and parts of Africa. Yet in many of these it may be little more than a façade, the shells of democratic life wrapped around *persistent authoritarian practices and institutions. More and more countries seem to be moving out of traditional authoritarianism, but it is unclear whether their transition to an illiberal regime is to be viewed positively as a "halfway house" to democracy, or rather a new incarnation of nondemocratic rule in a pseudo-democratic guise.*

Our next two pieces look at the relationship between authoritarianism and ideas. Jack Snyder and Karen Ballentine raise questions about the transition from authoritarianism to democracy in their 1996 work, "Nationalism and the Marketplace of Ideas." Scholars and policymakers who deal with political change and ethnic conflict often note that the former can lead to the latter (as discussed in Chapter 3), as the sudden shift in a regime and state power causes old or new conflicts between rival groups to emerge. The authors warn us to consider how the move from authoritarianism to democracy is not in itself a simple good. Without careful management, the transition may provide the opening for even worse outcomes.

If there are limits to democracy in generating peace, are there inherent limits to democracy as a whole? Are certain societies or cultures not amenable to democracy? In his 2002 piece "Islam and Democracy" Steven Fish tackles this touchy subject head on. Drawing on a range of data, Fish finds that Muslim countries are indeed highly prone to authoritarianism. The question is why? Standard explanations—that Muslim societies are more violent, less secular, or less trusting—are found not to stand up to scrutiny. Fish suggests that scholars should concentrate more on the status of women in Muslim societies and should consider how this may strengthen authoritarianism in various ways. Where women are disempowered and marginalized, democracy is weaker or less likely. This is a concern not just for Muslim countries, but also for the two most populous countries in the world, China and India, where pronounced gender disparity raises questions about their prospects for democracy.

JUAN J. LINZ AND ALFRED STEPAN

MODERN NONDEMOCRATIC REGIMES

Democratic transition and consolidation involve the movement from a nondemocratic to a democratic regime. However, specific polities may vary immensely in the *paths* available for transition and the unfinished *tasks* the new democracy must face before it is consoli-

dated. Our central endeavor in the next two chapters is to show how and why much—though of course not all—of such variation can be explained by prior regime type.

For over a quarter of a century the dominant conceptual framework among analysts interested in classifying the different political systems in the world has been the tripartite distinction between democratic, authoritarian, and totalitarian regimes. New paradigms emerge because they help analysts see commonalities and implications they had previously overlooked. When Juan Linz wrote his 1964 article "An Authoritarian Regime: Spain," he wanted to call attention to the fact that between what then were seen as the two major stable political poles—the democratic pole and the totalitarian pole—there existed a form of polity that had its own internal logic and was a steady regime type. Though this type was nondemocratic, Linz argued that it was fundamentally different from a totalitarian regime on four key dimensions—pluralism, ideology, leadership, and mobilization. This was of course what he termed an *authoritarian regime*. He defined them as: "political systems with limited, not responsible, political pluralism, without elaborate and guiding ideology, but with distinctive mentalities, without extensive nor intensive political mobilization, except at some points in their development, and in which a leader or occasionally a small group exercises power within formally ill-defined limits but actually quite predictable ones."[1]

In the 1960s, as analysts attempted to construct categories with which to compare and contrast all the systems in the world, the authoritarian category proved useful. As the new paradigm took hold among comparativists, two somewhat surprising conclusions emerged. First, it became increasingly apparent that more regimes were "authoritarian" than were "totalitarian" or "democratic" combined. Authoritarian regimes were thus the modal category of regime type in the modern world. Second, authoritarian regimes were not necessarily in transition to a different type of regime. As Linz's studies of Spain in the 1950s and early 1960s showed, the

From Juan J. Linz and Alfred Stepan, *Problems of Democratic Transition and Consolidation: Southern Europe, South America, and Post-Communist Europe* (Baltimore: Johns Hopkins University Press, 1996), pp. 38–54. Some of the authors' notes have been omitted.

four distinctive dimensions of an authoritarian regime—limited pluralism, mentality, somewhat constrained leadership, and weak mobilization—could cohere for a long period as a reinforcing and integrated system that was relatively stable.

Typologies rise or fall according to their analytic usefulness to researchers. In our judgment, the existing tripartite regime classification has not only become less useful to democratic theorists and practitioners than it once was, it has also become an obstacle. Part of the case for typology change proceeds from the implications of the empirical universe we need to analyze. Very roughly, if we were looking at the world of the mid-1980s, how many countries could conceivably be called "democracies" of ten years' duration? And how many countries were very close to the totalitarian pole for that entire period? Answers have, of course, an inherently subjective dimension, particularly as regards the evaluation of the evidence used to classify countries along the different criteria used in the typology. Fortunately, however, two independently organized studies attempt to measure most of the countries in the world as to their political rights and civil liberties. The criteria used in the studies are explicit, and there is a very high degree of agreement in the results. If we use these studies and the traditional tripartite regime type distinction, it turns out that more than 90 percent of modern nondemocratic regimes would have to share the same typological space—"authoritarian."[2] Obviously, with so many heterogenous countries sharing the same typological "starting place," this typology of regime type cannot tell us much about the extremely significant range of variation in possible transition paths and consolidation tasks that we believe in fact exists. Our purpose in the rest of this chapter is to reformulate the tripartite paradigm of regime type so as to make it more helpful in the analysis of *transition paths* and *consolidation tasks*. We propose therefore a revised typology, consisting of "democratic," "authoritarian," "totalitarian," "posttotalitarian," and "sultanistic" regimes.

Democracy

To start with the democratic type of regime, there are of course significant variations within democracy. However, we believe that such important categories as "consociational democracy" and "majoritarian democracy" are subtypes of democracy and not different regime types. Democracy as a regime type seems to us to be of sufficient value to be retained and not to need further elaboration at this point in the book.

Totalitarianism

We also believe that the concept of a totalitarian regime as an ideal type, with some close historical approximations, has enduring value. If a regime has eliminated almost all pre-existing political, economic, and social pluralism, has a unified, articulated, guiding, utopian ideology, has intensive and extensive mobilization, and has a leadership that rules, often charismatically, with undefined limits and great unpredictability and vulnerability for elites and nonelites alike, then it seems to us that it still makes historical and conceptual sense to call this a regime with strong totalitarian tendencies.

If we accept the continued conceptual utility of the democratic and totalitarian regime types, the area in which further typological revision is needed concerns the regimes that are clearly neither democratic nor totalitarian. By the early 1980s, the number of countries that were clearly totalitarian or were attempting to create such regimes had in fact been declining for some time. As many Soviet-type regimes began to change after Stalin's death in 1953, they no longer conformed to the totalitarian model, as research showed. This change created conceptual confusion. Some scholars argued that the totalitarian category itself was wrong. Others wanted to call post-Stalinist regimes authoritarian. Neither of these approaches seems to us fully satisfactory. Empirically, of course, most of

the Soviet-type systems in the 1980s were not totalitarian. However, the "Soviet type" regimes, with the exception of Poland * * *, could not be understood in their distinctiveness by including them in the category of an authoritarian regime.

The literature on Soviet-type regimes correctly drew attention to regime characteristics that were no longer totalitarian and opened up promising new studies of policy-making. One of these perspectives was "institutional pluralism." However, in our judgment, to call these post-Stalinist polities *pluralistic* missed some extremely important features that could hardly be called pluralistic. Pluralist democratic theory, especially the "group theory" variant explored by such writers as Arthur Bentley and David Truman, starts with *individuals in civil society* who enter into numerous freely formed interest groups that are relatively autonomous and often criss-crossing. The many groups in civil society attempt to aggregate their interests and compete against each other in political society to influence state policies. However, the "institutional pluralism" that some writers discerned in the Soviet Union was radically different, in that almost all the pluralistic conflict occurred in *regime-created organizations within the party-state* itself. Conceptually, therefore, this form of competition and conflict is actually closer to what political theorists call *bureaucratic politics* than it is to *pluralistic politics*.

Rather than forcing these Soviet-type regimes into the existing typology of totalitarian, authoritarian, and democratic regimes, we believe we should expand that typology by explicating a distinctive regime type that we will call *post-totalitarian*.[3] Methodologically, we believe this category is justified because on each of the four dimensions of regime type—pluralism, ideology, leadership, and mobilization—there can be a post-totalitarian ideal type that is different from a totalitarian, authoritarian, or democratic ideal type. Later in this chapter we will also rearticulate the argument for considering sultanism as a separate ideal-type regime.

To state our argument in bold terms, we first present a schematic presentation of how the five ideal-type regimes we propose—democratic, totalitarian, post-totalitarian, authoritarian, and sultanistic—differ from each other on each one of the four constituent characteristics of regime type (table 1). In the following chapter we make explicit what we believe are the implications of each regime type for democratic transition paths and the tasks of democratic consolidation.

Post-Totalitarianism

Our task here is to explore how, on each of the four dimensions of regime type, post-totalitarianism is different from totalitarianism, as well as different from authoritarianism. Where appropriate we will also call attention to some under-theorized characteristics of both totalitarian and post-totalitarian regimes that produce dynamic pressures for out-of-type change. We do not subscribe to the view that either type is static.

Post-totalitarianism, as table 1 implies, can encompass a continuum varying from "early post-totalitarianism," to "frozen post-totalitarianism," to "mature post-totalitarianism." Early post-totalitarianism is very close to the totalitarian ideal type but differs from it on at least one key dimension, normally some constraints on the leader. There can be frozen post-totalitarianism in which, despite the persistent tolerance of some civil society critics of the regime, almost all the other control mechanisms of the party-state stay in place for a long period and do not evolve (e.g., Czechoslovakia, from 1977 to 1989). Or there can be mature post-totalitarianism in which there has been significant change in all the dimensions of the post-totalitarian regime except that politically the leading role of the official party is still sacrosanct (e.g., Hungary from 1982 to 1988, which eventually evolved by late 1988 very close to an out-of-type change).

Concerning *pluralism*, the defining characteristic of totalitarianism is that there is no political, economic, or social pluralism in the polity and that pre-existing sources of pluralism have been uprooted or systematically repressed. In an authoritarian regime there is some limited political pluralism and often quite extensive economic and social pluralism. In an authoritarian regime, many of the manifestations of the limited political pluralism and the more extensive social and economic pluralism predate the authoritarian regime. How does pluralism in post-totalitarian regimes contrast with the near absence of pluralism in totalitarian regimes and the limited pluralism of authoritarian regimes?

In mature post-totalitarianism, there is a much more important and complex play of institutional pluralism within the state than in totalitarianism. Also, in contrast to totalitarianism, post-totalitarianism normally has a much more significant degree of social pluralism, and in mature post-totalitarianism there is often discussion of a "second culture" or a "parallel culture." Evidence of this is found in such things as a robust underground *samizdat* literature with multi-issue journals of the sort not possible under totalitarianism.[4] This growing pluralism is simultaneously a dynamic source of vulnerability for the post-totalitarian regime and a dynamic source of strength for an emerging democratic opposition. For example, this "second culture" can be sufficiently powerful that, even though leaders of the second culture will frequently be imprisoned, in a mature post-totalitarian regime opposition leaders can generate substantial followings and create enduring oppositional organizations in civil society. At moments of crisis, therefore, a mature post-totalitarian regime can have a cadre of a democratic opposition based in civil society with much greater potential to form a democratic political opposition than would be available in a totalitarian regime. A mature post-totalitarian regime can also feature the coexistence of a state-planned economy with extensive partial market

Table 1. Major Modern Regime Ideal Types and Their Defining Characteristics

Characteristic	Democracy	Authoritarianism	Totalitarianism	Post-totalitarianism	Sultanism
Pluralism	Responsible political pluralism reinforced by extensive areas of pluralist autonomy in economy, society, and internal life of organizations. Legally protected pluralism consistent with "societal corporatism" but not "state corporatism."	Political system with limited, not responsible political pluralism. Often quite extensive social and economic pluralism. In authoritarian regimes most of pluralism had roots in society before the establishment of the regime. Often some space for semiopposition.	No significant economic, social, or political pluralism. Official party has *de jure* and *de facto* monopoly of power. Party has eliminated almost all pretotalitarian pluralism. No space for second economy or parallel society.	Limited, but not responsible social, economic, and institutional pluralism. Almost no political pluralism because party still formally has monopoly of power. May have "second economy," but state still the overwhelming presence. Most manifestations of pluralism in "flattened polity" grew out of tolerated state structures or dissident groups consciously formed in opposition to totalitarian regime. In mature post-totalitarianism opposition often creates "second culture" or "parallel society."	Economic and social pluralism does not disappear but is subject to unpredictable and despotic intervention. No group or individual in civil society, political society, or the state is free from sultan's exercise of despotic power. No rule of law. Low institutionalization. High fusion of private and public.
Ideology	Extensive intellectual commitment to citizenship and procedural rules of contestation. Not teleological. Respect for rights of minorities, state of law, and value of individualism.	Political system without elaborate and guiding ideology but with distinctive mentalities.	Elaborate and guiding ideology that articulates a reachable utopia. Leaders, individuals, and groups derive most of their sense of mission, legitimation, and often specific policies from their commitment to some holistic conception of humanity and society.	Guiding ideology still officially exists and is part of the social reality. But weakened commitment to or faith in utopia. Shift of emphasis from ideology to programmatic consensus that presumably is based on rational decision-making and limited debate without too much reference to ideology.	Highly arbitrary manipulation of symbols. Extreme glorification of ruler. No elaborate or guiding ideology or even distinctive mentalities outside of despotic personalism. No attempt to justify major initiatives on the basis of ideology. Pseudo-ideology not believed by staff, subjects, or outside world.
Mobilization	Participation via autonomously generated organization of civil society and competing parties of political society guaranteed by a system of law. Value is on low regime mobilization but high citizen participation. Diffuse effort by regime to induce good citizenship and patriotism. Toleration of peaceful and orderly opposition.	Political system without extensive or intensive political mobilization except at some points in their development.	Extensive mobilization into a vast array of regime-created obligatory organizations. Emphasis on activism of cadres and militants. Effort at mobilization of enthusiasm. Private life is decried.	Progressive loss of interest by leaders and nonleaders involved in organizing mobilization. Routine mobilization of population within state-sponsored organizations to achieve a minimum degree of conformity and compliance. Many "cadres" and "militants" are mere careerists and opportunists. Boredom, withdrawal, and ultimately privatization of population's values become an accepted fact.	Low but occasional manipulative mobilization of a ceremonial type by coercive or clientelistic methods without permanent organization. Periodic mobilization of parastate groups who use violence against groups targeted by sultan.

Table 1. *(continued)*

Characteristic	Democracy	Authoritarianism	Totalitarianism	Post-totalitarianism	Sultanism
Leadership	Top leadership produced by free elections and must be exercised within constitutional limits and state of law. Leadership must be periodically subjected to and produced by free elections.	Political system in which a leader or occasionally a small group exercises power within formally ill-defined but actually quite predictable norms. Effort at cooptation of old elite groups. Some autonomy in state careers and in military.	Totalitarian leadership rules with undefined limits and great unpredictability for members and nonmembers. Often charismatic. Recruitment to top leadership highly dependent on success and commitment in party organization.	Growing emphasis by post-totalitarian political elite on personal security. Checks on top leadership via party structures, procedures, and "internal democracy." Top leaders are seldom charismatic. Recruitment to top leadership restricted to official party but less dependent upon building a career within party's organization. Top leaders can come from party technocrats in state apparatus.	Highly personalistic and arbitrary. No rational-legal constraints. Strong dynastic tendency. No autonomy in state careers. Leader unencumbered by ideology. Compliance to leaders based on intense fear and personal rewards. Staff of leader drawn from members of his family, friends, business associates, or men directly involved in use of violence to sustain the regime. Staff's position derives from their purely personal submission to the ruler.

experiments in the state sector that can generate a "red bourgeoisie" of state sector managers and a growing but subordinate private sector, especially in agriculture, commerce and services.

However, in a post-totalitarian regime this social and economic pluralism is different in degree and kind from that found in an authoritarian regime. It is different in degree because there is normally more social and economic pluralism in an authoritarian regime (in particular there is normally a more autonomous private sector, somewhat greater religious freedom, and a greater amount of above-ground cultural production). The difference in kind is typologically even more important. In a post-totalitarian society, the historical reference both for the power holders of the regime and the opposition is the previous totalitarian regime. By definition, the existence of a previous totalitarian regime means that most of the pre-existing sources of responsible and organized pluralism have been eliminated or repressed and a totalitarian order has been established. There is therefore an active effort at "detotalitarianization" on the part of oppositional currents in civil society. Much of the

emotional and organizational drive of the opposition in civil society is thus consciously crafted to forge alternatives to the political, economic, and social structures created by the totalitarian regime, structures that still play a major role in the post-totalitarian society. Much of the second culture therefore is not traditional in form but is found in new movements that arise out of the totalitarian experience. There can also be a state-led detotalitarianization in which the regime itself begins to eliminate some of the most extreme features of the monist experience. Thus, if there is growing "institutional pluralism," or a growing respect for procedure and law, or a newly tolerated private sector, it should be understood as a kind of pluralism that emerges *out of* the previous totalitarian regime.

However, it is typologically and politically important to stress that there are significant limits to pluralism in post-totalitarian societies. In contrast to an authoritarian regime, there is *no* limited and relatively autonomous pluralism in the explicitly political realm. The official party in all post-totalitarian regimes is still legally accorded the leading role in the polity. The institutional pluralism of a post-totalitarian regime should not be confused with political pluralism; rather, institutional pluralism is exercised within the party-state or within the newly tolerated second economy or parallel culture. The pluralism of the parallel culture or the second culture should be seen as a *social* pluralism that may have political implications. But we must insist that the party and the regime leaders in post-totalitarian regimes, unless they experience out-of-type change, accord *no* legitimacy or responsibility to nonofficial political pluralism.[5] Even the formal pluralism of satellite parties becomes politically relevant only in the final stages of the regime after the transition is in progress.

When we turn to the dimension of *leadership*, we also see central tendencies that distinguish totalitarian from authoritarian leadership. Totalitarian leadership is unconstrained by laws and procedures and is often charismatic. The leadership can come from the revolutionary party or movement, but members of this core are as vulnerable to the sharp policy and ideological changes enunciated by the leader (even more so in terms of the possibility of losing their lives) as the rest of the population. By contrast, in the Linzian scheme, authoritarian leadership is characterized by a political system in which a leader or occasionally a small group exercises power within formally ill-defined but actually quite predictable norms. There are often extensive efforts to co-opt old elite groups into leadership roles, and there is some autonomy in state careers and in the military.

As in a totalitarian regime, post-totalitarian leadership is still exclusively restricted to the revolutionary party or movement. However, in contrast to a totalitarian regime, post-totalitarian leaders tend to be more bureaucratic and state technocratic than charismatic. The central core of a post-totalitarian regime normally strives successfully to enhance its security and lessen its fear by reducing the range of arbitrary discretion allowed to the top leadership.

In contrast to those who say that the totali-

tarian regime concept is static, we believe that, when an opportunity presents itself (such as the death of the maximum leader), the top elite's desire to reduce the future leader's absolute discretion is predictably a dynamic source of pressure for out-of-type regime change from totalitarianism to post-totalitarianism. The post-totalitarian leadership is thus typologically closer in this respect to authoritarian leadership, in that the leader rules within unspecified but in reality reasonably predictable limits. However, the leadership in these two regime types still differs fundamentally. Post-totalitarian leadership is exclusively recruited from party members who develop their careers in the party organization itself, the bureaucracy, or the technocratic apparatus of the state. They all are thus recruited from the structures created by the regime. In sharp contrast, in most authoritarian regimes, the norm is for the regime to co-opt much of the leadership from groups that have some power, presence, and legitimacy that does not derive directly from the regime itself. Indeed, the authoritarian regime has often been captured by powerful fragments of the pre-existing society. In some authoritarian regimes, even access to top positions can be established not by political loyalties as much as by some degree of professional and technical expertise and some degree of competition through examinations that are open to the society as a whole. In mature post-totalitarian regimes, technical competence becomes increasingly important, but we should remember that the original access to professional training was controlled by political criteria. Also, the competences that are accepted or recognized in post-totalitarian systems are technical or managerial but do not include skills developed in a broader range of fields such as the law, religious organizations, or independent business or labor.

The limited party-bureaucratic-technocratic pluralism under post-totalitarianism does not give the regime the flexibility for change within the regime that co-optation of nonregime elites can give to many authoritarian regimes. The desire to resist the personalized leadership of the First Secretary–ideologue can be a source of change from totalitarian to post-totalitarian, but it can also lead eventually to the oligarchic leadership of aging men supported by the nomenklatura. Attempts at rejuvenation at the top by including or co-opting new men and women from the outside are normally very limited. In extreme cases (i.e., the GDR and post-1968 Czechoslovakia), frozen post-totalitarianism shows geriatric tendencies. Under crisis circumstances, the inability to renovate leadership, not so paradoxically, is a potential source of dynamic change in that a frozen post-totalitarian regime, with its old and narrow leadership base, has a very limited capacity to negotiate. Such a leadership structure, if it is not able to repress opponents in a crisis, is particularly vulnerable to *collapse*. One of the reasons why midlevel cadres in the once all-powerful coercive apparatus might, in time of crisis, let the regime collapse rather than fire upon the democratic opposition has to do with the role of ideology in post-totalitarianism.

The contrast between the role of *ideology* in a totalitarian system and in a post-totalitarian system is sharp, but it is more one of behavior and belief than one of official canon. In the area of ideology, the dynamic potential for change from a totalitarian to a post-totalitarian regime, both on the part of the cadres and on the part of the society, is the growing empirical disjunction between official ideological claims and reality. This disjunction produces lessened ideological commitment on the part of the cadres and growing criticism of the regime by groups in civil society. In fact, many of the new critics in civil society emerge out of the ranks of former true believers, who argue that the regime does not—or, worse, cannot—advance its own goals. The pressures created by this tension between doctrine and reality often contributes to an out-of-type shift from a totalitarian regime effort to mobilize enthusiasm to a post-totalitarian effort to maintain

acquiescence. In the post-totalitarian phase, the elaborate and guiding ideology created under the totalitarian regime still exists as the official state canon, but among many leaders there is a weakened commitment to and faith in utopia. Among much of the population, the official canon is seen as an obligatory ritual, and among groups in the "parallel society" or "second culture," there is constant reference to the first culture as a "living lie." This is another source of weakness, of the "hollowing out" of the post-totalitarian regime's apparent strength.

The role of ideology in a post-totalitarian regime is thus diminished from its role under totalitarianism, but it is still quite different from the role of ideology in an authoritarian regime. Most authoritarian regimes have diffuse nondemocratic mentalities, but they do not have highly articulated ideologies concerning the leading role of the party, interest groups, religion, and many other aspects of civil society, political society, the economy, and the state that still exist in a regime we would call post-totalitarian. Therefore, a fundamental contrast between a post-totalitarian and authoritarian regime is that in a post-totalitarian regime there is an important ideological legacy that cannot be ignored and that cannot be questioned officially. The state-sanctioned ideology has a *social presence* in the organizational life of the post-totalitarian polity. Whether it expresses itself in the extensive array of state-sponsored organizations or in the domain of incipient but still officially controlled organizations, ideology is part of the social reality of a post-totalitarian regime to a greater degree than in most authoritarian regimes.

The relative de-ideologization of post-totalitarian regimes and the weakening of the belief in utopia as a foundation of legitimacy mean that, as in many authoritarian regimes, there is a growing effort in a post-totalitarian polity to legitimate the regime on the basis of performance criteria. The gap between the original utopian elements of the ideology and the increasing legitimation efforts on the basis of efficacy, particularly when the latter fails, is one of the sources of weakness in post-totalitarian regimes. Since democracies base their claim to obedience on the procedural foundations of democratic citizenship, as well as performance, they have a layer of insulation against weak performance not available to most post-totalitarian or authoritarian regimes. The weakening of utopian ideology that is a characteristic of post-totalitarianism thus opens up a new dynamic of regime vulnerabilities—or, from the perspective of democratic transition, new opportunities—that can be exploited by the democratic opposition. For example, the discrepancy between the constant reiteration of the importance of ideology and the ideology's growing irrelevance to policymaking or, worse, its transparent contradiction with social reality contribute to undermining the commitment and faith of the middle and lower cadres in the regime. Such a situation can help contribute to the rapid collapse of the regime if midlevel functionaries of the coercive apparatus have grave doubts about their right to shoot citizens who are protesting against the regime and its ideology, as we shall see when we discuss events in 1989 in East Germany and Czechoslovakia.

The final typological difference we need to explore concerns *mobilization*. Most authoritarian regimes never develop complex, all-inclusive networks of association whose purpose is the mobilization of the population. They may have brief periods of intensive mobilization, but these are normally less intensive than in a totalitarian regime and less extensive than in a post-totalitarian regime. In totalitarian regimes, however, there is extensive and intensive mobilization of society into a vast array of regime-created organizations and activities. Because utopian goals are intrinsic to the regime, there is a great effort to mobilize enthusiasm to activate cadres, and most leaders emerge out of these cadres. In the totalitarian system, "privatized" bourgeois individuals at home with their family and friends and enjoying life in the small circle of their own choosing are decried.

In post-totalitarian regimes, the extensive array of institutions of regime-created mobilization vehicles still dominate associational life. However, they have lost their intensity. Membership is still generalized and obligatory but tends to generate more boredom than enthusiasm. State-technocratic employment is an alternative to cadre activism as a successful career path, as long as there is "correct" participation in official organizations. Instead of the mobilization of enthusiasm that can be so functional in a totalitarian regime, the networks of ritualized mobilization in a post-totalitarian regime can produce a "cost" of time away from technocratic tasks for professionals and a cost of boredom and flight into private life by many other people. When there is no structural crisis and especially when there is no perception of an available alternative, such privatization is not necessarily a problem for a post-totalitarian regime. Thus, Kadar's famous saying, "Those who are not against us are for us," is a saying that is conceivable only in a post-totalitarian regime, not in a totalitarian one. However, if the performance of a post-totalitarian as opposed to a totalitarian regime is so poor that the personal rewards of private life are eroded, then privatization and apathy may contribute to a new dynamic—especially if alternatives are seen as possible—of crises of "exit," "voice," and "loyalty."[6]

Let us conclude our discussion of post-totalitarianism with a summary of its political and ideological weaknesses. We do this to help enrich the discussion of why these regimes collapsed so rapidly once they entered into prolonged stagnation and the USSR withdrew its extensive coercive support. Indeed in chapter 17, "Varieties of Post-totalitarian Regimes," we develop a theoretical and empirical argument about why frozen post-totalitarian regimes are more vulnerable to collapse than are authoritarian or totalitarian regimes.

Totalitarianism, democracy, and even many authoritarian regimes begin with "genetic" legitimacy among their core supporters, given the historical circumstances that led to the establishment of these regimes. By contrast, post-totalitarianism regimes do not have such a founding genetic legitimacy because they emerge out of the routinization, decay, or elite fears of the totalitarian regime. Post-totalitarian regimes, because of coercive resources they inherit and the related weaknesses of organized opposition, can give the appearance of as much or more stability than authoritarian regimes; if external support is withdrawn, however, their inner loss of purpose and commitment make them vulnerable to collapse.

Post-totalitarian politics was a result in part of the moving away from Stalinism, but also of social changes in Communist societies. Post-totalitarian regimes did away with the worst aspects of repression but at the same time maintained most mechanisms of control. Although less bloody than under Stalinism, the presence of security services—like the Stasi in the GDR—sometimes became more pervasive. Post-totalitarianism could have led to moderate reforms in the economy, like those discussed at the time of the Prague Spring, but the Brezhnev restoration stopped dynamic adaptation in the USSR and in most other Soviet-type systems, except for Hungary and Poland.

Post-totalitarianism had probably less legitimacy for the ruling elites and above all the middle-level cadres than had a more totalitarian system. The loss of the utopian component of the ideology and the greater reliance on performance (which after some initial success did not continue) left the regimes vulnerable and ultimately made the use of massive repression less justifiable. Passive compliance and careerism opened the door to withdrawal into private life, weakening the regime so that the opposition could ultimately force it to negotiate or to collapse when it could not rely on coercion.

The weakness of post-totalitarian regimes has not yet been fully analyzed and explained but probably can be understood only by keeping in mind the enormous hopes and energies initially associated with Marxism-Leninism that in the past explained the emergence of totalitarianism and its appeal.[7] Many distinguished and influential Western intellectuals admired or excused Leninism and in the 1930s even Stalinism, but few Western intellectuals on the left could muster enthusiasm for post-totalitarianism in the USSR or even for perestroika and glasnost.

As we shall see in part 4, the emergence and evolution of post-totalitarianism can be the result of three distinct but often interconnected processes: (1) deliberate policies of the rulers to soften or reform the totalitarian system (detotalitarianism by choice), (2) the internal "hollowing out" of the totalitarian regimes' structures and an internal erosion of the cadres' ideological belief in the system (detotalitarianism by decay), and (3) the creation of social, cultural, and even economic spaces that resist or escape totalitarian control (detotalitarianism by societal conquest).

"Sultanism"

A large group of polities, such as Haiti under the Duvaliers, the Dominican Republic under Trujillo, the Central African Republic under Bokassa, the Philippines under Marcos, Iran under the Shah, Romania under Ceauşescu, and North Korea under Kim Il Sung, have had strong tendencies toward an extreme form of patrimonialism that Weber called *sultanism*. For Weber,

> *patrimonialism* and, in the extreme case, *sultanism* tend to arise whenever traditional domination develops an administration and a military force which are purely personal instruments of the master. . . . Where domination . . . operates primarily on the basis of discretion, it will be called *sultanism* . . . The non-traditional element is not, however, rationalized in impersonal terms, but consists only in the extreme development of the ruler's discretion. It is this which distinguishes it from every form of rational authority.[8]

Weber did not intend the word *sultanism* to imply religious claims to obedience. In fact, under Ottoman rule, the ruler held two distinct offices and titles, that of sultan and that of caliph. Initially, the Ottoman ruler was a sultan, and only after the conquest of Damascus did he assume the title of caliph, which entailed religious authority. After the defeat of Turkey in World War I and the proclamation of the republic, the former ruler lost his title of sultan but retained his religious title of caliph until Atatürk eventually forced him to relinquish even that title. Our point is that the secular and religious dimensions of his authority were conceptually and historically distinguished. Furthermore, the term *sultan* should not be analytically bound to the Middle East. Just as there are mandarins in New Delhi and Paris as well as in Peking and there is a macho style of politics in the Pentagon as well as in Buenos Aires, there are sultanistic rulers in Africa and the Caribbean as well as in the Middle East. What we do want the term *sultanism* to connote is a generic style of domination and regime rulership that is, as Weber says, an extreme form of patrimonialism. In sultanism, the private and the public are fused, there is a strong tendency toward familial power and dynastic succession, there is no distinction between a state career and personal service to the ruler, there is a lack of rationalized impersonal ideology, economic success depends on a personal relationship to the ruler, and, most of all, the ruler acts only according to his own unchecked discretion, with no larger, impersonal goals.

Table 1 gives substantial details on what a sultanistic type is in relation to pluralism, ideology, mobilization, and leadership. In this section we attempt to highlight differences between sultanism, totalitarianism, and authoritarianism because, while we believe they are distinct ideal types, in any concrete case a specific polity could have a mix of some sultanistic and some authoritarian tendencies (a combination that might open up a variety of transition options) or a mix of sultanistic and totalitarian tendencies (a combination that would tend to eliminate numerous transition options).

In his long essay, "Totalitarian and Authoritarian Regimes," Juan Linz discussed the special features that make sultanism a distinctive type of nondemocratic regime.[9] Since the sultanistic regime type has not been widely accepted in the literature, we believe it will be useful for us to highlight systematically its distinctive qualities so as to make more clear the implications of this type of regime for the patterns of democratic resistance and the problems of democratic consolidation.

In sultanism, there is a high fusion by the ruler of the private and the public. The sultanistic polity becomes the personal domain of the sultan. In this domain there is no rule of law and there is low institutionalization. In sultanism there may be extensive social and economic pluralism, but almost never political pluralism, because political power is so directly related to the ruler's person. However, the essential reality in a sultanistic regime is that all individuals, groups, and institutions are permanently subject to the unpredictable and despotic intervention of the sultan, and thus all pluralism is precarious.

In authoritarianism there may or may not be a rule of law, space for a semi-opposition, or space for regime moderates who might establish links with opposition moderates, and there are normally extensive social and economic activities that function within a secure framework of relative autonomy. Under sultanism, however, there is no rule of law, no space for a semiopposition, no space for regime moderates who might negotiate with democratic moderates, and no sphere of the economy or civil society that is not subject to the despotic exercise of the sultan's will. As we demonstrate in the next chapter, this critical difference between pluralism in authoritarian and sultanistic regimes has immense implications for the types of transition that are *available* in an authoritarian regime but *unavailable* in a sultanistic regime.

There is also a sharp contrast in the function and consequences of ideology between totalitarian and sultanistic regimes. In a totalitarian regime not only is there an elaborate and guiding ideology, but ideology has the function of legitimating the regime, and rulers are often somewhat constrained by their own value system and ideology. They or their followers, or both, believe in that ideology as a point of reference and justification for their actions. In contrast, a sultanistic ruler characteristically has no elaborate and guiding ideology. There may be highly personalistic statements with pretensions of being an ideology, often named after the sultan, but this ideology is elaborated after the ruler has assumed power, is subject to extreme manipulation, and, most importantly, is not believed to be constraining on the ruler and is relevant only as long as he practices it. Thus, there could be questions raised as to whether Stalin's practices and statements were consistent with Marxism-Leninism, but there would be no reason for anyone to debate whether Trujillo's statements were consistent with Trujilloism. The contrast between authoritarian and sultanistic regimes is less stark over ideology; however, the distinctive mentalities that are a part of most authoritarian alliances are normally more constraining on rulers than is the sultan's idiosyncratic and personal ideology.

The extensive and intensive mobilization that is a feature of totalitarianism is seldom found in a sultanistic regime because of its low degree of institutionalization and its low commitment to an overarching ideology. The low degree of organization means that any mobilization that does occur is uneven and sporadic. Probably the biggest difference between sultanistic mobilization and authoritarian mobilization is the tendency within sultanism (most dramatic in the case of the Duvalier's Tonton Macoutes in Haiti) to use para-state groups linked to the sultan to wield violence and terror against anyone who opposes the ruler's will. These para-state groups are not modern bureaucracies with generalized norms and procedures; rather, they are direct extensions of the sultan's will. They have no significant institutional autonomy. As Weber stressed,

they are purely "personal treatments of the master."

Finally, how does leadership differ in sultanism, totalitarianism, and authoritarianism? The essence of sultanism is *unrestrained personal rulership*. This personal rulership is, as we have seen, unconstrained by ideology, rational-legal norms, or any balance of power. "Support is based not on a coincidence of interest between preexisting privileged social groups and the ruler but on interests created by his rule, rewards he offers for loyalty, and the fear of his vengeance."[10]

In one key respect leadership under sultanism and totalitarianism is similar. In both regimes the leader rules with undefined limits on his power and there is great unpredictability for elites and nonelites alike. In this respect, a Stalin and a Somoza are alike. However, there are important differences. The elaborate ideology, with its sense of nonpersonal and public mission, is meant to play an important legitimating function in totalitarian regimes. The ideological pronouncements of a totalitarian leader are taken seriously not only by his followers and cadres, but also by the society and intellectuals, including—in the cases of Leninism, Stalinism, and Marxism (and even fascism)—by intellectuals outside the state in which the leader exercises control. This places a degree of organizational, social, and ideological constraint on totalitarian leadership that is not present in sultanistic leadership. Most importantly, the intense degree to which rulership is personal in sultanism makes the *dynastic* dimension of rulership normatively acceptable and empirically common, whereas the public claims of totalitarianism make dynastic ambition, if not unprecedented, at least aberrant.

The leadership dimension shows an even stronger contrast between authoritarianism and sultanism. As Linz stated in his discussion of authoritarianism, leadership is exercised in an authoritarian regime "with formally ill-defined but actually quite predictable" norms.[11] In most authoritarian regimes some bureaucratic entities play an important part. These bureaucratic entities often retain or generate their own norms, which imply that there are procedural and normative limits on what leaders can ask them to do in their capacity as, for example, military officers, judges, tax officials, or police officers. However, a sultanistic leader simply "demands unconditional administrative compliance, for the official's loyalty to his office is not an impersonal commitment to impersonal tasks that define the extent and content of his office, but rather a servant's loyalty based on a strictly personal relationship to the ruler and an obligation that in principle permits no limitation."[12]

We have now spelled our the central tendencies of five ideal-type regimes in the modern world, four of which are nondemocratic. We are ready for the next step, which is to explore why and how the *type* of prior nondemocratic regime has an important effect on the democratic transition paths available and the tasks to be addressed before democracy can be consolidated.

NOTES

1. Juan J. Linz, "An Authoritarian Regime: The Case of Spain," in Erik Allardt and Yrjö Littunen, eds., *Cleavages, Ideologies and Party Systems* (Helsinki: Transactions of the Westermarck Society, 1964), 291–342. Reprinted in Erik Allardt and Stein Rokkan, eds., *Mass Politics: Studies in Political Sociology* (New York: Free Press, 1970). The definition is found on 255.

2. We arrive at this conclusion in the following fashion. The annual survey coordinated by Raymond D. Gastil employs a 7-point scale of the political rights and civil liberties dimensions of democracy. With the help of a panel of scholars, Gastil, from 1978 to 1987, classified annually 167 countries on this scale. For our purposes if we call the universe of democracies those countries that from 1978 to 1987 never received a score of lower than 2 on the Gastil scale for political

rights and 3 for civil liberty, we come up with 42 countries. This is very close to the number of countries that Coppedge and Reinicke classify as "full polyarchies" in their independent study of the year 1985. Since our interest is in how countries become democracies we will exclude those 42 countries from our universe of analysis. This would leave us with 125 countries in the universe we want to explore.

If we then decide to call long-standing "totalitarian" regimes those regimes that received the lowest possible score on political rights and civil liberties on the Gastil scale for each year in the 1978–1987 period, we would have a total of nine countries that fall into the totalitarian classification. Thus, if one used the traditional typology, the Gastil scale would imply that 116 of 125 countries, or 92.8 percent of the universe under analysis, would have to be placed in the same typological space. See Gastil, *Freedom in the World*, 54–65.

3. Juan Linz, in his "Totalitarian and Authoritarian Regimes," in Fred I. Greenstein and Nelson W. Polsby, eds., *Handbook of Political Science* (Reading, Mass.: Addison-Wesley Publishing Co., 1975), 3:175–411, analyzed what he called "post-totalitarian authoritarian regimes," see 336–50. Here, with our focus on the available paths to democratic transition and the tasks of democratic consolidation, it seems to both of us that it is more useful to treat post-totalitarian regimes not as a subtype of authoritarianism, but as an ideal type in its own right.

4. For example, in mature post-totalitarian Hungary the most influential *samizdat* publication, *Beszélö*, from 1982 to 1989, was issued as a quarterly with publication runs of 20,000. Information supplied to Alfred Stepan by the publisher and editorial board member, Miklós Haraszti. Budapest, August 1994.

5. Hungary in 1988–89 represents a mature post-totalitarian regime which, by engaging

in extensive detotalitarianization and by increasingly recognizing the legitimacy of other parties, had experienced significant out-of-type changes even before the Communist Party lost power. See chapter 17.

6. The reference, of course, is to Albert Hirschman, *Exit, Voice and Loyalty* (Cambridge: Harvard University Press, 1970), 59. For a fascinating discussion of this dynamic in relation to the collapse of the GDR, see Hirschman, "Exit, Voice and the Fate of the German Democratic Republic: An Essay on Conceptual History," *World Politics* 45:2 (January 1993): 173–202.

7. On the ideological and moral attractiveness of revolutionary Marxist-Leninism as a total system and the "vacuum" left in the wake of its collapse, see Ernest Gellner, "Homeland of the Unrevolution," *Daedalus* (Summer 1993): 141–54.

8. Max Weber, *Economy and Society: An Outline of Interpretive Sociology*, ed. Guenther Roth and Claus Wittich (Berkeley: University of California Press, 1978), 1:231, 232. Italics in the original.

9. Linz, "*Totalitarian and Authoritarian Regimes*," 259–63.

10. Ibid., 260.

11. Ibid., 255.

12. Ibid., 260.

LARRY DIAMOND

THINKING ABOUT HYBRID REGIMES

Is Russia a democracy? What about Ukraine, Nigeria, Indonesia, Turkey, or Venezuela? There was a time when these were simple questions of regime classification. But the empirical reality in these countries is a lot messier than it was two decades ago, and so, in a way, is the never-ending dialogue on how to think about and classify regimes.

Few conceptual issues in political science have been subjected to closer or more prolific scrutiny in recent decades than this problem of "what democracy is . . . and is not,"[1] and which regimes are "democracies" and which not. We are replete with definitions and standards and tools of measurement. But the curious fact is that—a quarter-century into the "third wave" of democratization and the renaissance it brought in comparative democratic studies—we are still far from consensus on what constitutes "democracy." And we still struggle to classify ambiguous regimes.

Some insist on a fairly robust (though still procedural) definition of democracy, like Robert Dahl's "polarchy." By this conception, democracy requires not only free, fair, and competitive elections, but also the freedoms that make them truly meaningful (such as freedom of organization and freedom of expression), alternative sources of information, and institutions to ensure that government policies depend on the votes and preferences of citizens. Some measure democracy by a "minimalist" standard like Joseph Schumpeter's: a political system in which the principal positions of power are filled "through a competitive struggle for the people's vote."[2] Yet contemporary applications of this electoral conception heavily overlap with Dahl's polyarchy by also implying the civil and political freedoms necessary for political debate and electoral campaigning.

From *Journal of Democracy* 13, no. 2 (2002), pp. 21–35.

Even if we agree to apply a minimalist, electoral standard for democracy, vexing questions remain. If, following Samuel Huntington, a system is democratic when "its most powerful collective decision makers are selected through fair, honest, and periodic elections in which candidates freely compete for votes,"[3] what constitutes "fair, honest, and free" elections? How can we know that parties have had a fair chance to campaign and that voters around the country (especially countries as large and diverse as Russia, Nigeria, and Indonesia) have been able to exercise their will freely? How—especially where elections do not benefit from parallel vote tabulations[4]—can we know that the reported results accurately reflect the votes that were cast? And how do we know that the officials elected are really the "most powerful decision makers," that there are not significant "reserved domains" of military, bureaucratic, or oligarchical power?[5]

These questions have taken on a heightened relevance in recent years for several reasons. First, more regimes than ever before are adopting the *form* of electoral democracy, with regular, competitive, multiparty elections. Second, many of these regimes—indeed, an unprecedented proportion of the world's countries—have the form of electoral democracy but fail to meet the substantive test, or do so only ambiguously. And third, with heightened international expectations and standards for electoral democracy, including the rise of international election observing, there is closer international scrutiny of individual countries' democratic practices than ever before.

Yet even with this closer scrutiny, independent observers do not agree on how to classify regimes. Freedom House classifies all six regimes mentioned at the beginning of this essay as democracies. Yet by the logic of the three articles that follow, they are all (or mostly) something less than electoral democracies: competitive authoritarian systems, hegemonic-party systems, or hybrid regimes of some kind. At best, Ukraine, Nigeria, and Venezuela are *ambiguous* cases. We may not have enough information

now to know whether electoral administration will be sufficiently autonomous and professional, and whether contending parties and candidates will be sufficiently free to campaign, so as to give the political opposition a fair chance to defeat the government in the next elections. Regime classification must, in part, assess the previous election, but it must also assess the intentions and capacities of ambiguously democratic ruling elites, something that is very hard to do. Increasingly, independent observers view Russia as an electoral authoritarian regime. Many so view Nigeria as well, given the massive (and quite characteristic) fraud in the 1999 elections. Indonesia's constitutional assignment of some parliamentary seats to unelected military representatives contradicts a basic principle of democracy. But even if that provision were removed, the military would remain a major veto player (like the Turkish military, which has repeatedly forced the disqualification of a popular, moderately Islamist party).

These are hardly the only issues or anomalies in regime classification. In the 1970s and 1980s, scholars and observers debated whether Mexico, Senegal, and Singapore were really democracies (as their governments insisted). These debates fizzled once other countries in their respective regions began to experience true democratization and the democratic deficiencies of these one-party hegemonies became more blatantly apparent. More recently, a growing number of scholars are questioning the tendency to classify regimes as democratic simply because they have multiparty elections with some degree of competition and uncertainty. In an important conceptual contribution, focused on Eurasia and Latin America, Steven Levitsky and Lucan Way argue in the pages that follow that regimes may be *both* competitive *and* authoritarian.

This set of articles exemplifies a new wave of scholarly attention to the varieties of nondemocratic regimes and to the rather astonishing frequency with which contemporary authoritarian regimes manifest, at least superficially, a number of democratic features. This new intellectual upsurge partly reflects the exhaustion of the "third wave" of democratic transitions, which essentially crested in the mid-1990s.[6] For some years now, it has been apparent that a great many of the new regimes are not themselves democratic, or any longer "in transition" to democracy. Some of the countries that fall into the "political gray zone . . . between full-fledged democracy and outright dictatorship" are in fact electoral democracies, however "feckless" and poorly functioning, but many fall below the threshold of electoral democracy and are likely to remain there for a very long time.[7]

A Historical Perspective

Hybrid regimes (combining democratic and authoritarian elements) are not new. Even in the 1960s and 1970s, there existed multiparty, electoral, but undemocratic regimes. Of these electoral autocracies—Mexico, Singapore, Malaysia, Senegal, South Africa, Rhodesia, and Taiwan (which allowed *dangwai*, or "outside the party," competitors)—only the Malaysian and Singaporean regimes survive today. Historically, there have also been numerous cases in Europe and Latin America of limited (elite) party competition with a limited franchise. In Latin America, these nineteenth-century and early-twentieth-century "oligarchical" democracies "contributed to the ultimate development of full democracy" by establishing some of its major political institutions, as well as the principles of limitation and rotation of power.[8] Thus these countries epitomized Dahl's optimal path to stable polyarchy, with the rise of political competition preceding the expansion of participation, so that the culture of democracy first took root among a small elite and then diffused to the larger population as it was gradually incorporated into electoral politics.[9] In the contemporary world of mass participation, this gradualist path has been closed off, and anxious elites have thus sought out other ways to limit and control competition.

Until the past decade or two, most efforts at political control included a ban on opposition political parties (if not on electoral competition altogether) and severe limits on the organization of dissent and opposition in civil society as well. Thus Juan Linz's encyclopedic *Totalitarian and Authoritarian Regimes* (originally published in 1975) contains barely a mention of multiparty electoral competition *within* authoritarian regimes. Party politics figures within the framework of a single (typically mobilizational) party, and only brief mention is made of "pseudo-multiparty systems."[10] Certainly Linz does not identify, among his seven principal authoritarian regime types, anything like the "competitive authoritarian" regime type discussed by Levitsky and Way—and for good reason. This type of hybrid regime, which is now so common, is very much a product of the contemporary world.

One term for this phenomenon is "electoral authoritarianism." However, the term "pseudo-democracy" resonates distinctively with the contemporary era, in which democracy is the only broadly legitimate regime form, and regimes have felt unprecedented pressure (international and domestic) to adopt—or at least to mimic—the democratic form. Virtually all hybrid regimes in the world today are quite deliberately *pseudodemocratic*, "in that the existence of formally democratic political institutions, such as multiparty electoral competition, masks (often, in part, to legitimate) the reality of authoritarian domination."[11] All such regimes lack an arena of contestation sufficiently open, free, and fair so that the ruling party can readily be turned out of power if it is no longer preferred by a plurality of the electorate. While an opposition victory is not impossible in a hybrid regime, it requires a level of opposition mobilization, unity, skill, and heroism far beyond what would normally be required for victory in a democracy. Often, too, it requires international observation and intervention to preempt and prevent (as in Nicaragua in 1990) or to expose and delegitimate (as in the Philippines in 1986) the electoral manipulations and fraud of the authoritarian regime.

If scholarly treatment of hybrid or "electoral

authoritarian" regimes is relatively new, it is not without some intellectual foundations in the transitions paradigm and in other earlier comparative work on democracy. Guillermo O'Donnell and Philippe Schmitter emphasized the inherent uncertainty and variation in the outcomes of regime transitions. A transition from authoritarian rule could produce a democracy, or it could terminate with a liberalized authoritarian regime *(dictablanda)* or a restrictive, illiberal democracy *(democradura)*.[12] During the early wave of enthusiasm over the spread of democracy in Latin America, Terry Karl criticized the tendency to equate democracy with competitive multiparty elections. She argued that military domination and human rights abuses rendered the Central American regimes of the 1980s and early 1990s "hybrid regimes," not democracies.[13] Robert Dahl classified (circa 1969) as "near polyarchies" six competitive electoral regimes.[14] Juan Linz, Seymour Martin Lipset, and I labeled "semidemocratic" those regimes "where the effective power of elected officials is so limited, or political party competition so restricted, or the freedom and fairness of elections so compromised that electoral outcomes, while competitive, still deviate significantly from popular preferences; and/or where civil and political liberties are so limited that some political orientations and interests are unable to organize and express themselves."[15] Among our 26 cases, Senegal, Zimbabwe, Malaysia, and Thailand (during 1980–88, when the government was led by an unelected prime minister) fell into the category that Levitsky and Way call "competitive authoritarian." Mexico fit the model of a hegemonic party system, in which a relatively institutionalized ruling party monopolizes the political arena, using coercion, patronage, media control, and other means to deny formally legal opposition parties any real chance of competing for power.[16] Singapore remains a classic example of such a system.

The Rise of Pseudodemocracy

One of the most striking features of the "late period" of the third wave has been the unprecedented growth in the number of regimes that are neither clearly democratic nor conventionally authoritarian. If we use a very demanding standard of democracy, encompassing not only democratic elections but solid protection of civil liberties under a strong rule of law, then the proportion of intermediate regimes truly swells because so many of the new "democracies" of the third wave are "illiberal."[17] However, I believe a more analytically fruitful approach is to measure separately both *electoral democracy*, in the minimalist terms that Schumpeter, Huntington, and others have used, and *liberal democracy*.[18] We can also divide nondemocratic regimes into those with multiparty electoral competition of some kind (variously termed "electoral authoritarian," "pseudodemocratic," or "hybrid") and those that are *politically closed*. We can further divide electoral authoritarian regimes into the *competitive authoritarian* (following Levitsky and Way's formulation) and the uncompetitive or (following Schedler, and before him Giovanni Sartori) *hegemonic*. Tables 1 and 2 sort the world's regimes into these five categories, plus the residual one of *ambiguous regimes*.

During the third wave, both the number and proportion of democracies in the world have more than doubled. We find 104 democracies in the world at the end of 2001, seventeen fewer than Freedom House counts[19] but well over twice the 39 democracies at the start of the third wave; this accounts for 54 percent of the world's regimes, twice the proportion in 1974 (see Table 1). About seven in ten democracies may then be considered liberal (in that they have a fairly liberal Freedom House score of 2.0 or lower on the seven-point scale averaging political rights and civil liberties). Another 31 democracies are electoral but not liberal; some are clearly illiberal, with no more than a middling score on civil liberties. I consider 17 regimes "ambiguous" in

Table 1. Regime Types and Frequencies, End 2001

Regime Types	Countries Over One Million Population N (%)	Countries Under One Million Population N (%)	All Countries N (%)
Liberal Democracy (*FH Score 1-2.0*)	45 (30)	28 (66.7)	73 (38.0)
Electoral Democracy	29 (19.3)	2 (4.8)	31 (16.1)
Ambiguous Regimes	14 (9.3)	3 (7.1)	17 (8.9)
Competitive Authoritarian	19 (127)	2 (4.8)	21 (10.9)
Hegemonic Electoral Authoritarian	22 (14.7)	3 (7.1)	25 (13.0)
Politically Closed Authoritarian	21 (14)	4 (9.5)	25 (13.0)
Total	*150 (100)*	*42 (100)*	*192 (100)*

the sense that they fall on the blurry boundary between electoral democracy and competitive authoritarianism, with independent observers disagreeing over how to classify them.[20] Virtually all 17 could be classified as "competitive authoritarian." Doing so would raise the number of such regimes from 21 to as many as 38, and the proportion from 11 to 20 percent—quite a significant phenomenon. Another 25 regimes are electoral authoritarian but in a more hegemonic way. They do not exhibit the degrees and forms of competitiveness elucidated by Levitsky and Way and illustrated as well by some of the African cases discussed by Nicolas van de Walle in his essay. Their elections and other "democratic" institutions are largely façades, yet they may provide some space for political opposition, independent media, and social organizations that do not seriously criticize or challenge the regime. Finally, 25 regimes do not have any of the architecture of political competition and pluralism. These remain politically closed regimes.

The data in Table 1 and the underlying scheme of classification raise a number of interesting points and issues. The most stunning is the dwindling proportion of politically closed regimes in the world. This transformation is partly reflected in the steady overall rise of freedom in the world (with the average score on the combined seven-point Freedom House scale improving from 4.47 in 1974 to 3.47 in 2001). And it is partly seen in the shrinking number and proportion of states with the two most repressive

average freedom scores of 6.5 and 7.0. These most repressive regimes declined from 29 in 1974 to 21 in 2001, and as a proportion of all states, they shrank from one-fifth to barely a tenth (11 percent).

Thus the trend toward democracy has been accompanied by an even more dramatic trend toward pseudodemocracy. Only about half a dozen regimes in 1974 (less than 5 percent) would have met Schedler's criteria of electoral authoritarianism: undemocratic but with multiparty elections and some degree of political pluralism. The rest were all military, one-party, or personalist regimes. Today, at least 45 and perhaps as many as 60 are electoral authoritarian— roughly between a quarter and a third of all states. In proportional terms, authoritarian forms of multiparty electoral competition have increased during the third wave much more rapidly than democratic ones.

At the same time, military regimes have virtually disappeared as anything more than a transitional type of rule. Today, ambitious soldiers either legitimize their rule by running for president in contested, multiparty elections (however fraudulent, coerced, and manipulated), or they carve out large, autonomous spheres of political influence and economic domination behind the veil of civilian, multiparty rule. The first path has been taken by a number of African military strongmen, such as Jerry Rawlings in Ghana and most recently Yahya Jammeh in the Gambia. Nigerian dictator Sani Abacha was engaged in

Table 2. Classification of Regimes at the End of 2001

Liberal Democracy FH 1–2.0	Electoral Democracy FH >2.0	Ambiguous Regimes	Competitive Authoritarian	Hegemonic Electoral Authoritarian	Politically Closed Authoritarian
Western Democracies (28)					
24 West European states					
United States (1,1)					
Canada (1,1)					
Australia (1,1)					
New Zealand (1,1)					
Postcommunist (27)					
Czech Republic (1,2)	Moldova (2,4)	Armenia (4,4)	Bosnia-Herzegovina (5,4)*	Azerbaijan (6,5)	Turkmenistan (7,7)
Hungary (1,2)	Yugoslavia (3,3)	Georgia (4,4)	Russia (5,5)	Kazakhstan (6,5)	
Poland (1,2)	Albania (3,4)	Macedonia (4,4)	Belarus (6,6)	Kyrgyzstan (6,5)	
Slovakia (1,2)		Ukraine (4,4)		Tajikistan (6,6)	
Slovenia (1,2)				Uzbekistan (7,6)	
Estonia (1,2)					
Latvia (1,2)					
Lithuania (1,2)					
Bulgaria (1,3)					
Croatia (2,2)					
Romania (2,2)					
Latin America and the Caribbean (33)					
8 Caribbean states[1]	Argentina (2,3)	Venezuela (3,5)	Antigua & Barbuda (4,2)		Cuba (7,7)
Uruguay (1,1)	El Salvador (2,3)	Paraguay (4,3)	Haiti (6,6)		
Costa Rica (1,2)	Jamaica (2,3)	Colombia (4,4)			
Panama (1,2)	Mexico (2,3)				
Suriname (1,2)	Brazil (3,3)				
Bolivia (1,3)	Ecuador (3,3)				
Peru (1,3)	Honduras (3,3)				
Chile (2,2)	Nicaragua (3,3)				
Dominican Republic (2,2)	Trinidad & Tobago (3,3)				
Guyana (2,2)	Guatemala (3,4)				
Asia (E, SE, & S) (25)					
Japan (1,2)	India (2,3)	Indonesia (3,4)	East Timor (5,3)*	Singapore (5,5)	Brunei (7,5)
Taiwan (1,2)	Mongolia (2,3)		Malaysia (5,5)	Maldives (6,5)	Bhutan (7,6)
South Korea (2,2)	Philippines (2,3)			Cambodia (6,5)	China (7,6)
	Thailand (2,3)			Pakistan (6,5)[2]	Laos (7,6)
	Bangladesh (3,4)				Vietnam (7,6)

Table 2. Classification of Regimes at the End of 2001 (cont.)

	Liberal Democracy FH 1–2.0	Electoral Democracy FH >2.0	Ambiguous Regimes	Competitive Authoritarian	Hegemonic Electoral Authoritarian	Politically Closed Authoritarian
	Nepal (3,4)	Sri Lanka (3,4)			Afghanistan (7,7)	Burma (7,7) North Korea (7,7)
Pacific Islands (12)	8 Pacific island states[3]	Papua New Guinea (2,3) Solomon Islands (4,4)	Fiji (4,3) Tonga (5,3)**			
Africa (Sub-Sahara) (48)	Cape Verde (1,2) Mauritius (1,2) São Tomé & Príncipe (1,2) South Africa (1,2) Botswana (2,2)	Ghana (2,3) Mali (2,3) Namibia (2,3) Benin (3,2) Madagascar (2,4) Seychelles (3,3) Senegal (3,4) Malawi (4,3) Niger (4,4)	Mozambique (3,4) Tanzania (4,4) Nigeria (4,5) Djibouti (4,5) Sierra Leone (4,5) Zambia (5,4)	Lesotho (4,4) Central African Rep. (4,5) Guinea-Bissau (4,5) Côte d'Ivoire (5,4) Gabon (5,4) The Gambia (5,5) Togo (5,5) Ethiopia (5,6) Kenya (6,5) Cameroon (6,6) Zimbabwe (6,6)	Burkina Faso (4,4) Congo, Brazzaville (5,4) Comoros (6,4) Mauritania (5,5) Chad (6,5)[4] Guinea (6,5) Uganda (6,5) Angola (6,6) Liberia (6,6) Equatorial Guinea (6,7)	Swaziland (6,5)** Burundi (6,6) Congo, Kinshasa (6,6) Eritrea (7,6) Rwanda (7,6) Somalia (6,7) Sudan (7,7)
Middle East-North Africa (19)	Israel (1,3)		Turkey (4,5)	Lebanon (6,5) Iran (6,6) Yemen (6,6)	Kuwait (4,5)** Jordan (5,5)** Morocco (5,5)** Algeria (5,6) Tunisia (6,5) Egypt (6,6)	Bahrain (6,5)**[5] Oman (6,5)** United Arab Emirates (6,5)** Qatar (6,6)** Iraq (7,7) Libya (7,7) Saudi Arabia (7,7)** Syria (7,7)

Notes:
*International Protectorate.
**Traditional Monarchy. Tonga is a liberal autocracy, with only partial elective authority.
[1]Bahamas, Barbados, Belize, Dominica, Grenada, St. Kitts & Nevis, St. Lucia, St. Vincent & the Grenadines.
[2]Pakistan has not held elections since the October 1999 military coup. It is a transitional regime that is difficult to classify, since it is more open and pluralistic than closed authoritarian regimes.
[3]Kiribati, Marshall Islands, Micronesia, Nauru, Palau, Samoa, Tuvalu, Vanuatu.
[4]Technically a no-party regime, but with competitive and partially free elections.
[5]In transition to a more open and competitive political system.

such a maneuver when he was struck dead by a "heart attack" in 1998. General—now President—Pervez Musharraf may yet pursue a similar conversion in Pakistan, albeit perhaps with considerably more genuine popular support. The second course has been taken by the military in Indonesia, and to a lesser degree still characterizes the military in Turkey, Thailand, Nigeria, and parts of Latin America.

There is also a striking correlation between country size and regime type. As I noted a few years ago,[21] countries with populations under one million are much more likely to be both democracies and liberal democracies. Two-thirds of these countries are liberal democracies, while only 30 percent of countries with populations over one million are. Among the larger 150 countries, only half are democracies, while 70 percent of the small countries are. The countries with populations over one million are about twice as likely as small states to have an electoral authoritarian regime and half again as likely to have a closed authoritarian regime.

Electoral Democracy vs. Electoral Authoritarianism

Interesting issues revolve around the boundaries between regime types, which all the authors in this issue recognize to be blurry and controversial. When fitting messy and elusive realities against ideal types, it cannot be otherwise. This is why I classify so many regimes as ambiguous —a judgment, however, that only addresses the border between democracy and electoral authoritarianism. The distinctions between liberal and electoral democracy, and between competitive and hegemonic electoral authoritarianism, can also require difficult and disputable judgements. Thus the country classifications in Table 2 are offered more in an illustrative than a definitive spirit.

As Schedler elaborates, the distinction between electoral democracy and electoral authoritarianism turns crucially on the freedom, fairness,

inclusiveness, and meaningfulness of elections. Often particularly difficult are judgments about whether elections have been free and fair, both in the ability of opposition parties and candidates to campaign and in the casting and counting of the votes. Hence the frequency with which the validations by international observer missions of elections in ambiguous or electoral authoritarian regimes are, often convincingly, criticized as superficial, premature, and politically driven.

Elections are "free" when the legal barriers to entry into the political arena are low, when there is substantial freedom for candidates and supporters of different political parties to campaign and solicit votes, and when voters experience little or no coercion in exercising their electoral choices. Freedom to campaign requires some considerable freedom of speech, movement, assembly, and association in political life, if not fully in civil society. It is hard, however, to separate these two spheres, or to weigh the significance of particular violations. How many opposition candidates and supporters must be killed or arrested before one discerns a blatantly undemocratic pattern? Typically more than one murder is necessary, but fewer than the 21 deadly assaults committed during the two months prior to Cambodia's 1998 elections.[22] In India, election-related killings have a long history and have recently risen to alarming levels in some states. No major observer denies that India is a democracy, but particularly in states (like Bihar) where corruption, criminality, murder, and kidnapping heavily taint the electoral process, it is an illiberal and degraded one. A crucial consideration in assessing a regime is whether political violence is clearly and extensively organized by the state or ruling party as a means of punishing, terrorizing, and demoralizing opposition.

Assessments about whether elections are free or not thus require careful and nuanced judgments about the scale, pattern, and context of violations. The same is true for the dimension of electoral fairness. Levitsky and Way argue that political systems descend into electoral authoritarianism when violations of the "minimum criteria for democracy" are so serious that they create "an uneven playing field between government and opposition." Yet even in many liberal and established democracies, there is not a truly level playing field. Often, governing parties or executives enjoy advantages of incumbency—readier access to the media, an easier time raising money from business, and the ability (strictly legal or not) to use government transport and staff while campaigning. No system is a perfect democracy, all require constant vigilance, and scattered violations do not negate the overall democratic character of elections.

When evaluating elections, it is crucial to examine their systemic character. We have by now elaborate criteria to judge the fairness of elections. Elections are fair when they are administered by a neutral authority; when the electoral administration is sufficiently competent and resourceful to take specific precautions against fraud in the voting and vote counting; when the police, military, and courts treat competing candidates and parties impartially throughout the process; when contenders all have access to the public media; when electoral districts and rules do not systematically disadvantage the opposition; when independent monitoring of the voting and vote-counting is allowed at all locations; when the secrecy of the ballot is protected; when virtually all adults can vote; when the procedures for organizing and counting the vote are transparent and known to all; and when there are clear and impartial procedures for resolving complaints and disputes.[23] This is a long list, but serious efforts to compromise the freedom and fairness of elections form a pattern (beginning well before election day) that is visible across institutional arenas. The institutional biases and misdeeds are there for international observers to see if those observers have the time, experience, courage, and country expertise to do so.[24]

Degrees of Authoritarian Competitiveness

No less difficult is the challenge of distinguishing between competitive authoritarian regimes and hegemonic electoral authoritarian ones. Levitsky and Way posit four arenas in which "opposition forces may periodically challenge, weaken, and occasionally even defeat autocratic incumbents." While contestation in the judiciary and the mass media is hard to quantify, contestation in elections and legislatures does allow for more structured comparison.

Table 2 on the preceding pages classifies the world's regimes by the sixfold typology explained above. Regimes are considered democratic if they have free, fair, and open elections for all the principal positions of political power, as defined above and by Schedler in his contribution. In addition to the Freedom House scores, three types of data are drawn upon in my classification of nondemocratic regimes: the percentage of legislative seats held by the ruling party, the percentage of the vote won by the ruling party presidential candidate, and the years the incumbent ruler has continuously been in power. The latter, as van de Walle shows in his essay on Africa, can be a telling indicator of the degree to which a country has opened up, as well as a predictor of its future openness to democratic change. Although I do not use any mathematical formula to combine these three indicators and the Freedom House scores, a formal index of authoritarian competitiveness is worth developing.

One defining feature of competitive authoritarian regimes is significant parliamentary opposition. In regimes where elections are largely an authoritarian façade, the ruling or dominant party wins almost all the seats: repeatedly over 95 percent in Singapore, about 80 percent in Egypt in 2000 and Mauritania in 2001, 89 percent in Tanzania in 2000, and repeatedly over 80 percent in Tunisia during the 1990s.[25] In Cambodia the hegemonic character of rule by Hun Sen's Cambodian People's Party (CPP) was not apparent in the bare majority of parliamentary seats it won in 1998, but it became more blatant in early 2002 when the CPP won control of about 99 percent of the 1,621 local communes with about 70 percent of the vote.

Where, as in Kazakhstan and Kyrgyzstan, parties are so poorly developed that it is difficult to interpret legislative election results, presidential election returns offer other evidence of hegemony. After winning a presidential referendum with a 95 percent "yes" vote in 1995, Kazakhstan's President Nursultan Nazarbayev was re-elected with 80 percent of the vote in 1999. In 1995 and again in 2000, Kyrgyz president Askar Akayev, in whom the West placed early (and naïve) hopes for democratic progress, was re-elected with 75 percent of the vote. One clear sign of hegemony is when the president "wins" three-quarters or more of the popular vote. This also happened in Algeria in 1999, in Azerbaijan in 1998, in Burkina Faso in 1998, in Cameroon (with an opposition boycott) in 1997, in Djibouti in 1999, and in Tanzania in 2000.

At the extreme end of the continuum, the presidents of Egypt, Tunisia, and Yemen were all "reelected" in the 1990s with well over 90 percent of the vote. These men have been in power now for 21, 15, and 12 years, respectively, pointing to another sign of authoritarian hegemony: prolonged presidential tenure. Other examples include 23 years in Angola, 20 years in Cameroon, 35 years in Gabon, 18 years in Guinea, and 16 years in Uganda. Yet some long-ruling autocrats have had to fight for their political lives in the 1990s. Daniel arap Moi (who has finally pledged to step down this year after 24 years in power) was reelected twice during the 1990s with less than 42 percent of the vote. Zimbabwe's President Robert Mugabe, in power for 22 years, was resorting to massive violence and intimidation in his unpopular presidential reelection bid as this article went to press. His ruling party won only a bare majority of seats in a rough 2000 election that marked a breakthrough from numbing hegemony to competitive authoritarianism.

These data become more revealing when weighed with the annual Freedom House ratings of political rights and civil liberties. Generally, electoral authoritarian regimes range from 4.0 to 6.0 on the combined seven-point scale. Regimes closer to the less repressive score (4.0) allow more political pluralism and civic space, and hence are more likely to be competitive authoritarian. Some examples include Peru under Fujimori (4.5 in 1995), Senegal under the hegemonic Socialist Party (which averaged 4.0 or 4.5 during the 1990s), and Côte d'Ivoire (4.5 today, with competitive presidential and legislative elections in 2000). Many observers consider Tanzania a democracy, with its relatively benign regime (4.0), despite persistent electoral irregularities. Yet if one traces its pedigree back to President Julius Nyerere's original TANU party, the Chama Cha Mapizindi (CCM) is the only ruling party Tanzanians have known in nearly 40 years of independence.

The reason we must examine several variables is that levels of freedom and levels of electoral competitiveness do not always neatly align. Indeed, when longtime authoritarian rulers face serious challenges (as in Malaysia and Zimbabwe recently), they may turn to their nastiest levels of repression, deploying levels of violence and intimidation that are unnecessary when political domination can be more subtly secured at the ballot box. Tracking the interplay between changes in political competition and changes in political repression may thus help us understand when and how moments of possible transition open and close in electoral authoritarian regimes.

Black and White or Shades of Gray?

Comparative politics is returning with new concepts and data to a very old issue: the forms and dynamics of authoritarian rule. If nothing else, the three articles that follow show that these divergent forms do matter. As democracies differ among themselves in significant ways and degrees, so do contemporary authoritarian regimes, and if we are to understand the contemporary dynamics, causes, limits, and possibilities of regime change (including possible future democratization), we must understand the different, and in some respects new, types of authoritarian rule.

At the same time, we must appreciate that classificatory schemes like the ones in these articles impose an uneasy order on an untidy empirical world. We should not ignore the critics of "whole system" thinking, who eschew efforts at regime classification altogether and seek to identify the ways in which each political system combines democratic and undemocratic features.[26] These approaches remind us that most regimes are "mixed" to one degree or another.[27] Even many politically closed regimes have quasi-constitutional mechanisms to limit power and consult broader opinion. For example, although China lacks competitive elections at any significant level, it has taken some steps to rotate power and to check certain abuses of corrupt local and provincial officials. Every step toward political liberalization matters, both for the prospect of a transition to democracy and for the quality of political life as it is daily experienced by abused and aggrieved citizens. As Levitsky and Way imply, significant steps toward a more open, competitive, pluralistic, and restrained authoritarian system can emerge in arenas other than electoral ones.

Democratic regimes are also "mixed" forms of government, not only in the ways they empower institutions intentionally placed beyond the reach of elected officials (such as constitutional courts or central banks), but in less desirable respects as well. In their constant struggles to restrain corruption, and in their ongoing frustration in trying to contain the role of money in politics, even the world's most liberal democracies exhibit the pervasive imperfections of responsiveness that led Robert Dahl to adopt the term "polyarchy" instead of "democracy" for his seminal study. As we add the forms and dynamics of electoral authoritarianism to our long list of issues in comparative democratic studies, we should not neglect these imperfections in our own systems. The transformations of Taiwan, Mexico, and Senegal in the 1990s show that competitive authoritarian regimes can become democracies. But democracies, new and old, liberal and illiberal, can also become more democratic.

NOTES

1. Philippe C. Schmitter and Terry Lynn Karl, "What Democracy is . . . and Is Not," *Journal of Democracy* 2 (Summer 1991): 75–88.
2. Joseph Schumpeter, *Capitalism, Socialism, and Democracy*, 2nd ed. (New York: Harper, 1947), 269.
3. Samuel P. Huntington, *The Third Wave: Democratization in the Late Twentieth Century* (Norman: University of Oklahoma Press, 1991), 7.
4. Larry Garber and Glenn Cowan, "The Virtues of Parallel Vote Tabulations," *Journal of Democracy* 4 (April 1993): 95–107.
5. J. Samuel Valenzuela, "Democratic Consolidation in Post-Transitional Settings: Notion, Process, and Facilitating Conditions," in Scott Mainwaring, Guillermo O'Donnell, and J. Samuel Valenzuela, eds., *Issues in Democratic Consolidation: The New South American Democracies in Comparative Perspective* (Notre Dame: University of Notre Dame Press, 1992), 64–66.
6. Larry Diamond, *Developing Democracy: Toward Consolidation* (Baltimore: Johns Hopkins University Press, 1999), ch. 2.
7. Thomas Carothers, "The End of the Transition Paradigm," *Journal of Democracy* 13 (January 2002): 5–21, quoted from pp. 9 and 18.
8. Larry Diamond and Juan J. Linz, "Introduction: Politics, Society, and Democracy in Latin America," in Larry Diamond, Juan J. Linz, and Seymour Martin Lipset, eds., *Democracy in Developing Countries: Latin America* (Boulder, Colo.: Lynne Rienner, 1989), 8.
9. Robert Dahl, *Polyarchy: Participation and*

Opposition (New Haven: Yale University Press, 1971), 33–36.

10. Juan J. Linz, *Totalitarian and Authoritarian Regimes* (Boulder, Colo.: Lynne Rienner, 2000), 60.

11. Larry Diamond, Juan J. Linz, and Seymour Martin Lipset, *Democracy in Developing Countries*, xviii.

12. Guillermo O'Donnell and Philippe C. Schmitter, *Transitions from Authoritarian Rule: Tentative Conclusions about Uncertain Democracies* (Baltimore: Johns Hopkins University Press, 1986), 9.

13. Terry Lynn Karl, "The Hybrid Regimes of Central America," *Journal of Democracy* 6 (July 1995): 72–86. See also Terry Lynn Karl, "Dilemmas of Democratization in Latin America," *Comparative Politics* 23 (October 1990): 14–15.

14. Robert Dahl, *Polyarchy*, 248.

15. Larry Diamond, Juan J. Linz, and Seymour Martin Lipset, *Democracy in Developing Countries*, xvii.

16. Giovanni Sartori, *Parties and Party Systems: A Framework for Analysis* (Cambridge: Cambridge University Press, 1976): 230–38.

17. Guillermo O'Donnell, "Delegative Democracy," *Journal of Democracy* 5 (January 1994): 55–69; Larry Diamond, "Democracy in Latin America: Degrees, Illusions, and Directions for Consolidation," in Tom Farer, ed., *Beyond Sovereignty: Collectively Defending Democracy in the Americas* (Baltimore: Johns Hopkins University Press, 1996), 52–104; Larry Diamond, *Developing Democracy*, 42–50; Fareed Zakaria, "The Rise of Illiberal Democracy," *Foreign Affairs* 76 (November-December 1997):22–43.

18. Liberal democracy extends freedom, fairness, transparency, accountability, and the rule of law from the electoral process into all other major aspects of governance and interest articulation, competition, and representation. See Larry Diamond, *Developing Democracy*, 10–13.

19. See Adrian Karatnycky, "The 2001 Freedom House Survey," *Journal of Democracy* 13 (January 2002): 99.

20. The only exception in this ambiguous group is Tonga, the lone "liberal autocracy"—a nondemocracy with a Freedom House score on civil liberties better than the mid-point of 4—and thus difficult to classify in this framework.

21. Larry Diamond, *Developing Democracy*, 117–19.

22. Freedom House, *Freedom in the World: The Annual Survey of Political Rights and Civil Liberties, 2000–2001* (New York: Freedom House, 2001), 121.

23. This draws from Jørgen Elklit and Palle Svensson, "What Makes Elections Free and Fair?" *Journal of Democracy* 8 (July 1997): 32–46. See also the essays on electoral administration in Andreas Schedler, Larry Diamond, and Marc F. Plattner, eds., *The Self-Restraining State: Power and Accountability in New Democracies* (Boulder, Colo.: Lynne Rienner, 1999): 75–142.

24. For a thoughtful critique of international election observation, see Thomas Carothers, "The Rise of Election Monitoring: The Observers Observed," *Journal of Democracy* 8 (July 1997): 16–31.

25. Space does not permit presentation of the detailed election data in this article. Two tables with these detailed results for selected ambiguous and electoral authoritarian regimes may be found on the *Journal of Democracy* website at *www.journalofdemocracy.org*.

26. For a classic critical treatment in this vein, see Richard L. Sklar, "Developmental Democracy," *Comparative Studies in Society and History* 29 (October 1987): 686–724.

27. For an Africanist perspective, see Richard L. Sklar, "The Significance of Mixed Government in Southern African Studies: A Preliminary Assessment," in Toyin Falola, ed., *African Politics in Postimperial Times: The Essays of Richard L. Sklar* (Trenton, N.J.: Africa World Press, 2002), 479–87.

JACK SNYDER AND KAREN BALLENTINE

NATIONALISM AND THE MARKETPLACE OF IDEAS

The conventional wisdom among human rights activists holds that a great deal of the ethnic conflict in the world today is caused by propagandistic manipulations of public opinion. Human Rights Watch, for example, points the finger at unscrupulous governments who try to save their own skins by "playing the communal card." As antidotes, such groups prescribe democratization, wide-open debate in civil society, and greater freedom of the press.[1] Scholars likewise argue that a major stimulus to belligerent nationalism is the state's manipulation of mass media and mass education to infuse the nation with a sense of in-group patriotism and out-group rivalry. They, too, prescribe greater freedom of speech.

We agree that media manipulation often plays a central role in promoting nationalist and ethnic conflict, but we argue that promoting unconditional freedom of public debate in newly democratizing societies is, in many circumstances, likely to make the problem worse. Historically and today, from the French Revolution to Rwanda, sudden liberalizations of press freedom have been associated with bloody outbursts of popular nationalism. The most dangerous situation is precisely when the government's press monopoly begins to break down.[2] During incipient democratization, when civil society is burgeoning but democratic institutions are not fully entrenched, the state and other elites are forced to engage in public debate in order to compete for mass allies in the struggle for power. Under those circumstances, governments and their opponents often have the motive and the opportunity to play the nationalist card.

When this occurs, unconditional freedom of

speech is a dubious remedy. Just as economic competition produces socially beneficial results only in a well-institutionalized marketplace, where monopolies and false advertising are counteracted, so too increased debate in the political marketplace leads to better outcomes only when there are mechanisms to correct market imperfections. Many newly democratizing states lack institutions to break up governmental and non-governmental information monopolies, to professionalize journalism, and to create common public forums where diverse ideas engage each other under conditions in which erroneous arguments will be challenged. In the absence of these institutions, an increase in the freedom of speech can create an opening for nationalist mythmakers to hijack public discourse.

In developing these arguments, we first define nationalist mythmaking and explain the scope of our claims. Second, we present our concept of the marketplace of ideas and offer hypotheses about conditions that facilitate nationalist mythmaking, illustrating these propositions with examples from that classic hotbed of nationalist mythmaking, the Weimar Republic, and from other recent and historical cases. Third, we test our argument against two hard cases, ethnic conflict in the former Yugoslavia and in Rwanda, both dramatic clashes that seem superficially to fit the conventional view that a government media monopoly is the problem, and unfettered speech the antidote. Fourth, we explore cases with comparatively moderate outcomes to determine the conditions under which democratization does not produce intense nationalist mythmaking. We conclude with suggestions for better institutionalizing public debate in new democracies.

From *International Security* 21, no. 2 (Fall 1996), pp. 5–40. Some of the authors' notes have been omitted.

Nationalist Mythmaking

Conventional wisdom is right in focusing on inflammatory propaganda as a cause of nationalism and ethnic conflicts. The archetype for this notion is the stem-winding oratory of Adolf Hitler, with its renowned pied-piper effect on malleable audiences. Likewise, the world's first instance of aggressive nationalism, the Wars of the French Revolution, was sparked by an outpouring of warlike commentary in France's newly free press, which swept the demagogic journalist Jacques Pierre Brissot into power. Recent reincarnations of this phenomenon, stressed in analyses by nongovernmental organizations (NGOs) and by scholars, include the Hutu "hate radio" stations that encouraged genocide against Rwanda's Tutsi minority, as well as President Slobodan Milošević's use of the television monopoly to foster an embattled, surly mentality among Serbs.

Conventional wisdom is one-sided, however, when it blames nationalist demagogy primarily on governmental media monopolies and consequently prescribes unfettered free speech as the remedy. A 1995 report by Human Rights Watch, for example, concluded that in ten of the hottest contemporary ethnic conflicts, manipulative governments had "played the communal card" as a way to forestall declining popularity or to pursue strategies of divide-and-rule. "Dictatorship offers the ideal condition for playing the 'communal card,'" because "official control of information makes public opinion highly manipulable." Yet almost all of the countries studied in the report—India, Israel, South Africa, Romania, Sri Lanka, the former Yugoslavia, Lebanon, Russia, Armenia, and Azerbaijan—had recently held openly contested elections where powerful opposition groups were more nationalist than the government. In addition, Human Rights Watch argued that, because "conditions for polarization along communal lines are less propitious in a society where public debate is encouraged," where past human rights abuses are vigorously prosecuted, and where there is "free participation in a broad range of voluntary and public associa-tions," the cure is "vigorous civic debate" in a "well developed civil society."[3] But in fact, the Hindu fundamentalist Bharatiya Janata Party, the Armenian Karabakh Committee, and most of the instigators of ethnic conflict in the Human Rights Watch cases *are* "civil society," that is, voluntary organizations not created by the state. The Weimar Republic had record numbers of newspapers per capita, choral societies, and grassroots nationalist organizations, all indicators of a vigorous civil society; likewise, the nationalistic Jacobin Clubs of the French Revolution were spontaneous emanations of civil society.[4]

Conventional analyses fail to emphasize that a "well developed" civil society is not simply a matter of many clamoring voices, but also the set of institutions and social norms that make pluralism a civil process of persuasion and reconciling of differences. No matter how well-intentioned and knowledgeable, non-governmental organizations promoting human rights tend to understate the tension between their ideal of an open society and the difficulty of establishing its preconditions in newly democratizing societies. As a consequence, their remedies may sometimes fuel nationalist mythmaking rather than dampen it. It is understandable that such groups are reluctant to explore the trade-offs entailed in promoting free speech, since there is undoubtedly a risk that qualifications to the argument for free speech can be exploited by dictators who wish to snuff out freedom of expression entirely. Nonetheless, because the risks of uncritical advocacy of unconditional free speech can be very high, these trade-offs must be analyzed forthrightly.

Defining Nationalism and Myths

Nationalism, according to the most widely accepted definition, is the doctrine that the state and the nation should be congruent. Nationalism holds that legitimate rule is based on the sovereignty of a culturally or historically distinctive people in a polity that expresses and protects those distinctive characteristics. We examine under this definition both the state-seeking activity of ethnic groups in multi-ethnic states and also the rivalries of established and more ethnically homogeneous nation-states, insofar as their leaders seek to legitimate their power and appeal for popular support for their policies by claiming to fulfill the historical mission or cultural identity of the nation.

"Myths," for our purposes, are assertions that would lose credibility if their claim to a basis in fact or logic were exposed to rigorous, disinterested public evaluation. The assertion that the Holocaust never happened is an example of a myth, in this sense. Nationalist mythmaking, then, is the attempt to use dubious arguments to mobilize support for nationalist doctrines or to discredit opponents. For some scholars, nationalist mythmaking is understood exclusively in this sense of promoting demonstrable falsehoods: in Ernest Renan's words, "getting its history wrong is part of being a nation."[5] Other scholars of nationalism, however, conceive of myth in the sense of *mythomoteur*, that is, as a story about the origins, special character, and destiny of the "nation."[6] The values embodied in such mythomoteurs are not subject to falsification, no matter how astutely they are scrutinized. Assertions like "it is good to be Ruritanian" or "Ruritanians deserve their own state" cannot be falsified, not because they are irrational, but because they are normative claims which exist independently of objective standards of argumentation. Nationalist mythomoteurs can, on occasion, lead to conflict: for example, when both Ruritanians and Megalomanians identify the same territory as "our historic homeland," and each claims to "deserve" exclusive, sovereign control over it. Because of the non-falsifiability of national mythomoteurs, even a well-constituted marketplace of ideas cannot provide iron-clad restraints against this kind of mythology. A well-constituted marketplace can, however, effectively mitigate the propagation of falsifiable nationalist myths. This capacity is of no small consequence since, typically, nationalist conflict is not the spontaneous emanation of vague mythomoteurs but the product of deliberate elite efforts to mobilize latent solidarities behind a particular political program, which falsifiable myths are used to justify. Thus, some of the justifications offered for why Ruritanians deserve to rule a territory (e.g., "we ruled it six centuries ago") or why they should preventively attack the Megalomanians (e.g., "they were able to kill ten million of us during the last war, because we let our guard down") entail empirical claims or causal inferences that are subject to objective scrutiny and perhaps verification or refutation.

We do not contend that all nationalist ideas are myths, let alone falsifiable ones. Nor do we argue that nationalists are uniquely prone to political mythmaking, nor that nationalism and nationalist conflict stem only from mythmaking. Besides myths, scholars have identified many factors that plausibly contribute to nationalism or nationalist conflict: the rise of the modern state, economic change, political repression, socio-economic inequality, security threats, and so forth. Our focus on mythmaking is not intended to compete with these approaches, but to complement them. We argue that these factors work their effects on nationalism through the process of persuasion and mythmaking in the marketplace of ideas. As many scholars have stressed, whatever background factors may contribute to nationalism, nationalist agitation and propaganda are always necessary conditions to the development of a mass nationalist movement.

Though nationalism and nationalist myths are not the only cause of conflict between nations, we do argue that a tendency to breed conflict is inherent in typical nationalist myths, because they overemphasize the cultural and historical distinctiveness of the national group, exaggerate the threat posed to the nation by other groups, ignore the degree to which the nation's own actions provoked such threats, and play down the costs of seeking national goals through militant means. Nationalist mobilization against alleged threats from other national groups, whether within the state or abroad, heightens the risk of conflict by stereotyping opponents as irremediably hostile, yet inferior and vulnerable to vigilant preventive attack. Whether such myths can be successfully sold depends in large measure on the structure of the marketplace of ideas in which they are advanced.

Imperfect Markets and Nationalist Mythmaking

Liberal conventional wisdom, steeped in John Stuart Mill's argument that truth is most likely to emerge from no-holds-barred debate, optimistically expects the invisible hand of free competition to check the mythmaking of nationalist demagogues. Under conditions of "perfect competition" in the political marketplace, it may indeed be true that, on balance, unfettered debate tends to discredit ill-founded myths by revealing their factual inaccuracies, their logical contradictions, or the hidden costs of acting on their implications. That is probably one reason why mature democracies never fight wars against each other. However, when waning authoritarian power is newly challenged by the forces of mass politics, competition in the marketplace of ideas is likely to be highly imperfect, and opportunities for nationalist mythmaking abound.

In the political marketplace, governmental and non-governmental elites advance arguments about the benefits of policies and commit themselves to these policies in order to gain political support. Consumers in the marketplace decide whom to support based in part on the persuasiveness of the arguments of elite entrepreneurs and on the credibility of the elites' commitments to implement desired policies. Middlemen in the marketplace (journalists and policy experts) and market institutions (the media, analytical institutions, and the laws regulating them) convey political entrepreneurs' commitments and argu-

ments to consumers in ways that provide varying degrees of information about their credibility and accuracy. The better institutionalized the market, the better it scrutinizes arguments and forces ideas to confront each other in common forums, and therefore the better the information the market provides. The media that comprise the marketplace include not only instruments of mass communication like television and newspapers, but also local networks of face-to-face persuasion, as well as elite publications and discourse that generate ideas for mass dissemination.

Thus, the commodities exchanged in the market are consumers' political support and suppliers' policy commitments. The role that ideas play in the "marketplace of ideas" is not that of goods, but that of advertisements for political support. Ideas put forward in the marketplace convey purported information about values and interests, and also about facts and causal inferences from facts. Thus, the supplier uses advertising to convince the consumer to want what the supplier has to offer: for example, to believe that the fulfillment of the nation's destiny is rightful and valuable, and that the consumer's personal interests and values will be served by it. The supplier also tries to convince the consumer that the offered policies will produce the advertised benefits with a high probability at a low cost, and that alternative policies will lead to worse results. To accomplish this, the suppliers' advertising includes claims about, for example, the nature of the nation's opponents, the likelihood of cooperation with other national groups, the history of past interactions with them, and the prospects of success from nationalist mobilization or armed conflict.

Our conception of the marketplace of ideas is based on the description of economic markets provided by standard economic analysis. The structure of the market consists of the degree of concentration of supply, the degree of segmentation of demand, and the strength of institutions regulating market interactions, including those that provide information or regulate advertising.

Imperfect competition occurs when there are few sellers because of large scale economies and high barriers to entry, and when products are differentiated for sale to segmented markets. Market segmentation may occur as a result of consumers' distinctive tastes for differentiated products, the artificial inculcation of differentiated preferences through targeted advertising, transportation costs or other advantages in distribution and marketing to a particular set of consumers, or political barriers to exchange between market segments. Under these conditions, sellers tend to engage either in competitive advertising, collusion to divide up market share, or a combination of the two. Rivalry is more likely when barriers to entry are falling, or in a "young industry," where "sellers may not have learned what to expect of rivals" and "may be scrambling to secure an established place in the industry, in the process inadvertently starting a price war."[7] To achieve socially beneficial outcomes under imperfect competition, regulation is needed to break up trusts, prohibit collusion, and insure truth in advertising.

The marketplace of ideas in newly democratizing states often mirrors that of a young, poorly regulated industry, where barriers to entry are falling, competition is imperfect, and oligopolistic elites exploit partial media monopolies in intense competition to win mass support in a segmented market. This kind of imperfectly competitive market may yield the worst of both worlds: elites are driven to compete for the mobilization of mass support, but by targeting niche markets, they can avoid debating in a common forum where ideas are publicly held up to rigorous scrutiny by competitors and expert evaluators. In these circumstances, nationalism may help elites to gain support in an ethnic market niche and also to maintain high barriers to entry by diverting demands for civic participation into mobilization for national goals. Thus, market conditions in newly democratizing states often create both the incentive for nationalist advertising and the conditions for its success, as we explain below.

Partial Monopolies of Supply

What human rights advocates fear most is a complete governmental monopoly over the press. In this situation, the government can propagate any nationalist myth without having to face countervailing arguments. While we agree that perfect monopoly is hardly desirable, we argue that it is not the only—and perhaps not the most—dangerous condition for nationalist mythmaking. Conditions of perfect monopoly make the audience skeptical. In communist and other authoritarian states, for example, people tend to discount propaganda precisely because they know that it comes from a monopolistic source, and typically turn to informal networks and stratagems for reading between the lines of official discourse. Moreover, perfect monopolists often lack a motive to mobilize their population's nationalism. Facing no active opposition and ruling without popular consent, they face little need to compete for the mantle of popular legitimacy by whipping up mass enthusiasms. Indeed, unleashing mass nationalism would only hinder their goal of depoliticizing domestic politics and would introduce needless complications into their management of foreign relations. For this reason, dictatorships play the nationalist card only under two conditions: when their ability to monopolize power and discourse is slipping, like that of the Argentine junta on the eve of the Falklands War, or when their ascent to power, and hence their legitimacy, have been based on the use of popular nationalism to prevail in an initially pluralistic setting, such as Bonaparte after the French Revolution, Hitler after the Weimar Republic, or the Japanese military regime after the collapse of the Taisho democracy of the 1920s.

Especially prone to nationalist mythmaking are situations of partial monopoly over supply in the marketplace of ideas, which often occur during the earliest stages of democratization. In such conditions of intra-elite competition, governments and other elite interests often enjoy residual market power as the legacy of authoritarian monopoly control: the state or economic elites of the threatened ruling circles may still control key components of the mass media or have the resources to shape its content. Nationalist militaries may invoke their monopoly of specialized expertise to exaggerate foreign threats; the government may tendentiously regulate broadcast media in what it calls "the public interest"; private economic lobbies may buy journalists, supposedly neutral experts, and media access. For example, Alfred Hugenberg, the chairman of the board of directors of Krupp Steel during World War I and the chairman of the German National People's Party during the Weimar Republic, established the Telegraph Union wire service, which gave him control over half of Germany's press.[8] By providing loans, reduced-rate newsprint, and accounting services to inflation-ridden papers, Hugenberg achieved substantial control over many papers while maintaining their facades of independence. Though even small cities often had multiple newspapers, Hugenberg's service fed them all the same nationalist-slanted copy.

As a democratizing political system opens up, old elites and rising counter-elites must compete for the support of new entrants into the marketplace through popular appeals, including appeals to the purported common interests of elites and mass groups in pursuing nationalistic aims against out-groups. In many instances, including the case of Serbian President Slobodan Milošević, these elites evince little interest in nationalism until rising pressure for mass political participation gives them an incentive to do so.[9] This strategy worked extremely well, for example, for the Kaiser-appointed governments of Bismarckian and Wilhelmine Germany, which faced the dilemma of winning budgetary approval from a Reichstag elected by universal suffrage. Five times between the founding of the Reich and 1914 the government chose to fight elections on what it styled as "national" issues— the Kulturkampf against the Catholics in 1874, the campaign of 1878 tarring socialists as antinational, the campaigns to support bills to strengthen the army in 1887 and in 1893, and the "Hottentot election" on German colonial policy in 1907. Each time elections were fought on "national" grounds, voter turnout increased and more rightist candidates were elected, in part because conservative candidates got more votes overall and in part because coalitions of right-wing parties were more cohesive. Hidden financing of nationalist movements and publications by the Navy and by industrial interests, combined with prosecutions of opposition voices under a restrictive press law, played an essential part in this strategy.

Rising counter-elites also tend to play the nationalist card; indeed, they often make the initial move in a spiral of nationalist outbidding. From the French revolution to contemporary Armenia, Azerbaijan, Georgia, and Croatia, it has often been elites from outside the ruling circles who pushed nationalist issues to the fore of the public debate, asserting a right to rule on the grounds that old elites were lax in pursuing the national or ethnic interest. In principle, populist counter-elites in conditions of incipient democratization can opt for any of several ideological stances *vis-à-vis* the old authoritarian regime. They can pursue a liberal strategy, criticizing the old elites' denial of individual civic rights; a socialist line, criticizing class domination; an ethnic line, criticizing the old elite for favoring a particular cultural group; or a more inclusive nationalist line, arguing that the narrow, venal old elite was ignoring the broader national interest. Nationalism is often attractive to rising counter-elites in part for the same reason that old ruling elites adopt it: unlike liberalism or socialism, nationalism allows the aspiring elite to make claims in the name of the masses without necessarily committing itself to a policy of sharing power and wealth with the masses once it has seized control of the state. Other incentives may depend more on context: e.g., which ideologies are discredited by association with the hated *ancien régime*, whether cultural differences are already salient and thus available to be politicized as ethno-nationalism, and whether the rising counter-elite has some particular comparative advantage as the standard bearer for a distinctive national culture, as might be the case with literary or religious elites. Also important, however, is whether the structure of demand in the marketplace of ideas is highly segmented, and thus permissive for nationalist mythmaking.

Segmentation of Demand

A well-constituted marketplace of ideas depends not only on the expression of diverse views by different groups in society, but also on individuals' exposure to diverse ideas. A highly segmented marketplace has the former, but not the latter. In a segmented marketplace of ideas, individuals in one market segment lack exposure to ideas expressed in other segments, or exposure is filtered through sources that distort those ideas.

Demand in the marketplace of ideas is likely to be segmented in newly democratizing states. A common sphere of democratic discourse depends on the development of unifying institutions, such as state-wide non-partisan media, which take time to construct. In many cases, the authoritarian states or colonial powers that were the democratizing states' predecessors leave a legacy of divisive institutions and ideas that were elements in a strategy of divide-and-rule. In other cases, democracy and freedom of expression are newly thrust upon traditional societies whose political horizons have historically been local and communal. Even in democratizing post-communist states with a legacy of hyper-centralization, the media's financial vulnerability often leaves it vulnerable to capture by partisan segments, thus spoiling it as a neutral forum for debate.

Narrow market segments magnify the effects of oligopolistic control over supply, because they are more susceptible to domination by a single, myth-purveying supplier. Unlike true monopolists, oligopolists *are* forced to compete, but they often do so by increasing sales to consumers in segments of the market that they can monopolize, rather than in market segments where they

face strong competitors. When this happens, there is no common marketplace of ideas, in which contending discourses and evidence confront each other directly on an even playing field. Instead, the existence of parallel monopoly discourses creates the illusion of market pluralism and free choice of ideas and, by vitiating skepticism, makes oligopolistic propaganda more effective than under pure monopoly.[10] Thus, the more segmented the market, the more the effects of partial monopolies of supply are magnified, and the more feasible is mythmaking.

Nationalist groups in the newly democratic Weimar Republic, including those backed by heavy industrial cartels, competed for mass electoral support against labor parties and liberals not so much by preaching to the constituencies of their opponents as by exploiting partial propaganda monopolies to mobilize their own. Hugenberg had only 50 percent of the overall Weimar media market, but he enjoyed a virtual monopoly over the flow of news to papers in Germany's small cities and towns, the locations that later voted most heavily for Hitler.[11] Exploiting Hugenberg's priming of middle class opinion, Hitler's successes came not from winning over liberal, socialist, or undecided opinion in open debate, but by cornering the nationalist market segment through skillful penetration of grassroots voluntary organizations, such as veterans groups and beer-drinking societies. Since Hitler attained a dominant position in the Reichstag with only one-third of the vote, and used this as a platform for an unconstitutional seizure of the media and other state powers, monopolizing one segment of the market was enough to be decisive in a splintered polity.

Segmented markets of ideas in democratizing states are conducive to nationalism for several reasons. The most fundamental reason is that elites have an incentive to promote nationalist populism as a substitute for true democratization. Segmented markets allow elite oligopolists to carve out a market niche where their nationalist ideas are not held up to systematic scrutiny. This is true even if the segmental divisions do not follow linguistic, ethnic, or communal lines. The nationalist market niches in Weimar Germany and in contemporary Russia, for example, reflect segmental cleavages *within* the majority ethnic group, such as those between urban and rural groups, between large cities and small towns, between soldiers or veterans and civilians, between economic strata, or between age groups. In these cases, mobilization of support by nationalists and by nationalistic Russian communists relied more heavily on face-to-face ward-heeling, handbills, and pamphlets targeted to specialized constituencies than on open media debate aimed at a broader range of society.

Market segmentation in newly democratizing states sometimes follows communal or linguistic lines. Language differences and exclusive face-to-face social networks may channel the dissemination of ideas along ethnic lines. These ethnic segments rarely start out with a highly developed sense of national political identity or nationalist political goals. On the contrary, ethnicity typically becomes politicized as nationalism only after the emergence of mass political discourse. Still less do ethnic market segments start out with consumer preferences for militant, xenophobic nationalism, based on "ancient hatreds." An ethnically differentiated market segment may, however, share a set of common experiences and a common, parochial discourse, which mythmakers can exploit.[12]

Propaganda is most effective when it taps into the audience's predispositions or when it can link a new idea to attitudes that the audience already holds. Thus, Milošević's success in mobilizing Serbian ethnic sentiment was due not only to his monopoly over Belgrade television but also to the historical legacy of ethnic conflict and the tense situation between Albanians and Serbs in Kosovo, which left his Serbian audience primed to accept his divisive and uncontested message. In this situation, there was positive feedback between supply and demand, in that segmented public opinion was ripe for national-

ist appeals, which in turn increased nationalism and deepened the segmentation of the market.

Even those scholars who tout the rationality of public opinion attach two crucial qualifications, one on the supply side and one on the demand side: the public responds rationally to events within the limits of the information and analysis that it receives, and given its predispositions. John Zaller, for example, shows that American voters rely for their opinions on perceived experts whom they believe share their own values.[13] In this view, experts do not tell people what to care about, but they do shape people's estimates of the costs and feasibility of various means for pursuing the ends that they value. Consequently, demand reflects not only the preferences of consumers but also the extent to which consumers with similar predispositions are isolated in separate market segments, each dominated by a single supplier.

Often the ethnic or communal segmentation of the market is not a spontaneous reflection of language or traditional social organization, but rather the modern artifact of elite strategies of divide and rule. For example, European colonial rulers—whether Stalin in Central Asia or Belgians in Rwanda—often highlighted or even created ethnic cleavages in order to split local populations and insure the dependence of native functionaries. Even in the heart of Europe, Bismarck and his successors concocted the segmentation of the German marketplace of ideas through their nationalistic agenda-setting and electoral propaganda, which divided the middle classes from socialists and Catholics, who were stigmatized as "enemies of the Reich." The belligerent tone of the bourgeois press, pressure groups and associations like the Navy League and Colonial Society, and political parties were all shaped by the nationalist themes around which elections were fought. Militarist ideas promoted in these campaigns and fostered by the middle-class, Protestant, patriotic organizations they spawned—including the notions of a need for *Lebensraum*, victimization by the encircling great powers, the superiority of German culture, and the spiritual benefits of war—became standard fare in right-wing thinking. In this way, electoral tactics erected high walls between segments of German society, which continued to shape political discourse and electoral strategies down through the Weimar period.

Sometimes elites segment the marketplace in a way that inadvertently loads the dice in favor of nationalist ideas. Tito's decentralizing reforms of the 1960s, which were intended in part to assuage and defuse ethno-nationalism, put Yugoslavia's media in the hands of regional leaderships, which in the 1980s fell into the hands of nationalists like Milošević. This federalization of power left pan-Yugoslav reformers like Ante Marković with no instrument for transcending the Serb and Croat nationalists' media monopoly over their respective ethnic niche markets.

While governmental elites in democratizing states are segmenting the emerging marketplace of ideas, counter-elites and consumers are rarely passive. Often, elite manipulations produce unintended consequences, and nationalist mobilization spins out of control. In Wilhelmine Germany, for example, the strategy of popular nationalism became less and less manageable for the "iron and rye" coalition of heavy industrialists and landed aristocrats. Numerically, the working class grew faster than other constituencies, shrinking the base from which the government could mobilize a majority. Moreover, the conservative elites' mass allies increasingly tried to use nationalist issues to push the old elites aside. After Germany's supposed humiliation by France in the Moroccan Crisis of 1911, mass nationalist groups and middle-class military officers claimed that the old elites running the German state lacked the dynamism to meet the looming challenge from Germany's enemies. To stay ahead of this tide of popular criticism, even the Junker aristocrats leading the Conservative party felt compelled to slam the weak policy of the Bethmann Hollweg government. The elites had unleashed a power that they were unable to control.

Segmentation of demand, in short, may be shaped by a number of factors: the pre-existing preferences or experiences of groups sharing a common outlook; differentiated preferences induced by targeted advertising; division of media markets by language or region; or divisions imposed by political boundaries, as in federal systems. Such factors may be overridden, however, if political discourse is channeled into a wider framework by strong catchall parties or nonpartisan media institutions.

Media Institutions and Norms

Where markets are imperfect, increased freedom of speech will tend to exacerbate nationalist mythmaking unless institutions and norms correct the flaws in the market. A well-institutionalized marketplace of ideas requires anti-trust and equal time regulations guaranteeing media access, the training of journalists in the verification of sources and the separation of fact from opinion, and the development of expert evaluative institutions whose prestige depends on maintaining a reputation for objectivity. Without such regulatory institutions, free speech by itself will not guarantee that a range of voices is effectively heard, that competing arguments are forced to confront each other on their merits, that participants in debate are held accountable for the accuracy of their statements, that factual claims are scrutinized, that experts' credentials are verified, that hidden sources of bias are exposed, or that violators of the norms of fair debate are held up to public censure.[14]

Regulation entails some risk of abuse, the severity of which depends in part on how it is carried out. In centralized forms of regulation, a state official or governmental body decides who has access to the media and what are the ground rules for its use. In contrast, decentralized regulation is achieved through routines of professional behavior in institutions such as the professional media, universities, think tanks, and legislative oversight bodies. Both forms of regulation may be useful antidotes to market imperfections, and both may be used in combination. Decentralized regulation is generally preferable, since centralized regulation creates the risk that the state will exploit its regulatory power to establish its own media monopoly. However, where decentralized institutions are weak or lack the required professional norms, centralized regulation, especially if it is subject to democratic control or held accountable to international standards, may be preferable to an imperfect, unregulated marketplace.

Similarly, the regulation of the content of speech, such as the banning of hate speech, is more subject to abuse than the establishment of norms of debate, which set standards for how people are expected to argue their cases. The latter would include the professional journalist's norm of distinguishing facts from opinion, the scholar's norm of citing sources of alleged facts, and the League of Women Voters' norm of expecting candidates to debate issues in a common forum in front of a panel of disinterested expert questioners. Establishing strong norms of debate is generally preferable to regulating the content of speech, but when norms are weak, content regulation may also be needed. Like centralized regulation, content limits should be accountable to democratic oversight or international standards.

Regulation is not a panacea. Indeed, skeptics doubt how well media institutions structure public debate even in the most mature democracies. Nevertheless, there is substantial evidence that effective evaluative institutions do have an impact on public views. Studies show that, apart from the influence of a popular president, American public opinion is swayed most strongly by the media testimony of experts who are perceived to be credible and unbiased.

If the marketplace of ideas is imperfect even in mature democracies, its flaws are still more grave in new democracies. An integrated public

sphere, in which each idea confronts every other idea on its merits, does not get created overnight. Without the functional equivalents of institutions like the *New York Times*, the *MacNeil-Lehrer News Hour*, the Brookings Institution, and the Congressional Budget Office, discussion may be open, but an exchange and evaluation of contending views before a common audience may not occur. In many newly democratizing societies, press laws are biased and capriciously enforced. The middlemen of the marketplace of ideas—journalists, public intellectuals, and public-interest watchdogs—tend to perform poorly in the initial stages of the expansion of press freedom. Instead of digging out the truth and blowing the whistle on fallacious arguments, journalists in emerging markets are often beholden to a particular party or interest group, make little attempt to distinguish between fact and opinion, and lack training in the standards of journalistic professionalism. While Thomas Jefferson said that if forced to choose, he would rather have a free press than a democratic government, in assessing the actual state of the press in young America, he remarked that "a suppression of the press could not more completely deprive the nation of its benefits, than is done by its abandoned prostitution to falsehood. Nothing can now be believed which is seen in a newspaper. Truth itself becomes suspicious by being put into that polluted vehicle."[15]

Even if a new democracy has a responsible elite press, its ability to impose a coherent structure on discourse may not penetrate to the grassroots level. Weimar's liberal, Jewish-owned, mass circulation newspapers were objective and even erudite, but their ideas failed to penetrate beyond Berlin or Hamburg. Even in those urban centers, workers read the liberal press only for the sports, feature stories, and movie listings, ignoring the political views of the "class enemy." Today, India's elite English-language press has a laudable system of self-regulation and responsible coverage of communal conflict, but the populist vernacular press remains immune to these high standards. In newly democratizing states, the penetration of ideas to the grassroots often requires face-to-face contacts. In India, at least before Indira Gandhi's time, this was accomplished by the moderate, secularist political machine of the Congress Party. In contrast, at the dawn of Sri Lankan democracy in the 1950s, only Sinhalese Buddhist priests, who fiercely opposed toleration of the Tamil Hindu minority, had networks for persuading voters at the crucial village level.

Market Forces That Promote Nationalist Mythmaking

In summary, under conditions of incipient democratization, the increased openness of public debate often fosters nationalist mythmaking and ethnic conflict because opportunistic governmental and non-governmental elites exploit partial monopolies of supply, segmented demand, and the weakness of regulatory institutions in the marketplace of ideas. We argue that the greater these market imperfections (that is, the greater the rivalry between oligopolistic elites, the greater the consumer segmentation, and the more dependent and partisan are media institutions), then the greater the likelihood for nationalist mythmaking to dominate public discourse, and the greater the likelihood for mythmaking to promote conflict. Conversely, the more perfect the marketplace and the more integrated the public sphere, the less effective is nationalist mythmaking. These hypotheses are probabilistic, not invariant relationships or sufficient causes. This article does not present a systematic test of all these propositions. As a first step towards evaluating them, however, we examine two hard cases, Yugoslavia and Rwanda, which are often invoked on behalf of the conventional wisdom that governments are largely responsible for nationalist mythmaking and that unconditional free speech is the best antidote.

Monopolizing Market Segments in the Former Yugoslavia

On the surface, the story of the media in the Yugoslav conflict may seem to fit the Human Rights Watch analysis quite well. Government officials in the republics of Serbia and Croatia used their near-monopoly control of the news media to fuel their publics' ethnic prejudices, mobilizing a popular nationalist constituency to support their rule while discrediting more liberal opponents. However, the media monopoly merely gave elites in the republics the tools to sell nationalist myths. The motive and the opportunity were created by the Serbian elite's fear of democratization, by the plausibility of these myths to consumers in a segmented market, and by the unevenness of journalistic standards. Under these highly imperfect market conditions, the weakening of the central Yugoslav state created a potential opening for increased political pluralism, which threatened the oligarchs who ruled the federal republics and also created an opportunity for political entrepreneurs—including politicians, journalists, and intellectuals—to exploit their media market power in the competition for mass support. Tito's dispersion of control over television to the republics in the 1960s and 1970s, under the theory that a federalist devolution of power would dampen underlying ethnic tensions, turned out to have been a grave mistake. By 1989, when Yugoslav Prime Minister Ante Marković finally embarked on the creation of an all-Yugoslav television network, it was already too little, too late. This suggests that NGOs' standard prescription of reducing centralized state media power needs strong qualifications.

In 1987, Slobodan Milošević, head of the Serbian Central Committee of the League of Communists, mounted a systematic campaign using his control over the Serbian state television monopoly to convince the Serbian people that Serbs residing in Kosovo province, the historic cradle of Serbdom, were suffering discrimination, repression, and rape at the hands of the Albanian majority there. He chose the television correspondent who would report to Belgrade from Pristina, the capital of Kosovo, and personally phoned the station almost daily to tell the editors what stories to highlight. After Milošević's April 1987 speech in Kosovo, Belgrade TV showed the local Albanian police clubbing the Serbian crowd, and Milošević saying "From now on, no one has the right to beat you," but it left out the pictures of the crowd stoning the police.[16] Exploiting the wave of chauvinist sentiment touched off by this media campaign, Milošević used the Kosovo issue as a pretext to purge anti-Milošević journalists, charging them with issuing "one-sided and untrue reports," and to consolidate conservative domination in party circles in Belgrade. Thus, nationalist media manipulation was the centerpiece of Milošević's successful strategy for defeating liberal reformers in the scramble for both mass and elite support as power devolved from the center in the post-Tito period. Milošević never achieved an absolute monopoly over the Serb media, but he controlled its commanding heights, the state television station and Belgrade's three major daily newspapers. An independent TV station and the semi-independent *Borba* newspaper were prevented by low wattage and limited newsprint from reaching beyond the Belgrade suburbs into Milošević's stronghold in rural Serbia.[17]

Because of Yugoslavia's decentralized federal structure, republican television stations were totally independent of the central government, but were monopolized by the republican Communist parties. The Yugoslav media, like most other aspects of Yugoslav life, had become by the 1980s "an alliance of regional oligarchies."[18] Republican television stations would not even show Prime Minister Marković's speeches. To combat this, Marković established an all-Yugoslav network, Yutel, in 1989. However, the central government's financial limitations, themselves a consequence of Yugoslavia's federal structure,

left Yutel dependent on army surplus equipment and the sufferance of local broadcasters. After only four months on the air, Croatia pulled the plug on Yutel over a sensitive story on Slavonia, and most other republics followed suit. As the *coup de grace*, Serbian nationalist thugs trashed Yutel's Belgrade office. Thus, the ability of republican government leaders to manipulate the mass media reflected the collapse of the multinational Yugoslav state.

However, the ethnic segmentation of the media market cannot be blamed entirely on republican governments. Journalists and scholars also played the ethnic card, in some cases well before Milošević. Many Serbian intellectuals were obsessed with the Albanian threat in Kosovo even before Milošević began his media campaign on the issue. In 1986, for example, a large number of prominent members of the Serbian Academy of Sciences published a memorandum on the "genocide" being perpetrated against Serbs in Kosovo. This document was condemned by the Serbian Central Committee and the mainstream Belgrade press, still operating under traditional Yugoslav norms of comity between ethnic groups, though Milošević urged them to keep the condemnation secret. Some of these nationalist intellectuals and a portion of the Serbian journalistic community may have been acting partly out of sincere concerns. But in the view of some analysts, these intellectuals saw the Kosovo issue as a vehicle for breaking down communist limitations on intellectual freedom and for press "liberalization."[19] This reflected the necessity for all Yugoslav elites to reposition themselves on a new foundation of ideological legitimacy in the context of the waning of centralized communist authority. In this setting, the professional journalistic community split, some choosing the nationalist route and energetically aiding the Milošević takeover, some resisting it and ultimately being forced out. Mark Thompson of the journalism NGO Article 19, though generally a strong partisan of Yugoslavia's independent journalists, describes the Milošević takeover in the fall of 1987 as "a collusion among Serbia's Communist politicians, its bureaucracy, its intellectual class, and its news media."

Thus, organized forces in "civil society," no less than in government, saw the benefits of the strategy of monopolizing media control within a market niche. They were sometimes even willing to conspire explicitly with the ethnic archfoe to accomplish it. For example, after Serb, Croat, and Muslim nationalist parties emerged as the winners of Bosnia's 1991 elections, the three nationalist foes tried to collude to divide up among them the assets of Bosnia's integrated, civic television service, and to exclude the moderate parties of their respective ethnic groups.

The success of media propaganda depended both on monopoly of supply and also on the nature of demand, including the plausibility of the message in light of consumers' predispositions. Some propaganda campaigns were strikingly successful. For example, the Serbs enjoyed a six-month period of television monopoly in northern Bosnia, which they used to prime their population for the 1992 campaign of "ethnic cleansing" by repeatedly charging that Muslims were plotting to establish an Islamic fundamentalist state. Later, Serbs guarding prison camps accused their Muslim captives of precisely the charges that had been reiterated on the news. Similarly, as a result of Serb propaganda, 38 percent of Belgrade residents in a July 1992 poll thought that it was the Muslim-Croat forces who had recently been shelling the Bosnian capital of Sarajevo, versus only 20 percent who knew it had been the Serbs.[20] However, viewers refused to swallow every lie whole. When the popular nationalist Vuk Drašković mounted a mass anti-war rally in March 1991, the government-controlled media's attempts to portray him as in league with the Croats and Albanians fizzled as too implausible. The following year, only 8 percent of Serbian respondents thought that state television kept them "well informed," versus 43 percent for the independent media.[21]

Thus, the impact of the supply of nationalist propaganda must be assessed in light of the demand for it. As Mark Thompson put it: "People's bedrock attitudes toward the wars in Croatia and Bosnia are not created by the state media; rather, the media play variations upon those attitudes, which derive from other sources (national history, family background, education, oral culture). Media did not inject their audiences with anti-Muslim prejudice or exploitable fear of Croatian nationalism. The prejudice and fear were widespread, latently at least; there was a predisposition to believe 'news' which elicited and exploited the prejudice; without the media, however, Serbia's leaders could not have obtained public consent and approval of its nationalist politics."[22]

The importance of underlying predispositions is demonstrated by comparing the propaganda strategies that Milošević tailored for the Serbs and those Tudjman adopted for the Croats. Belgrade television portrayed the Serbs as always on the defensive, the perennial victims of every battle. Dead Serbs were favored imagery. This was thought to strike the right chord in a people who glorify a defeat at the hands of the Turks half a millennium ago in the battle of Kosovo. In contrast, government propaganda directives told Croatian television to soft-pedal defeats, never show footage of destroyed Croat towns, and "always finish such reports with optimistic declarations and avowals."[23] The government feared that Croats, lacking as firm a tradition of statehood as the Serbs had, might simply give up hope if they knew the odds they faced.

What was lacking in the Yugoslav case was not just free speech, but strong institutions to counteract market imperfections and to promote a professional, unbiased, pan-Yugoslav mass media. Standard antidotes to state power would have been of doubtful effectiveness in this case, even though it is true that media monopolies in the hands of republican governments caused most of the damage. Federalism, that standard remedy for constraining state exploitation of ethnic minorities, was in fact one of the main problems. Moreover, "consociational" power-sharing, which is often prescribed as a complement to federalism, was also troublesome. In the Bosnian media, for example, the practice of allotting equal time for each group's biases made the evening news a series of stories with different slants, while the true story of the Yugoslav army's role in the attacks on Sarajevo, for example, was suppressed as a violation of consociational comity. Likewise, providing piecemeal subsidies to individual newspapers in the capital city, as the International Federation of Journalists did for *Borba*, failed to go to the heart of the problem, since the backbone of support for nationalism lay in the Serb countryside, where Milošević's media monopoly was uncontested. Finally, simply prescribing maximum freedom of speech would have been unavailing, given the inclinations and the capacity of various elite strata, both inside and outside the government, to exploit the population's predispositions to ethnic anxiety.

Rwandan Hate Radio

The 1994 mass murder of some 800,000 Tutsi and moderate Hutu organized by extremist Hutu in top circles of the Rwandan government is another case that may seem to fit the Human Rights Watch analysis perfectly. Officials of the authoritarian regime of President Juvénal Habyarimana, feeling their power endangered, used their monopoly control of mass media and university appointments to create a "finely tuned propaganda machine" that played on Hutu fears of the former Tutsi elite and purveyed false, inflammatory versions of the history of relations between the two groups. In April 1994, the Hutu official clique unleashed militias trained in the techniques of genocide. Independent journalists were a special target in the first wave of the killings. At the same time, Radio-Télévision Libre des Mille Collines, a pseudo-private station established by Habyarimana's wife, spread the word that Tutsi rebels were about to rise up and

kill Hutu, and consequently that all Hutu should join the militias in a campaign of preventive killing. Militias threatened to kill Hutu who did not participate in the genocide, so it is difficult to judge how much of the killing was triggered by the radio propaganda *per se*.[24] Nonetheless, all sources agree that the hate broadcasts played a significant role in the second phase of the killing, after the initial militia sweeps. Holly Burkhalter, the Washington director of Human Rights Watch, argued that jamming the hate radio was "the one action that, in retrospect, might have done the most to save Rwandan lives." The radios instead withdrew from the advancing Tutsi army into the safe haven of the French army zone, where they continued to broadcast.[25]

NGOs such as Human Rights Watch and Africa Rights, as well as many independent scholars, drew the lesson that the international community needs to encourage Rwanda and Burundi to democratize, to foster an independent press, and to bring the perpetrators of genocide to justice.[26] However, upon closer examination, their prescriptions are contradicted by their own highly persuasive analyses of the causes of the Rwanda genocide. After the genocide, NGOs continue to advocate precisely those measures that their analyses show to have triggered the killings: an increase in political pluralism, the prospect of trials of the guilty, and the promotion of anti-government media.

In the late 1980s and early 1990s, falling coffee prices and economic disruptions caused by fighting with Uganda-based Tutsi rebels put the Habyarimana regime on the defensive. Under intense pressure from the domestic Hutu opposition and from international aid donors, the regime agreed under the 1993 Arusha Accords to a limited political opening, involving power-sharing with opposition groups, the legalization of numerous opposition political parties calling for democratic elections and, as an Africa Rights report puts it, "an explosion in the number of newspapers and journals" published by anti-government groups after the abandonment of the press monopoly in July 1990.[27] "A vibrant press had been born almost overnight," says Gérard Prunier, but its biased commentary was written "in terrible bad faith."[28] Hutu extremists attached to the regime continued to monopolize the radio, a key asset among a population that was 60 percent illiterate. After a Tutsi rebel attack on the capital in 1993 was parried only with the help of French troops, Habyarimana had had no alternative but to accept the Arusha agreement, which provided for Tutsi participation in government, a rebel military unit to provide security for Tutsi politicians in the capital, and the exclusion of Hutu extremists from the joint Hutu-Tutsi government. Moderate Hutu from southern Rwanda, where "Hutu" and "Tutsi" were racially almost indistinguishable, began to mobilize politically against Hutu extremists in the government clique and their northern Rwanda social base.

As part of the settlement, an international commission named names of highly placed Hutu extremists who were complicit in small-scale killings of Tutsi. "Individuals named were promised an amnesty," says Africa Rights's Alex de Waal, "but knew that their actions were under scrutiny," and so distrusted these guarantees. Human rights groups were active in this period of internationally sponsored power-sharing and pluralization. "Rwanda had one of the most vigorous human-rights movements in Africa," says de Waal. "Six independent human rights organizations cooperated in exposing abuses by government and rebel forces."[29]

In this setting, the clique around Habyarimana had every reason to fear democratization and calls for justice from the international community. To forestall a fall from power and judicial accountability, these officials developed the plan for a mass genocide. "The extremists' aim," says Africa Rights, "was for the entire Hutu populace to participate in the killing. That way, the blood of genocide would stain everybody. There could be no going back for the Hutu population."[30] But there was a flaw in this plan. Habyarimana, heavily dependent on foreign aid to prop up his system of official patronage, balked at implementing a bloodbath that he knew would cut

him off from foreign funds. The president's extremist allies in the military and security services had no such qualms. From January to March 1994, their unofficial journal *Kangura*, an example of the "flowering" of Rwandan media in the period of pluralism and incipient power-sharing, warned Habyarimana not to flinch from the destruction of the Tutsi and predicted with astonishing accuracy the details of his assassination: Habyarimana was killed in April by his own presidential guard upon returning from a meeting at Dar Es Salaam where he made renewed concessions to international donors, the UN, and the Organization of African Unity. As de Waal aptly states, "Habyarimana was a victim of the international peace industry."[31]

Despite the clear evidence that NGO analysts themselves recite, they fail to acknowledge that the very solutions they continue to promote are the same as the steps that caused the killings. Human Rights Watch correctly notes that the "free and fair" election of Burundi's first Hutu president in October 1993 set the stage for the killing of some 50,000 Hutu and Tutsi. The Tutsi military, fearing that the elected government's power-sharing scheme would neutralize the army as a security guarantee for the Tutsi minority, launched a coup to protect its monopoly of force, touching off a series of reprisals. Yet Human Rights Watch urges democratic accountability and prosecution of the killers "to deter further slaughter," despite the fact that it was precisely the threat of such accountability that provoked the slaughter in Rwanda and Burundi in the first place.[32]

Both the Rwanda and Burundi cases show that the ideals of democratic rights, uncompromising justice, and free speech must make pragmatic accommodations to recalcitrant reality. Recognizing this, *Reporters sans Frontières* warns that the "error committed in Rwanda, which consisted of applying the rule of 'laissez faire' in the name of the principle of liberty of the press, must not be repeated in Burundi." While working to reconstitute the private news media in both countries and to bring journalists implicated in the genocide campaign to justice, the French NGO acknowledges that the thirteen newspapers that it is helping in Rwanda are short on personnel, paper, and facilities; have a circulation under 1,000 each; cost a day's wage to buy one issue; and consist primarily of opinions, not news. Realistically skeptical about some of the journalists it supports, *Reporters sans Frontières* conditions aid on a pledge to forswear ethnic hate speech. In Burundi, *Reporters sans Frontières* notes the paradox that many journalists working under a new law on press freedom are calling for an ethnic dictatorship that would shut down non-official expression of views. Since the invisible hand of the marketplace of ideas is so unreliable in such circumstances, *Reporters sans Frontières* relies also on the visible hand of two international radio stations broadcasting into Rwanda and Burundi from Zaire.

Conditions for Successful Liberalization of the Marketplace of Ideas

In numerous recent cases, such as South Africa, increases in press freedom and democratic participation in politics spawned no sanguinary outbursts of nationalism. Historically, Britain democratized and evolved a free press without developing German-style populist nationalism. These cases had better outcomes because their elites had weaker motivations to propound nationalist myths, because their markets were not as segmented, or because effective institutions of free debate were in place before the democratization of political participation. If elites believe that the expansion of free speech and democratic participation poses little threat to their interests, nationalism will be moderate. This pattern suggests that activists should target their efforts at patiently putting in place these preconditions of constructive public discourse, rather than clamoring for no-holds-barred press freedom

across the board. Institutional foundations of free debate are achieved either by historical evolution or by conscious design, not instantaneously by the invisible hand of competition.

The paradigm-setting case for these conditions is Great Britain. England did fight an intense civil war in the seventeenth century shortly after a dramatic increase in the number of newspapers and the freedom of political expression in them. However, by the dawn of the age of mass nationalism in the late eighteenth and early nineteenth centuries, Britain had already achieved a set of well-established norms of free speech among wide circles of the elite. The decisive move to end censorship in Britain came at the beginning of the eighteenth century, at a time when the political position of the Whig aristocracy was at its strongest and the proportion of the British population who could vote in parliamentary elections was actually declining. In that same era, Britain's integration of the Scottish and Welsh peoples into a centralized state before the era of mass democracy prevented ethnic segmentation of the market, at least in the core of the realm. By the mid-nineteenth century, when the penny press and the expansion of the electoral franchise further widened the scope of political debate to include the middle class, existing journalistic institutions and norms of debate provided a structure to channel and regulate the exchange of ideas. Moreover, Britain's traditional ruling class shared many commercial interests with the rising middle class, and so had little reason to "play the nationalist card" to forestall democratic policies like the repeal of tariffs on imported food. In a limited way, some aristocratic demagogues, most notably Lord Palmerston on the eve of the Crimean War, succeeded in diverting public opinion away from political reform towards a foreign policy of nationalist expansion, but these adventures were moderate in scope. Though Britain conquered vast portions of the globe, it generally did so in a cost-conscious way: it appeased foes strategically, pulled back from overcommitments, and never placed its nationalism beyond the pale of rational discussion weighing the costs and benefits of imperial policies.

Several contemporary success cases of relatively peaceful democratization and media liberalization share one or more of these characteristics of the British case: that is, guarantees of the interests of powerful elites, no ethnic segmentation of the market, or thorough institutionalization of the marketplace of ideas before democratization. Indeed, some of these moderate cases are former British colonies, which inherited along with the English language a tradition of professionalized journalism from the colonial period. One factor in the smooth South African transition, for example, was the well-established English-language opposition press, exemplified by the Rand *Daily Mail* and its successors, which for decades had been consistently more liberal than many of its readers. The political opening in the 1990s permitted the English-language press to report more freely, and a new black press was funded by churches and through Danish and Norwegian subsidies. Television and especially print news, already staffed with a professional cadre, moved quickly toward international norms. This allowed the divisions between Afrikaner, English, and black media that had prevailed under apartheid to be overcome rapidly. Moreover, Nelson Mandela's moderate rhetoric reassured whites about the consequences of free speech, as does their residual power to veto threatening developments.

India is another case in which a balanced marketplace of ideas was well institutionalized long before the transition to democratic politics, and in which the central ruling elite saw its interests as served by moderate, secular policies rather than divisive, ethno-communal ones. By the turn of the century, the English-language Indian press was already able to use the pressure of open public debate to constrain the non-elected British regime's policies. By the time of independence, a number of highly professional, major urban newspapers had developed a voluntary press code for reporting on communal riots, which abjured inflammatory headlines, refrained from specifying casualty figures during the heat of the moment, scrupulously cited sources, and dug for accurate information on the causes of riots. These informal codes were institutionalized in the Press Council, modeled on its British forebear. The Council was given the same statutory powers to investigate violations as a civil court. Smaller, partisan papers sometimes inflamed communal tensions, however, and during the 1947 riots a restrictive press ordinance with pre-publication censorship was temporarily adopted. In provincial towns, publishers and journalists are highly dependent on the support of local business elites, and expedience often gets in the way of truth in reporting on communal tensions. The vernacular (i.e., non-English) press commonly circulates false reports, inflated death figures, and unevaluated statements by communal leaders. This gap between the restrained, professional, state-wide press and the inflammatory communal press has been growing over the past two decades, as a result of economic change and the growth of literacy in provincial areas. Social change, sharply rising newspaper readership, and the emergence of a local intelligentsia has played a central role in reigniting communal conflict in Kashmir, for example.

In the heyday of the Congress Party's centralized, secular leadership, local Congress notables kept a short leash on the expression of communal prejudices. In the 1970s, however, Indira Gandhi sought to free herself from Congress's grassroots organizational structure through direct appeals not only to religious groups, but also to increasingly politicized lower-caste and lower-class segments of Indian society. As Human Rights Watch argues correctly, these segmental appeals touched off an increasing communalization of Indian politics.[33] However, the problem nowadays is hardly that the central, secular elites, including the elite media, are too demagogic, but that their power was weakened *vis-à-vis* nationalist challengers by the de-institutionalization of the Congress Party.

In other contemporary cases, the nationalist dogs are not barking because old elites have found a safe haven in the new regime. In many of the democratizing post-communist states of Eastern Europe, former apparatchiks have profited from the privatization of industry, attracted a mass constituency based on appeals to economic security rather than nationalism, and still rule many of these countries. Likewise, in Latin America, former military elites have been given "golden parachutes," and journalistic institutions were already well established as the result of earlier periods of democratization.[34]

Prescriptions for an Integrated Marketplace of Ideas

Democratization and free speech can be made compatible with ethnic harmony and the moderation of nationalist sentiment only under favorable conditions of supply, demand, and institutional regulation. If these conditions do not exist, they need to be created before, or at least along with, the unfettering of speech and political participation.

On the supply side, the international community may be needed to help break up information monopolies, especially in states with very weak journalistic traditions and a weak civil society. In Cambodia, for example, the UN's successful media and information program was designed, according to the UN commander, to "bypass the propaganda of the Cambodian factions" by directly disseminating information about the elections.[35] The breakup of monopoly power over politics and discourse must coincide, however, with measures to reduce elites' incentives for nationalist mythmaking or to eliminate their capacity to make trouble. As our cases show, it is reckless for the international community to threaten elites with across-the-board exposure and prosecution of past crimes, unless there exists the will and capability to render harmless the likely backlash from elites that are pushed to the wall. Otherwise, elites that are potentially threatened by democratization and the end of censorship should be guaranteed a soft landing

in the emerging open society. Many Latin American and East European countries have done well by keeping prosecutions limited. In contrast, fine moral declarations without effective actions are the worst possible policy.

On the demand side, ethnically segmented markets should be counteracted by the promotion of civic-territorial conceptions of national identity, as in Ukraine. Inclusive national identities can be fostered through an integrative press, which expresses a variety of outlooks on the same pages. All too often, international aid goes to the opposition press in democratizing countries regardless of its journalistic quality, on the grounds that creating a pluralism of voices is the essential objective. In Romania, for example, the U.S. Agency for International Development has subsidized anti-government newspapers that fail to meet even the most minimal standards of accuracy in reporting.[36] Instead, aid should go to forums that present varied ideas, not a single line, in a setting that fosters effective interchange and factual accuracy. In post-1945 Germany, for example, American occupiers licensing newspapers showed a strong preference for editorial teams whose members spanned diverse political orientations. This approach extends Donald Horowitz's critique of Arend Lijphart's strategy of "consociational" representation of communal power blocs into the realm of public discourse. Whereas Lijphart's approach rewards politicians who mobilize support along ethnic lines, Horowitz advises electoral rules that reward vote-pooling, in order to promote cross-ethnic political alliances and to break down the communal segmentation of politics. Applying Horowitz's principles to the marketplace of ideas, we counsel idea-pooling through integrative public forums, to break down the intellectual boundaries between ethnically exclusive "imagined communities."[37]

For this reason, we urge NGOs and other aid donors to reconsider projects to provide ethnic minorities with their "own" media. Instead, we suggest supporting media that strive to attract a politically and ethnically diverse audience, invite the expression of various viewpoints, and hold news stories to rigorous standards of objectivity. This can be done by expanding existing NGO programs to train journalists from newly democratizing countries, such as those of the International Press Institute in Vienna, and by providing quality news organizations with equipment, subsidized newsprint, or other logistical support. Special efforts should be made to encompass the regional and local press in these efforts. In case after case—Weimar, Germany, India, Sri Lanka, and contemporary Russia—key vehicles of nationalist mythmaking have been face-to-face networks and rough-hewn periodicals. To provide an effective alternative to these, media projects should focus on the inclusion of local journalists in the activities of state-wide media associations, mid-career training sabbaticals for grassroots journalists, and financial subsidies to make a high quality local press independent and affordable.

Major efforts should be made to promote the institutionalization of effective norms of elite discourse, journalistic professionalism, and independent evaluative bodies *before* the full opening of mass political participation. Whenever possible, market imperfections should be counteracted by decentralized institutions, not centralized regulatory directives, and by the promotion of norms of fair debate, not by restrictions on the content of speech. In some cases, however, certain kinds of constraints on speech may be necessary in multi-ethnic societies while these institutions are being built. This may be ethically uncomfortable for Western liberals; moreover, it is politically difficult to design constraints on democracy and free speech that do not play into the hands of elites who want to squelch freedom entirely. When electoral polarization touched off communal riots in Malaysia in 1969, for example, Malay elites banned public discussion of ethnic issues and imposed a regime of ethnic coexistence that insured Malay political domination and economic prosperity for the Chinese business community. After a quarter-century of tight press controls, the un-easy communal peace still holds, but this interlude, which might have been used to prepare an institutional infrastructure for a more durable, democratic solution, has been squandered.

Neither the ethnic strife unleashed by unchecked democratization in cases like Sri Lanka nor the temporary, repressive communal cease-fire in cases like Malaysia is desirable. One element of a better solution is for international donors to offer incentives to political and economic to elites to prepare the institutionalization of open discourse, while tolerating some limits on free expression, including limits on ethnic hate speech, in the short run. Another element is direct aid to professionalize those elements of the media that are attempting to create an integrated forum for responsible, accurate debate. But when these remedies are unavailing, those who value both unfettered speech and peace must, without illusions, assess the tradeoff between them.

NOTES

1. Human Rights Watch, *Playing the "Communal Card"* (New York: Human Rights Watch, April 1995), reprinted as *Slaughter among Neighbors: The Political Origins of Communal Violence* (New Haven, Conn.: Yale University Press, 1995); Human Rights Watch, " 'Hate Speech' and Freedom of Expression," *Free Expression Project*, Vol. 4, No. 3 (March 1992).

2. Van Evera, "Hypotheses," p. 33. Human Rights Watch, *Playing the "Communal Card,"* p. viii, points this out, but disregards it when drawing conclusions. According to Freedom House's ratings, civil liberties, which include freedom of speech, improved in Yugoslavia, Rwanda, and Burundi shortly before the recent outbreaks of massive ethnic violence there. Raymond Gastil and R. Bruce McColm, eds., *Freedom in the World* (New York: Freedom House, 1988–93), pp. 411–412 (1988), 272–274 (1989–90), 104–105,

313–315 (1990–91), and 153–155, 429–431 (1992–93).

3. Human Rights Watch, *Playing the "Communal Card,"* xiv, xvii. For a more nuanced NGO view, see Bruce Allyn and Steven Wilkinson, *Guidelines for Journalists Covering Ethnic Conflict* (Cambridge, Mass.: Conflict Management Working Paper, January 1994).

4. Pierre Birnbaum, *States and Collective Action* (Cambridge, U.K.: Cambridge University Press, 1988), pp. 39–40; Peter Fritzsche, *Rehearsals for Fascism: Populism and Political Mobilization in Weimar Germany* (New York: Oxford University Press, 1990), p. 75. Robert Putnam, *Making Democracy Work* (Princeton, N.J.: Princeton University Press, 1993), fails to address the Weimar case.

5. Quoted in Hobsbawm, *Nations and Nationalism*, p. 12.

6. Anthony D. Smith, *The Ethnic Origins of Nations* (Oxford, U.K.: Blackwell, 1986), pp. 15, 24; John Armstrong, *Nations before Nationalism* (Chapel Hill: University of North Carolina Press, 1982).

7. Richard Leftwich and Ross Eckert, *The Price System and Resource Allocation*, 9th ed. (Chicago: Dryden, 1985), p. 407. The same uncertainty that fuels rivalrous behavior in a "young industry" typically characterizes periods of democratization and, in the absence of shared norms or effective enforcement mechanisms, often produces the same results. See Adam Przeworski, *Democracy and the Market* (Cambridge, U.K.: Cambridge University Press, 1991).

8. Modris Eksteins, *The Limits of Reason: The German Democratic Press and the Collapse of Weimar Democracy* (London: Oxford University Press, 1975).

9. Laura Silber and Allan Little, *Yugoslavia: Death of a Nation* (New York: TV Books, 1996), pp. 38–39.

10. For related arguments, see Edward S. Herman and Noam Chomsky, *Manufacturing Consent* (New York: Pantheon, 1988).

11. Eksteins, *Limits of Reason*, pp. 80–81; Thomas Childers, *The Nazi Voter* (Chapel Hill: University of North Carolina Press, 1983), pp. 157–159.

12. Susanne Hoeber Rudolph and Lloyd Rudolph, "Modern Hate," *New Republic*, Vol. 208, No. 12 (March 22, 1993), pp. 24–29; Milton Esman, *Ethnic Politics* (Ithaca, N.Y.: Cornell University Press, 1994), pp. 28–31.

13. John Zaller, *The Nature and Origins of Mass Opinion* (Cambridge, U.K.: Cambridge University Press, 1992).

14. For various approaches to regulating speech and media, see Judith Lichtenberg, ed., *Democracy and the Mass Media* (Cambridge, U.K.: Cambridge University Press, 1990), esp. pp. 52, 127–128, 144–145, 186–201.

15. Letter to John Norvell, June 14, 1807, in Merrill D. Peterson, ed., *The Portable Thomas Jefferson* (New York: Viking, 1975), p. 505.

16. Velko Vujacic, "Serbian Nationalism, Slobodan Milosevic and the Origins of the Yugoslav War," *The Harriman Review*, Vol. 8, No. 4 (December 1995), p. 29; Thompson, *Forging War*, p. 20.

17. Gagnon, "Ethnic Nationalism and International Conflict: The Case of Serbia"; Susan Woodward, *Balkan Tragedy* (Washington, D.C.: Brookings, 1995), pp. 99, 230–232, 293; Branka Magaš *The Destruction of Yugoslavia* (London: Verso, 1993), pp. 3–76; Thompson, *Forging War*, p. 56, 65–66, 114–116, 124.

18. Thompson, *Forging War*, pp. 6–7, 16.

19. Milivojević, "The Media in Serbia," p. 164; Thompson, *Forging War*, p. 54; Silber and Little, *Yugoslavia*, p. 33; see also Magaš, *Destruction*, pp. 49–76.

20. Changes in media content were also used successfully to shift opinion in favor of peace. On April 9, 1993, 70 percent of Serbian respondents said they opposed the Vance-Owen peace plan, but on April 27, af-

ter a reversal of policy by the Serbian government and media, only 20 percent opposed it, and 39 percent were in favor. Thompson, *Forging War*, pp. 127–128, 209, 264.

21. Nonetheless, even the independent media found itself caught in the self-fulfilling prophecies generated by nationalist myth-making. As Serbian journalist Stojan Cerovic said in May 1992, "Anybody who explains the truth can do so only at his own cost. Reality sounds like the blackest anti-Serbian propaganda, and anyone who describes it will frighten people and turn them against him." Thompson, *Forging War*, pp. 73–75, 127–129. For a dissenting view which stresses the limited success of appeals to Serbian nationalism, see Gagnon, "Ethnic Conflict as Demobilizer."

22. Thompson, *Forging War*, pp. 127–128.

23. Thompson, *Forging War*, pp. 105–111, 161.

24. Quotation from Africa Rights, *Rwanda*, p. 35; also pp. vi, 37–38, 63–64, 69–72, 150; Human Rights Watch, *Playing the "Communal Card,"* pp. 7, 9.

25. Holly Burkhalter, "The Question of Genocide," *World Policy Journal*, Vol. 11, No. 4 (Winter 1994–95), pp. 44–54, esp. 51, 53.

26. Human Rights Watch, *Playing*, pp. 16–17; Africa Rights, *Rwanda*, p. 720; Reporters sans Frontières, *Rwanda: L'impasse? La liberté de las presse après le génocide, 4 juillet 1994–28 août 1995* (Paris: Reporters sans Frontières, 1995), pp. 48–50; Alison Des Forges, "The Rwandan Crisis," paper prepared for a conference on Sources of Conflict in Rwanda (Washington, D.C.: U.S. Department of State, October 17, 1994).

27. Africa Rights, *Rwanda*, p. 150.

28. Prunier, *The Rwanda Crisis*, chap. 4, "Slouching towards Democracy," esp. pp. 131–133, 157, on the low quality and extremism of these new entrants into public discourse.

29. Alex de Waal, "The Genocidal State," *Times Literary Supplement*, July 1, 1994, pp. 3–4; see also Africa Rights, *Rwanda*, pp. 30–32.

30. Africa Rights, *Rwanda*, p. v; also pp. 568–596; Prunier, *The Rwanda Crisis*, p. 170; Jones, "Arusha."

31. De Waal, "The Genocidal State," p. 4; also Jones, "Arusha." On Habyarimana's death, see Prunier, *Rwanda Crisis*, pp. 213–229.

32. Human Rights Watch, *Playing*, pp. 16–17.

33. Human Rights Watch, *Playing the "Communal Card,"* p. 21.

34. Article 19, *Guidelines for Election Broadcasting*, p. 5.

35. Michael W. Doyle, *UN Peacekeeping in Cambodia: UNTAC's Civil Mandate* (Boulder, Colo.: Lynne Rienner, 1995), pp. 54–55. For other cases, see Dan Lindley, "Collective Security Organizations and Internal Conflict," in Michael E. Brown, ed., *The International Dimensions of Internal Conflict* (Cambridge, Mass.: MIT Press, 1996), pp. 562–567.

36. Thomas Carothers, *Assessing Democratic Assistance: The Case of Romania* (Washington, D.C.: Carnegie Endowment for International Peace, 1996), pp. 80–89.

37. Horowitz, *A Democratic South Africa?* chaps. 4 and 5; Arend Lijphart, *Democracy in Plural Societies* (New Haven, Conn.: Yale University Press, 1977). On common media as a precondition for an integrated national consciousness, see Benedict Anderson, *Imagined Communities* (London: Verso, 1983).

M. STEVEN FISH

ISLAM AND AUTHORITARIANISM

Are predominantly Muslim societies distinctly disadvantaged in democratization? Some observers, noting what appears to be an especially high incidence of authoritarianism in the Islamic world, have held that Islam may be incompatible with open government. Others have argued that Islam is not necessarily antithetical to democratization. Yet few studies have attempted to establish empirically whether a democratic deficit really exists and, if so, how it can be explained.

The present article offers a straightforward cross-national examination of the relationship between Islam and regime type. After briefly sketching my conception of democracy, I conduct an empirical test of the determinants of political regime. The test provides strong support for the hypothesis that Muslim countries are democratic underachievers. The causal connection between Islam and regime type is then explored. Many conventional assumptions about Islam and politics do not withstand scrutiny. Muslim societies are not more prone to political violence; nor are they less "secular" than non-Muslim societies; and interpersonal trust is not necessarily lower in Muslim societies. But one factor does help explain the democratic deficit: the subordination of women. I furnish elements of a provisional theory linking the station of females and regime type and I discuss the implications of the findings for democracy. I further contend that patriarchal social order in Muslim societies has an ironic character, since it cannot be accounted for in scriptural terms.

* * *

From *World Politics* 55 (October 2002), pp. 4–37. Some of the author's notes have been omitted.

Determinants of Regime Type: Hypotheses

I test only hypotheses that are tractable to quantitative analysis and that are manifestly distinct from the dependent variable. Thus, I examine only what are commonly regarded as structural and cultural variables, as well as several historical variables that are amenable to coding in "yes" or "no" terms. A further limitation of my study arises from the problem of case selection. Including all countries of the world with populations over half a million helps mitigate the problem, but the analysis is not free from selection bias. I test only relationships that obtain in contemporary politics. As I do not use a random sample from all of history, I cannot confidently extend inferences from my sample to the world at other times. Whether or not a study of, say, the interwar period or the late nineteenth century would turn up similar findings is an empirical problem that deserves attention, but one that cannot be addressed here. In short, this inquiry is bounded in terms of both the hypotheses it tests and the period of time to which it applies. If the present article has anything to offer at all, its contribution is provisional and temporally specific. The aim is to assess whether the hypothesis that links Islam to authoritarianism enjoys empirical support when one controls for other possible determinants of political regime.

* * *

The most widely embraced causal hypothesis in the study of political regimes posits a positive relationship between *economic development* and democratic attainment. Analysts associate higher levels of economic development with lower levels of social conflict, more sophisticated populations, and broader and deeper social support for popular rule.[1] Some recent empirical studies have found that economic development does not inexorably generate democracy but that the durability of democracy, once established, is greater in wealthier countries.[2] A standard measure of economic development is gross domestic product (GDP) per capita. * * *

What may be dubbed the *sociocultural division* hypothesis is embraced almost as reflexively as the economic development hypothesis. Ethnically diverse societies are usually seen as disadvantaged and homogenous ones as fortunate. According to this logic, ethnic differences divide society and make compromise and consensus difficult. Ethnic heterogeneity raises the risk of intercommunal violence, which can quickly undermine democracy. To measure sociocultural division, I use the ethnolinguistic fractionalization scores generated by the Ethnologue project. 0 represents complete uniformity and 1 represents highest fractionalization. * * *

Economic performance is often held to influence political regime. Strong economic performance may protect fledgling democracies. Bad performance may generate popular dissatisfaction, alienate powerful social groups, and damage the cross-class alliances that stabilize democracy. Yet the stability of authoritarian regimes may also be vulnerable to economic performance, meaning that bad performance may open possibilities for democratization. The legitimacy of authoritarian regimes often rests on the promise of better economic performance alone, while open regimes also enjoy the legitimacy conferred by popular selection of the rulers and the state's respect for rights. Prolonged prosperity under an authoritarian regime may have contradictory effects. It might generate good will for the regime; but it might also raise popular expectations and increase the costs of repression as populations become more sophisticated. It may thereby ultimately undermine authoritarianism. There is no logical reason to expect strong economic performance in a democracy, by contrast,

ever to undermine the democratic regime. The preponderance of theory therefore suggests that sustained high rates of economic growth will help democratic regimes and may either help or hurt authoritarian regimes. On balance, one would expect strong performance to be conducive to democratization. * * *

British colonial heritage has long been considered a boon for the prospects for popular rule. Myron Weiner asserted that the most empirically persuasive explanation for democracy in the developing world is British colonial heritage. According to Weiner, "The British tradition of imposing limits on government, of establishing norms for the conduct of those who exercise power, and of creating procedures for the management of conflict has had a powerful influence on the creation of democratic systems in the Third World."[3] The British are often also credited with leaving behind the Westminster model of parliamentarism, which some analysts regard as a strong constitutional basis for democracy.[4] * * *

Since the beginning of the 1990s, another type of legacy has also been seen as important: a *communist heritage*. Most scholars regard the effects of communist legacy as negative. According to many, communist party rule bequeathed an antidemocratic political culture.[5] Soviet-type regimes, to a greater extent than other types of authoritarianism, destroyed political and civil society,[6] leaving behind what Juan Linz and Alfred Stepan have called a "flattened landscape," a condition that "creates problems for political representation" in the post-Soviet period.[7] * * *

Natural resource endowment has been regarded as influencing political regime. Abundance of natural resources, and particularly of oil, has often been regarded as democracy's antagonist. It may enable the state to buy off society with low taxation and high welfare spending and thereby allay popular demand for political accountability. So too may it reduce political competition to a fight over control of the agencies that manage the distribution of oil rents. It may enable the state to sustain a large and powerful internal security apparatus capable of repressing challengers. Resource abundance may also distort modernization, spurring expansion of national income without inducing the socio-economic changes that usually accompany an increase in wealth and that may favor democracy.[8]

* * *

Analysis of Data

Results

* * *

The negative results are as interesting as the positive ones. British colonial heritage does not necessarily provide significant advantages; nor does a Soviet-type past pose insurmountable disadvantages. Economic performance is not shown to be of great importance. Greater ethnic uniformity does not provide a firmer basis for a more open political regime than does greater heterogeneity.

The strong, positive relationship between democracy and economic development is consistent with long-standing social-scientific thinking and is therefore unsurprising. The negative relationship between democracy and OPEC membership supports the hypothesis that abundance of oil may conduce authoritarianism.

Due perhaps to cultural sensitivity or to an understandable reluctance to characterize nearly one-third of the world's polities as intractably resistant to popular rule, scholars have tended to treat the relationship between Islam and democracy circumspectly and have steered clear of examining it rigorously. The evidence presented here, however, reveals a link that is too stark and robust to ignore, neglect, or dismiss.

The Connection between Islam and Authoritarianism: Some Plausible but Unsatisfactory Ideas

Some claims may be dispensed with based on the above analysis. One is that there is no link between democratic deficit and Islam per se but that Muslim countries are far poorer than others and that underdevelopment therefore explains the relationship between Islam and authoritarianism. Muslim countries are indeed poorer than non-Muslim countries on average, but the empirical analysis controlled for development and Muslim countries still scored much lower . . . FH scores and Polity scores. So too did the analysis control for economic performance; this variable is not decisive. OPEC membership was also included. While the variable for OPEC was substantively and statistically significant, it clearly did not account for all the effects of Islam; oil rents alone probably do not explain the democratic deficit. Ethnic fractionalization was included as well. Predominantly Muslim countries are, on average, somewhat more ethnically diverse than non-Muslim countries. But the factor is not decisive in determining political regime; Muslim countries are not less democratic because they are more heterogeneous. The dummy variable for Islam is not picking up the effects of or serving as a proxy for any other variable tested here.

Some other possible explanations for the tie between Islam and authoritarianism, however, cannot be ruled out based on the preceding quantitative analysis. Here I inspect these ideas.

Are Muslim Societies More Prone to Political Violence?

Over two and a half centuries ago, Montesquieu asserted that Islam had a violent streak that predisposed Muslim societies to authoritarianism: "The Christian religion is remote from pure despotism; the gentleness so recommended in the gospel stands opposed to the despotic fury with which a prince would mete out his own jus-

Table 4. Bivariate Regressions of Polity Scores on Hypothesized Determinants[a]

Variable	Coefficient	Adj.R²	Number of Cases
Islamic religious tradition (dummy variable)	–7.97***	.29	153
Economic development (log GDP per capita $_{1990}$)	4.34***	.18	154
Sociocultural division (Ethnologue ethnolinguistic fractionalization index)	–6.88***	.09	154
Economic performance (growth of GDP per capita $_{1975-98\ ave\ annual\ change\ \%}$)	0.64***	.06	148
British colonial heritage (dummy variable)	0.33	.00	154
Communist heritage (dummy variable)	1.42	.00	154
OPEC membership (dummy variable)	–9.01***	.11	154

*p<0.05; **p<0.01; ***p<0.001
[a]Entries are unstandardized regression coefficients.

tice and exercise his cruelties. . . . The Mohammedan religion, which speaks only with a sword, continues to act on men with the destructive spirit that founded it."[9] Some scholars still embrace Montesquieu's assessment. Samuel Huntington, for example, holds that Muslim societies are especially prone to political violence. If he is right, given the hazards that violence poses to popular rule, this problem may help explain democratic underachievement.[10]

Is Huntington right? Monty Marshall has assembled a comprehensive list of incidents of political violence in the world during the post-war period.[11] By Marshall's account, there have been 207 episodes of major intrastate political violence. All of them occurred in countries included in the universe of cases under examination here. Of these events, 72—or 35 percent of the total— took place in Muslim countries. The data show that the Muslim world has had its fair share of political violence—indeed, a bit more than its fair share. But only a bit more. Since 30 percent of the world's polities are predominantly Muslim, the evidence does not show that the Islamic world has been the site of a grossly disproportionate amount of political violence.

Another useful source of data is the set of "governance indicators" that Daniel Kaufmann and colleagues have created based on extensive surveys.[12] One of their governance indictors is

"political stability/lack of violence." Scores range from about –2.5 to 2.5, with higher values corresponding to better outcomes (less violence and political instability born of violence). The data are imperfect but provide another window on the problem.

To assess Muslim countries in comparative context, I conducted an analysis of variance test (ANOVA), comparing the mean scores on the stability/lack of violence index for Muslim and Catholic countries. * * * I use Catholic countries as a comparative referent in part because they, like Muslim countries, have often been characterized as resistant to democracy (as well as to good governance, economic development, and other desirable things).[13] Furthermore, like Muslim countries, Catholic countries, which include many nations of Latin America and Africa as well as of Southern and Eastern Europe, constitute a large and extremely diverse group.

The results are shown in left-side column of numbers in Table 6. There is a statistically significant difference between the categories, with Muslim countries suffering from more violence. But when one controls for level of economic development the difference loses statistical significance. * * * Economic development is indeed related to stability/lack of violence, with higher income associated with greater stability/less violence. But the Islam variable is not statistically

Table 6. Difference in Mean Stability/Lack of Violence and Trust Scores for Catholic and Muslim Countries[a]

	Stability/Lack of Violence Score	Trust Score (Mean Percentage of Respondents Saying That People Can Be Trusted)
Muslim countries	-0.45	20.3
Catholic countries	0.22	24.9
F	11.11	0.80

Sources: Data for stability/lack of violence index: Daniel Kaufmann, Aart Kraay, and Pablo Zoido-Lobaton, "Composite Indicator Dataset" from "Governance Matters," World Bank Policy Research Department Working Paper no. 2195 (worldbank.org/wbi/gov ernance/gov_data, accessed May 2001). For trust scores: *World Values Survey*; data provided by Ronald Inglehart, chair of the World Values Surveys Executive Committee, 2002.

[a]Sample for stability/lack of violence analysis is 84 countries (43 Muslim); sample for trust analysis is 36 countries (7 Muslim).

significant. When one controls for economic development, the evidence for a link between Islam and violence is weak at best.

How, then, does Huntington reach his conclusions, which my own findings contradict? Huntington has different standards for the evaluation of data. He arrives at "overwhelming" evidence for the greater violence of Muslim societies by totaling up "ethnopolitical conflicts" in 1993–94 and "ethnic conflicts" in 1993, then within each group dividing the site of strife into Muslim and non-Muslim societies. Huntington emphasizes "intercivilizational" violence, by which he means conflict between Muslim and non-Muslim countries. His evidence on intercivilizational strife seems unequivocal: two-thirds of conflicts (thirty-six of fifty-one cases) were between Muslim and non-Muslim countries. But Huntington takes the further step of saying that "intracivilizational" conflict is also much more common in the Muslim world. He not only argues that "Islam's borders are bloody" but also adds, "and so are its innards." Its innards are most important for our purposes. But here the data are ambiguous. In the category of "intracivilizational" strife, only eighteen of fifty-eight conflicts—or 31 percent—were in Muslim societies. Given that 30 percent of the world's polities are predominantly Muslim, Huntington's evidence is less than overwhelming. Indeed, his evidence on intracivilizational conflict provides no support

for his argument, though he does not allow this detail to interfere with his generalizations. Finally, Huntington fails to control for any other variables. Simple correlation, presented in the form of unanalyzed descriptive statistics, serves as his empirical evidence.[14]

Is Interpersonal Trust Lower in Muslim Societies?

Many social scientists have linked interpersonal trust and democracy. Ronald Inglehart has found a positive correlation between the percentage of respondents who say in the World Values Surveys that people can be trusted, on the one hand, and country averages on FH scores from 1972 to 1997, on the other.[15] I used the data from the most recent available wave of World Values Surveys, which were conducted in the 1990s, to measure trust. An ANOVA test using the seven Muslim countries and the twenty-nine Catholic countries for which data are available shows that the level of trust in Muslim countries is not substantially lower than in Catholic countries, as is shown in the right-hand column of Table 6. * * *

Are Muslim Polities Less "Secular"?

A commonly embraced but rarely scrutinized argument holds that religious and secular authority are joined in Islamic societies, both in the popular imagination and in institutional practice, and that this fusion helps explain the democratic deficit. Jamal al-Suwaidi asserts that "Muslims have continued to assume that only a 'religious leader' can provide good government for the Muslim community."[16] According to Huntington, "God and Caesar, church and state, spiritual and temporal authority, have been a prevailing dualism in Western culture." In contrast, "In Islam God is Caesar."[17]

Two assumptions underlie this thinking. The first is that religion is more important to Muslims than it is to adherents of other faiths and that this difference is reflected in political preferences and authority structures. Muslims are more Muslim than Christians are Christian, and political life in predominantly Muslim societies is far more heavily saturated with religion. The second assumption is that religiosity per se is the ally of authoritarianism, and secularism of democracy.

Brief examination leaves room for skepticism regarding both assumptions. First, the notion that Muslims are more "religious" is completely dependent on subjective perspective. To a New Yorker in Mecca or a Berliner in Teheran, the idea that Islam is more deeply ingrained in Muslim societies than Christianity is in Christian societies may seem irrefutable. But to a Mississippian in Kazakhstan, a South African in Azerbaijan, a Pole in Syria, or an Irish person in Java, the situation might not be so clear. Indeed, it may be equally unclear to a Kazakh in Mississippi, an Azeri in South Africa, a Syrian in Poland, or a Javanese in Ireland. The fundaments of one's own culture, at any rate, naturally seem less conspicuous, imposing, and exotic—indeed, less "fundamental"—than do those of other cultures. The present author, who was raised in small cities in the American South and Midwest, does not view churches blanketing the landscape or Christian television and radio networks filling the airwaves as particularly striking. While traveling in Muslim countries, however, the author regards the sight of people facing Mecca together in prayer as a formidable demonstration of mass religiosity. Some of the author's associates who

grew up in predominantly Muslim societies have a different view. While in the United States, they regard what the author sees as unobtrusive manifestations of everyday social life as signs that American society is saturated with (Christian) religious influence. Their outlook is akin to that of As'ad AbuKhalil, who has rightly criticized "the mistaken association between secularism and Christianity."[18]

One may also question Huntington's notion that political and religious authority are strictly separated in the West and fused in the Muslim world. The separation of God and Caesar is far less complete in predominantly Christian countries than many Americans realize. Until 1995 all long-standing European democracies with a substantial Lutheran majority had established state churches. In Germany church and state are intertwined in education, taxation, social service provision, and finance. Nor does a rigorous separation between church and state prevail in many countries where Catholic traditions predominate. One would be hard pressed to find it in Poland, Ireland, Brazil, or Chile. Nor, needless to say, are religion and the state separated in Israel. What is more, the extent to which "God is Caesar" in the Muslim world is often greatly exaggerated. Religious and political power may be joined in, say, Iran and Taliban-era Afghanistan. But these polities are atypical. It is difficult to state with confidence that the fusion of sacred and temporal power is substantially and consistently greater in former Soviet Central Asia, North Africa, Muslim West Africa, Muslim Southeast Asia, Bangladesh, Iraq, Syria, Turkey, Azerbaijan, and Albania than it is in non-Muslim countries. If, moreover, al-Suwaidi is correct to say that Muslims seek a religious leader to guide the political community, one would expect most political heroes in the Islamic world to be religious leaders. But many of the Muslim world's most popular politicians—including Indonesia's Sukarno and Megawati Sukarnoputri, Pakistan's Zulfikar Ali Bhutto and Benazir Bhutto, Malaysia's Mohamad Mahathir, Senegal's Léopold Senghor, Mali's Alpha Oumar Konaré, and

Egypt's Gamal Abd al-Nasir—hardly fit that profile. If by "religious leader" al-Suwaidi means not a religious authority but merely a person who professes to hold some religious belief, he is on firmer ground. But in this case, Muslims are unexceptional. What are the chances of a self-proclaimed atheist becoming president of Costa Rica, the Philippines, or the United States? Social scientists in predominantly Christian societies may ignore candidates' religion; much of the rest of the electorate does not.

In short, the assumption that religion is consistently more important to Muslims than it is to adherents of other faiths and that this difference is clearly reflected in social and political life is open to doubt.

Of course I might be wrong. The evidence I have adduced on this point is the best I can muster, but it is scarcely definitive. Rigorously assessing the weight of religion in popular consciousness is exceedingly difficult; here we truly see through a glass darkly. The shortage of data is acute. The World Values Surveys query people on their religious activities and the importance of religion in their lives. But to date there still are precious little data on Muslim countries; the data available on religion in the surveys are almost all from predominantly Christian societies. Perhaps religion is really more important in Muslim countries than it is elsewhere. Would this fact then explain the greater incidence of authoritarianism in Islamic countries? This question touches on the second assumption mentioned above—namely, that religiosity per se is the ally of authoritarianism, and secularism of democracy. In some classical theories of modernization, secularization is often portrayed as progress itself—a claim rarely questioned and hence seldom examined in social science. But how sound is it?

Examining countries outside the advanced industrial world helps shed some light on the matter. As of 1994, 110 of the 157 countries under examination here had annual incomes per capita at purchasing power parity that did not exceed $6000. They account for about four-fifths of the world's population. Among these countries, only nine maintained FH scores in each of the ten annual surveys between 1991–92 and 2000–2001 that qualified them as "free" polities. All of them —Benin, Botswana, Bulgaria, Costa Rica, Jamaica, Lithuania, Mongolia, Namibia, and Poland—are exceptions to the "rule" that democracy is a luxury that only rich countries can afford or can sustain for longer than a fleeting spell.

This is a diverse group; its members are united by little other than their exceptionally open politics. If secularism were especially conducive to democratization, however, one would expect to find another regularity within this group: a preponderance of relatively secular societies.

But the reality is inconsistent with this expectation. Benin is the world's stronghold of Vodou, which permeates the country's social life and politics. Religion also occupies a prominent place in Botswana. As in Benin, traditional native religions are of great importance, though successful efforts by missionaries among the chiefs in the mid- and late nineteenth century established a tradition of strong Christian religiosity among the elite. Costa Rica is deeply religious; over two-thirds of the population are practicing Catholics. Jamaica is a confessional mosaic in which most people actively practice their religion. Namibia is, as Philip Steenkamp notes, "the most Christian of African countries"; an absolute majority is active in churches. Poland and Lithuania are arguably the most religious societies in the postcommunist world. Catholicism, deeply rooted in both, played a central organizational and spiritual role in the anticommunist resistance. Bulgaria and Mongolia, which are in fact relatively secular societies, are the exceptions to the pattern of high religiosity among the developing world's most open polities.

In sum, there are ample grounds for skepticism regarding the claim that people in predominantly Muslim societies are more observant religionists than people elsewhere; so too is there plenty of room for questioning the usual association of secularism with democracy and religiosity with authoritarianism. At the very least, it would seem wise to heed Alfred Stepan's

Table 8. Difference in Mean Literacy Gap, Sex Ratio, Women in Government, and the Gender Empowerment Measure for Catholic and Muslim Countries[a]

	Literacy Gap, 1990 (Male Literacy Rate Minus Female Literacy Rate)	Sex Ratio, 2000 (Mean Number of Males per 100 Females)	Women in Government, 1998 (Mean Percent of Ministerial and Subministerial Officials)	Gender Empowerment Measure, 1998
Muslim countries	18.7	102	5.2	.29
Catholic countries	4.3	97	12.2	.50
F	60.80	13.05	38.12	74.59

[a]Sample for literacy gap analysis is 89 countries (46 Muslim); sample for sex ratio analysis is 88 countries (45 Muslim); sample for women in government is 90 countries (47 Muslim); sample for Gender Empowerment Measure is 54 countries (20 Muslim).

caveat that "the concept of secularism must be radically rethought" as it relates to modernity and democracy.

Thus, the question remains unanswered: how does Islam disfavor democracy?

The Connection between Islam and Authoritarianism: A Hypothesis that Works

The Problem of Female Subordination

In one demonstrable way, Muslim societies are distinct in a manner that may affect politics: the treatment and status of women and girls. Some scholars, relying on ethnographic research and deep knowledge of specific societies, have noted what appears to be an unusual degree of subordination of women in Muslim societies. Some have suggested that this factor may affect life not only in the family and immediate community but also at higher levels as well. Several scholars have begun subjecting the problem of women's status and democracy to rigorous investigation, but they have relied mostly on public opinion surveys. Such studies are potentially of great value. Here, however, I rely on indicators other than those gleaned from either in-depth ethnography or opinion surveys.

I use multiple indicators to assess the station of women. The first is the difference between male and female literacy rates. I assume that a larger gap in favor of males reflects lower esteem for the education of girls and negatively affects the life chances of females relative to males. I use data for literacy rates in 1990. The first (leftmost) column of Table 8 shows the ANOVA test for Catholic and Muslim countries. The difference between the groups is large and statistically significant. * * * The Islam variable is statistically significant and its coefficient is large. The gap in literacy rates between men and women is on average over six percentage points larger in Muslim countries than in non-Muslim countries, controlling for income per capita.

* * *

The Link between the Station of Females and Political Regime: Some Provisional Theory

Precisely how the status and treatment of women and girls affects political regime must be the subject of a great deal more research before firm conclusions may be drawn. Here I can suggest only several tentative ideas. Sociological, psychological, and demographic explanations offer some promise. Differentials between male and female literacy rates and sex-ratio imbalances reflect social relations in the family and the immediate community, and the character of these relations may reproduce themselves at higher levels. Several leading writers have argued that the repressiveness and unquestioned dominance of the father in the family and of the male in relations between men and women replicate themselves in broader society, creating a culture of domination, intolerance, and dependency in social and political life.[19] The notion of isomorphism between primary social relations and those that obtain in broader society has a long history in social science. One must of course approach the idea with caution; some culturalist theories that assumed congruence between the family and the polity have not fared well in light of evidence. Still, the possibility of a connection should not be ignored. Individuals who are more accustomed to rigidly hierarchical relations in their personal lives may be less prone to resist such patterns of authority in politics. The generalization applies to the wielders of authority as much as to the objects. One of Martin Luther King's favorite sayings was that in order to hold a man down, one needed to stay down there with him. One might reformulate the adage as, in order to hold women down, a man needed to stay down there with them—meaning, of course, that oppression as a habit of life blocks the oppressor's own advancement and freedom.

Furthermore, men behave differently under organizational conditions in which women are present and under those in which they are not. Segregation of the sexes in the school, the workplace, and places of leisure creates a fundamentally different setting for social relations—and for authority relations among males—than does integration. What is more, the social marginalization of women may remove distinctive voices and influences from politics. Some political psychologists have found that women are superior to men in some aspects of building consensus.[20] Other researchers have shown that men hold attitudes that are more conducive to authoritarianism. An important recent study showed that men have a stronger "social dominance" orientation than women; women are generally less comfortable with hierarchy and inequality.[21] Some scholars have found that women tend to be more averse to extremism and violence in politics.[22] If such findings are valid, the relegation of women to the sidelines of public life—which illiteracy has the effect of doing and which the women-in-government variable and the GEM help measure—circumscribes the influence of antiauthoritarian voices. The question is not whether Margaret Thatcher or Indira Gandhi governed with a feminine touch that distinguished her from her male colleagues; it is, instead, whether gaping sex differentials in literacy rates in the general population may shape social life in a manner that influences politics.

Patriarchy's purely demographic manifestations may also affect politics. Sex ratios, analyzed above, have not heretofore attracted much attention in political science, but they may prove crucial for understanding politics in coming decades. Of the thirty-two countries with sex ratios that exceed 102/100, twenty-two are predominantly Muslim. In a few oil-rich countries of the Persian Gulf, imbalances may be attributed to large numbers of (mostly male) guest workers. Most of the foreign workers are themselves from other Muslim countries, however, and their absence from home lowers the sex ratio for their home countries. It is not clear precisely to what extent labor migrations affect overall sex ratios. In any case, in most countries with high sex ratios labor migrations do not affect the numbers. In Afghanistan, Bangladesh, Iran, and Pakistan, for example, all of which have sex ratios over 104/100, the imbalance cannot be explained without reference to neglect of girls' health care and nutrition and sex-selective abortion. Extremely high sex ratios themselves make for a social time bomb and may dim the prospects for popular rule. They may create conditions under which young men are more likely to join militant groups and engage in threatening, anomic behavior that provokes official repression. Late marriages for males, who in some Muslim countries must by custom be economically capable of supporting wives who do not work, may contribute to male aggression and frustration, but sheer numbers exacerbate the problem. Countries with sex ratios that exceed 103/100—which include Afghanistan, Iran, Jordan, Kuwait, Libya, Pakistan, Saudi Arabia, Somalia, Sudan, and Syria —are not bereft of mass social stress and movements of militant religious brotherhoods.

Just as understanding the causal mechanism linking female subordination and authoritarianism requires a great deal more study, so too is further investigation necessary to grasp fully the link between Islam and authoritarianism more generally. Even as the above analysis provides evidence that the station of women helps explain the relationship between Islam and regime type, it by no means furnishes a complete picture. * * * The treatment of women and girls may be an important part of the story, but it is very likely only one of several factors. Natural resource endowment may explain some of the problem as well, as the analysis showed above. Some candidate factors that are often adduced to explain political regime type, such as a British colonial past and sociocultural diversity, were shown to have little explanatory power. Others, however, are much harder to test statistically and were not included in the analysis. The structure of social networks is one such factor. Some writers have noted what appears to be the unusual tenacity of clan and tribal relations in Muslim societies and have argued that such ties are inimical to democracy.[23] Other scholars have shown that Soviet-type regimes decimated familialism in non-Muslim areas but could not do so in predominantly Muslim parts of the communist world.[24] One social scientist has recently investigated how specific facets of kin-based political power affect the position of women. In a rigorous qualitative comparison of three North African countries, she has illuminated how variation in state-formation, state-building, and nation-building experiences may affect kin-based political power and help account for cross-national differences in women's status.[25]

The resilience and durability of primordial ties may help explain the resistance of Muslim countries to democratization. But some specialists have argued, by contrast, that clan cleavages and networks may furnish social bases for the growth of civic associations and the extension of citizenship rights and may, under some circumstances, promote democratization.[26] Advancement of understanding will undoubtedly require a great deal more research, including both cross-national analysis and single-country and small-N studies. There is still a lot to explain.

Implications for Democracy

The findings may hold implications for democracy's prospects, both within and outside the Muslim world. First, they point to the need to study variation in the extent of sex disparities across Muslim countries. Some countries have sex ratios of 104/100 or higher, gaps between male and female literacy rates of 20 or more percentage points, and rates of women's participation in high office that do not exceed the mean for all Muslim countries. They include Afghanistan, Bangladesh, Côte d'Ivoire, Libya, Oman, Pakistan, Saudi Arabia, Somalia, and Syria. In some other polities conditions are less starkly unfavorable but on balance still inauspicious. Algeria, Egypt, Iraq, Nigeria, Sudan, Tunisia, Turkey, and Yemen each have sex ratios in the 102–3/100 range and large literacy gaps, and only in Turkey is women's participation in government well above the Muslim mean. Morocco does not have an unbalanced sex ratio, but the literacy gap is wide and women's participation in government is not substantially above the Muslim average. In Iran and Jordan the literacy gap is not as severe as in many other Muslim countries, but women are virtually absent from high politics and the sex ratio is dramatically unbalanced. Several of these countries—most notably, Bangladesh, Pakistan, Nigeria, and Turkey—have some traditions and institutions of open government and are often seen as the Islamic world's leading candidates for thoroughgoing, lasting democratization. The present analysis provides grounds for skepticism regarding the chances for robust democracy in any of these polities.

Democracy's prospects may be more favorable elsewhere. Despite the prominence of Megawati Sukarnoputri, whose inherited personal authority carried her to the pinnacle of state, women are not well represented in high government in Indonesia. But other conditions are more auspicious: the sex ratio is not unbalanced and the literacy gap is smaller than the Muslim average. The picture is mixed in other countries as well. Malaysia's sex ratio is only mildly unbalanced, the literacy gap is moderate, and women are relatively well represented in government. In the small, wealthy states of the Persian Gulf, sex ratios are extremely lopsided and women are absent or virtually absent from high politics. But in these countries the literacy gap is moderate or even nonexistent—a condition that might provide a substantial advantage for possible future democratization. Burkina Faso, Gambia, and Mali have no sex ratio problem and, by Muslim standards, only moderate literacy gaps. They also have high rates of female political participation in government. These countries, or some portion of them, may help soften the link between Islam and authoritarianism—in part because they do not bear the full complement of stark sexual inequalities common in many other Muslim countries. Other factors, including levels of economic development and dependence on oil exports, will of course affect democracy's prospects as well.

In addition to directing attention to potentially important variation within the Muslim world, the present article raises questions regarding democracy's future in some non-Muslim countries. Large literacy gaps, lopsided, male-dominant sex ratios, and scarcity of women in high politics are especially acute in Muslim countries, but these conditions are by no means distinctively Muslim. The world's two largest polities, neither of them predominantly Muslim, suffer from all three conditions. In India the literacy gap in 1990 was 26 percentage points; in China, 19. Women's participation in government in both countries is meager. In India the proportion of women in high officialdom is the same as the mean for Muslim countries; in China it is even lower. The sex ratio in each country exceeds 106/100. In India infanticide and neglect of girls' health is rampant, and child mortality for girls greatly exceeds that for boys. There is controversy over the rate of infanticide in present-day China, but little question that neglect of girls' health care remains dire. What is more, sex-selective abortion has risen steeply since the widespread introduction of ultrasound and amniocentesis in the 1980s. The at-birth sex ratio in China now stands at an astoundingly disproportionate 117/100. In neither India nor China are rates of infanticide, neglect of girls' health care and education, or prenatal sex selection markedly lower among the majority Hindus and Han Chinese than among the Muslim minorities. In neither country is imbalance in the sex ratio a new phenomenon. Further, in both the problem is growing more acute rather than abating, as urbanization and other aspects of modernization have not done anything to mitigate the problem.[27]

India's open politics would seem to challenge the arguments advanced in this article. Indeed, the Indian experience shows that the problems of patriarchy analyzed here do not necessarily spell doom for open government. India has a well-established reputation for violating social-scientific generalizations; perhaps it is unsurprising that it is also exceptional in terms of the link between societal patriarchy and political regime. Nonetheless, the findings of this article furnish grounds for skepticism regarding the viability of democracy in India. Ethnic divisions and poverty are usually seen as the most formidable challenges to Indian democracy. The findings reported here suggest the merits of adding sex ratio and the sex gap in literacy rates to the list of challenges. Sex ratio has become the focus of intense discussion in India. Many Indian scholars, journalists, and government officials consider the problem, which is growing more acute by the year with the spread of inexpensive ultrasound machines, a social catastrophe in the making. They are working to force the issue to the top of the public agenda.[28] If conditions in India may darken the prospects for the endurance of democracy, those in China may undermine possibilities for its emergence. Sex ratio in some regions of China now exceeds 140/100 and the sex disparity nationally is widening rapidly. "Bachelor villages," inhabited predominantly by men, already cover parts of the Chinese countryside in several regions. Police officials report a steep rise in crime in these areas, as well as an explosion of trade in kidnapped women and trafficking in women from Vietnam and North Korea. While Chinese leaders are perhaps less concerned than some of their Indian counterparts about the implications for democracy, they are indeed alarmed by threats to social order.[29]

Finally, the findings presented in this article highlight a fundamental difference between two types of societies: on the one hand, those that have a reputation for male dominance and emphasis on clan and family honor but that nevertheless do not exhibit large sex disparities in basic indicators, and, on the other hand, those that do exhibit such disparities. Southern Europe and countries with Iberian colonial heritage are often regarded as highly patriarchal. But in few places in these areas does one find gaping differentials in the basic indicators used here. Levels of economic development as well as *overall* illiteracy rates are broadly similar in Turkey, Mexico, and Brazil. Yet the literacy gap in these countries is 22, 5, and 2 percent, respectively; the sex ratio is 102/100 in Turkey and 97/100 in both Mexico and Brazil. Levels of economic development and overall literacy rates are higher in Jordan and Iran than they are in Honduras and Nicaragua. Yet the literacy gap is 18 percent in both Jordan and Iran, while there is virtually no literacy gap in Honduras or Nicaragua. Sex ratio is 105/100 in both Jordan and Iran; it is 100/100 in Honduras and 97/100 in Nicaragua. Women make up about 1 percent of high officialdom in the former countries and

over 10 percent in the latter. Syria and the Philippines have nearly identical national incomes per capita. In Syria the sex ratio is 104/100, the literacy gap is 35 percentage points, and women fill one in thirty high-ranking posts in government. In the Philippines the sex ratio is 99/100, the literacy gap is 1 percent, and women occupy one in six top government jobs. These examples are in no way exceptional; they are representative and broadly illustrative. In short, patriarchy varies. A culture may in some senses be male dominated but still eschew prenatal sex selection and value the health and basic education of girls as much or nearly as much as the health and basic education of boys. Alternatively, a culture may assign disparate weights to the value of male and female life. The difference may have implications for political regime.

The Irony of Female Subordination

Nothing could be less heartening to democratic idealists than the notion that a particular religion is inimical to democracy. Religious traditions are usually constants within societies; they are variables only across societies. Societies usually are "stuck" with their religious traditions and the social and psychological orientations they encode and reproduce.

Yet religious practices and the salience of particular beliefs can change. Even if Muslim countries are more male dominated in some respects than non-Muslim countries, there is no logical reason why such a state of affairs must be immutable. Rigid segregation according to sex and male domination does not have a firm scriptural basis.[30] The Koran provides no justification whatsoever for practices such as female genital mutilation and it condemns all infanticide as a heinous sin, even if it is motivated by a fear of want (17:31; 81:1–14). Much of the Koran's instruction on marriage, divorce, and other aspects of relations between the sexes (for example, 2:222–41; 4:3; 4:128; 33:1–5; 58:1–4) is more liberal than the *sharia* (religious law) as practiced in some modern-day Muslim societies. It is therefore as dubious to try to locate the sources of social practice and order in scripture in Islamic settings as it is to try to locate them there in Christian and Jewish settings, because as with all holy injunction based on sacred text, interpretive traditions are powerful and ultimately determine practice. The status of women in Muslim societies is thus both paradoxical and mutable.

At the present time, however, the evidence shows that Muslim countries are markedly more authoritarian than non-Muslim societies, even when one controls for other potentially influential factors; and the station of women, more than other factors that predominate in Western thinking about religious systems and politics, links Islam and the democratic deficit.

NOTES

1. Seymour Martin Lipset, *Political Man* (Garden City, N.Y.: Doubleday, 1960); Andrew C. Janos, *East Central Europe in the Modern World* (Stanford, Calif.: Stanford University Press, 2000); Valerie Bunce, "Comparative Democratization: Big and Bounded Generalizations," *Comparative Political Studies* 33 (August–September 2000); Andreas Schedler, "Measuring Democratic Consolidation," *Studies in Comparative International Development* 36 (Spring 2001).

2. Adam Przeworski, Michael E. Alvarez, José Antonio Cheibub, and Fernando Limongi, *Democracy and Development* (Cambridge: Cambridge University Press, 2000).

3. Myron Weiner, "Empirical Democratic Theory," in Myron Weiner and Ergun Özbudun, eds., *Competitive Elections in Developing Countries* (Durham, N.C.: Duke University Press, 1987), 20.

4. Guy Lardeyret, "The Problem with PR," in Larry Diamond and Marc F. Plattner, eds., *The Global Resurgence of Democracy*, 2d ed. (Baltimore: Johns Hopkins University Press,

1996), 175–80; Anthony Payne, "Westminster Adapted: The Political Order of the Commonwealth Caribbean," in Domingez, Pastor, and Worrell (fn. 9).

5. Ken Jowitt, "The Leninist Legacy," in Ivo Banac, ed., *Eastern Europe in Revolution* (Ithaca, N.Y.: Cornell University Press, 1992).

6. Marc Morjé Howard, "Free Not to Participate: The Weakness of Civil Society in Post-Communist Europe," Studies in Public Policy no. 325 (Glasgow: University of Stathclyde, 2000); M. Steven Fish, *Democracy from Scratch: Opposition and Regime in the New Russian Revolution* (Princeton: Princeton University Press, 1995).

7. Linz and Stepan (fn. 11), 247.

8. Michael L. Ross, "Does Oil Hinder Democracy?" *World Politics* 53 (April 2001); Terry Lynn Karl, *The Paradox of Plenty: Oil Booms and Petro-States* (Berkeley: University of California Press, 1997).

9. Charles Louis de Secondat (Montesquieu), *The Spirit of the Laws*, ed. Anne M. Cohler, Basia Carolyn Miller, and Harold Samuel Stone (Cambridge: Cambridge University Press, 1995), 461–62.

10. Samuel P. Huntington, *The Clash of Civilizations and the Remaking of the Modern World* (New York: Simon and Schuster, 1996).

11. Monty G. Marshall, "Major Episodes of Political Violence, 1946–1999" (members.aol. com/CSPmgm/warlist, accessed December 2001).

12. Daniel Kaufmann, Aart Kraay, and Pablo Zoido-Lobaton, "Composite Indicator Dataset," from "Governance Matters," World Bank Policy Research Department Working Paper no. 2195 (world-bank.org/wbi/ governance/gov_data, accessed May 2001).

13. Lipset (fn. 5); Rafael La Porta, Florencio Lopez-De-Silanes, Andrei Shleifer, and Robert Vishney, "The Quality of Government," *Journal of Law, Economics and Organization* 15 (April 1999); Samuel P. Huntington, "Will More Countries Become

Democratic?" *Political Science Quarterly* 99 (Summer 1984).

14. Huntington (fn. 23), 256–58.

15. Inglehart, "Trust, Well-Being and Democracy," in Mark E. Warren, ed., *Democracy and Trust* (Cambridge: Cambridge University Press, 1999).

16. Al-Suwaidi, "Arab and Western Conceptions of Democracy," in David Garnham and Mark Tessler, eds., *Democracy, War, and Peace in the Middle East* (Bloomington: Indiana University Press, 1995), 87.

17. Huntington (fn. 23), 70. For a similar argument, see Bernard Lewis, "Islam and Liberal Democracy: A Historical Overview," *Journal of Democracy* 7 (April 1996).

18. AbuKhalil, "Against the Taboos of Islam," in Charles E. Butterworth and I. William Zartman, eds., *Between the State and Islam* (Cambridge: Cambridge University Press, 2001), 115.

19. Sharabi (fn. 34); Abdellah Hammoudi, *The Victim and Its Masks* (Chicago: University of Chicago Press, 1988), 46–47, 150–51; idem, *Master and Disciple: The Cultural Foundations of Moroccan Authoritarianism* (Chicago: University of Chicago Press, 1997); David S. Landes, *The Wealth and Poverty of Nations: Why Some Are So Rich and Some So Poor* (New York: Norton, 1999), 410–15.

20. Rose McDermott and Jonathan A. Cowden, "The Effects of Uncertainty and Sex in a Crisis Simulation Game," *International Interactions* 27, no. 4 (2001).

21. Felicia Pratto, L. M. Stallworth, and Jim Sidanius, "The Gender Gap: Differences in Political Attitudes and Social Dominance Orientation," *British Journal of Social Psychology* 36 (March 1997).

22. Pamela Johnston Conover and Virginia Sapiro, "Gender, Feminist Consciousness and War," *American Journal of Political Science* 37 (November 1993); Carol Gilligan, "In a Different Voice: Women's Conceptions of Self and Morality," in Diana Tietjens Meyers, *Feminist Social Thought* (New York: Rout-

ledge, 1997); Janet Flammang, *Women's Political Voice* (Philadelphia: Temple University Press, 1997); Barbara Crossette, "Living in a World without Women," *New York Times*, November 4, 2001.

23. Saad Eddin Ibrahim, cited in Iliya Harik, "Democratic Thought in the Arab World," in Butterworth and Zartman (fn. 31), 143–44.

24. Pauline Jones Luong, *Institutional Change and Political Continuity in Post-Soviet Central Asia* (Cambridge: Cambridge University Press, 2002); Muriel Atkin, "Thwarted Democratization in Tajikistan," in Karen Dawisha and Bruce Parrot, eds., *Conflict, Cleavage, and Change in Central Asia and the Caucasus* (Cambridge: Cambridge University Press, 1997); Kathleen Collins, *Clans, Pacts, and Politics: Understanding Regime Change in Central Asia* (Ph.D. diss., Stanford University, 1999).

25. Mounira M. Charrad, *States and Women's Rights: The Making of Postcolonial Tunisia, Algeria, and Morocco* (Berkeley: University of California Press, 2001).

26. Eva Bellin, "Civil Society: Effective Tool for the Analysis of Middle East Politics?" *PS: Political Science and Politics* 27 (September 1994); Sheila Carapico, *Civil Society in Yemen* (Cambridge: Cambridge University Press, 1998); Dennis Galvan, "Political Turnover and Social Change in Senegal," *Journal of Democracy* 12 (July 2001); Linda L. Layne, "Tribesmen as Citizens," in Layne, ed., *Elections in the Middle East* (Boulder, Colo.: Westview, 1987); Timothy J. Piro, "Liberal Professionals in the Arab World," in Butterworth and Zartman (fn. 31).

27. Fred Arnold, Minja Kim Choe, and T. K. Roy, "Son Preference, the Family-Building Process and Child Mortality in India," *Population Studies* 52 (November 1998); Sabu M. George and Ranbir S. Dahiya, "Female Foeticide in Rural Haryana," *Economic and Political Weekly* 33, 32 (August 14, 1998), 2191–98; Monica Das Gupta and P. N. Mari Bhat, "Fertility Decline and Increased Mani-

festation of Sex Bias in India," *Population Studies* 51 (November 1997); Gita Aravamudan, "Chilling Deaths," *Week* (India), January 24, 1999 (the-week.com, accessed December 2001); Gilbert Rozman, *Population and Marketing Settlements in Ch'ing China* (New York: Cambridge University Press, 1982); Yi Zeng et al., "Causes and Implications of the Recent Increase in the Reported Sex-Ratio at Birth in China," *Population and Development Review* 19 (June 1993); Sten Johansson and Ola Nygren, "The Missing Girls of China," *Population and Development Review* 17 (March 1991); Erik Eckholm, "Desire for Sons Drives Use of Prenatal Scans in China," *New York Times*, June 22, 2002; J. H. Chu, "Prenatal Sex Determination and Sex-Selective Abortion in Rural Central China," *Population and Development Review* 27 (June 2001).

28. Malini Karkal, "Invisibility of the Girl Child in India," *Indian Journal of Social Work* 52 (January 1991); "Female Infanticide Continues Unchecked, Unheard," *Times of India*, November 6, 2000; Sudha Ramachandran, "New Technologies, Old Prejudices Blamed for India's Vanishing Girls," *Panos* (London), September 2001 (panos.org.uk, accessed March 2002); Sampath Kumar, "Changing Views on Female Infanticide," *BBC News*, December 11, 2001 (news. bbc.co.uk, accessed April 2002); R. P. Ravindra, "The Campaign against Sex Determination Tests," in Chhaya Datar, ed., *The Struggle against Violence* (Calcutta: Shree, 1993).

29. Xingwang Zhou, "Artificial Sex Selection Can Create Disorder in Society: There Is a Natural Ratio of Males to Females," *Worker's Daily* [*Gongren Ribao*], August 9, 1999 (usembassy-china.org.cn, accessed March 2002); State Family Planning Commission of China, "Further Efforts to Seek Solutions for Problems in the Population Structure" (2001) (sfpc.gov.cn, accessed March 2002); John Pomfret, "In China's Countryside, 'It's a Boy!' Too Often," *Washington Post*, May 29, 2001; Maureen J. Graham, Ulla Larsen, and Xiping Xu, "Son Preference in Anhui Province, China," *International Family Planning Perspectives* 24 (June 1998).

30. See Fazlur Rahman, *Islam*, 2d ed. (Chicago: Chicago University Press, 1979), 38–40, 231–32; idem, *Islam and Modernity: Transformation of an Intellectual Tradition* (Chicago: University of Chicago Press, 1984), 13–20; Fatima Mernissi, *The Veil and the Male Elite* (Cambridge, Mass.: Perseus, 1992); Farid Esack, *Qur'an Liberation and Pluralism* (Oxford: Oneworld, 1997); Amina Wadud, *Qur'an and Woman* (Oxford: Oxford University Press, 1999).

6 DEMOCRACY

If democracy is something positive to be strived for, how does it come about and what are its necessary components? The readings in this section try to address these questions by considering the origins and institutions of democracy as well as the dangers that democracy faces. Much of this work has emerged in the past fifteen years, following the end of the Cold War and the subsequent wave of democratization throughout much of the world.

Fareed Zakaria's "A Brief History of Human Liberty" (2003) builds on our earlier discussion of the state in Chapter 2 to help us understand why modern democracy first emerged in Europe. With the collapse of the Roman Empire, Europe broke into an enormous number of rival political units, leading to diversity, competition, and interstate conflict that would help forge the modern state. These early states were often highly decentralized, leaving power in the hands of a local elite, who could check a monarch's ability to gather absolute power. At the same time, the early division of church and state also weakened the ability of any leader to claim both spiritual and earthly authority, something reinforced by the Protestant Reformation. This decentralization of power allowed for greater individual liberties, helping to foster both capitalist development and the idea of democratic control. In the end, Zakaria concludes that democracy requires the development of the entrenched habits of liberty—individual rights supported by the rule of law—something not easily or intentionally created. His comments in many ways reflect Diamond's discussion of hybrid regimes in Chapter 5.

While Zakaria focuses on the origins of democracy, other scholars are concerned with how its institutions are actually constructed, and to what effect. In their widely cited work "What Democracy Is . . . and Is Not" (1991), Schmitter and Karl provide an overview of some of the most important elements, among them government accountability, public competition, and the mechanisms of elections and majority rule. Democracy is not just a set of mechanisms, however; it is also a set of agreed-upon principles promising that the members of the democracy will abide by the competitive outcome. But beyond these basic elements there is a wide array of democratic types, differing in such areas as how majorities are structured, the nature of executive power, the kinds of checks and balances that will be used to stabilize power, or the way power is decentralized. There is no one necessary mix for democracy, and how these institutions are combined or modified depends on the historical circumstances and the contemporary challenges of the country in question.

However, some scholars do believe that certain kinds of democratic combinations are more stable or responsive than others. Lijphart (1996) investigates two of the most important differences among democracies: presidential versus parliamentary rule, and proportional representation (PR) versus plurality (also known as single-member district or first past the post) elections. Presidentialism and plurality elections promote majoritarian or a "winner take all" form of government; proportional representation tends to generate more consensus in politics. Is one a better form than the other? Lijphart concludes that the parliamentary-PR system is superior to the presidential-plurality system found in the United States in terms of minority rights, participation, and economic equality. So, how democracies are constructed can have a distinct impact on the kinds of policies and outcomes they produce.

Finally, we turn to a consideration of social capital. This concept has become widely discussed in political science and policy circles, due largely to the work of Robert Putnam and his 2000 book, Bowling Alone. *Drawing from research conducted in both the United States and Italy (which appeared in an earlier work entitled* Making Democracy Work)*, Putnam has described the notion of social capital as networks and "norms of reciprocity" that make people active participants in democratic life. Where social capital is strong, Putnam argues, democracy is sustained by this web of interconnections that promotes civic life. In the United States (and perhaps elsewhere), however, civic organization is declining, leading to a weakened democracy that is disconnected from the public. Yet while Putnam lauds social capital and laments its decline, Sheri Berman (1997) warns us that the mere presence or growth of social capital is not an unmitigated good. In her study of Germany after World War I, she found a society where social capital was flourishing in the form of numerous organizations, all competing for power. But in the absence of a strong state to process these demands, politics broke down, paving the way for extremism and fascism. Social capital without channels for participation can be just as dangerous as no social capital at all.*

FAREED ZAKARIA

A BRIEF HISTORY OF HUMAN LIBERTY

It all started when Constantine decided to move. In A.D. 324 the leader of the greatest empire in the world went east, shifting his capital from Rome to Byzantium, the old Greek colony, at the mouth of the Black Sea, which he promptly renamed Constantinople. Why abandon Rome, the storied seat of the empire? Constantine explained that he did it "on command of God." You can't really argue with that kind of logic, though vanity and ambition surely played some part as well. Constantine desperately wanted to leave behind a grand legacy and, short of winning a war, what better way to do so than to build a new capital city? The move was also politically smart. Constantinople was closer to the great cultural and economic centers of the day, such as Athens, Thessalonika, and Antioch. (Rome in those days was considered a backwater.) And Constantinople was a more strategic point from which to defend the empire against its enemies, mainly Germanic tribes and Persian armies. In the fourth century, the pivots of history lay in the east.

Emperors don't travel light, and Constantine was no exception. He shifted not just the capital but tens of thousands of its inhabitants and commandeered immense quantities of food and wine from Egypt, Asia Minor, and Syria to feed his people. He sent his minions across the empire to bring art for the "new Rome." Such was the pillage that the historian Jacob Burckhardt described it as "the most disgraceful and extensive thefts of art in all history . . . committed for the purpose of decorating [Constantinople]."[1] Senators and other notables were given every inducement to move; exact replicas of their homes were

waiting for them in the new city. But although he took most of his court, Constantine left one person behind: the bishop of Rome. This historic separation between church and state was to have fateful, and beneficial, consequences for humankind.

Although the bishop of Rome had nominal seniority—because the first holder of that office, Peter, was the senior apostle of Christ—Christianity had survived by becoming a decentralized religion, comprising a collection of self-governing churches. But Rome was now distant from the imperial capital. Other important priests, such as the bishop of Byzantium and those of nearby Antioch, Jerusalem, and Alexandria, now lived in the shadow of the emperor and quickly became appendages of state authority. But, far from palace power and intrigue, the Roman church flourished, asserting an independence that eventually allowed it to claim the mantle of spiritual leadership of the Christian peoples. As a result of this separation, the great English classical scholar Ernest Barker observed, the East (Byzantium) fell under the control of the state and the West (Rome) came under the sovereignty of religion. It would be more accurate to say that in the West sovereignty was contested; for 1,500 years after Constantine's move, European history was marked by continual strife between church and state. From the sparks of those struggles came the first fires of human liberty.

Liberty, Old and New

Obviously it is an oversimplification to pick a single event to mark the beginnings of a complex historical phenomenon—in this case, the development of human liberty—but stories have to

From Fareed Zakaria, *The Future of Freedom* (New York: W. W. Norton, 2003), pp. 29–58. Some of the author's notes have been omitted.

start somewhere. And the rise of the Christian Church is, in my view, the first important source of liberty in the West—and hence the world. It highlights the central theme of this chapter, which is that liberty came to the West centuries before democracy. Liberty led to democracy and not the other way around. It also highlights a paradox that runs through this account: whatever the deeper structural causes, liberty in the West was born of a series of power struggles. The consequences of these struggles—between church and state, lord and king, Protestant and Catholic, business and the state—embedded themselves in the fabric of Western life, producing greater and greater pressures for individual liberty, particularly in England and, by extension, in the United States.

Some might contest this emphasis on the Christian Church, pointing fondly to ancient Greece as the seedbed of liberty. They will think of Pericles' famous funeral oration, delivered in 431 B.C., which conjured a stirring vision of the Athens of his day, dedicated to freedom, democracy, and equality. For much of the nineteenth century British and German university curricula assumed that the greatest flowering of human achievement took place in the city-states of Greece around the fifth century B.C. (The study of ancient Greece and Rome at Oxford and Cambridge is still colloquially called "Greats.") But the Victorian obsession with Greece was part fantasy. Ancient Greece was an extraordinary culture, fertile in philosophy, science, and literature. It was the birthplace of democracy and some of its associated ideas, but these were practiced in only a few, small city-states for at most a hundred years and died with the Macedonian conquest of Athens in 338 B.C. Over a millennium later, Greece's experiment became an inspiration for democrats, but in the intervening centuries, it left no tangible or institutional influences on politics in Europe.

More to the point, Greece was not the birthplace of liberty as we understand it today. Liberty in the modern world is first and foremost the freedom of the individual from arbitrary authority, which has meant, for most of history, from the brute power of the state. It implies certain basic human rights: freedom of expression, of association, and of worship, and rights of due process. But ancient liberty, as the enlightenment philosopher Benjamin Constant explained, meant something different: that everyone (actually, every male citizen) had the right to participate in the governance of the community. Usually all citizens served in the legislature or, if this was impractical, legislators were chosen by lottery, as with American juries today. The people's assemblies of ancient Greece had unlimited powers. An individual's rights were neither sacred in theory nor protected in fact. Greek democracy often meant, in Constant's phrase, "the subjection of the individual to the authority of the community."[2] Recall that in the fourth century B.C. in Athens, where Greek democracy is said to have found its truest expression, the popular assembly—by democratic vote—put to death the greatest philosopher of the age because of his teachings. The execution of Socrates was democratic but not liberal.

If the Greek roots of Western liberty are often overstated, the Roman ones are neglected. When Herodotus wrote that the Greeks were "a free people" he meant that they were not slaves under foreign conquest or domination—an idea we would today call "national independence" or "self-determination." (By this definition, the North Koreans today are a free people.) The Romans emphasized a different aspect of freedom: that all citizens were to be treated equally under the law. This conception of freedom is much closer to the modern Western one, and the Latin word for it, *libertas*, is the root of ours. Whereas Greece gave the world philosophy, literature, poetry, and art, Rome gave us the beginnings of limited government and the rule of law. The Roman Republic, with its divided government (three branches), election of officials to limited terms, and emphasis on equality under law has been a model for governments ever since, most consciously in the founding of the American Republic. To this day Roman political concepts and terms endure throughout the Western world: senate, republic, constitution, prefecture. Western law is so filled with Roman legacies that until the early twentieth century, lawyers had to be well versed in Latin. Most of the world's laws of contract, property, liability, defamation, inheritance, and estate and rules of procedure and evidence are variations on Roman themes. For Herbert Asquith, the gifted amateur classicist who became prime minister of the United Kingdom, Rome's greatest gift to the ages was that "she founded, developed and systematized the jurisprudence of the world."[3]

The gaping hole in Roman law, however, was that as a practical matter, it didn't apply to the ruling class, particularly as the republic degenerated into a monarchy by the first century. Emperors such as Nero, Vitellius, and Galba routinely sentenced people to death without trial, pillaged private homes and temples, and raped and murdered their subjects. Caligula famously had his horse appointed senator, an act that probably violated the implicit, if not explicit, rules of that once-august body. Traditions of law that had been built carefully during Rome's republican years crumbled in the decadence of empire. The lesson of Rome's fall is that, for the rule of law to endure, you need more than the good intentions of the rulers, for they may change (both the intentions and the rulers). You need institutions within society whose strength is independent of the state. The West found such a countervailing force in the Catholic Church.

The Paradox of Catholicism

Rome's most concrete legacy has been the Roman Catholic Church, which the English philosopher Thomas Hobbes called "the ghost of the deceased Roman Empire sitting crowned upon [its] grave."[4] The culture of Rome became the culture of Catholicism. Through the church were transmitted countless traditions and ideas—and, of course, Latin which gave educated people all

over Europe a common language and thus strengthened their sense of being a single community. To this day the ideas and structure of the Catholic Church—its universalism, its hierarchy, its codes and laws—bear a strong resemblance to those of the Roman Empire.

The Catholic Church might seem an odd place to begin the story of liberty. As an institution it has not stood for freedom of thought or even, until recently, diversity of belief. In fact, during the Middle Ages, as it grew powerful, it became increasingly intolerant and oppressive, emphasizing dogma and unquestioning obedience and using rather nasty means to squash dissent (recall the Spanish Inquisition). To this day, its structure remains hierarchical and autocratic. The church never saw itself as furthering individual liberty. But from the start it tenaciously opposed the power of the state and thus placed limits on monarchs' rule. It controlled crucial social institutions such as marriage and birth and death rites. Church properties and priests were not subject to taxation—hardly a small matter since at its height the church owned one-third of the land in Europe. The Catholic Church was the first major institution in history that was independent of temporal authority and willing to challenge it. By doing this it cracked the edifice of state power, and in nooks and crannies individual liberty began to grow.

The struggles between church and state began just over fifty years after Constantine's move. One of Constantine's successors, the emperor Theodosius, while in a nasty dispute with the Thessalonians, a Greek tribe, invited the whole tribe to Milan—and orchestrated a bloodcurdling massacre of his guests: men, women, and children. The archbishop of Milan, a pious priest named Ambrose, was appalled and publicly refused to give the emperor Holy Communion. Theodosius protested, resorting to a biblical defense. He was guilty of homicide, he explained, but wasn't one of the Bible's heroic kings, David, guilty not just of homicide but of adultery as well? The archbishop was unyielding, thundering back, in the English historian

Edward Gibbon's famous account, "You have imitated David in his crime, imitate then his repentance."[5] To the utter amazement of all, for the next eight months the emperor, the most powerful man in the world, periodically dressed like a beggar (as David had in the biblical tale) and stood outside the cathedral at Milan to ask forgiveness of the archbishop.

As the Roman Empire crumbled in the East, the bishop of Rome's authority and independence grew. He became first among the princes of the church, called "Il Papa," the holy father. In 800, Pope Leo III was forced to crown the Frankish ruler Charlemagne as Roman emperor. But in doing so, Leo began the tradition of "investiture," whereby the church had to bless a new king and thus give legitimacy to his reign. By the twelfth century, the pope's power had grown, and he had become a pivotal player in Europe's complex political games. The papacy had power, legitimacy, money, and even armies. It won another great symbolic battle against Holy Roman Emperor Henry IV, who in 1077 challenged—unsuccessfully—Pope Gregory VII's expansion of the power of investiture. Having lost the struggle, Henry, so the legend goes, was forced to stand barefoot in the snow at Canossa to seek forgiveness from the holy father. Whether or not that tale is true, by the twelfth century the pope had clearly become, in power and pomp, a match for any of Europe's kings, and the Vatican had come to rival the grandest courts on the continent.

The Geography of Freedom

The church gained power in the West for a simple reason: after the decline of the Roman Empire, it never again faced a single emperor of Europe. Instead, the Catholic Church was able to play one European prince against another, becoming the vital "swing vote" in the power struggles of the day. Had one monarch emerged across the continent, he could have crushed the church's independence, turning it into a handmaiden of state power. That is what happened to the Greek Orthodox Church and later the Russian Orthodox Church (and, for that matter, to most religions around the world). But no ruler ever conquered all of Europe, or even the greater part of it. Over the millennia only a few tried—Charlemagne, Charles V, Napoleon, Kaiser Wilhelm, and Hitler. All were thwarted, most fairly quickly.

What explains this? Probably mountains and rivers. Europe is riven with barriers that divide its highlands into river valleys bordered by mountain ranges. Its rivers flow into sheltered, navigable bays along the long, indented Mediterranean coastline—all of which means that small regions could subsist, indeed thrive, on their own. Hence Europe's long history of many independent countries. They are hard to conquer, easy to cultivate, and their rivers and seas provide ready trade routes. Asia, by contrast, is full of vast flatlands—the steppes in Russia, the plains in China—through which armies could march unhindered. Not surprisingly, these areas were ruled for millennia by centralized empires.

Europe's topography made possible the rise of communities of varying sizes—city-states, duchies, republics, nations, and empires. In 1500 Europe had within it more than 500 states, many no larger than a city. This variety had two wondrous effects. First, it allowed for diversity. People, ideas, art, and even technologies that were unwelcome or unnoticed in one area would often thrive in another. Second, diversity fueled constant competition between states, producing innovation and efficiency in political organization, military technology, and economic policy. Successful practices were copied; losing ways were cast aside. Europe's spectacular economic and political success—what the economic historian Eric Jones has termed "the European miracle"— might well be the result of its odd geography.[6]

Lords and Kings

Geography and history combined to help shape Europe's political structure. The crumbling of the Roman Empire and the backwardness of the German tribes that destroyed it resulted in decentralized authority across the continent; no ruler had the administrative capacity to rule a far-flung kingdom comprising so many independent tribes. By contrast, in their heyday, Ming and Manchu China, Mughal India, and the Ottoman Empire controlled vast lands and diverse peoples. But in Europe local landlords and chieftains governed their territories and developed close ties with their tenants. This became the distinctive feature of European feudalism—that its great landowning classes were independent. From the Middle Ages until the seventeenth century, European sovereigns were distant creatures who ruled their kingdoms mostly in name. The king of France, for example, was considered only a duke in Brittany and had limited authority in that region for hundreds of years. In practice if monarchs wanted to do anything—start a war, build a fort—they had to borrow and bargain for money and troops from local chieftains, who became earls, viscounts, and dukes in the process.

Thus Europe's landed elite became an aristocracy with power, money, and legitimacy—a far cry from the groveling and dependent courtier-nobles in other parts of the world. This near-equal relationship between lords and kings deeply influenced the course of liberty. As Guido de Ruggiero, the great historian of liberalism, wrote, "Without the effective resistance of particular privileged classes, the monarchy would have created nothing but a people of slaves."[7] In fact monarchs did just that in much of the rest of the world. In Europe, on the other hand, as the Middle Ages progressed, the aristocracy demanded that kings guarantee them certain rights that even the crown could not violate. They also established representative bodies—parliaments, estates general, diets—to give permanent voice to their claims. In these medieval bargains lie the foundations of what we today call "the rule of law." Building on Roman traditions, these rights were secured and strengthened by the power of the nobility. Like the clash between church and state, the conflict between the aristocracy and the monarchy is the second great power struggle of European history that helped provide, again unintentionally, the raw materials of freedom.

The English aristocracy was the most independent in Europe. Lords lived on their estates, governing and protecting their tenants. In return, they extracted taxes, which kept them both powerful and rich. It was, in one scholar's phrase, "a working aristocracy": it maintained its position not through elaborate courtly rituals but by taking part in politics and government at all levels.[8] England's kings, who consolidated their power earlier than did most of their counterparts on the continent, recognized that their rule depended on co-opting the aristocracy—or at least some part of it. When monarchs pushed their luck they triggered a baronial backlash. Henry II, crowned king in 1154, extended his rule across the country, sending judges to distant places to enforce royal decrees. He sought to unify the country and create a common, imperial law. To do this he had to strip the medieval aristocracy of its powers and special privileges. His plan worked but only up to a point. Soon the nobility rose up in arms—literally—and after forty years of conflict, Henry's son, King John, was forced to sign a truce in 1215 in a field near Windsor Castle. That document, Magna Carta, was regarded at the time as a charter of baronial privilege, detailing the rights of feudal lords. It also had provisions guaranteeing the freedom of the church and local autonomy for towns. It came out (in vague terms) against the oppression of any of the king's subjects. Over time the document was interpreted more broadly by English judges, turning it into a quasi constitution that enshrined certain individual rights. But even in its day, Magna Carta was significant, being the first written limitation on royal authority in Europe. As such, the historian Paul Johnson noted, it is "justly classified as the first of the English Statutes of the Realm, from which English, and thus American, liberties can be said to flow."[9]

Rome versus Reform

After church versus state and king versus lord, the next great power struggle, between Catholics and Protestants, was to prove the longest and bloodiest, and once again it had accidental but revolutionary implications for freedom. Its improbable instigator was a devout German monk who lived in a small backwater town called Wittenberg. It was the early sixteenth century, and across Europe there was already great dissatisfaction with the papacy, which had become extraordinarily powerful and corrupt. Rome's most scandalous practice was the widespread sale of indulgences: papal certificates absolving the buyer of sins, even those not yet committed. The money financed the church's never-ending extravagance, which even by the glittering standards of the Baroque era was stunning. Its newest project was the largest, grandest cathedral ever known to man—St. Peter's in Rome. Even today, when one walks through the acres of marble in the Vatican, gazing at gilt, jewels, tapestries, and frescos from wall to wall and floor to ceiling, it is easy to imagine the pious rage of Martin Luther.

There had been calls for reform before Luther—Erasmus, for one, had urged a simpler, stripped down form of worship—but none had frontally challenged the authority of the church. Luther did so in ninety-five tightly reasoned theses, which he famously nailed to the door of the Castle Church in Wittenberg on the morning of October 31, 1517. Luther may have had right on his side, but he also had luck. His heresy came at an opportune moment in the history of technology. By the time the Catholic Church reacted and responded to his action, strictly forbidding the dissemination of his ideas, the new printing presses had already circulated Luther's document all over Europe. The Reformation had begun. One hundred and fifty bloody years later, almost half of Europe was Protestant.

Were Martin Luther to see Protestantism today, with its easygoing doctrines that tolerate much and require little, he would probably be horrified. Luther was not a liberal. On the contrary, he had accused the Vatican of being too lax in its approach to religion. In many ways he was what we would today call a fundamentalist, demanding a more literal interpretation of the Bible. Luther's criticisms of the papacy were quite similar to those made today by Islamic fundamentalists about the corrupt, extravagant regimes of the Middle East that have veered from the true, devout path. Luther was attacking the pope from the conservative end of the theological spectrum. In fact some have said that the clash between Catholicism and Protestantism illustrates the old maxim that religious freedom is the product of two equally pernicious fanaticisms, each canceling the other out.

Most of the sects that sprang up as a consequence of the Reformation were even more puritanical than Lutheranism. The most influential of them was a particularly dour creed, Calvinism, which posited the wretched depravity of man and the poor chances of salvation for all but a few, already chosen by God. But the various Protestant sects converged in rejecting the authority of the papacy and, by implication, all religious hierarchy. They were part of a common struggle against authority and, although they didn't know it at the time, part of the broader story of liberty.

For all their squabbles, these small Protestant sects in northern Europe opened up the possibility of a personal path to truth, unmediated by priests. To the extent that they imagined any clergy at all, it was to be elected by a self-governing congregation. Often minority sects within a larger community, they fought for the rights of all minorities to believe and worship as they chose. Together, they opened up the space for religious freedom in the Western world. They helped shape modern ideas about not only freedom of conscience and of speech but also critical scientific inquiry, first of religious texts such as the Bible, then of all received wisdom. Science, after all, is a constant process of challenging authority and contesting dogma. In that sense modern science owes an unusual debt to sixteenth-century religious zealots.

The more immediate, political effect of Protestantism was to give kings and princes an excuse to wrest power away from the increasingly arrogant Vatican, something they were looking to do anyway. The first major assault took place not in support of Protestant ideals but for the less-exalted reason that a restless monarch wanted an heir. Henry VIII of England asked Pope Clement VII to annul his marriage to Catherine of Aragon because she had not produced an heir to the throne. (Not for lack of effort: in eight years she had given birth to one daughter and five infants who had died, and had miscarried twice.) The pope refused and King Henry broke with the Vatican, proclaiming himself head of the Church of England. Henry had no doctrinal dispute with the Catholic Church. In fact he had defended the pope against Luther in an essay, for which the Vatican honored him as "Defender of the Faith," a title his successor, strangely, bears to this day. The newly independent Anglican Church was thus Catholic in doctrine—except for the small matter of the pope.

The English break was the first and most prominent of a series of religious revolts and wars against the Vatican involving virtually every state in Europe and lasting almost 150 years after Luther's act of defiance. The wars resulting from the Reformation came to an end in 1648. The Peace of Westphalia, as it was called, ended the Thirty Years' War among the Germans and rendered unto Caesar that which was Caesar's—plus a good bit of that which used to be God's (actually, the pope's). It revived a 1555 idea—*cuius regio eius religio* (whoever's domain, his religion prevails)—that princes could choose their state religions, and it explicitly permitted religious toleration and migration. The year 1648 is not a clean point of separation between church and state, but it does symbolize an important shift in Western history. Westphalia laid to rest the idea that Europe was one great Christian community—"Christendom"—governed spiritually by the Catholic Church and temporally by the holy Roman emperor. The future belonged to the state.

The Enlightened State

By the seventeenth century, the real challenge to princely power came not from religion but from local authorities: the princes, dukes, barons, and counts. But over the course of this century the prince would best his rivals. He strengthened his court and created a central government—a state—that dwarfed its local rivals. The state triumphed for several reasons: technological shifts, heightened military competition, the stirrings of nationalism, and the ability to centralize tax collection. One consequence, however, is worth noting. The strengthening of the state was not good for liberty. As the power of monarchs grew, they shut down most of the medieval parliaments, estates, assemblies, and diets. When France's Estates General were summoned in the spring of 1789—on the eve of the revolution—it was their first assembly in 175 years! The newly powerful royals also began abolishing the multilayered system of aristocratic privileges, regional traditions, and guild protections in favor of a uniform legal code, administered by the monarch. The important exception was the English Parliament, which actually gained the upper hand in its struggle with the monarchy after the Glorious Revolution of 1688.[10]

On the face of it the weakening of the aristocracy might seem a victory for equality under law, and it was presented as such at the time. As Enlightenment ideas swept through seventeenth century Europe, philosophers such as Voltaire and Diderot fantasized about the "rationalization" and "modernization" of government. But in practice these trends meant more power for the central government and the evisceration of local and regional authority. "Enlightened absolutism," as it was later called, had some progressive elements about it. Rulers such as Frederick II of Prussia, Catherine II of Russia, and Joseph II of Austria tolerated religious dissent, enacted legal reforms, and lavished money and attention on artists, musicians, and writers (which might help explain the good press they received). But the shift in power weakened the only groups in society capable of checking royal authority and excess. Liberty now depended on the largesse of the ruler. When under pressure from abroad or at home, even the most benign monarch—and his not-so-benign successors—abandoned liberalization and squashed dissent. By the end of the eighteenth century, with war, revolution, and domestic rebellion disturbing the tranquility of Europe, enlightened absolutism became more absolutist than enlightened.

The monarchy reached its apogee in France under Louis XIV. Feudalism in France had always been different from that in England. Sandwiched between hostile neighbors, France was perpetually mobilizing for war, which kept its central government strong. (Louis XIV was at war for thirty of his fifty-four years of rule.) The monarchy exploited these geopolitical realities to keep the nobles distant from their power base, which was their land. Building on the foundation laid by the brilliant Cardinal Richelieu, Louis XIV edged nobles out of local administration and put in their place his own regional officials. He also downgraded regional councils and assemblies. Louis was called the "Sun King" not because of his gilded possessions, as is often thought, but because of his preeminent position in the country. All other forces paled in comparison. Louis XIV brought France's aristocrats to Paris permanently, luring them with the most glittering court in Europe. His purpose was to weaken them. The legendary excess of the French monarchy—the ceaseless games, balls, hunts, and court rituals, the wonder of Versailles—was at one level a clever political device to keep the lords in a gilded cage. Behind the sumptuous silks and powdered wigs, the French aristocracy was becoming powerless and dependent.[11]

The French Revolution (1789) changed much in the country, but not these centripetal tendencies. Indeed, the revolution only centralized the country further. In contrast to England's Glorious Revolution (1688), which had strengthened the landed aristocracy, the French Revolution destroyed it. It also crippled the church and weakened local lords, parishes, and banks. As the great nineteenth century scholar-politician Lord Acton observed, the revolution was not so much about the limitation of central power as about the abrogation of all other powers that got in the way. The French, he noted, borrowed from Americans "their theory of revolution not their theory of government—their cutting but not their sewing." Popular sovereignty took on all the glory and unchecked power of royal sovereignty. "The people" were supreme, and they proclaimed their goals to be *liberté, égalité, fraternité*. Once dependent on royal largesse, liberty now depended on the whims of "the citizens," represented of course by the leaders of the revolution.

But there was another model of liberty and it took a Frenchman to see it. Montesquieu—actually Charles-Louis de Secondat, baron de La Brède et de Montesquieu—like many Enlightenment liberals in the eighteenth century admired England for its government. But Montesquieu went further, identifying the genius of the English system: that it guaranteed liberty in fact rather than proclaiming it in theory. Because government was divided between the king, aristocrats (House of Lords), and commoners (House of Commons), no one branch could grow too strong. This "separation of powers" ensured that civil liberties would be secure and religious dissent tolerated. Montesquieu did not put blind faith in the mechanics of government and constitutions; his major work was titled, after all, *The Spirit of the Laws*.

In fact, over the centuries, the British monarch's powers had been so whittled away that by the late eighteenth century, Britain, although formally a monarchy, was really an aristocratic republic, ruled by its landed elite. Montesquieu's flattering interpretation strongly influenced the British themselves. The preeminent English jurist of the era, William Blackstone, used

Montesquieu's ideas when writing his commentaries on English law. The American political philosopher Judith Shklar pointed out that during the founding of the American Republic "Montesquieu was an oracle." James Madison, Thomas Jefferson, John Adams, and others consciously tried to apply his principles in creating a new political system. He was quoted by them more than any modern author (only the Bible trumped him). His appeal was so widespread, noted Shklar, that "both those who supported the new constitution and those who opposed it relied heavily on Montesquieu for their arguments."[12]

The Consequences of Capitalism

By the eighteenth century, Britain's unusual political culture gained a final, crucial source of strength: capitalism. If the struggles between church and state, lords and kings, and Catholics and Protestants cracked open the door for individual liberty, capitalism blew the walls down. Nothing has shaped the modern world more powerfully than capitalism, destroying as it has millennia-old patterns of economic, social, and political life. Over the centuries it has destroyed feudalism and monarchism with their emphasis on bloodlines and birth. It has created an independent class of businesspeople who owe little to the state and who are now the dominant force in every advanced society in the world. It has made change and dynamism—rather than order and tradition—the governing philosophy of the modern age. Capitalism created a new world, utterly different from the one that had existed for millennia. And it took root most firmly in England.

It started elsewhere. By the fourteenth century, trade and commerce, frozen during much of the Middle Ages, was once again thriving in parts of Europe. A revolution in agricultural technology was producing surpluses of grain, which had to be sold or bartered. Market towns and port cities—Antwerp, Brussels, Venice, Genoa—became centers of economic activity.

Double-entry bookkeeping, the introduction of Arabic numerals, and the rise of banking turned money-making from an amateur affair into a systematic business. Soon the commercial impulse spread inland from the port cities, mostly in the Low Countries and later in England, where it was applied to all kinds of agriculture, crafts, manufacturing, and services. Why capitalism spread to these areas first is still debated, but most economic historians agree that a competent state that protected private property was an important factor. Where capitalism succeeded it was "in the main due to the type of property rights created," write the leading historians on the subject, Douglass North and Robert Thomas.[13] By the sixteenth century a consensus was developing across Europe that "Property belongs to the family, sovereignty to the prince and his magistrates." A fifteenth-century jurist in Spain had explained, "To the king is confided solely the administration of the kingdom and not dominion over things."[14] Only in England, however, was a king (Charles I) actually executed, in large part for levying arbitrary taxes.

The systematic protection of property rights transformed societies. It meant that the complex web of feudal customs and privileges—all of which were obstacles to using property efficiently—could be eliminated. The English landed elite took a leading role in modernizing agriculture. Through the enclosures system, a brutal process of asserting their rights over the pastures and commons of their estates, they forced the peasants and farmers who had lived off these lands into more specialized and efficient labors. The pastures were then used for grazing sheep, to service the highly profitable wool trade. By adapting to the ongoing capitalist revolution, the English landed classes secured their power but also helped modernize their society. The French aristocrats, in contrast, were absentee landlords who did little to make their properties more productive and yet continued to extract hefty feudal dues from their tenants. Like many continental aristocracies, they disdained commerce.

Beyond enterprising nobles, capitalism also created a new group of wealthy and powerful men who owed their riches not to land grants from the crown but to independent economic activity. Ranging from minor aristocrats to enterprising peasants, these English "yeomen" were, in the words of one historian, "a group of ambitious, aggressive small capitalists."[15] They were the first members of the bourgeoisie, the industrious property-owning class that Karl Marx defined as "the owners of the means of production of a society and employer of its laborers." Marx accurately recognized that this class was the vanguard of political liberalization in Europe. Since its members benefited greatly from capitalism, the rule of law, free markets, and the rise of professionalism and meritocracy, they supported gradual reforms that furthered these trends. In a now-legendary work of social science, the Harvard scholar Barrington Moore, Jr., studied the pathways to democracy and dictatorship around the world and presented his central conclusion in four words: "No bourgeoisie, no democracy."[16]

British politics was revolutionized as entrepreneurial activity became the principal means of social advancement. The House of Commons, which had wrested power from the king in the seventeenth century and ran the country, now swelled with newly rich merchants and traders. The number of titled nobles in Britain was always tiny: fewer than 200 by the end of the eighteenth century.[17] But beneath them lay a broad class, often called the "English gentry." The gentry usually had some connection to the aristocracy and often took on responsibilities in local government, but it ultimately drew its prestige and power from business, professional work, or efficient farming. Many of these men entered public life, and with a healthy distance from the old order, pushed for progressive reforms such as free trade, free markets, individual rights, and freedom of religion.

The three most powerful British prime ministers of the nineteenth century—Robert Peel, William Gladstone, and Benjamin Disraeli—all came from the ranks of the gentry. This newly powerful class adopted many of the traits of the aristocracy—manor houses, morning coats, hunting parties—but it was more fluid. "Gentlemen" were widely respected and, even more than lords, became the trendsetters of their society. Indeed, by the eighteenth century, the English gentleman became an almost mythic figure toward which society aspired. A nurse is said to have asked King James I to make her son a gentleman. The monarch replied, "A gentleman I could never make him, though I could make him a lord." A visiting Frenchman ridiculed the tendency of the English aristocracy to ape the gentry: "At London, masters dress like their valets and duchesses copy after their chambermaids."[18] Today the English gentleman is remembered mostly as a dandy, whose aesthetic sensibility is marketed worldwide by Ralph Lauren. But his origins are intimately connected with the birth of English liberty.

Anglo-America

Despite the rise of capitalism, limited government, property rights, and constitutionalism across much of Europe by the eighteenth century, England was seen as unique. It was wealthier, more innovative, freer, and more stable than any society on the continent. As Guido de Ruggiero noted, "The liberties of the individual, especially security of person and property, were solidly assured. Administration was decentralized and autonomous. The judiciary bodies were wholly independent of the central government. The prerogatives of the crown were closely restricted. . . . [P]olitical power was concentrated in the hands of Parliament. What similar spectacle could the continent offer?" Many observers at the time drew similar conclusions, praising England's constitution and national character. Some focused more specifically on economics. For Voltaire, "commerce which has enriched the citizens of England has helped make them free . . . that liberty has in turn expanded commerce."

Rather than cultivating the decadent pleasures of its nobility, the observant French clergyman Abbe Coyer remarked, the English government had helped "the honest middle class, that precious portion of nations."[19] Free markets helped enrich the middle class, which then furthered the cause of liberty. It seemed a virtuous circle.

The lands most like England were its colonies in America. The colonists had established governments that closely resembled those they had left behind in Tudor England. In 1776, when they rebelled against George III, the colonists couched their revolution as a call for the return of their rights as Englishmen. As they saw it, their long-established liberties had been usurped by a tyrannical monarch, forcing them to declare independence. In some ways it was a replay of England's own Glorious Revolution, in which Parliament rebelled against an arbitrary monarch whose chief sin was also to have raised taxes without the consent of the governed— or rather, the taxed. The winners in both 1688 and 1776 were the progressive, modernizing, and commercially minded elites. (The losers, in addition to the king, were the old Tories, who remained loyal to the crown both in seventeenth-century England and eighteenth-century America.)

But if England was exceptional, America was a special case of a special case. It was England without feudalism. Of course America had rich, landed families, but they were not titled, had no birth-rights, and were not endowed with political power comparable to that of the members of the House of Lords. To understand eighteenth-century America, the historian Richard Hofstadter wrote, one had to imagine that unique possibility, "a middle class world."[20] Aristocratic elements in the economy and society, though present, rarely dominated. In the North, they began to wane by the close of the eighteenth century. The historian Gordon Wood noted, "In the 1780s we can actually sense the shift from a premodern society to a modern one where business interests and consumer tastes of ordinary people were coming to dominate." The American Revolution, which produced, in Wood's words, "an explosion of entrepreneurial power," widened the gulf between America and Europe.[21] America was now openly bourgeois and proud of it. Days after arriving in the United States in 1831, Tocqueville noted in his diary that in America "the whole society seems to have melted into a middle class."

The American path to liberal democracy was exceptional. Most countries don't begin their national experience as a new society without a feudal past. Free of hundreds of years of monarchy and aristocracy, Americans needed neither a powerful central government nor a violent social revolution to overthrow the old order. In Europe liberals feared state power but also fantasized about it. They sought to limit it yet needed it to modernize their societies. "The great advantage of the Americans," Tocqueville observed famously, "is that they have arrived at a state of democracy without having to endure a democratic revolution. . . . [T]hey are born equal without having to become equal."

By the early nineteenth century in the United Kingdom and the United States, for the most part, individual liberty flourished and equality under law ruled. But neither country was a democracy. Before the Reform Act of 1832, 1.8 percent of the adult population of the United Kingdom was eligible to vote. After the law that figure rose to 2.7 percent. After further widening of the franchise in 1867, 6.4 percent could vote, and after 1884, 12.1 percent.[22] Only in 1930, once women were fully enfranchised, did the United Kingdom meet today's standard for being democratic: universal adult suffrage. Yet it was widely considered the model of a constitutional liberal state—one that protected liberty and was governed by law.

The United States was more democratic than the United Kingdom, but not by as much as people think. For its first few decades, only white male property owners were eligible to vote—a system quite similar to that in the country whose rule it had just thrown off. In 1824—48 years after independence—only 5 percent of adult Americans cast a ballot in the presidential election. That number rose dramatically as the Jacksonian revolution spread and property qualifications were mostly eliminated. But not until the eve of the Civil War could it even be said that every white man in the United States had the right to vote. Blacks were enfranchised in theory in 1870, but in fact not until a century later in the South. Women got the vote in 1920. Despite this lack of democracy, for most of the nineteenth century, the United States and its system of laws and rights were the envy of the world. And with time, constitutional liberalism led to democracy, which led to further liberty, and so it went.

The rest of Europe followed a more complex path to liberal democracy than did the United Kingdom and the United States, but it eventually got there. What happened in Britain and America slowly and (mostly) peacefully happened on the continent in a jerky and bloody fashion (as will be discussed in the next chapter). Still, most became liberal democracies by the late 1940s and almost all the rest have done so since 1989, with consolidation taking place fast and firmly. The reason is clear: all Western countries shared a history that, for all its variations, featured the building of a constitutional liberal tradition. The English case is what scholars call the "ideal type," which makes it useful to highlight. But by the eighteenth century, even the most retrograde European power was a liberal regime when compared with its counterparts in Asia or Africa. Citizens had explicit rights and powers that no non-Western subject could imagine. Monarchs were restrained by law and tradition. A civil society of private enterprise, churches, universities, guilds, and associations flourished without much interference from the state. Private property was protected and free enterprise flowered. Often these freedoms were stronger in theory than in practice, and frequently they were subject to abuse by autocratic monarchs. But compared with the rest of the world the West was truly the land of liberty.

Culture as Destiny

This brief history of liberty might seem a discouraging guide. It suggests that any country hoping to become a liberal democracy should probably relocate to the West. And without a doubt, being part of the Western world—even if on the periphery—is a political advantage. Of all the countries that gained independence after the Soviet empire collapsed, those that have shared what one might call "the Western experience"—the old lands of the Austrian and German empires—have done best at liberal democracy. The line that separated Western and Eastern Christendom in 1500 today divides successful liberal regimes from unsuccessful, illiberal ones. Poland, Hungary, and the Czech Republic, which were most securely a part of Europe, are furthest along in consolidating their democracies; the Baltic states are next in line. Even in the Balkans, Slovenia and Croatia, which fall on the western side of that East-West line, are doing well while Serbia and Albania (on the east) are having a far more troubled transition.

Does this mean that culture is destiny? This powerful argument has been made by distinguished scholars from Max Weber to Samuel Huntington. It is currently a trendy idea. From business consultants to military strategists, people today talk about culture as the easy explanation to most puzzles. Why did the U.S. economy boom over the last two decades? It's obvious: our unique entrepreneurial culture. Why is Russia unable to adapt to capitalism? Also obvious: it has a feudal, antimarket culture. Why is Africa mired in poverty? And why is the Arab world breeding terrorists? Again, culture.

But these answers are too simple. After all, American culture also produced stagflation and the Great Depression. And the once-feudal cultures of Japan and Germany seem to have adapted to capitalism well, having become the second- and third-richest countries in the world, respectively. A single country can succeed and fail at different times, sometimes just a few decades apart, which would suggest that something other than its culture—which is relatively unchanging—is at work.

Singapore's brilliant patriarch Lee Kuan Yew once explained to me that if you want to see how culture works, compare the performance of German workers and Zambian workers anywhere in the world. You will quickly come to the conclusion that there is something very different in the two cultures that explains the results. Scholars make similar arguments: in his interesting work *Tribes*, Joel Kotkin argues that if you want to succeed economically in the modern world, the key is simple—be Jewish, be Indian, but above all, be Chinese.

Lee and Kotkin are obviously correct in their observation that certain groups—Chinese, Indians, Jews—do superbly in all sorts of settings. (In fact I find this variant of the culture theory particularly appealing, since I am of Indian origin.) But if being Indian is a key to economic success, what explains the dismal performance of the Indian economy over the first four decades after its independence in 1947—or, for that matter, for hundreds of years before that? Growing up in India I certainly did not think of Indians as economically successful. In fact I recall the day a legendary member of the Indian parliament, Piloo Mody, posed the following question to Indira Gandhi during the prime minister's "question hour" in New Delhi: "Can the prime minister explain why Indians seem to thrive economically under every government in the world except hers?"

Similar questions might be asked of China, another country that did miserably in economic terms for hundreds of years until two decades ago. If all you need are the Chinese, China has billions of them. As for Jews, although they have thrived in many places, the one country where they are a majority, Israel, was also an economic mess until recently. Interestingly, the economic fortunes of all three countries (India, China, Israel) improved markedly around the 1980s. But this was not because they got themselves new cultures, but because their governments changed specific policies and created a more market-friendly system. China is today growing faster than India, but that has more to do with the fact that China is reforming its economy more extensively than India is, than with any supposed superiority of the Confucian ethic over the Hindu mind-set.

It is odd that Lee Kuan Yew is such a fierce proponent of cultural arguments. Singapore is culturally not very different from its neighbor Malaysia. It is more Chinese and less Malay but compared to the rest of the world, the two countries share much in common. But much more than its neighbors, Singapore has had an effective government that has pursued wise economic policies. That surely, more than innate cultural differences, explains its success. The key to Singapore's success, in other words, is Lee Kuan Yew, not Confucius. The point is not that culture is unimportant; on the contrary it matters greatly. It represents the historical experience of a people, is embedded in their institutions, and shapes their attitudes and expectations about the world. But culture can change. German culture in 1939 was very different from what it became in 1959, just twenty years later. Europe, once the heartland of hypernationalism, is now postnationalist, its states willing to cede power to supranational bodies in ways that Americans can hardly imagine. The United States was once an isolationist republic with a deep suspicion of standing armies. Today it is a hegemon with garrisons around the world. The Chinese were once backward peasants; now they are smart merchants. Economic crises, war, political leadership—all these things change culture.

A hundred years ago, when East Asia seemed immutably poor, many scholars—most famously Max Weber—argued that Confucian-based cultures discouraged all the attributes necessary for success in capitalism.[23] A decade ago, when East Asia was booming, scholars had turned this explanation on its head, arguing that Confucianism actually emphasized the traits essential for economic dynamism. Today the wheel has turned again and many see in "Asian values" all the ingredients of crony capitalism. In his study Weber linked northern Europe's economic success to its "Protestant ethic" and predicted that the Catholic south would stay poor. In fact, Italy and France have grown faster than Protestant Europe over the last half-century. One may use the stereotype of shifty Latins and a *mañana* work ethic to explain the poor performance of some countries, but then how does one explain Chile? Its economy is doing as well as that of the strongest of the Asian "tigers." Its success is often attributed to another set of Latin values: strong families, religious values, and determination.

In truth we cannot find a simple answer to why certain societies succeed at certain times. When a society does succeed it often seems inevitable in retrospect. So we examine successful societies and search within their cultures for the seeds of success. But cultures are complex; one finds in them what one wants. If one wants to find cultural traits of hard work and thrift within East Asia, they are there. If you want instead to find a tendency toward blind obedience and nepotism, these too exist. Look hard enough and you will find all these traits in most cultures.

Culture is important. It can be a spur or a drag, delaying or speeding up change. It can get codified in institutions and practices, which are often the real barriers to success. Indian culture may or may not hurt its chances for economic growth, but Indian bureaucracy certainly does. The West's real advantage is that its history led to the creation of institutions and practices that, although in no sense bound up with Western genes, are hard to replicate from scratch in other societies. But it can be done.

The East Asian Model

Looking at the many non-Western transitions to liberal democracy over the last three decades one can see that the countries that have moved furthest toward liberal democracy followed a version of the European pattern: capitalism and the rule of law first, and then democracy. South Korea, Taiwan, Thailand, and Malaysia were all governed for decades by military juntas or single-party systems. These regimes liberalized the economy, the legal system, and rights of worship and travel, and then, decades later, held free elections. They achieved, perhaps accidentally, the two essential attributes of good government that James Madison outlined in the Federalist Papers. First, a government must be able to control the governed, then it must be able to control itself. Order plus liberty. These two forces will, in the long run, produce legitimate government, prosperity, and liberal democracy. Of course, it's easier said than done.

In the 1950s and 1960s, most Western intellectuals scorned East Asia's regimes as reactionary, embracing instead popular leaders in Asia and Africa who were holding elections and declaring their faith in the people—for example in Ghana, Tanzania, and Kenya. Most of these countries degenerated into dictatorships while East Asia moved in precisely the opposite direction. It should surely puzzle these scholars and intellectuals that the best-consolidated democracies in Latin America and East Asia—Chile, South Korea, and Taiwan—were for a long while ruled by military juntas. In East Asia, as in western Europe, liberalizing autocracies laid the groundwork for stable liberal democracies.

In almost every case the dictatorships opened the economy slowly and partially, but this process made the government more and more liberal. "An unmistakable feature in East Asia since World War II," wrote a leading scholar of East Asia, Minxin Pei,

> is the gradual process of authoritarian institutionalization. . . . At the center of this process was the slow emergence of modern political institutions exercising formal and informal constraining power through dominant parties, bureaucracies, semi-open electoral procedures, and a legal system that steadily acquired a measure of autonomy. The process had two beneficial outcomes—a higher level of stability and security of property rights (due to increasing constraints placed on rulers by the power of market forces and new political norms)."[24]

East Asia is still rife with corruption, nepotism, and voter fraud—but so were most Western democracies, even fifty years ago. Elections in Taiwan today are not perfect but they are probably more free and fair than those in the American South in the 1950s (or Chicago in the 1960s). Large conglomerates (*chaebols*) have improper influence in South Korean politics today, but so did their equivalents in Europe and the United States a century ago. The railroads, steel companies, shipbuilders, and great financiers of the past were probably more powerful than any East Asian tycoon today. They dominated America during its late-nineteenth-century Gilded Age. (Can you even name the political contemporaries of J. P. Morgan, E. H. Harriman, and John D. Rockefeller?) One cannot judge new democracies by standards that most Western countries would have flunked even thirty years ago. East Asia today is a mixture of liberalism, oligarchy, democracy, capitalism, and corruption—much like the West in, say, 1900. But most of East Asia's countries are considerably more liberal and democratic than the vast majority of other non-Western countries.

An even more striking proof that a constitutional liberal past can produce a liberal democratic present was identified by the late political scientist Myron Weiner in 1983. He pointed out that, as of then, "every single country in the Third World that emerged from colonial rule since the Second World War with a population of at least one million (and almost all the smaller colonies as well) with a continuous democratic experience is a former British colony."[25] British rule meant not democracy—colonialism is almost by definition undemocratic—but limited constitutional liberalism and capitalism. There are now other Third World democracies but Weiner's general point still holds. To say this is not to defend colonialism. Having grown up in a postcolonial country I do not need to be reminded of the institutionalized racism and the abuse of power that was part of the imperial legacy. But it is an undeniable fact that the British Empire left behind a legacy of law and capitalism that has helped strengthen the forces of liberal democracy in many of its former colonies—though not all. France, by contrast, encouraged little constitutionalism or free markets in its occupied lands, but it did enfranchise some of its colonial populations in northern Africa. Early democratization in all those cases led to tyranny.

The Western path has led to liberal democracy far from the Western world. But the sequence and timing of democratization matter. Most Third World countries that proclaimed themselves democracies immediately after their independence, while they were poor and unstable, became dictatorships within a decade. As Giovanni Sartori, Columbia University's great scholar of democracy, noted about the path from constitutional liberalism to democracy, "the itinerary is not reversible." Even European deviations from the Anglo-American pattern—constitutionalism and capitalism first, only then democracy—were far less successful in producing liberal democracy. To see the complications produced by premature democratization, we could return to the heart of Europe—back in time to the early twentieth century.

NOTES

1. Jacob Burckhardt, *The Age of Constantine the Great*, tr. Moses Hadas (Berkeley: University of California Press, 1983), 351.

2. Benjamin Constant, "The Liberty of the Ancients Compared with That of the Moderns" (1819), in *Benjamin Constant: Political Writings*, Biancamaria Fontana, ed. (New York: Cambridge University Press, 1988).

3. Herbert Asquith, "Introduction," in Ernest Barker, *The Legacy of Rome* (Oxford, Clarendon Press, 1923), vii.

4. Quoted in David Gress, *From Plato to NATO: The Idea of the West and Its Opponents* (New York: Free Press, 1998), 125. I am particularly indebted to this fascinating and important book for its discussion of Rome and the Catholic Church.

5. Edward Gibbon, *The Decline and Fall of the Roman Empire*, vol. 3, chapter 27, part 4. Again, thanks to David Gress for this story and source.

6. E. L. Jones, *The European Miracle: Environments, Economies, and Geopolitics in the History of Europe and Asia* (New York: Cambridge University Press, 1981). This is a wonderfully broad and suggestive book, but Jones places greater weight on culture than I do.

7. Guido de Ruggiero, *The History of European Liberalism* (Oxford: Oxford University Press, 1927). A wonderful book that deserves to be a classic.

8. Daniel A. Baugh, ed., *Aristocratic Government and Society in Eighteenth Century England* (New York: New Viewpoints, 1975).

9. Paul Johnson, "Laying Down the Law," *Wall Street Journal*, March 10, 1999.

10. In the historian J. H. Plumb's words, "the Revolution of 1688 was a monument raised by the gentry to its own sense of independence." J. H. Plumb, *The Growth of Political Stability in England, 1675–1725* (London: Macmillan, 1967), 29–30.

11. Jacques Barzun, *From Dawn to Decadence: 1500 to the Present* (New York: HarperCollins, 2000), 287–89.

12. Judith Shklar, *Montesquien* (New York: Oxford University Press, 1987), 121.

13. Douglass North and Robert Thomas, *The Rise of the Western World: A New Economic History* (Cambridge: Cambridge University Press, 1973), x.

14. Richard Pipes, *Property and Freedom* (New York: Knopf, 1999), 111.

15. Mildred Campbell, *The English Yeomen under Elizabeth and the Early Stuarts* (New York: A. M. Kelley, 1968), cited in Barrington Moore, *Social Origins of Dictatorship and Democracy: Lord and Peasant in the Making of the Modern World* (Boston: Beacon Press, 1966).

16. Moore, *Social Origins*, 418. The original says "bourgeois" not "bourgeoisie," but it is often quoted as the latter, which is what I have done.

17. J. M. Roberts, *The Penguin History of the World* (New York: Penguin, 1997), 553.

18. E. J. Hobsbawm, *Industry and Empire* (New York: Penguin, 1969), 26.

19. Hobsbawm, *Industry*, 48.

20. Richard Hofstadter, *America at 1750: A Social Portrait* (New York: Knopf, 1971), 131.

21. Gordon Wood, *The Radicalism of the American Revolution* (New York: Random House, 1993), p. 348.

22. Voting percentages calculated using B. R. Mitchell, *Abstract of British Historical Statistics* (Cambridge: Cambridge University Press, 1962); The Great Britain Historical G.I.S., University of Essex, available at www.geog.port.ac.uk/gbhgis/db; and E. J. Evans, *The Forging of the Modern Industrial State: Early Industrial Britain, 1783–1870* (New York: Longman, 1983). Also see Gertrude Himmelfarb, "The Politics of Democracy: The English Reform Act of 1867," *Journal of British Studies* 6 (1966).

23. Max Weber, *The Protestant Ethic and the Spirit of Capitalism* (New York: Scribner's, 1958).

24. Minxin Pei, "Constructing the Political Foundations for Rapid Economic Growth," in Henry Rowen, ed., *Behind East Asia's Growth: The Political and Social Foundations of an Economic Miracle* (London: Routledge, 1997), 39–59.

25. Myron Weiner, "Empirical Democratic Theory," in Myron Weiner and Ergun Ozbudun, eds., *Competitive Elections in Developing Countries* (Durham, N.C.: Duke University Press, 1987), 20.

PHILIPPE C. SCHMITTER AND TERRY LYNN KARL

WHAT DEMOCRACY IS . . . AND IS NOT

For some time, the word democracy has been circulating as a debased currency in the political marketplace. Politicians with a wide range of convictions and practices strove to appropriate the label and attach it to their actions. Scholars, conversely, hesitated to use it—without adding qualifying adjectives—because of the ambiguity that surrounds it. The distinguished American political theorist Robert Dahl even tried to introduce a new term, "polyarchy," in its stead in the (vain) hope of gaining a greater measure of conceptual precision. But for better or worse, we are "stuck" with democracy as the catchword of contemporary political discourse. It is the word that resonates in people's minds and springs from their lips as they struggle for freedom and a better way of life; it is the word whose meaning we must discern if it is to be of any use in guiding political analysis and practice.

The wave of transitions away from autocratic rule that began with Portugal's "Revolution of the Carnations" in 1974 and seems to have crested with the collapse of communist regimes across Eastern Europe in 1989 has produced a welcome convergence toward [a] common definition of democracy.[1] Everywhere there has been a silent abandonment of dubious adjectives like "popular," "guided," "bourgeois," and "formal" to modify "democracy." At the same time, a remarkable consensus has emerged concerning the minimal conditions that polities must meet in order to merit the prestigious appellation of "democratic." Moreover, a number of international organizations now monitor how well these standards are met; indeed, some countries even consider them when formulating foreign policy.[2]

From *Journal of Democracy* (Summer 1991), pp. 67–73.

What Democracy Is

Let us begin by broadly defining democracy and the generic *concepts* that distinguish it as a unique system for organizing relations between rulers and the ruled. We will then briefly review *procedures*, the rules and arrangements that are needed if democracy is to endure. Finally, we will discuss two operative *principles* that make democracy work. They are not expressly included among the generic concepts or formal procedures, but the prospect for democracy is grim if their underlying conditioning effects are not present.

One of the major themes of this essay is that democracy does not consist of a single unique set of institutions. There are many types of democracy, and their diverse practices produce a similarly varied set of effects. The specific form democracy takes is contingent upon a country's socioeconomic conditions as well as its entrenched state structures and policy practices.

Modern political democracy is a system of governance in which rulers are held accountable for their actions in the public realm by citizens, acting indirectly through the competition and cooperation of their elected representatives.[3]

A *regime or system of governance* is an ensemble of patterns that determines the methods of access to the principal public offices; the characteristics of the actors admitted to or excluded from such access; the strategies that actors may use to gain access; and the rules that are followed in the making of publicly binding decisions. To work properly, the ensemble must be institutionalized—that is to say, the various patterns must be habitually known, practiced, and accepted by most, if not all, actors. Increasingly, the preferred mechanism of institutionalization is a written body of laws undergirded by a written constitution, though many enduring political norms can have an informal, prudential, or traditional basis.[4]

For the sake of economy and comparison, these forms, characteristics, and rules are usually bundled together and given a generic label. Democratic is one; others are autocratic, authoritarian, despotic, dictatorial, tyrannical, totalitarian, absolutist, traditional, monarchic, obligarchic, plutocratic, aristocratic, and sultanistic.[5] Each of these regime forms may in turn be broken down into subtypes.

Like all regimes, democracies depend upon the presence of *rulers*, persons who occupy specialized authority roles and can give legitimate commands to others. What distinguishes democratic rulers from nondemocratic ones are the norms that condition how the former come to power and the practices that hold them accountable for their actions.

The *public realm* encompasses the making of collective norms and choices that are binding on the society and backed by state coercion. Its content can vary a great deal across democracies, depending upon preexisting distinctions between the public and the private, state and society, legitimate coercion and voluntary exchange, and collective needs and individual preferences. The liberal conception of democracy advocates circumscribing the public realm as narrowly as possible, while the socialist or social-democratic approach would extend that realm through regulation, subsidization, and, in some cases, collective ownership of property. Neither is intrinsically more democratic than the other— just *differently* democratic. This implies that measures aimed at "developing the private sector" are no more democratic than those aimed at "developing the public sector." Both, if carried to extremes, could undermine the practice of democracy, the former by destroying the basis for satisfying collective needs and exercising legitimate authority; the latter by destroying the

basis for satisfying individual preferences and controlling illegitimate government actions. Differences of opinion over the optimal mix of the two provide much of the substantive content of political conflict within established democracies.

Citizens are the most distinctive element in democracies. All regimes have rulers and a public realm, but only to the extent that they are democratic do they have citizens. Historically, severe restrictions on citizenship were imposed in most emerging or partial democracies according to criteria of age, gender, class, race, literacy, property ownership, tax-paying status, and so on. Only a small part of the total population was eligible to vote or run for office. Only restricted social categories were allowed to form, join, or support political associations. After protracted struggle—in some cases involving violent domestic upheaval or international war—most of these restrictions were lifted. Today, the criteria for inclusion are fairly standard. All native-born adults are eligible, although somewhat higher age limits may still be imposed upon candidates for certain offices. Unlike the early American and European democracies of the nineteenth century, none of the recent democracies in southern Europe, Latin America, Asia, or Eastern Europe has even attempted to impose formal restrictions on the franchise or eligibility to office. When it comes to informal restrictions on the effective exercise of citizenship rights, however, the story can be quite different. This explains the central importance (discussed below) of procedures.

Competition has not always been considered an essential defining condition of democracy. "Classic" democracies presumed decision making based on direct participation leading to consensus. The assembled citizenry was expected to agree on a common course of action after listening to the alternatives and weighing their respective merits and demerits. A tradition of hostility to "faction," and "particular interests" persists in democratic thought, but at least since *The Federalist Papers* it has become widely accepted that competition among factions is a necessary evil in democracies that operate on a more-than-local scale. Since, as James Madison argued, "the latent causes of faction are sown into the nature of man," and the possible remedies for "the mischief of faction" are worse than the disease, the best course is to recognize them and to attempt to control their effects.[6] Yet while democrats may agree on the inevitability of factions, they tend to disagree about the best forms and rules for governing factional competition. Indeed, differences over the preferred modes and boundaries of competition contribute most to distinguishing one subtype of democracy from another.

The most popular definition of democracy equates it with regular *elections*, fairly conducted and honestly counted. Some even consider the mere fact of elections—even ones from which specific parties or candidates are excluded, or in which substantial portions of the population cannot freely participate—as a sufficient condition for the existence of democracy. This fallacy has been called "electoralism" or "the faith that merely holding elections will channel political action into peaceful contests among elites and accord public legitimacy to the winners"—no matter how they are conducted or what else constrains those who win them.[7] However central to democracy, elections occur intermittently and only allow citizens to choose between the highly aggregated alternatives offered by political parties, which can, especially in the early stages of a democratic transition, proliferate in a bewildering variety. During the intervals between elections, citizens can seek to influence public policy through a wide variety of other intermediaries: interest associations, social movements, locality groupings, clientelistic arrangements, and so forth. *Modern democracy, in other words, offers a variety of competitive processes and channels for the expression of interests and values—associational as well as partisan, functional as well as territorial, collective as well as individual. All are integral to its practice.*

Another commonly accepted image of democracy identifies it with *majority rule*. Any governing body that makes decisions by combining the votes of more than half of those eligible and present is said to be democratic, whether that majority emerges within an electorate, a parliament, a committee, a city council, or a party caucus. For exceptional purposes (e.g., amending the constitution or expelling a member), "qualified majorities" of more than 50 percent may be required, but few would deny that democracy must involve some means of aggregating the equal preferences of individuals.

A problem arises, however, when *numbers* meet *intensities*. What happens when a properly assembled majority (especially a stable, self-perpetuating one) regularly makes decisions that harm some minority (especially a threatened cultural or ethnic group)? In these circumstances, successful democracies tend to qualify the central principle of majority rule in order to protect minority rights. Such qualifications can take the form of constitutional provisions that place certain matters beyond the reach of majorities (bills of rights); requirements for concurrent majorities in several different constituencies (confederalism); guarantees securing the autonomy of local or regional governments against the demands of the central authority (federalism); grand coalition governments that incorporate all parties (consociationalism); or the negotiation of social pacts between major social groups like business and labor (neocorporatism). The most common and effective way of protecting minorities, however, lies in the everyday operation of interest associations and social movements. These reflect (some would say, amplify) the different intensities of preference that exist in the population and bring them to bear on democratically elected decision makers. Another way of putting this intrinsic tension between numbers and intensities would be to say that "in modern democracies, votes may be counted, but influences alone are weighted."

Cooperation has always been a central feature of democracy. Actors must voluntarily make collective decisions binding on the polity as a whole. They must cooperate in order to compete. They must be capable of acting collectively through parties, associations, and movements in order to select candidates, articulate preferences, petition authorities, and influence policies.

But democracy's freedoms should also encourage citizens to deliberate among themselves, to discover their common needs, and to resolve their differences without relying on some supreme central authority. Classical democracy emphasized these qualities, and they are by no means extinct, despite repeated efforts by contemporary theorists to stress the analogy with behavior in the economic marketplace and to reduce all of democracy's operations to competitive interest maximization. Alexis de Tocqueville best described the importance of independent groups for democracy in his *Democracy in America*, a work which remains a major source of inspiration for all those who persist in viewing democracy as something more than a struggle for election and re-election among competing candidates.[8]

In contemporary political discourse, this phenomenon of cooperation and deliberation via autonomous group activity goes under the rubric of "civil society." The diverse units of social identity and interest, by remaining independent of the state (and perhaps even of parties), not only can restrain the arbitrary actions of rulers, but can also contribute to forming better citizens who are more aware of the preferences of others, more self-confident in their actions, and more civic-minded in their willingness to sacrifice for the common good. At its best, civil society provides an intermediate layer of governance between the individual and the state that is capable of resolving conflicts and controlling the behavior of members without public coercion. Rather than overloading decision makers with increased demands and making the system ungovernable,[9] a viable civil society can mitigate conflicts and improve the quality of citizenship—without relying exclusively on the privatism of the marketplace.

Representatives—whether directly or indirectly elected—do most of the real work in modern democracies. Most are professional politicians who orient their careers around the desire to fill key offices. It is doubtful that any democracy could survive without such people. The central question, therefore, is not whether or not there will be a political elite or even a professional political class, but how these representatives are chosen and then held accountable for their actions.

As noted above, there are many channels of representation in modern democracy. The electoral one, based on territorial constituencies, is the most visible and public. It culminates in a parliament or a presidency that is periodically accountable to the citizenry as a whole. Yet the sheer growth of government (in large part as a byproduct of popular demand) has increased the number, variety, and power of agencies charged with making public decisions and not subject to elections. Around these agencies there has developed a vast apparatus of specialized representation based largely on functional interests, not territorial constituencies. These interest associations, and not political parties, have become the primary expression of civil society in most stable democracies, supplemented by the more sporadic interventions of social movements.

The new and fragile democracies that have sprung up since 1974 must live in "compressed time." They will not resemble the European democracies of the nineteenth and early twentieth centuries, and they cannot expect to acquire the multiple channels of representation in gradual historical progression as did most of their predecessors. A bewildering array of parties, interests, and movements will all simultaneously seek political influence in them, creating challenges to the polity that did not exist in earlier processes of democratization.

Procedures That Make Democracy Possible

The defining components of democracy are necessarily abstract, and may give rise to a considerable variety of institutions and subtypes of democracy. For democracy to thrive, however, specific procedural norms must be followed and civic rights must be respected. Any polity that fails to impose such restrictions upon itself, that fails to follow the "rule of law" with regard to its own procedures, should not be considered democratic. These procedures alone do not define democracy, but their presence is indispensable to its persistence. In essence, they are necessary but not sufficient conditions for its existence.

Robert Dahl has offered the most generally accepted listing of what he terms the "procedural minimal" conditions that must be present for modern political democracy (or as he puts it, "polyarchy") to exist:

1. Control over government decisions about policy is constitutionally vested in elected officials.
2. Elected officials are chosen in frequent and fairly conducted elections in which coercion is comparatively uncommon.
3. Practically all adults have the right to vote in the election of officials.
4. Practically all adults have the right to run for elective offices.
5. Citizens have a right to express themselves without the danger of severe punishment on political matters broadly defined. . . .
6. Citizens have a right to seek out alternative sources of information. Moreover, alternative sources of information exist and are protected by law.
7. . . . Citizens also have the right to form relatively independent associations or organizations, including independent political parties and interest groups.[10]

These seven conditions seem to capture the essence of procedural democracy for many theorists, but we propose to add two others. The first might be thought of as a further refinement of item (1), while the second might be called an implicit prior condition to all seven of the above.

1. Popularly elected officials must be able to exercise their constitutional powers without

being subjected to overriding (albeit informal) opposition from unelected officials. Democracy is in jeopardy if military officers, entrenched civil servants, or state managers retain the capacity to act independently of elected civilians or even veto decisions made by the people's representatives. Without this additional caveat, the militarized polities of contemporary Central America, where civilian control over the military does not exist, might be classified by many scholars as democracies, just as they have been (with the exception of Sandinista Nicaragua) by U.S. policy makers. The caveat thus guards against what we earlier called "electoralism"—the tendency to focus on the holding of elections while ignoring other political realities.
2. The polity must be self-governing; it must be able to act independently of constraints imposed by some other overarching political system. Dahl and other contemporary democratic theorists probably took this condition for granted since they referred to formally sovereign nation-states. However, with the development of blocs, alliances, spheres of influence, and a variety of "neocolonial" arrangements, the question of autonomy has been a salient one. Is a system really democratic if its elected officials are unable to make binding decisions without the approval of actors outside their territorial domain? This is significant even if the outsiders are relatively free to alter or even end the encompassing arrangement (as in Puerto Rico), but it becomes especially critical if neither condition [pertains] (as in the Baltic states).

Principles That Make Democracy Feasible

Lists of component processes and procedural norms help us to specify what democracy is, but they do not tell us much about how it actually functions. The simplest answer is "by the consent of the people"; the more complex one is "by the contingent consent of politicians acting under conditions of bounded uncertainty."

In a democracy, representatives must at least informally agree that those who win greater electoral support or influence over policy will not use their temporary superiority to bar the losers from taking office or exerting influence in the future, and that in exchange for this opportunity to keep competing for power and place, momentary losers will respect the winners' right to make binding decisions. Citizens are expected to obey the decisions ensuing from such a process of competition, provided its outcome remains contingent upon their collective preferences as expressed through fair and regular elections or open and repeated negotiations.

The challenge is not so much to find a set of goals that command widespread consensus as to find a set of rules that embody contingent consent. The precise shape of this "democratic bargain," to use Dahl's expression,[11] can vary a good deal from society to society. It depends on social cleavages and such subjective factors as mutual trust, the standard of fairness, and the willingness to compromise. It may even be compatible with a great deal of dissensus on substantive policy issues.

All democracies involve a degree of uncertainty about who will be elected and what policies they will pursue. Even in those polities where one party persists in winning elections or one policy is consistently implemented, the possibility of change through independent collective action still exists, as in Italy, Japan, and the Scandinavian social democracies. If it does not, the system is not democratic, as in Mexico, Senegal, or Indonesia.

But the uncertainty embedded in the core of all democracies is bounded. Not just any actor can get into the competition and raise any issue he or she pleases—there are previously established rules that must be respected. Not just any policy can be adopted—there are conditions that

must be met. Democracy institutionalizes "normal," limited political uncertainty. These boundaries vary from country to country. Constitutional guarantees of property, privacy, expression, and other rights are a part of this, but the most effective boundaries are generated by competition among interest groups and cooperation within civil society. Whatever the rhetoric (and some polities appear to offer their citizens more dramatic alternatives than others), once the rules of contingent consent have been agreed upon, the actual variation is likely to stay within a predictable and generally accepted range.

This emphasis on operative guidelines contrasts with a highly persistent, but misleading theme in recent literature on democracy—namely, the emphasis upon "civic culture." The principles we have suggested here rest on rules of prudence, not on deeply ingrained habits of tolerance, moderation, mutual respect, fair play, readiness to compromise, or trust in public authorities. Waiting for such habits to sink deep and lasting roots implies a very slow process of regime consolidation—one that takes generations—and it would probably condemn most contemporary experiences *ex hypothesi* to failure. Our assertion is that contingent consent and bounded uncertainty can emerge from the interaction between antagonistic and mutually suspicious actors and that the far more benevolent and ingrained norms of a civic culture are better thought of as a *product* and not a producer of democracy.

How Democracies Differ

Several concepts have been deliberately excluded from our generic definition of democracy, despite the fact that they have been frequently associated with it in both everyday practice and scholarly work. They are, nevertheless, especially important when it comes to distinguishing subtypes of democracy. Since no single set of actual institutions, practices, or values embodies democracy, polities moving away from authoritarian rule can mix different components to produce different democracies. It is important to recognize that these do not define points along a single continuum of improving performance, but a matrix of potential combinations that are *differently* democratic.

1. *Consensus*: All citizens may not agree on the substantive goals of political action or on the role of the state (although if they did, it would certainly make governing democracies much easier).

2. *Participation*: All citizens may not take an active and equal part in politics, although it must be legally possible for them to do so.

3. *Access*: Rulers may not weigh equally the preferences of all who come before them, although citizenship implies that individuals and groups should have an equal opportunity to express their preferences if they choose to do so.

4. *Responsiveness*: Rulers may not always follow the course of action preferred by the citizenry. But when they deviate from such a policy, say on grounds of "reason of state" or "overriding national interest," they must ultimately be held accountable for their actions through regular and fair processes.

5. *Majority rule*: Positions may not be allocated or rules may not be decided solely on the basis of assembling the most votes, although deviations from this principle usually must be explicitly defended and previously approved.

6. *Parliamentary sovereignty*: The legislature may not be the only body that can make rules or even the one with final authority in deciding which laws are binding, although where executive, judicial, or other public bodies make that ultimate choice, they too must be accountable for their actions.

7. *Party government*: Rulers may not be nominated, promoted, and disciplined in their activities by well-organized and program-matically coherent political parties, although where they are not, it may prove more difficult to form an effective government.

8. *Pluralism*: The political process may not be based on a multiplicity of overlapping, voluntaristic, and autonomous private groups. However, where there are monopolies of representation, hierarchies of association, and obligatory memberships, it is likely that the interests involved will be more closely linked to the state and the separation between the public and private spheres of action will be much less distinct.

9. *Federalism*: The territorial division of authority may not involve multiple levels and local autonomies, least of all ones enshrined in a constitutional document, although some dispersal of power across territorial and/or functional units is characteristic of all democracies.

10. *Presidentialism*: The chief executive officer may not be a single person and he or she may not be directly elected by the citizenry as a whole, although some concentration of authority is present in all democracies, even if it is exercised collectively and only held indirectly accountable to the electorate.

11. *Checks and Balances*: It is not necessary that the different branches of government be systematically pitted against one another, although governments by assembly, by executive concentrations, by judicial command, or even by dictatorial fiat (as in time of war) must be ultimately accountable to the citizenry as a whole.

While each of the above has been named as an essential component of democracy, they should instead be seen either as indicators of this or that type of democracy, or else as useful standards for evaluating the performance of particular regimes. To include them as part of the generic definition of democracy itself would be to mistake the American polity for the universal model of democratic governance. Indeed, the parliamentary, consociational, unitary, corporatist, and concentrated arrangements of continental Europe may have some unique virtues for guiding polities through the uncertain transition from autocratic to democratic rule.[12]

What Democracy Is Not

We have attempted to convey the general meaning of modern democracy without identifying it with some particular set of rules and institutions or restricting it to some specific culture or level of development. We have also argued that it cannot be reduced to the regular holding of elections or equated with a particular notion of the role of the state, but we have not said much more about what democracy is not or about what democracy may not be capable of producing.

There is an understandable temptation to load too many expectations on this concept and to imagine that by attaining democracy, a society will have resolved all of its political, social, economic, administrative, and cultural problems. Unfortunately, "all good things do not necessarily go together."

First, democracies are not necessarily more efficient economically than other forms of government. Their rates of aggregate growth, savings, and investment may be no better than those of nondemocracies. This is especially likely during the transition, when propertied groups and administrative elites may respond to real or imagined threats to the "rights" they enjoyed under authoritarian rule by initiating capital flight, disinvestment, or sabotage. In time, depending upon the type of democracy, benevolent long-term effects upon income distribution, aggregate demand, education, productivity, and creativity may eventually combine to improve economic and social performance, but it is certainly too much to expect that these improvements will occur immediately—much less that they will be defining characteristics of democratization.

Second, democracies are not necessarily more efficient administratively. Their capacity to make decisions may even be slower than that of the regimes they replace, if only because more actors must be consulted. The costs of getting things done may be higher, if only because "payoffs" have to be made to a wider and more resourceful set of clients (although one should never underestimate the degree of corruption to be found within autocracies). Popular satisfaction with the new democratic government's performance may not even seem greater, if only because necessary compromises often please no one completely, and because the losers are free to complain.

Third, democracies are not likely to appear more orderly, consensual, stable, or governable than the autocracies they replace. This is partly a byproduct of democratic freedom of expression, but it is also a reflection of the likelihood of continuing disagreement over new rules and institutions. These products of imposition or compromise are often initially quite ambiguous in nature and uncertain in effect until actors have learned how to use them. What is more, they come in the aftermath of serious struggles motivated by high ideals. Groups and individuals with recently acquired autonomy will test certain rules, protest against the actions of certain institutions, and insist on renegotiating their part of the bargain. Thus the presence of antisystem parties should be neither surprising nor seen as a failure of democratic consolidation. What counts is whether such parties are willing, however reluctantly, to play by the general rules of bounded uncertainty and contingent consent.

Governability is a challenge for all regimes, not just democratic ones. Given the political exhaustion and loss of legitimacy that have befallen autocracies from sultanistic Paraguay to totalitarian Albania, it may seem that only democracies can now be expected to govern effectively and legitimately. Experience has shown, however, that democracies too can lose the ability to govern. Mass publics can become disenchanted with their performance. Even more threatening is the temptation for leaders to fiddle with procedures and ultimately undermine the principles of contingent consent and bounded uncertainty. Perhaps the most critical moment comes once the politicians begin to settle into the more predictable roles and relations of a consolidated democracy. Many will find their expectations frustrated; some will discover that the new rules of competition put them at a disadvantage; a few may even feel that their vital interests are threatened by popular majorities.

Finally, democracies will have more open societies and polities than the autocracies they replace, but not necessarily more open economies. Many of today's most successful and well-established democracies have historically resorted to protectionism and closed borders, and have relied extensively upon public institutions to promote economic development. While the long-term compatibility between democracy and capitalism does not seem to be in doubt, despite their continuous tension, it is not clear whether the promotion of such liberal economic goals as the right of individuals to own property and retain profits, the clearing function of markets, the private settlement of disputes, the freedom to produce without government regulation, or the privatization of state-owned enterprises necessarily furthers the consolidation of democracy. After all, democracies do need to levy taxes and regulate certain transactions, especially where private monopolies and oligopolies exist. Citizens or their representatives may decide that it is desirable to protect the rights of collectivities from encroachment by individuals, especially propertied ones, and they may choose to set aside certain forms of property for public or cooperative ownership. In short, notions of economic liberty that are currently put forward in neoliberal economic models are not synonymous with political freedom—and may even impede it.

Democratization will not necessarily bring in its wake economic growth, social peace, administrative efficiency, political harmony, free markets, or "the end of ideology." Least of all will it bring about "the end of history." No doubt some

of these qualities could make the consolidation of democracy easier, but they are neither prerequisites for it nor immediate products of it. Instead, what we should be hoping for is the emergence of political institutions that can peacefully compete to form governments and influence public policy, that can channel social and economic conflicts through regular procedures, and that have sufficient linkages to civil society to represent their constituencies and commit them to collective courses of action. Some types of democracies, especially in developing countries, have been unable to fulfill this promise, perhaps due to the circumstances of their transition from authoritarian rule.[13] The democratic wager is that such a regime, once established, will not only persist by reproducing itself within its initial confining conditions, but will eventually expand beyond them.[14] Unlike authoritarian regimes, democracies have the capacity to modify their rules and institutions consensually in response to changing circumstances. They may not immediately produce all the goods mentioned above, but they stand a better chance of eventually doing so than do autocracies.

NOTES

1. For a comparative analysis of the recent regime changes in southern Europe and Latin America, see Guillermo O'Donnell, Philippe C. Schmitter, and Laurence Whitehead, eds., *Transitions from Authoritarian Rule*, 4 vols. (Baltimore: Johns Hopkins University Press, 1986). For another compilation that adopts a more structural approach see Larry Diamond, Juan Linz, and Seymour Martin Lipset, eds., *Democracy in Developing Countries*, vols. 2, 3, and 4 (Boulder, Colo.: Lynne Rienner, 1989).

2. Numerous attempts have been made to codify and quantify the existence of democracy across political systems. The best known is probably Freedom House's *Freedom in the*

World: Political Rights and Civil Liberties, published since 1973 by Greenwood Press and since 1988 by University Press of America. Also see Charles Humana, *World Human Rights Guide* (New York: Facts on File, 1986).

3. The definition most commonly used by American social scientists is that of Joseph Schumpeter: "that institutional arrangement for arriving at political decisions in which individuals acquire the power to decide by means of a competitive struggle for the people's vote." *Capitalism, Socialism, and Democracy* (London: George Allen and Unwin, 1943), 269. We accept certain aspects of the classical procedural approach to modern democracy, but differ primarily in our emphasis on the accountability of rulers to citizens and the relevance of mechanisms of competition other than elections.

4. Not only do some countries practice a stable form of democracy without a formal constitution (e.g., Great Britain and Israel), but even more countries have constitutions and legal codes that offer no guarantee of reliable practice. On paper, Stalin's 1936 constitution for the USSR was a virtual model of democratic rights and entitlements.

5. For the most valiant attempt to make some sense out of this thicket of distinctions, see Juan Linz, "Totalitarian and Authoritarian Regimes" in *Handbook of Political Science*, eds. Fred I. Greenstein and Nelson W. Polsby (Reading Mass.: Addison Wesley, 1975), 175–411.

6. "Publius" (Alexander Hamilton, John Jay, and James Madison), *The Federalist Papers* (New York: Anchor Books, 1961). The quote is from Number 10.

7. See Terry Karl, "Imposing Consent? Electoralism versus Democratization in El Salvador," in *Elections and Democratization in Latin America, 1980–1985*, eds. Paul Drake and Eduardo Silva (San Diego: Center for Iberian and Latin American Studies, Center for US/Mexican Studies, University of California, San Diego, 1986), 9–36.

8. Alexis de Tocqueville, *Democracy in America*, 2 vols. (New York: Vintage Books, 1945).

9. This fear of overloaded government and the imminent collapse of democracy is well reflected in the work of Samuel P. Huntington during the 1970s. See especially Michel Crozier, Samuel P. Huntington, and Joji Watanuki, *The Crisis of Democracy* (New York: New York University Press, 1975). For Huntington's (revised) thoughts about the prospects for democracy, see his "Will More Countries Become Democratic?," *Political Science Quarterly* 99 (Summer 1984): 193–218.

10. Robert Dahl, *Dilemmas of Pluralist Democracy* (New Haven: Yale University Press, 1982), 11.

11. Robert Dahl, *After the Revolution: Authority in a Good Society* (New Haven: Yale University Press, 1970).

12. See Juan Linz, "The Perils of Presidentialism," *Journal of Democracy* 1 (Winter 1990): 51–69, and the ensuing discussion by Donald Horowitz, Seymour Martin Lipset, and Juan Linz in *Journal of Democracy* 1 (Fall 1990): 73–91.

13. Terry Lynn Karl, "Dilemmas of Democratization in Latin America" *Comparative Politics* 23 (October 1990): 1–23.

14. Otto Kirchheimer, "Confining Conditions and Revolutionary Breakthroughs," *American Political Science Review* 59 (1965): 964–974.

AREND LIJPHART

CONSTITUTIONAL CHOICES FOR NEW DEMOCRACIES

Two fundamental choices that confront architects of new democratic constitutions are those between plurality elections and proportional representation (PR) and between parliamentary and presidential forms of government. The merits of presidentialism and parliamentarism were extensively debated by Juan J. Linz, Seymour Martin Lipset, and Donald L. Horowitz in the Fall 1990 issue of the *Journal of Democracy*.[1] I strongly concur with Horowitz's contention that the electoral system is an equally vital element in democratic constitutional design, and therefore that it is of crucial importance to evaluate these two sets of choices in relation with each other. Such an analysis, as I will try to show, indicates that the combination of parliamentarism with proportional representation should be an especially attractive one to newly democratic and democratizing countries.

The comparative study of democracies has shown that the type of electoral system is significantly related to the development of a country's party system, its type of executive (one-party vs. coalition cabinets), and the relationship between its executive and legislature. Countries that use the plurality method of election (almost always applied, at the national level, in single-member districts) are likely to have two-party systems, one-party governments, and executives that are dominant in relation to their legislatures. These are the main characteristics of the Westminster or *majoritarian* model of democracy, in which power is concentrated in the hands of the majority party. Conversely, PR is likely to be associated with multiparty systems, coalition governments (including, in many cases, broad and inclusive

From Larry Diamond and Marc F. Plattner, eds. *The Global Resurgence of Democracy* (Baltimore: Johns Hopkins University Press, 1996), pp. 162–74.

coalitions), and more equal executive-legislative power relations. These latter characteristics typify the *consensus* model of democracy, which, instead of relying on pure and concentrated majority rule, tries to limit, divide, separate, and share power in a variety of ways.[2]

Three further points should be made about these two sets of related traits. First, the relationships are mutual. For instance, plurality elections favor the maintenance of a two-party system; but an existing two-party system also favors the maintenance of plurality, which gives the two principal parties great advantages that they are unlikely to abandon. Second, if democratic political engineers desire to promote either the majoritarian cluster of characteristics (plurality, a two-party system, and a dominant, one-party cabinet) or the consensus cluster (PR, multipartism, coalition government, and a stronger legislature), the most practical way to do so is by choosing the appropriate electoral system. Giovanni Sartori has aptly called electoral systems "the most specific manipulative instrument of politics."[3] Third, important variations exist among PR systems. Without going into all the technical details, a useful distinction can be made between *extreme* PR, which poses few barriers to small parties, and *moderate* PR. The latter limits the influence of minor parties through such means as applying PR in small districts instead of large districts or nationwide balloting, and requiring parties to receive a minimum percentage of the vote in order to gain representation, such as the 5-percent threshold in Germany. The Dutch, Israeli, and Italian systems exemplify extreme PR and the German and Swedish systems, moderate PR.

The second basic constitutional choice, between parliamentary and presidential forms of government, also affects the majoritarian or consensus character of the political system. Presidentialism yields majoritarian effects on the party system and on the type of executive, but a consensus effect on executive-legislative relations. By formally separating the executive and legislative powers, presidential systems generally promote a rough executive-legislative balance of power. On the other hand, presidentialism tends to foster a two-party system, as the presidency is the biggest political prize to be won, and only the largest parties have a chance to win it. This advantage for the big parties often carries over into legislative elections as well (especially if presidential and legislative elections are held simultaneously), even if the legislative elections are conducted under PR rules. Presidentialism usually produces cabinets composed solely of members of the governing party. In fact, presidential systems concentrate executive power to an even greater degree than does a one-party parliamentary cabinet—not just in a single *party* but in a single *person*.

Explaining Past Choices

My aim is not simply to describe alternative democratic systems and their majoritarian or consensus characteristics, but also to make some practical recommendations for democratic constitutional engineers. What are the main advantages and disadvantages of plurality and PR and of presidentialism and parliamentarism? One way to approach this question is to investigate why contemporary democracies made the constitutional choices they did.

Figure 1 illustrates the four combinations of basic characteristics and the countries and regions where they prevail. The purest examples of the combination of presidentialism and plurality are the United States and democracies heavily influenced by the United States, such as the Philippines and Puerto Rico. Latin American countries have overwhelmingly opted for presidential-PR systems. Parliamentary-plurality systems exist in the United Kingdom and many

former British colonies, including India, Malaysia, Jamaica, and the countries of the so-called Old Commonwealth (Canada, Australia, and New Zealand). Finally, parliamentary-PR systems are concentrated in Western Europe. Clearly, the overall pattern is to a large extent determined by geographic, cultural, and colonial factors—a point to which I shall return shortly.

Very few contemporary democracies cannot be accommodated by this classification. The major exceptions are democracies that fall in between the pure presidential and pure parliamentary types (France and Switzerland), and those that use electoral methods other than pure PR or plurality (Ireland, Japan, and, again, France).[4]

Two important factors influenced the adoption of PR in continental Europe. One was the problem of ethnic and religious minorities; PR was designed to provide minority representation and thereby to counteract potential threats to national unity and political stability. "It was no accident," Stein Rokkan writes, "that the earliest moves toward proportional representation (PR) came in the ethnically most heterogeneous countries." The second factor was the dynamic of the democratization process. PR was adopted "through a convergence of pressures from below and from above. The rising working class wanted to lower the thresholds of representation in order to gain access to the legislatures, and

Figure 1—Four Basic Types of Democracy

	Presidential	*Parliamentary*
Plurality Elections	*United States* *Philippines*	*United Kingdom* *Old Commonweath* *India* *Malaysia* *Jamaica*
Proportional Representation	*Latin America*	*Western Europe*

the most threatened of the old-established parties demanded PR to protect their position against the new waves of mobilized voters created by universal suffrage."[5] Both factors are relevant for contemporary constitution making, especially for the many countries where there are deep ethnic cleavages or where new democratic forces need to be reconciled with the old antidemocratic groups.

The process of democratization also originally determined whether parliamentary or presidential institutions were adopted. As Douglas V. Verney has pointed out, there were two basic ways in which monarchical power could be democratized: by taking away most of the monarch's personal political prerogatives and making his cabinet responsible to the popularly elected legislature, thus creating a parliamentary system; or by removing the hereditary monarch and substituting a new, democratically elected "monarch," thus creating a presidential system.[6]

Other historical causes have been voluntary imitations of successful democracies and the dominant influence of colonial powers. As Figure 1 shows very clearly, Britain's influence as an imperial power has been enormously important. The U.S. presidential model was widely imitated in Latin America in the nineteenth century. And early in the twentieth century, PR spread quickly in continental Europe and Latin America, not only for reasons of partisan accommodation and minority protection, but also because it was widely perceived to be the most democratic method of election and hence the "wave of the democratic future."

This sentiment in favor of PR raises the controversial question of the *quality* of democracy achieved in the four alternative systems. The term "quality" refers to the degree to which a system meets such democratic norms as representativeness, accountability, equality, and participation. The claims and counterclaims are too well-known to require lengthy treatment here, but it is worth emphasizing that the differences between the opposing camps are not as great as is often supposed. First of all, PR and plurality advocates disagree not so much about the respective effects of the two electoral methods as about the weight to be attached to these effects. Both sides agree that PR yields greater proportionality and minority representation and that plurality promotes two-party systems and one-party executives. Partisans disagree on which of these results is preferable, with the plurality side claiming that only in two-party systems can clear accountability for government policy be achieved.

In addition, both sides argue about the *effectiveness* of the two systems. Proportionalists value minority representation not just for its democratic quality but also for its ability to maintain unity and peace in divided societies. Similarly, proponents of plurality favor one-party cabinets not just because of their democratic accountability but also because of the firm leadership and effective policy making that they allegedly provide. There also appears to be a slight difference in the relative emphasis that the two sides place on quality and effectiveness. Proportionalists tend to attach greater importance to the *representativeness* of government, while plurality advocates view the *capacity to govern* as the more vital consideration.

Finally, while the debate between presidentialists and parliamentarists has not been as fierce, it clearly parallels the debate over electoral systems. Once again, the claims and counterclaims revolve around both quality and effectiveness. Presidentialists regard the direct popular election of the chief executive as a democratic asset, while parliamentarists think of the concentration of executive power in the hands of a single official as less than optimally democratic. But here the question of effectiveness has been the more seriously debated issue, with the president's strong and effective leadership role being emphasized by one side and the danger of executive-legislative conflict and stalemate by the other.

Evaluating Democratic Performance

How can the actual performance of the different types of democracies be evaluated? It is extremely difficult to find quantifiable measures of democratic performance, and therefore political scientists have rarely attempted a systematic assessment. The major exception is G. Bingham Powell's pioneering study evaluating the capacity of various democracies to maintain public order (as measured by the incidence of riots and deaths from political violence) and their levels of citizen participation (as measured by electoral turnout).[7] Following Powell's example, I will examine these and other aspects of democratic performance, including democratic representation and responsiveness, economic equality, and macroeconomic management.

Due to the difficulty of finding reliable data outside the OECD countries to measure such aspects of performance, I have limited the analysis to the advanced industrial democracies. In any event, the Latin American democracies, given their lower levels of economic development, cannot be considered comparable cases. This means that one of the four basic alternatives—the presidential-PR form of democracy prevalent only in Latin America—must be omitted from our analysis.

Although this limitation is unfortunate, few observers would seriously argue that a strong case can be made for this particular type of democracy. With the clear exception of Costa Rica and the partial exceptions of Venezuela and Colombia, the political stability and economic performance of Latin American democracies have been far from satisfactory. As Juan Linz has argued, Latin American presidential systems have been particularly prone to executive-legislative deadlock and ineffective leadership.[8] Moreover, Scott Mainwaring has shown persuasively that this problem becomes especially serious when presidents do not have majority support in their legislatures.[9] Thus the Latin American model of presidentialism combined with PR legislative elections remains a particularly unattractive option.

The other three alternatives—presidential-plurality, parliamentary-plurality, and parliamentary-PR systems—are all represented among the firmly established Western democracies. I focus on the 14 cases that unambiguously fit these three categories. The United States is the one example of presidentialism combined with plurality. There are four cases of parliamentarism-plurality (Australia, Canada, New Zealand, and the United Kingdom), and nine democracies of the parliamentary-PR type (Austria, Belgium, Denmark, Finland, Germany, Italy, the Netherlands, Norway, and Sweden). Seven long-term, stable democracies are excluded from the analysis either because they do not fit comfortably into any one of the three categories (France, Ireland, Japan, and Switzerland), or because they are too vulnerable to external factors (Israel, Iceland, and Luxembourg).

Since a major purpose of PR is to facilitate minority representation, one would expect the PR systems to outperform plurality systems in this respect. There is little doubt that this is indeed the case. For instance, where ethnic minorities have formed ethnic political parties, as in Belgium and Finland, PR has enabled them to gain virtually perfect proportional representation. Because there are so many different kinds of ethnic and religious minorities in the democracies under analysis, it is difficult to measure systematically the *degree* to which PR succeeds in providing more representatives for minorities than does plurality. It is possible, however, to compare the representation of women—a minority in political rather than strictly numerical terms—systematically across countries. The first column of Table 1 shows the percentages of female members in the lower (or only) houses of the national legislatures in these 14 democracies during the early 1980s. The 16.4-percent average for the parliamentary-PR systems is about four times higher than the 4.1 percent for the United States or the 4.0-percent average for the

Table 1. Women's Legislative Representation, Innovative Family Policy, Voting Turnout, Income Inequality, and the Dahl Rating of Democratic Quality

	Women's Repr. 1980–82	Family Policy 1976–80	Voting Turnout 1971–80	Income Top 20% 1985	Dahl Rating 1969
Pres.-Plurality (N=1)	4.1	3.00	54.2%	39.9%	3.0
Parl.-Plurality (N=4)	4.0	2.50	75.3	42.9	4.8
Parl.-PR (N=9)	16.4	7.89	84.5	39.0	2.2

Note: The one presidential-plurality democracy is the United States; the four parliamentary-plurality democracies are Australia, Canada, New Zealand, and the United Kingdom; and the nine parliamentary-PR democracies are Austria, Belgium, Denmark, Finland, Germany, Italy, the Netherlands, Norway, and Sweden.

Sources: Based on Wilma Rule, "Electoral Systems, Contextual Factors and Women's Opportunity for Election to Parliament in Twenty-Three Democracies," *Western Political Quarterly* 40 (September 1987): 483; Harold L. Wilensky, "Common Problems, Divergent Policies: An 18-Nation Study of Family Policy," *Public Affairs Report* 31 (May 1990): 2; personal communication by Harold L. Wilensky to the author, dated 18 October 1990; Robert W. Jackman, "Political Institutions and Voter Turnout in the Industrial Democracies," *American Political Science Review* 81 (June 1987): 420; World Bank, *World Development Report 1989* (New York: Oxford University Press, 1989), 223; Robert A. Dahl, *Polyarchy: Participation and Opposition* (New Haven: Yale University Press, 1971), 232.

parliamentary-plurality countries. To be sure, the higher social standing of women in the four Nordic countries accounts for part of the difference, but the average of 9.4 percent in the five other parliamentary-PR countries remains more than twice as high as in the plurality countries.

Does higher representation of women result in the advancement of their interests? Harold L. Wilensky's careful rating of democracies with regard to the innovativeness and expansiveness of their family policies—a matter of special concern to women—indicates that it does.[10] On a 13-point scale (from a maximum of 12 to a minimum of 0), the scores of these countries range from 11 to 1. The differences among the three groups (as shown in the second column of Table 1) are striking: the PR countries have an average score of 7.89, whereas the parliamentary-plurality countries have an average of just 2.50, and the U.S. only a slightly higher score of 3.00. Here again, the Nordic countries have the highest scores, but the 6.80 average of the non-Nordic PR countries is still well above that of the plurality countries.

The last three columns of Table 1 show indicators of democratic quality. The third column lists the most reliable figures on electoral participation (in the 1970s); countries with compulsory voting (Australia, Belgium, and Italy) are not included in the averages. Compared with the extremely low voter turnout of 54.2 percent in the United States, the parliamentary-plurality systems perform a great deal better (about 75 percent). But the average in the parliamentary-PR systems is still higher, at slightly above 84 percent. Since the maximum turnout that is realistically attainable is around 90 percent (as indicated by the turnouts in countries with compulsory voting), the difference between 75 and 84 percent is particularly striking.

Another democratic goal is political equality, which is more likely to prevail in the absence of great economic inequalities. The fourth column of Table 1 presents the World Bank's percentages of total income earned by the top 20 percent of households in the mid-1980s.[11] They show a slightly less unequal distribution of income in the parliamentary-PR than in the parliamentary-plurality systems, with the United States in an intermediate position.

Finally, the fifth column reports Robert A. Dahl's ranking of democracies according to ten indicators of democratic quality, such as freedom of the press, freedom of association, competitive party systems, strong parties and interest groups, and effective legislatures.[12] The stable democracies range from a highest rating of 1 to a low of 6. There is a slight pro-PR bias in Dahl's ranking (he includes a number-of-parties variable that rates multiparty systems somewhat higher than two-party systems), but even when we discount this bias we find striking differences between the parliamentary-PR and parliamentary-plurality countries: six of the former are given the highest score, whereas most of the latter receive the next to lowest score of 5.

No such clear differences are apparent when we examine the effect of the type of democracy on the maintenance of public order and peace. Parliamentary-plurality systems had the lowest incidence of riots during the period 1948–77, but the highest incidence of political deaths; the latter figure, however, derives almost entirely from the high number of political deaths in the United Kingdom, principally as a result of the Northern Ireland problem. A more elaborate statistical analysis shows that societal division is a much more important factor than type of democracy in explaining variation in the incidence of political riots and deaths in the 13 parliamentary countries.[13]

A major argument in favor of plurality systems has been that they favor "strong" one-party governments that can pursue "effective" public policies. One key area of government activity in which this pattern should manifest itself is the management of the economy. Thus advocates of plurality systems received a rude shock in 1987 when the average per capita GDP in Italy (a PR and multiparty democracy with notoriously uncohesive and unstable governments) surpassed that of the United Kingdom, typically regarded as the very model of strong and effective government. If Italy had discovered large amounts of oil in the Mediterranean, we would undoubtedly explain its superior economic performance in terms of this fortuitous factor. But it was not Italy but Britain that discovered the oil!

Economic success is obviously not solely determined by government policy. When we examine economic performance over a long period of time, however, the effects of external influences are minimized, especially if we focus on countries with similar levels of economic development. Table 2 presents OECD figures from the 1960s through the 1980s for the three most important aspects of macroeconomic performance—average annual economic growth, inflation, and unemployment rates.

Although Italy's economic growth has indeed been better than that of Britain, the parliamentary-plurality and parliamentary-PR countries as groups do not differ much from each other or from the United States. The slightly higher growth rates in the parliamentary-PR systems cannot be considered significant. With regard to inflation, the United States has the best record, followed by the parliamentary-PR systems. The most sizable differences appear in unemployment levels; here the parliamentary-PR countries

Table 2. Economic Growth, Inflation, and Unemployment (in percent)

	Economic Growth 1961–88	Inflation 1961–88	Unemployment 1965–88
Pres.-Plurality (N=1)	3.3	5.1	6.1
Parl.-Plurality (N=4)	3.4	7.5	6.1
Parl.-PR (N=9)	3.5	6.3	4.4

Sources: *OECD Economic Outlook*, No. 26 (December 1979), 131; No. 30 (December 1981), 131, 140, 142; No. 46 (December 1989), 166, 176, 182.

perform significantly better than the plurality countries.[14] Comparing the parliamentary-plurality and parliamentary-PR countries on all three indicators, we find that the performance of the latter is uniformly better.

Lessons for Developing Countries

Political scientists tend to think that plurality systems such as the United Kingdom and the United States are superior with regard to democratic quality and governmental effectiveness—a tendency best explained by the fact that political science has always been an Anglo-American-oriented discipline. This prevailing opinion is largely contradicted, however, by the empirical evidence presented above. Wherever significant differences appear, the parliamentary-PR systems almost invariably post the best records, particularly with respect to representation, protection of minority interests, voter participation, and control of unemployment.

This finding contains an important lesson for democratic constitutional engineers: the parliamentary-PR option is one that should be given serious consideration. Yet a word of caution is also in order, since parliamentary-PR democracies differ greatly among themselves. Moderate PR and moderate multipartism, as in Germany and Sweden, offer more attractive models than the extreme PR and multiparty systems of Italy and the Netherlands. As previously noted, though, even Italy has a respectable record of democratic performance.

But are these conclusions relevant to newly democratic and democratizing countries in Asia, Africa, Latin America, and Eastern Europe, which are trying to make democracy work in the face of economic underdevelopment and ethnic divisions? Do not these difficult conditions require strong executive leadership in the form of a powerful president or a Westminster-style, dominant one-party cabinet?

With regard to the problem of deep ethnic cleavages, these doubts can be easily laid to rest.

Divided societies, both in the West and elsewhere, need peaceful coexistence among the contending ethnic groups. This requires conciliation and compromise, goals that in turn require the greatest possible inclusion of representatives of these groups in the decision-making process. Such power sharing can be arranged much more easily in parliamentary and PR systems than in presidential and plurality systems. A president almost inevitably belongs to one ethnic group, and hence presidential systems are particularly inimical to ethnic power sharing. And while Westminster-style parliamentary systems feature collegial cabinets, these tend not to be ethnically inclusive, particularly when there is a majority ethnic group. It is significant that the British government, in spite of its strong majoritarian traditions, recognized the need for consensus and power sharing in religiously and ethnically divided Northern Ireland. Since 1973, British policy has been to try to solve the Northern Ireland problem by means of PR elections and an inclusive coalition government.

As Horowitz has pointed out, it may be possible to alleviate the problems of presidentialism by requiring that a president be elected with a stated minimum of support from different groups, as in Nigeria.[15] But this is a palliative that cannot compare with the advantages of a truly collective and inclusive executive. Similarly, the example of Malaysia shows that a parliamentary system can have a broad multiparty and multiethnic coalition cabinet in spite of plurality elections, but this requires elaborate preelection pacts among the parties. These exceptions prove the rule: the ethnic power sharing that has been attainable in Nigeria and Malaysia only on a limited basis and through very special arrangements is a natural and straightforward result of parliamentary-PR forms of democracy.

PR and Economic Policy Making

The question of which form of democracy is most conducive to economic development is more difficult to answer. We simply do not have enough cases of durable Third World democracies representing the different systems (not to mention the lack of reliable economic data) to make an unequivocal evaluation. However, the conventional wisdom that economic development requires the unified and decisive leadership of a strong president or a Westminster-style dominant cabinet is highly suspect. First of all, if an inclusive executive that must do more bargaining and conciliation were less effective at economic policy making than a dominant and exclusive executive, then presumably an authoritarian government free of legislative interference or internal dissent would be optimal. This reasoning—a frequent excuse for the overthrow of democratic governments in the Third World in the 1960s and 1970s—has now been thoroughly discredited. To be sure, we do have a few examples of economic miracles wrought by authoritarian regimes, such as those in South Korea or Taiwan, but these are more than counterbalanced by the sorry economic records of just about all the nondemocratic governments in Africa, Latin America, and Eastern Europe.

Second, many British scholars, notably the eminent political scientist S.E. Finer, have come to the conclusion that economic development requires not so much a *strong* hand as a *steady* one. Reflecting on the poor economic performance of post-World War II Britain, they have argued that each of the governing parties indeed provided reasonably strong leadership in economic policy making but that alternations in governments were too "absolute and abrupt," occurring "between two sharply polarized parties each eager to repeal a large amount of its predecessor's legislation." What is needed, they argue, is "greater stability and continuity" and "greater moderation in policy," which could be provided by a shift to PR and to coalition governments much more likely to be centrist in orientation.[16] This argument would appear to be equally applicable both to developed and developing countries.

Third, the case for strong presidential or Westminster-style governments is most compelling where rapid decision making is essential. This means that in foreign and defense policy parliamentary-PR systems may be at a disadvantage. But in economic policy making speed is not particularly important—quick decisions are not necessarily wise ones

Why then do we persist in distrusting the economic effectiveness of democratic systems that engage in broad consultation and bargaining aimed at a high degree of consensus? One reason is that multiparty and coalition governments *seem* to be messy, quarrelsome, and inefficient in contrast to the clear authority of strong presidents and strong one-party cabinets. But we should not let ourselves be deceived by these superficial appearances. A closer look at presidential systems reveals that the most successful cases—such as the United States, Costa Rica, and pre-1970 Chile—are at least equally quarrelsome and, in fact, are prone to paralysis and deadlock rather than steady and effective economic policy making. In any case, the argument should not be about governmental aesthetics but about actual performance. The undeniable elegance of the Westminster model is not a valid reason for adopting it.

The widespread skepticism about the economic capability of parliamentary-PR systems stems from confusing governmental strength with effectiveness. In the short run, one-party cabinets or presidents may well be able to formulate economic policy with greater ease and speed. In the long run, however, policies supported by a broad consensus are more likely to be successfully carried out and to remain on course than policies imposed by a "strong" government against the wishes of important interest groups.

To sum up, the parliamentary-PR form of democracy is clearly better than the major alternatives in accommodating ethnic differences, and it has a slight edge in economic policy making as well. The argument that considerations of governmental effectiveness mandate the rejection of parliamentary-PR democracy for developing countries is simply not tenable. Constitution makers in new democracies would do themselves and their countries a great disservice by ignoring this attractive democratic model.

NOTES

1. Donald L. Horowitz, "Comparing Democratic Systems," Seymour Martin Lipset, "The Centrality of Political Culture," and Juan J. Linz, "The Virtues of Parliamentarism," *Journal of Democracy* 1 (Fall 1990): 73–91. A third set of important decisions concerns institutional arrangements that are related to the difference between federal and unitary forms of government: the degree of government centralization, unicameralism or bicameralism, rules for constitutional amendment, and judicial review. Empirical analysis shows that these factors tend to be related: federal countries are more likely to be decentralized, to have significant bicameralism, and to have "rigid" constitutions that are difficult to amend and protected by judicial review.

2. For a fuller discussion of the differences between majoritarian and consensus government, see Arend Lijphart, *Democracies: Patterns of Majoritarian and Consensus Government in Twenty-One Countries* (New Haven: Yale University Press, 1984).

3. Giovanni Sartori, "Political Development and Political Engineering," in *Public Policy* vol. 17, eds. John D. Montgomery and Alfred O. Hirschman (Cambridge: Harvard University Press, 1968), 273.

4. The first scholar to emphasize the close connection between culture and these constitutional arrangements was G. Bingham Powell, Jr. in his *Contemporary Democracies Participation, Stability, and Violence* (Cambridge: Harvard University Press, 1982), 67. In my previous writings, I have sometimes classified Finland as a presidential or semi-presidential system, but I now agree with Powell (pp. 56–57) that, although the directly elected Finnish president has special authority in foreign policy, Finland operates like a parliamentary system in most other respects. Among the exceptions, Ireland is a doubtful case; I regard its system of the single transferable vote as mainly a PR method, but other authors have classified it as a plurality system. And I include Australia in the parliamentary-plurality group, because its alternative-vote system, while not identical with plurality, operates in a similar fashion.

5. Stein Rokkan, *Citizens, Elections, Parties: Approaches to the Comparative Study of the Processes of Development* (Oslo: Universitetsforlaget, 1970), 157.

6. Douglas V. Verney, *The Analysis of Political Systems* (London: Routledge and Kegan Paul, 1959), 18–23, 42–43.

7. Powell, op. cit., esp. 12–29 and 111–74.

8. Juan J. Linz, "The Perils of Presidentialism," *Journal of Democracy* 1 (Winter 1990): 51–69.

9. Scott Mainwaring, "Presidentialism in Latin America," *Latin American Research Review* 25 (1990): 167–70.

10. Wilensky's ratings are based on a five-point scale (from 4 to 0) "for each of three policy clusters: existence and length of maternity and parental leave, paid and unpaid; availability and accessibility of public daycare programs and government effort to expand daycare; and flexibility of retirement systems. They measure government action to assure care of children and maximize choices in balancing work and family demands for everyone." See Harold L. Wilensky, "Common Problems, Divergent Policies: An 18-Nation Study of Family Policy," *Public Affairs Report* 31 (May 1990): 2.

11. Because of missing data, Austria is not included in the parliamentary-PR average.

12. Robert A. Dahl, *Polyarchy: Participation and Opposition* (New Haven: Yale University Press, 1971), 231–45.

13. This multiple-correlation analysis shows

that societal division, as measured by the degree of organizational exclusiveness of ethnic and religious groups, explains 33 percent of the variance in riots and 25 percent of the variance in political deaths. The additional explanation by type of democracy is only 2 percent for riots (with plurality countries slightly more orderly) and 13 percent for deaths (with the PR countries slightly more peaceful).

14. Comparable unemployment data for Austria, Denmark, and New Zealand are not available, and these countries are therefore not included in the unemployment figures in Table 2.
15. Horowitz, op. cit., 76–77.
16. S.E. Finer, "Adversary Politics and Electoral Reform," in *Adversary Politics and Electoral Reform*, ed. S.E. Finer (London: Anthony Wigram, 1975), 30–31.

ROBERT D. PUTNAM

TUNING IN, TUNING OUT: THE STRANGE DISAPPEARANCE OF SOCIAL CAPITAL IN AMERICA

It is a daunting honor to deliver the inaugural Pool Lecture. Ithiel de Sola Pool was a brilliant, broad-gauged scholar whose interests ranged from the Nazi elite to direct satellite broadcasting, from the first rigorous computer simulation of electoral behavior to the development of network theory, from which he invented "small world" research. He helped found the field of political communications. A graduate of the University of Chicago's political science department during its classic golden age, and first chair of the MIT political science department, Pool must also have been a remarkable teacher, for his students continue to contribute to our understanding of technology, communications, and political behavior. When I accepted this honor, I did not guess how close my own inquiry would lead me to Pool's own professional turf. I shall return to the contemporary relevance of Pool's insights at the conclusion of this talk.

For the last year or so, I have been wrestling with a difficult mystery. It is, if I am right, a puzzle of some importance to the future of American democracy. It is a classic brain-teaser, with a corpus delicti, a crime scene strewn with clues, and many potential suspects. As in all good detective stories, however, some plausible miscreants turn out to have impeccable alibis, and some important clues hint at portentous developments that occurred long before the curtain rose. Moreover, like Agatha Christie's *Murder on the Orient Express*, this crime may have had more than one perpetrator, so that we shall need to sort out ringleaders from accomplices. Finally, I need to make clear at the outset that I am not yet sure that I have solved the mystery. In that sense, this lecture represents work-in-progress. I have a prime suspect that I am prepared to indict, but the evidence is not yet strong enough to convict, so I invite your help in sifting clues.

From *PS: Political Science & Politics* (December 1995), pp. 664–83.

Theories and Measures of Social Capital

Allow me to set the scene by saying a word or two about my own recent work.[1] Several years ago I conducted research on the arcane topic of local government in Italy (Putnam 1993). That study concluded that the performance of government and other social institutions is powerfully influenced by citizen engagement in community affairs, or what (following Coleman 1990) I termed *social capital*. I am now seeking to apply that set of ideas and insights to the urgent problems of contemporary American public life.

By "social capital," I mean features of social life—networks, norms, and trust—that enable participants to act together more effectively to pursue shared objectives. Whether or not their shared goals are praiseworthy is, of course, entirely another matter. To the extent that the norms, networks, and trust link substantial sectors of the community and span underlying social cleavages—to the extent that the social capital is of a "bridging" sort—then the enhanced cooperation is likely to serve broader interests and to be widely welcomed. On the other hand, groups like the Michigan militia or youth gangs also embody a kind of social capital, for these networks and norms, too, enable members to cooperate more effectively, albeit to the detriment of the wider community.

Social capital, in short, refers to social connections and the attendant norms and trust. Who benefits from these connections, norms, and trust—the individual, the wider community, or some faction within the community—must be

Figure 1—Membership Trends (1974–1994) by Type of Group (education controlled)

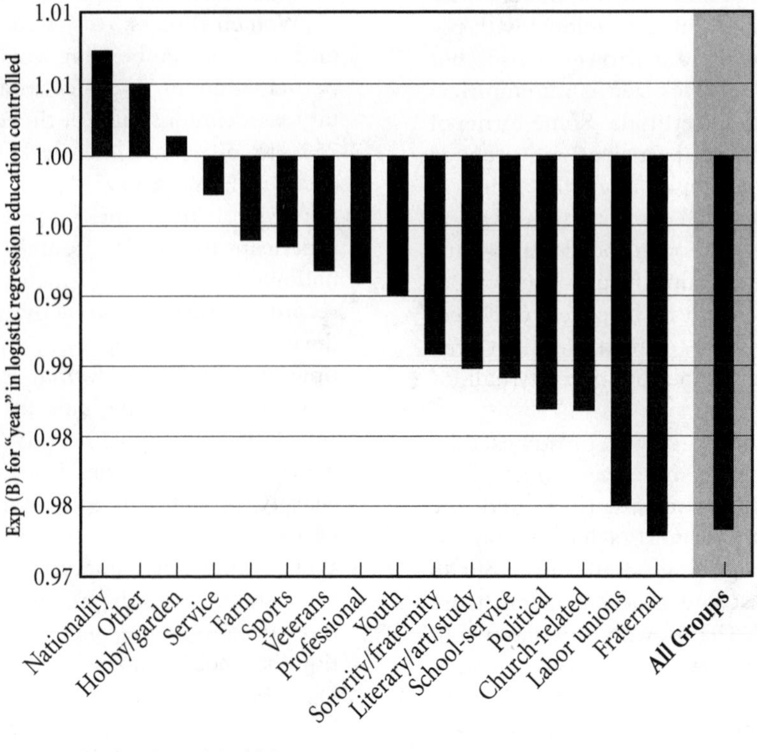

Source: General Social Survey, 1974–1994

determined empirically, not definitionally.[2] Sorting out the multiple effects of different forms of social capital is clearly a crucial task, although it is not one that I can address here. For present purposes, I am concerned with forms of social capital that, generally speaking, serve civic ends.

Social capital in this sense is closely related to political participation in the conventional sense, but these terms are not synonymous. Political participation refers to our relations with political institutions. Social capital refers to our relations with one another. Sending a check to a PAC is an act of political participation, but it does not embody or create social capital. Bowling in a league or having coffee with a friend embodies and creates social capital, though these are not acts of political participation. (A grassroots political movement or a traditional urban machine is a social capital-intensive form of political participation.) I use the term "civic engagement" to refer to people's connections with the life of their communities, not merely with politics. Civic engagement is correlated with political participation in a narrower sense, but whether they move in lock-step is an empirical question, not a logical certitude. Some forms of individualized political participation, such as check-writing, for example, might be rising at the same time that social connectedness was on the wane. Similarly, although social trust—trust in other people—and political trust—trust in political authorities—might be empirically related, they are logically quite distinct. I might well trust my neighbors without trusting city hall, or vice versa.

The theory of social capital presumes that, generally speaking, the more we connect with other people, the more we trust them, and vice versa. At least in the contexts I have so far explored, this presumption generally turns out to be true: social trust and civic engagement are strongly correlated. That is, with or without controls for education, age, income, race, gender, and so on, people who join are people who trust.[3] Moreover, this is true across different countries, and across different states in the

United States, as well as across individuals, and it is true of all sorts of groups.[4] Sorting out which way causation flows—whether joining causes trusting or trusting causes joining—is complicated both theoretically and methodologically, although John Brehm and Wendy Rahn (1995) report evidence that the causation flows mainly from joining to trusting. Be that as it may, civic connections and social trust move together. Which way are they moving?

Bowling Alone: Trends in Civic Engagement

Evidence from a number of independent sources strongly suggests that America's stock of social capital has been shrinking for more than a quarter century.

- Membership records of such diverse organizations as the PTA, the Elks club, the League of Women Voters, the Red Cross, labor unions, and even bowling leagues show that participation in many conventional voluntary associations has declined by roughly 25% to 50% over the last two to three decades (Putnam 1995, 1996).
- Surveys of the time budgets of average Americans in 1965, 1975, and 1985, in which national samples of men and women recorded every single activity undertaken during the course of a day, imply that the time we spend on informal socializing and visiting is down (perhaps by one quarter) since 1965, and that the time we devote to clubs and organizations is down even more sharply (probably by roughly half) over this period.[5]
- While Americans' interest in politics has been stable or even growing over the last three decades, and some forms of participation that require moving a pen, such as signing petitions and writing checks, have increased significantly, many measures of collective participation have fallen sharply

(Rosenstone and Hansen 1993; Putnam 1996), including attending a rally or speech (off 36% between 1973 and 1993), attending a meeting on town or school affairs (off 39%), or working for a political party (off 56%).

- Evidence from the General Social Survey demonstrates, at all levels of education and among both men and women, a drop of roughly one-quarter in group membership since 1974 and a drop of roughly one-third in social trust since 1972.[6] Moreover, as Figure 1 illustrates, slumping membership has afflicted all sorts of groups, from sports clubs and professional associations to literary discussion groups and labor unions.[7] Only nationality groups, hobby and garden clubs, and the catch-all category of "other" seem to have resisted the ebbing tide. Furthermore, Gallup polls report that church attendance fell by roughly 15% during the 1960s and has remained at that lower level ever since, while data from the National Opinion Research Center suggest that the decline continued during the 1970s and 1980s and by now amounts to roughly 30% (Putnam 1996).

Each of these approaches to the problem of measuring trends in civic engagement has advantages and drawbacks. Membership records offer long-term coverage and reasonable precision, but they may underrepresent newer, more vibrant organizations. Time budgets capture real investments of time and energy in both formal and informal settings, not merely nominal membership, but the available data are episodic and drawn from relatively small samples that are not entirely comparable across time. Surveys are more comprehensive in their coverage of various types of groups, but (apart from church attendance) comparable trend data are available only since the mid-1970s, a decade or more after the putative downturn began, so they may understate the full decline. No single source is perfect for testing the hypothesized decline in social con-

nectedness, although the consistency across different measuring rods is striking.

A fuller audit of American social capital would need to account for apparent counter-trends.[8] Some observers believe, for example, that support groups and neighborhood watch groups are proliferating, and few deny that the last several decades have witnessed explosive growth in interest groups represented in Washington. The growth of "mailing list" organizations, like the American Association of Retired People or the Sierra Club, although highly significant in political (and commercial) terms, is not really a counter-example to the supposed decline in social connectedness, however, since these are not really associations in which members meet one another. Their members' ties are to common symbols and ideologies, but not to each other. These organizations are sufficiently different from classical "secondary" associations as to deserve a new rubric—perhaps "tertiary" associations. Similarly, although most secondary associations are not-for-profit, most prominent nonprofits (from Harvard University to the Metropolitan Opera) are bureaucracies, not secondary associations, so the growth of the "Third Sector" is not tantamount to a growth in social connectedness. With due regard to various kinds of counter-evidence, I believe that the weight of the available evidence confirms that Americans today are significantly less engaged with their communities than was true a generation ago.

Of course, lots of civic activity is still visible in our communities. American civil society is not moribund. Indeed, evidence suggests that America still outranks many other countries in the degree of our community involvement and social trust (Putnam 1996). But if we compare ourselves, not with other countries but with our parents, the best available evidence suggests that we are less connected with one another.

This prologue poses a number of important questions that merit further debate:

- Is it true that America's stock of social capital has diminished?

- Does it matter?
- What can we do about it?

The answer to the first two questions is, I believe, "yes," but I cannot address them further in this setting. Answering the third question—which ultimately concerns me most—depends, at least in part, on first understanding the *causes* of the strange malady afflicting American civic life. This is the mystery I seek to unravel here: Why, beginning in the 1960s and accelerating in the 1970s and 1980s, did the fabric of American community life begin to fray? Why are more Americans bowling alone?

Explaining the Erosion of Social Capital

Many possible answers have been suggested for this puzzle:

- Busyness and time pressure
- Economic hard times (or, according to alternative theories, material affluence)
- Residential mobility
- Suburbanization
- The movement of women into the paid labor force and the stresses of two-career families
- Disruption of marriage and family ties
- Changes in the structure of the American economy, such as the rise of chain stores, branch firms, and the service sector
- The Sixties (most of which actually happened in the Seventies), including
  —Vietnam, Watergate, and disillusion with public life
  —The cultural revolt against authority (sex, drugs, and so on)
- Growth of the welfare state
- The civil rights revolution
- Television, the electronic revolution, and other technological changes

Most respectable mystery writers would hesitate to tally up this many plausible suspects, no matter how energetic the fictional detective. I am not yet in a position to address all these theories—certainly not in any definitive form—but we must begin to winnow the list. To be sure, a social trend as pervasive as the one we are investigating probably has multiple causes, so our task is to assess the relative importance of such factors as these.

A solution, even a partial one, to our mystery must pass several tests.

Is the proposed explanatory factor correlated with trust and civic engagement? If not, it is difficult to see why that factor should even be placed in the lineup. For example, many women have entered the paid labor force during the period in question, but if working women turned out to be more engaged in community life than housewives, it would be harder to attribute the downturn in community organizations to the rise of two-career families.

Is the correlation spurious? If parents, for example, were more likely to be joiners than childless people, that might be an important clue. However, if the correlation between parental status and civic engagement turned out to be entirely spurious, due to the effects of (say) age, we would have to remove the declining birth rate from our list of suspects.

Is the proposed explanatory factor changing in the relevant way? Suppose, for instance, that people who often move have shallower community roots. That could be an important part of the answer to our mystery *only if* residential mobility itself had risen during this period.

Is the proposed explanatory factor vulnerable to the claim that it might be the result *of civic disengagement, not the cause?* For example, even if newspaper readership were closely correlated with civic engagement across individuals and across time, we would need to weigh the possibility that reduced newspaper circulation is the result (not the cause) of disengagement.

Against that set of benchmarks, let us consider various potential influences on social capital formation.

Education

Human capital and social capital are closely related, for education has a very powerful effect on trust and associational membership, as well as many other forms of social and political participation. Education is by far the strongest correlate that I have discovered of civic engagement in all its forms, including social trust and membership in many different types of groups.[9] In fact, as Figure 2 illustrates, the relationship between education and civic engagement is a curvilinear one of increasing returns. The last two years of college make twice as much difference to trust and group membership as the first two years of high school. The four years of education between 14 and 18 total years have *ten times more impact* on trust and membership than the first four years of formal education. The same basic pattern applies to both men and women,

and to all races and generations. Education, in short, is an extremely powerful predictor of civic engagement.

Sorting out just why education has such a massive effect on social connectedness would require a book, not a mere lecture.[10] Education is in part a proxy for social class and economic differences, but when income, social status, and education are used together to predict trust and group membership, education continues to be the primary influence. (Income and satisfaction with one's personal financial situation both have a significant independent effect.) In short, highly educated people are much more likely to be joiners and trusters, partly because they are better off economically, but mostly because of the skills, resources, and inclinations that were imparted to them at home and in school.

It is widely recognized that Americans today are better educated than our parents and grandparents. It is less often appreciated how

Figure 2—Social Trust and Group Membership by Years of Education

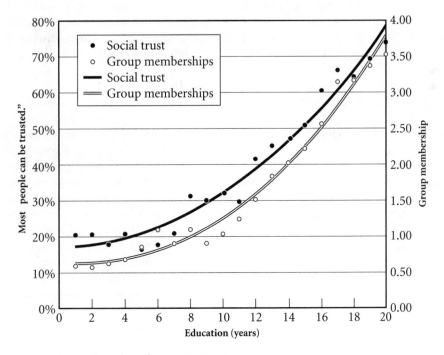

Source: General Social Survey, 1972–1994

massively and rapidly this trend has transformed the educational composition of the adult population during just the last two decades. Since 1972, the proportion of all adults with fewer than 12 years of education has been cut in half, falling from 40% to 18%, while the proportion with more than 12 years has nearly doubled, rising from 28% to 50%, as the generation of Americans educated around the turn of this century (most of whom did not finish high school) passed from the scene and were replaced by the baby boomers and their successors (most of whom attended college).

Thus, education boosts civic engagement sharply, and educational levels have risen massively. Unfortunately, these two undeniable facts only deepen our central mystery. By itself, the rise in educational levels should have *increased* social capital during the last 20 years by 15–20%, even assuming that the effects of education were merely linear. (Taking account of the curvilinear effect in Figure 1, the rise in trusting and joining should have been even greater, as Americans moved up the accelerating curve.) By contrast, however, the actual GSS figures show a net *decline* since the early 1970s of roughly the same magnitude (trust by about 20–25%, memberships by about 15–20%). The relative declines in social capital are similar *within* each educational category—roughly 25% in group memberships and roughly 30% in social trust since the early 1970s, and probably even more since the early 1960s.

Thus, this first investigative foray leaves us more mystified than before. We may nevertheless draw two useful conclusions from these findings, one methodological and one substantive:

1. Since education has such a powerful effect on civic engagement and social trust, we need to take account of educational differences in our exploration of other possible factors, in order to be sure that we do not confuse the consequences of education with the possible effects of other variables.[11]

2. Whatever forces lie behind the slump in civic engagement and social trust, those forces have affected all levels in American society.[12] Social capital has eroded among the one in every twelve Americans who have enjoyed the advantages (material and intellectual) of graduate study; it has eroded among the one in every eight Americans who did not even make it into high school; and it has eroded among all the strata in between. The mysterious disengagement of the last quarter century seems to have afflicted all echelons of our society.

Pressures of Time and Money

Americans certainly *feel* busier now than a generation ago: the proportion of us who report feeling "always rushed" jumped by half between the mid-1960s and the mid-1990s (Robinson and Godbey 1995). Probably the most obvious suspect behind our tendency to drop out of community affairs is pervasive busyness. And lurking nearby in the shadows are those endemic economic pressures so much discussed nowadays —job insecurity and declining real wages, especially among the lower two-thirds of the income distribution.

Yet, however culpable busyness and economic insecurity may appear at first glance, it is hard to find any incriminating evidence. In fact, the balance of the evidence argues that pressures of time and money are apparently *not* important contributors to the puzzle we seek to solve.

In the first place, time budget studies do *not* confirm the thesis that Americans are, on average, working longer than a generation ago. On the contrary, Robinson and Godbey (1995) report a five-hour per week *gain* in free time for the average American between 1965 and 1985, due partly to reduced time spent on housework and partly to earlier retirement. Their claim that Americans have more leisure time now than several decades ago is, to be sure, contested by other observers. Schor (1991), for example, reports evidence that our work hours are lengthening, especially for women. Whatever the resolution of that controversy, however, the thesis that attributes civic disengagement to longer workdays is rendered much less plausible by looking at the correlation between work hours, on the one hand, and social trust and group membership, on the other.

The available evidence strongly suggests that, in fact, long hours on the job are *not* associated with lessened involvement in civic life or reduced social trust. Quite the reverse: results from the General Social Survey show that employed people belong to somewhat *more* groups than those outside the paid labor force. Even more striking is the fact that among workers, longer hours are linked to *more* civic engagement, not less.[13] This surprising discovery is fully consistent with evidence from the time budget studies. Robinson (1990a) reports that, unsurprisingly, people who spend more time at work do feel more rushed, and these harried souls do spend less time eating, sleeping, reading books, engaging in hobbies, and just doing nothing. Compared to the rest of the population, they also spend a lot less time watching television—almost 30% less. However, they do *not* spend less time on organizational activity. In short, those who work longer forego *Nightline*, but not the Kiwanis club, *ER*, but not the Red Cross.

I do not conclude from the positive correlation between group membership and work hours that working longer actually *causes* greater civic involvement—there are too many uncontrolled variables here for that—but merely that hard work does not *prevent* civic engagement. Moreover, the nationwide falloff in joining and trusting is perfectly mirrored among full-time workers, among part-time workers, and among those outside the paid labor force. So if people are dropping out of community life, long hours do not seem to be the reason.

If time pressure is not the culprit we seek, how about financial pressures? It is true that people with lower incomes and those who feel financially strapped are less engaged in community life and less trusting than those who are better off, even holding education constant. On the other hand, the downtrends in social trust and civic engagement are entirely visible at all levels in the income hierarchy, with no sign whatever that they are concentrated among those who have borne the brunt of the economic distress of the last two decades. Quite the contrary, the declines in engagement and trust are actually somewhat greater among the more affluent segments of the American public than among the poor and middle-income wage-earners. Furthermore, controlling for both real income and financial satisfaction does little to attenuate the fall in civic engagement and social trust. In short, neither objective nor subjective economic well-being has inoculated Americans against the virus of civic disengagement; if anything, affluence has slightly exacerbated the problem.

I cannot absolutely rule out the possibility that some part of the erosion of social capital in recent years might be linked to a more generalized sense of economic insecurity that may have affected all Americans, nor do I argue that economic distress *never* causes disengagement. Studies of the unemployed during and after the Great Depression (Jahoda, Lazarsfeld, and Zeisel 1933; Ginzberg 1943; Wilcock and Franke 1963) have described a tendency for them to disengage from community life. However, the basic patterns in the contemporary evidence are inconsistent with any simple economic explanation for our central puzzle. Pressures of time and money may be a part of the backdrop, but neither can be a principal culprit.[14]

Mobility and Suburbanization

Many studies have found that residential stability and such related phenomena as homeownership are associated with greater civic engagement. At an earlier stage in this investigation (Putnam 1995, 30), I observed that "mobility, like frequent repotting of plants, tends to disrupt root systems, and it takes time for an uprooted individual to put down new roots." I must now report, however, that further inquiry fully exonerates residential mobility from any responsibility for our fading civic engagement. Data from the U.S. Bureau of the Census 1995 (and earlier years) show that rates of residential mobility have been remarkably constant over the last half century. In fact, to the extent that there has been any change at all, both long-distance and short-distance mobility have *declined* over the last five decades. During the 1950s, 20% of Americans changed residence each year and 6.9% annually moved across county borders; during the 1990s, the comparable figures are 17% and 6.6%. Americans, in short, are today slightly *more* rooted residentially than a generation ago. If the verdict on the economic distress interpretation had to be nuanced, the verdict on mobility is unequivocal. This theory is simply wrong.

But if moving itself has not eroded our social capital, what about the possibility that we have moved to places—especially the suburbs—that are less congenial to social connectedness? To test this theory, we must first examine the correlation between place of residence and social capital. In fact, social connectedness does differ by community type, but the differences turn out to be modest and in directions that are inconsistent with the theory.

Controlling for such demographic characteristics as education, age, income, work status, and race, citizens of the nation's 12 largest metropolitan areas (particularly their central cities, but also their suburbs) are roughly 10% less trusting and report 10–20% fewer group memberships than residents of other cities and towns (and their suburbs). Meanwhile, residents of very small towns and rural areas are (in accord with some hoary stereotypes) slightly more trusting and civically engaged than other Americans. Unsurprisingly, the prominence of different *types* of groups does vary significantly by location: major cities have more political and nationality clubs; smaller cities more fraternal, service, hobby, veterans, and church groups; and rural areas more agricultural organizations. But over-

all rates of associational memberships are not very different.

Moreover, this pallid pattern cannot account for our central puzzle. In the first place, there is virtually no correlation between gains in population and losses in social capital, either across states or across localities of different sizes. Even taking into account the educational and social backgrounds of those who have moved there, the suburbs have faintly higher levels of trust and civic engagement than their respective central cities, a fact that *ceteris paribus* should have produced growth, not decay, in social capital over the last generation. The central point, however, is that the downtrends in trusting and joining are virtually identically everywhere—in cities, big and small, in suburbs, in small towns, and in the countryside.

There are, of course, suburbs and suburbs. Evanston is not Levittown is not Sun City. The evidence available does not allow us to determine whether different types of suburban living have different effects on civic connections and social trust. However, these data do rule out the thesis that suburbanization per se has caused the erosion of America's social capital. In this respect, size of place is like mobility—a cross-sectional correlate that cannot explain our trend. Both where we live and how long we've lived there matter for social capital, but neither explains why it is eroding everywhere.

The Changing Role of Women

Most of our mothers were housewives, and most of them invested heavily in social capital formation—a jargony way of referring to untold, unpaid hours in church suppers, PTA meetings, neighborhood coffee klatches, and visits to friends and relatives. The movement of women out of the home and into the paid labor force is probably the most portentous social change of the last half century. However welcome and overdue the feminist revolution may be, it is hard to believe that it has had no impact on social connectedness. Could this be the primary reason for the decline of social capital over the last generation?

Some patterns in the available survey evidence seem to support this claim. All things considered, women belong to somewhat fewer voluntary associations than men (Edwards, Edwards, and Watts 1984 and the sources cited there; more recent GSS data confirm this finding). On the other hand, time budget studies suggest that women spend more time on those groups and more time in informal social connecting than men (Robinson and Godbey 1995). Although the absolute declines in joining and trusting are approximately equivalent among men and women, the relative declines are somewhat greater among women. Controlling for education, memberships among men have declined at a rate of about 10–15% a decade, compared to about 20–25% a decade for women. The time budget data, too, strongly suggest that the decline in organizational involvement in recent years is concentrated among women. These sorts of facts, coupled with the obvious transformation in the professional role of women over this same period, led me in previous work to suppose that the emergence of two-career families might be the most important single factor in the erosion of social capital.

As we saw earlier, however, work status itself seems to have little net impact on group membership or on trust. Housewives belong to different types of groups than do working women (more PTAs, for example, and fewer professional associations), but in the aggregate working women are actually members of slightly more voluntary associations.[15] Moreover, the overall declines in civic engagement are somewhat greater among housewives than among employed women. Comparison of time budget data between 1965 and 1985 (Robinson and Godbey 1995) seems to show that employed women as a group are actually spending more time on organizations than before, while nonemployed women are spending less. This same study suggests that the major decline in informal socializing since 1965 has also been concentrated among nonemployed women. The central fact, of course, is that the overall trends are down for all categories of women (and for men, too—even bachelors), but the figures suggest that women who work full-time actually may have been more resistant to the slump than those who do not.

Thus, although women appear to have borne a disproportionate share of the decline in civic engagement over the last two decades, it is not easy to find any micro-level data that tie that fact directly to their entry into the labor force. It is hard to control for selection bias in these data, of course, because women who have chosen to enter the workforce doubtless differ in many respects from women who have chosen to stay home. Perhaps one reason that community involvement appears to be rising among working women and declining among housewives is that precisely the sort of women who, in an earlier era, were most involved with their communities have been disproportionately likely to enter the workforce, thus simultaneously lowering the average level of civic engagement among the remaining homemakers and raising the average among women in the workplace. Obviously, we have not been running a great national controlled experiment on the effects of work on women's civic engagement, and in any event the patterns in the data are not entirely clear. Contrary to my own earlier speculations, however, I can find little evidence to support the hypothesis that the movement of women into the workplace over the last generation has played a major role in the reduction of social connectedness and civic engagement. On the other hand, I have no clear alternative explanation for the fact that the relative declines are greater among women than among men. Since this evidence is at best circumstantial, perhaps the best interim judgment here is the famous Scots verdict: not proven.

Marriage and Family

Another widely discussed social trend that more or less coincides with the downturn in civic engagement is the breakdown of the traditional family unit—mom, dad, and the kids. Since the family itself is, by some accounts, a key form of social capital, perhaps its eclipse is part of the explanation for the reduction in joining and trusting in the wider community. What does the evidence show?

First of all, evidence of the loosening of family bonds is unequivocal. In addition to the century-long increase in divorce rates (which accelerated in the mid-1960s to the mid-1970s and then leveled off), and the more recent increase in single-parent families, the incidence of one-person households has more than doubled since 1950, in part because of the rising number of widows living alone (Caplow, Bahr, Modell, and Chadwick 1991, 47, 106, 113). The net effect of all these changes, as reflected in the General Social Survey, is that the proportion of all American adults who are currently unmarried climbed from 28% in 1974 to 48% in 1994.

Second, married men and women do rank somewhat higher on both our measures of social capital. That is, controlling for education, age, race, and so on, single people—both men and women, divorced, separated, and never-married—are significantly less trusting and less engaged civically than married people.[16] Roughly speaking, married men and women are about a third more trusting and belong to about 15–25% more groups than comparable single men and women. (Widows and widowers are more like married people than single people in this comparison.)

In short, successful marriage (especially if the family unit includes children) is statistically associated with greater social trust and civic engagement. Thus, some part of the decline in both trust and membership is tied to the decline in marriage. To be sure, the direction of causality behind this correlation may be complicated, since it is conceivable that loners and paranoids are harder to live with. If so, divorce may in some degree be the consequence, not the cause, of lower social capital. Probably the most reasonable summary of these arrays of data, however, is that the decline in successful marriage is

a significant, though modest part of the reason for declining trust and lower group membership. On the other hand, changes in family structure cannot be a major part of our story, since the overall declines in joining and trusting are substantial even among the happily married. My own verdict (based in part on additional evidence to be introduced later) is that the disintegration of marriage is probably an accessory to the crime, but not the major villain of the piece.

The Rise of the Welfare State

Circumstantial evidence, particularly the timing of the downturn in social connectedness, has suggested to some observers (for example, Fukuyama 1995, 313–314) that an important cause—perhaps even *the* cause—of civic disengagement is big goverment and the growth of the welfare state. By "crowding out" private initiative, it is argued, state intervention has subverted civil society. This is a much larger topic than I can address in detail here, but a word or two may be appropriate.

On the one hand, some government policies have almost certainly had the effect of destroying social capital. For example, the so-called "slum clearance" policies of the 1950s and 1960s replaced physical capital, but destroyed social capital, by disrupting existing community ties. It is also conceivable that certain social expenditures and tax policies may have created disincentives for civic-minded philanthropy. On the other hand, it is much harder to see which government policies might be responsible for the decline in bowling leagues and literary clubs.

One empirical approach to this issue is to examine differences in civic engagement and public policy across different political jurisdictions to see whether swollen government leads to shriveled social capital. Among the U.S. states, however, differences in social capital appear essentially uncorrelated with various measures of welfare spending or government size.[17] Citizens in free-spending states are no less trusting or engaged than citizens in frugal ones. Cross-national comparison can also shed light on this question. Among 19 OECD countries for which data on social trust and group membership are available from the 1990–1991 World Values Survey, these indicators of social capital are, if anything, *positively* correlated with the size of the state.[18] This simple bivariate analysis, of course, cannot tell us whether social connectedness encourages welfare spending, whether the welfare state fosters civic engagement, or whether both are the result of some other unmeasured factor(s). Sorting out the underlying causal connections would require much more thorough analysis. However, even this simple finding is not easily reconciled with the notion that big government undermines social capital.

Race and the Civil Rights Revolution

Race is such an absolutely fundamental feature of American social history that nearly every other feature of our society is connected to it in some way. Thus, it seems intuitively plausible that race might somehow have played a role in the erosion of social capital over the last generation. In fact, some observers (both black and white) have noted that the decline in social connectedness and social trust began just after the greatest successes of the civil rights revolution of the 1960s. To some, that coincidence has suggested the possibility of a kind of sociological "white flight," as legal desegregation of civic life led whites to withdraw from community associations.

Like the theory about the welfare state, this racial interpretation of the destruction of social capital is highly controversial and can hardly be settled within the compass of these brief remarks. Nevertheless, the basic facts are these.

First, racial differences in associational membership are not large. At least until the 1980s, controlling for educational and income differences, blacks actually belonged to more associations on average than whites, essentially be-

cause they were more likely than comparably situated whites to belong to religious and ethnic organizations and no less likely to belong to any other type of group.[19] On the other hand, racial differences in social trust are very large indeed, even taking into account differences in education, income, and so on. On average, during the 1972–94 period, controlling for educational differences, about 17% of blacks endorsed the view that "most people can be trusted," as compared to about 45% of whites, and about 27% of respondents of other races.[20] These racial differences in social trust, of course, reflect not collective paranoia, but real experiences over many generations.

Second, the erosion of social capital has affected all races. In fact, during the 1980s the downturns in both joining and trusting were even greater among blacks (and other racial minorities) than among the white majority. This fact is inconsistent with the thesis that "white flight" is a significant cause of civic disengagement, since black Americans have been dropping out of religious and civic organizations at least as rapidly as white Americans. Even more important, the pace of disengagement among whites has been uncorrelated with racial intolerance or support for segregation. Avowedly racist or segregationist whites have been no quicker to drop out of community organizations during this period than more tolerant whites. Figure 3 presents illustrative evidence, its three parallel slopes showing that the decline in group membership is essentially identical among whites who favor segregation, whites who oppose it, and blacks.[21]

This evidence is far from conclusive, of course, but it does shift the burden of proof onto those who believe that racism is a primary explanation for growing civic disengagement over the last quarter century, however virulent racism continues to be in American society.[22] This evidence also suggests that reversing the civil rights gains of the last 30 years would do nothing to reverse the social capital losses.

Figure 3—Group Membership by Race and Racism, 1974–1994 (Education controlled)

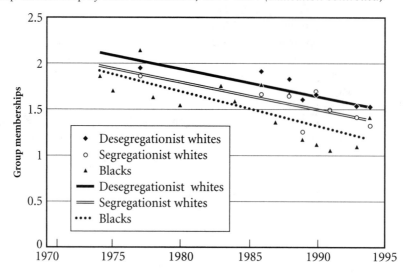

Source: General Social Survey, 1972–1994
Equal weighting of three educational categories.
White segregationism measured by support for racial segregation in social club.

Generational Effects

Our efforts thus far to localize the sources of civic disengagement have been singularly unfruitful. The downtrends are uniform across the major categories of American society—among men and among women; in central cities, in suburbs, and in small towns; among the wealthy, the poor, and the middle class; among blacks, whites, and other ethnic groups; in the North, in the South, on both coasts and in the heartland. One notable exception to this uniformity, however, involves age. In all our statistical analyses, age is second only to education as a predictor of all forms of civic engagement and trust. Older people belong to more organizations than young people, and they are less misanthropic. Older Americans also vote more often and read newspapers more frequently, two other forms of civic engagement closely correlated with joining and trusting.

Figure 4 shows the basic pattern—civic involvement appears to rise more or less steadily from early adulthood toward a plateau in middle age, from which it declines only late in life. This humpback pattern, familiar from many analyses of social participation, including time-budget studies (Robinson and Godbey 1995), seems naturally to represent the arc of life's engagements. Most observers have interpreted this pattern as a life cycle phenomenon, and so, at first, did I.

Evidence from the General Social Survey (GSS) enables us to follow individual cohorts as they age. If the rising lines in Figure 4 represent deepening civic engagement with age, then we should be able to track this same deepening engagement as we follow, for example, the first of the baby boomers—born in 1947—as they aged from 25 in 1972 (the first year of the GSS) to 47 in 1994 (the latest year available). Startlingly, however, such an analysis, repeated for successive birth cohorts, produces virtually no evidence of such life cycle changes in civic engagement. In fact, as various generations moved through the period between 1972 and 1994, their levels of trust and membership more often fell than rose, reflecting a more or less simultaneous decline in civic engagement among young and old alike,

Figure 4—Civic Engagement by Age (education controlled)

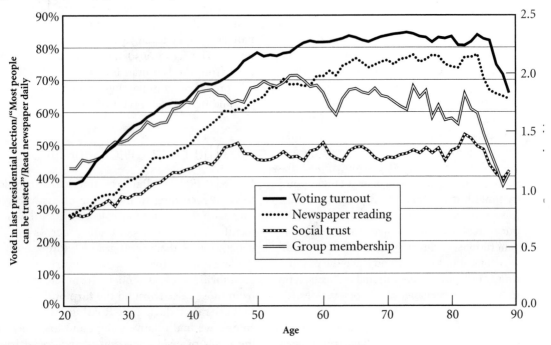

Source: General Social Survey, 1972–1994
Respondents aged 21–89. Three-year moving averages.
Equal weighting of three educational categories.

particularly during the second half of the 1980s. But that downtrend obviously cannot explain why, throughout the period, older Americans were always more trusting and engaged. In fact, the only reliable life cycle effect visible in these data is a withdrawal from civic engagement very late in life, as we move through our 80s.

The central paradox posed by these patterns is this: Older people are consistently more engaged and trusting than younger people, yet we do not become more engaged and trusting as we age. What's going on here?

Time and age are notoriously ambiguous in their effects on social behavior. Social scientists have learned to distinguish three contrasting phenomena:

1. *Life-cycle effects* represent differences attributable to stage of life. In this case individu-

als change as they age, but since the effects of aging are, in the aggregate, neatly balanced by the "demographic metabolism" of births and deaths, life cycle effects produce no aggregate change. Everyone's close-focus eyesight worsens as we age, but the aggregate demand for reading glasses changes little.

2. *Period effects* affect all people who live through a given era, regardless of their age.[23] Period effects can produce both individual and aggregate change, often quickly and enduringly, without any age-related differences. The sharp drop in trust in government between 1965 and 1975, for example, was almost entirely this sort of period effect, as Americans of all ages changed their minds about their leaders' trustworthiness. Similarly, as just noted, a modest portion of the

decline in social capital during the 1980s appears to be a period effect.

3. *Generational effects*, as described in Karl Mannheim's classic essay on "The Problem of Generations," represent the fact that "[i]ndividuals who belong to the same generation, who share the same year of birth, are endowed, to that extent, with a common location in the historical dimension of the social process" (Mannheim 1952, 290). Like life cycle effects (and unlike typical period effects), generational effects show up as disparities among age groups at a single point in time, but like period effects (and unlike life cycle effects) generational effects produce real social change, as successive generations, enduringly "imprinted" with divergent outlooks, enter and leave the population. In pure generational effects, no individual ever changes, but society does.

At least since the landmark essay by Converse (1976), social scientists have recognized that to sort out life cycle, period, and generational effects requires sensitivity to a priori plausibility, "side knowledge," and parsimony, not merely good data and sophisticated math. In effect, cohort analysis inevitably involves more unknowns than equations. With some common sense, some knowledge of history, and some use of Ockham's razor, however, it is possible to exclude some alternatives and focus on more plausible interpretations.

Returning to our conundrum, how could older people today be more engaged and trusting, if they did not become more engaged and trusting as they aged? The key to this paradox, as David Butler and Donald Stokes (1974) observed in another context, is to ask, not *how old people are*, but *when they were young*. Figure 5 addresses this reformulated question, displaying various measures of civic engagement according to the respondents' year of birth.[24] (Figure 5 includes data on voting from the National Election Studies, since Miller 1992 and Miller and Shanks 1995 have drawn on that data to demonstrate

powerful generational effects on turnout, and it is instructive to see how parallel are the patterns that they discovered for voting turnout and the patterns for civic engagement that concern us here.[25] The figure also includes data on social trust from the National Election Studies, which will prove useful in parsing generational, life cycle, and period interpretations.)

The Long Civic Generation

In effect, Figure 5 lines up Americans from left to right according to their date of birth, beginning with those born in the last third of the nineteenth century and continuing across to the generation of their great-grandchildren, born in the last third of the twentieth century. As we begin moving along this queue from left to right—from those raised around the turn of the century to those raised during the Roaring Twenties, and so on—we find relatively high and unevenly rising levels of civic engagement and social trust. Then rather abruptly, however, we encounter signs of reduced community involvement, starting with men and women born in the early 1930s. Remarkably, this downward trend in joining, trusting, voting, and newspaper reading continues almost uninterruptedly for nearly 40 years. The trajectories for the various different indicators of civic engagement are strikingly parallel: each shows a high, sometimes rising plateau for people born and raised during the first third of the century; each shows a turning point in the cohorts born around 1930; and each then shows a more or less constant decline down to the cohorts born during the 1960s.[26]

By any standard, these intergenerational differences are extraordinary. Compare, for example, the generation born in the early 1920s with the generation of their grandchildren born in the late 1960s. Controlling for educational disparities, members of the generation born in the 1920s belong to almost twice as many civic associations as those born in the late 1960s (roughly 1.9 memberships per capita, compared to roughly

Figure 5—Social Capital and Civic Engagement by Generation (education controlled)

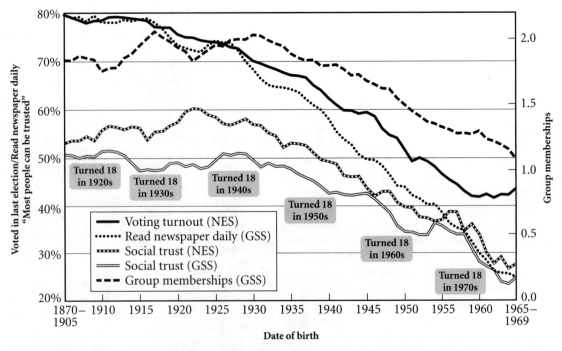

Source: General Social Survey (GSS), 1972–1994, and National Election Studies (NES), 1952–1992
Respondents aged 25–80. Five-year moving averages.
Equal weighting of three educational categories.

1.1 memberships per capita). The grandparents are more than twice as likely to trust other people (50–60%, compared with 25% for the grandchildren). They vote at nearly double the rate of the most recent cohorts (roughly 75% compared with 40–45%), and they read newspapers almost three times as often (70–80% read a paper daily compared with 25–30%). And bear in mind that we have found no evidence that the youngest generation will come to match their grandparent's higher levels of civic engagement as they grow older.

Thus, read not as life cycle effects, but rather as generational effects, the age-related patterns in our data suggest a radically different interpretation of our basic puzzle. Deciphered with this key, Figure 5 depicts a long "civic" generation, born roughly between 1910 and 1940, a broad group of people substantially more engaged in community affairs and substantially more trusting than those younger than they.[27] The culminating point of this civic generation is the cohort born in 1925–1930, who attended grade school during the Great Depression, spent World War II in high school (or on the battle field), first voted in 1948 or 1952, set up housekeeping in the 1950s, and watched their first television when they were in the late twenties. Since national surveying began, this cohort has been exceptionally civic: voting more, joining more, reading newspapers more, trusting more. As the distinguished sociologist Charles Tilly (born in 1928) said in commenting on an early version of this essay, "we are the last suckers."

To help in interpreting the historical contexts within which these successive generations of Americans matured, Figure 5 also indicates the decade within which each cohort came of age.

Thus, we can see that each generation who reached adulthood since the 1940s has been less engaged in community affairs than its immediate predecessor.

Further confirmation of this *generational* interpretation comes from a comparison of the two parallel lines that chart responses to an identical question about social trust, posed first in the National Election Studies (mainly between 1964 and 1976) and then in the General Social Survey between 1972 and 1994.[28] If the greater trust expressed by Americans born earlier in the century represented a *life cycle* effect, then the graph from the GSS surveys (conducted when these cohorts were, on average, 10 years older) should have been some distance *above* the NES line. In fact, the GSS line lies about 5–10% *below* the NES line. That downward shift almost surely represents a *period* effect that depressed social trust among all cohorts during the 1980s.[29] That downward period effect, however, is substantially more modest than the large generational differences already noted.

In short, the most parsimonious interpretation of the age-related differences in civic engagement is that they represent a powerful reduction in civic engagement among Americans who came of age in the decades after World War II, as well as some modest additional disengagement that affected all cohorts during the 1980s. These patterns hint that being raised after World War II was a quite different experience from being raised before that watershed. It is as though the post-war generations were exposed to some mysterious X-ray that permanently and increasingly rendered them less likely to connect with the community. Whatever that force might have been, *it*—rather than anything that happened during the 1970s and 1980s—accounts for most of the civic disengagement that lies at the core of our mystery.

But if this reinterpretation of our puzzle is correct, why did it take so long for the effects of that mysterious X-ray to become manifest? If the underlying causes of civic disengagement can be traced to the 1940s and 1950s, why did the effects become conspicuous in PTA meetings and Masonic lodges, in the volunteer lists of the Red Cross and the Boy Scouts, and in polling stations and church pews and bowling alleys across the land only during the 1960s, 1970s, and 1980s?

The visible effects of this generational disengagement were delayed for several decades by two important factors:

1. The postwar boom in college enrollments boosted massive numbers of Americans up the sloping curve of civic engagement traced in Figure 2. Miller and Shanks (1995) observe that the postwar expansion of educational opportunities "forestalled a cataclysmic drop" in voting turnout, and it had a similar delaying effect on civic disengagement more generally.

2. The full effects of generational developments generally appear several decades after their onset, because it takes that long for a given generation to become numerically dominant in the adult population. Only after the mid-1960s did significant numbers of the "post-civic generation" reach adulthood, supplanting older, more civic cohorts. Figure 6 illustrates this generational accounting. The long civic generation (born between 1910 and 1940) reached its zenith in 1960, when it comprised 62% of those who chose between John Kennedy and Richard Nixon. By the time that Bill Clinton was elected president in 1992, that cohort's share in the electorate had been cut precisely in half. Conversely, over the last two decades (from 1974 to 1994) boomers and X-ers (that is, Americans born after 1946) have grown as a fraction of the adult population from 24% to 60%.

In short, the very decades that have seen a national deterioration in social capital are the same decades during which the numerical dominance of a trusting and civic generation has been replaced by the dominion of "post-civic" cohorts. Moreover, although the long civic generation has enjoyed unprecedented life expectancy, allowing its members to contribute more than their share

Figure 6—The Rise and Decline of a "Civic" Generation

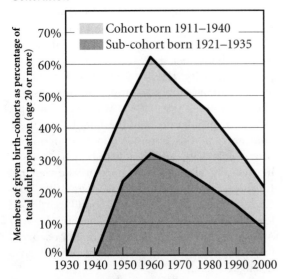

Source: Calculated from U.S. Census Bureau, current population reports.

to American social capital in recent decades, they are now passing from the scene. Even the youngest members of that generation will reach retirement age within the next few years. Thus, a generational analysis leads almost inevitably to the conclusion that the national slump in trust and engagement is likely to continue, regardless of whether the more modest "period effect" depression of the 1980s continues.

More than two decades ago, just as the first signs of disengagement were beginning to appear in American politics, Ithiel de Sola Pool (1973, 818–21) observed that the central issue would be—it was then too soon to judge, as he rightly noted—whether the development represented a temporary change in the weather or a more enduring change in the climate. It now appears that much of the change whose initial signs he spotted did in fact reflect a climatic shift. Moreover, just as the erosion of the ozone layer was detected only many years after the proliferation of the chlorofluorocarbons that caused it, so too the erosion of America's social capital became visible only several decades after the un-

derlying process had begun. Like Minerva's owl that flies at dusk, we come to appreciate how important the long civic generation has been to American community life just as its members are retiring. Unless America experiences a dramatic upward boost in civic engagement (a favorable "period effect") in the next few years, Americans in 2010 will join, trust, and vote even less than we do today.

The Puzzle Reformulated

To say that civic disengagement in contemporary America is in large measure generational merely reformulates our central puzzle. We now know that much of the cause of our lonely bowling probably dates to the 1940s and 1950s, rather than to the 1960s and 1970s. What could have been the mysterious anti-civic "X-ray" that affected Americans who came of age after World War II and whose effects progressively deepened at least into the 1970s?[30]

A number of superficially plausible candidates fail to fit the timing required by this new formulation of our mystery.

- Family instability seems to have an ironclad alibi for what we have now identified as the critical period, for the generational decline in civic engagement began with the children of the maritally stable 1940s and 1950s.[31] The divorce rate in America actually fell after 1945, and the sharpest jump in the divorce rate did not occur until the 1970s, long after the cohorts who show the sharpest declines in civic engagement and social trust had left home. Similarly, working mothers are exonerated by this re-specification of our problem, for the plunge in civicness among children of the 1940s, 1950s, and 1960s happened while mom was still at home.

- Our new formulation of the puzzle opens the possibility that the *Zeitgeist* of national unity and patriotism that culminated in 1945 might have reinforced civic-mindedness. On the other hand, it is hard to assign any consistent role to the Cold War and the Bomb, since the anti-civic trend appears to have deepened steadily from the 1940s to the 1970s, in no obvious harmony with the rhythms of world affairs. Nor is it easy to construct an interpretation of Figure 5 in which the cultural vicissitudes of "the Sixties" could play a significant role.

■ Neither economic adversity nor affluence can easily be tied to the generational decline in civic engagement, since the slump seems to have affected in equal measure those who came of age in the placid Fifties, the booming Sixties, and the busted Seventies.

I have discovered only one prominent suspect against whom circumstantial evidence can be mounted, and in this case, it turns out, some directly incriminating evidence has also turned up. This is not the occasion to lay out the full case for the prosecution, nor to review rebuttal evidence for the defense. However, I want to illustrate the sort of evidence that justifies indictment. The culprit is television.

First, the timing fits. The long civic generation was the last cohort of Americans to grow up without television, for television flashed into American society like lightning in the 1950s. In 1950 barely 10% of American homes had television sets, but by 1959 90% did, probably the fastest diffusion of a technological innovation ever recorded. The reverberations from this lightning bolt continued for decades, as viewing hours per capita grew by 17–20% during the 1960s and by an additional 7–8% during the 1970s. In the early years, TV watching was concentrated among the less educated sectors of the population, but during the 1970s the viewing time of the more educated sectors of the population began to converge upward. Television viewing increases with age, particularly upon retirement, but each generation since the introduction of television has begun its life cycle at a higher starting point. By 1995, viewing per TV household was more than 50% higher than it had been in the 1950s.[32]

Most studies estimate that the average American now watches roughly four hours per day.[33] Robinson (1990b), using the more conservative time-budget technique for determining how people allocate their time, offers an estimate closer to three hours per day, but concludes that as a primary activity, television absorbs 40% of the average American's free time, an increase of about one-third since 1965. Moreover, multiple sets have proliferated: by the late 1980s, three quarters of all U.S. homes had more than one set (Comstock 1989), and these numbers too are rising steadily, allowing ever more private viewing. In short, as Robinson and Godbey 1995 conclude, "television is the 800-pound gorilla of leisure time." This massive change in the way Americans spend our days and nights occurred precisely during the years of generational civic disengagement.

Evidence of a link between the arrival of television and the erosion of social connections is, however, not merely circumstantial. The links between civic engagement and television viewing can instructively be compared with the links between civic engagement and newspaper reading. The basic contrast is straightforward: newspaper reading is associated with high social capital, TV viewing with low social capital.

Controlling for education, income, age, race, place of residence, work status, and gender, TV viewing is strongly and negatively related to social trust and group membership, whereas the same correlations with newspaper reading are positive. Figure 7 shows that within every educational category, heavy readers are avid joiners, whereas Figure 8 shows that heavy viewers are more likely to be loners.[34] Viewing and reading are themselves uncorrelated—some people do lots of both, some do little of either—but Figure 9 shows that (controlling for education, as always) "pure readers" (that is, people who watch less TV than average and read more newspapers than average) belong to 76% more civic organizations than "pure viewers." Precisely the same pattern applies to other indicators of civic engagement, including social trust and voting

Figure 7—Group Membership by Newspaper Readership and Education

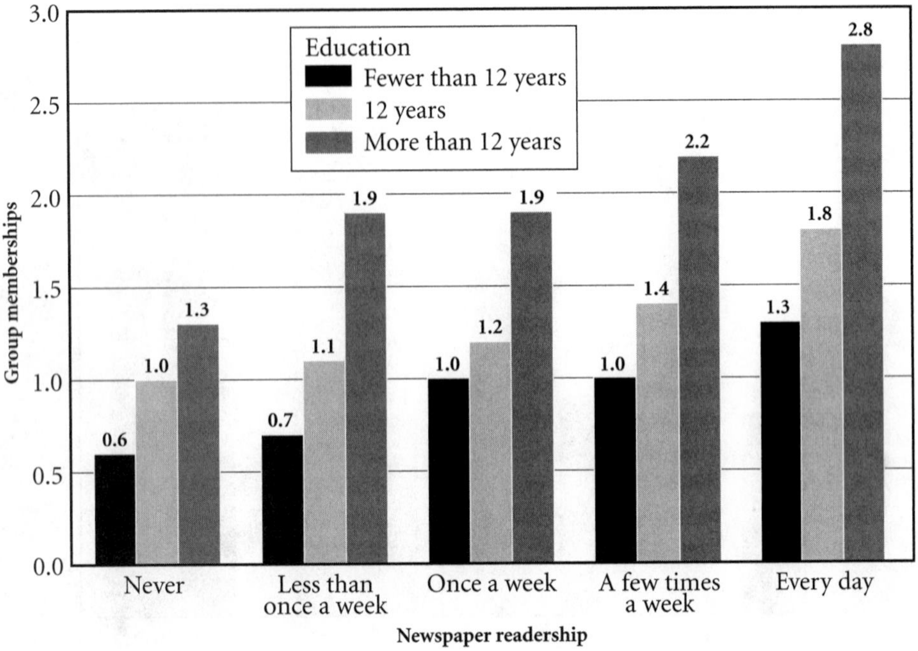

Source: General Social Survey, 1974–1994

turnout. "Pure readers," for example, are 55% more trusting than "pure viewers."[35]

In other words, each hour spent viewing television is associated with less social trust and less group membership, while each hour reading a newspaper is associated with more. An increase in television viewing of the magnitude that the United States has experienced in the last four decades might directly account for as much as one-quarter to one-half of the total drop in social capital, even without taking into account, for example, the indirect effects of television viewing on newspaper readership or the cumulative effects of "life-time" viewing hours.[36]

How might television destroy social capital?

- *Time displacement.* Even though there are only 24 hours in everyone's day, most forms of social and media participation are positively correlated. People who listen to lots of classical music are more likely, not less

likely, than others to attend Cubs games. Television is the principal exception to this generalization—the only leisure activity that seems to inhibit participation outside the home. TV watching comes at expense of nearly every social activity outside the home, especially social gatherings and informal conversations (Comstock et al 1978; Comstock 1989; Bower 1985; and Robinson and Godbey 1995). TV viewers are homebodies.

Most studies that report a negative correlation between television watching and community involvement (including my Figure 7) are ambiguous with respect to causality, because they merely compare different individuals at a single time. However, one important quasi-experimental study of the introduction of television in three Canadian towns (Williams 1986) found the same pattern at the aggregate level across time: a major effect of television's arrival was the

Figure 8—Group Membership by Television Viewing and Education

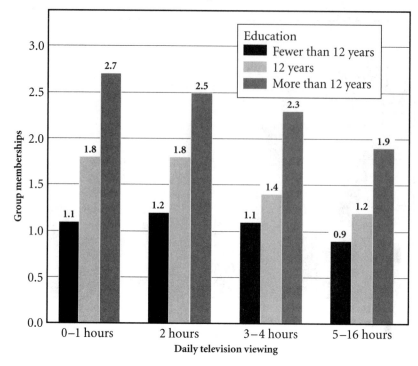

Source: General Social Survey, 1974–1994

reduction in participation in social, recreational, and community activities among people of all ages. In short, television is privatizing our leisure time.

- *Effects on the outlooks of viewers.* An impressive body of literature, gathered under the rubric of the "mean world effect," suggests that heavy watchers of TV are unusually skeptical about the benevolence of other people—overestimating crime rates, for example. This body of literature has generated much debate about the underlying causal patterns, with skeptics suggesting that misanthropy may foster couch-potato behavior rather than the reverse. While awaiting better experimental evidence, however, a reasonable interim judgment is that heavy television watching may well increase pessimism about human nature (Gerbner et al 1980; Dobb and MacDonald 1979; Hirsch 1980;

Hughes 1980; and Comstock 1989, 265–69). Perhaps, too, as social critics have long argued, both the medium and the message have more basic effects on our ways of interacting with the world and with one another. Television may induce passivity, as Postman (1985) has claimed, and it may even change our fundamental physical and social perceptions, as Meyrowitz (1985) has suggested.

- *Effects on children.* TV occupies an extraordinary part of children's lives—consuming about 40 hours per week on average. Viewing is especially high among pre-adolescents, but it remains high among younger adolescents: time-budget studies (Carnegie Council on Adolescent Development 1993, 5, citing Timmer et al. 1985) suggest that among youngsters aged 9–14 television consumes as much time as *all other discretionary activities combined*, including playing, hobbies, clubs, out-

Figure 9—Group Membership by Media Usage (education controlled)

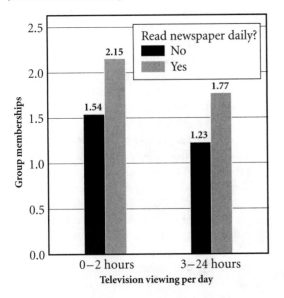

Source: General Social Survey, 1974–1994
Entries based on three equally weighted
educational categories.

door activities, informal visiting, and just hanging out. The effects of television on childhood socialization have, of course, been hotly debated for more than three decades. The most reasonable conclusion from a welter of sometimes conflicting results appears to be that heavy television watching probably increases aggressiveness (although perhaps not actual violence), that it probably reduces school achievement, and that it is statistically associated with "psychosocial malfunctioning," although how much of this effect is self-selection and how much causal remains much debated (Condry, 1993). The evidence is, as I have said, not yet enough to convict, but the defense has a lot of explaining to do.

Conclusion

Ithiel de Sola Pool's posthumous book, *Technologies Without Borders* (1990), is a prescient work, astonishingly relevant to our current national debates about the complicated links among technology, public policy, and culture. Pool defended what he called "soft technological determinism." Revolutions in communications technologies have profoundly affected social life and culture, as the printing press helped bring on the Reformation. Pool concluded that the electronic revolution in communications technology, whose outlines he traced well before most of us were even aware of the impending changes, was the first major technological advance in centuries that would have a profoundly decentralizing and fragmenting effect on society and culture.

Pool hoped that the result might be "community without contiguity." As a classic liberal, he welcomed the benefits of technological change for individual freedom, and, in part, I share that enthusiasm. Those of us who bemoan the decline of community in contemporary America need to be sensitive to the liberating gains achieved during the same decades. We need to avoid an uncritical nostalgia for the Fifties. On the other hand, some of the same freedom-friendly technologies whose rise Pool predicted may indeed be undermining our connections with one another and with our communities. I suspect that Pool would have been open to that argument, too, for one of Pool's most talented protégés, Samuel Popkin (1991, 226–31) has argued that the rise of television and the correlative decline of social interaction have impaired American political discourse. The last line in Pool's last book (1990, 262) is this: "We may suspect that [the technological trends that we can anticipate] will promote individualism and will make it harder, not easier, to govern and organize a coherent society."

Pool's technological determinism was "soft" precisely because he recognized that social values can condition the effects of technology. In the end this perspective invites us not merely to consider how technology is privatizing our lives—if, as it seems to me, it is—but to ask whether we entirely like the result, and if not, what we might do about it. But that is a topic for another day.

NOTES

1. I wish to thank several researchers for sharing valuable unpublished work on related themes: John Brehm and Wendy Rahn (1995); Warren Miller and Merrill Shanks (1995), John Robinson and Geoffrey Godbey (1995); and Eric Uslaner (1995). Professor Uslaner was generous in helping track down some elusive data and commenting on an earlier draft. I also wish to thank a fine team of research assistants, including Jay Braatz, Maryann Barakso, Karen Ferree, Archon Fung, Louise Kennedy, Jeff Kling, Kimberly Lochner, Karen Rothkin, and Mark Warren. Support for the research project from which this study derives has been provided by the Aspen Institute, Carnegie Corporation, the Ford, Kovler, Norman, and Rockefeller foundations, and Harvard University.

2. In this respect I deviate slightly from James Coleman's "functional" definition of social capital. See Coleman (1990): 300–21.

3. The results reported in this paragraph and throughout the paper, unless otherwise indicated, are derived from the General Social Survey. These exceptionally useful data derive from a series of scientific surveys of the adult American population, conducted nearly every year since 1972 by the National Opinion Research Center, under the direction of James A. Davis and Tom W. Smith. The cumulative sample size is approximately 32,000, although the questions on trust and group membership that are at the focus of our inquiry have not been asked of all respondents in all years. Our measure of trust derives from this question: "Generally speaking, would you say that most people can be trusted, or that you can't be too careful in dealing with people": for this question, N = 22390. For evidence confirming the power of this simple measure of social trust, see Uslaner (1995). Our measure of group membership derives from this question: "Now we would like to know something about the groups or organizations to which individuals belong. Here is a list of various organizations. Could you tell me whether or not you are a member of each type?" The list includes fraternal groups, service clubs, veterans' groups, political clubs, labor unions, sports groups, youth groups, school service groups, hobby or garden clubs, social fraternities or sororities, nationality groups, farm organizations, literary, arts, discussion or study groups, professional or academic societies, church-affiliated groups, and any other groups. For this question, N = 19326. Neither of these questions, of course, is a perfect measure of social capital. In particular, our measure of multiple memberships refers not to total groups, but to total *types* of groups. On the other hand, "noise" in data generally depresses observed correlations below the "true" value, so our findings are more likely to understate than to exaggerate patterns in the "real world."

4. Across the 35 countries for which data are available from the World Values Survey (1990–91), the correlation between the average number of associational memberships and endorsement of the view that "most people can be trusted" is r .65. Across the 42 states for which adequate samples are available in the General Social Survey (1972–1994), the comparable correlation is r .71. Across individuals in the General Social Survey (1972–1994), controlling for education, race, and age, social trust is significantly and separately correlated with membership in political clubs, literary groups, sports clubs, hobby and garden clubs, youth groups, school service groups, and other associations. The correlation with social trust is insignificant only for veterans groups, labor unions, and nationality groups.

5. The 1965 sample, which was limited to non-retired residents of cities between 30,000 and 280,000 population, was not precisely equivalent to the later national samples, so

appropriate adjustments need to be made to ensure comparability. For the 1965–1975 comparison, see Robinson (1981, 125). For the 1975–1985 comparison (but apparently without adjustment for the 1965 sampling peculiarities), see Cutler (1990). Somewhat smaller declines are reported in Robinson and Godbey (1995), although it is unclear whether they correct for the sampling differences. Additional work to refine these cross-time comparisons is required and is currently underway.

6. Trust in political authorities—and indeed in many social institutions—has also declined sharply over the last three decades, but that is conceptually a distinct trend. As we shall see later, the etiology of the slump in social trust is quite different from the etiology of the decline in political trust.

7. For reasons explained below, Figure 1 reports trends for membership in various types of groups, *controlling for* the respondent's education level.

8. Some commentaries on "Bowling Alone" have been careless, however, in reporting apparent membership growth. *The Economist* (1995, 22), for example, celebrated a recent rebound in total membership in parent-teacher organizations, without acknowledging that this rebound is almost entirely attributable to the growing number of children. The fraction of parents who belong to PTAs has regained virtually none of the 50% fall that this metric registered between 1960 and 1975. Despite talk about the growth of "support groups," another oft-cited counterexample. I know of no statistical substantiation for this claim. One might even ask whether the vaunted rise in neighborhood watch groups might not represent only a partial, artificial replacement for the vanished social capital of traditional neighborhoods—a kind of sociological Astroturf, suitable only where you can't grow the real thing. See also Glenn (1987, S124) for survey evidence of "an increased tendency for individuals to withdraw allegiance from . . . anything outside of themselves."

9. The only exceptions are farm groups, labor unions, and veterans' organizations, whose members have slightly less formal education than the average American. Interestingly, sports clubs are *not* an exception; college graduates are nearly three times more likely to belong to a sports group than are high school drop-outs. Education is uncorrelated with church attendance, but positively correlated with membership in church-related groups.

10. For a thorough recent investigation of the role of education in accounting for differences in political participation, see Verba, Schlozman, and Brady (1995).

11. As a practical matter, all subsequent statistical presentations here implement this precept by equally weighing respondents from three broad educational categories—those with fewer than 12 years formal schooling, those with exactly 12 years, and those with more than 12 years. Conveniently, this categorization happens to slice the 1972–1994 GSS sample into nearly equal thirds. The use of more sophisticated mathematical techniques to control for educational differences would alter none of the central conclusions of this essay.

12. The downturns in both joining and trusting seem to be somewhat greater among Americans on the middle rungs of the educational ladder—high school graduates and college dropouts—than among those at the very top and bottom of the educational hierarchy, but the differences are not great, and the trends are statistically significant at all levels.

13. This is true with or without controls for education and year of survey. The patterns among men and women on this score are not identical, for women who work part-time appear to be somewhat more civically engaged and socially trusting than either those who work full-time or those who do not work outside the home at all. Whatever

we make of this intriguing anomaly, which apparently does not appear in the time budget data (Robinson and Godbey 1995) and which has no counterpart in the male half of the population, it cannot account for our basic puzzle, since female part-time workers constitute a relatively small fraction of the American population, and the fraction is growing, not declining. Between the first half of the 1970s and the first half of the 1990s, according to the GSS data, the fraction of the total adult population constituted by female part-time workers rose from about 8% to about 10%.

14. Evidence on generational differences presented below reinforces this conclusion.

15. Robinson and Godbey (1995); however, report that nonemployed women still spend more time on activity in voluntary associations than their employed counterparts.

16. Multivariate analysis hints that one major reason why divorce lowers connectedness is that it lowers family income, which in turn reduces civic engagement.

17. I have set aside this issue for fuller treatment in later work. However, I note for the record that (1) state-level differences in social trust and group membership are substantial, closely intercorrelated and reasonably stable, at least over the period from the 1970s to the 1990s, and (2) those differences are surprisingly closely correlated (R^2 = .52) with the measure of "state political culture" invented by Elazar (1966), and refined by Sharkansky (1969), based on descriptive accounts of state politics during the 1950s and traceable in turn to patterns of immigration during the nineteenth century and before.

18. Public expenditure as a percentage of GDP in 1989 is correlated r – .29 with 1990–1991 trust and r – .48 with 1990–1991 associational memberships.

19. For broadly similar conclusions, see Verba, Schlozman, and Brady (1995, 241–47) and the sources cited there.

20. As elsewhere in this essay, "controlling for educational differences" here means averaging the average scores for respondents with fewer than 12 years of schooling, with exactly 12 years, and with more than 12 years, respectively.

21. White support for segregation in Figure 3 is measured by responses to this question in the General Social Survey: "If you and your friends belonged to a social club that would not let Blacks join, would you try to change the rules so that Blacks could join?" Essentially identical results obtain if we measure white racism instead by support for antimiscegenation laws or for residential segregation.

22. As we shall see in a moment, much civic disengagement actually appears to be generational, affecting people born after 1930, but not those born before. If this phenomenon represented white flight from integrated community life after the civil rights revolution, it is difficult to see why the trend should be so much more marked among those who came of age in the more tolerant 1960s and 1970s, and hardly visible at all among those who came of age in the first half of the century, when American society was objectively more segregated and subjectively more racist.

23. Period effects that affect only people of a specific age shade into generational effects, which is why Converse, when summarizing these age-related effects, refers to "two-and-a-half" types, rather than the conventional three types.

24. To exclude the life cycle effects in the last years of life, Figure 5 excludes respondents over 80. To avoid well-known problems in reliably sampling young adults, as discussed by Converse (1976), Figure 5 also excludes respondents aged under 25. To offset the relatively small year-by-year samples and to control for educational differences, Figure 5 charts five-year moving averages across the

three educational categories used in this essay.

25. I learned of the Miller/Shanks argument only after discovering generational differences in civic engagement in the General Social Survey data, but their findings and mine are strikingly consistent.

26. Too few respondents born in the late nineteenth century appear in surveys conducted in the 1970s and 1980s for us to discern differences among successive birth cohorts with great reliability. However, those scant data (not broken out in Figure 5) suggest that the turn of the century might have been an era of rising civic engagement. Similarly, too few respondents born after 1970 have yet appeared in national surveys for us to be confident about their distinctive generational profile, although the slender results so far seem to suggest that the 40-year generational plunge in civic engagement might be bottoming out. However, even if this turns out to be true, it will be several decades before that development could arrest the aggregate drop in civic engagement, for reasons subsequently explained in the text.

27. Members of the 1910–1940 generation also seem more civic than their elders, at least to judge by the outlooks of the relatively few men and women born in the late nineteenth century who appeared in our samples.

28. The question on social trust appeared biennially in the NES from 1964 to 1976 and then reappeared in 1992. I have included the 1992 NES interviews in the analysis in order to obtain estimates for cohorts too young to have appeared in the earlier surveys.

29. Additional analysis of indicators of civic engagement in the GSS, not reported in detail here, confirms this downward shift during the 1980s.

30. I record here one theory attributed variously to Robert Salisbury (1985), Gerald Gamm, and Simon and Garfunkel. Devotees of our national pastime will recall that Joe DiMag-

gio signed with the Yankees in 1936, just as the last of the long civic generation was beginning to follow the game, and he turned center field over to Mickey Mantle in 1951, just as the last of "the suckers" reached legal maturity. Almost simultaneously, the Braves, the Athletics, the Browns, the Senators, the Dodgers, and the Giants deserted cities that had been their homes since the late nineteenth century. By the time Mantle in turn left the Yankees in 1968, much of the damage to civic loyalty had been done. This interpretation explains why Mrs. Robinson's plaintive query that year about Joltin' Joe's whereabouts evoked such widespread emotion. A deconstructionist analysis of social capital's decline would highlight the final haunting lamentation, "our nation turns its *lonely* eyes to you" [emphasis added].

31. This exoneration applies to the possible effects of divorce on children, not to its effects on the couple themselves, as discussed earlier in this essay.

32. For introductions to the massive literature on the sociology of television, see Bower (1985), Comstock et al. (1978), Comstock (1989), and Grabner (1993). The figures on viewing hours in the text are from Bower (1985, 33) and *Public Perspective* (1995, 47). Cohort differences are reported in Bower 1985, 46.

33. This figure excludes periods in which television is merely playing in the background. Comstock (1989, 17) reports that "on any fall day in the late 1980s, the set in the average television owning household was on for about eight hours.")

34. In fact, multiple regression analysis, predicting civic engagement from television viewing and education, suggests that heavy TV watching is one important reason *why* less educated people are less engaged in the life of their communities. Controlling for differential TV exposure significantly reduces the correlation between education and engagement.

35. Controlling for education, 45% of respondents who watch TV two hours or less a day and read newspapers daily say that "most people can be trusted," as compared to 29% of respondents who watch TV three hours or more a day and do not read a newspaper daily.

36. Newspaper circulation (per household) has dropped by more than half since its peak in 1947. To be sure, it is not clear which way the tie between newspaper reading and civic involvement works, since disengagement might itself dampen one's interest in community news. But the two trends are clearly linked.

REFERENCES

Bower, Robert T. 1985. *The Changing Television Audience in America*. New York: Columbia University Press.

Brehm, John, and Wendy Rahn. 1995. "An Audit of the Deficit in Social Capital." Durham, NC: Duke University. Unpublished manuscript.

Butler, David, and Donald Stokes. 1974. *Political Change in Britain: The Evolution of Electoral Choice*, 2nd ed. New York: St. Martin's.

Caplow, Theodore, Howard M. Bahr, John Modell, and Bruce A. Chadwick. 1991. *Recent Social Trends in the United States: 1960–1990*. Montreal: McGill-Queen's University Press.

Carnegie Council on Adolescent Development. 1993. *A Matter of Time: Risk and Opportunity in the Nonschool Hours: Executive Summary*. New York: Carnegie Corporation of New York.

Coleman, James. 1990. *Foundations of Social Theory*. Cambridge, MA: Harvard University Press.

Comstock, George, Steven Chaffee, Natan Katzman, Maxwell McCombs, and Donald Roberts. 1978. *Television and Human Behavior*. New York: Columbia University Press.

Comstock, George. 1989. *The Evolution of American Television*. Newbury Park, CA: Sage.

Condry, John. 1993. "Thief of Time, Unfaithful Servant: Television and the American Child," *Daedalus* 122 (Winter): 259–78.

Converse, Philip E. 1976. *The Dynamics of Party Support: Cohort-Analyzing Party Identification*. Beverly Hills, CA: Sage.

Cutler, Blaine. 1990. "Where Does the Free Time Go?" *American Demographics* (November): 36–39.

Davis, James Allan, and Tom W. Smith. *General Social Surveys. 1972–1994*. [machine readable data file]. Principal Investigator, James A. Davis; Director and Co-Principal Investigator, Tom W. Smith. NORC ed. Chicago: National Opinion Research Center, producer, 1994; Storrs, CT: The Roper Center for Public Opinion Research, University of Connecticut, distributor.

Dobb, Anthony N., and Glenn F. Macdonald. 1979. "Television Viewing and Fear of Victimization: Is the Relationship Causal?" *Journal of Personality and Social Psychology* 37: 170–79.

Edwards, Patricia Klobus, John N. Edwards, and Ann DeWitt Watts, "Women, Work, and Social Participation." *Journal of Voluntary Action Research* 13 (January–March, 1984), 7–22.

Elazar, Daniel J. 1966. *American Federalism: A View from the States*. New York: Crowell.

Fukuyama, Francis. 1995. *Trust: The Social Virtues and the Creation of Prosperity*. New York: The Free Press.

Gerbner, George, Larry Gross, Michael Morgan, and Nancy Signorielli. 1980. "The 'Mainstreaming' of America: Violence Profile No. 11," *Journal of Communication* 30 (Summer): 10–29.

Ginzberg, Eli. *The Unemployed*. 1943. New York: Harper and Brothers.

Glenn, Norval D. 1987. "Social Trends in the United States: Evidence from Sample Surveys." *Public Opinion Quarterly* 51: S109–S126.

Grabner, Doris A. 1993. *Mass Media and American Politics*. Washington, D.C.: CQ Press.

Hirsch, Paul M. "The 'Scary World' of the Non-viewer and Other Anomalies: A Re-analysis of Gerbner et al.'s Findings on Cultivation Analysis, Part I," *Communication Research* 7 (October): 403–56.

Hughes, Michael. 1980. "The Fruits of Cultivation Analysis: A Re-examination of the Effects of Television Watching on Fear of Victimization, Alienation, and the Approval of Violence." *Public Opinion Quarterly* 44: 287–303.

Jahoda, Marie, Paul Lazarsfeld, and Hans Zeisel. 1933. *Marienthal*. Chicago: Aldine-Atherton.

Mannheim, Karl. 1952. "The Problem of Generations." In *Essays on the Sociology of Knowledge*, ed. Paul Kecsckemeti. New York: Oxford University Press: 276–322.

Meyrowitz, Joshua. 1985. *No Sense of Place: The Impact of Electronic Media on Social Behavior*. New York: Oxford University Press.

Miller, Warren F., and J. Merrill Shanks. 1995. *The American Voter Reconsidered*. Tempe, AZ: Arizona State University. Unpublished manuscript.

Miller, Warren E. 1992. "The Puzzle Transformed: Explaining Declining Turnout." *Political Behavior* 14: 1–43.

Pool, Ithiel de Sola. 1973. "Public Opinion." In *Handbook of Communication*, ed. Ithiel de Sola Pool et al. Chicago: Rand McNally: 779–835.

Pool, Ithiel de Sola. 1990. *Technologies Without Boundaries: On Telecommunications in a Global Age*. Cambridge, MA: Harvard University Press.

Popkin, Samuel L. 1991. *The Reasoning Voter*. Chicago: University of Chicago Press.

Postman, Neil. 1985. *Amusing Ourselves to Death: Public Discourse in the Age of Show Business*. New York: Viking-Penguin Books.

Public Perspective. 1995. "People, Opinion, and Polls: American Popular Culture." 6 (August/September): 37–48.

Putnam, Robert D. 1993. *Making Democracy Work: Civic Traditions in Modern Italy*. Princeton, NJ: Princeton University Press.

Putnam, Robert D. 1995. "Bowling Alone, Revisited," *The Responsive Community* (Spring): 18–33.

Putnam, Robert D. 1996. "Bowling Alone: Democracy in America at the End of the Twentieth Century," forthcoming in a collective volume edited by Axel Hadenius. New York: Cambridge University Press.

Robinson, John. 1981. "Television and Leisure Time: A New Scenario," *Journal of Communication* 31 (Winter): 120–30.

Robinson, John. 1990a. "The Time Squeeze." *American Demographics* (February).

Robinson, John. 1990b. "I Love My TV." *American Demographics* (September): 24–27.

Robinson, John, and Geoffrey Godbey, 1995. *Time for Life*. College Park, MD: University of Maryland. Unpublished manuscript.

Rosenstone, Steven J., and John Mark Hansen. 1993. *Mobilization, Participation, and Democracy in America*. New York: Macmillan.

Salisbury, Robert H. 1985. "Blame Dismal World Conditions on . . . Baseball. *Miami Herald* (May 18): 27A.

Schor, Juliet. 1991. *The Overworked American*. New York: Basic Books.

Sharkansky, Ira. 1969. "The Utility of Elazar's Political Culture." *Polity* 2: 66–83.

The Economist. 1995. "The Solitary Bowler." 334 (18 February): 21–22.

Timmer, S. G., J. Eccles, and I. O'Brien. 1985. "How Children Use Time." In *Time, Goods, and Well-Being*, ed. F. T. Juster and F. B. Stafford. Ann Arbor, MI: University of Michigan, Institute for Social Research.

U.S. Bureau of the Census. 1995 (and earlier years). *Current Population Reports*. Washington, D.C.

Uslaner, Eric M. 1995. "Faith, Hope, and Charity: Social Capital, Trust, and Collective Action." College Park, MD: University of Maryland. Unpublished manuscript.

Verba, Sidney, Kay Lehman Schlozman, and Henry E. Brady. 1995. *Voice and Equality: Civic Volunteerism in American Politics*. Cambridge, MA: Harvard University Press.

Wilcock, Richard, and Walter H. Franke. 1963. *Unwanted Workers*. New York: Free Press of Glencoe.

Williams, Tannis Macbeth, ed. 1986. *The Impact of Television: A Natural Experiment in Three Communities*. New York: Academic Press.

SHERI BERMAN

CIVIL SOCIETY AND THE COLLAPSE OF THE WEIMAR REPUBLIC

Practically everywhere one looks, from social science monographs to political speeches to *People* magazine, the concept of "civil society" is in vogue. A flourishing civil society is considered to have helped bring down the Evil Empire and is held to be a prerequisite for the success of post-Soviet democratic experiments; a civil society in decline is said to threaten democracy in America. Tocqueville is the theorist of the decade, having noted a century and a half ago that "Americans of all ages, all stations in life, and all types of disposition are forever forming associations." Further, he linked such behavior to the robustness of the nation's representative institutions. "Nothing," he claimed, "more deserves attention than the intellectual and moral associations in America. . . . In democratic countries the knowledge of how to combine is the mother of all other forms of knowledge; on its progress depends that of all the others."[1]

Today neo-Tocquevilleans such as Robert Putnam argue that civil society is crucial to "making democracy work,"[2] while authors like Francis Fukuyama and Benjamin Barber (who differ on everything else) agree that it plays a key role in driving political, social, and even economic outcomes.[3] This new conventional wisdom, however, is flawed. It is simply not always

true that, as Putnam (for example) puts it, "Tocqueville was right: Democratic government is strengthened, not weakened, when it faces a vigorous civil society."[4] This essay will show how a robust civil society actually helped scuttle the twentieth century's most critical democratic experiment, Weimar Germany.

Associational life flourished in Germany throughout the nineteenth and early in the twentieth century. Yet in contrast to what neo-Tocquevillean theories would predict, high levels of associationism, absent strong and responsive national government and political parties, served to fragment rather than unite German society. It was weak political institutionalization rather than a weak civil society that was Germany's main problem during the Wilhelmine and Weimar eras. As Samuel Huntington noted almost three decades ago, societies with highly active and mobilized publics and low levels of political institutionalization often degenerate into instability, disorder, and even violence;[5] German political development provides a classic example of this dynamic in action. During the interwar period in particular, Germans threw themselves into their clubs, voluntary associations, and professional organizations out of frustration with the failures of the national government and political parties, thereby helping to undermine the Weimar Republic and facilitate Hitler's rise to power. In addition,

From *World Politics* 49, no. 3 (1997), pp. 401–29. Some of the author's notes have been omitted.

Weimar's rich associational life provided a critical training ground for eventual Nazi cadres and a base from which the National Socialist German Workers' Party (NSDAP) could launch its *Machtergreifung* (seizure of power). Had German civil society been weaker, the Nazis would never have been able to capture so many citizens for their cause or eviscerate their opponents so swiftly.

A striking implication of this analysis is that a flourishing civil society does not necessarily bode well for the prospects of liberal democracy. For civil society to have the beneficial effects neo-Tocquevilleans posit, the political context has to be right: absent strong and responsive political institutions, an increasingly active civil society may serve to undermine, rather than strengthen, a political regime. Political institutionalization, in other words, may be less chic a topic these days than civil society, but it is logically prior and historically more important. As Huntington put it, a well-ordered civic polity requires "a recognizable and stable pattern of institutional authority . . . political institutions [must be] sufficiently strong to provide the basis of a legitimate political order and working political community." Without such political institutions, societies will lack trust and the ability to define and realize their common interests.[6] Political scientists need to remember that Tocqueville himself considered Americans' political associations to be as important as their nonpolitical ones, and they need to examine more closely how the two interact in different situations.

Neo-Tocquevillean Theories

The logic of neo-Tocquevillean theories bears closer examination. Contemporary scholars, it turns out, are not the first to "rediscover" the great Frenchman, nor even the first to link group bowling and political development. After World War II several social scientists also claimed to have found in associational life a key to understanding democracy's success or failure.

During the 1950s and 1960s social scientists such as William Kornhauser and Hannah Arendt helped turn the concept of "mass society" into a powerful theory for explaining the disintegration of democracy and the rise of totalitarianism in Europe. This school believed that Europe's slide into barbarism was greased by, among other factors, the collapse of intermediate associations across much of the Continent during the interwar years; the epigraph to Kornhauser's *Politics of Mass Society* was Tocqueville's warning that "if men are to remain civilized or to become so, the art of associating together must grow and improve in the same ratio in which the equality of conditions is increased." Drawing on Durkheim, and to a lesser degree on Marx, the mass society theorists argued that industrialization and modernity estranged citizens from one another, leaving them rootless and searching for ways of belonging. Ripped from their traditional moorings, masses were available for mobilization by extremist movements—unless, that is, individuals could develop communal bonds through organizational affiliations and involvement. Without "a multiplicity of independent and often conflicting forms of association," Kornhauser wrote, "people lack the resources to restrain their own behavior as well as that of others. Social atomization engenders strong feelings of alienation and anxiety, and therefore the disposition to engage in extreme behavior to escape from these tensions."[7]

Civil society, according to these theorists, was an antidote to the political viruses that afflicted mass society. Participation in organizations not only helped bring citizens together, bridging cleavages and fostering skills necessary for democratic governance, but it also satisfied their need to belong to some larger grouping. According to this view, a key reason for the collapse of the Weimar Republic was its status as a classic mass society, which made it susceptible to the blandishments of totalitarian demagoguery. Hitler's supporters were drawn primarily from alienated individuals who lacked a wide range of associational memberships and saw in the NSDAP a way of integrating themselves into a larger community; had German civil society been stronger, the republic might not have fallen.

The empirical evidence did not support such a causal sequence. For this and other reasons (such as the advent of newer and trendier theories), by the late 1960s social scientists had moved on and the concept of mass society had fallen out of vogue. Beginning in the 1970s, however, a third wave of democratization swept across the globe,[8] and scholars sought to identify its causes, as well as those factors that determined democratic success more generally. Several were drawn to the same Tocquevillean insights that had attracted Kornhauser, Arendt and others a few decades earlier. Putnam's *Making Democracy Work* was particularly important for the revival of interest in the role played by private, voluntary associations in sustaining vibrant democracy.

Like the mass society theorists, recent neo-Tocquevillean analyses stress the way individuals relate to each other and their society when explaining why democratic regimes function well. To measure and explain the success of democracy, Putnam, for example, uses the concepts of civic community and social capital; for both of these the key indicator is what might be termed associationism, the propensity of individuals to form and join a wide range of organizations spontaneously. According to Putnam:

> Civil associations contribute to the effectiveness and stability of democratic government . . . both because of their "internal" effects on individual members and because of their "external" effects on the wider polity. Internally, associations instill in their members habits of cooperation, solidarity, and public spiritedness. . . . Externally . . . a dense network of secondary associations . . . [enhances the articulation and aggregation of interests and] contributes to effective social collaboration.[9]

Associations "broaden the participants' sense of self, developing the 'I' into the 'We.'" "Networks of civic engagement," meanwhile, "foster sturdy norms of generalized reciprocity and encourage the emergence of social trust," which help re-solve dilemmas of collective action and smooth economic and political negotiations.[10] For Putnam almost any type of secondary association will serve these functions, as long as it is not organized around vertical bonds of authority and dependency. As he puts it: "The manifest purpose of the association [need not] be political."[11] "Taking part in a choral society or a bird-watching club can teach self-discipline and an appreciation for the joys of successful collaboration," he writes, thus contributing to the efficiency of regional government in Italy; the decline of league bowling, similarly, signals the decay of democracy in the United States. In sum, for Putnam and others in the new generation of neo-Tocquevillean analysts, associationism is both an indicator of healthy democracy and a prerequisite for it.

*   *   *

This essay now proceeds to explore the internal and external effects of German associationism, focusing on the Protestant middle classes in particular because of the critical role they played in the disintegration of the Weimar Republic and the rise of the Nazis. The results show that the postwar neo-Tocquevilleans were wrong in their assertion that an absence of civil society paved the way for the collapse of democracy and the rise of totalitarianism in Germany. I find, to the contrary, that participation in organizations of civil society *did* link individuals together and help mobilize them for political participation (just as current neo-Tocquevillean scholars claim), but in the German case this served not to strengthen democracy but to weaken it. And finally, I show that the NSDAP rose to power, not by attracting alienated, apolitical Germans, but rather by recruiting highly activist individuals and then exploiting their skills and associational affiliations to expand the party's appeal and consolidate its position as the largest political force in Germany. The essay concludes by probing the broader implications of the German case for theories of political development.

Civil Society in Bismarckian and Wilhelmine Germany

German associational life grew rapidly during the late eighteenth and nineteenth centuries. Spurred by changes in the legal code, the breakdown of preindustrial corporate traditions, and growing social wealth and diversification, an increasingly dense network of private voluntary associations spread throughout the country. This trend was pronounced enough for many to comment that Germany was in the grips of an "associational passion" on the eve of the 1848 revolutions. Voluntary associations were active in public life, in areas ranging from education to land preservation policy; in particular, they helped a growing and self-assertive bourgeoisie pursue its social and economic interests. Many historians, therefore, have interpreted German associational life from the mid-eighteenth to the mid-nineteenth century as a "symptom of the rise of bourgeois society and . . . a factor serving to accelerate" its development.[12]

The next spurt of German associational growth began in the 1870s. One contributing factor was the constitution adopted by the new German Reich in 1871: the granting of universal suffrage encouraged a wide variety of groups to form organizations in order to give themselves a voice in the political sphere. More importantly, just as the institutional structure of the Reich was prompting certain kinds of organizational activity, the prolonged economic downturn that began in the late 1870s highlighted the vulnerability of different groups and increased demands for state aid. During the following two decades almost all sectors of German society engaged in a frenzy of associational activity, with heavy industry, small business, the *Mittelstand*, and white-collar groups all forming their own organizations. The fight over protectionism was certainly a key reason for the emergence of new associations, but the Great Depression, as contemporaries referred to it, did more than merely highlight the divergent interests of different socioeconomic groups. It led many to recognize that Germany was at a historical turning point, poised between a traditional agricultural existence and industrialized modernity. The tension between these two visions stimulated the formation of a wide variety of organizations, many of which (such as patriotic societies, sports and reading clubs, and neighborhood associations) were designed to foster certain values and lifestyles, rather than directly engage the political process.

*   *   *

By the end of the nineteenth century, therefore, a distinct and troubling pattern had already begun to appear in Germany—the growth of civic associations during periods of strain. When national political institutions and structures proved either unwilling or unable to address their citizens' needs, many Germans turned away from them and found succor and support in the institutions of civil society instead. Because weak national political institutions reinforced social cleavages instead of helping to narrow them, moreover, associational activity generally occurred within rather than across group lines. Under these circumstances, associational life served not to integrate citizens into the political system, as neo-Tocquevilleans would predict, but rather to divide them further or mobilize them outside—and often against—the existing political regime.

As the liberal parties stumbled, their natural constituencies were left unorganized, and many of their natural activists found themselves adrift and in search of alternative ways of becoming involved in public affairs. As one observer has noted, "Members of the middle strata may have looked with disdain on parties and elections, but they participated with extraordinary vigor in a dense network of other institutions through which they sought political influence, social identity and economic advantage."[13] Many of these activists played critical roles in forming and staffing the nationalist associations that became so popular in Germany in the decades before World War I.

*   *   *

On the eve of World War I, practically all Germans were discontented with national political life. The then chancellor Bethmann-Hollweg would later write of this period:

> While the storm-clouds gathered ever more heavily on the world horizon, an almost inexplicable pressure weighed on the political life of Germany. . . . [M]alaise and dejection imparted a depressing tone to political party activity, which lacked any progressive impulse. The word Reichsverdrossenheit [dissatisfaction with the imperial state] rose up out of the darkness.[14]

With the national government unresponsive to calls for economic and political change and traditional political parties unable to adjust to the era of mass politics, civil society offered an outlet for the demands and aspirations of an increasingly restive German populace. This growth of associations during these years did not signal a growth in liberal values or democratic political structures; instead, it reflected and furthered the fragmentation of German political life and the delegitimization of national political institutions. State-society relations thus took an ominous turn during the Wilhelmine era, with consequences that would plague the Weimar Republic in later decades.

Civil Society in the Weimar Republic

The democratization of Germany at the end of World War I opened up a new phase in the country's associational life. Hitherto unrepresented and unorganized groups began to form their own organizations, and the Weimar years witnessed feverish associational activity at practically every level. The number of local voluntary associations grew throughout the 1920s, reaching extremely high levels as measured by both historical and comparative standards.[15] National associations also grew rapidly, and participation in professional organizations reached very high levels among the middle classes in particular. Yet, as in Wilhelmine Germany, the rise in associationism signaled, not the spread of liberal values or the development of healthy democratic political institutions, but rather the reverse. The parties of the bourgeois middle had reconstituted themselves after the war and proclaimed their commitment to becoming true "people's parties" and reintegrating German society. But these parties found it increasingly difficult to hold on to their constituencies in the face of growing economic, political, and social conflicts during the 1920s. Once again this created a vicious circle. The weakness of the bourgeois parties and national political structures drove many citizens looking for succor and support into civil society organizations, which were organized primarily along group lines rather than across them. The vigor of associational life, in turn, served to further undermine and delegitimize the republic's political structures. The result was a highly organized but vertically fragmented and discontented society that proved to be fertile ground for the Nazi's rise and eventual *Machtergreifung*.

The German revolution raised hope among the middle classes that the "divisive" and "unrepresentative" parties of the Wilhelmine era would be replaced by a single *Volkspartei* capable of unifying the nation's patriotic bourgeoisie and confronting the menace of social democracy. Popular support for such a course was strong, but institutional jealousies and elite divisions prevented its adoption. Instead, Weimar's early years saw, along with a strengthened conservative movement, the formation of two main liberal parties (the German Democratic Party [DDP] and the German People's Party [DVP]) and of several smaller regional parties, as well as reconsolidation of the Catholic Zentrum. The nonsocialist portion of Germany's political spectrum was thus permanently divided among a large (and eventually increasing) number of parties, which soon began to squabble among themselves.

The failure of the bourgeois parties to form a single movement or even to agree on important issues of the day did not dull the desire of the German middle classes for some form of antisocialist unity and a greater role in the political, social, and economic life of the republic. Throughout the 1920s "burghers from all social stations [continued] to demand more effective representation and a more direct political voice" and refused to abandon the ideals of bourgeois unity and community. In this context, bourgeois social life took on a renewed vigor and sense of urgency. "More voluntary associations attracted more members and did so in a more active fashion than ever before. Just as retailers, bakers, and commercial employees had organized into economic interest groups, so also did gymnasts, folklorists, singers and churchgoers gather into clubs, rally new members, schedule meetings, and plan a full assortment of conferences and tournaments."[16]

At first, this activity occurred in conjunction with, or at least parallel to, traditional party politics, since the newly reconstituted liberal parties tried to improve their grassroots organization, cultivate broader ties, and even achieve the status of a "people's party." By the middle of the decade, however, the attempt to reshape the relationship between national political life and civil society had failed, with the Great Inflation of 1922–23 being the turning point. Economic historians may disagree over which socioeconomic groups suffered the most, but there is little doubt that the middle classes suffered greatly, even if the pain was more psychological than material. This was followed by the crushing stabilization of 1923–24, which hit white-collar workers and the middle classes particularly hard. "By the end of the 1920s the economic position of the independent middle class had deteriorated to such an extent that it was no longer possible to distinguish it from the proletariat on the basis of income as a criterion."

The economic dislocations made all groups more jealous of their socioeconomic interests and more strident and narrow in their political demands, while making the middle classes increasingly resentful of both workers and big business, who were seen as having a disproportionate influence over the national government and political parties. By fighting for measures such as the eight-hour day and better wages, the SPD was considered to be serving the class interests of its core constituency above all else; the contrast between real (if limited) SPD success and the political impotence of the middle classes generated further paroxysms of antisocialist fervor.

Middle-class groups also became increasingly frustrated with the unwillingness or inability of liberal and conservative parties such as the DDP, DVP and DNVP (German National People's Party) to recognize their needs and act as their representatives on the national political stage. These parties came to be seen as the tools of big capitalists and financial interests, and the ideal of the people's party faded as the traditional parties of the middle and right seemed to be run by and for an unrepresentative elite. Local-level organizations and associational affiliations, furthermore, were allowed to languish or break away. Not surprisingly, the vote share of the traditional bourgeois parties dropped precipitously throughout the 1920s. In 1924 the DVP and DDP together managed to attract only about 15 percent, and splinter parties were forming to capture their increasingly alienated and fragmented constituency. By 1928—the high point of economic stabilization and supposedly the "golden age" of the Weimar Republic—the splinter parties were outpolling the traditional parties of the middle.

As before, middle-class tension and frustration sparked a growth in associational activity. During the 1920s middle-class Germans threw themselves into their clubs, community groups, and patriotic organizations while increasingly abandoning the seemingly ineffectual liberal parties. By the middle of the decade both the style and the substance of bourgeois social life in Germany had begun to change:

Spurred by growing political tensions, social organizations helped to lead an unprecedented surge of apoliticism that escaped the control of bourgeois elites. . . . [M]any spokesman for Weimar apoliticism argued that social organizations would do more than cushion political strife—they would bind together a moralistic, antisocialist, "folk community" of disparate classes and strata. . . . [T]he middle and late 1920s . . . thus saw not only an acceleration of tensions that had originated in the Empire but also an unprecedented rupture between the social and the political authority of the local bourgeoisie.[17]

What occurred in Germany was no less than an inversion of neo-Tocquevillean theory; not only did participation in civil society organizations fail to contribute to republican virtue, but it in fact subverted it. "[A]s the middle class became more and more disenchanted with and hostile towards the republic, their energies ceased to be channeled into proto political organizations and party political organizations of the center and right which the old elites had traditionally headed. Instead the radicalized troops of the middle class deserted these organizations and their leaders."[18]

*   *   *

The Rise of the NSDAP

During the 1920s the Nazi Party (the NSDAP) was stagnant—low on funds and unable to fill meeting halls or amass a significant share of the vote. By 1926 the situation had become so dire that the party began to move toward a major shift in strategy. Where previously the NSDAP had focused primarily on urban areas and working-class voters, it now reoriented its appeal toward the middle classes, nonvoters, and farmers, while proclaiming itself above the group divisions that plagued the country. Thus, as late as the 1928 elections the Nazis polled only 2.6 percent, whereas four years later they were the largest party in the Weimar Republic. What enabled the Nazis to make such spectacular

inroads into the German electorate? The depression, the weak response to it from mainstream parties, Hitler's charisma and political savvy—all these clearly played a role. A significant part of the answer, however, lies with contemporary German civil society.

As voters abandoned traditional bourgeois parties during the 1920s and then grappled with the ravages of the depression, a political vacuum opened up in German politics, a vacuum that offered the Nazis a golden opportunity to assemble an unprecedented coalition. To this end, the NSDAP exploited its increasingly strong position in Weimar's rich associational life. The dense networks of civic engagement provided the Nazis with cadres of activists who had the skills necessary to spread the party's message and increase recruitment. Those networks also served as a fifth column, allowing the NSDAP to infiltrate and master a significant sector of bourgeois society before emerging to seize control of Germany's national political structures. As one scholar notes:

> Path-breaking work in recent years on the rise of National Socialism has stressed the importance of local newspapers, municipal notables, and voluntary associations, and points to the buoyancy and vigor of civic traditions. Had bourgeois community life been overly disoriented and fragmented, the body of new evidence indicates, the Nazis would never have been able to marshal the resources or plug into the social networks necessary to their political success.[19]

During the second half of the 1920s the Nazis concentrated on attracting bourgeois "joiners" who had become disillusioned with traditional party politics. Like the neo-Tocquevilleans, Hitler recognized that participation in associational life provided individuals with the kinds of leadership skills and social ties that could be very useful in the political arena. Civil society activists formed the backbone of the Nazis' grassroots propaganda machine. The party also skillfully exploited their organizational contacts and social expertise to gain insight into the fears and needs of particular groups and to tailor new appeals to them—using them, in other words, as "focus groups." The activists, finally, provided the movement with unparalleled local organizations. In contrast to the other bourgeois parties, the Nazis were able to develop flexible and committed local party chapters that enabled full and accurate two-way communication between the national party and its frontline troops.

Recent research into local life in interwar Germany details the crucial role played by bourgeois "joiners" in paving the way for the Nazi rise to power. Rudy Koshar's excellent study of Marburg, for example, shows that party members were an unusually activist bunch. "Before September 1930 there existed at least 46 Nazi party members with 73 cross-affiliations. For the period before 30 January 1933 overall, there were at least 84 Nazi students and 116 nonstudent party adherents with 375 cross-affiliations to occupational associations, sports clubs, nonparty municipal electoral states, civic associations, student fraternities and other local voluntary groups." By January 1933 there was at least one Nazi Party member in one out of every four voluntary groups in the city.[20] The Nazi elite was even more well connected.

Koshar describes the key role of civil society activists in creating a powerful and dynamic Nazi organization in Marburg. By the time of the Nazi breakthrough in the 1930 elections, the NSDAP had representatives in a wide range of civic associations working to spread the movement's message, get out the vote, and discredit political opponents. "The 1930–31 electoral victories were more lasting than expected, because the NSDAP was gaining control over a field of social organizations wider than that supporting bourgeois parties."[21] The activists not only created a powerful electoral machine but also helped the NSDAP to anchor itself in local communities in a way no other bourgeois party could match. The Nazis used their local organization to design propaganda and political events that would mesh with and appeal to Marburg's particular social rhythms, making the NSDAP

seem sympathetic and responsive by contrast with elitist and out-of-touch liberals and conservatives.

> [T]he party was attractive in part because of its positive image in conversations in the marketplace, local stores, university classrooms, fraternity houses, meeting halls, soccer fields, and homes. Hitler's seemingly mysterious mass appeal could hardly have been so extensive without the unplanned propaganda of daily social life. . . . Through infiltration, the NSDAP gained moral authority over organizations in which it also established a material base. It was becoming the political hub, the focus of legitimacy and material power, that bourgeois constituencies had lacked.[22]

The Nazis did not merely exploit their cadres' preexisting associational bonds; they even deliberately infiltrated activists into a wide range of bourgeois organizations in order to eliminate potential opponents from positions of power within them. Without the opportunity to exploit Weimar's rich associational network, in short, the Nazis would not have been able to capture important sectors of the German electorate so quickly and efficiently.

*   *   *

The Nazis had infiltrated and captured a wide range of national and local associations by the early 1930s, finally bridging the gap between bourgeois civil society and party politics that had plagued Germany for half a century. From this base Hitler was able to achieve two goals that had long eluded German politicians—the creation of an effective political machine and a true cross-class coalition. With these in Nazi hands and bourgeois competitors eliminated, Hindenburg found it increasingly difficult to ignore Hitler's demands for a change of course. By the end of 1932 Schleicher had lost Hindenburg's confidence; two days after Schleicher was forced to resign, Hitler was named chancellor.

Conclusions: Germany, Associationism, and Political Development

The German case reveals a distinct pattern of associationism that does not conform to the predictions of neo-Tocquevillean theories. German civil society was rich and extensive during the nineteenth and early twentieth centuries, and this nation of joiners should accordingly have provided fertile soil for a successful democratic experiment. Instead, it succumbed to totalitarianism. This does not mean that civil society was disconnected from German political development; it was, rather, connected in ways that the reigning neo-Tocquevillean theories ignore.

The vigor of German civil society actually developed in inverse relation to the vigor and responsiveness of national political institutions and structures. Instead of helping to reduce social cleavages, Germany's weak and poorly designed political institutions exacerbated them; instead of responding to the demands of an increasingly mobilized population, the country's political structures obstructed meaningful participation in public life. As a result, citizens' energies and interests were deflected into private associational activities, which were generally organized within rather than across group boundaries. The vigor of civil society activities then continued to draw public interest and involvement away from parties and politics, further sapping their strength and significance. Eventually the Nazis seized the opportunities afforded by such a situation, offering a unifying appeal and bold solutions to a nation in crisis. The NSDAP drew its critical cadres precisely from among bourgeois civil society activists with few ties to mainstream politics, and it was from the base of bourgeois civil society that the party launched its swift *Machtergreifung*. In short, one cannot understand the rise of the Nazis without an appreciation of the role played by German civil society, and one cannot understand the contours of that civil society without reference to the country's weak political institutionalization.

*   *   *

On the eve of the Great Depression, Germany found itself in a precarious political situation—its civil society was highly developed but segmented, and its mainstream bourgeois parties were disintegrating. Many citizens active in secondary associations were politically frustrated and dissatisfied; when the depression added economic and political chaos to the mix, the result was a golden opportunity for a new political force. The Nazis stepped into the breach, reaching out to the disaffected bourgeois civil society activists and using the country's organizational infrastructure to make inroads into various constituencies. The dense network of German associations enabled the NSDAP to create in a remarkably short time a dynamic political machine and cross-class coalition unlike anything Germany had ever before seen—one to which it soon succumbed.

The German case should make us skeptical of many aspects of neo-Tocquevillean theory. In particular, German political development raises questions about what has by now become practically conventional wisdom, namely, that there is a direct and positive relationship between a rich associational life and stable democracy. Under certain circumstances, clearly the very opposite is the case: associationism and the prospects for democratic stability can actually be inversely related. Furthermore, many of the consequences of associationism stressed by neo-Tocquevillean scholars—providing individuals with political and social skills, creating bonds between citizens, facilitating mobilization, decreasing barriers to collective action—can be turned to antidemocratic ends as well as to democratic ones. Perhaps, therefore, associationism should be considered a politically neutral multiplier—neither inherently good nor inherently bad, but rather dependent for its effects on the wider political context.

The neo-Tocquevilleans have in fact already

been criticized for their inability to predict whether civil society activity will have negative or positive consequences for political development. Some, for example, have taken Putnam to task for praising the long-term salutory effect of civil society activity in Northern Italy while ignoring the fact that this selfsame activity proved to be consistent with Fascism.[23] What the analysis presented here seems to indicate is that if we want to know *when* civil society activity will take on oppositional or even antidemocratic tendencies, we need to ground our analyses in concrete examinations of political reality. If a country's political institutions and structures are capable of channeling and redressing grievances and the existing political regime enjoys public support and legitimacy, then associationism will probably buttress political stability by placing its resources and beneficial effects in the service of the status quo. This is the pattern Tocqueville described.

If, on the contrary, political institutions and structures are weak and/or the existing political regime is perceived to be ineffectual and illegitimate, then civil society activity may become an alternative to politics, increasingly absorbing citizens' energies and satisfying their basic needs. In such situations, associationism will probably undermine political stability, by deepening cleavages, furthering dissatisfaction, and providing rich soil for oppositional movements. Flourishing civil society activity in these circumstances signals governmental and party failure and may bode ill for the regime's future.

This latter pattern fits Germany in the late nineteenth and early twentieth centuries, as we have seen, but it may be applicable to many other cases as well, with provocative implications. The weakening of communist regimes in Eastern Europe, for example, was hastened by a rise in civil society activity there in the 1980s; parts of the contemporary Arab world are witnessing a remarkable growth in Islamist civil society activity that feeds on the citizenry's frustration with the region's unrepresentative and unresponsive authoritarian governments. In

such situations civil society may not necessarily promote liberal democracy, as the neo-Tocquevilleans would have it, but rather may simply corrode the foundations of the current political order while providing an organizational base from which it can be challenged. From this perspective, the fact that a militant Islamist movement, for example, provides its supporters with religious classes, professional associations, and medical services tells us little about what might happen should the movement ever gain power; it tells us much more about the political failure and gloomy prospects of the nation's existing regime.

Unfortunately, one need not look so far abroad to find examples of this pattern. The *New York Times* noted in a recent report on the District of Columbia, for example, that for many of Washington's residents home rule "has come to mean a patronage-bloated, ineffective city payroll offering phantom services." The weakness and failure of Washington's local government and political system, in turn, has spurred both a rise in associational activity and a fragmentation of social consciousness and communal identity. "Volunteerism [is] growing stronger in the face of the dwindling services, mismanagement and budget shortfalls that bedevil the city," according to one neighborhood activist. "Gradually," says another, "people come to feel they have to take care of themselves and not worry about the other guy."[24] Another observer proclaims: "Amid widespread disillusionment with government and its ability to solve the nation's most pervasive problems, a loosely formed social movement promoting a return to 'civil society' has emerged . . . drawing a powerful and ideologically diverse group of political leaders."[25] When associationism and communitarian activities flourish in such a context, it would seem that there is cause, not for celebration, but rather for deep concern about the failure of the community's political institutions.

Finally, if neo-Tocquevilleans have misunderstood the true connections between civic and political institutions, the policy advice they offer should be called into question. Responding to current public dissatisfaction with the state of democracy in America, many have argued that the remedy lies in fostering local associational life. This prescription may prove to be both misguided and counterproductive, however. If a population increasingly perceives its government, politicians, and parties to be inefficient and unresponsive, diverting public energies and interest into secondary associations may only exacerbate the problem, fragment society, and weaken political cohesion further. American democracy would be better served if its problems were addressed directly rather than indirectly. Increased bird watching and league bowling, in other words, are unlikely to have positive effects unless the nation's political institutions are also revitalized.

NOTES

1. Aexis de Tocqueville, *Democracy in America* (New York: Harper and Row, 1988), 513, 517.

2. Putnam, *Making Democracy Work: Civic Traditions in Modern Italy* (Princeton: Princeton University Press, 1993); see also idem, "Bowling Alone: America's Declining Social Capital," *Journal of Democracy* 6 (January 1995); idem, "The Prosperous Community," *American Prospect*, no. 13 (Spring 1993); and idem, "The Strange Disappearance of Civic America," *American Prospect*, no. 24 (Winter 1996).

3. Fukuyama, *Trust: Social Virtues and the Creation of Prosperity* (New York: Free Press, 1995); and Barber, *Jihad vs. McWorld: How the Planet Is Both Falling Apart and Coming Together—and What This Means for Democracy* (New York: NY Times Books, 1995).

4. Putnam (fn. 2, *Making Democracy Work*), 182.

5. Samuel P. Huntington, *Political Order in Changing Societies* (New Haven: Yale University Press, 1968).

6. Ibid., 82–83, 5–25.

7. William Kornhauser, *The Politics of Mass Society* (Glencoe, Ill.: Free Press, 1959), 32.

8. Samuel P. Huntington, *The Third Wave: Democratization in the Late Twentieth Century* (Norman: University of Oklahoma Press, 1991).

9. Putnam (fn. 2, *Making Democracy Work*), 89–90. On social capital, see also James Coleman, *Foundations of Social Theory* (Cambridge: Belknap Press of Harvard University, 1990).

10. Putnam (fn. 2, 1995), 67. See also idem, "Tuning In, Tuning Out: The Strange Disappearance of Social Capital in America," *PS* (December 1995); and idem (fn. 2, "The Prosperous Community").

11. Putnam (fn. 2, *Making Democracy Work*), 90. For a separate argument on the consequences of organizations' internal structures, see Harry Eckstein, "A Theory of Stable Democracy," in Eckstein, *Division and Cohesion in Democracy: A Study of Norway* (Princeton: Princeton University Press, 1966).

12. Thomas Nipperdey, "Verein als soziale Struktur in Deutschland im späten 18. und frühen 19. Jahrhundert: Eine Fallstudie zur Modernisierung," in Nipperdey, *Gesellschaft, Kultur, Theorie: Gesammelte Aufsätze zur neueren Geschichte* (Göttingen: Vandenhoeck und Ruprecht, 1976).

13. James J. Sheehan, *German Liberalism in the Nineteenth Century* (Atlantic Highlands, N.J.: Humanities Press, 1995), 236.

14. Theobald von Bethmann-Hollweg, *Betrachtungen zum Weltkrieg*, vol. 1 (Berlin: R. Hubbing, 1919–21).

15. William Sheridan Allen, *The Nazi Seizure of Power: The Experience of a Single German Town, 1922–1945* (New York: 1984); Peter Fritzsche, *Rehearsals for Fascism: Populism and Political Mobilization in Weimar Germany* (New York: Oxford University Press, 1990); and Koshar, *Social Life, Local Politics, and Nazism: Marburg, 1880–1935* (Chapel

Hill: University of North Carolina Press, 1986). For cross-national comparisions of the impact of civil society activity on democracy, see Nancy Bermeo, "Getting Mad or Going Mad? Citizens, Scarcity, and the Breakdown of Democracy in Interwar Europe" (Paper presented at the annual meeting of the APSA, San Francisco, 1996); Nancy Bermeo and Phil Nord, eds., "Civil Society before Democracy" (Manuscript, Princeton University, 1996); and Dietrich Rueschemeyer, Evelyne Huber Stephens, and John D. Stephens, *Capitalist Development and Democracy* (Chicago: University of Chicago Press, 1992), esp. 113–14.

16. Fritzsche (fn. 15), 76.

17. Koshar (fn. 15), 166.

18. Detlev J. K. Peukert, *The Weimar Republic* (New York: Hill and Wang, 1989), 230.

19. Fritzsche (fn. 15), 13.

20. Koshar, "Contentious Citadel: Bourgeois Crisis and Nazism in Marburg/Lahn, 1880–1933," in Thomas Childers, *The Nazi Voter: The Social Foundations of Fascism in Germany* (Chapel Hill: University of North Carolina Press, 1983), 24, 28–29. See also Koshar (fn. 17); Allen (fn. 15); and idem, "The Nazification of a Town," in John L. Snell, ed., *The Nazi Revolution: Hitler's Dictatorship and the German Nation* (Lexington, Mass.: D. C. Heath, 1973).

21. Koshar (fn. 17), 202.

22. Ibid., 204, 202.

23. See Sidney Tarrow, "Making Social Science Work across Space and Time: A Critical Reflection on Robert Putnam's Making Democracy Work," *American Political Science Review* 90 (June 1996). Interestingly, Tarrow also criticizes Putnam for failing to recognize that much of the civil society activity he finds was directly or indirectly created by Italian political parties. According to Tarrow, in other words, civil society may not be an *independent* variable (as Putnam claims) but rather an *intermediary* variable, along the lines suggested by the analysis presented here.

24. Ward 3 block-watch organizer Kathy Smith and Cleveland Park Citizens Association president Stephen A. Koczak, respectively, quoted in Francis X. Clines, "Washington's Troubles Hit Island of Affluence," *New York Times*, July 26, 1996, p. A19.

25. "Promoting a Return to 'Civil Society,' Diverse Group of Crusaders Looks to New Solutions to Social Problems," *Washington Post*, December 15, 1996.

7 ADVANCED DEMOCRACIES

This chapter explores some of the aspects and challenges of **advanced democracies,** *countries that have stable democratic regimes, a high level of economic development, and extensive civil rights and liberties. It focuses specifically on three questions:*

1. *What enables advanced democracies to emerge and thrive?*
2. *How do institutional differences among advanced democracies affect their politics and policy?*
3. *Can advanced democracies continue to promote* **equality**—*for example, through generous welfare states—in the twenty-first century?*

By most measures the northern states of the United States were the first "advanced democracy." Universal male suffrage—albeit almost always restricted to white males—had been achieved by the 1830s in almost all U.S. states (in Britain, even the 1832 Reform Act extended the franchise to only about one in five adult males), institutionalization was advanced, and per capita income (according to the economic historian Angus Maddison) already exceeded that of contemporary France. The liberal French nobleman, intellectual, and politician Alexis de Tocqueville visited the United States in 1831 and set out to explain to his European compatriots why and how American democracy worked. He came to two firm conclusions, well set out in his own Introduction to his 1835 classic, Democracy in America: (a) social equality led inevitably to democracy, and (b) equality, at least in Europe and America, was everywhere increasing.

Tocqueville saw economic growth and prosperity as but one of the causes of social equalization, and thus of democracy. The sociologist and political scientist Seymour Martin Lipset, in his classic Political Man (1960), first perceived what is now taken as a commonplace: that while other factors still matter, richer countries are highly likely to be both more equal and more democratic. Wealth alone, through a series of processes that Lipset explored, leads normally to democracy. (In the readings for Chapter 9 we shall see an important modification of Lipset's thesis.)

As discussed in Chapter 6, democracies divide between "majoritarian" and "proportional" (PR) electoral systems. Advanced democracies also differ on this dimension: the United States, the United Kingdom, Canada, Australia, France, Japan, and Italy are majoritarian (or mostly so), while most of the other advanced democracies (including virtually all of the smaller ones) use PR. An interesting sidelight is that several of the advanced democracies have recently changed their electoral systems: France used PR for one election in 1986, then reverted to a majoritarian system; and in the early 1990s Italy and Japan switched from mostly proportional systems to mostly majoritarian ones, while New Zealand switched from a "first-past-the-post" majoritarian system to a proportional one.

What are countries actually choosing when they adopt (or retain) one electoral system or another? As was emphasized in Chapter 6, above all a majoritarian system normally (as in the United States) allows only two major parties to survive, while PR encourages a multiplicity of parties. This regularity is so powerful and has such strong causal properties that it is called (after its discoverer) **Duverger's Law**—*one of the very few causal laws known to political science. Duverger's original (1951) explanation of it has never really been surpassed, and its essence is presented here.*

You may recall from Chapter 4 that PR seems to have one other important effect: it makes for much more generous welfare states and hence for considerably greater economic equality. But why? Perhaps voters in some countries inherently prefer greater equality and choose both a welfare state and *PR; or it might be either that PR gives voters* more *welfare than they really want, or that majoritarian electoral systems give them* less *welfare than they desire. One way to phrase this question is simple: which system comes closer to giving the* **median voter**—*the one at exactly the 50th percentile on a left-right ordering, and presumably the one who, in a democracy, should prevail—exactly what she wants? In a pioneering 1994 study of the advanced democracies, Huber and Powell reached a surprising conclusion that subsequent research (some of it by Powell) has only reinforced:* **proportional** *systems, on average, produce policy outcomes much closer to what the median voter wants. Indeed, subsequent work has shown that* **majoritarian** *systems produce outcomes considerably to the political right—including less redistribution, less welfare, and less equality—than their median voters desire.*

Can the generous (mostly PR) welfare states survive in an increasingly competitive global economy? While the conventional wisdom holds that they cannot because the high taxes that fund generosity make their products too expensive to compete, the 2001 article from The Economist, *"Is Government Disappearing?" contends that "big government" is far from being doomed— not least because, precisely in the most trade-exposed societies, citizens actually want* more *welfare (and, at least under PR, get what they want).*

ALEXIS DE TOCQUEVILLE

AUTHOR'S INTRODUCTION

Among the novel objects that attracted my attention during my stay in the United States, nothing struck me more forcibly than the general equality of condition among the people. I readily discovered the prodigious influence that this primary fact exercises on the whole course of society; it gives a peculiar direction to public opinion and a peculiar tenor to the laws; it imparts new maxims to the governing authorities and peculiar habits to the governed.

I soon perceived that the influence of this fact extends far beyond the political character and the laws of the country, and that it has no less effect on civil society than on the government; it creates opinions, gives birth to new sentiments, founds novel customs, and modifies whatever it does not produce. The more I advanced in the study of American society, the more I perceived that this equality of condition is the fundamental fact from which all others seem to be derived and the central point at which all my observations constantly terminated.

I then turned my thoughts to our own hemisphere, and thought that I discerned there something analogous to the spectacle which the New World presented to me. I observed that equality of condition, though it has not there reached the extreme limit which it seems to have attained in the United States, is constantly approaching it; and that the democracy which governs the American communities appears to be rapidly rising into power in Europe.

Hence I conceived the idea of the book that is now before the reader.

It is evident to all alike that a great democratic revolution is going on among us, but all do not look at it in the same light. To some it appears to be novel but accidental, and, as such, they hope it may still be checked; to others it seems irresistible, because it is the most uniform, the most ancient, and the most permanent tendency that is to be found in history.

I look back for a moment on the situation of France seven hundred years ago, when the territory was divided among a small number of families, who were the owners of the soil and the rulers of the inhabitants; the right of governing descended with the family inheritance from generation to generation; force was the only means by which man could act on man; and landed property was the sole source of power.

Soon, however, the political power of the clergy was founded and began to increase: the clergy opened their ranks to all classes, to the poor and the rich, the commoner and the noble; through the church, equality penetrated into the government, and he who as a serf must have vegetated in perpetual bondage took his place as a priest in the midst of nobles, and not infrequently above the heads of kings.

The different relations of men with one another became more complicated and numerous as society gradually became more stable and civilized. Hence the want of civil laws was felt; and the ministers of law soon rose from the obscurity of the tribunals and their dusty chambers to appear at the court of the monarch, by the side of the feudal barons clothed in their ermine and their mail.

While the kings were ruining themselves by their great enterprises, and the nobles exhausting their resources by private wars, the lower orders were enriching themselves by commerce. The influence of money began to be perceptible in state affairs. The transactions of business opened a new road to power, and the financier

From Alexis de Tocqueville, *Democracy in America* (New York: A. A. Knopf, 1945), pp. 3–16. Author's notes have been omitted.

rose to a station of political influence in which he was at once flattered and despised.

Gradually enlightenment spread, a reawakening of taste for literature and the arts became evident; intellect and will contributed to success; knowledge became an attribute of government, intelligence a social force; the educated man took part in affairs of state.

The value attached to high birth declined just as fast as new avenues to power were discovered. In the eleventh century, nobility was beyond all price; in the thirteenth, it might be purchased. Nobility was first conferred by gift in 1270, and equality was thus introduced into the government by the aristocracy itself.

In the course of these seven hundred years it sometimes happened that the nobles, in order to resist the authority of the crown or to diminish the power of their rivals, granted some political power to the common people. Or, more frequently, the king permitted the lower orders to have a share in the government, with the intention of limiting the power of the aristocracy.

In France the kings have always been the most active and the most constant of levelers. When they were strong and ambitious, they spared no pains to raise the people to the level of the nobles; when they were temperate and feeble, they allowed the people to rise above themselves. Some assisted democracy by their talents, others by their vices. Louis XI and Louis XIV reduced all ranks beneath the throne to the same degree of subjection; and finally Louis XV descended, himself and all his court, into the dust.

As soon as land began to be held on any other than a feudal tenure, and personal property could in its turn confer influence and power, every discovery in the arts, every improvement in commerce of manufactures, created so many new elements of equality among men. Henceforward every new invention, every new want which it occasioned, and every new desire which craved satisfaction were steps towards a general leveling. The taste for luxury, the love of war, the rule of fashion, and the most superficial as well as the deepest passions of the human heart seemed to cooperate to enrich the poor and to impoverish the rich.

From the time when the exercise of the intellect became a source of strength and of wealth, we see that every addition to science, every fresh truth, and every new idea became a germ of power placed within the reach of the people. Poetry, eloquence, and memory, the graces of the mind, the fire of imagination, depth of thought, and all the gifts which Heaven scatters at a venture turned to the advantage of democracy; and even when they were in the possession of its adversaries, they still served its cause by throwing into bold relief the natural greatness of man. Its conquests spread, therefore, with those of civilization and knowledge; and literature became an arsenal open to all, where the poor and the weak daily resorted for arms.

In running over the pages of our history, we shall scarcely find a single great event of the last seven hundred years that has not promoted equality of condition.

The Crusades and the English wars decimated the nobles and divided their possessions: the municipal corporations introduced democratic liberty into the bosom of feudal monarchy; the invention of firearms equalized the vassal and the noble on the field of battle; the art of printing opened the same resources to the minds of all classes; the post brought knowledge alike to the door of the cottage and to the gate of the palace; and Protestantism proclaimed that all men are equally able to find the road to heaven. The discovery of America opened a thousand new paths to fortune and led obscure adventures to wealth and power.

If, beginning with the eleventh century, we examine what has happened in France from one half-century to another, we shall not fail to perceive that at the end of each of these periods a twofold revolution has taken place in the state of society. The noble has gone down the social ladder, and the commoner has gone up; the one descends as the other rises. Every half-century brings them nearer to each other, and they will soon meet.

Nor is this peculiar to France. Wherever we look, we perceive the same revolution going on throughout the Christian world.

The various occurrences of national existence have everywhere turned to the advantage of democracy: all men have aided it by their exertions, both those who have intentionally labored in its cause and those who have served it unwittingly; those who have fought for it and even those who have declared themselves its opponents have all been driven along in the same direction, have all labored to one end; some unknowingly and some despite themselves, all have been blind instruments in the hands of God.

The gradual development of the principle of equality is, therefore, a providential fact. It has all the chief characteristics of such a fact: it is universal, it is lasting, it constantly eludes all human interference, and all events as well as all men contribute to its progress.

Would it, then, be wise to imagine that a social movement the causes of which lie so far back can be checked by the efforts of one generation? Can it be believed that the democracy which has overthrown the feudal system and vanquished kings will retreat before tradesmen and capitalists? Will it stop now that it has grown so strong and its adversaries so weak?

Whither, then, are we tending? No one can say, for terms of comparison already fail us. There is greater equality of condition in Christian countries at the present day than there has been at any previous time, in any part of the world, so that the magnitude of what already has been done prevents us from foreseeing what is yet to be accomplished.

The whole book that is here offered to the public has been written under the influence of a kind of religious awe produced in the author's mind by the view of that irresistible revolution which has advanced for centuries in spite of every obstacle and which is still advancing in the midst of the ruins it has caused.

It is not necessary that God himself should speak in order that we may discover the unquestionable signs of his will. It is enough to ascertain what is the habitual course of nature and the constant tendency of events. I know, without special revelation, that the planets move in the orbits traced by the Creator's hand.

If the men of our time should be convinced, by attentive observation and sincere reflection, that the gradual and progressive development of social equality is at once the past and the future of their history, this discovery alone would confer upon the change the sacred character of a divine decree. To attempt to check democracy would be in that case to resist the will of God; and the nations would then be constrained to make the best of the social lot awarded to them by Providence.

The Christian nations of our day seem to me to present a most alarming spectacle; the movement which impels them is already so strong that it cannot be stopped, but it is not yet so rapid that it cannot be guided. Their fate is still in their own hands; but very soon they may lose control.

The first of the duties that are at this time imposed upon those who direct our affairs is to educate democracy, to reawaken, if possible, its religious beliefs; to purify its morals; to mold its actions; to substitute a knowledge of statecraft for its inexperience, and an awareness of its true interest for its blind instincts, to adapt its government to time and place, and to modify it according to men and to conditions. A new science of politics is needed for a new world.

This, however, is what we think of least; placed in the middle of a rapid stream, we obstinately fix our eyes on the ruins that may still be descried upon the shore we have left, while the current hurries us away and drags us backward towards the abyss.

In no country in Europe has the great social revolution that I have just described made such rapid progress as in France; but it has always advanced without guidance. The heads of the state have made no preparation for it, and it has advanced without their consent or without their knowledge. The most powerful, the most intelligent, and the most moral classes of the nation have never attempted to control it in order to guide it. Democracy has consequently been abandoned to its wild instincts, and it has grown up like those children who have no parental guidance, who receive their education in the public streets, and who are acquainted only with the vices and wretchedness of society. Its existence was seemingly unknown when suddenly it acquired supreme power. All then servilely submitted to its caprices; it was worshipped as the idol of strength; and when afterwards it was enfeebled by its own excesses, the legislator conceived the rash project of destroying it, instead of instructing it and correcting its vices. No attempt was made to fit it to govern, but all were bent on excluding it from the government.

The result has been that the democratic revolution has taken place in the body of society without that concomitant change in the laws, ideas, customs, and morals which was necessary to render such a revolution beneficial. Thus we have a democracy without anything to lessen its vices and bring out its natural advantages; and although we already perceive the evils it brings, we are ignorant of the benefits it may confer.

While the power of the crown, supported by the aristocracy, peaceably governed the nations of Europe, society, in the midst of its wretchedness, had several sources of happiness which can now scarcely be conceived or appreciated. The power of a few of his subjects was an insurmountable barrier to the tyranny of the prince; and the monarch, who felt the almost divine character which he enjoyed in the eyes of the multitude, derived a motive for the just use of his power from the respect which he inspired. The nobles, placed high as they were above the people, could take that calm and benevolent interest in their fate which the shepherd feels towards his flock; and without acknowledging the poor as their equals, they watched over the destiny of those whose welfare Providence had entrusted to their care. The people, never having

conceived the idea of a social condition different from their own, and never expecting to become equal to their leaders, received benefits from them without discussing their rights. They became attached to them when they were clement and just and submitted to their exactions without resistance or servility, as to the inevitable visitations of the Deity. Custom and usage, moreover, had established certain limits to oppression and founded a sort of law in the very midst of violence.

As the noble never suspected that anyone would attempt to deprive him of the privileges which he believed to be legitimate, and as the serf looked upon his own inferiority as a consequence of the immutable order of nature, it is easy to imagine that some mutual exchange of goodwill took place between two classes so differently endowed by fate. Inequality and wretchedness were then to be found in society, but the souls of neither rank of men were degraded.

Men are not corrupted by the exercise of power or debased by the habit of obedience, but by the exercise of a power which they believe to be illegitimate, and by obedience to a rule which they consider to be usurped and oppressive.

On the one side were wealth, strength, and leisure, accompanied by the pursuit of luxury, the refinements of taste, the pleasures of wit, and the cultivation of the arts; on the other were labor, clownishness, and ignorance. But in the midst of this coarse and ignorant multitude it was not uncommon to meet with energetic passions, generous sentiments, profound religious convictions, and wild virtues.

The social state thus organized might boast of its stability, its power, and, above all, its glory.

But the scene is now changed. Gradually the distinctions of rank are done away with; the barriers that once severed mankind are falling; property is divided, power is shared by many, the light of intelligence spreads, and the capacities of all classes tend towards equality. Society becomes democratic, and the empire of democracy is slowly and peaceably introduced into institutions and customs.

I can conceive of a society in which all men would feel an equal love and respect for the laws of which they consider themselves the authors; in which the authority of the government would be respected as necessary, and not divine; and in which the loyalty of the subject to the chief magistrate would not be a passion, but a quiet and rational persuasion. With every individual in the possession of rights which he is sure to retain, a kind of manly confidence and reciprocal courtesy would arise between all classes, removed alike from pride and servility. The people, well acquainted with their own true interests, would understand that, in order to profit from the advantages of the state, it is necessary to satisfy its requirements. The voluntary association of the citizens might then take the place of the individual authority of the nobles, and the community would be protected from tyranny and license.

I admit that, in a democratic state thus constituted, society would not be stationary. But the impulses of the social body might there be regulated and made progressive. If there were less splendor than in an aristocracy, misery would also be less prevalent; the pleasures of enjoyment might be less excessive, but those of comfort would be more general; the sciences might be less perfectly cultivated, but ignorance would be less common; the ardor of the feelings would be constrained, and the habits of the nation softened; there would be more vices and fewer crimes.

In the absence of enthusiasm and ardent faith, great sacrifices may be obtained from the members of a commonwealth by an appeal to their understanding and their experience; each individual will feel the same necessity of union with his fellows to protect his own weakness; and as he knows that he can obtain their help only on condition of helping them, he will readily perceive that his personal interest is identified with the interests of the whole community. The nation, taken as a whole, will be less brilliant, less glorious, and perhaps less strong; but the majority of the citizens will enjoy a greater degree of prosperity, and the people will remain peaceable, not because they despair of a change for the better, but because they are conscious that they are well off already.

If all the consequences of this state of things were not good or useful, society would at least have appropriated all such as were useful and good; and having once and forever renounced the social advantages of aristocracy, mankind would enter into possession of all the benefits that democracy can offer.

But here it may be asked what we have adopted in the place of those institutions, those ideas, and those customs of our forefathers which we have abandoned.

The spell of royalty is broken, but it has not been succeeded by the majesty of the laws. The people have learned to despise all authority, but they still fear it; and fear now extorts more than was formerly paid from reverence and love.

I perceive that we have destroyed those individual powers which were able, single-handed, to cope with tyranny; but it is the government alone that has inherited all the privileges of which families, guilds, and individuals have been deprived; to the power of a small number of persons, which if it was sometimes oppressive was often conservative, has succeeded the weakness of the whole community.

The division of property has lessened the distance which separated the rich from the poor; but it would seem that, the nearer they draw to each other, the greater is their mutual hatred and the more vehement the envy and the dread with which they resist each other's claims to power; the idea of right does not exist for either party, and force affords to both the only argument for the present and the only guarantee for the future.

The poor man retains the prejudices of his forefathers without their faith, and their ignorance without their virtues; he has adopted the doctrine of self-interest as the rule of his actions without understanding the science that puts it to use; and his selfishness is no less blind than was formerly his devotion to others.

If society is tranquil, it is not because it is conscious of its strength and its well-being, but because it fears its weakness and its infirmities; a single effort may cost it its life. Everybody feels the evil, but no one has courage or energy enough to seek the cure. The desires, the repinings, the sorrows, and the joys of the present time lead to nothing visible or permanent, like the passions of old men, which terminate in impotence.

We have, then, abandoned whatever advantages the old state of things afforded, without receiving any compensation from our present condition; we have destroyed an aristocracy, and we seem inclined to survey its ruins with complacency and to accept them.

The phenomena which the intellectual world presents are not less deplorable. The democracy of France, hampered in its course or abandoned to its lawless passions, has overthrown whatever crossed its path and has shaken all that it has not destroyed. Its empire has not been gradually introduced or peaceably established, but it has constantly advanced in the midst of the disorders and the agitations of a conflict. In the heat of the struggle each partisan is hurried beyond the natural limits of his opinions by the doctrines and the excesses of his opponents, until he loses sight of the end of his exertions, and holds forth in a way which does not correspond to his real sentiments or secret instincts. Hence arises the strange confusion that we are compelled to witness.

I can recall nothing in history more worthy of sorrow and pity than the scenes which are passing before our eyes. It is as if the natural bond that unites the opinions of man to his tastes, and his actions to his principles, was now broken; the harmony that has always been observed between the feelings and the ideas of mankind appears to be dissolved and all the laws of moral analogy to be abolished.

Zealous Christians are still found among us, whose minds are nurtured on the thoughts that pertain to a future life, and who readily espouse the cause of human liberty as the source of all moral greatness. Christianity, which has declared that all men are equal in the sight of God, will not refuse to acknowledge that all citizens are equal in the eye of the law. But, by a strange coincidence of events, religion has been for a time entangled with those institutions which democracy destroys; and it is not infrequently brought to reject the equality which it loves, and to curse as a foe that cause of liberty whose efforts it might hallow by its alliance.

By the side of these religious men I discern others whose thoughts are turned to earth rather than to heaven. These are the partisans of liberty, not only as the source of the noblest virtues, but more especially as the root of all solid advantages; and they sincerely desire to secure its authority, and to impart its blessings to mankind. It is natural that they should hasten to invoke the assistance of religion, for they must know that liberty cannot be established without morality, nor morality without faith. But they have seen religion in the ranks of their adversaries, and they inquire no further; some of them attack it openly, and the rest are afraid to defend it.

In former ages slavery was advocated by the venal and slavish-minded, while the independent and the warm-hearted were struggling without hope to save the liberties of mankind. But men of high and generous character are now to be met with, whose opinions are directly at variance with their inclinations, and who praise that servility and meanness which they have themselves never known. Others, on the contrary, speak of liberty as if they were able to feel its sanctity and its majesty, and loudly claim for humanity those rights which they have always refused to acknowledge.

There are virtuous and peaceful individuals whose pure morality, quiet habits, opulence, and talents fit them to be the leaders of their fellow men. Their love of country is sincere, and they are ready to make the greatest sacrifices for its welfare. But civilization often finds them among its opponents; they confound its abuses with its benefits, and the idea of evil is inseparable in their minds from that of novelty.

Near these I find others whose object is to materialize mankind, to hit upon what is expedient without heeding what is just, to acquire knowledge without faith, and prosperity apart from virtue; claiming to be the champions of modern civilization, they place themselves arrogantly at its head, usurping a place which is abandoned to them, and of which they are wholly unworthy.

Where are we, then?

The religionists are the enemies of liberty, and the friends of liberty attack religion; the high-minded and the noble advocate bondage, and the meanest and most servile preach independence; honest and enlightened citizens are opposed to all progress, while men without patriotism and without principle put themselves forward as the apostles of civilization and intelligence.

Has such been the fate of the centuries which have preceded our own? and has man always inhabited a world like the present, where all things are not in their proper relationships, where virtue is without genius, and genius without honor; where the love of order is confused with a taste for oppression, and the holy cult of freedom with a contempt of law; where the light thrown by conscience on human actions is dim, and where nothing seems to be any longer forbidden or allowed, honorable or shameful, false or true?

I cannot believe that the Creator made man to leave him in an endless struggle with the intellectual wretchedness that surrounds us. God destines a calmer and a more certain future to the communities of Europe. I am ignorant of his designs, but I shall not cease to believe in them because I cannot fathom them, and I had rather mistrust my own capacity than his justice.

There is one country in the world where the great social revolution that I am speaking of seems to have nearly reached its natural limits. It has been effected with ease and simplicity; say rather that this country is reaping the fruits of the democratic revolution which we are undergoing, without having had the revolution itself.

The emigrants who colonized the shores of America in the beginning of the seventeenth century somehow separated the democratic principle from all the principles that it had to contend with in the old communities of Europe, and transplanted it alone to the New World. It has there been able to spread in perfect freedom and peaceably to determine the character of the laws by influencing the manners of the country.

It appears to me beyond a doubt that, sooner or later, we shall arrive, like the Americans, at an almost complete equality of condition. But I do not conclude from this that we shall ever be necessarily led to draw the same political consequences which the Americans have derived from a similar social organization. I am far from supposing that they have chosen the only form of government which a democracy may adopt; but as the generating cause of laws and manners in the two countries is the same, it is of immense interest for us to know what it has produced in each of them.

It is not, then, merely to satisfy a curiosity, however legitimate, that I have examined America; my wish has been to find there instruction by which we may ourselves profit. Whoever should imagine that I have intended to write a panegyric would be strangely mistaken, and on reading this book he will perceive that such was not my design; nor has it been my object to advocate any form of government in particular, for I am of the opinion that absolute perfection is rarely to be found in any system of laws. I have not even pretended to judge whether the social revolution, which I believe to be irresistible, is advantageous or prejudicial to mankind. I have acknowledged this revolution as a fact already accomplished, or on the eve of its accomplishment; and I have selected the nation, from among those which have undergone it, in which its development has been the most peaceful and the most complete, in order to discern its natural consequences and to find out, if possible, the means of rendering it profitable to mankind. I confess that in America I saw more than America; I sought there the image of democracy itself, with its inclinations, its character, its prejudices, and its passions, in order to learn what we have to fear or to hope from its progress.

In the first part of this work I have attempted to show the distinction that democracy, dedicated to its inclinations and tendencies and abandoned almost without restraint to its instincts, gave to the laws the course it impressed on the government, and in general the control which it exercised over affairs of state. I have sought to discover the evils and the advantages which it brings. I have examined the safeguards used by the Americans to direct it, as well as those that they have not adopted, and I have undertaken to point out the factors which enable it to govern society.

My object was to portray, in a second part, the influence which the equality of conditions and democratic government in America exercised on civil society, on habits, ideas, and customs; but I grew less enthusiastic about carrying out this plan. Before I could have completed the task which I set for myself, my work would have become purposeless. Someone else would before long set forth to the public the principal traits of the American character and, delicately cloaking a serious picture, lend to the truth a charm which I should not have been able to equal.

I do not know whether I have succeeded in making known what I saw in America, but I am certain that such has been my sincere desire, and that I have never, knowingly, molded facts to ideas, instead of ideas to facts.

Whenever a point could be established by the aid of written documents, I have had recourse to the original text, and to the most authentic and reputable works. I have cited my authorities in the notes, and anyone may verify them. Whenever opinions, political customs, or remarks on the manners of the country were concerned, I have endeavored to consult the most informed men I met with. If the point in question was important or doubtful, I was not satisfied with one witness, but I formed my opinion on the evidence of several witnesses. Here the reader must necessarily rely upon my word. I could frequently have cited names which either are known to him or deserve to be so in support of my assertions; but I have carefully abstained from this practice. A stranger frequently hears important truths at the fireside of his host, which the latter would perhaps conceal from the ear of friendship; he consoles himself with his guest for the silence to which he is restricted, and the shortness of the traveler's stay takes away all fear of an indiscretion. I carefully noted every conversation of this nature as soon as it occurred, but these notes will never leave my writing-case. I had rather injure the success of my statements than add my name to the list of those strangers who repay generous hospitality they have received by subsequent chagrin and annoyance.

*   *   *

SEYMOUR MARTIN LIPSET

ECONOMIC DEVELOPMENT AND DEMOCRACY

*   *   *

Economic Development in Europe and the Americas

Perhaps the most common generalization linking political systems to other aspects of society has been that democracy is related to the state of economic development. The more well-to-do a nation, the greater the chances that it will sustain democracy. From Aristotle down to the present, men have argued that only in a wealthy society in which relatively few citizens lived at the level of real poverty could there be a situation in which the mass of the population intelligently participate in politics and develop the self-restraint necessary to avoid succumbing to the appeals of irresponsible demagogues. A society divided between a large impoverished mass and a small favored elite results either in oligarchy (dictatorial rule of the small upper stratum) or in tyranny (popular-based dictatorship). To give these two political forms modern labels, tyranny's face today is communism or Peronism; while oligarchy appears in the traditionalist dictatorships found in parts of Latin America, Thailand, Spain, or Portugal.

To test this hypothesis concretely, I have used various indices of economic development—wealth, industrialization, urbanization, and education—and computed averages (means) for the countries which have been classified as more or less democratic in the Anglo-Saxon world and Europe, and in Latin America.

In each case, the average wealth, degree of

From Seymour Martin Lipset, *Political Man* (Garden City, N.Y.: Doubleday, 1960), pp. 31–51. Some of the author's notes have been omitted.

industrialization and urbanization, and level of education is much higher for the more democratic countries, as the data in Table I indicate. If I had combined Latin America and Europe in one table, the differences would have been even greater.

The main indices of *wealth* used are per capita income, number of persons per motor vehicle and thousands of persons per physician, and the number of radios, telephones, and newspapers per thousand persons. The differences are striking on every score (See Table I). In the more democratic European countries, there are 17 persons per motor vehicle compared to 143 for the less democratic. In the less dictatorial Latin-American countries there are 99 persons per motor vehicle versus 274 for the more dictatorial.[1] Income differences for the groups are also sharp, dropping from an average per capita income of $695 for the more democratic countries of Europe to $308 for the less democratic; the corresponding difference for Latin America is from $171 to $119. The ranges are equally consistent, with the lowest per capita income in each group falling in the "less democratic" category, and the highest in the "more democratic."

Industrialization, to which indices of wealth are of course clearly related, is measured by the percentage of employed males in agriculture and the per capita commercially produced "energy" being used in the country (measured in terms of tons of coal per person per year). Both of these show equally consistent results. The average percentage of employed males working in agriculture and related occupations was 21 in the "more democratic" European countries and 41 in the "less democratic"; 52 in the "less dictatorial" Latin-American countries and 67 in the "more dictatorial." The differences in per capita energy employed are equally large.

The degree of *urbanization* is also related to the existence of democracy.[2] Three different indices of urbanization are available from data compiled by International Urban Research (Berkeley, California): the percentage of the population in communities of 20,000 and over, the percentage in communities of 100,000 and over, and the percentage residing in standard metropolitan areas. On all three of these indices the more democratic countries score higher than the less democratic for both of the areas under investigation.

Many people have suggested that the higher the *education* level of a nation's population, the better the chances for democracy, and the comparative data available support this proposition. The "more democratic" countries of Europe are almost entirely literate: the lowest has a rate of 96 per cent; while the "less democratic"[3] nations have an average rate of 85 per cent. In Latin America the difference is between an average rate of 74 per cent for the "less dictatorial" countries and 46 per cent for the "more dictatorial."[3] The educational enrollment per thousand total population at three different levels—primary, post-primary, and higher educational—is equally consistently related to the degree of democracy. The tremendous disparity is shown by the extreme cases of Haiti and the United States. Haiti has fewer children (11 per thousand) attending school in the primary grades than the United States has attending colleges (almost 18 per thousand).

The relationship between education and democracy is worth more extensive treatment since an entire philosophy of government has seen increased education as the basic requirement of democracy.[4] As James Bryce wrote, with special reference to South America, "education,

Table 1. A Comparison of European, English-speaking, and Latin-American Countries, Divided into Two Groups, "More Democratic" and "Less Democratic," by Indices of Wealth, Industrialization, Education, and Urbanization

A. Indices of Wealth

Means	Per Capita Income	Thousands of Persons per Doctor	Persons per Motor Vehicle
European and English-speaking Stable Democracies	U.S.$ 695	.86	17
European and English-speaking Unstable Democracies and Dictatorships	308	1.4	143
Latin-American Democracies and Unstable Dictatorships	171	2.1	99
Latin-American Stable Dictatorships	119	4.4	274
Ranges			
European Stable Democracies	420–1,453	.7–1.2	3–62
European Dictatorships	128–482	.6–4	10–538
Latin-American Democracies	112–346	.8–3.3	31–174
Latin-American Stable Dictatorships	40–331	1.0–10.8	38–428

Table 1. A Comparison of European, English-speaking, and Latin-American Countries, Divided into Two Groups, "More Democratic" and "Less Democratic," by Indices of Wealth, Industrialization, Education, and Urbanization (cont.)

Means	Telephones per 1,000 Persons	Radios per 1,000 Persons	Newspaper Copies per 1,000 Persons
European and English-speaking Stable Democracies	205	350	341
European and English-speaking Unstable Democracies and Dictatorships	58	160	167
Latin-American Democracies and Unstable Dictatorships	25	85	102
Latin-American Stable Dictatorships	10	43	43
Ranges			
European Stable Democracies	43–400	160–995	242–570
European Dictatorships	7–196	42–307	46–390
Latin-Amercian Democracies	12–58	38–148	51–233
Latin-American Stable Dictatorships	1–24	4–154	4–111

1B. Indices of Industrialization

Means	Percentage of Males in Agriculture	Per Capita Energy Consumed
European Stable Democracies	21	3.6
European Dictatorships	41	1.4
Latin-American Democracies	52	.6
Latin-American Stable Dictatorships	67	.25
Ranges		
European Stable Democracies	6–46	1.4–7.8
European Dictatorships	16–60	.27–3.2
Latin-American Democracies	30–63	.30–0.9
Latin-American Stable Dictatorships	46–87	.02–1.27

1C. Indices of Education

Means	Percentage Literate	Primary Education Enrollment per 1,000 Persons	Post-Primary Enrollment per 1,000 Persons	Higher Education Enrollment per 1,000 Persons
European Stable Democracies	96	134	44	4.2
European Dictatorships	85	121	22	3.5
Latin-American Democracies	74	101	13	2.0
Latin-American Dictatorships	46	72	8	1.3
Ranges				
European Stable Democracies	95–100	96–179	19–83	1.7–17.83
European Dictatorships	55–98	61–165	8–37	1.6–6.1
Latin-American Democracies	48–87	75–137	7–27	.7–4.6
Latin-American Dictatorshps	11–76	11–149	3–24	.2–3.1

1D. Indices in Urbanization

Means	Per Cent in Cities over 20,000	Per Cent in Cities over 100,000	Per Cent in Metropolitan Areas
European Stable Democracies	43	28	38
European Dictatorships	24	16	23
Latin-American Democracies	28	22	26
Latin-American Stable Dictatorships	17	12	15
Ranges			
European Stable Democracies	28–54	17–51	22–56
European Dictatorships	12–44	6–33	7–49
Latin-American Democracies	11–48	13–37	17–44
Latin-American Stable Dictatorships	5–36	4–22	7–26

if it does not make men good citizens, makes it at least easier for them to become so."[5] Education presumably broadens man's outlook, enables him to understand the need for norms of tolerance, restrains him from adhering to extremist doctrines, and increases his capacity to make rational electoral choices.

The evidence on the contribution of education to democracy is even more direct and strong on the level of individual behavior *within* countries than it is in cross-national correlations. Data gathered by public opinion research agencies which have questioned people in different countries about their beliefs on tolerance for the opposition, their attitudes toward ethnic or racial minorities, and their feelings for multiparty as against one-party systems have showed that the most important single factor differentiating those giving democratic responses from the others has been education. The higher one's education, the more likely one is to believe in democratic values and support democratic practices.[6] All the relevant studies indicate that education is more significant than either income or occupation.

These findings should lead us to anticipate a far higher correlation between national levels of education and political practice than we in fact find. Germany and France have been among the best educated nations of Europe, but this by itself did not stabilize their democracies.[7] It may be, however, that their educational level has served to inhibit other anti-democratic forces.

If we cannot say that a "high" level of education is a *sufficient* condition for democracy, the available evidence suggests that it comes close to being a *necessary* one. In Latin America, where widespread illiteracy still exists, only one of all the nations in which more than half the population is illiterate—Brazil—can be included in the "more democratic" group.

Lebanon, the one member of the Arab League which has maintained democratic institutions since World War II, is also by far the best educated (over 80 per cent literacy). East of the Arab world, only two states, the Philippines and Japan, have since 1945 maintained democratic regimes without the presence of large anti-democratic parties. And these two countries, although lower than most European states in per capita income, are among the world's leaders in educational attainment. The Philippines actually rank second to the United States in the proportion of people attending high schools and universities, and Japan has a higher educational level than any European nation.[8]

Although the evidence has been presented separately, all the various aspects of economic development—industrialization, urbanization, wealth, and education—are so closely interrelated as to form one major factor which has the political correlate of democracy.[9] A recent study of the Middle East further substantiates this. In 1951–52, a survey of Turkey, Lebanon, Egypt, Syria, Jordan, and Iran, conducted by Daniel Lerner and the Bureau of Applied Social Research, found a close connection between urbanization, literacy, voting rates, media consumption and production, and education.[10] Simple and multiple correlations between the four basic variables were computed for all countries for which United Nations statistic were available (in this case 54) with the following results:[11]

Dependent Variable	Multiple Correlation Coefficient
Urbanization	.61
Literacy	.91
Media Participation	.84
Political Participation	.82

In the Middle East, Turkey and Lebanon score higher on most of these indices than do the other four countries analyzed, and Daniel Lerner, in reporting on the study, points out that the "great post-war events in Egypt, Syria, Jordan and Iran have been the violent struggles for the control of power—struggles notably absent in Turkey and Lebanon [until very recently] where the control of power has been decided by elections."[12]

Lerner further points out the effect of disproportionate development, in one area or another, for over-all stability, and the need for co-ordinated changes in all of these variables. Comparing urbanization and literacy in Egypt and Turkey, he concludes that although Egypt is far more urbanized than Turkey, it is not really "modernized," and does not even have an adequate base for modernization, because literacy has not kept pace. In Turkey, all of the several indices of modernization have kept pace with each other, with rising voting participation (36 per cent in 1950), balanced by rising literacy, urbanization, etc. In Egypt, the cities are full of "homeless illiterates," who provide a ready audience for political mobilization in support of extremist ideologies. On Lerner's scale, Egypt should be twice as literate as Turkey, since it is twice as urbanized. The fact that it is only half as literate explains, for Lerner, the "imbalances" which "tend to become circular and to accelerate social disorganization," political as well as economic.[13]

Lerner introduces one important theoretical addition—the suggestion that these key variables in the modernization process may be viewed as historical phases, with democracy part of later developments, the "crowning institution of the participant society" (one of his terms for a modern industrial society). His view on the relations between these variables, seen as stages, is worth quoting at some length:

> The secular evolution of a participant society appears to involve a regular sequence of three phases. Urbanization comes first, for cities alone have developed the complex of skills and resources which characterize the modern industrial economy. Within this urban matrix develop both of the attributes which distinguish the next two phases—literacy and media growth. There is a close reciprocal relationship between these, for the literate develop the media which in turn spread literacy. But, literacy performs the key function in the second phase. The capacity to read, at first acquired by relatively few people, equips them to perform the varied tasks required in the modernizing society. Not until the third phase, when the elaborate technology of industrial development is fairly well advanced, does a society begin to produce newspapers, radio networks, and motion pictures on a massive scale. This, in turn, accelerates the spread of literacy. Out of this interaction develop those institutions of participation (e.g., voting) which we find in all advanced modern societies.[14]

Lerner's thesis, that these elements of modernization are functionally interdependent, is by no means established by his data. But the material presented in this chapter offers an opportunity for research along these lines. Deviant cases, such as Egypt, where "lagging" literacy is associated with serious strains and potential upheaval, may also be found in Europe and Latin America, and their analysis—a task not attempted here—will further clarify the basic dynamics of modernization and the problem of social stability in the midst of institutional change.

Economic Development and the Class Struggle

Economic development, producing increased income, greater economic security, and widespread higher education, largely determines the form of the "class struggle," by permitting those in the lower strata to develop longer time perspectives and more complex and gradualist views of politics. A belief in secular reformist gradualism can be the ideology of only a relatively well-to-do lower class. Striking evidence for this thesis may be found in the relationship between the patterns of working-class political action in different countries and the national income, a correlation that is almost startling in view of the many other cultural, historical, and juridical factors which affect the political life of nations.

In the two wealthiest countries, the United States and Canada, not only are communist parties almost nonexistent but socialist parties have never been able to establish themselves as major forces. Among the eight next wealthiest countries—New Zealand, Switzerland, Sweden, United Kingdom, Denmark, Australia, Norway, Belgium, Luxembourg and Netherlands—all of whom had a per capita income of over $500 a year in 1949 (the last year for which standardized United Nations statistics exist), moderate socialism predominates as the form of leftist politics. In none of these countries did the Communists secure more than 7 per cent of the vote, and the actual Communist party average among them has been about 4 per cent. In the eight European countries which were below the $500 per capita income mark in 1949—France, Iceland, Czechoslovakia, Finland, West Germany, Hungary, Italy, and Austria—and which have had at least one postwar democratic election in which both communist and noncommunist parties could compete, the Communist party has had more than 16 per cent of the vote in six, and an over-all average of more than 20 per cent in the eight countries as a group. The two low-income countries in which the Communists are weak—Germany and Austria—have both had direct experience with Soviet occupation.[15]

Leftist extremism has also dominated working-class politics in two other European nations which belong to the under $500 per capita income group—Spain and Greece. In Spain before Franco, anarchism and left socialism were much stronger than moderate socialism; while in Greece, whose per capita income in 1949 was only $128, the Communists have always been much stronger than the socialists, and fellow-traveling parties have secured a large vote in recent years.

The inverse relationship between national economic development as reflected by per capita income and the strength of Communists and other extremist groups among Western nations is seemingly stronger than the correlations between other national variables like ethnic or religious factors.[16] Two of the poorer nations with large Communist movements—Iceland and Finland—are Scandinavian and Lutheran. Among the Catholic nations of Europe, all the poor ones except Austria have large Communist or anarchist movements. The two wealthiest Catholic democracies—Belgium and Luxembourg—have few Communists. Though the French and Italian can-

tons of Switzerland are strongly affected by the cultural life of France and Italy, there are almost no Communists among the workers in these cantons, living in the wealthiest country in Europe.

The relation between low per capita wealth and the precipitation of sufficient discontent to provide the social basis for political extremism is supported by a recent comparative polling survey of the attitudes of citizens of nine countries. Among these countries, feelings of personal security correlated with per capita income (.45) and with per capita food supply (.55). If satisfaction with one's country, as measured by responses to the question, "Which country in the world gives you the best chance of living the kind of life you would like to live?" is used as an index of the amount of discontent in a nation, then the relationship with economic wealth is even higher. The study reports a rank order correlation of .74 between per capita income and the degree of satisfaction with one's own country.[17]

This does not mean that economic hardship or poverty *per se* is the main cause of radicalism. There is much evidence to sustain the argument that stable poverty in a situation in which individuals are not exposed to the possibilities of change breeds, if anything, conservatism.[18] Individuals whose experience limits their significant communications and interaction to others on the same level as themselves will, other conditions being equal, be more conservative than people who may be better off but who have been exposed to the possibilities of securing a better way of life.[19] The dynamic in the situation would seem to be exposure to the possibility of a better way of life rather than poverty as such. As Karl Marx put it in a perceptive passage: "A house may be large or small; as long as the surrounding houses are equally small it satisfies all social demands for a dwelling. But if a palace arises beside the little house, the little house shrinks into a hut."[20]

With the growth of modern means of communication and transportation both within and among countries, it seems increasingly likely that the groups in the population that are poverty-stricken but are isolated from knowledge of better ways of life or unaware of the possibilities for improvement in their condition are becoming rarer and rarer, particularly in the urban areas of the Western world. One may expect to find such stable poverty only in tradition-dominated societies.

Since position in a stratification system is always relative and gratification or deprivation is experienced in terms of being better or worse off than other people, it is not surprising that the lower classes in all countries, regardless of the wealth of the country, show various signs of resentment against the existing distribution of rewards by supporting political parties and other organizations which advocate some form of redistribution.[21] The fact that the form which these political parties take in poorer countries is more extremist and radical than it is in wealthier ones is probably more related to the greater degree of inequality in such countries than to the fact that their poor are actually poorer in absolute terms. A comparative study of wealth distribution by the United Nations "suggest[s] that the richest fraction of the population (the richest 10th, 5th, etc.) generally receive[s] a greater proportion of the total income in the less developed than in the more developed countries."[22] The gap between the income of professional and semi-professional personnel on the one hand and ordinary workers on the other is much wider in the poorer than in the wealthier countries. Among manual workers, "there seems to be a greater wage discrepancy between skilled and unskilled workers in the less developed countries. In contrast the leveling process, in several of the developed countries at least, has been facilitated by the over-all increase of national income . . . not so much by reduction of the income of the relatively rich as by the faster growth of the incomes of the relatively poor."[23]

The distribution of consumption goods also tends to become more equitable as the size of national income increases. The wealthier a country, the larger the proportion of its population which owns automobiles, telephones, bathtubs,

refrigerating equipment, and so forth. Where there is a dearth of goods, the sharing of such goods must inevitably be less equitable than in a country in which there is relative abundance. For example, the number of people who can afford automobiles, washing machines, decent housing, telephones, good clothes, or have their children complete high school or go to college still represents only a small minority of the population in many European countries. The great national wealth of the United States or Canada, or even to a lesser extent the Australasian Dominions or Sweden, means that there is relatively little difference between the standards of living of adjacent social classes, and that even classes which are far apart in the social structure will enjoy more nearly similar consumption patterns than will comparable classes in Southern Europe. To a Southern European, and to an even greater extent to the inhabitant of one of the "underdeveloped" countries, social stratification is characterized by a much greater distinction in ways of life, with little overlap in the goods the various strata own or can afford to purchase. It may be suggested, therefore, that the wealthier a country, the less is status inferiority experienced as a major source of deprivation.

Increased wealth and education also serve democracy by increasing the lower classes' exposure to cross-pressures which reduce their commitment to given ideologies and make them less receptive to extremist ones. The operation of this process will be discussed in more detail in the next chapter, but it means involving those strata in an integrated national culture as distinct from an isolated lower-class one.

Marx believed that the proletariat was a revolutionary force because it had nothing to lose but its chains and could win the whole world. But Tocqueville, analyzing the reasons why the lower strata in America supported the system, paraphrased and transposed Marx before Marx ever made his analysis by pointing out that "only those who have nothing to lose ever revolt."[24]

Increased wealth also affects the political role of the middle class by changing the shape of the stratification structure from an elongated pyramid, with a large lower-class base, to a diamond with a growing middle class. A large middle class tempers conflict by rewarding moderate and democratic parties and penalizing extremist groups.

The political values and style of the upper class, too, are related to national income. The poorer a country and the lower the absolute standard of living of the lower classes, the greater the pressure on the upper strata to treat the lower as vulgar, innately inferior, a lower caste beyond the pale of human society. The sharp difference in the style of living between those at the top and those at the bottom makes this psychologically necessary. Consequently, the upper strata in such a situation tend to regard political rights for the lower strata, particularly the right to share power, as essentially absurd and immoral. The upper strata not only resist democracy themselves; their often arrogant political behavior serves to intensify extremist reactions on the part of the lower classes.

The general income level of a nation also affects its receptivity to democratic norms. If there is enough wealth in the country so that it does not make too much difference whether some redistribution takes place, it is easier to accept the idea that it does not matter greatly which side is in power. But if loss of office means serious losses for major power groups, they will seek to retain or secure office by any means available. A certain amount of national wealth is likewise necessary to ensure a competent civil service. The poorer the country, the greater the emphasis on nepotism—support of kin and friends. And this in turn reduces the opportunity to develop the efficient bureaucracy which a modern democratic state requires.[25]

Intermediary organizations which act as sources of countervailing power seem to be similarly associated with national wealth. Tocqueville and other exponents of what has come to be known as the theory of the "mass society"[26] have argued that a country without a multitude of organizations relatively independent of the central

state power has a high dictatorial as well as revolutionary potential. Such organizations serve a number of functions: they inhibit the state or any single source of private power from dominating all political resources; they are a source of new opinions; they can be the means of communicating ideas, particularly opposition ideas, to a large section of the citizenry; they train men in political skills and so help to increase the level of interest and participation in politics. Although there are no reliable data on the relationship between national patterns of voluntary organization and national political systems, evidence from studies of individual behavior demonstrates that, regardless of other factors, men who belong to associations are more likely than others to give the democratic answer to questions concerning tolerance and party systems, to vote, or to participate actively in politics. Since the more well-to-do and better educated a man is, the more likely he is to belong to voluntary organizations, the propensity to form such groups seems to be a function of level of income and opportunities for leisure within given nations.[27]

The Politics of Rapid Economic Development

The association between economic development and democracy has led many Western statesmen and political commentators to conclude that the basic political problem of our day is produced by the pressure for rapid industrialization. If only the underdeveloped nations can be successfully started on the road to high productivity, the assumption runs, we can defeat the major threat to newly established democracies, their domestic Communists. In a curious way, this view marks the victory of economic determinism or vulgar Marxism within democratic political thought. Unfortunately for this theory, political extremism based on the lower classes, communism in particular, is not to be found only in low-income countries but also in newly industrializing nations. This correlation is not, of course, a recent phenomenon. In 1884, Engels noted that explicitly socialist labor movements had developed in Europe during periods of rapid industrial growth, and that these movements declined sharply during later periods of slower change.

The pattern of leftist politics in northern Europe in the first half of the twentieth century in countries whose socialist and trade-union movements are now relatively moderate and conservative illustrates this point. Wherever industrialization occurred *rapidly*, introducing sharp *discontinuities* between the pre-industrial and industrial situation, more rather than less extremist working-class movements emerged. In Scandinavia, for example, the variations among the socialist movements of Denmark, Sweden, and Norway can be accounted for in large measure by the different timing and pace of industrialization, as the economist Walter Galenson has pointed out.[28] The Danish Social Democratic movement and trade-unions have always been in the reformist, moderate, and relatively non-Marxist wing of the international labor movement. In Denmark, industralization developed as a slow and gradual process. The rate of urban growth was also moderate, which had a good effect on urban working-class housing conditions. The slow growth of industry meant that a large proportion of Danish workers all during the period of industrialization were men who had been employed in industry for a long time, and, consequently, newcomers who had been pulled up from rural areas and who might have supplied the basis for extremist factions were always in a minority. The left-wing groups which gained some support in Denmark were based on the rapidly expanding industries.

In Sweden, on the other hand, manufacturing industry grew very rapidly from 1900 to 1914. This caused a sudden growth in the number of unskilled workers, largely recruited from rural areas, and the expansion of industrial rather than craft unions. Paralleling these developments in industry, a left-wing movement arose within the trade-unions and the Social Democratic party which opposed the moderate policies

that both had developed before the great industrial expansion. A strong anarcho-syndicalist movement also emerged in this period. Here again, these aggressive left-wing movements were based on the rapidly expanding industries.[29]

Norway, the last of the three Scandinavian countries to industrialize, had an even more rapid rate of growth. As a result of the emergence of hydroelectric power, the growth of an electrochemical industry, and the need for continued construction, Norway's industrial workers doubled between 1905 and 1920. And as in Sweden, this increase in the labor force meant that the traditional moderate craft-union movement was swamped by unskilled and semiskilled workers, most of whom were young migrants from rural areas. A left wing emerged within the Federation of Labor and the Labor party, capturing control of both in the latter stages of World War I. It should be noted that Norway was the only Western European country which was still in its phase of rapid industrialization when the Comintern was founded, and its Labor party was the only one which went over almost intact to the Communists.

In Germany before World War I, a revolutionary Marxist left wing, in large measure derived from workers in the rapidly growing industries, retained considerable support within the Social Democratic party, while the more moderate sections of the party were based on the more stable established industries.[30]

The most significant illustration of the relationship between rapid industrialization and working-class extremism is the Russian Revolution. In Czarist Russia, the industrial population jumped from 16 million in 1897 to 26 million in 1913.[31] Trotsky in his *History of the Russian Revolution* has shown how an increase in the strike rate and in union militancy paralleled the growth of industry. It is probably not coincidental that two nations in Europe in which the revolutionary left gained control of the dominant section of the labor movement before 1920—Russia and Norway—were also countries in which the processes of rapid capital accumulation and basic industrialization were still going on.[32]

The revolutionary socialist movements which arise in response to strains created by rapid industrialization decline, as Engels put it, wherever "the transition to large-scale industry is more or less completed . . . [and] the conditions in which the proletariat is placed become stable."[33] Such countries are, of course, precisely the industrialized nations where Marxism and revolutionary socialism exist today only as sectarian dogmas. In those nations of Europe where industrialization never occurred, or where it failed to build an economy of efficient large-scale industry with a high level of productivity and a constant increase in mass-consumption patterns, the conditions for the creation or perpetuation of extremist labor politics also exist.

A different type of extremism, based on the small entrepreneurial classes (both urban and rural), has emerged in the less developed and often culturally backward sectors of more industrialized societies. The social base of classic fascism seems to arise from the ever present vulnerability of part of the middle class, particularly small businessmen and farm owners, to large-scale capitalism and a powerful labor movement. Chapter 5 analyzes this reaction in detail as it is manifest in a number of countries.

It is obvious that the conditions related to stable democracy discussed here are most readily found in the countries of northwest Europe and their English-speaking offspring in America and Australasia; and it has been suggested, by Weber among others, that a historically unique concatenation of elements produced both democracy and capitalism in this area. Capitalist economic development, the basic argument runs, had its greatest opportunity in a Protestant society and created the burgher class whose existence was both a catalyst and a necessary condition for democracy. Protestantism's emphasis on individual responsibility furthered the emergence of democratic values in these countries and resulted in an alignment between the

burghers and the throne which preserved the monarchy and extended the acceptance of democracy among the conservative strata. Men may question whether any aspect of this interrelated cluster of economic development, Protestantism, monarchy, gradual political change, legitimacy, and democracy is primary, but the fact remains that the cluster does not hang together.

NOTES

1. It must be remembered that these figures are means, compiled from census figures for the various countries. The data vary widely in accuracy, and there is no way of measuring the validity of compound calculated figures such as those presented here. The consistent direction of all these differences, and their large magnitude, is the main indication of validity.

2. Urbanization has often been linked to democracy by political theorists. Harold J. Laski asserted that "organized democracy is the product of urban life," and that it was natural therefore that it should have "made its first effective appearance" in the Greek city states, limited as was their definition of "citizen." See his article "Democracy" in the *Encyclopedia of the Social Sciences* (New York: Macmillan, 1937), Vol. V, pp. 76–85. Max Weber held that the city, as a certain type of political community, is a peculiarly Western phenomenon, and traced the emergence of the notion of "citizenship" from social developments closely related to urbanization. For a partial statement of his point of view, see the chapter on "Citizenship" in *General Economic History* (Glencoe: The Free Press, 1950), pp. 315–38.

3. The pattern indicated by a comparison of the averages for each group of countries is sustained by the ranges (the high and low extremes) for each index. Most of the ranges overlap; that is, some countries which are in

the "less democratic" category are higher on any given index than some which are "more democratic." It is noteworthy that in both Europe and Latin America, the nations which are lowest on any of the indices presented in the table are also in the "less democratic" category. Conversely, almost all countries which rank at the top of any of the indices are in the "more democratic" class.

4. See John Dewey, *Democracy and Education* (New York: Macmillan, 1916).

5. James Bryce, *South America: Observations and Impressions* (New York: Macmillan, 1912), p. 546.

6. See G. H. Smith, "Liberalism and Level of Information," *Journal of Educational Psychology*, 39 (1948), pp. 65–82; Martin A. Trow, *Right Wing Radicalism and Political Intolerance* (Ph.D. thesis, Department of Sociology, Columbia University, 1957), p. 17; Samuel A. Stouffer, *Communism, Conformity, and Civil Liberties* (New York: Doubleday & Co., Inc., 1955); Kotaro Kido and Masataka Sugi, "A Report of Research on Social Stratification and Mobility in Tokyo" (III), *Japanese Sociological Review*, 4 (1954), pp. 74–100.

7. Dewey has suggested that the character of the educational system will influence its effect on democracy, and this may shed some light on the sources of instability in Germany. The purpose of German education, according to Dewey, writing in 1916, was one of "disciplinary training rather than of personal development." The main aim was to produce "absorption of the aims and meaning of existing institutions," and "thoroughgoing subordination" to them. See John Dewey, *op. cit.*, pp. 108–10.

8. Ceylon, which shares the distinction with the Philippines and Japan of being the only democratic countries in South and Far East Asia in which the communists are unimportant electorally, also shares with them the distinction of being the only countries in this area in which a *majority* of the popula-

tion is literate. It should be noted, however, that Ceylon does have a fairly large Trotskyist party, now the official opposition, and while its educational level is high for Asia, it is much lower than either Japan or the Philippines.

9. This statement is a "statistical" statement, which necessarily means that there will be many exceptions to the correlation. Thus we know that poorer people are more likely to vote for the Democratic or Labor parties in the U.S. and England. The fact that a large minority of the lower strata vote for the more conservative party in these countries does not challenge the proposition that stratification position is a main determinant of party choice.

10. The study is reported in Daniel Lerner's *The Passing of Traditional Society* (Glencoe: The Free Press, 1958). These correlations are derived from census data; the main sections of the survey dealt with reactions to and opinions about the mass media, with inferences as to the personality types appropriate to modern and to traditional society.

11. *Ibid.*, p. 63. The index of political participation was the per cent voting in the last five elections. These results cannot be considered as independent verification of the relationships presented in this paper, since the data and variables are basically the same, but the identical results using three entirely different methods, the phi coefficient, multiple correlations, and means and ranges, show decisively that the relationships cannot be attributed to artifacts of the computations. It should also be noted that the three analyses were made without knowledge of each other.

12. *Ibid.*, pp. 84–85.

13. *Ibid.*, pp. 87–89. Other theories of underdeveloped areas have also stressed the circular character of the forces sustaining a given level of economic and social development, and in a sense this paper may be regarded as an effort to extend the analysis of the com-

plex of institutions constituting a "modernized" society to the political sphere.

14. Lerner, *op. cit.*, p. 60.

15. It should be noted that before 1933–34, Germany had one of the largest Communist parties in Europe; while the Socialist party of Austria was the most left-wing and Marxist European party in the Socialist International.

16. The relationship expressed above can be presented in another way. The seven European countries in which Communist or fellow-traveling parties have secured large votes in free elections had an average per capita income in 1949 of $330. The ten European countries in which the Communists have been a failure electorally had an average per capita income of $585.

17. William Buchanan and Hadley Cantril, *How Nations See Each Other* (Urbana: University of Illinois Press, 1953), p. 35.

18. See Emile Durkheim, *Suicide: A Study in Sociology* (Glencoe: The Free Press, 1951), pp. 253–54; see also Daniel Bell, "The Theory of Mass Society," *Commentary*, 22 (1956), p. 80.

19. There is also a considerable body of evidence which indicates that those occupations which are economically vulnerable and those workers who have experienced unemployment are prone to be more leftist in their outlook.

20. Karl Marx, "Wage-Labor and Capital," in *Selected Works*, Vol. I (New York: International Publishers, 1933), pp. 268–69. "Social tensions are an expression of unfulfilled expectations," Daniel Bell, *op. cit.*, p. 80.

21. A summary of the findings of election studies in many countries shows that, with few exceptions, there is a strong relationship between lower social position and support of "leftist" politics. There are, of course, many other characteristics which are also related to left voting, some of which are found among relatively well paid but socially isolated groups. Among the population as a whole, men are much more likely to vote for the left than women, while members of minority religious and ethnic groups also display a leftist tendency.

22. *United Nations Preliminary Report on the World Social Situation* (New York: 1952), pp. 132–33. Gunnar Myrdal, the Swedish economist, has recently pointed out: "It is, indeed, a regular occurrence endowed almost with the dignity of an economic law that the poorer the country, the greater the difference between poor and rich." *An International Economy* (New York: Harper & Bros., 1956), p. 133.

23. *United Nations Preliminary Report . . . , ibid.* A recently completed comparison of income distribution in the United States and a number of western European countries concludes that "there has not been any great difference" in patterns of income distribution among these countries. These findings of Robert Solow appear to contradict those reported above from the U.N. Statistics Office, although the latter are dealing primarily with differences between industrialized and underdeveloped nations. In any case, it should be noted that Solow agrees that the relative position of the lower strata in a poor as compared with a wealthy country is quite different. As he states, "in comparing Europe and America, one may ask whether it makes sense to talk about relative income inequality independently of the absolute level of income. An income four times another income has different content according as the lower income means malnutrition on the one hand or provides some surplus on the other." Robert M. Solow, *A Survey of Income Inequality Since the War* (Stanford: Center for Advanced Study in the Behavioral Sciences, 1958, mimeographed), pp. 41–44, 78.

24. Alexis de Tocqueville, *Democracy in America*, Vol. I (New York: Alfred A. Knopf, Vintage ed., 1945), p. 258.

25. For a discussion of this problem in a new state, see David Apter, *The Gold Coast in*

Transition (Princeton: Princeton University Press, 1955), esp. Chaps. 9 and 13. Apter shows the importance of efficient bureaucracy, and the acceptance of bureaucratic values and behavior patterns for the existence of a democratic political order.

26. See Emil Lederer, *The State of the Masses* (New York: Norton, 1940); Hannah Arendt, *Origins of Totalitarianism* (New York: Harcourt, Brace & Co., 1951); Max Horkheimer, *Eclipse of Reason* (New York: Oxford University Press, 1947); Karl Mannheim, *Man and Society in an Age of Reconstruction* (New York: Harcourt, Brace & Co., 1940); Philip Selznick, *The Organizational Weapon* (New York: McGraw-Hill Book Co., 1952); José Ortega y Gasset, *The Revolt of the Masses* (New York: Norton, 1932); William Kornhauser, *The Politics of Mass Society* (Glencoe: The Free Press, 1959).

27. See Edward Banfield, *The Moral Basis of a Backward Society* (Glencoe: The Free Press, 1958), for an excellent description of the way in which abysmal poverty serves to reduce community organization in southern Italy. The data which do exist from polling surveys conducted in the United States, Germany, France, Great Britain, and Sweden show that somewhere between 40 and 50 per cent of the adults in these countries belong to voluntary associations, without lower rates of membership for the less stable democracies, France and Germany, than among the more stable ones, the United States, Great Britain, and Sweden. These results seemingly challenge the general proposition, although no definite conclusion can be made, since most of the studies employed noncomparable categories. This point bears further research in many countries.

28. See Walter Galenson, *The Danish System of Labor Relations* (Cambridge: Harvard University Press, 1952); see also Galenson, "Scandinavia," in Galenson, ed., *Comparative Labor Movements* (New York: Prentice-Hall, 1952), esp. pp. 105–20.

29. See Rudolf Heberle, *Zur Geschichte der Arbeiter-bewegung in Schweden*, Vol. 39 of *Probleme der Weltwirtschaft* (Jena: Gustav Fischer, 1925).

30. See Ossip Flechtheim, *Die KPD in der Weimarer Republik* (Offenbach am Main: Bollwerk-Verlag Karl Drott, 1948), pp. 213–14; see also Rose Laub Coser, *An Analysis of the Early German Socialist Movement* (unpublished M.A. thesis, Department of Sociology, Columbia University, 1951).

31. Colin Clark, *The Conditions of Economic Progress* (London: Macmillan, 1952), p. 421.

32. The Communists also controlled the Greek trade-unions and Socialist Labor party. The Greek case while fitting this pattern is not completely comparable, since no real pre-Communist labor movement existed and a pro-Bolshevik movement arose from a combination of the discontents of workers in the war-created new industry and the enthusiasm occasioned by the Russian Revolution.

33. Friedrich Engels, "Letter to Karl Kautsky," Nov. 8, 1884, in Karl Marx and Friedrich Engels, *Correspondence 1846–1895* (New York: International Publishers, 1946), p. 422; see also Val R. Lorwin, "Working-class Politics and Economic Development in Western Europe," *American Historical Review*, 63 (1958), pp. 338–51; for an excellent discussion of the effects of rapid industrialization on politics, see also Reinhold Niebuhr, *The Irony of American History* (New York: Charles Scribner's Sons, 1952), pp. 112–18.

MAURICE DUVERGER

THE NUMBER OF PARTIES

*   *   *

Only individual investigation of the circumstances in each country can determine the real origins of the two-party system. The influence of such national factors is certainly very considerable; but we must not in their *favour* underestimate the importance of one general factor of a technical kind, the electoral system. Its effect can be expressed in the following formula: *the simple-majority single-ballot system favours the two-party system.* Of all the hypotheses that have been defined in this book, this approaches the most nearly perhaps to a true sociological law. An almost complete correlation is observable between the simple-majority single-ballot system and the two-party system: dualist countries use the simple-majority vote and simple-majority vote countries are dualist. The exceptions are very rare and can generally be explained as the result of special conditions.

We must give a few details about this coexistence of the simple-majority and the two-party systems. First let us cite the example of Great Britain and the Dominions: the simple-majority system with a single ballot is in operation in all; the two-party system operates in all, with a Conservative-Labour antagonism tending to replace the Conservative-Liberal antagonism. It will be seen later that Canada, which appears to present an exception, in fact conforms to the general rule.[1] Although it is more recent and more restricted in time the case of Turkey is perhaps more impressive. In this country, which had been subjected for twenty years to the rule of a single party, divergent tendencies were manifest as early as 1946; the secession of the Na-

tionalist party, which broke away from the opposition Democratic party in 1948, might have been expected to give rise to a multi-party system. On the contrary, at the 1950 elections the simple-majority single-ballot system, based on the British pattern (and intensified by list-voting), gave birth to a two-party system: of 487 deputies in the Great National Assembly only ten (i.e. 2.07%) did not belong to one or other of the two major parties, Democrats and Popular Republicans. Nine were Independents and one belonged to the Nationalist party. In the United States the traditional two-party system also co-exists with the simple-majority single-ballot system. The American electoral system is, of course, very special, and the present-day development of primaries introduces into it a kind of double poll, but the attempt sometimes made to identify this technique with the "second ballot" is quite mistaken. The nomination of candidates by an internal vote inside each party is quite a different thing from the real election. The fact that the nomination is open makes no difference: the primaries are a feature of party organization and not of the electoral system.

The American procedure corresponds to the usual machinery of the simple-majority single-ballot system. The absence of a second ballot and of further polls, particularly in the presidential election, constitutes in fact one of the historical reasons for the emergence and the maintenance of the two-party system. In the few local elections in which proportional representation has from time to time been tried it shattered the two-party system: for example in New York between 1936 and 1947, where there were represented on the City Council 5 parties in 1937 (13 Democrats, 3 Republicans, 5 American Labor, 3 City Fusionists, 2 dissident Democrats), 6 parties in 1941 (by the addition of 1 Commu-

From Maurice Duverger, *Political Parties: Their Organization and Activity in the Modern State* (New York: Wiley, 1954), pp. 217–28.

Fig. 1. Disparity between percentage of votes and percentage of seats in Great Britain.

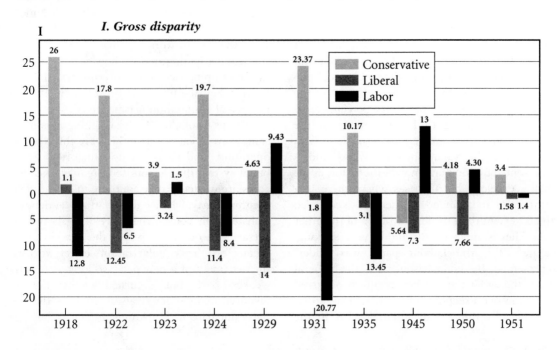

I. Gross disparity

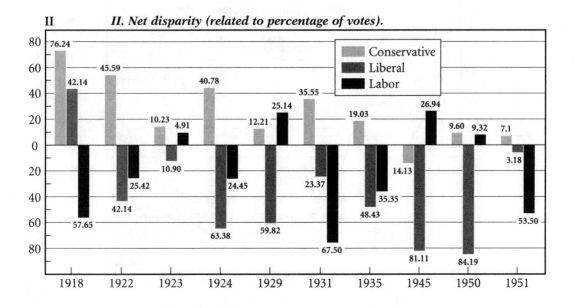

II. Net disparity (related to percentage of votes).

nist), and 7 parties in 1947 (as a result of an internal split in the American Labor party supported by the Garment Trade Unions).

*   *   *

Elimination [of third parties] is itself the result of two factors working together: a mechanical and a psychological factor. The mechanical factor consists in the "under-representation" of the third, i.e. the weakest party, its percentage of seats being inferior to its percentage of the poll. Of course in a simple-majority system with two parties the vanquished is always under-represented by comparison with the victor, as we shall see below, but in cases where there is a third party it is under-represented to an even greater extent than the less favoured of the other two. The example of Britain is very striking: before 1922, the Labour party was under-represented by comparison with the Liberal party; thereafter the converse regularly occurred (with the one exception of 1931, which can be explained by the serious internal crisis in the

Labour party and the crushing victory of the Conservatives); in this way the third party finds the electoral system mechanically unfair to it (Fig. 1). So long as a new party which aims at competing with the two old parties still remains weak the system works against it, raising a barrier against its progress. If, however, it succeeds in outstripping one of its forerunners, then the latter takes its place as third party and the process of elimination is transferred.

The psychological factor is ambiguous in the same way. In cases where there are three parties operating under the simple-majority single-ballot system the electors soon realize that their votes are wasted if they continue to give them to the third party: whence their natural tendency to transfer their vote to the less evil of its two adversaries in order to prevent the success of the greater evil. This "polarization" effect works to the detriment of a new party so long as it is the weakest party but is turned against the less favoured of its older rivals as soon as the new party outstrips it. It operates in fact in the same

Fig. 2. Elimination of Liberal Party in Great Britain

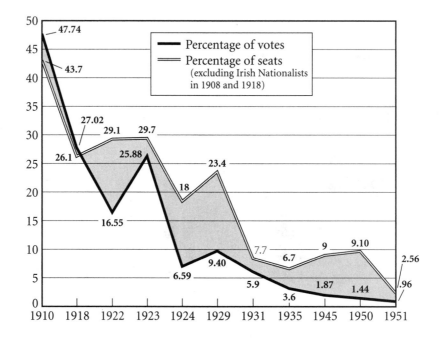

way as "under-representation." The reversal of the two effects does not always occur at the same moment, under-representation generally being the earlier, for a certain lapse of time is required before the electors become aware of the decline of a party and transfer their votes to another. The natural consequence is a fairly long period of confusion during which the hesitation of the electors combines with the transposition of the "under-representation" effect to give an entirely false picture of the balance of power amongst the parties: England experienced such drawbacks between 1923 and 1935. The impulse of the electoral system towards the creation of bipartism is therefore only a long-term effect.

The simple-majority single-ballot system appears then to be capable of maintaining an established dualism in spite of schisms in old parties and the birth of new parties. For a new party to succeed in establishing itself firmly it must have at its disposal strong backing locally or great and powerful organization nationally. In the first case, moreover, it will remain circum-

scribed within the geographical area of its origin and will only emerge from it slowly and painfully, as the example of Canada demonstrates. Only in the second case can it hope for a speedy development which will raise it to the position of second party, in which it will be favoured by the polarization and under-representation effects. Here perhaps we touch upon one of the deep-seated reasons which have led all Anglo-Saxon Socialist parties to organize themselves on a Trade Union basis; it alone could put at their disposal sufficient strength for the "take-off," small parties being eliminated or driven back into the field of local campaigns. The simple-majority system seems equally capable of re-establishing dualism when it has been destroyed by the appearance of a third party. The comparison between Great Britain and Belgium offers a striking contrast: in both countries a traditional two-party system was broken up at the beginning of the century by the emergence of Socialism. Fifty years later the majority system restored bipartism in Great Britain by the elimi-

Fig. 3. "Rescue" of Belgian Liberal Party by P.R. (No. of seats in Chamber of Deputies.)

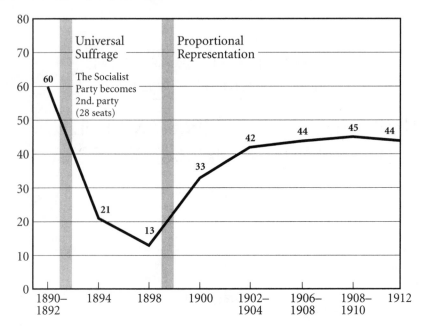

nation of the Liberals (Fig. 2), whereas in Belgium proportional representation saved the Liberal party and later made possible the birth of the Communist party, without counting a few other parties between the wars (Fig. 3).

Can we go further and say that the simple-majority system is capable of producing bipartism in countries where it has never existed? If they already show a fairly clear tendency towards two parties, the answer would unquestionably be in the affirmative. The establishment of the simple-majority single-ballot system in Western Germany would undoubtedly have the effect of gradually destroying the small and medium-sized parties, leaving the Socialists and Christian Democrats face to face; there is undoubtedly no country in which the technical conditions more nearly approach those required for the establishment of a parliamentary system after the British pattern. In Italy an electoral reform of the same kind would have the same results—with the sole difference that the Communists would be one of the two parties, which would greatly imperil the future of the democratic system. However, the brutal application of the single-ballot system in a country in which multipartism has taken deep root, as in France, would not produce the same results, except after a very long delay. The electoral system works in the direction of bipartism; it does not necessarily and absolutely lead to it in spite of all obstacles. The basic tendency combines with many others which attenuate it, check it, or arrest it. With these reserves we can nevertheless consider that dualism of parties is the "brazen law" (as Marx would have said) of the simple-majority single-ballot electoral system.

*   *   *

NOTES

1. Australia too offers an exception since the development of the *Country party*. But the system of preferential voting in operation there profoundly modifies the machinery of the simple-majority poll and makes it more like a two-ballot system by allowing a regrouping of the scattered votes. It is moreover a striking fact that the appearance of the Country party coincided with the introduction of the preferential vote.

JOHN D. HUBER AND
G. BINGHAM POWELL, JR.

CONGRUENCE BETWEEN CITIZENS AND POLICYMAKERS IN TWO VISIONS OF LIBERAL DEMOCRACY

A more reasonable justification for democracy, then, is that, to a substantially greater degree than any alternative to it, a democratic government provides an orderly and peaceful process by means of which a majority of citizens can induce the government to do what they most want it to do and to avoid doing what they most want it not to do.

—*Robert A. Dahl*
Democracy and Its Critics

From *World Politics* 46 (April 1994), pp. 291–326. Some of the authors' notes have been omitted.

Liberal democracy claims to establish connections between citizens and policymakers. The repeated processes of electoral competition and legislative bargaining are supposed to ensure that policymakers do what citizens want them to do. There are, however, at least two quite different visions of the democratic processes that can create congruence between citizen preferences and public policies.

In what we call the *Majority Control vision*, democratic elections are designed to create strong, single-party majority governments that are essentially unconstrained by other parties in the policymaking process. Policymakers are likely to do what citizens want them to do because the party that controls the government has won majority support in the election. Its announced policy comments, previous record, or both were preferred to the partisan alternative by a majority of the citizens. In the other vision, which we call the *Proportionate Influence vision*, elections are designed to produce legislatures that reflect the preferences of all citizens. After the election legislative bargaining between parties is necessary for policymaking, and the influences of the various parties in post-election bargaining processes determine the extent to which policymakers do what citizens want them to do.

In this paper, we offer a simple way to conceptualize the degree of congruence between citizens and their governments, comparing citizen self-placements on the left-right scale with the placement of the governing political parties on the same scale by expert observers. We then attempt to give explicit theoretical form to the Majority Control and Proportionate Influence visions, to link them empirically to specific types of modern democracies, and to measure their successes and failures at creating congruence. We want to know in particular how such theoretically critical features as responsible incumbent governments at the time of the election, identifiable future governments in electoral competition, proportional representation in electoral outcomes, and the formation of majority governments after the election are related to levels of congruence.

Congruence, of course, is not the only democratic virtue: some of the processes treated here as intervening may be highly valued in their own right.[1] Voters oriented to control may wish to see

government formations that change in response to even small vote shifts. Voters may prefer to have very distinctive choices. Voters may prefer that policy-making be highly efficient. Permanent minorities may prefer proportionate representation and consultative legislative bargaining, especially if other processes directly impose the preferences of the majority. We therefore do not propose that congruence between citizen preferences and public policy should be the only grounds for choosing or supporting one vision over the other. We do think, however, that congruence between the preferences of citizens and the actions of policy-makers constitutes a major claim and goal of liberal democracy. Thus, Dahl's "reasonable justification for democracy" posits that "a majority of citizens can induce the government to do what they most want it to do and to avoid doing what they most want it not to do."[2] This is not a unique position but rather articulates more clearly than most a common assumption of those who theorize about liberal democracy. Hence, although congruence is only a part of our general interest in democratic processes, it is an important part.

Conceptualizing and Measuring the Congruence between Preferences of Citizens and Policymakers

Dahl's justification of democracy directs our attention to identifying the policy position that is in some sense "most preferred" by the voters. We believe that the position that has the best claim to represent this "most preferred" policy is the position of the median voter. On a single issue or a single-issue dimension, if we assume that the preferences of voters are single-peaked, the position of the median voter is the only policy that is preferred to all others by a majority of voters.[3] Thus, the relationship between the positions of policymakers and the position of the median voter is central to the study of congruence.

To see the importance of the median voter's preferences in another light, imagine that the voters did not elect representatives but rather voted directly on policy. We should expect these voters to adopt (eventually) a policy position that corresponds to the policy position of the median voter because the median voter's position is the only one that cannot be defeated by a majority. If some position other than the median is adopted, then a minority has prevailed over a majority. Indeed, as the adopted policy position moves farther away from the median voter, the size of the majority that prefers some other policy grows larger and the size of the prevailing minority grows smaller. As the concept of democracy depends on minorities not prevailing over majorities, the position of the median voter has notable normative significance.[4]

Unfortunately, there are fundamental theoretical, as well as practical, problems that constrain our ability to use the position of the median voter as the solution to the congruence problem. In particular, social choice theory seems to demonstrate that the preferences of citizens are almost always collectively uninterpretable if they form more than one dimension. Regardless of the distribution of preferences or the relative weight citizens assign to the different dimensions, there is no single position that a majority prefers to all other positions. In fact, a process of sequentially pitting one position against another can almost always lead to any outcome.[5] These very general and very powerful results lead William Riker to argue that it is impossible to compare what citizens "prefer" with any set of government policies.[6]

Although these theoretical results severely constrain the meaning of any claim that democracies can give citizens "what they want," there is nonetheless at least one answer that satisfies both the claims of social choice theory and the claims of traditional democratic theory: that it is frequently possible to understand "what citizens want" as a distribution of preferences on a single-issue dimension that may include many specific issues.[7] Indeed, it may be that the ability

of students of legislative voting behavior to describe voting over long periods of time in a single dimension and the ability of students of electoral behavior to describe party competition in many different countries using a single dimension reflect the need for democratic debate to reduce conflict to a single dimension in order to make it intelligible.[8] Without something like this single dimension for competition and discourse, it is at best very difficult—perhaps even conceptually impossible—to compare citizen preferences with the promises and actions of the policymakers.

The most common single dimension in modernized democracies is almost certainly the left-right ideological continuum. The language of "left" and "right" creates a unidimensional discourse that can assimilate the various issues and alternatives that continuously appear before the electorate.[9] Studies show that elites, political experts, and mass publics are able to think about political issues using the language of left and right.[10]

Existing studies also show that when surveyed, most citizens can place themselves reasonably meaningfully on a left-right scale. Citizen self-placement on left-right scales is determined by attitudes toward the issues of the day and by perceptions of the party system.[11] Although the substantive content of the scale positions varies from country to country, the distance between scale points seems to reflect roughly similar differences in attitudes toward important issues.[12]

Left-right scales therefore provide an obvious tool for analyzing congruence. One can measure the position of the median voter using opinion surveys that have asked citizens in many countries to place themselves on a left-right continuum (which usually ranges from 1 to 10). And one can measure the position of governments and policymakers using a 1982 survey conducted by Castles and Mair that asked experts, academics, and journalists to place the parties in their country of expertise on a 0–10 left-right scale.[13] We can then measure congruence by analyzing the distance between the position of the policymaking parties and the position of the median

Table 1. Characteristics for Majority Control, Mixed, and Proportionate Influence Systems
1968–87
(1978–85)[a]

	System Type		
	Majority Control: Australia, Great Britain, New Zealand	*Mixed: France, Germany, Ireland, Spain, Sweden*	*Proportionate Influence: Belgium, Denmark, Italy, Netherlands*
Electoral competition			
identifiability	100 (100)	80 (75)	36 (45)
past government status	.67 (.80)	.17 (.06)	0 (0)
effective no. of parties	2.2 (2.2)	3.1 (3.0)	5.1 (5.4)
Election outcomes			
percentage of elections won by a single party or a preelection coalition	95 (100)	66 (58)	7 (10)
proportionality	85 (83)	92 (93)	95 (96)
Legislative bargaining			
percentage of committee systems that permit opposition influence	0 (0)	60 (60)	80 (80)
Number of elections	29 (5)	29 (12)	27 (10)

[a]The top number in each cell is for the period 1968–87. The figure in parentheses is for the period 1978–85 (the period for which we analyze congruence). The top number in the "Proportionality" row is calculated using the figures in Mackie and Rose, *The International Almanac of Electoral History*, 3d ed. (Washington, D.C.: CQ Press, 1991), 510, which are calculated using only the last election reported in their study.

citizen: the larger the distance, the less the congruence; the smaller the distance, the greater the congruence.

Our study is obviously related to and influenced by those empirical studies of political representation that built on the seminal work of Miller and Stokes and that examined relationships between the positions of citizens and the positions or behavior of their representatives.[14] However, our work diverges from this tradition in three important respects. First, we treat parties as units in assessing policymaker positions;[15] given the high levels of unified party voting in most parliamentary systems, this is an essential starting point.[16] Second, we do not analyze connections between groups of voters and their chosen representatives; rather, we analyze those between the citizenry as a whole and the collective policymakers. Third, although our measures of congruence are closely related to Achen's "centrism" measure (which is the *squared* difference between the representative and the citizen mean), we focus on the citizen median rather than the citizen mean.[17] Our reason for using the median is theoretical: if the median and the mean do not coincide, a majority will always prefer the median to the mean. Moreover, since the mean minimizes the sum of the squared distances, it gives greater weight to cases more distant from the center. We see no justification in democratic theory for permitting minorities to prevail over majorities or for giving greater weight to ideologically extreme citizens. Indeed, there is no evidence to suggest that ideologically extreme citizens hold their positions more intensely, which might be the one possible, but hotly debatable, justification for weighting them more heavily. For those unpersuaded by our theoretical argument, however, we can report that all the subsequent results hold equally well using means, rather than medians, for citizens.

*   *   *

In Table 1 we . . . classify political systems into three categories: Majority Control, Mixed, and Proportionate Influence.[18] In the first category we place Australia, New Zealand, and Britain. These systems score high on each of the measures associated with Majority Control systems: voters almost always had a strong sense of the future governments, responsibility for policy was usually very clear (as measured both by past government single-party majorities and by the absence of committee arrangements guaranteeing a role for the opposition), and a single party or preelection coalition nearly always won a majority. At the same time, these systems did poorly on the measure associated with the Proportionate Influence vision: the effective number of parties was near two, proportionality of representation, was relatively poor, and the governments dominated policy-making.

At the other extreme, we place the systems of Belgium, Denmark, Italy, and the Netherlands as most closely approximating the Proportionate Influence systems. In these systems, the effective number of parties was high, giving the voters a wide range of party choice. Proportionality was also high in these systems, assuring many citizens or groups of representation in the legislature. Finally, the committee systems gave the opposition a strong role in three of the countries, while in Italy the incohesion of the Christian Democrats (DC) and decentralization in the legislature frequently gave the opposition a role in policy-making. Not surprisingly, these systems did poorly on most of the measures associated with the Majority Control vision.

In the middle we find the five cases of France, Germany, Ireland, Spain, and Sweden. A good case can be made for classifying each one way or another—France and Ireland have some notable majoritarian properties, and Sweden has some strong proportional influence properties— but each case also has some features that diminish the fit. France has multiple parties, and in both France and Ireland the key property of high identifiability shifts from election to election. Sweden, in the other direction, offered through preelection coalitions some tight voter-government connections. Germany is an almost perfect mix of the usually conflicting properties of the two approaches (except for substantial power sharing that weakens clarity).

*   *   *

Citizens, Governments, and Ideological Congruence in Majoritarian and Proportionate Influence Systems

We develop two measures, called Government Distance I and Government Distance II, of the congruence between the position of the government and the estimated position of the median voter.[19] For both measures if the government

Table 2. Congruence between Government and Citizen Left-Right Orientations[a]

| | System Type | | |
	Majority Control	Mixed	Proportional Influence:
Government Distance I	1.61	1.43	.96
	(28%)	(23%)	(20%)
Government Distance II	1.61	1.55	1.03
	(28%)	(25%)	(20%)
N	5	16	17

[a]Government Distance I measures the difference between the weighted mean left-right position of the government and the left-right position of the median voter. Government Distance II measures the difference between the left-right position of the median party in the government coalition and the left-right position of the median citizen. The numbers in parentheses give the percentage of voters between the government and the median citizen. Positions of the partes are taken from Castles and Mair (fn.10).

contains only a single party, the expert placement of that party becomes the placement of the government and the measure of congruence is the absolute distance between that party and the median citizen. In the case of multiparty coalition governments, we include all parties holding cabinet seats in the government. Government Distance I takes the average position of all the parties in the government weighted by the size of the respective parties. This measure seems intuitively reasonable and is consistent with research by Browne and Fanklin, Gamson, and Schofield and Laver, who show that the share of ministry portfolios received by a government party is generally proportional to its share of legislative seats among the parties in the government coalition.[20]

Since the number of portfolios a party receives may not be a good measure of its influence in the coalition, we developed an alternative measure, Government Distance II. This second measure assumes that the left-right position of the government coalition is dominated by the placement of the median party within it. Hence, Government Distance II is simply the left-right position of the median party within the government. Which of these two measures is more appropriate depends, of course, on whatever theory we might have about how policymaking goes on within the government. As we

shall see, however, the results for both measures are quite similar.[21]

Comparing Congruence between Citizens and Governments in the Three Types of Systems

Table 2 shows the average distance scores for the three types of systems using our two different measures of the position of the government. The data show that the two measures of distance work quite similarly. It is also clear that the Majority Control and Mixed systems have governments that are on average substantially farther from the median voter than are governments in the Proportionate Influence systems: the average government in the Majority Control and the Mixed system is over 1.5 points from the median; the average government in the Proportional Influence system is about 1 point away. Even with so few cases, the difference between the mean of the Proportionate Influence systems and the mean of the Majority Control systems is statistically significant at .05 (one-tailed test).

In parentheses in Table 2 we show the percentage of voters between the government and the median citizen. This figure depends on both the absolute distance and the distribution of voters on the left-right scale. If the voters were more dispersed in the Majority Control systems, for example, a larger distance might affect the same number of voters as does a smaller distance in the Proportionate Influence systems. However, we see the same pattern as in the absolute distances. The Majority Control systems find, on average, 28 percent of the electorate between the government and the median, whereas the figures are 23–25 percent in Mixed systems and 20 percent in the Proportionate Influence systems.

The advantage of the Proportionate Influence systems in offering greater congruence between governments and voters is somewhat theoretically unexpected. We expected that governments in the Majority Control systems would be close to the median as the direct result of party competition and voter choices (under either Downsian theory or some of the nonstrategic or partially strategic alternatives). We also expected coalition bargaining in the Proportional Influence systems might result in governments that are often farther away from the median voter. But the converse is true. The reason for the poorer performance of the Majority Control systems is basically that the two main parties in Britain and Australia are far from the median (over 2 points) during the period of our study. The closer of the two large parties does come to power, but it is still rather extreme.[22] In New Zealand the Majority Control vision seems to work better; in fact both major parties are fairly close to the median (about 1 point).

A similar problem is evident in the Mixed systems, although it is less theoretically surprising in the multiparty situations. A common pattern here is the formation of formal or informal preelection coalitions that pit right against left. These coalitions frequently fail to converge, but the one that gets a majority forms a government without bargaining with the opposition. In France, especially, both major alternative governments are very far from the median voter. In 1978 the winning conservative coalition was 2.75 from the median—the farthest in our sample. In Germany, Spain, and Sweden, too, the alterna-

tives are rather far apart, each around 1.5 points from the median. Only in Ireland are both of the two alternatives quite close to the median.

*　　*　　*

Concluding Comments

We have attempted to bring into more precise focus two general visions of the processes that link citizens and policymakers in contemporary democracies. We should stress that the generality of our results is constrained by our research design: it may be that a different slice of time would reveal majoritarian electoral competition in which the parties are not so extreme and proportionate influence bargaining is less centrist. Moreover, we are well aware that the "commitments" of governments and their actual policy outcomes are not necessarily the same. This difference would be especially troubling for our results if policies diverged further from promises in the Proportionate Influence systems than in the Majoritarian ones. The difficulty of identifying clear responsibility for policy in the former creates prima facie grounds for concern.

With these caveats said, the results of our analysis seem clear and consistent. In the simple comparison, contrary to our expectations from the theoretical arguments about creating congruence connections in each approach, the governments in the Proportionate Influence systems are on average significantly closer to their median voter than are governments in the Majority Control and Mixed systems.

*　　*　　*

NOTES

1. Some of these other virtues are more fully described and elaborated in G. Bingham Powell, Jr., "Elections as Instruments of Democracy" (Manuscript, University of Rochester, 1993).

2. Robert A. Dahl, *Democracy and Its Critics* (New Haven, Conn.: Yale University Press, 1989), 95. In a similar vein, see Hanna Pitkin, *The Concept of Representation* (Berkeley: University of California Press, 1967), 234.

3. See Duncan Black, "On the Rationale of Group Decision Making," *Journal of Political Economy* 56 (February 1948).

4. On the general importance of majorities for democratic theory, see Carl Cohen, *Democracy* (Athens: University of Georgia Press, 1971), 68–71; and Dahl (fn. 2), 135–53. To recognize the importance of majority positions in democratic theory is, of course, not to deny that taking account of intense minorities is an important theoretical and practical problem for democracy. We do not pretend to deal with it here.

5. See Richard D. McKelvey, "Intrasitivities in Multidimensional Voting Models," *Journal of Economic Theory* 12 (June 1976); idem, "General Conditions for Global Intransitivities in Formal Voting Models," *Econometrica* 47 (September 1979); McKelvey and Norman Schofield, "Generalized Symmetry Conditions at a Core Point," *Econometrica* 55 (July 1987); and Charles Plott, "A Notion of Equilibrium and Its Possibility under Majority Rule," *American Economic Review* 57 (September 1967). For some recent challenges, see Ken Kollman, John H. Miller, and Scott E. Page, "Adaptive Parties in Spatial Elections," *American Political Science Review* 86 (December 1992); and Craig Tovey, "The Instability of Instability" (Manuscript, Georgia Institute of Technology, 1991).

6. Riker, "Implications from the Disequilibrium of Majority Rule for the Study of Institutions," *American Political Science Review* 74 (June 1980); and idem, *Liberalism against Populism* (San Francisco: W. H. Freeman, 1982).

7. There might also be an issue or issue dimension that citizens agree is so important that in comparison to it all other issues or dimensions can be ignored. Part of the power of democracy may, indeed, lie in the fact that a majority would reject the idea of officeholders looting the national treasury for their personal benefit, regardless of what other feasible policy promises were offered. Such an issue might never appear on the agenda of party competition, but its elimination as a possible outcome would be a powerful contribution of democracy.

8. On legislative voting behavior, see Keith T. Poole and Howard Rosenthal, "A Spatial Model for Legislative Role Call Analysis," *American Journal of Political Science* 29 (May 1985); and idem, "Patterns of Congressional Voting," *American Journal of Political Science* 35 (February 1991). On party competition, see the contributions in Ian Budge, David Robertson, and Derek Hearl, eds., *Ideology, Strategy, and Party Change: Spatial Analyses of Post-war Election Programmes in Nineteen Democracies* (Cambridge: Cambridge University Press, 1987).

9. See Budge, Robertson, and Hearl (fn. 8); and Ronald Inglehart, *Culture Shift in Advanced Industrial Democracy* (Princeton: Princeton University Press, 1990), 273–74.

10. See Samuel H. Barnes, *Representation in Italy: Institutionalized Tradition and Electoral Choice* (Chicago: University of Chicago Press, 1977); Francis Castles and Peter Mair, "Left-Right Political Scales: Some Expert Judgments," *European Journal of Political Research* 29 (March 1984); Philip E. Converse and Roy Pierce, *Political Representation in France* (Cambridge: Harvard University Press, 1986); Russell J. Dalton, "Political Parties and Political Representation: Party Supporters and Party Elites in Nine Nations," *Comparative Political Studies* 18 (October 1985); Dalton, Scott C. Flanagan, and Paul Allen Beck, eds., *Electoral Change in Advanced Industrial Societies: Realignment or Dealignment?* (Princeton: Princeton University Press, 1984); and Inglehart (fn. 9).

11. See John D. Huber, "Values and Partisanship in Left-Right Orientations: Measuring Ideology," *European Journal of Political Re-*

search 17 (September 1989); Inglehart, "The Changing Structure of Political Cleavages in Western Society," in Dalton, Flanagan, and Beck (fn. 10); and Inglehart and Hans Klingemann, "Party Identification, Ideological Preference and the Left-Right Dimension among Mass Publics," in Ian Budge, Ivor Crewe, and Dennis Fairlie, eds., *Party Identification and Beyond* (London: Wiley, 1976).

12. Huber (fn. 11).

13. See fn. 10. Most of our estimates of the positions of the median voters are taken from the Eurobarometer surveys, which use a scale that ranges from 1 to 10. We also use citizen surveys taken in Sweden, Australia, and New Zealand. We convert the scales from these surveys, as well as those from the Castles and Mair expert survey, to the 10-point scale used by the Eurobarometer. Our analysis assumes that the experts on the country used a scale whose meaning was similar to that used by citizens in that country and that the distance between scale numbers was roughly the same for the experts and citizens in all countries.

14. Warren E. Miller and Donald E. Stokes, "Constituency Influence in Congress," *American Political Science Review* 57 (March 1963). See also Christopher H. Achen, "Measuring Representation: Perils of the Correlation Coefficient," *American Journal of Political Science* 21 (November 1977); idem, "Measuring Representation," *American Journal of Political Science* 22 (May 1978); Barnes (fn. 10); Converse and Pierce (fn. 10); Dalton (fn. 10); Morris Fiorina, *Representatives, Roll Calls, and Constituencies* (Lexington, Mass.: D. C. Heath, 1974); Warren E. Miller, "Majority Rule and the Representative System of Government," in Erik Allardt and Yrjo Littunen, eds., *Cleavages, Ideologies and Party Systems* (Helsinki: Academic Bookstore, 1964); and Lynda Powell, "Issue Representation in Congress," *Journal of Politics* 44 (August 1982).

15. Dalton (fn. 10) also uses parties as the unit of analysis.

16. For linkage analysis confirming this point, see Converse and Pierce (fn. 10); and Barnes (fn. 10).

17. Achen (fn. 14, 1978).

18. Table 1 gives figures for both the larger time period (1968–87) and the narrower time period (1978–85). The data reassure us that system characteristics during the time period that we study below do not differ substantially from the system characteristics during the larger time period.

19. Since the left-right scales have discrete boundaries between the different cells, we approximate the location of the median voter using a technique described in Thomas H. Wonnacott and Ronald J. Wonnacott, *Introductory Statistics for Business and Economics*, 3d ed. (New York: John Wiley, 1984), 671.

20. Eric Browne and Mark Franklin, "Aspects of Coalition Payoffs in European Parliamentary Democracies," *American Political Science Review* 67 (June 1973); Peter Gamson, "A Theory of Coalition Formation," *American Sociological Review* 26 (April 1961); Norman Schofield and Michael Laver, "Bargaining Theory and Portfolio Payoffs in European Coalition Government, 1945–83," *British Journal of Political Science* 15 (April 1985).

21. The mean scores by country for Government Distance I (II) are Australia 1.35 (1.35), Belgium .74 (.74), Denmark 1.36 (1.46), France 1.96 (2.15), West Germany 1.55 (1.81), Ireland .47 (.84), Italy .92 (1.24), Netherlands .90 (.50), New Zealand .95 (.95), Sweden 1.28 (1.17), Great Britain 2.39 (2.39), and Spain 1.94 (1.94).

22. In Britain the closest parties to the median voter were the Liberals in 1979 and the Alliance in 1983, but neither of these parties won as much as a quarter of the votes, and both were heavily penalized by the election laws. The Conservatives were somewhat closer to the median than was Labour, but both large parties were rather far away.

THE ECONOMIST

IS GOVERNMENT DISAPPEARING?

Not As Quickly As One Might Wish

Economists are often accused of greeting some item of news with the observation, "That may be so in practice, but is it true in theory?" Sceptics too seem much more interested in superficially plausible theories about the diminishing power of the state than in the plain facts.

In practice, though perhaps not in theory, governments around the world on average are now collecting slightly more in taxes—not just in absolute terms, but as a proportion of their bigger economies—than they did ten years ago. This is true of the G7 countries, and of the smaller OECD economies as well (see chart 1). The depredations of rampant capitalists on the overall ability of governments to gather income and do good works are therefore invisible. These findings are so strange in theory that many economic analysts have decided not to believe them.

Tax burdens vary a lot from country to country—something else which is wrong in theory. Despite the variations, governments in all the advanced economies are well provided for. The United States is invoked by some European anti-globalists as the land of naked capitalism, the nadir of "private affluence and public squalor" to which other countries are being driven down. Well, its government collected a little over 30% of GDP in taxes last year: an average of some $30,000 per household, adding up to roughly $3 trillion. This is a somewhat larger figure than the national income of Germany, and it goes a long way if spent wisely.

At the other extreme is Sweden, despite its celebrated taxpayer revolt of the early 1990s. Last year its taxes came to 57% of GDP, a savage

From *The Economist* (September 27, 2001), pp. 14–18.

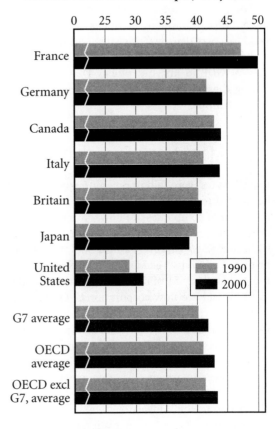

Chart 1   Onward and Upward
General Government Receipts, % of GDP

Source: OECD

reduction of three percentage points since 1990. Next comes Denmark, on 53%, fractionally higher than in 1990. And here's a funny thing. Sweden and Denmark are among the most open economies in the world, far more open than the United States. Denmark's ratio of imports to national income is 33%, compared with America's 14%. And in common with other advanced economies, neither of these Scandinavian countries has capital controls to keep investment penned in.

Harvard's Dani Rodrik, one of the more careful and persuasive globalisation sceptics, has written: "Globalisation has made it exceedingly difficult for government to provide social insurance . . . At present, international economic integration is taking place against the background of receding governments and diminished social obligations. The welfare state has been under attack for two decades." Sweden, admittedly, is reeling, its government now able to collect only 57% of GDP in tax. But plucky Denmark is resisting these attacks well, and so is most of the rest of Europe.

Money Isn't Everything

Even if taxes were falling precipitously, it would be absurd to claim, as many globalisation sceptics do, that companies are nowadays more powerful than governments. It is routine to be told, as in *The Silent Takeover*, a new book by a Cambridge University academic, Noreena Hertz, things like this: "51 of the 100 biggest economies in the world are now corporations." Quite what that implies is never explained: readers are invited to draw their own conclusion about the relative power of governments and companies.

Before you even think about whether it makes sense to weigh corporate power against state power, you can see that this particular comparison, which measures the size of companies by their sales, is bogus. National income is a measure of value added. It cannot be compared with a company's sales (equal to value added plus the cost of inputs). But even if that tiresome, endlessly repeated error were corrected, there would be no sense in comparing companies with governments in terms of their power over people.

The power of even the biggest companies is nothing compared with that of governments—no matter how small or poor the country concerned. The value added of Microsoft is a little over $20 billion a year, about the same as the national income of Uruguay. Does this make it remotely plausible that Bill Gates has more sway over the people of Uruguay than their government does? Or take Luxembourg—another small economy with, presumably, a correspondingly feeble state. Can Microsoft tax the citizens of Luxembourg (whose government collected 45% of GDP from them last year), conscript them if it has a mind to, arrest and imprison them for behaviour it disapproves of, or deploy physical force against them at will? No, not even using Windows XP.

But those are specious comparisons, you might reply. Of course Bill Gates is less powerful than the government of Uruguay in Uruguay, but Mr. Gates exercises his power, such as it is, globally. Well then, where, exactly, is Mr. Gates supposed to be as powerful in relation to the government as the alarming comparison between value added and national income implies? And if Bill Gates does not have this enormous power in any particular country or countries, he does not have it at all. In other words, the power that Mr. Gates exercises globally is over Microsoft. Every government he ever meets is more powerful than he is in relation to its own citizens.

In a war between two countries, national income is relevant as a measure of available resources. If companies raised armies and fought wars, their wealth would count for something. But they don't, and couldn't: they lack the power. Big companies do have political influence. They have the money to lobby politicians and, in many countries, to corrupt them. Even so, the idea that companies have powers over citizens remotely as great as those of governments—no matter how big the company, no matter how small or poor the country—is fatuous. Yet it is never so much as questioned by anti-globalists.

Any power to tax, however limited, gives a country more political clout than Microsoft or General Electric could dream of. But how can a small, exceptionally open economy such as Denmark manage to collect more than 50% of GDP in taxes, in utter defiance of the logic of global capitalism? The answer seems inescapable: Denmark no longer exists, and questions are starting to be asked about the existence of many other European countries. At least, that is how it looks in theory; in practice, the theory needs to be looked at again.

The Limits of Government

The alleged squeeze on government arises from the fact that, in a world of integrated economies, again in Mr. Rodrik's words, "owners of capital, highly skilled workers, and many professionals . . . are free to take their resources where they are most in demand." The people Mr. Rodrik refers to have high incomes. Through the taxes they pay, they make an indispensable contribution to the public finances. If economic integration allows capital and skills to migrate to low-tax jurisdictions, the tax base will shrink. Governments will find themselves unable to finance social programmes, safety nets or redistribution of income. Anticipating this flight of capital and skills, governments have to cut taxes and dismantle the welfare state before the migration gets under way. Markets triumph over democracy.

That is the theory. Experience largely refutes it, but it is not entirely wrong. In a variety of ways, economic integration does put limits on what governments can do. However, some of those constraints are eminently desirable. Integration makes it harder to be a tyrant. Governments have been known to oppress their subjects. Oppression is more difficult with open borders: people can leave and take their savings with them. In such cases, global markets are plainly an ally of human rights.

The affinity of totalitarianism and economic isolation was obvious in the case of the Soviet Union and communist Eastern Europe; it is still plain today in the case of North Korea, say. But democracies are capable of oppression too. It would therefore be wrong to conclude that integration is undesirable merely because it limits the power of government, even if the government concerned is democratic. One needs to recognise that some constraints on democracy are desirable, and then to ask whether the constraints imposed by markets are too tight.

These issues are rarely, if ever, addressed by the critics of globalisation: it is simpler to deplore the notion of "profits before people." The sceptics either insist, or regard it as too obvious even to mention, that the will of the people, democratically expressed, must always prevail. This is amazingly naive. Even the most elementary account of democracy recognises the need for checks and balances, including curbs on the majoritarian "will of the people." Failing those, democracies are capable of tyranny over minorities.

The sceptics are terribly keen on "the people." Yet the idea that citizens are not individuals with different goals and preferences, but an undifferentiated body with agreed common interests, defined in opposition to other monolithic interests such as "business" or "foreigners," is not just shallow populism, it is proto-fascism. It is self-contradictory, as well. The sceptics would not hesitate to call for "the people" to be overruled if, for instance, they voted for policies that violated human rights, or speeded the extermination of endangered species, or offended against other values the sceptics regard as more fundamental than honouring the will of the majority.

The possibility that people might leave is not the only curb that economic integration puts on government. The global flow of information, a by-product of the integration of markets, also works to that effect. It lets attention be drawn to abuses of all kinds: of people especially, but also of the environment or of other things that the sceptics want to protect. Undeniably, it also fosters a broader kind of policy competition among governments. This works not through the sort of mechanical market arbitrage that would drive down taxes regardless of what citizens might want, but through informing voters about alternatives, thus making them more demanding.

The fashion for economic liberalisation in recent years owes something to the remarkable success of the American economy during the 1990s: a success which, thanks to globalisation, has been seen and reflected upon all over the world. Growing knowledge about the West helped precipitate the liberation of Eastern Europe. But information of this kind need not always favour the market. For instance, the failure of the American government to extend adequate health care to all its citizens has been noticed as well, and voters in countries with universal publicly financed health-care systems do not, on the whole, want to copy this particular model. The global flow of knowledge creates, among other things, better-informed voters, and therefore acts as a curb on government power. This does nothing but good.

The anti-globalists themselves, somewhat self-contradictorily, use the information-spreading aspect of globalisation to great effect. Organising a worldwide protest movement would be much harder without the World Wide Web, but the web itself is merely one dimension of globalisation. The economic integration that sceptics disapprove of is in many ways necessary for effective resistance to the more specific things they object to—not all of which, by any means, are themselves the products of globalisation.

Still, all this is to acknowledge that economic integration does limit the power of government, including democratic government. The question is whether it limits it too much, or in undesirable ways. So far as far public spending is concerned, the answer seems clear. Given that even in conditions of economic integration people are willing to tolerate tax burdens approaching 60% of GDP, and that tax burdens of between 40% and 55% of GDP are routine in industrial economies other than the United States, the limits are plainly not that tight. These figures say that democracy has plenty of room for manoeuvre.

The Mystery of the Missing Tax Cut

One puzzle remains: why are taxes not coming down? There are several answers. One is that in-

ternational integration is far from complete, and is likely to remain so. Technology has caused distance to shrink, but not to disappear. National borders still matter as well, even more than mere distance, and far more than all the interest in globalisation might lead you to expect. For all but the smallest economies, trade and investment are still disproportionately intranational rather than international. Especially in the developed world, borders still count not so much because of overt protectionist barriers, but because countries remain jurisdictionally and administratively distinct. This is not likely to change in the foreseeable future.

For instance, if a supplier defaults on a contract to sell you something, it is much easier to get legal redress if your seller is in the same country (and subject to the same legal authority) than it would be if you had to sue in a foreign court. Because of these difficulties in contracting, trading across borders still calls for much more trust between buyers and sellers than trading within borders—so much so as to rule out many transactions. This remains true even in systems such as the European Union's, where heroic efforts have been made to overcome inadvertent obstacles to trade, suggesting that they will prove even more durable everywhere else.

You would expect the international mobility of capital to be especially high, given that the costs of physically transporting the stuff are virtually zero, yet it is surprising just how relatively immobile even capital remains. In the aggregate, the flow of capital into or out of any given country can be thought of as balancing that country's saving and investment. If the country invests more than it saves (that is, if it runs a current-account deficit), capital flows in; if it saves more than it invests (a current-account surplus), the country must lend capital to the rest of the world. Perfect capital mobility would imply that, country by country, national saving and investment would move freely in relation to each other. Very large inflows or outflows of capital in relation to national income would be the order of the day. In fact they are not. Nowadays, a sur-

Chart 2   *Count the Ways*
OECD Tax Mix, % of GDP

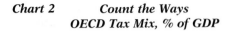

- ▮ Non-tax receipts
- ▮ Other taxes including property taxes
- ▮ Consumption taxes
- ▮ Taxes on corporate income
- ▮ Taxes on personal income
- ▮ Social security and payroll taxes

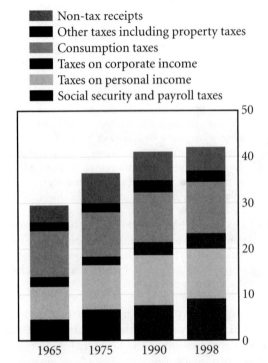

plus or deficit of just a few percentage points of GDP is regarded as big.

Still, capital is much more mobile than labour—and mobile enough, to be sure, to have given rise to some tax competition among governments. So far this competition has affected the structure of tax codes rather than overall tax burdens; total yields have been unaffected. In an effort to attract inflows of capital, and especially inflows of foreign direct investment, governments have been lowering their tax rates for corporate income and raising them for personal income, or relying more on a variety of indirect taxes, or both (see chart 2). But it is easy to exaggerate the extent even of this structural shift, never mind the effect on total taxation. This is because taxes on corporate income were small to begin with, so not much was at stake. In fact, heavy reliance on corporate taxes is bad policy even in a closed economy. Indeed, in a closed

economy, you can make a respectable case on efficiency grounds for excluding corporate income from taxes altogether.

Taxes on company profits, the argument goes, are taxes on shareholders' income—ultimately, that is, taxes on a particular category of personal income. In the end, although it is politically convenient to pretend otherwise, "the people" pay all the taxes: companies are mere intermediaries. There is no reason to tax the income people receive as shareholders any differently from the income they receive as owners of bank deposits or as workers. In a closed economy, you might as well abolish the corporate-income tax and instead tax profits when they turn up as dividends in the incomes of individual taxpayers: it is simpler, and it is less likely to affect investment decisions in unintended ways.

In an open economy, however, company ownership is to some extent in the hand of foreigners, not just the citizens of the country where the company is based. This makes it more tempting to tax corporate income, because this allows the government to bring foreigners within the scope of its tax base. Seen this way, it is odd to blame globalisation for downward pressure on corporate-tax rates. Were it not for globalisation, there would be no reason to have corporate taxes in the first place. But it is true that once you are collecting corporate taxes, greater capital mobility limits your take. Economic integration rationalises, and at the same time limits, reliance on corporate-income taxes. The issue is subtler than it seems.

Staying Put

But what matters far more than corporate tax policy is that most people, skilled as well as unskilled, are reluctant to move abroad. Since workers tend to stay put, governments can tax them at surprisingly high rates without provoking flight. In all but extreme cases, the democratic constraint (the need to secure a broad measure of popular support for tax increases) binds governments long before the economic constraint imposed by international integration (the risk that groups facing very high taxes will leave). In the case of taxes on profits, it is true that the economic constraint will bind before the democratic one, and that globalisation serves to tighten the economic constraint further—but this does not matter. There is no need for high taxes on profits if people are willing to hand over 50% or more of what they produce in the form of taxes on income and consumption.

To simple-minded believers in the most desiccated branch of neoclassical economics, all this may seem surprising. Their theories regard people as "rational economic men," narrow utility-maximisers with no ties to family, place or culture. Presumably, these ciphers would shop around for low-tax jurisdictions. Oddly, the same benighted view of human nature must be shared by many globalisation sceptics—otherwise, why would they fear taxpayer flight on a scale sufficient to abolish the European welfare state? But in real life, it is better to take a fuller, broader view of the human condition. Since people seem to choose to be tied down, indeed to relish it, governments, within broad limits, can carry on taxing them regardless of globalisation. If it seems prudent to cut taxes on profits in order to attract inflows of foreign investment, no problem. Taxes on people will still be sufficient to finance generous public spending of every kind.

Be Very Afraid

Many anti-globalists have strangely little confidence in the merits of the policies they are anxious to sustain. Fearing what may be lost if globalisation continues uncurbed, Mr. Rodrik writes:

> If it was the 19th century that unleashed capitalism in its full force, it was the 20th century that tamed it and boosted its productivity by supplying the institutional underpinnings of market-based economies. Central banks to regulate credit and

the supply of liquidity, fiscal policies to stabilise aggregate demand, antitrust and regulatory authorities to combat fraud and anti-competitive behaviour, social insurance to reduce lifetime risk, political democracy to make the above institutions accountable to the citizenry—these were all innovations that firmly took root in today's rich countries only during the second half of the 20th century. That the second half of the century was also a period of unprecedented prosperity for Western Europe, the United States, Japan and some other parts of East Asia is no coincidence. These institutional innovations greatly enhanced the efficiency and legitimacy of markets and in turn drew strength from the material advancement unleashed by market forces . . . The dilemma that we face as we enter the 21st century is that markets are striving to become global while the institutions needed to support them remain by and large national . . . The desire by producers and investors to go global weakens the institutional base of national economies.

The argument, presumably, is that international capital will flow away from countries with the high public spending and taxes that these highly developed institutions involve. One answer is that international investment, as already noted, is much less important in most countries than domestic investment. But a more fundamental question is this: why should foreign capital flow away from countries that have equipped themselves with these institutions, if, as Mr. Rodrik emphasises, those arrangements have "boosted . . . productivity" and "greatly enhanced the efficiency . . . of markets"—so much so that the most ambitious period of national institution-building was also a time of growing and "unprecedented" prosperity for the nations that joined in?

If public spending boosts productivity, then competition among governments for inward investment is likely to favour more public spending (and the taxes needed to pay for it), not less. Suppose, as seems plausible, that public spending on education raises productivity by increasing the supply of skilled workers. Then you would expect international investment to be drawn to countries that invest heavily in top-quality schools and universities. Suppose, as may also be true, that public spending on social programmes such as health and welfare raises productivity, by producing a healthier and more contented workforce, with better labour relations and greater labour mobility. If so, again international capital will be drawn to countries that spend money on those things. Globalisation, surely, will not frown on policies whose net effect is to foster productivity and efficiency.

But what about policies that do not serve those goals? Many would argue, for instance, that welfare policies, especially if too generous, encourage idleness and reduce economy-wide productivity. Suppose that is true. Also suppose that, knowing it to be true, most people want such policies anyway. You might feel that they are entitled to that opinion, and in a democracy they are entitled to get their way. Another example might be policies to limit working hours. Suppose that they reduce productivity, but that people vote for them anyway. Must globalisation overrule democracy?

Globalisation v. Democracy

The answer even in this case is no—and to see why is to understand why so many of the fears about globalisation and democracy are groundless. Policies that reduce productivity do, in the first instance, cut a country's feasible standard of living, narrowly defined in terms of GDP per head. But what happens after that? If a country that is open to international trade and capital flows adopts some such policies, perhaps on the ground that they will raise living standards according to some broader definition, wages and profits will fall relative to what they would otherwise have been. Next, investment will fall and the capital stock will shrink, again compared with what they would otherwise have been. This will continue until the scarcity of capital drives the rate of profit back up, at the margin, to the rate prevailing in the global capital market.

All this time the economy will grow more slowly than if the policies had not been followed. Once the economy has adjusted, however, it remains as "competitive" as it was at the outset: lower wages have restored labour costs per unit of output, and a smaller stock of capital has restored the return on capital. The economy has grown more slowly for a spell. It is less prosperous than it would have been. But in due course, once wages and profits have adjusted, the economy will again be as attractive, or unattractive, to foreign investors as it was at the outset. The government's adoption of policies that compromise efficiency is not punished by excommunication from the global economy, or with an accelerating spiral of decline; the only penalty is compromised efficiency and lower measured incomes, which is what the country chose in the first place.

Would the economy have fared any better without globalisation? Had it been closed to international flows of goods and capital, could it have adopted those productivity-cutting policies and paid no price at all? The answer is no. Even in a closed economy, policies that reduce productivity would cause wages and profits to fall, as in the open-economy case. The return on capital would be lower, so saving and investment would decline, relative to what they would have been (there would be no cross-border capital flows in this case, so saving and investment must always be equal). The capital stock would shrink and growth would be held back until the scarcity of capital drove the return back up. As in the open-economy case, the result would be a spell of slower growth and a standard of living permanently lower than it would otherwise have been.

The main difference is probably that in the closed-economy case, the losses would be subtracted from an economy that is already very much poorer than its open-economy counterpart, because it is closed. Conceivably, this would make further losses politically easier to sustain. But that is the most you can say in defence of the view that globalisation forbids social policies which jeopardise productivity. "Stay poor, because once you start to get rich you may find that you like it." Not exactly compelling, is it?

You might well conclude from all this that globalisation, if anything, will lead to higher rather than lower social spending. As argued earlier, globalisation raises aggregate incomes but at the same time increases economic insecurity for certain groups. Both of these consequences tend to raise social spending. Generous social spending is a "superior good": as countries grow richer, they want to spend more of their incomes on it, and can afford to. At the same time, quite separately, greater economic insecurity directly spurs demand for social spending.

Given that globalisation increases the demand for social spending; given that it does not rule out any decision to increase such spending which harms productivity, any more than a closed economy would; given that increases in social spending which raise productivity will be rewarded with inflows of capital; given all this, should globalisation and the generous social spending that democracies favour not go hand in hand? They should, and indeed rising social spending alongside faster, deeper globalisation is exactly what the figures for the past several decades show.

Governments in rich countries need to look again at their social policies, partly to make sure that temporary and longer-term losers from globalisation, and from economic growth in general, get well-designed help. But there is no reason whatever to fear that globalisation makes social policies more difficult to finance. In the end, by raising incomes in the aggregate, it makes them easier to finance. It creates additional economic resources, which democracies can use as they see fit.

COMMUNISM AND POST-COMMUNISM

This section traces the concept of communism, its limitations, collapse, and future prospects. We begin with the most commonly read work of Karl Marx and Friedrich Engels, Manifesto of the Communist Party (1848), where they lay out their understanding of human history and its dynamics, and the inevitability of the communist revolution to come. For Marx and Engels, economic relations are the driving force of all human relations, and it is these changes in economic relations that drive history. History is a succession of revolutions by those who are exploited against those who exploit them. At the midpoint of the nineteenth century, with the Industrial Revolution just under way, the authors predicted that the limitations of capitalism would soon bring about its overthrow and replacement by a system in which resources and wealth were equally shared. Marx and Engels thus combined research with activism, and their ideas would go on to spark communist movements across the globe, and revolutions in such places as Russia and China.

But communism in practice was more challenging than Marx or Engels anticipated. The idea of eliminating private property and market forces led to an economy administered by the state and backed by authoritarian rule. In addition to denying democratic freedoms, communism also grew increasingly unable to provide material needs and economic growth. By the 1980s, attempts to reform this ossified structure in the Soviet Union and Eastern Europe quickly led to its undoing. In an early evaluation of the collapse of communism, Adam Przeworski, an American political scientist originally from Poland, attempts in his prologue to Democracy and the Market (1991) to understand why this system fell apart and fell apart so quickly. Unable to trade freedom for economic development, a cynical party leadership remained in power only through the threat of force. When this evaporated, so did communism. Writing so soon after the collapse, Przeworski is skeptical about the prospects for these countries.

With respect to Eastern Europe, at least, Przeworski was overly pessimistic. In fact, many of these countries went on to build strong democratic institutions. Other countries, however, particularly those that were formerly *part of the Soviet Union, have fared less well. Why this difference? Valerie Bunce's "Rethinking Recent Democratization" (2003) draws upon these cases as well as earlier examples of political transition in southern Europe and Latin America to deepen our understanding of successful political change. Historical factors, popular mobilization, nationalism, the role of the military, and the degree of uncertainty about the prospects for change all contributed to different paths away from communism, allowing some countries to break decisively from the past while other transitions were much more constrained. Bunce reminds us that there is no uniform path of political transitions, and that the constraints and opportunities that might exist in one region (such as Latin America or southern Europe) may be quite different from those that exist in another.*

Bunce's cross-national approach leads us to think about how such changes might occur in the last major country controlled by the Communist Party: China. Lucian Pye's "Traumatized Political Cultures" (2002) looks at China in comparison to Russia and draws some comparisons about their different trajectories of reform. Pye, whose work on Asia stretches back fifty years, concurs with Bunce that political change is constrained by the particular context, while emphasizing in particular the role of political culture. Comparing China and Russia, Pye argues that both countries are burdened by political cultures that have been traumatized by totalitarianism, so that the norms and social ties necessary for civil society have been largely shattered. Yet Pye, like Ian Buruma in his piece "What Beijing Can Learn from Moscow," (2001) takes a position quite the opposite from most observers of Russia and China. China, with its dynamic economy, seems poised to transform itself into a developed country and a major player in world politics, while Russia seems to be in economic and political decline. But Pye and Buruma both conclude that while China may be experiencing dramatic economic changes, its resistance to political reform will force it to face a much more difficult and dangerous political transition in the future. Buruma worries that in the absence of any representative institutions, even of the limited sort found in Russia, China will experience increasing political violence as those marginalized by rapid change vent their anger. Pye adds to this discussion by observing that nationalism is increasingly filling the void left by communist ideology as a means of state control over the public. Increasing unrest could lead not to liberalization, but to an increasingly repressive Chinese regime.

KARL MARX AND FRIEDRICH ENGELS

MANIFESTO OF THE COMMUNIST PARTY

A spectre is haunting Europe—the spectre of communism. All the powers of old Europe have entered into a holy alliance to exorcise this spectre: Pope and Tsar, Metternich and Guizot, French Radicals and German police-spies.

Where is the party in opposition that has not been decried as communistic by its opponents in power? Where is the opposition that has not hurled back the branding reproach of communism, against the more advanced opposition parties, as well as against its reactionary adversaries?

Two things result from this fact:

I. Communism is already acknowledged by all European powers to be itself a power.

II. It is high time that Communists should openly, in the face of the whole world, publish their views, their aims, their tendencies, and meet this nursery tale of the spectre of communism with a manifesto of the party itself.

To this end, Communists of various nationalities have assembled in London and sketched the following manifesto, to be published in the English, French, German, Italian, Flemish and Danish languages.

I—Bourgeois and Proletarians

The history of all hitherto existing society is the history of class struggles.

Freeman and slave, patrician and plebian, lord and serf, guild-master and journeyman, in a word, oppressor and oppressed, stood in constant opposition to one another, carried on an uninterrupted, now hidden, now open fight, a fight that each time ended, either in a revolutionary reconstitution of society at large, or in the common ruin of the contending classes.

In the earlier epochs of history, we find almost everywhere a complicated arrangement of society into various orders, a manifold gradation of social rank. In ancient Rome we have patricians, knights, plebians, slaves; in the Middle Ages, feudal lords, vassals, guild-masters, journeymen, apprentices, serfs; in almost all of these classes, again, subordinate gradations.

The modern bourgeois society that has sprouted from the ruins of feudal society has not done away with class antagonisms. It has but established new classes, new conditions of oppression, new forms of struggle in place of the old ones.

Our epoch, the epoch of the bourgeoisie, possesses, however, this distinct feature: it has simplified class antagonisms. Society as a whole is more and more splitting up into two great hostile camps, into two great classes directly facing each other—bourgeoisie and proletariat.

From the serfs of the Middle Ages sprang the chartered burghers of the earliest towns. From these burgesses the first elements of the bourgeoisie were developed.

The discovery of America, the rounding of the Cape, opened up fresh ground for the rising bourgeoisie. The East-Indian and Chinese markets, the colonisation of America, trade with the colonies, the increase in the means of exchange and in commodities generally, gave to commerce, to navigation, to industry, an impulse never before known, and thereby, to the revolutionary element in the tottering feudal society, a rapid development.

The feudal system of industry, in which in-

From Karl Marx and Friedrich Engels, *Selected Works in Three Volumes*, Vol. 1 (Moscow, USSR: Progress Publishers, 1969), pp. 98–137.

dustrial production was monopolized by closed guilds, now no longer suffices for the growing wants of the new markets. The manufacturing system took its place. The guild-masters were pushed aside by the manufacturing middle class; division of labor between the different corporate guilds vanished in the face of division of labor in each single workshop.

Meantime, the markets kept ever growing, the demand ever rising. Even manufacturers no longer sufficed. Thereupon, steam and machinery revolutionized industrial production. The place of manufacture was taken by the giant, MODERN INDUSTRY; the place of the industrial middle class by industrial millionaires, the leaders of the whole industrial armies, the modern bourgeois.

Modern industry has established the world market, for which the discovery of America paved the way. This market has given an immense development to commerce, to navigation, to communication by land. This development has, in turn, reacted on the extension of industry; and in proportion as industry, commerce, navigation, railways extended, in the same proportion the bourgeoisie developed, increased its capital, and pushed into the background every class handed down from the Middle Ages.

We see, therefore, how the modern bourgeoisie is itself the product of a long course of development, of a series of revolutions in the modes of production and of exchange.

Each step in the development of the bourgeoisie was accompanied by a corresponding political advance in that class. An oppressed class under the sway of the feudal nobility, an armed and self-governing association of medieval commune: here independent urban republic (as in Italy and Germany); there taxable "third estate" of the monarchy (as in France); afterward, in the period of manufacturing proper, serving either the semi-feudal or the absolute monarchy as a counterpoise against the nobility, and, in fact, cornerstone of the great monarchies in general— the bourgeoisie has at last, since the establishment of Modern Industry and of the world

market, conquered for itself, in the modern representative state, exclusive political sway. The executive of the modern state is but a committee for managing the common affairs of the whole bourgeoisie.

The bourgeoisie, historically, has played a most revolutionary part.

The bourgeoisie, wherever it has got the upper hand, has put an end to all feudal, patriarchal, idyllic relations. It has pitilessly torn asunder the motley feudal ties that bound man to his "natural superiors," and has left no other nexus between people than naked self-interest, than callous "cash payment." It has drowned out the most heavenly ecstacies of religious fervor, of chivalrous enthusiasm, of philistine sentimentalism, in the icy water of egotistical calculation. It has resolved personal worth into exchange value, and in place of the numberless indefeasible chartered freedoms, has set up that single, unconscionable freedom—Free Trade. In one word, for exploitation, veiled by religious and political illusions, it has substituted naked, shameless, direct, brutal exploitation.

The bourgeoisie has stripped of its halo every occupation hitherto honored and looked up to with reverent awe. It has converted the physician, the lawyer, the priest, the poet, the man of science, into its paid wage laborers.

The bourgeoisie has torn away from the family its sentimental veil, and has reduced the family relation into a mere money relation.

The bourgeoisie has disclosed how it came to pass that the brutal display of vigor in the Middle Ages, which reactionaries so much admire, found its fitting complement in the most slothful indolence. It has been the first to show what man's activity can bring about. It has accomplished wonders far surpassing Egyptian pyramids, Roman aqueducts, and Gothic cathedrals; it has conducted expeditions that put in the shade all former exoduses of nations and crusades.

The bourgeoisie cannot exist without constantly revolutionizing the instruments of production, and thereby the relations of production, and with them the whole relations of society. Conservation of the old modes of production in unaltered form, was, on the contrary, the first condition of existence for all earlier industrial classes. Constant revolutionizing of production, uninterrupted disturbance of all social conditions, everlasting uncertainty and agitation distinguish the bourgeois epoch from all earlier ones. All fixed, fast frozen relations, with their train of ancient and venerable prejudices and opinions, are swept away, all new-formed ones become antiquated before they can ossify. All that is solid melts into air, all that is holy is profaned, and man is at last compelled to face with sober senses his real condition of life and his relations with his kind.

The need of a constantly expanding market for its products chases the bourgeoisie over the entire surface of the globe. It must nestle everywhere, settle everywhere, establish connections everywhere.

The bourgeoisie has, through its exploitation of the world market, given a cosmopolitan character to production and consumption in every country. To the great chagrin of reactionaries, it has drawn from under the feet of industry the national ground on which it stood. All old-established national industries have been destroyed or are daily being destroyed. They are dislodged by new industries, whose introduction becomes a life and death question for all civilized nations, by industries that no longer work up indigenous raw material, but raw material drawn from the remotest zones; industries whose products are consumed, not only at home, but in every quarter of the globe. In place of the old wants, satisfied by the production of the country, we find new wants, requiring for their satisfaction the products of distant lands and climes. In place of the old local and national seclusion and self-sufficiency, we have intercourse in every direction, universal interdependence of nations. And as in material, so also in intellectual production. The intellectual creations of individual nations become common property. National one-sidedness and narrow-mindedness become more and more impossible, and from the numerous national and local literatures, there arises a world literature.

The bourgeoisie, by the rapid improvement of all instruments of production, by the immensely facilitated means of communication, draws all, even the most barbarian, nations into civilization. The cheap prices of commodities are the heavy artillery with which it forces the barbarians' intensely obstinate hatred of foreigners to capitulate. It compels all nations, on pain of extinction, to adopt the bourgeois mode of production; it compels them to introduce what it calls civilization into their midst, i.e., to become bourgeois themselves. In one word, it creates a world after its own image.

The bourgeoisie has subjected the country to the rule of the towns. It has created enormous cities, has greatly increased the urban population as compared with the rural, and has thus rescued a considerable part of the population from the idiocy of rural life. Just as it has made the country dependent on the towns, so it has made barbarian and semi-barbarian countries dependent on the civilized ones, nations of peasants on nations of bourgeois, the East on the West.

The bourgeoisie keeps more and more doing away with the scattered state of the population, of the means of production, and of property. It has agglomerated population, centralized the means of production, and has concentrated property in a few hands. The necessary consequence of this was political centralization. Independent, or but loosely connected provinces, with separate interests, laws, governments, and systems of taxation, became lumped together into one nation, with one government, one code of laws, one national class interest, one frontier, and one customs tariff.

The bourgeoisie, during its rule of scarce one hundred years, has created more massive and more colossal productive forces than have all preceding generations together. Subjection of nature's forces to man, machinery, application of chemistry to industry and agriculture, steam navigation, railways, electric telegraphs, clearing of whole continents for cultivation, canalization or rivers, whole populations conjured out of the ground—what earlier century had even a presentiment that such productive forces slumbered in the lap of social labor?

We see then: the means of production and of exchange, on whose foundation the bourgeoisie built itself up, were generated in feudal society. At a certain stage in the development of these means of production and of exchange, the conditions under which feudal society produced and exchanged, the feudal organization of agriculture and manufacturing industry, in one word, the feudal relations of property became no longer compatible with the already developed productive forces; they became so many fetters. They had to be burst asunder; they were burst asunder.

Into their place stepped free competition, accompanied by a social and political constitution adapted in it, and the economic and political sway of the bourgeois class.

A similar movement is going on before our own eyes. Modern bourgeois society, with its relations of production, of exchange and of property, a society that has conjured up such gigantic means of production and of exchange, is like the sorcerer who is no longer able to control the powers of the nether world whom he has called up by his spells. For many a decade past, the history of industry and commerce is but the history of the revolt of modern productive forces against modern conditions of production, against the property relations that are the conditions for the existence of the bourgeois and of its rule. It is enough to mention the commercial crises that, by their periodical return, put the existence of the entire bourgeois society on its trial, each time more threateningly. In these crises, a great part not only of the existing products, but also of the previously created productive forces, are periodically destroyed. In these crises, there breaks out an epidemic that, in all earlier epochs, would have seemed an absurdity—the epidemic of over-production. Society suddenly finds itself

put back into a state of momentary barbarism; it appears as if a famine, a universal war of devastation, had cut off the supply of every means of subsistence; industry and commerce seem to be destroyed. And why? Because there is too much civilization, too much means of subsistence, too much industry, too much commerce. The productive forces at the disposal of society no longer tend to further the development of the conditions of bourgeois property; on the contrary, they have become too powerful for these conditions, by which they are fettered, and so soon as they overcome these fetters, they bring disorder into the whole of bourgeois society, endanger the existence of bourgeois property. The conditions of bourgeois society are too narrow to comprise the wealth created by them. And how does the bourgeoisie get over these crises? On the one hand, by enforced destruction of a mass of productive forces; on the other, by the conquest of new markets, and by the more thorough exploitation of the old ones. That is to say, by paving the way for more extensive and more destructive crises, and by diminishing the means whereby crises are prevented.

The weapons with which the bourgeoisie felled feudalism to the ground are now turned against the bourgeoisie itself.

But not only has the bourgeoisie forged the weapons that bring death to itself; it has also called into existence the men who are to wield those weapons—the modern working class—the proletarians.

In proportion as the bourgeoisie, i.e., capital, is developed, in the same proportion is the proletariat, the modern working class, developed— a class of laborers, who live only so long as they find work, and who find work only so long as their labor increases capital. These laborers, who must sell themselves piecemeal, are a commodity, like every other article of commerce, and are consequently exposed to all the vicissitudes of competition, to all the fluctuations of the market.

Owing to the extensive use of machinery, and to the division of labor, the work of the proletarians has lost all individual character, and, consequently, all charm for the workman. He becomes an appendage of the machine, and it is only the most simple, most monotonous, and most easily acquired knack, that is required of him. Hence, the cost of production of a workman is restricted, almost entirely, to the means of subsistence that he requires for maintenance, and for the propagation of his race. But the price of a commodity, and therefore also of labor, is equal to its cost of production. In proportion, therefore, as the repulsiveness of the work increases, the wage decreases. What is more, in proportion as the use of machinery and division of labor increases, in the same proportion the burden of toil also increases, whether by prolongation of the working hours, by the increase of the work exacted in a given time, or by increased speed of machinery, etc.

Modern Industry has converted the little workshop of the patriarchal master into the great factory of the industrial capitalist. Masses of laborers, crowded into the factory, are organized like soldiers. As privates of the industrial army, they are placed under the command of a perfect hierarchy of officers and sergeants. Not only are they slaves of the bourgeois class, and of the bourgeois state; they are daily and hourly enslaved by the machine, by the overlooker, and, above all, in the individual bourgeois manufacturer himself. The more openly this despotism proclaims gain to be its end and aim, the more petty, the more hateful and the more embittering it is.

The less the skill and exertion of strength implied in manual labor, in other words, the more modern industry becomes developed, the more is the labor of men superseded by that of women. Differences of age and sex have no longer any distinctive social validity for the working class. All are instruments of labor, more or less expensive to use, according to their age and sex.

No sooner is the exploitation of the laborer by the manufacturer, so far at an end, that he receives his wages in cash, than he is set upon by the other portion of the bourgeoisie, the landlord, the shopkeeper, the pawnbroker, etc.

The lower strata of the middle class—the small tradespeople, shopkeepers, and retired tradesmen generally, the handicraftsmen and peasants—all these sink gradually into the proletariat, partly because their diminutive capital does not suffice for the scale on which Modern Industry is carried on, and is swamped in the competition with the large capitalists, partly because their specialized skill is rendered worthless by new methods of production. Thus, the proletariat is recruited from all classes of the population.

The proletariat goes through various stages of development. With its birth begins its struggle with the bourgeoisie. At first, the contest is carried on by individual laborers, then by the work of people of a factory, then by the operative of one trade, in one locality, against the individual bourgeois who directly exploits them. They direct their attacks not against the bourgeois condition of production, but against the instruments of production themselves; they destroy imported wares that compete with their labor, they smash to pieces machinery, they set factories ablaze, they seek to restore by force the vanished status of the workman of the Middle Ages.

At this stage, the laborers still form an incoherent mass scattered over the whole country, and broken up by their mutual competition. If anywhere they unite to form more compact bodies, this is not yet the consequence of their own active union, but of the union of the bourgeoisie, which class, in order to attain its own political ends, is compelled to set the whole proletariat in motion, and is moreover yet, for a time, able to do so. At this stage, therefore, the proletarians do not fight their enemies, but the enemies of their enemies, the remnants of absolute monarchy, the landowners, the non-industrial bourgeois, the petty bourgeois. Thus, the whole historical movement is concentrated in the hands of the bourgeoisie; every victory so obtained is a victory for the bourgeoisie.

But with the development of industry, the

proletariat not only increases in number; it becomes concentrated in greater masses, its strength grows, and it feels that strength more. The various interests and conditions of life within the ranks of the proletariat are more and more equalized, in proportion as machinery obliterates all distinctions of labor, and nearly everywhere reduces wages to the same low level. The growing competition among the bourgeois, and the resulting commercial crises, make the wages of the workers ever more fluctuating. The increasing improvement of machinery, ever more rapidly developing, makes their livelihood more and more precarious; the collisions between individual workmen and individual bourgeois take more and more the character of collisions between two classes. Thereupon, the workers begin to form combinations (trade unions) against the bourgeois; they club together in order to keep up the rate of wages; they found permanent associations in order to make provision beforehand for these occasional revolts. Here and there, the contest breaks out into riots.

Now and then the workers are victorious, but only for a time. The real fruit of their battles lie not in the immediate result, but in the ever expanding union of the workers. This union is helped on by the improved means of communication that are created by Modern Industry, and that place the workers of different localities in contact with one another. It was just this contact that was needed to centralize the numerous local struggles, all of the same character, into one national struggle between classes. But every class struggle is a political struggle. And that union, to attain which the burghers of the Middle Ages, with their miserable highways, required centuries, the modern proletarian, thanks to railways, achieve in a few years.

This organization of the proletarians into a class, and, consequently, into a political party, is continually being upset again by the competition between the workers themselves. But it ever rises up again, stronger, firmer, mightier. It compels legislative recognition of particular interests of the workers, by taking advantage of the divisions among the bourgeoisie itself. Thus, the Ten-Hours Bill in England was carried.

Altogether, collisions between the classes of the old society further in many ways the course of development of the proletariat. The bourgeoisie finds itself involved in a constant battle. At first with the aristocracy; later on, with those portions of the bourgeoisie itself, whose interests have become antagonistic to the progress of industry; at all time with the bourgeoisie of foreign countries. In all these battles, it sees itself compelled to appeal to the proletariat, to ask for help, and thus to drag it into the political arena. The bourgeoisie itself, therefore, supplies the proletariat with its own elements of political and general education, in other words, it furnishes the proletariat with weapons for fighting the bourgeoisie.

Further, as we have already seen, entire sections of the ruling class are, by the advance of industry, precipitated into the proletariat, or are at least threatened in their conditions of existence. These also supply the proletariat with fresh elements of enlightenment and progress.

Finally, in times when the class struggle nears the decisive hour, the progress of dissolution going on within the ruling class, in fact within the whole range of old society, assumes such a violent, glaring character, that a small section of the ruling class cuts itself adrift, and joins the revolutionary class, the class that holds the future in its hands. Just as, therefore, at an earlier period, a section of the nobility went over to the bourgeoisie, so now a portion of the bourgeoisie goes over to the proletariat, and in particular, a portion of the bourgeois ideologists, who have raised themselves to the level of comprehending theoretically the historical movement as a whole.

Of all the classes that stand face to face with the bourgeoisie today, the proletariat alone is a genuinely revolutionary class. The other classes decay and finally disappear in the face of Modern Industry; the proletariat is its special and essential product.

The lower middle class, the small manufacturer, the shopkeeper, the artisan, the peasant, all these fight against the bourgeoisie, to save from extinction their existence as fractions of the middle class. They are therefore not revolutionary, but conservative. Nay, more, they are reactionary, for they try to roll back the wheel of history. If, by chance, they are revolutionary, they are only so in view of their impending transfer into the proletariat; they thus defend not their present, but their future interests; they desert their own standpoint to place themselves at that of the proletariat.

The "dangerous class," the social scum, that passively rotting mass thrown off by the lowest layers of the old society, may, here and there, be swept into the movement by a proletarian revolution; its conditions of life, however, prepare it far more for the part of a bribed tool of reactionary intrigue.

In the condition of the proletariat, those of old society at large are already virtually swamped. The proletarian is without property; his relation to his wife and children has no longer anything in common with the bourgeois family relations; modern industry labor, modern subjection to capital, the same in England as in France, in America as in Germany, has stripped him of every trace of national character. Law, morality, religion, are to him so many bourgeois prejudices, behind which lurk in ambush just as many bourgeois interests.

All the preceding classes that got the upper hand sought to fortify their already acquired status by subjecting society at large to their conditions of appropriation. The proletarians cannot become masters of the productive forces of society, except by abolishing their own previous mode of appropriation, and thereby also every other previous mode of appropriation. They have nothing of their own to secure and to fortify; their mission is to destroy all previous securities for, and insurances of, individual property.

All previous historical movements were movements of minorities, or in the interest of minorities. The proletarian movement is the self-conscious, independent movement of the immense majority, in the interest of the immense majority. The proletariat, the lowest stratum of our present society, cannot stir, cannot raise itself up, without the whole superincumbent strata of official society being sprung into the air.

Though not in substance, yet in form, the struggle of the proletariat with the bourgeoisie is at first a national struggle. The proletariat of each country must, of course, first of all settle matters with its own bourgeoisie.

In depicting the most general phases of the development of the proletariat, we traced the more or less veiled civil war, raging within existing society, up to the point where that war breaks out into open revolution, and where the violent overthrow of the bourgeoisie lays the foundation for the sway of the proletariat.

Hitherto, every form of society has been based, as we have already seen, on the antagonism of oppressing and oppressed classes. But in order to oppress a class, certain conditions must be assured to it under which it can, at least, continue its slavish existence. The serf, in the period of serfdom, raised himself to membership in the commune, just as the petty bourgeois, under the yoke of the feudal absolutism, managed to develop into a bourgeois. The modern laborer, on the contrary, instead of rising with the process of industry, sinks deeper and deeper below the conditions of existence of his own class. He becomes a pauper, and pauperism develops more rapidly than population and wealth. And here it becomes evident that the bourgeoisie is unfit any longer to be the ruling class in society, and to impose its conditions of existence upon society as an overriding law. It is unfit to rule because it is incompetent to assure an existence to its slave within his slavery, because it cannot help letting him sink into such a state, that it has to feed him, instead of being fed by him. Society can no longer live under this bourgeoisie, in other words, its existence is no longer compatible with society.

The essential conditions for the existence and for the sway of the bourgeois class is the formation and augmentation of capital; the condition for capital is wage labor. Wage labor rests exclusively on competition between the laborers. The advance of industry, whose involuntary promoter is the bourgeoisie, replaces the isolation of the laborers, due to competition, by the revolutionary combination, due to association. The development of Modern Industry, therefore, cuts from under its feet the very foundation on which the bourgeoisie produces and appropriates products. What the bourgeoisie therefore produces, above all, are its own grave-diggers. Its fall and the victory of the proletariat are equally inevitable.

II—Proletarians and Communists

In what relation do the Communists stand to the proletarians as a whole? The Communists do not form a separate party opposed to the other working-class parties.

They have no interests separate and apart from those of the proletariat as a whole.

They do not set up any sectarian principles of their own, by which to shape and mold the proletarian movement.

The Communists are distinguished from the other working-class parties by this only:

1. In the national struggles of the proletarians of the different countries, they point out and bring to the front the common interests of the entire proletariat, independently of all nationality.
2. In the various stages of development which the struggle of the working class against the bourgeoisie has to pass through, they always and everywhere represent the interests of the movement as a whole.

The Communists, therefore, are on the one hand practically, the most advanced and resolute section of the working-class parties of every country, that section which pushes forward all others; on the other hand, theoretically, they have over the great mass of the proletariat the advantage of clearly understanding the lines of march, the conditions, and the ultimate general results of the proletarian movement.

The immediate aim of the Communists is the same as that of all other proletarian parties: Formation of the proletariat into a class, overthrow of the bourgeois supremacy, conquest of political power by the proletariat.

The theoretical conclusions of the Communists are in no way based on ideas or principles that have been invented, or discovered, by this or that would-be universal reformer.

They merely express, in general terms, actual relations springing from an existing class struggle, from a historical movement going on under our very eyes. The abolition of existing property relations is not at all a distinctive feature of communism.

All property relations in the past have continually been subject to historical change consequent upon the change in historical conditions.

The French Revolution, for example, abolished feudal property in favor of bourgeois property.

The distinguishing feature of communism is not the abolition of property generally, but the abolition of bourgeois property. But modern bourgeois private property is the final and most complete expression of the system of producing and appropriating products that is based on class antagonisms, on the exploitation of the many by the few.

In this sense, the theory of the Communists may be summed up in the single sentence: Abolition of private property.

We Communists have been reproached with the desire of abolishing the right of personally acquiring property as the fruit of a man's own labor, which property is alleged to be the groundwork of all personal freedom, activity and independence.

Hard-won, self-acquired, self-earned property! Do you mean the property of petty artisan and of the small peasant, a form of property that preceded the bourgeois form? There is no need to abolish that; the development of industry has to a great extent already destroyed it, and is still destroying it daily.

Or do you mean the modern bourgeois private property?

But does wage labor create any property for the laborer? Not a bit. It creates capital, i.e., that kind of property which exploits wage labor, and which cannot increase except upon conditions of begetting a new supply of wage labor for fresh exploitation. Property, in its present form, is based on the antagonism of capital and wage labor. Let us examine both sides of this antagonism.

To be a capitalist, is to have not only a purely personal, but a social STATUS in production. Capital is a collective product, and only by the united action of many members, nay, in the last resort, only by the united action of all members of society, can it be set in motion.

Capital is therefore not only personal; it is a social power.

When, therefore, capital is converted into common property, into the property of all members of society, personal property is not thereby transformed into social property. It is only the social character of the property that is changed. It loses its class character.

Let us now take wage labor.

The average price of wage labor is the minimum wage, i.e., that quantum of the means of subsistence which is absolutely requisite to keep the laborer in bare existence as a laborer. What, therefore, the wage laborer appropriates by means of his labor merely suffices to prolong and reproduce a bare existence. We by no means intend to abolish this personal appropriation of the products of labor, an appropriation that is made for the maintenance and reproduction of human life, and that leaves no surplus wherewith to command the labor of others. All that we want to do away with is the miserable character of this appropriation, under which the laborer lives merely to increase capital, and is allowed to live only in so far as the interest of the ruling class requires it.

In bourgeois society, living labor is but a means to increase accumulated labor. In communist society, accumulated labor is but a means to widen, to enrich, to promote the existence of the laborer.

In bourgeois society, therefore, the past dominates the present; in communist society, the present dominates the past. In bourgeois society, capital is independent and has individuality, while the living person is dependent and has no individuality.

And the abolition of this state of things is called by the bourgeois, abolition of individuality and freedom! And rightly so. The abolition of bourgeois individuality, bourgeois independence, and bourgeois freedom is undoubtedly aimed at.

By freedom is meant, under the present bourgeois conditions of production, free trade, free selling and buying.

But if selling and buying disappears, free selling and buying disappears also. This talk about free selling and buying, and all the other "brave words" of our bourgeois about freedom in general, have a meaning, if any, only in contrast with restricted selling and buying, with the fettered traders of the Middle Ages, but have no meaning when opposed to the communist abolition of buying and selling, or the bourgeois conditions of production, and of the bourgeoisie itself.

You are horrified at our intending to do away with private property. But in your existing society, private property is already done away with for nine-tenths of the population; its existence for the few is solely due to its non-existence in the hands of those nine-tenths. You reproach us, therefore, with intending to do away with a form of property, the necessary condition for whose existence is the non-existence of any property for the immense majority of society.

In one word, you reproach us with intending to do away with your property. Precisely so; that is just what we intend.

From the moment when labor can no longer be converted into capital, money, or rent, into a social power capable of being monopolized, i.e., from the moment when individual property can no longer be transformed into bourgeois property, into capital, from that moment, you say, individuality vanishes.

You must, therefore, confess that by "individual" you mean no other person than the bourgeois, than the middle-class owner of property. This person must, indeed, be swept out of the way, and made impossible.

Communism deprives no man of the power to appropriate the products of society; all that it does is to deprive him of the power to subjugate the labor of others by means of such appropriations.

It has been objected that upon the abolition of private property, all work will cease, and universal laziness will overtake us.

According to this, bourgeois society ought long ago to have gone to the dogs through sheer idleness; for those who acquire anything, do not work. The whole of this objection is but another expression of the tautology: There can no longer be any wage labor when there is no longer any capital.

All objections urged against the communistic mode of producing and appropriating material products, have, in the same way, been urged against the communistic mode of producing and appropriating intellectual products. Just as to the bourgeois, the disappearance of class property is the disappearance of production itself, so the disappearance of class culture is to him identical with the disappearance of all culture.

That culture, the loss of which he laments, is, for the enormous majority, a mere training to act as a machine.

But don't wrangle with us so long as you apply, to our intended abolition of bourgeois property, the standard of your bourgeois notions of freedom, culture, law, etc. Your very ideas are but the outgrowth of the conditions of your bourgeois production and bourgeois property, just as your jurisprudence is but the will of your class made into a law for all, a will whose essential character and direction are determined by the economical conditions of existence of your class.

The selfish misconception that induces you to transform into eternal laws of nature and of reason the social forms stringing from your present mode of production and form of property— historical relations that rise and disappear in the progress of production—this misconception you share with every ruling class that has preceded you. What you see clearly in the case of ancient property, what you admit in the case of feudal property, you are of course forbidden to admit in the case of your own bourgeois form of property.

Abolition of the family! Even the most radical flare up at this infamous proposal of the Communists.

On what foundation is the present family, the bourgeois family, based? On capital, on private gain. In its completely developed form, this family exists only among the bourgeoisie. But this state of things finds its complement in the practical absence of the family among proletarians, and in public prostitution.

The bourgeois family will vanish as a matter of course when its complement vanishes, and both will vanish with the vanishing of capital.

Do you charge us with wanting to stop the exploitation of children by their parents? To this crime we plead guilty.

But, you say, we destroy the most hallowed of relations, when we replace home education by social.

And your education! Is not that also social, and determined by the social conditions under which you educate, by the intervention direct or indirect, of society, by means of schools, etc.? The Communists have not intended the intervention of society in education; they do but seek to alter the character of that intervention, and to rescue education from the influence of the ruling class.

The bourgeois claptrap about the family and education, about the hallowed correlation of parents and child, becomes all the more disgusting, the more, by the action of Modern Industry, all the family ties among the proletarians are torn asunder, and their children transformed into simple articles of commerce and instruments of labor.

But you Communists would introduce community of women, screams the bourgeoisie in chorus.

The bourgeois sees his wife a mere instrument of production. He hears that the instruments of production are to be exploited in common, and, naturally, can come to no other conclusion that the lot of being common to all will likewise fall to the women.

He has not even a suspicion that the real point aimed at is to do away with the status of women as mere instruments of production.

For the rest, nothing is more ridiculous than the virtuous indignation of our bourgeois at the community of women which, they pretend, is to be openly and officially established by the Communists. The Communists have no need to introduce free love; it has existed almost from time immemorial.

Our bourgeois, not content with having wives and daughters of their proletarians at their disposal, not to speak of common prostitutes, take the greatest pleasure in seducing each other's wives. (Ah, those were the days!)

Bourgeois marriage is, in reality, a system of wives in common and thus, at the most, what the Communists might possibly be reproached with is that they desire to introduce, in substitution for a hypocritically concealed, an openly legalized system of free love. For the rest, it is self-evident that the abolition of the present system of production must bring with it the abolition of free love springing from that system, i.e., of prostitution both public and private.

The Communists are further reproached with desiring to abolish countries and nationality.

The workers have no country. We cannot take from them what they have not got. Since the proletariat must first of all acquire political supremacy, must rise to be the leading class of the nation, must constitute itself *the* nation, it is,

so far, itself national, though not in the bourgeois sense of the word.

National differences and antagonism between peoples are daily more and more vanishing, owing to the development of the bourgeoisie, to freedom of commerce, to the world market, to uniformity in the mode of production and in the conditions of life corresponding thereto.

The supremacy of the proletariat will cause them to vanish still faster. United action of the leading civilized countries at least is one of the first conditions for the emancipation of the proletariat.

In proportion as the exploitation of one individual by another will also be put an end to, the exploitation of one nation by another will also be put an end to. In proportion as the antagonism between classes within the nation vanishes, the hostility of one nation to another will come to an end.

The charges against communism made from a religious, a philosophical and, generally, from an ideological standpoint, are not deserving of serious examination.

Does it require deep intuition to comprehend that man's ideas, views, and conception, in one word, man's consciousness, changes with every change in the conditions of his material existence, in his social relations and in his social life?

What else does the history of ideas prove, than that intellectual production changes its character in proportion as material production is changed? The ruling ideas of each age have ever been the ideas of its ruling class.

When people speak of the ideas that revolutionize society, they do but express that fact that within the old society the elements of a new one have been created, and that the dissolution of the old ideas keeps even pace with the dissolution of the old conditions of existence.

When the ancient world was in its last throes, the ancient religions were overcome by Christianity. When Christian ideas succumbed in the eighteenth century to rationalist ideas, feudal society fought its death battle with the then revolutionary bourgeoisie. The ideas of religious liberty and freedom of conscience merely gave expression to the sway of free competition within the domain of knowledge.

"Undoubtedly," it will be said, "religious, moral, philosophical, and juridicial ideas have been modified in the course of historical development. But religion, morality, philosophy, political science, and law, constantly survived this change."

"There are, besides, eternal truths, such as Freedom, Justice, etc., that are common to all states of society. But communism abolishes eternal truths, it abolishes all religion, and all morality, instead of constituting them on a new basis; it therefore acts in contradiction to all past historical experience."

What does this accusation reduce itself to? The history of all past society has consisted in the development of class antagonisms, antagonisms that assumed different forms at different epochs.

But whatever form they may have taken, one fact is common to all past ages, viz., the exploitation of one part of society by the other. No wonder, then, that the social consciousness of past ages, despite all the multiplicity and variety it displays, moves within certain common forms, or general ideas, which cannot completely vanish except with the total disappearance of class antagonisms.

The communist revolution is the most radical rupture with traditional relations; no wonder that its development involved the most radical rupture with traditional ideas.

But let us have done with the bourgeois objections to communism.

We have seen above that the first step in the revolution by the working class is to raise the proletariat to the position of ruling class to win the battle of democracy.

The proletariat will use its political supremacy to wrest, by degree, all capital from the bourgeoisie, to centralize all instruments of production in the hands of the state, i.e., of the proletariat organized as the ruling class; and to increase the total productive forces as rapidly as possible.

Of course, in the beginning, this cannot be effected except by means of despotic inroads on the rights of property, and on the conditions of bourgeois production; by means of measures, therefore, which appear economically insufficient and untenable, but which, in the course of the movement, outstrip themselves, necessitate further inroads upon the old social order, and are unavoidable as a means of entirely revolutionizing the mode of production.

These measures will, of course, be different in different countries.

Nevertheless, in most advanced countries, the following will be pretty generally applicable.

1. Abolition of property in land and application of all rents of land to public purposes.
2. A heavy progressive or graduated income tax.
3. Abolition of all rights of inheritance.
4. Confiscation of the property of all emigrants and rebels.
5. Centralization of credit in the banks of the state, by means of a national bank with state capital and an exclusive monopoly.
6. Centralization of the means of communication and transport in the hands of the state.
7. Extension of factories and instruments of production owned by the state; the bringing into cultivation of waste lands, and the improvement of the soil generally in accordance with a common plan.
8. Equal obligation of all to work. Establishment of industrial armies, especially for agriculture.
9. Combination of agriculture with manufacturing industries; gradual abolition of all the distinction between town and country by a more equable distribution of the populace over the country.
10. Free education for all children in public schools. Abolition of children's factory labor in its present form. Combination of education with industrial production, etc.

When, in the course of development, class distinctions have disappeared, and all production has been concentrated in the hands of a vast association of the whole nation, the public power will lose its political character. Political power, properly so called, is merely the organized power of one class for oppressing another. If the proletariat during its contest with the bourgeoisie is compelled, by the force of circumstances, to organize itself as a class; if, by means of a revolution, it makes itself the ruling class, and, as such, sweeps away by force the old conditions of production, then it will, along with these conditions, have swept away the conditions for the existence of class antagonisms and of classes generally, and will thereby have abolished its own supremacy as a class.

In place of the old bourgeois society, with its classes and class antagonisms, we shall have an association in which the free development of each is the condition for the free development of all.

*   *   *

IV—Position of the Communists in Relation to the Various Existing Opposition Parties

Section II has made clear the relations of the Communists to the existing working-class parties, such as the Chartists in England and the Agrarian Reformers in America.

The Communists fight for the attainment of the immediate aims, for the enforcement of the momentary interests of the working class; but in the movement of the present, they also represent and take care of the future of that movement. In France, the Communists ally with the Social Democrats against the conservative and radical bourgeoisie, reserving, however, the right to take up a critical position in regard to phases and illusions traditionally handed down from the Great Revolution.

In Switzerland, they support the Radicals, without losing sight of the fact that this party consists of antagonistic elements, partly of Democratic Socialists, in the French sense, partly of radical bourgeois.

In Poland, they support the party that insists on an agrarian revolution as the prime condition for national emancipation, that party which fomented the insurrection of Krakow in 1846.

In Germany, they fight with the bourgeoisie whenever it acts in a revolutionary way, against the absolute monarchy, the feudal squirearchy, and the petty-bourgeoisie.

But they never cease, for a single instant, to instill into the working class the clearest possible recognition of the hostile antagonism between bourgeoisie and proletariat, in order that the German workers may straightway use, as so many weapons against the bourgeoisie, the social and political conditions that the bourgeoisie must necessarily introduce along with its supremacy, and in order that, after the fall of the reactionary classes in Germany, the fight against the bourgeoisie itself may immediately begin.

The Communists turn their attention chiefly to Germany, because that country is on the eve of a bourgeois revolution that is bound to be carried out under more advanced conditions of European civilization and with a much more developed proletariat than that of England was in the seventeenth, and France in the eighteenth century, and because the bourgeois revolution in Germany will be but the prelude to an immediately following proletarian revolution.

In short, the Communists everywhere support every revolutionary movement against the existing social and political order of things.

In all these movements, they bring to the front, as the leading question in each, the property question, no matter what its degree of development at the time.

Finally, they labor everywhere for the union and agreement of the democratic parties of all countries.

The Communists disdain to conceal their views and aims. They openly declare that their ends can be attained only by the forcible over-throw of all existing social conditions. Let the ruling classes tremble at a communist revolu-tion. The proletarians have nothing to lose but their chains. They have a world to win.

Proletarians of all countries, unite!

ADAM PRZEWORSKI

A PROLOGUE: THE FALL OF COMMUNISM

Transitions to democracy occurred in South-ern Europe—in Greece, Portugal, and Spain—in the mid 1970s. They were launched in the Southern Cone of Latin Amer-ica, except for Chile—in Argentina, Brazil, and Uruguay—in the early 1980s. And they were in-augurated in Eastern Europe during the "Au-tumn of the People" of 1989. Can we draw on the earlier experiences to understand the later ones? Are there lessons to be learned from history?

In spite of the waves of democratization in Southern Europe and Latin America, the fall of communism took everyone by surprise. No one had expected that the communist system, styled by some as totalitarian precisely because it was supposed to be immutable, would collapse sud-denly and peacefully. What made the transition to democracy in Eastern Europe possible? What made it happen so quickly and so smoothly?

Since the fall of communism in Eastern Eu-rope is the prologue to the analyses that follow, let me reconstruct the story as I see it. Yet first we need a warning against facile analyses. The "Autumn of the People" was a dismal failure of political science. Any retrospective explanation of the fall of communism must not only account for the historical developments but also identify the theoretical assumptions that prevented us from

From Adam Przeworski, *Democracy and the Market: Political and Economic Reforms in Eastern Europe and Latin America* (New York: Cambridge University Press, 1991), pp. 1–9.

anticipating these developments. For if we are wise now, why were we not equally sage before?

Most terminal cancer patients die of pneu-monia. And social science is not very good at sorting out underlying causes and precipitating conditions; witness the fifty years of controversy over the fall of Weimar. For the response to the question "Why did communism collapse?" is not the same as to "Why did it collapse in the au-tumn of 1989?" It is easier to explain why com-munism had to fall than why it did.

"Totalitarianism" could not answer either question: It could not diagnose the cancer and hence the vulnerability to pneumonia. The total-itarian model was more ideological than the so-cieties it depicted as such. This model denied the possibility of conflict within communist societies because it saw them as based on dogma and re-pression. Yet from the late 1950s, ideology was no longer the cement, to use Gramsci's expres-sion, that held these societies together. I remem-ber how startled I was by the leading slogan of May Day 1964 in Poland: "Socialism is a guaran-tee of our borders." Socialism—the project for a new future—was no longer the end; it had be-come an instrument of traditional values. And by the 1970s, repression had subsided: As the com-munist leadership became bourgeoisified, it could no longer muster the self-discipline re-quired to crush all dissent. Party bureaucrats were no longer able to spend their nights at meetings, to wear working-class uniforms, to march and shout slogans, to abstain from ostentatious consumption. What had developed was "goulash communism," "Kadarism," "Brezhnevism": an implicit social pact in which elites offered the prospect of material welfare in exchange for silence. And the tacit premise of this pact was that socialism was no longer a model of a new future but an underdeveloped something else. Khrushchev set it as the goal of the Soviet Union to catch up with Great Britain; by the 1970s, Western Europe had become the standard of comparison, and the comparisons became increasingly humiliating.

As Polish and Hungarian surveys showed, the outcome was a society that was highly materialistic, atomized, and cynical. It was a society in which people uttered formulas they did not believe and that they did not expect anyone else to believe. Speech became a ritual. I am haunted by a Soviet joke. A man is distributing leaflets in Red Square. He is stopped by a policeman, who confiscates them, only to discover that they are blank. "What are you spreading? They are blank. Nothing is written!" the surprised guardian of order exclaims. "Why write?" is the answer. "Everybody knows . . ."

Words became dangerous, so dangerous that the five armies to invade Czechoslovakia in 1968 cited as one reason Ludvik Vaculik's "Two Thousand Words." And most subversive were the very ideals that founded this social order: rationality, equality, even the working class. As early as the 1960s, Polish surveys showed that engineering students were most radical in criticizing the socialist economy; they were the ones imbued with the value of rationality. Polish dissidents adopted in the mid 1970s a simple strategy to subvert the political system: They decided to use the rights proclaimed by the Communist constitution. And the decisive threat to this system originated from those on behalf of whom it had always claimed legitimacy: the working class. Communist ideology became a threat to the social order in which it was embodied. People need some modicum of cognitive consistency; when their thoughts and their words perpetually diverge, life becomes intolerable.

This is why the cry for "truth" became at least as important in imploding this system as the clamor for bread, why history became an obsession when the regime began to crumble, why a leading opponent of the Communist regime in the Soviet Union has been the director of the National Archive, why high school history examinations were suspended for two years in the Soviet Union, why writers and intellectuals became the leaders of the postcommunist regimes.

But those of us who saw no reason to distinguish between authoritarianism and totalitarianism, those of us who found in the transition to democracy in Spain, Greece, Argentina, Brazil, or the Philippines a ready-made model for Hungary, Poland, or the Soviet Union, were looking for the symptoms of pneumonia but did not diagnose the cancer. We knew how to analyze the dynamic of conflicts once they flared up, but not the conditions ensuring that they would. Although Timothy Garton Ash (1990: 252) cautiously wrote, in September of 1988, about the possibility of the "Ottomanization"—"emancipation by decay"—of the Soviet empire, no one sensed how feeble the communist system had become, no one expected that just a little push would cause it to collapse.

The "Autumn of the People" constitutes one event, or perhaps one and a half. Henry Kissinger's domino theory triumphed; all he missed was the direction in which the dominoes would fall. What happened in Romania was caused by what had occurred in Czechoslovakia; what ensued in Czechoslovakia resulted from the breakdown in East Germany; what stimulated masses of people to fill the streets in East Germany followed the political changes in Hungary; what showed Hungarians a way out was the success of the negotiations in Poland. I know that hundreds of macrohistorical comparative sociologists will write thousands of books and articles correlating background conditions with outcomes in each country, but I think they will be wasting their time, for the entire event was one single snowball. I mean it in a technical sense: As developments took place in one country, people elsewhere were updating their probabilities of success, and as the next country went over the brink, the calculation was becoming increasingly reassuring. And I have no doubt that the last holdouts will follow.

The open rebellion began in Poland in 1976 and flared up for the first time in 1980. The first instance of collapse of a communist system does not date to 1989 but to December 13, 1981. The coup d'état of General Jaruzelski was proof that Communist parties could no longer rule with passive acquiescence, that from now on power must be based on force. As the economic strategy of the 1970s collapsed, as intellectuals found their voices and workers took over their factories, party bureaucrats were unable to preserve their rule. To continue to enjoy privileges, they had to abdicate political power in favor of organized forces of repression. Communist rule became militarized because only in this form could it survive the revolt of the society.

From then on it was only the fear of physical force, external and internal, that held the system together. Even this force turned out to be insufficient when Polish workers struck again in the summer of 1988, and it is to the credit of General Jaruzelski that he understood it. The decision to compromise with the opposition was imposed on the Polish party by the military. The Hungarian party split from the top, without the same pressure from below and without being coerced by the armed forces. The success of the Polish negotiations in the spring of 1989 showed Hungarians a road to peaceful transfer of power. By that time party bureaucrats in both countries began to realize that if they could hold onto political power, perhaps they could, to use Elemer Hankiss's felicitous phrase, "convert it" into economic power before it was too late.

The spark that ignited the subsequent chain of events was the Hungarian decision to let East German refugees proceed to West Germany. Having learned that the road was open from Budapest, East Germans tried Prague. At this moment, the East German leadership made a fatal mistake. They agreed that the refugees could

transit to the West but decided to "humiliate" them. They had them pass by train through East Germany to be exposed to the scorn of organized demonstrations. But instead of condemning the refugees, the masses turned the demonstrations against the regime, as they would later do in Bulgaria and Romania. The rest is history. Once hundreds of thousands of people had flooded the streets of Leipzig, Dresden, and Berlin, once the wall had fallen, the pressure on Czechoslovakia was irresistible, and all the Bulgarian communists could do was to limit the damage.

The Gorbachev revolution in the Soviet Union obviously played a crucial role in unleashing the events in Eastern Europe. It was the single precipitating event, the pneumonia. But this platitude easily leads to confusion.

The threat of Soviet intervention, imprinted in the memories of 1956 in Hungary and 1968 in Czechoslovakia, was the constraint on internal developments in Eastern Europe. But it was only that: the constraint, a dam placed against pressing waters. When this dam cracked, it was the pent-up waters that overran its remains. The change in the Soviet Union did not propel transformations in Hungary and Poland; what it did was to remove the crucial factor that had been blocking them. The constraint was external, but the impetus was internal. This is why the "Soviet factor" does not render invalid the application of Latin American models to Eastern Europe.

Moreover, the Gorbachev revolution was not a fluke of history. The Soviet Union was not exempt—in retrospect it is obvious—from the same pressures that made the system crack in Eastern Europe. Unable to persuade, incapable of silencing dissident voices, inept at feeding its own people, impotent against an amalgam of tribes in the mountains of Afghanistan, indolent in international technological competition—was this not the Soviet Union of 1984? And had we made this list, would we not have concluded, whatever theoretical differences divide us, that no such system could last?

Could the Soviet Union have invaded Poland

in 1981? Could it have maintained its empire? At what cost to its internal peace and prosperity? In my view, the changes in the Soviet Union, including the shift of the Soviet strategic posture with regard to Eastern Europe, were to a large extent endogenous; that is, they were brought about in part by the developments in Eastern Europe, by the increasing political and economic costs of maintaining the empire.

Everyone, not only marxists, used to believe that political change of this magnitude could only be violent. Yet except in Romania and in the nationalistic flare-ups in the Soviet Union and Yugoslavia, not a single person was killed in this revolution. Why?

The reasons the system collapsed so rapidly and so quietly are to be found both in the realm of ideology and in the realm of physical force. For me, again the most striking aspect of this collapse is that party bureaucrats had nothing to say to defend their power. They were simply mute; they did not speak about socialism, progress, the future, prosperity, rationality, equality, the working class. They only calculated how many thousands of people they could beat up if they persevered, how many ministerial posts they would have to yield if they compromised, how many jobs they could retain if they surrendered. The most they could muster were declarations of patriotic commitment, but their credentials were dubious. And even now, when the relabeled or transformed Communist parties declare their devotion to democratic socialism, they still do not mean what they say: The founding Program of the Polish Social Democratic Party begins with the statement that Poland is the highest value the party adheres to, affirms its commitment to political democracy, and goes on to express the preference for "whatever forms of property . . . are economically most efficient." These declarations may serve the party in finding a place in the new system, but these are not the values with which it could have defended the old one. By 1989, party bureaucrats did not believe in their speech. And to shoot, one must believe in something. When those who hold the trigger have absolutely nothing to say, they have no force to pull it.

Moreover, they did not have the guns. In no country did the army, as distinct from the police forces, come to the rescue. In Poland, the armed forces led the reforms; only when three generals walked out of the February 1989 meeting of the Central Committee did party bureaucrats understand that their days were over. In all the other countries, including Romania, the army refused to repress. I have a cynical view of the reason for this posture, although I admit that perhaps patriotic motivations did play a role. Educated by the Latin American experience, I find the canonical phrase uttered by the generals all over Eastern Europe foreboding. When the military proclaim, "The army does not serve a political party, but the nation," I see them jumping at the chance to free themselves from civilian control, to establish themselves as the arbiter of the national fate. Yet whether or not I am correct, in fact party bureaucrats did not control the guns. I cannot stop myself from recounting a Polish joke that encapsulates the entire story. An older man ventures to buy meat. A long line has already formed. The delivery is not coming; people are getting impatient. The man begins to swear: at the leader, at the party, at the system. Another man approaches him and remarks, pointing to his head: "You know, comrade, if you said things like this in the old days, we would just go 'Paf' and it would all be over." The old man returns home empty-handed. His wife asks, "They have no more meat?" "It is worse than that," the man replies; "they have no more bullets."

What was it that collapsed in Eastern Europe? "Communism" is a neutral answer to this question, since it is a label that has no more advocates. But was it not socialism? Many of those who believe that there can be no socialism without democracy contend that the system that failed in Eastern Europe was perhaps Stalinism, statism, bureaucracy, or communism, but not socialism. Yet I fear that the historical lesson is more radical, that what died in Eastern Europe is the very idea of rationally administering things to satisfy human needs—the feasibility of implementing public ownership of productive resources through centralized command; the very project of basing a society on disinterested cooperation—the possibility of dissociating social contributions from individual rewards. If the only ideas about a new social order originate today from the Right, it is because the socialist project—the project that was forged in Western Europe between 1848 and 1891 and that had animated social movements all over the world since then—failed, in the East and in the West. True, the values of political democracy and of social justice continue to guide social democrats such as myself, but social democracy is a program to mitigate the effects of private ownership and market allocation, not an alternative project of society.

Now several countries in Eastern Europe, again led by Poland, have ventured or are about to venture into the greatest experiment in history since the forced Stalinist industrialization of 1929. Although the prevailing mood follows Adenauer's dictum of *keine Experimenten*, the economic transformations envisaged in these countries ironically mirror the communist project. They implement an intellectual blueprint, a blueprint developed within the walls of American academia and shaped by international financial institutions. They are radical; they are intended to turn upside down all the existing social relations. And they offer a single panacea, a magic wand that, once waved, will cure all ills. Replace "nationalization of the means of production" with "private property" and "plan" with "market," and you can leave the structure of the ideology intact. Perhaps revolutions are shaped by the very systems against which they are directed?

What, then, is the future of Eastern Europe? As I see it, Eastern European societies can follow three roads: their own, that of Southern Europe, or that of Latin America and other countries of the capitalist South. This is what future discussions of Eastern Europe will be all about: Which of these three roads is most likely?

The Left sees in these countries a historic chance to realize what used to be called the third and today should be counted as the second way: a chance to develop a social system alternative to both capitalism and communism. This system would be democratic market socialism: democracy in the political realm and an economy that combines a large cooperative sector with allocation by markets. Although blueprints for this system animate political discussions in Czechoslovakia, Hungary, and Poland, I believe that if such a system does develop it will be mainly by default. Plans for selling the entire public sector to private owners are simply unrealistic, given the low level of domestic savings and fears of foreign domination. Hence, a large number of firms may either remain in state hands or be transferred to employees for lack of private buyers. Whether this property structure will have profound consequences for firm performance, for the role of workers in the enterprise, for their political organization outside the firm, and for political institutions is still a matter of controversy. I remain skeptical.

Whatever mix of ownership patterns emerges, the road the new elites and the people in Eastern Europe want to take is the one that leads to Europe. "Democracy, market, Europe" is the banner. The optimistic scenario is to retrace the path of Spain. Since 1976, in only fifteen years Spain has succeeded in irreversibly consolidating democratic institutions, allowing peaceful alternation in power; in modernizing its economy and making it internationally competitive; in imposing civilian control over the military; in solving complicated national questions; in extending citizenship rights; and in inducing cultural changes that made it part of the European community of nations. And this is what everyone in Eastern Europe expects to happen. Eastern Europeans deeply believe that if it had not been for "the system," they would have been like Spain. And now this system is gone. They will thus reenter Europe. They will become a part of the West.

But Spain is a miracle: one of a handful of

countries that since World War I have escaped the economics, the politics, and the culture of poor capitalism. Portugal did not match this achievement; Greece is experiencing profound economic difficulties and a shaky political situation. And note the case of Turkey, which tried and failed to generate the economic, political, and cultural transformations that would have brought it into Europe.

Should we, then, expect these hopes to be fulfilled? Is Eastern Europe on its way to the West, or will the Hungarians, the Poles, and the Romanians join billions of people who inhabit the capitalist South?

VALERIE BUNCE

RETHINKING RECENT DEMOCRATIZATION: LESSONS FROM THE POST-COMMUNIST EXPERIENCE

Recent Democratization

Our understanding of recent democratization—of such issues as the origins and the consolidation of new democracies—has been heavily influenced by the experiences of Latin America and southern Europe. This is not surprising. The third wave of democratization, as Samuel Huntington termed it, began in southern Europe and then moved quickly to Latin America. Moreover, given the political oscillations of the region they study, specialists in Latin American politics were unusually well positioned to address questions of regime transition. Finally, combining the experiences of these two regions offered a comparative advantage. They contained a large number of countries, virtually all of which had redemocratized over the course of a decade and a half; they shared some commonalities in terms of history and culture; and yet they varied with respect to the timing and mode of transition. It is precisely such a mix of similarities and differences that makes for instructive comparison.

From *World Politics* 55 (January 2003), pp. 167–92. Some of the author's notes have been omitted.

The breakdown of state socialism in the Soviet Union and Eastern Europe between 1989 and 1991 and the subsequent rise of new regimes and new states throughout this region provide us with an opportunity to broaden the discussion of recent democratization. By broadening, I refer, most obviously, to the geography of the conversation. If recent democratization is, indeed, a global process, then the terrain of these studies should better reflect that fact. Moreover, only by expanding the geographical horizons can we know whether our conceit as social scientists—that is, our presumption of generalizability—is well founded.

There are, in addition, three other aspects of broadening. One is the familiar argument, central to the ideology of pluralism, that more voices are preferable to fewer in producing quality outcomes. This is particularly important in comparative politics, given the correlation between geographical and intellectual boundaries. As we all know, the concepts used, the questions asked, and the theories evaluated all tend to take on a regional cast.

Just as familiar is a second consideration. Stepping outside our familiar terrain often alerts us to new factors and new relationships—more generally, new thinking, to borrow from Gorbachev. As already suggested, this is not just a matter of reaping intellectual benefits from liberalization of trade among scholarly cultures. This is also a function of the new issues that additional cases often introduce. For example, with the rise of new states and new economic and political regimes in the former communist world came heightened sensitivity among scholars to a series of previously overlooked concerns. These include the impact of economic regime transition on the democratic project; the critical distinction between founding genuinely new democracies (as in most postcommunist states) versus redemocratization (as with much of Latin America and southern Europe); the impact of identity politics and the state on democratization; the consequences for democratic politics of deficiencies in civil and political society; and the role of international institutions in founding, sustaining, and/or undermining new democracies.

A final benefit of broadening is methodological. The most illuminating comparisons are those that restrain the universe of causes while expanding the range of results. In the case of comparative democratization, while Latin America and southern Europe go far in meeting the first condition, they are less helpful on the second—though recent threats to democracy in, say, Peru, Venezuela, Colombia, and perhaps Argentina have provided greater variation in dependent variables. By contrast, the postcommunist region of East-Central Europe and the former Soviet Union is unusually useful on both counts, given, for example, similarities in institutional legacies and in both the timing and the agenda of transformation alongside the sheer diversity of the region's economic and political pathways—what Charles King has aptly termed the "mercurial dependent variables" of postcommunism.[1]

The appeal of this region as an ideal laboratory for comparative inquiry has not been lost on analysts. There are thus a number of studies that use cases from the postcommunist area to address such questions as why democracies either do or do not arise and why some of the new democracies succeed, whereas others break down; whether variations in economic performance reflect historical or more recent influences and geographical, economic, or political factors; and why transitions to democracy are sometimes accompanied by nationalist protests, why some states dissolve in reaction to these protests, and why state dissolution is either violent or peaceful.

Comparing New Democracies

This article aims to use the postcommunist experience in East-Central Europe and the former Soviet Union—twenty-seven cases in all—to rethink our understanding of recent democratization. It does so by conducting a conversation between two bodies of research: (1) studies of Latin America and southern Europe, which collectively have constituted the reigning wisdom in the field, and (2) research on postcommunist politics. The discussion will focus on two relationships central to discussions in the field—between transitional politics and subsequent regime trajectories and between the consolidation and the sustainability of democracy. We will see that the postcommunist experience challenges the way both issues have been understood.

In particular, I argue the following. First, the degree of uncertainty in democratic transitions varies considerably. This in turn affects the strategies of transition and their payoffs. Second, mass mobilization can contribute to both the founding and the consolidation of democracy. Third, under certain conditions the democratic project is furthered by transitions that involve both nationalist protest and changes in state boundaries. Fourth, while rapid progress in democratic consolidation improves the prospects for democratic survival in the future, it does not follow that unconsolidated democracies are necessarily less sustainable. Indeed, compromising democracy (and the state) may *contribute* to democratic survival. Finally, while comparisons among new democracies can identify the optimal *conditions* for democratization, they may have less to say about optimal *strategies* for democratization.

Transitions to Democracy: Assumptions and Arguments

The analysis of recent democratization has been premised on some core assumptions about transitions from dictatorship to democracy—with the transitional period understood as beginning with an evident weakening of authoritarian rule and ending with the first competitive elections. These assumptions include the following: (1) that immediate influences are more important than historical considerations in shaping transitional dynamics; (2) that transitions are inherently quite uncertain; (3) that the central dynamic in a transition is bargaining between authoritarian leaders and leaders of the democratic opposition, with outcomes a function of their relative power; and (4) that the key issues on the table during the transition are breaking with authoritarian rule, building democratic institutions, and eliciting the cooperation of authoritarians.[2]

These assumptions, coupled with comparative studies of Latin America and southern Europe, have produced several generalizations about what constitutes the ideal approach to transition. First, as Dankwart Rustow argued more than thirty years ago, successful democratization seems to require at the very least a prior settlement of the national and state questions.[3] Second, bargaining about the rules of the transition and the new political order should be limited to a small group of authoritarian elites and representatives of the democratic opposition. Finally, given the uncertainty of transitions, it is useful to forge compromises that promote political stability during the construction of a democratic order. In practice, this means pacting; reducing the range of issues on the bargaining

table (for example, avoiding reforms of the state and, if possible, major and inherently destabilizing economic reforms); demobilizing publics (which also limits the issues on the table, while depriving the authoritarians of a rationale for sabotaging democratization); forming interim governments with leaders agreeable to both sides; giving the military some room for political maneuver in the constitution; and holding a competitive election that produces a government broadly representative of both authoritarians and democrats.

Mass Mobilization

The postcommunist experience seems to challenge many of these assumptions about transitional strategies. Let us begin by addressing the role of mass publics in the transition. It is widely agreed among specialists and confirmed by the rankings over time by Freedom House that the most successful transitions to democracy in the postcommunist region have been in the Czech Republic, Estonia, Hungary, Latvia, Lithuania, Poland, and Slovenia. The transition to democracy in every one of these cases, except Hungary, began with mass protests.[4] Moreover, if we restrict our focus to those countries that show significant improvement in their democratic performance over time, or Bulgaria and Romania, we see the same pattern: mass mobilization at the beginning of the transition.

Why was mass mobilization so often helpful to the democratic transition in the postcommunist context? The answer is that political protests performed a number of valuable functions. They signaled the breakdown of the authoritarian order; created a widespread sense that there were alternatives to that order; pushed authoritarian leaders (and sometimes even leaders of the opposition, as with Walesa in Poland) to the bargaining table; created (and sometimes restored) a large opposition united by its rejection of the incumbent regime; and gave opposition leaders a resource advantage when bargaining with authoritarian elites. Finally, mass mobilization created a mandate for radical change that subsequently translated into a large victory for the democratic forces in the first competitive elections and, following that, led to the introduction of far-reaching economic and political reforms.

Uncertainty

If we accept that mass mobilization during the transition can further the democratic project, then we necessarily confront additional challenges to the received wisdom about recent democratization. First, it can be argued that in many cases such mobilization in the postcommunist region reduced the uncertainty of the transition—by providing a clear reading of mass sentiments, by strengthening the bargaining power of opposition leaders, and by forcing the communists to give up their defense of the old order, either stepping aside quickly (as in Czechoslovakia) or, when thinking prospectively, joining the movement for democracy (as in Poland, Slovenia, and the Baltic states).[5] At the same time, mass mobilization promised—and delivered—a popular mandate for democracy in the first competitive elections.

Most of the transitions to democracy in the postcommunist world were, of course, highly uncertain. This is evidenced by the fact that the first competitive election in most of the countries in the region led to a communist victory. Indeed, the larger the victory, the more likely that authoritarian rule continued. Moreover, even ten years after the transition began, only one-third of the postcommunist regimes were ranked fully free. Although this is the highest number since state socialism fell, it is a percentage much lower than what one finds at a comparable point in the Latin American and southern European transitions. When combined with the earlier observations, these patterns suggest that the uncertainty surrounding postcommunist political trajectories varied significantly.[6] In some cases, a democratic outcome was relatively pre-

dictable; in most others, the political options after communism were far more open-ended.

Strategic Implications of Uncertainty

The existence of a more certain political environment in some countries calls into question both the necessity and the logic, outlined earlier, of safeguarding the new democracy by forging compromises between authoritarians and democrats. It is precisely the absence of pressure to do so in the Polish, the Czech, and the other highly successful transitions that explains another contrast between the "East" and the "South." It is true that many of the most successful transitions in the postcommunist area included pacting (though rarely as elaborate as the Spanish experience) and that some also evidenced for a brief time broadly representative interim governments. It is also true, however, that the transitions in the postcommunist region that combined pacting with demobilized publics—or what has been asserted to be the preferred approach in the South—were precisely the transitions that were most likely to continue authoritarian rule in the postcommunist region. Moreover, the other compromises that were deemed so beneficial for the southern European and Latin American transitions were rejected by opposition leaders in Poland, Hungary, Slovenia, and the like. Instead, they were strongly positioned to favor an immediate and sharp break with the authoritarian past. Thus, in every highly successful case of democratization in the region, the military was excluded from political influence from the start; the first elections involved a radical break with the political leadership of the past; and major changes in the economy were introduced quickly. Just as important was the commitment in each of these cases to reforming the state, including in most of them its very boundaries. For the Czech Republic, Hungary, Poland, Slovenia, and the Baltic states, then, the agenda of transition was unusually ambitious.

Postcommunist transition dynamics therefore ask us to amend the familiar formulation drawn from the South. It was precisely because mass mobilization was so threatening to authoritarians that leaders of the opposition in some of these countries were free to carry out radical political and economic reforms. Put differently: because of popular mobilization or, in the Hungarian case, reform communism and collaboration between democrats and authoritarians, opposition leaders in what became the most sustainable and full-scale democracies in the East could proceed quickly in breaking with authoritarian rule and building democratic (and, for that matter, capitalist) institutions without worrying as much as their counterparts elsewhere about appeasing authoritarian interests.

This, in turn, altered the strategies of transition and their payoffs. While bridging between the old and the new order constituted by all accounts the most successful approach to democratization in Latin America and southern Europe, the most successful strategy in the postcommunist region was the opposite—severing ties.

The Role of the Military

Also contributing to these interregional contrasts in the optimal strategies of transition was the very different role of the military in Latin America and southern Europe, on the one hand, and in the communist area, on the other hand. Specialists in the South have argued with essentially one voice that the biggest threat to democracy today, as in the past, is the military. One has only to recall, for example, the long history of military interventions in Latin American politics, most of which terminated democracy (though some of them oversaw a return to democratic governance, as also occurred in unusually circuitous fashion, in the Portuguese transition). There is, in addition, the attempted military coup d'état in Spain in 1982. Indeed, precisely because of its long importance in politics, the

military has been awarded remarkable powers in many Latin American constitutions, their democratic claims notwithstanding. When combined, these examples carry an obvious message: the military in these contexts can make or break regimes. It is precisely this capacity that contributed to the uncertainty of the transitions in the South and that necessitated compromises with authoritarian forces.

In much of the postcommunist world, by contrast, there is a long tradition of civilian control over the military—a tradition that goes far back in Russian history and that, following the Bolshevik Revolution and the demilitarization after the Civil War, was maintained at home and then after World War II was projected outward to the members of the Soviet bloc. Civil-military relations, in short, constituted one area where the authoritarian past proved to be beneficial, rather than a burden, for democratization after state socialism.

With the military less threatening in the postcommunist context and with mass publics in some cases mobilized in support of democracy, authoritarian elites in the postcommunist region were indeed under siege. This was particularly the case in East-Central Europe, where domestic control over the military (and the secret police)—except in Yugoslavia, Romania, and Albania—had been ceded to the Soviet Union after 1968. All this left the opposition in what came to be the most successful democracies in the region with unusual freedom of maneuver—a freedom enhanced by public support in the streets. As a result, both the effects of mass mobilization *and* the most successful strategies of transition were different in the postcommunist context from what they had been in Latin America and southern Europe.

Nationalist Mobilization

The analysis thus far has sidestepped an issue of considerable importance in the transitions from state socialism: the distinction between protests against the regime and protests against the state. Here, the postcommunist region exhibits another surprising pattern. While popular protest in both the Czech lands and Poland targeted the regime, the Baltic and Slovene demonstrations are better understood as both liberal and nationalist. In the latter cases, then, nationalism supported democratic governance, even when nationalist concerns grew out of and were in part responsible for the disintegration of a state.

There also seems to be another positive linkage between nationalist mobilization and successful, sustained democratization. The republics that made up the Soviet Union, Yugoslavia, and Czechoslovakia varied considerably from each other with respect to whether publics protested, whether the opposition was strong and united, and whether publics, the opposition, and, indeed, even the communists were committed to democratization. With the breakup of these three ethnofederal states along republican lines, those republics with the best conditions for democratic governance were liberated from a political and economic context that made such an outcome unlikely, if not impossible. Thus, not just Slovenia and the Baltic republics, but also Macedonia, Moldova, Russia, and Ukraine were better positioned to pursue a democratic course following state disintegration.

How can we reconcile these observations with the familiar argument that nationalist mobilization poses a threat to democracy on the grounds that the logics of state building and democratization are contradictory? This argument, moreover, has empirical support in the post-communist world, given the deleterious effects of nationalism on political developments after state socialism in Bosnia, Croatia, Georgia, Serbia and Montenegro (and Kosovo), and Slovakia. In each of these cases the nationalist movement excluded minorities residing within the republic; transformed some communists into nationalists, who then used nationalism to maintain authoritarian control; and constructed illiberal successor regimes while deconstructing successor states. What explains these divergent consequences of nationalism?

When nationalism enters the discussion, parsimonious arguments often give way to thick explanations. In this instance, however, there seems to be a relatively simple distinction: *when* nationalist demonstrations began in the republics. Late nationalist mobilization—or nationalist demonstrations that first appeared when the communist regime and state were disintegrating—is associated in virtually every instance with a rapid transition to democracy and progress since that time in building a stable—or at least increasingly stable—democratic order. This describes, in particular, not just the cases of Estonia, Latvia, Lithuania, and Slovenia, but also the far more flawed, but nonetheless durable democracies of Moldova, Russia, and Ukraine.

By contrast, nationalist demonstrations that first occurred before the regime and state began to unravel are associated with very different political pathways after state socialism—either democratic breakdown or a delayed transition to democracy. There were five republics and one autonomous province that experienced such demonstrations by their titular nation during the 1970s or at the beginning of the 1980s: Armenia, Croatia, Georgia, Kosovo, Slovakia, and, to a more limited extent, Serbia. In every one of these cases the subsequent transition to democracy was undermined, as was the successor state in most cases.

Why is timing so important? The key seems to be differences in regime context. In the "early" cases, nationalist mobilization arose in response to two conditions: a strong sense of identity on the part of members and especially the self-appointed leaders of the republic's titular nation (reflecting earlier developments, such as the experience of statehood prior to communist party rule) coupled with republican political dynamics that featured domination by the titular nation along with significant autonomy from the center. Once demonstrations began, three developments followed: minorities within these republics (except homogeneous Armenia) defended themselves from titular domination by building countermovements while allying with the center; the center, fearing that nationalist protests would spread and thereby challenge both the regime and the state, suppressed the titular national protesters, purged the republican party, and empowered minorities as a counterweight to the titular nation; and the republican party fissured in the face of irreconcilable demands from local nationalists versus central communists.

As a result, by the time state socialism began to dissolve, the stage was already set for an unusually problematic transition to both democratic rule and independent statehood. Two insurmountable divides were in place. The first was between nationalists, who dominated the political scene, and liberals, who had been demobilized. The second was between leaders of the majority nation and leaders of minority communities. The national identities of these groups were well defined and exclusivist, and their competing identities were joined with competing interests, political alliances, and preferences for the future. Moreover, the communist leaders of these republics, facing the loss of both their institutional and their ideological bases for ruling, did not have the option their Slovenian counterparts had, of defecting to an opposition that embraced both independent statehood and liberal democracy. Instead, they could either become nationalists or, if adopting a liberal position, face political marginalization.

By contrast, when nationalist mobilization began only later, in response to the weakening of the regime and the state, all these conditions were absent—or at least less well defined. This meant that the majority and the minorities were free to coalesce around the issues of republican sovereignty and liberal democracy. Thus, in these contexts a liberal agenda combined with a nationalist agenda; and not only opposition forces but even many communists embraced that agenda.

We can now conclude our discussion of transitions in the South versus the East. The experiences of the latter region suggest the following, all running counter to the received wisdom about Latin America and southern Europe. First, historical factors are critical in shaping the resources and especially the preferences of elites during the transition, as well as, more generally, transition trajectories. Second, one proximate and positive influence, lying outside the high politics of the transition, is mass mobilization. Third, transitions seem to vary in their degree of uncertainty, and this affects what constitutes the most successful path. In the postcommunist world, where some transitions were less uncertain, the most successful approach was one that moved quickly on both political and economic fronts. Fourth, democratization can be successful when it is combined with nationalist mobilization and the founding of a new state. This is particularly so when such mobilization first begins with the weakening of the state and the regime.

Finally, if we divide the transitions in the postcommunist world into two types—where nationalist mobilization was present and where it was not—we find two simple stories. One has already been noted—the consequences for democratization of timing—when nationalist mobilization begins. The second story describes the remaining countries in the region. Here, the key issue appears to be the strength of the opposition, as indicated by their competitiveness in the first election. Put succinctly, the better their electoral performance, the more successful the transition to democracy.

*   *   *

Conclusions

Research on democratization, particularly the founding and performance of new democracies, is largely a literature about the choices political leaders have made and the consequences of those choices. It is also largely a literature based on the return to democracy in Latin America and southern Europe. The purpose of this article has been both to question and to complicate the focus on elites and the generalizations that have been made about transitions to democracy, democratic consolidation, and democratic sustainability. I have done so by adding an additional region to the empirical equation—the twenty-seven countries that make up the Eurasian postcommunist region.

Several conclusions emerged. First, transitions to democracy seem to vary considerably with respect to the uncertainty surrounding the process. This variance in turn affects the strategies of transition and their payoffs. In the postcommunist region it was widely assumed that the uncertainty surrounding these transitions was unusually high, given, for example, the absence in most cases of a democratic past together, the extraordinary economic and political penetration of state socialism, and the seeming tensions among democratization, state building, the construction of a capitalist economy, and the radically changed relationship of the state to the international system. It turns out, however, that for a number of countries in the region the transition to democracy was in fact not so uncertain, for two reasons. First, the military was eliminated from the transition. Second, there was present a powerful opposition that gained strength from popular mobilization against the regime (often also against the state) (as with the Baltic, Slovenian, Czech, and Polish cases) and/or reform communists who collaborated with an opposition committed to democracy (as with the Baltic countries, Slovenia, Poland, and Hungary).

Because uncertainty was lower, moreover, the transition in all of these cases produced a sharp break with the state socialist past—for example, through founding elections that gave the opposition a large mandate, rapid progress in constructing democratic institutions, quick introduction of far-reaching economic reforms, and, in most of the cases, the construction of a new state. By contrast, transition was far more uncertain where the military was engaged in the transition, where mass mobilization focused on leaving the state but not building democracy,

and/or where the communists were able to command considerable support in the first election. As a result, the break with the authoritarian past was less definitive—in terms of both political leadership and public policy.

These contrasts have several implications. One is that, while the most successful transitions in the South involved bridging, the most successful transitions in the East involved breakage. Indeed, it is precisely the bridging approach in the East that produced the most fragile democracies. The other is that the contrast between bridging and breakage—and the costs and benefits of each approach—in large measure reflected differences in uncertainty.

Another conclusion is that mass mobilization can play a very positive role in the transition, as it did, for example, in the Baltic, Polish, Czech, and Slovenian cases and, most recently, in Serbia and Montenegro. This is largely because mass mobilization can reduce uncertainty, thereby influencing the preferences of the communists, as well as the division of power between them and the opposition.

Nationalist mobilization and the disintegration of the state can also influence the democratic project. Whether this occurs seems to reflect a key distinction: whether such protests first arose when the regime and state were unraveling or whether the demonstrations at that time were the culmination of a longer history of such protests. In the first case, which describes Slovenia, the Baltic countries, Russia, Ukraine, and Moldova, the transition produced sustainable democratic orders, albeit of varying quality. By contrast, in every transition where nationalist protest had a longer lineage, both the old and the new state, as well as the democratic project, experienced continuing contestation.

This leads to another conclusion. If we divide the twenty-seven cases into two groups—where the transition was accompanied by significant nationalist mobilization and where it was not— we find two sets of stories. As already noted, the first story is about the timing of nationalist mobilization. In the second group, the key issue is the strength of the opposition, which is indicated, for example, by the outcome of the first election.

This brings us to our final set of arguments. It is true, when adding the amendments already discussed, that political leaders—their preferences, their power, and their actions—are critical to the founding and the sustainability of democracy. However, it does not then follow that leaders in different countries have the same menu from which to choose; that similar choices in different contexts necessarily have the same consequences; that there are, as a result, optimal choices that are generally applicable; or that compromising the democratic project and the state during and after the transition necessarily reduces the sustainability of democracy. There are two basic distinctions here: between conditions and strategies and between the consolidation of democracy and sustaining it.

In the first distinction, the key point is that some transitions are more constrained—or more uncertain—than others, and it is precisely the degree of uncertainty that defines both the strategies available to political leaders and the consequences of those strategies. Thus, "easy" transitions feature very different matrices of choices and payoffs than do "hard" transitions. In the postcommunist world there were transitions, as noted above, where the opposition was powerful and the authoritarians either marginalized or collaborative and where, as a result, there could be a radical break with the past. These transitions then produced a quick consolidation of both democracy and capitalism and, when accompanied by state disintegration, even the state. They also set the standard for what constituted the ideal approach—in economics, as well as in politics.

Most transitions in the postcommunist world did not fall into this category, however. Instead, uncertainty was higher, and the best result was a compromised democracy, capitalism, and state. Nonetheless, this did not necessarily mean that leaders in these contexts adopted the wrong strategies. Rather, they merely faced the "wrong"

conditions. Moreover, if they had pretended otherwise and opted for breaking over bridging, thereby emulating their more successful counterparts, they might very well have ended up with no state, democracy, or capitalism. Thus, strategies and their particular payoffs are defined by contexts, not by other cases—unless those cases have similar contexts.

This leads, in turn, to the relationship between the consolidation and sustainability of democracy. It is certainly true that consolidated democracies are very likely to sustain themselves. But it does not follow that unconsolidated democracies are necessarily less sustainable or that policies and behaviors that compromise the consolidation of democracy necessarily detract from its sustainability. Indeed, as the Russian case suggests, it may be precisely the limits to democracy, as well as to the state and capitalism, and the policies that contributed to those limits that sustain all three.

We are now in a position to address some issues of broader concern. First, as this article reinforces, the cases chosen do indeed seem to determine the conclusions drawn. This is particularly the case, one can argue, when case selection reduces variation in dependent variables. Moreover, case selection also seems to shape assumptions and therefore analytical approaches. Second, as noted in the introduction, it can be costly to restrict our regional reach. As we have discovered, expanding regional horizons can introduce new variables and new issues, while challenging common assumptions, approaches, and arguments. However, given the repeated contrasts between the South and the East that emerged in this article, an obvious question presents itself: do these contrasts mean that political dynamics are regionally defined?

It is tempting to concur with this statement. After all, for the postcommunist cases in particular, the notion of regional effects is logical—given, for instance, the structural similarities forged by the political economy of state socialism and the Soviet bloc; the common origins of all the new states as a result of disintegration of the ethnofederal states in the region along republican lines; and the similarities in the timing as well as the key players involved in the transition to democracy. However, I would nonetheless argue against the notion that political dynamics respond to regional effects.

First and most obviously, a major rationale for analyzing the postcommunist cases is their extraordinary variability, not their similarities. Indeed, it is ironic that the variable practices of authoritarianism in Latin America and southern Europe and the variable timing of their transitions to democracy seem to have produced less variation in transition dynamics and in the quality and sustainability of the democratic project than we see in the postcommunist context. Second, like urban-rural distinctions and even some nongeographical cleavages, such as gender and class, that analysts habitually employ, region only begs the question about the factors actually at work. As Adam Przeworski and Henry Teune argued more than thirty years ago: the purpose of comparative analysis is to replace place-names with variables.[7] Indeed, this is precisely what this article has attempted to do by framing the discussion in terms of variations (1) in the timing of nationalist mobilization, (2) in the historical role of the military in politics, (3) in the strength of the opposition, (4) in the uncertainty built into the transition, and (5) in the range of policy options available to political leaders and their payoffs.

Thus, region is merely a summary of factors that have taken on geographical form. For this reason and because regions can provide not just new factors and variation in those factors, cross-regional studies can be quite helpful in contesting or complicating those assumptions and arguments that were derived from the analysis of one or several similar regions.[8] This is particularly the case when regions are very different from one another in culture, historical development, and relationship to the international system; when they add new causal considerations to the analysis; when they vary the timing of the political dynamics of interest; and when they evidence considerable variation in dependent variables. It is precisely for these reasons—and not because region itself matters—that it is advisable where possible to expand our geographical horizons. This is particularly the case for democratization, given its global reach.

NOTES

1. Charles King, "Post-Postcommunism: Transition, Comparison, and the End of 'Eastern Europe,'" *World Politics* 53 (October 2000). On the divergent political and economic dynamics of the postcommunist region, see Valerie Bunce, "The Political Economy of Postsocialism," *Slavic Review* 58 (Winter 1999); www.freedomhouse.org/ratings/index; Karen Dawisha, "Post-Communism's Troubled Steps toward Democracy: An Aggregate Analysis of Progress in the Twenty-seven New States" (Manuscript, Center for the Study of Post-Communist Societies, University of Maryland, September 1997).

2. O'Donnell, Schmitter, and Whitehead (fn. 1); Terry Lynn Karl, "Dilemmas of Democratization in Latin America," *Comparative Politics* 23 (Spring 1990); Guiseppe Di Palma, *To Craft Democracy* (Berkeley: University of California Press, 1990).

3. Rustow, "Transitions to Democracy: Toward a Dynamic Model," *Comparative Politics* 2 (April 1970).

4. In Hungary mass mobilization was understood to be politically risky (and turned out ultimately to be unnecessary), given the brutal suppression of the Hungarian Revolution in 1956, on the one hand, and the willingness of the reform communists, even before the roundtable, to jump on the democratic bandwagon, on the other hand. See Patrick H. O'Neil, "Revolution from Within: Institutional Analysis, Transitions from Authoritarianism, and the Case of Hungary," *World Politics* 48 (July 1996).

5. See Anna M. Grzymala-Busse, *Redeeming*

the Communist Past: The Regeneration of Communist Parties in East-Central Europe (Cambridge: Cambridge University Press, 2002).

6. Because Poland was the first country in the region to break with communist party rule, its transition was somewhat more uncertain. Given the character of the Soviet bloc, however, developments in Poland during the first half of 1989 lowered the risks of transition for other members of the bloc.

7. Przeworski and Teune, *The Logic of Social Inquiry* (New York: John Wiley, 1970).

8. See, for example, Doug McAdam, Sidney Tarrow, and Charles Tilly, *Dynamics of Contention* (Cambridge: Cambridge University Press, 2001).

LUCIAN W. PYE

TRAUMATIZED POLITICAL CULTURES: THE AFTER EFFECTS OF TOTALITARIANISM IN CHINA AND RUSSIA

Developments in both China and Russia are a challenge to political science, and more particularly to theories of political culture. Both countries are engaged in profound processes of transition involving the abandonment of totalitarianism and the adoption of market-based economies. It is, however, far from clear what form their political systems will eventually take. They are currently following strikingly different paths. Are the differences a reflection of their distinctive cultures? Or, are the differences more structural, a manifestation of their respective stages of economic and social development? Or, are they merely the consequences of the idiosyncratic choices and policy decisions of the two leaderships?

No doubt a full answer to the question of where China and Russia are headed would require the examination of all these questions and some others as well. For our purposes here the focus will be limited to critical concerns about the stresses the political cultures have gone through. Our attention will be primarily directed to the Chinese case, with references to Russia serving mainly to gain the benefits of a comparative perspective. Keeping in mind Russian developments is of value because Russia has gone further down the road of abandoning Communism and hence its experiences may foreshadow what is in store for China.

Our emphasis will be on political culture because developments in this realm will, in a fundamental fashion, determine the emerging norms of legitimacy and the content of the new national identities. Political scientists have a special obligation to explore these developments since they will provide the foundations for the future constitutional orders of the two countries. Since the fall of Communism in Russia and the introduction of the reforms in China, political scientists have largely concentrated on analyzing on-going policy decisions, and especially the economic problems of the two countries. Consequently they have conspicuously ignored what should be one of the discipline's most fundamental concerns: the all-important question of the

From *Japanese Journal of Political Science* 1 (May 2000), pp. 113–28. Some of the author's notes have been omitted.

norms of legitimacy which frame the constitutional order and give government its authority to rule. The norms and values, the ideals and principles which give governments legitimacy are a manifestation of their political cultures. These are matters that should command the attention of political scientists as much as, if not more than, say, the fate of the failed state owned enterprises (SOEs) in China or the activities of Russia's robber barons.

This is a big challenge for political culture theory, but in recent years there has been a revival of interest in political culture precisely because it has turned out to be a valuable approach for finding answers to the truly big questions in comparative politics and international relations theory. These include such questions as: Why are some countries rich and others poor? Why have some been more successful in becoming stable democracies? In the post-Cold War world, where will the most likely lines of international conflict be drawn? These are the questions addressed in important new books, all of which find their answers in the realm of culture. Thus, David Landes's (1998) *The Wealth and Poverty of Nations* concludes that 'culture is the key' for explaining why some countries have become rich and others remain poor; Thomas Sowell's (1998) *Conquest and Culture* sees culture as the critical factor in explaining Western civilization's dominant role in world history; Robert Putnam's (1993) *Making Democracy Work* traces the relative successes and failures at democracy of the different regional governments of Italy to their cultural traditions; and Samuel P. Huntington's (1996) *Clash of Civilizations* holds that cultural factors will determine the fault lines of international conflicts after the collapse of Communism.

The challenge of discerning the future bases of legitimacy in China and Russia is, however, greater than the problems confronted in these recent studies because in the cases of Russia and China it is precisely the political cultures that are in the process of uncertain change. The authors of all of the above studies could treat cul-

ture as a fixed independent variable, operating with the almost magical powers of enduring 'History'. In the case of Putnam's study of Italian regional differences, twentieth-century practices were, it seems, determined by thirteenth-century practices. With contemporary China and Russia we are dealing with systems that are in the midst of profound transitions, and it is therefore not possible to treat their traditional political cultures as being still fully intact.

The big challenge in determining the essence of the changes and the degrees of continuity is to identify what aspects of the cultures were the most severely damaged during their experiences with totalitarianism. The decades of Communism brought not just change from their traditional cultures but, as we shall argue, traumatic shock to their respective national psyches.

In analyzing the post-totalitarian circumstances it is also appropriate to focus on the prospects for democracy because in the post-Cold War world the attainment of pluralistic democracy and a market economy have become the widely accepted standard for national development. The goal of democracy is the appropriate yardstick for measuring national progress because at present there is no other generally recognized alternatives to democracy such as there were in the 1930s and 1940s when fascism and Communism had their appeals. If either China or Russia fail at democracy they may produce an alternative, but it would emerge out of a failed effort at democracy.

Since we will be guided by concerns about the prospects for democracy we will employ two of the most important concepts in political culture theory: the concepts of civic culture—that is, the values basic to stable democracy, and civil society—that is the development of autonomous associations that can represent the interests of society. The question of how the Chinese and Russian political cultures, so severely damaged by their totalitarian experience, now measure up with respect to these two concepts will tell a great deal about the directions in which they are headed.

Enduring Individual Identities but Weak Collective Identities

It is significant that in China and Russia today cultural continuity is to be found mainly at the level of individual behavior, and not at the collective level of the community and the nation. The processes of liberalization in both cases exposed the astonishing fact that the decades of indoctrination to create 'New Men' had not changed the individual Chinese or Russian nearly as much as might have been expected. When Deng Xiaoping's reforms gave the Chinese people a chance to be more themselves they quickly manifested behavior patterns consistent with pre-Communist Chinese culture. All of Mao Zedong's efforts to change Chinese national character have had little lasting effect. Similarly Stalin's massive effort to make 'New Soviet Men' failed fundamentally to change Russians as individuals.

But the story of their collective identities, which give substance to their national psyches, is quite different. In both China and Russia the break with their experiments with totalitarianism has not brought an automatic revival of their traditional political cultures. In both countries it is still hard to discern what is taking shape in the formulation of new senses of collective identity, but it is clear that there will be no reversion to their respective earlier national identities. The only significant continuity is that both countries seem to be back at the point of their pre-Communist ambivalence about modernization: the Russians torn between Westernizers and Slavophiles, the Chinese between traditionalists and advocates of Western ways. The old issues are there, but the terms of the debate will have to be significantly different given the new circumstances and their failed experiences with totalitarianism. For over a century both Chinese and Russians have had deep ambivalence about fitting into the modern world. They wanted the benefits of modernity but they did not want to simply copy the West. They still have not found a way to resolve that dilemma.

This contrast between the level of the individual and that of the collectivity is troublesome because it strikes at what has always been a vulnerable area in political culture theory. This is the micro–macro problem, which is the problem of the connection between individual psychology and group psychology. Central to this problem is the question of how valid is it to apply knowledge about individual psychology to group behavior. It is one of the paradoxes of political psychology that we have a great deal more solid knowledge about individual psychology than about group or collective behavior. Given the richness of our knowledge about the individual, it is tempting to jump from the individual to the collectivity, but a national political culture is not just the sum of the attitudes, values, and habits of all the individuals involved. A collectivity, such as a nation, has to have its distinctive norms, that is its shared values, myths, and ideals which together constitute the community's distinctive spirit or psyche.

The experiences with totalitarianism, and the shocks that accompanied its ending, profoundly affected the lives of individual Chinese and Russians, but the damage has been far more severe with respect to precisely those sentiments and attitudes that are fundamental for the effectiveness of collective behavior. In both countries there has been a dramatic breakdown in the norms essential for any form of civil society. It is no exaggeration to say that a moral vacuum exists in both countries. Moreover, the level of trust critical for constructive impersonal relationships, which was never particularly high in either Russia or China, has now largely evaporated. Lives have become more private as people turn inward to look after their individual interests, focusing on family ties and personal friendships. The level of social capital is shockingly low and hence there is little potential for creating effective civil societies. The erosion of collective values has undermined the foundations of legitimacy of the governments and consequently corruption abounds.

The situation has been described by some as a breakdown in morals and ethics, while others speak of a crisis of faith. These are true descriptions, but in seeking to be more precise, our interpretation is that both political cultures have been traumatized. That is, there has been profound damage to the norms and beliefs that give structure and content to the national political culture. Individually Russians and Chinese have been psychologically scarred, but the damage to the collective norms has been much more severe. These are the norms that govern society–state relations and that make effective collective action possible. More particularly, the damage has been the greatest in destroying the basis for trust in social relations, so cynicism now reigns. This situation has profound consequences for the task of arriving at appropriate new national identities.

In both China and Russia, even before the shock of the collapse of Communism, the people had experienced tremendous suffering and psychological devastation caused by the very institutions which should have been nurturing and protecting them, their political systems. No society could possibly have gone through the hell of Chinese and Russian totalitarianism without having their social system profoundly disturbed and disoriented. In China the very process of recruiting leaders involved induction into a world in which fear was a dominant emotion. Cadres were always vulnerable to charges of 'incorrectness', and purges could sweep the system, indiscriminately destroying both good people and bad. The Russian elite had its years of terror. The Chinese cadres were in a constant state of anxiety over whom to trust and how to deal with their fears. Over 34,000 cadres met their deaths, including Politburo members Liu Shaoqi, Tao Zhu, Peng Dehuai, and He Long Teiwes and Sun (1996). In both countries those who set the tone had the deepest fears and the least trust. Understandably people who have gone through such experiences will be quick to grasp at the opportunities for corruption offered by even a small degree of liberalization.

For Russians there has been in addition to the horrendous losses of two world wars, revolution and civil war, the terror of the Stalin years. It has been argued that the West exaggerated the intensity of Soviet totalitarianism because many Russians were able to privatize their lives even during Stalin's rule and have a life devoid of politics. The very practice of escaping into their private lives and trying to blank out all thought about public affairs is, however, evidence of the very trauma we have been describing.

China from the beginning of the twentieth century has been plagued with constant turmoil and wars, both civil and international. With the collapse of the Qing Dynasty, China lost the chance for a smooth transition to democracy by making a gradual transition by way of a constitutional monarchy, such as Japan and the ruling houses of Europe were able to do. Instead China was instantly declared to be a republic, but of course it lacked all the cultural norms and institutional arrangements essential for such a form of government, and hence it disintegrated into the War Lord era. In 1927 the Nationalist briefly united the country, but in less than five years Japan took over Manchuria, and in five more years the Sino-Japanese war put the country into turmoil. During that war China was divided between Occupied and Free China, a division that was more complete than that of France between Vichy and Free France. When peace came, China did not have enough time to heal its divisions before it was again torn apart by the struggle between the Nationalists and the Communists. The years of Communist rule devastated whole categories of Chinese society. First with land reform, the rural establishment was exterminated; then with the Hundred Flowers and the Anti-Rightist campaigns the intellectuals were left in a state of shock, too timid thereafter to assert their traditional role. Then came the Great Leap and the worst famine in human history, and finally the horrors of the Cultural Revolution. Mao's policies resulted in more deaths than the combined numbers of deaths caused by Stalin and Hitler (Short, 2000). The cumulating effect has been an end of faith in Marxism–Leninism–Mao Zedong

Thought, but the power structure of the Communist Party still stands as a monument to greed, abuse, and corruption. Stripped of any faith in the ludicrous ideology they had been mouthing for decades, the people can only see the Party as an institution of crass power, intent only in looking after its own, while repressing any opposition.

Thus the critical bonds of the respective cultures which gave structure to social relations have eroded, and the values essential for a well-functioning social order are very weak. The guiding principles for coherent and disciplined social behavior have been subverted. As a result there are weak foundations for a civil society. In such a situation people feel it essential to look after their own interests and to act opportunistically. The result is rampant corruption, 'crony capitalism', and all manner of fraud and cheating.

The trauma is particularly acute with respect to the feelings about authority, leadership, and government in general. The Chinese have had to live through a period in which they were given exaggerated notions about the potency of leadership, but they were shockingly disillusioned as they learned how awful leaders can be, what troubles authority can cause, and how frightening government can be. Not surprising, politics and government are seen in a negative light, an evil force to be avoided.

The shock is particularly devastating because both societies before they went down the road of totalitarianism were not far removed from their traditional states in which social relations were highly structured, firmly disciplined, and ruled by custom. The disruptions that go with modernization have thus been exaggerated by the trauma of their experiences with totalitarianism. The domain of public morality is a wasteland.

National Trauma and the Evaporation of Trust

In China the leadership seems to believe that it can simply wait out the crisis and hope that as living conditions improve people will come to accept as legitimate a somewhat moderated and liberalized form of Communist Party rule. By suppressing all forms of spontaneous popular politics at the national level, and opening a small crack for local village elections, they hope that in time the system will gain new life. Paradoxically, the still repressive Chinese political system has in a perverse way operated to give individuals some degree of guidance as to what they should do to get rewards and avoid punishment. The rigidity of the political system has thus provided what amounts to the functional equivalent of social norms for helping people manage their lives. This short-term advantage, however, is likely to be negated in the longer run by the fact that the repressive power of the political system also prevents the Chinese people from working out for themselves any new norms which would reflect their best interests, and which they could internalize as the basis for a smooth functioning post-Communist society.

Thus, while in the short run it may seem that China has been able to avoid the troubles that engulfed Russia after the collapse of the Soviet system, in the longer run China may not be able to escape the same fate, if they fail to develop a new set of social norms which individuals can internalize as a part of their new national identity. China at the end of the twentieth century remained an empire awaiting the fate of all other empires, including the Soviet empire.

We should note here that the norms basic to a collectivity constitute, on the one hand, the structural framework for the society, and, on the other hand, they provide the individual with guidelines for effective social relations beyond the realm of private relationships. Thus the structures of social systems have a dual character as they provide both the objective framework that is the outcome of routinized social actions, and also the medium that individuals employ to advance their goals in society. The breakdown of the norms that we have been speaking of for China thus produces double confusion: confusion over the rules that make up the social system as a whole, and confusion for the individual over how to be socially effective.

This confusion over norms complicates the task of establishing new norms of legitimacy for the state. Moreover, compared to most countries the Chinese have a particularly serious problem in establishing the normative foundations for state legitimacy. This is because in modern times they have not had a shared religion that could serve as the basis for their national identity. Other countries generally have a common religion, or compatible religions, which can either directly provide the transcendental values for defining legitimacy, or give structure for a parallel secular set of transcendental values. Thus, as a part of the American national identity, such secular legitimizing values as freedom, justice, equality easily take on a sacred dimension. The Chinese since the erosion of Confucianism as a binding force have had no common shared transcendental framework of values which could be tapped for legitimizing the state. The effort to give Marxism–Leninism such a legitimizing force helped only to weaken Confucianism even further and to leave the country void of either a sacred or a secular framework of values.

The Russians have no such problem, given the speedy revival of the Orthodox church. Instead, the Russians, as always in their history, have little tendency for half measures; and thus they totally abandoned Communism and expected to achieve democracy and capitalism instantly. Now the hope is that by working through the challenge of confusion and disorder the people will in time sort out their interests, establish new social norms, and thereby form a workable pluralistic democracy. In the meantime it is hoped that somehow a system of rule by law can be established to check corruption and regulate the opportunistic industrial vultures. Their traumatized political culture makes it hard for them to achieve effective public order, as seen in the confusion of going from elections with only one party to a December, 1999, election with 26 parties. Indeed, the Russians deserve much credit for successfully carrying out somewhat fair elec-

tions which have usefully sorted out power among the contenders in the new political elite. What the elections so far have failed to do is to give greater content to the ideals that the Russians want as the basis for their new national identity. Unable to resolve their traumatized political culture, much of the Russian public have unfortunately become cynical about liberal democracy, not willing to give it enough time to become institutionalized, but blaming it for all of Russia's current problems.

The symptoms of trauma run very deep in both countries, and wishful thinking of either the Chinese or Russian variety will not bring satisfactory solutions. Both populations are acutely aware of how they have been grossly mistreated by the normal workings of their political system. Governments and ruling parties which pretended to be warm and friendly turned out to be ruthless and destructive. As the peoples fail to work out their troubles from the past there has been a marked tendency for self pity. In China in the early years of the reforms there was an outpouring of stories about the sufferings the authors had endured during the Cultural Revolution. Bookstores were filled with what was called the 'wounded' literature, largely accounts of personal tragedies, especially during the Cultural Revolution. The authorities did not censor such works because at the time they were trying to blame China's problems on the 'Gang of Four' even at the risk of tainting the image of the just deceased Chairman Mao. The public telling of horror stories seemingly worked as a catharsis for both author and reader.

*   *   *

What makes the search a response to true trauma is that the Chinese are not just aware that their political system mistreated them and caused them great suffering, but at a deeper and more psychologically repressed level, they are still in denial of the fact that they themselves individually once supported and enthusiastically participated in the very actions which caused such grievous suffering. Hence they are not themselves without blame for their troubles. They were able in the 'wounded' literature to speak out about their misfortunes, but, as yet, with a few notable exceptions, they have not been able to articulate the crimes that they committed against innocent others as they sought to be more Red than those they attacked as 'capitalist roaders' and faint-hearted revolutionaries.

This problem of repressed self-blame is peculiarly acute for the Chinese because their culture is famously strong in socializing its members to a high degree of need for achievement. The experience of growing up Chinese, especially under the unrelenting demands of Maoism, produced people with a compulsive need to excel. The resulting character formation has, understandably, profound problems with confronting suppressed self blame. This deep repression of guilt does however surface in the form of a reinforcement of the Chinese propensity to adopt a martyr complex. Feeling discounted and ill at ease with themselves their knee-jerk tendency is to claim that they have been mistreated.

The solution to this psychological problem demands that they must go further than just denounce the bad leaders of the past. They need to find a new basis for their identity, new standards for their achievement goals, and absolution from their guilt and martyr complexes.

At the level of ethnic identity the Chinese have no problems about knowing who they are. However, when it comes to national identity there are serious difficulties because the Chinese no longer believe in the official doctrine of Marxism–Leninism–Mao Thought and there are no alternatives. The continued repression by the Party prevents the people from engaging in a dialogue which might give them a new set of ideals, values, and principles that would help define them as a unique national culture. For more than half a century their government, led by the Communist Party, has used its considerable propaganda powers to denounce, as an ultimate evil, China's Confucian traditions. Today in the wake of the Reforms they feel that others are not giving them the respect that should be their due,

especially in the light of their remarkable economic successes. When asked, however, what others should respect China for, and what does China stand for internationally, they find it hard to answer. The slogan, 'To Get Rich Is Glorious' is hardly an appropriate one for the heirs of one of the world's greatest civilizations.

As a result of these difficulties with their sense of national identity the Chinese now have a shallow, thin-skinned, xenophobic form of nationalism, a 'we against them' view of the world. They are quick to take offense, and they suspect hostile designs behind the actions of the other states. The depth of their feelings of being mistreated are such that they are easily transposed to the international scene where they quickly feel that other states are mistreating China. The Chinese propensity for self-pity is such that the leadership does not feel silly when it denounces the actions of other states as 'Hurting the feelings of 1.2 billion Chinese people'. The state encourages this type of nationalism by dwelling on China's 'century of humiliation'. Consequently, the Chinese, who were less dominated by colonial rule than most Asian countries, now wail the most over having been mistreated by Western imperialism. Complaining about mistreatment by foreign powers diverts attention from the fact that most of China's sufferings has come from the actions of their own governments. The public however easily goes along with the official view because they do feel that they have been mistreated. Evidence of how widespread such insecurities are was revealed in the popular reactions to the accidental bombing of the Chinese embassy in Belgrade. It is a mentality that provides fertile ground for conspiracy theories. Indeed, given profound uncertainties caused by the trauma of totalitarianism and Communism, there is a hunger for the certainties that conspiracy theories provide. Such theories explain everything and provide an explicit reason for why things happen as they have.

Finally, the combination of this form of shallow, xenophobic nationalism and the weak basis of legitimacy makes the Chinese, and also the

Russian, rulers inordinately passionate about state sovereignty and the principle of non-intervention in domestic affairs. At a time when the forces of globalization are making borders ever more porous, their problems of legitimacy and identity cause the Chinese and Russian leaders to seem quaint but shrill as they complain about interference in their 'domestic affairs'. It was not surprising that China was the only conspicuous defender of Russia over its Chechnya operations, arguing that it was an internal matter and the business of no one else.

Blocked Memories and Stunted Imaginations

Again, the solution to these problems of a xenophobic nationalism and weak legitimacy calls for the establishment of a new sense of national identity that will be consistent with both Chinese traditions and the current international standards of state behavior. The molding of such a new identity requires that the Chinese reflect on their history and bring into consciousness those elements of their past that they can feel most proud of, and for which they want others to respect them. The process will call for the creation of a new set of constructive and unifying national myths.

It might seem that this should not be such a difficult task because the Chinese have a rich history of dramatic events that should be able to provide all the necessary symbols, slogans, and imagery to give content to such new national myths.[1] Yet, in spite of the fact that nearly every year the Chinese calendar is filled with anniversaries of modern political events which historians can point to as being worthy of collective respect, the Chinese people themselves seem to have no collective memories of those events. Their traumatized political culture has left them with a shocking lack of vivid shared memories. The year 1999 dramatized the extent to which China is a society with anniversaries but not memories. It was the 100th anniversary of the first reform

movement, but there is no collective memory of that initial attempt to modernize China: it was the 80th anniversary of the May Fourth Movement, but there is no popular basis for recollecting those once exciting times; it was the 50th anniversary of the establishment of the PRC, but that only reminded people of their ambivalence about Mao's rule; it was the 20th anniversary of Democracy Wall but no Chinese can speak loudly of that; and it was the 10th anniversary of Tiananmen and, needless to say, the regime wants to quash any memories of that event.

Thus, what is striking is not that the Chinese have so many anniversaries, but rather that they have so many blocked or repressed memories. The nature of modern Chinese politics has been such that it has been impossible for the Chinese people to collectively share their memories and weld them together to form enduring and inspiring myths for succeeding generations. The absence of a collective memory for a nation is as serious a liability as the repression of memory is for the individual. Clinical psychology tells us traumatic experiences can block the memory, and that repression of memory decisively inhibits the imagination, and this in turn stifles creativity. Individuals who have blanked out memories because of traumatic experiences will also lose their powers of imagination and creativity. The result is a kind of rootlessness of the personality.

What is true for the individual is also true for a national culture. The richness of modern Chinese history has not generated a creative process of bringing together the emotions and the imagery of collective memories to produce an inspired sense of national identity. The numerous repressions of collective memories have left China with an ill-formed nationalism. * * * Hackneyed calls to 'carrying on the revolution' have lost all meaning. Dwelling on humiliation has not produced collective pride. State-sponsored attempts at national myth making never really work, as the efforts of innumerable Third World countries prove. The uplifting visions of true national myths can only come out of the collective imaginations of a whole people who are able to build on their freely shared memories. Instead, politically, China today is, in Matthew Arnold's imagery, a blocked society suspended between a world which is dead and a world which is powerless to be born.

The Chinese are not the only people in Asia with problems of blocked memories and inadequate myths of national identity. The Japanese, for example, also have a problem of repressed collective memories so that they have difficulties with their symbols of nationalism. They are confused and ambivalent about their national flag and anthem. However, the Chinese problems are far and away more severe, for theirs are rooted in their traumatized political culture.

No Easy Solutions

The task of the political scientist is to identify the sources of national political problems and often to suggest possible solutions. It is not to predict what will happen, for prudent political scientists operate under the rule that 'Prophecy is voluntary folly', and hence is to be avoided.

The current scenes in Russia and China make it clear that in their different ways the two countries are still encumbered by their traumatized political cultures. In Russia the process of open politics and elections has provided a means for working through a part of the problem. Yet to date the norms for a stable civic culture and civil society have yet to be formed. The behavior of the leading political figures remains erratic, and relationships are not stable or enduring. Opportunism rules, not loyalties. There is a lack of national vision, but the direction in which salvation lies is discernible. The national urge is toward becoming a pluralistic democracy, but a decade of troubles has tarnished the concept of liberal democracy for many Russians. However, the political elite is overwhelmingly committed to achieving free market democracy. Therefore the Russian problem is over the means to achieve their national goal and not over the goal itself.

The situation in China is, as we have indicated, harder to judge because there has been little progress on political reforms. Hence there is no basis for determining what the Chinese reactions will be if, and when, the system is opened up for a popular effort at defining a new Chinese national identity, and new foundations for state legitimacy. The main obstacle to progress, as throughout modern Chinese history, has been the operations of the government and the behavior of those with power. It is an extremely significant fact that as individuals the Chinese are able to perform at the highest standards of the modern world whenever they are not hobbled by the destructive influences of the practices of power and authority typical of their culture. The problems arise directly from the burdens that Chinese power practices impose on the people. If it were not for the perverse nature of the Chinese political realm, the Chinese would be among the world's most productive and creative peoples.

Yet, the prospects for democracy are not particularly favorable because in addition there are difficulties stemming from the character of Chinese norms of civility, which are important because they provide the bases of both a civic culture and civil society. In particular such norms are especially weak with respect to impersonal relationships, the very relationships most essential for democratic behavior. Traditional Chinese culture had elaborate rules for face-to-face relations but not for more impersonal ones, especially those among strangers. It is significant that of the five basic relationships which Confucius said constituted the foundations of human society, three deal with family relations, another with neighbor-to-neighbor, and the fifth was ruler-to-subject, none governed the huge realm of impersonal relations with non-acquaintances. It is of course precisely such relations that are the foundations of any civil society. Almost as a way of trying to make up for such a vast void, the Chinese have perfected the practice of declaring any new acquaintance to be instantly an 'old friend', *lao pengyou*.

The Chinese are, however, masters at building social networks which can be exploited for political or commercial purposes. The Chinese system of *guanxi*, or connections, consists of highly particularistic relationships in which people who, for example, come from the same town, country, or even province, or who were classmates or went to the same school, or who served in the same organization are expected to be mutually supportive. It does not matter how close they may have been or even whether they particularly liked each other, they are still expected to respond to appeals for help.

It might seem that *guanxi* could provide the social capital necessary for a civil society. Individually the networks bring together some people, but they also encourage distrust of all outsiders. The Chinese today, moreover, feel that there is something improper and old-fashioned about their dependence upon *guanxi*, and hence they treat is as necessary but shameful feature of their culture. Modern Chinese generally insist that for China to modernize it will have to get rid of *guanxi*. They generally fail to appreciate that norms of reciprocity are essential in all societies. The problem has been that the Chinese have never tried to distinguish 'good' and 'bad' forms of *guanxi* in order to designate some as honorable and worth retaining and others as shameful which should be abandoned. It is the latter category that has been the basis of the pervasive corruption in contemporary China.

The spirit of *guanxi* is such that, while associations may be formed among intimates, their focus is usually on seeking favors from those in power and not in becoming citizen groups making demands on the government. Thus, the institutions and associations that are now taking form in what might appear to be a civil society tend to avoid overt political action and instead they seek special treatment from the authorities. Traditionally well-established associations in China, such as merchant guilds and clan associations, never sought to apply pressure on the government in support of their interests, but rather they operated as protective associations seeking special favors from officials in the appli-

cation of the law, often giving in return a 'slight consideration', or what in the West would be considered an inappropriate bribe. For the Chinese it was considered morally inappropriate for citizens to presume to want to change the laws in their favor. The tradition still holds as in the case of those who have prospered in Hong Kong have generally not been middle-class champions of democracy, as might be expected in classical political theory. Instead they are mainly docile apologists for the PRC, who, not wanting to stir the political waters, quietly seek special favors from the Beijing authorities.

What this means is that even though the associational bases for pluralistic politics may be evolving in China, it is not necessarily certain that emerging groups and institutions will openly perform as agents of competing political interests. The practice of deferring to authority will be hard to break. At the same time we can expect the Chinese to continue to engage in their great traditional political game which I have called 'feigned compliance', in which the central authorities proclaim grand policies and issue authoritative decrees while the local powers extol the greatness of the central authorities, not openly challenging the orders, but then quietly doing what makes sense locally. The center hesitates to enforce its orders for fear of exposing its impotence. This pattern of feigned compliance has worked over the centuries to hold China together as an enduring entity while allowing local and regional differences to be accomodated. It has operated throughout the Communist period and it still operates today.

What is most troubling is that the after effects of totalitarianism in China will make the Chinese more disinclined than they traditionally were to become politically assertive in challenging their rulers. The two groups that historically went counter to this general cultural pattern were the students and workers. After the horrors of Tiananmen the students have chosen to modernize their own thinking but not to assert themselves politically. Worker unrest has increased but it is geographically limited because the closing of failed state-owned enterprises has been uneven throughout the country. Thus, the process of healing the traumatized political culture has advanced only very, very slowly.

Viewed in these general terms about the nature of Chinese social traditions, the prospects for democratic development may not seem bright. Indeed, some version of a fascistic-nationalism may seem more likely. However, the decisive factor could easily be that of individual leadership: China could have new leaders, their Gorbachev and their Yeltsin, flawed leaders as they were, or closer to home their Chiang Ching-kuo. Transitions to democracy depend upon far more than just socioeconomic developments, for they are profoundly political processes, and the movement of politics always depends upon the actions of individuals. Farsighted leaders can overcome traditional cultural obstacles. If China in time has such visionary leaders it could open their society to the creative process of forming a dynamic, modern Chinese national identity. That sense of identity would have to capture much that was great in China's historic civilization, but also much that is of the essence of a modern pluralistic democracy. There is considerable evidence that the Chinese people long for such an escape from their current traumatized political culture.

NOTE

1. The analysis that follows is based on Pye (1996a, 1996b).

REFERENCES

Almond, Gabriel A. and S. Verba (1963), *The Civic Culture: Political Attitudes and Democracy in Five Nations*, Princeton: Princeton University Press.

Barme, Geremie (1996), *Shades of Mao: The Posthumous Cult of the Great Leader*, New York: Armonk.

Chao, Linda and Ramon Myers (1998), *Taiwan Gets It Right*, Baltimore: Johns Hopkins University Press.

Cohen Stephen (1985), *Rethinking the Soviet Experience: Politics and History since 1917*, New York: Oxford University Press.

Deak, Istvan, Jan T. Gross, and Tony Judt (eds.) (2000), *The Politics of Retribution in Europe: World War II and Its Aftermath*, Princeton: Princeton University Press.

Gellner, Ernest (1994), *Condition of Liberty*, New York: Allen Lane/Penguin.

Giddens, Anthony (1979), *Central Problems in Social Theory: Action, Structure and Contradiction in Social Analysis*, Berkeley, CA: University of California Press.

Goldman, Merle (1994), *Sowing the Seeds of Democracy in China: Political Reform in Deng Xiaoping's Era*, Cambridge: Cambridge University Press.

Huntington, P. (1996), *Clash of Civilizations*, New York: Simon & Schuster.

Lagrou, Pieter (2000), *The Legacy of Nazi Occupation: Patriotic Memory and National Recovery in Western Europe, 1945–1965*, Cambridge: Cambridge University Press.

Landes, David (1998), *The Wealth and Poverty of Nations*, New York: W. W. Norton.

Malia, Martin (1999), *Russia under Western Eyes: From the Bronze Horsemen to the Lenin Mausoleum*, Cambridge, MA: Harvard University Press.

McClelland, David C. (1961), *The Need Achieving Society*, Princeton: Princeton University Press.

Min Lin (1999), *The Search for Modernity: Chinese Intellectuals and the Cultural Discourse in the Post-Mao Era*, New York: St Martins Press.

Putnam, Robert (1993), *Making Democracy Work*, Princeton: Princeton University Press.

Putnam, Robert (1994), 'Bowling Alone', *Journal of Democracy*, January.

Pye, Lucian W. (1999a), 'Memory, Imagination, and National Myths', in Gerrit W. Gong (ed.), *Remembering and Forgetting: The Legacy of War and Peace in East Asia*, Washington,

DC: Center for Strategic and International Studies.

Pye, Lucian W. (1999b), 'A Calender of Anniversaries, but a Dearth of Memories', *Harvard Asia Quarterly*, 3 (3, Summer).

Short, Philip (2000), *Mao: A Life*, New York: Henry Holt, p. 631.

Sowell, Thomas (1998), *Conquest and Culture*, New York: Basic Books.

Teiwes, Frederick C. and Warren Sun (1996),

The Tragedy of Lin Biao: Riding the Tiger during the Cultural Revolution, Bathurst: Crawford House, p. 22.

Wood, Nancy (2000), *Vectors of Memory: Legacies of Trauma in Post-War Europe*, Oxford: Oxford University Press.

Yang, Mayfair Mei (1994), *Gifts, Favors, and Banquets: The Art of Social Relations in China*, Ithaca: Cornell University Press.

IAN BURUMA

WHAT BEIJING CAN LEARN FROM MOSCOW

Just how much the world has changed, at least on the surface, becomes clear to me somewhere above Irkutsk, on board an Air China flight from Beijing to Moscow. My fellow passengers are mostly Chinese with a scattering of Russians. The inflight entertainment consists of contemporary Chinese soap operas and old movies about revolutionary heroes battling various fascist enemies. But above Irkutsk we are provided with a History Channel documentary about the superiority of United States Navy destroyers. Phrases like "fighting for freedom" and "the American spirit" come gushing through our headphones as Navy helicopters release torpedoes and the guns of freedom boom. I look around to gauge Russian and Chinese reactions. Most people are fast asleep.

The reason for flying this route is to test a hypothesis, or rather, a commonly received opinion, which is that the Chinese are managing their transition from Communism to capitalism better than the Russians. Russia is a mess, its economy wrecked in the Yeltsin years by

ideology-driven shock treatment and grasping oligarchs, its daily life made a misery by widespread corruption and criminal rackets. China, on the other hand, is believed to have learned its lesson from the Russian experience. Mikhail Gorbachev's "failure" serves as a warning to the Chinese leaders against political reforms that would diminish the party's grip on power. Bolstered by enormous amounts of overseas Chinese investment, they have concentrated on economic reforms instead. Almost nobody in China, including most party cadres, actually believes in Communism. But an authoritarian one-party state fits the Chinese tradition, and most Chinese prefer it to the potential disorder of hasty democratization.

This is the story I heard over and over from foreign businessmen and diplomats. China's president, Jiang Zemin, echoed their views in a recent interview. "Should China apply the parliamentary democracy of the Western world, the only result will be that 1.2 billion Chinese people will not have enough food to eat," he said. "The result will be great chaos."

Of course, China with its huge rural population is not like Russia, which is more urban,

From *The New York Times Magazine* (September 2, 2001), pp. 32–36.

highly educated, rich in natural resources and close to Europe. And while China's economy is far more vibrant than Russia's, a mixture of insolvent banks, ravaged natural resources, bankrupt state firms, widespread unemployment and official corruption is storing up vast problems. The question is whether the Chinese experiment with party-controlled, authoritarian capitalism is likely in the long run to be more stable than Russia's stumbling democracy.

Beijing no longer looks like a city under Communist rule. You are greeted on arrival at the superb new international airport by pictures of traditional Chinese attractions—the Great Wall, the Forbidden City and Chinese dancers. There are no references to Communism in sight, and almost no slogans about class struggle or proletarian dictatorship. "Leadership of the party" is promoted, but in the sense that following the party is a patriotic more than a revolutionary duty. Now, even capitalist entrepreneurs are welcome to join the party.

The vast expanse of Tiananmen Square, with Mao's portrait on one side and Mao's mausoleum on the other, still looks menacing and bears the stamp of state authority. But it seems anachronistic in a city increasingly dominated by shopping malls, discothèques, international hotels, big banks and franchises of McDonald's and Starbucks. And there is a palpable nervousness that is a far cry from revolutionary celebration. Worshipers of the Falun Gong spiritual movement are arrested here as soon as they raise their arms in ritual exercise. Police are watching from every corner, in uniform and plainclothes.

It so happens that this year of Beijing's successful Olympic bid coincides with the 80th anniversary of the founding of the Chinese Communist Party. The People's Daily, the official party newspaper, announced all manner of celebrations, but again patriotism set the tone: operas "expressing the Chinese people's spirit of longing for the unification of the Chinese motherland" and the like. I decide to go and see an ex-

hibition at the new Millennium Monument of 80 years of party history.

Groups of people, many of them in military uniform, are lining up to get in. They look bored, as if this is a duty to be endured, which, for most of them, it is. I am stopped at the door. No individual tickets are available. But I am interested in history, I say. I would like to get in. Go and talk to the official in charge, I am told. The official, a puffed-up figure in a blue suit, is suspicious. Who am I? Which organization do I belong to? Why am I so interested in Communist Party history? The idea that anyone should want to look at the exhibit seems baffling to him. Finally, after some telephone calls to a superior official, I am allowed in, accompanied by a smiling young guide and a photographer, who takes a picture every time I point at something.

The exhibition has a peculiar contemporary bias. Party history begins with Mao Zedong, his humble origins, his struggle to "liberate" China and his triumph in 1949. But then history takes a major jump. There are some photographs of industrial enterprises in the 1950's, and there is a model of the first Chinese car. But there are no references to the Great Leap Forward of the late 1950's, when more than 30 million people died of famine, or to the Cultural Revolution of the 1960's or indeed to any other political purge or man-made convulsion.

The focus, instead, is entirely on Deng Xiaoping's economic reforms in the 1980's and on trade and technology in the 1990's. What is being celebrated here is not Communism but technocracy. One-party rule is justified, not by political dogma, but by economic efficiency and progress, precisely what many Western businessmen admire about China and often compare favorably with the Russian mess.

The combination of political dictatorship and a more or less capitalist economy looks attractive to foreign investors. What could be better, after all? No unions to cause trouble, and there are none of those messy elections that make democratic systems so unpredictable. This combination is not unique to the People's Republic of China, of course. The model is Gen. Augusto Pinochet's Chile.

It would be difficult for a Communist Party to openly cite Pinochet as an example to follow, but in private, I am told, he is much admired by people in the so-called mainstream of the party. The debate in Chinese government circles is not between political liberals and autocrats, but between those who favor the Pinochet model and "leftists" who, not unreasonably, see capitalism as a betrayal of socialist ideals. The current leadership would seem to be in the Pinochet camp.

It is possible to meet liberals in China who see things differently and argue for democratic reforms, but they are marginalized. This does not necessarily involve jail sentences anymore, or physical violence. Such methods are reserved for those who are brave or foolish enough to engage in organized opposition. Today, dissident thinkers are silenced in public by stopping them from teaching or publishing their thoughts.

One such person is Qin Hui, professor of economic history at Qinghai University in Beijing, a man of great learning and liberal views; he is no longer allowed to teach. Another is Liu Xiaobo, a famous literary critic, who spent years in prisons and labor camps for supporting the students in Tiananmen Square in 1989 and for promoting civil liberties. His writings are banned. A famous economic journalist, He Qinglian, wrote a best-selling book in 1998, "China's Pitfalls," about the dangers of capitalism without political freedoms. Since then she has been silenced and was forced into exile earlier this year.

Apologists for China's one-party rule dismiss such dissident intellectuals as irrelevant or, worse, as threats to stability. Indeed, China, for all the outward modernity of Beijing, may not be nearly as stable as it looks, and there is good reason to believe that the one-party system is itself the main source of instability.

For one thing, official corruption is endemic to the system. Without opposition, party cadres can do more or less what they like in the semi-capitalist casino of contemporary China. State officials buy natural resources at fixed government prices and sell them for huge profits on the private market. Or they "privatize" state industries by dismissing workers without pay and picking the enterprises clean of their assets. Anyone who dares to protest can be swiftly arrested. The result is a mafia economy, described in He Qinglian's book, where the difference between political bosses and criminal dons is hard to detect.

Corruption is perhaps inevitable in any transition to capitalism. Russia, obviously, is riddled with it. But systemic corruption unchecked by any political representation has already caused rebellions in China. It is what started the Tiananmen demonstrations in 1989, and why farmers and workers protest, sometimes violently, whenever they have a chance. The government knows this and launches periodic campaigns against corrupt officials. But since the main players in the mafia economy are party bosses and their dependents, such campaigns are little more than purges aimed at political rivals. They do little to enhance the cause of stable government or the rule of law; indeed, the lack of institutional checks on government power only makes things worse.

It is often claimed that economic freedoms create a middle class, which produces a "civil society," which in the long term will lead to democracy. This claim is made about China too, hence the common view that the Chinese government is right to concentrate on economic reforms first. The rise of a new middle class is plainly visible in Beijing, if crowded restaurants and discothèques are the yardstick. But every attempt to produce anything resembling a civil society is quashed—independent labor unions, political parties, student unions, religious communities. Indeed, *any* organization outside party control is forbidden.

Liu Xiaobo, the literary critic, has consistently spoken up for human rights, freedom of speech, democracy and most daringly of all, self-determination for Tibet. He did so, not only in private conversations, but also publicly, on

Tiananmen Square in 1989, and later in petitions to the government. He was released from prison in 1999.

I meet him in the coffee shop of a shabby hotel near his apartment, not far from the Millennium Monument. Like Qin Hui, Liu thinks the Russians are in many ways better off than the Chinese, not materially perhaps, but at least "they live in a democracy and can speak freely." The problem in China, he says, is not that people don't have enough to eat. The problem is that "any kind of popular initiative, not under government control, is made impossible. Workers and farmers cannot have organized representation. And as soon as a magazine or newspaper publishes something the government doesn't like, the editors are fired or the publication is shut down. What is the point of having opinions in private if they can't be made public?"

Liu Xiaobo is disgusted by the effect centuries of political authoritarianism has had on his people. As with so many Chinese intellectuals in the last hundred years or so, his political criticism has curdled into a sense of cultural despair. His recent writings are full of attacks on the Chinese character, the cowardice of Chinese intellectuals, the crass materialism of the common people. "The frightening thing about China," he says, "is that almost everyone says one thing in private and the opposite in public." Why frightening? "Because of the psychological damage," he says. "It corrupts society. It offends human dignity."

Liu is right, but cultural despair is not the solution to China's political problems; it is a symptom of them. A one-party dictatorship cannot peacefully resolve the conflicts of interest that exist in any society, especially one as large and complex as China. First, the Chinese Communist Party reduced the problem to a crude and brutal class struggle. Then, when people were sick of Maoism, they were lulled by the promise of universal prosperity, guaranteed by a technocratic elite. Since that dream cannot come true for many, if not most people, they are now subjected to aggressive nationalist propaganda. The objec-

tive, it seems, is to disguise conflicting domestic interests with constant national campaigns to make China great, to stand up to American imperialism, to get the Olympics to Beijing, to win more gold medals and so on.

Campaigns and exhortations are a traditional form of social control in east Asia, and it is possible that the fear of chaos will prop up the one-party state for some time. But the fundamental problems of official corruption and conflicting interests remain unsolved. When all peaceful channels of opposition are cut off, violence is all that remains.

This may not yet be visible in Beijing. But violent rebellion, especially in the countryside, where trouble is brewing once again, has been a feature of Chinese history for thousands of years. Economic technocracy cannot by itself lend legitimacy to the government. Once the people revolt, in an economic crisis, when millions could lose their livelihoods, there will be no way to contain them. Mikhail Gorbachev made many mistakes, but the least one can say about his political reforms is that they ended authoritarian rule with a minimum of bloodshed. China has yet to face that test.

As soon as I arrive in Moscow, I call Tatyana Tolstaya, the novelist and political essayist. I tell her that I have been to Budapest, Prague and Warsaw, but never to the heart of the old Soviet empire. She says: "Ah, those are European cities. This is Asia." When I ask another Russian about the lack of Internet cafes in Moscow, I am told the same thing: "This is Asia." But there are many Internet cafes in Asia, I say. "Not in our Asia" is the reply.

"Asia" is not always a positive term. It is sometimes used as a proud badge of anti-Western defiance, to be sure, but here it means backward, inefficient, sluggish, corrupt; the non-European face of Russia. It is a form of national self-denigration, an expression, perhaps, of what a Russian sociologist has called the "experience of failure," the idea that Russia is always lagging behind the West. When Mikhail Gorbachev embarked on his political reforms in the 1980's, he was trying to save socialism, but he was also playing to a Western gallery. Like other liberal reformers before him, he wanted Russia to join the West. He basked in his Western popularity, even as many Russians blamed him for yet another experience of failure: the collapse of the Soviet Empire.

Chinese are touchy about perceived Western superiority, too. But their nationalism is not based so much on a complex of peripheral inferiority as on a sense of humiliation, because the Middle Kingdom's weakness was exposed by 19th-century Western imperialism. Chinese nationalism has a pumped-up, grandiose quality, visible in Beijing's monumental new buildings, great national showcases of granite and glass often topped, rather absurdly, with mock Chinese roofs. Moscow has few monumental new buildings, but many old ones are being restored in an effort to reconnect with a more gracious, more European pre-Communist past. And unlike in Beijing, where Chairman Mao's destruction of the past has been almost completed by helter-skelter modernization, there is much visible history left in Moscow.

Olga Aleksakova, a Russian architect working in Rotterdam, tells me the restoration of pre-Communist Moscow buildings is an attempt to continue cultural trends that Stalinism cut short. Hence the love affair, not only with 18th- and 19th-century architecture, which influenced Stalinist building too, but with Art Nouveau and Art Deco. Much postmodern building in Moscow is in a quasi-Deco or Nouveau style.

We have dinner at her parents' place in a scruffy gray apartment block near the center of Moscow. Olga's father, Aleksandr Aleksakov, a designer of nuclear power stations, shows me how he copes with the inconveniences of Russian life: a home-made boiler in the bathroom provides hot water when only cold water is available, which happens every summer for several weeks. There are photographs in the hall of recent holidays in Spain.

Olga's mother, Tatyana Goloubkina, is in the insurance business, but her passion is French literature. She talks about her first trip to the West, in 1989, when she was 36. The memory of crossing at night from the darkness of East Berlin into the bright lights of the West still brings tears to her eyes. As we savor the meal of red caviar and delicious cold meats, washed down with vodka, Aleksandr remarks that life in Russia has changed so fast that young people cannot even imagine what it was like under Communism. "We forget what it was like," he says. "I never forget," says his wife. Her worst nightmare is that the borders of Russia will be closed once again.

The relative prosperity of Moscow—the abundance of excellent restaurants, the lively cafes, the well-stocked stores—is of course misleading. Just as Beijing is richer than most places in China, the rest of Russia is a long way from catching up with Moscow. And the problems of Russia's struggling democracy are not always as visible as Moscow's shopping arcades. As long as the brutal war in Chechnya continues, Russians can hardly fault the Chinese on human rights, and President Putin's attempts to curb the independent press are too close for comfort to Chinese methods.

But the main problem for Muscovites is lawlessness. One aspect of this is highly visible. Several times in one week I witnessed the same procedure. A traffic policeman pulls a car over, orders the driver to hand over his papers and charges him with a spurious traffic offense—a corner taken too fast, a white line crossed, whatever. The driver plucks a bill from his wallet, hands it to the cop and that, usually, is the end of the affair. But if the cop is greedy, or just in a bad mood, he might accuse his victim of being a drug dealer and exact a far heavier price.

Tolstaya tells me a few things about life in Moscow. We are sitting in a little park under a statue of Feliks Dzerzhinsky, Lenin's secret police chief and founder of the Gulag, which for years stood guard in front of the K.G.B. headquarters in Moscow. "Nobody gets paid enough," she says, "so everyone must make money on the side through bribes or payoffs of one kind or another. People create their own rules, which actually make more sense than those that the government tries to impose."

The Communist government was also corrupt, of course, as it is in China. That is one reason Gorbachev started his reforms. What has happened since the collapse of the Soviet system is that one mafia, that is, the party itself, has been replaced by many competing mafias. I ask Tolstaya whether this has made life any easier. "Everything is easier," she says. "With one gang in charge, all initiatives were stifled. People were always depressed. Life was terrible. It is incomparably better now."

I ask Yegor Gaidar the same question. The moon-faced Gaidar, as Boris Yeltsin's former deputy prime minister and finance minister, was responsible for price liberalization and other economic reforms that caused widespread misery in the 1990's. He decided then that shock therapy was the only way to "drag the patient off his bed." Alas, in the process, the patient was stripped of most of his assets. Gaidar, who now runs a liberal policy center, is still a deeply unpopular man. He smacks his red lips in thought and says: "At least in Russia corruption is out in the open. Politicians accuse each other of all kinds of dirty stuff. Many accusations are false. But at least it is openly discussed. This helps us understand the problem and, hopefully, to deal with it."

When Yegor Gaidar was still a young economist in the early 1980's, discussing neoclassical economic theory in clandestine meetings with other dissidents ("market economy" was still a forbidden phrase), the idea that Russia would become a democracy was still a fantasy. Back then Russian reformists still looked to China as a possible model. Chinese economic policies under Deng Xiaoping were in fact more liberal than Russia's, especially in agriculture. But when Gorbachev took everybody, including the young dissidents, by surprise and called for political reforms, China ceased to be an example for liberal reformists.

The only ones who still see China as a positive model are old Communists and the kind of people (some of whom are allies of President Putin) who like the idea of Pinochet's Chile. It is a curious phenomenon that the one thing authoritarian Russian thinkers and Chinese Communists have in common is admiration for General Pinochet. "Yes," says Yegor Gaidar, "that is still a trend. We are a young democracy. The first one in Russian history. There is a consensus about the market economy, but not yet about democracy." What would strengthen the support for democracy? Mr. Gaidar looks at me, smiles a little wistfully and says, "Life."

Sergei Tikhvinsky, honorary chairman of the Sino-Russian Friendship Association, former K.G.B. station chief in London and a diplomat in China in the 1950's, when Russia was still China's official "big brother," is the kind of man who thinks the Chinese got it right and the Russians got it wrong. I drink Chinese tea with him at his large Moscow apartment, filled with Chinese knickknacks, not all of the highest quality.

His favorite word is "efficient." Gorbachev's political reforms were "not efficient." He agrees that reforms were necessary in the 1980's, since the party had become corrupt and the Politburo was "inefficient," but keeping government control in party hands is the "efficient" way to move from Communism to a market economy. That is why the Chinese have done better. Hearing Tikhvinsky talk, I realize how close technocracy is to the K.G.B. mind. He is not a Communist ideologue, just an authoritarian who thinks that strong state control is essential for solving human problems.

Like most Western sinologues, Tikhvinsky analyzes Chinese politics mainly in cultural terms. He admires Deng Xiaoping, because he "restored contact between Confucianism and Marxism." Classical Marxism, he says, is out of date. "You have to adjust. This is the Chinese tradition. It is very efficient." But admiration does not all go one way. "There is growing interest in China in President Putin's policies, in a positive sense."

What do the Chinese regard as most positive about President Putin? "His efforts to strengthen central control of the regions and stop separatism, that is the main thing. And the Chinese still buy many Russian armaments. That, too, is important." Not freedom of the press? I ask, a little facetiously. Tikhvinsky sputters into his china teacup in disgust. "I'm very critical of the mass media," he says. "There is nothing positive about them. The Chinese know how to restrict all the negative influences . . . crime, pornography, sex. In our country they are not yet restricted."

An old K.G.B. man like Tikhvinsky is perhaps no more representative of Russian opinion than a convinced liberal like Gaidar. But then it is hard to tell who or what is representative in Russia, or any other society, for that matter. That is why in a free society people vote and argue in public through the mass media. Most Russians may not believe in democracy in the way Gaidar does, but according to opinion polls they do wish to hang on to their new freedoms.

In this sense, President Putin's confused politics might well be representative of public opinion. Many people share his distrust of the press, his wish to end the institutional chaos of the Yeltsin years by strengthening the state, but also his desire to maintain a multiparty system. Russia could end up going back to an authoritarian regime, but that has not happened yet. And as for the Pinochet model, Gaidar put it well back in 1991: people who believe that Russia can follow the example of Chile don't know the difference between the chaotic, ill-disciplined and economically illiterate Soviet Army and the sophisticated Chilean military elite.

Faith, in any case, is not a fundamental factor in democratic government. But it is vital in a one-party state. Since people cannot vote, they are required to express faith. What other justification can one leader or one party have to monopolize government power? And faith in the old party dogmas is just what is lacking in China today. Unless one believes that Chinese are naturally obedient to authority, this makes the

Chinese system brittle. Moscow might be less efficient than Beijing. The Russian economy is still a disaster in many ways. But efficiency isn't everything. At the beginning of the 20th century, Germany was efficient, proud of its industrial prowess, less than democratic and wallowing in resentful nationalism. And we all know what happened there.

Before leaving Moscow, I call up an old China hand by the name of Vladimir Skossyrev. He is now a journalist for Vremya MN, but he was a student in China in the late 1950's. In 1992, he was back there as a reporter for Izvestia. It was an unsettling experience, he says. He felt envious, worried and strangely alienated. These feelings were especially strong when he attended the 1992 Chinese Communist Party Congress. By that time Russians had abandoned all the Communist symbols of the past. Gaidar had started his free-market reforms, the statue of Dzerzhinsky was gone from in front of the Lubyanka, the Communist coup had failed. And there, in Beijing, Skossyrev saw it all again: men in suits singing the Internationale, holding forth in the old "wooden language," mouthing the same slogans, "just as in Russia before." It was all too reminiscent of the Brezhnev era, when the Soviet Union had stagnated in a decadent torpor. He was deeply shaken.

I ask him why he was envious. "Because the Chinese had carried out economic reforms more efficiently." And why worried? Well, he says, "we were warmly received, but everything was stage-managed. Every Chinese played his role. What worries me is that Chinese always obey orders. They never object. Every morning they are told what to do by their bosses. Now, relations with Russia are good. But there are still problems with the Sino-Russian borders. What if times change, and they want to reclaim Russian territory?"

There is a hint here of ancient Russian fears of Genghis Khan and the yellow hordes. A war with Russia is in fact unlikely. But Skossyrev is plainly wrong in his assertion that Chinese are always obedient. They are not. They can also be rebellious and anarchic. The Russians, like the people of India, at least have the institutions, however fragile and flawed, to give voice to their discontents. Russian democracy is far from perfect, and it could still come to grief. But so far it has proved more resilient than many people expected. In China, there is no institutional way for people to protest, and that is why China could easily explode one day, even as the poor, inefficient Russians stumble on.

9 LESS-DEVELOPED AND NEWLY INDUSTRIALIZING COUNTRIES

Few people in any developed country can imagine the grinding burden of poverty, and the horrible moral dilemmas it brings, in the typical "less-developed" country. Do famine-stricken parents, themselves the only support for several children, feed themselves or their children first? Do they sell or abandon some children to keep the others alive? We recoil at even contemplating such choices. William Easterly, a World Development Bank economist, confronts us directly with such images—both from the present-day Third World and from our own past—in the opening chapter of his important book, The Elusive Quest for Growth *(2000).*

*The intellectual puzzle of Third World poverty is that according to all our standard economic models, it should not persist. Investment in poor countries should earn much higher returns than in rich ones—a phenomenon known technically as "declining marginal productivity of capital"—and hence investment rates and economic growth should also be much higher. This standard result of economic theory is usually called the **theory of convergence**, and it holds that initially poor countries should grow so much faster than rich ones that their growth rates (and, allowing for random variation, their levels of wealth) should very quickly "converge" on those of rich countries. In a sentence, all poor countries should be duplicating the experience of the Asian "tigers." Korea, Taiwan, and China should be the rule, not the exception. More shockingly perhaps, rapid growth and rapid convergence should occur especially where poorer countries are open to foreign investment (since foreign investors will want those higher returns) and even more under imperialism (since it opens countries to foreign investment and guarantees foreign investors' property rights).*

It seems at first self-evident that nothing like this has happened in the real world, and Lant Pritchett, a development economist at the World Bank, argues forcefully in his influential article "Divergence, Big-Time" that virtually all of the predictions of convergence theory have been wrong over the last century and more: countries have diverged, not converged, in their rates of growth and levels of wealth. On the other hand, the editors of The Economist *magazine argue in "Liberty's Great Advance," that convergence has occurred over the last fifty years in those countries that adopted pro-growth policies, particularly free trade and openness to foreign investment. In this view, most Third World poverty is self-inflicted: regimes choose bad policies, which discourage growth that otherwise would occur automatically.*

Sub-Saharan Africa, the region that has grown most slowly (indeed, some African countries today are poorer than they were at independence), proves an important laboratory for weighing the relative importance of "policy" versus "destiny," and of external versus internal factors. In their own highly influential article, Paul Collier (another World Bank economist) and Jan Willem Gunning (an Oxford University economist who specializes in Africa) carefully weigh the evidence and conclude that mostly "policy"—in the past, external economic policy, more recently internal policy—is to blame.

How does democracy relate to economic growth, and to government policy generally? Most rich countries are democratic, and most democracies are rich; but is a democratic government likelier to adopt pro-growth policies? Some have argued that less-developed countries will actually grow more quickly under "enlightened" dictatorships. Robert Barro and Adam Przeworski and his associates address this question and find at best a weak link: while wealth makes countries democratic, democracy normally does not make them rich; but neither does democracy inhibit growth. Przeworski and his associates do however find another important effect of democracy: under democratic governments, workers receive a much higher share of what society produces. Others have argued convincingly for a related effect: democracies spend far more on the kinds of "public goods" that matter to average citizens—above all education and public health—while dictatorships spend more on "rents" (corrupt and noncorrupt prerequisites of office) for the rulers themselves and for their cronies. This effect emerges even in the relatively short run: spending on public goods rises dramatically in the first few years after a dictatorship yields to a democracy.[1]

Does it matter, then, if a less-developed country is a democracy? In the short term, democracy will not cause growth (but neither will it hinder it). In the longer term, many now argue, democracies' higher rate of investment in "human capital" (i.e., in education) will provide the basis for higher growth. And in the meantime, democracies certainly provide more to average citizens, both in wages and in public goods.

NOTE

1. See, in particular, David A. Lake and Matthew A. Baum, "The Invisible Hand of Democracy," from *Comparative Political Studies* 34 (2001), pp. 587–621, and David A. Brown and Wendy Hunter, "Democracy and Human Capital Formation," from *Comparative Political Studies* 37 (2004), pp. 842–64.

WILLIAM EASTERLY

TO HELP THE POOR

When I see another child eating, I watch him, and if he doesn't give me something I think I'm going to die of hunger.
—*A ten-year-old child in Gabon, 1997*

I am in Lahore, a city of 6 million people in Pakistan, on a World Bank trip as I write this chapter. Last weekend I went with a guide to the village of Gulvera, not far outside Lahore. We entered the village on an impossibly narrow paved road, which the driver drove at top speed except on the frequent occasions that cattle were crossing the road. We continued as the road turned into a dirt track, where there was barely enough space between the village houses for the car. Then the road seemed to dead-end. But although I could not detect any road, the guide pointed out to the driver how he could make a sharp right across an open field, then regain a sort of a road—flat dirt anyway. I hated to think what would happen to these dirt roads in rainy season.

The "road" brought us to the community center for the village, where a number of young and old men were hanging out (no women, on which more in a moment). The village smelled of manure. The men were expecting us and were extremely hospitable, welcoming us in to the brick-and-mortar community center, everyone grasping each of our right hands with their two hands and seating us on some rattan benches. They provided pillows for us to lean on or with which to otherwise make ourselves comfortable. They served us a drink of lassi, a sort of yogurt-milk mixture. The lassi pitcher was thickly covered with flies, but I drank my lassi anyway.

The men said that during the week, they worked all day in the fields, then came to the community center in the evenings to play cards and talk. The women couldn't come, they said, because they still had work to do in the evenings. Flocks of flies hummed everywhere, and some of the men had open sores on their legs. There was one youngish but dignified man nicknamed Deenu to whom everyone seemed to defer. Most of the men were barefoot, wearing long dusty robes. A crowd of children hung around the entrance watching us—only boys, no girls.

I asked Deenu what the main problems of Gulvera village were. Deenu said they were glad to have gotten electricity just six months before. Imagine getting electricity after generations spent in darkness. They were glad to have a boys' elementary school. However, they still lacked many things: a girls' elementary school, a doctor, drainage or sewerage (everything was dumped into a pool of rancid water outside the community center), telephone connections, paved roads. The poor sanitary conditions and lack of access to medical care in villages like Gulvera may help explain why a hundred out of every thousand babies die before their first birthday in Pakistan.

I asked Deenu if we could see a house. He walked with us over to his brother's house. It was an adobe-walled dirt-floor compound, which had two small rooms where they lived, stalls for the cattle, an outside dung-fired oven built into a wall, piles of cattle dung stacked up to dry, and a hand pump hooked up to a well. Children were everywhere, including a few girls finally, staring curiously at us. Deenu said his brother had seven children. Deenu himself had six brothers and seven sisters. The brothers all lived in the village; the sisters had married into other villages. The women in the household hung back near the two small rooms. We were not introduced to them.

From William Easterly, *The Elusive Quest for Growth: Economists' Adventures and Misadventures in the Tropics* (Cambridge, Mass.: MIT Press, 2001), pp. 5–19. Author's notes have been omitted.

Women's rights have not yet come to rural Pakistan, a fact reflected in some grim statistics: there are 108 men for every 100 women in Pakistan. In rich countries, women slightly outnumber men because of their greater longevity. In Pakistan, there are what Nobel Prize winner Amartya Sen called "missing women," reflecting some combination of discrimination against girls in nutrition, medical care, or even female infanticide. Oppression of women sometimes takes an even more violent turn. There was a story in the Lahore newspaper of a brother who had killed his sister to preserve the family honor; he had suspected her of an illicit affair.

Violence in the countryside is widespread in Pakistan, despite the peaceful appearance of Gulvera. Another story in the Lahore paper described a village feud in which one family killed seven members of another family. Bandits and kidnappers prey on travelers in parts of the countryside in Pakistan.

We walked back to the community center, passing a group of boys playing a game, where they threw four walnuts on the ground and then tried to hit one of the walnuts with another one. Deenu asked us if we would like to stay for lunch, but we politely declined (I didn't want to take any of their scarce food), said our goodbyes, and drove away. One of the villagers rode away with us, just to have an adventure. He told us that they had arranged for two cooks to prepare our lunch. I felt bad about having declined the lunch invitation.

We drove across the fields to where four brothers had grouped their compounds into a sort of a village and went through the same routine: the men greeting us warmly with two hands and seating us on rattan benches outside. No women were to be seen. The children were even more numerous and uninhibited than in Gulvera; they were mostly boys but this time also a few girls. They crowded around us watching everything we did, frequently breaking into laughter at some unknown faux pas by one of us. The men served us some very good milky sweet tea. I saw a woman peeking out from inside the house, but when I looked in her direction, she pulled back out of sight.

We walked into one of the brothers' compounds. Many women stood at the doors into their rooms, hanging back but watching us. The men showed us a churn that they used to make butter and yogurt. One of the men tried to show us how to use it, but he himself didn't know; this was woman's work. The children nearly passed out from laughing. The men brought us some butter to taste. They said they melted the butter to make ghee—clarified butter—which was an important ingredient in their cooking. They said if you ate a lot of ghee, it made you stronger. Then they gave us some ghee to taste. Most of their food seemed to consist of dairy products.

I asked what problems they faced. They had gotten electricity just one month before. They otherwise had the same unfulfilled needs as Gulvera: no telephone, no running water, no doctor, no sewerage, no roads. This was only a kilometer off the main road just outside Lahore, so we weren't in the middle of nowhere. They were poor, but these were relatively well-off villagers compared to more remote villages in Pakistan. The road leading to their minivillage was a half-lane track constructed of bricks that they had made themselves.

The majority of people in Pakistan are poor: 85 percent live on less than two dollars a day and 31 percent live in extreme poverty at less than one dollar a day. The majority of the world's people live in poor nations like Pakistan, where people live in isolated poverty even close to a major city. The majority of the world's people live in poor nations where women are oppressed, far too many babies die, and far too many people don't have enough to eat. We care about economic growth for the poor nations because it makes the lives of poor people like those in Gulvera better. Economic growth frees the poor from hunger and disease. Economy-wide GDP growth per capita translates into rising incomes for the poorest of the poor, lifting them out of poverty.

The Deaths of the Innocents

The typical rate of infant mortality in the richest fifth of countries is 4 out of every 1,000 births; in the poorest fifth of countries, it is 200 out of every 1,000 births. Parents in the poorest countries are fifty times more likely than in the richest countries to know grief rather than joy from the birth of a child. Researchers have found that a 10 percent decrease in income is associated with about a 6 percent higher infant mortality rate.

The higher rates of babies dying in the poorest countries reflect in part the higher rates of communicable and often easily preventable diseases such as tuberculosis, syphillis, diarrhea, polio, measles, tetanus, meningitis, hepatitis, sleeping sickness, schistosomiasis, river blindness, leprosy, trachoma, intestinal worms, and lower respiratory infections. At low incomes, disease is more dangerous because of lower medical knowledge, lower nutrition, and lower access to medical care.

Two million children die every year of dehydration from diarrhea. Another 2 million children die annually from pertussis, polio, diphtheria, tetanus, and measles.

Three million children die annually from bacterial pneumonia. Overcrowding of housing and indoor wood or cigarette smoke make pneumonia among children more likely. Malnourished children are also more likely to develop pneumonia than well-fed children. Bacterial pneumonia can be cured by a five-day course of antibiotics, like cotrimoxazole, that costs about twenty-five cents.

Between 170 million and 400 million children annually are infected with intestinal parasites like hookworm and roundworm, which impair cognition and cause anemia and failure to thrive.

Deficiency of iodine causes goiters—swelling of the thyroid gland at the throat—and lowered mental capacity. About 120,000 children born each year suffer from mental retardation and physical paralysis caused by iodine deficiency. About 10 percent of the world's population, adults and children both, suffer from goiter.

Vitamin A deficiency causes blindness in about half a million children and contributes to the deaths of about 8 million children each year. It is not independent of the other diseases discussed here; it makes death more likely from diarrhea, measles, and pneumonia.

Medicines that would alleviate these diseases are sometimes surprisingly inexpensive, a fact that UNICEF often uses to dramatize the depths of poverty of these suffering people. Oral rehydration therapy, at a cost of less than ten cents for each dose, can alleviate dehydration. Vaccination against pertussis, polio, diphtheria, measles, and tetanus costs about fifteen dollars per child. Vitamin A can be added to diets through processing of salt or sugar or administered directly through vitamin A capsules every six months. Vitamin A capsules cost about two cents each. Iodizing salt supplies, which costs about five cents per affected person per year, alleviates iodine deficiency. Intestinal parasites can be cured with inexpensive drugs like albendazole and praziquantel.

Wealthier and Healthier

Lant Pritchett, from Harvard's Kennedy School of Government, and Larry Summers, the former U.S. secretary of the treasury, found a strong association between economic growth and changes in infant mortality. They pointed out that a third factor that was unchanging over time for each country, like "culture" or "institutions," could not be explaining the simultaneous change in income and change in infant mortality. Going further, they argued that the rise in income was causing the fall in mortality rather than the other way around. They used a statistical argument that we will see more of later in this book. They observed some income increases that were probably unrelated to mortality, like income increases due to rises in a country's export prices.

They traced through the effect of such an income increase, finding that it still did result in a fall in infant mortality. If an income increase that has nothing to do with mortality changes is still associated with a fall in mortality, this suggests that income increases are causing reduced mortality.

Pritchett and Summers's findings, if we can take them literally, imply huge effects of income growth on the death of children. The deaths of about half a million children in 1990 would have been averted if Africa's growth in the 1980s had been 1.5 percentage points higher.

The Poorest of the Poor

The statistics presented so far are national averages. Behind the averages of even the poorest nation, there is still regional variation. Mali is one of the poorest nations on earth. The countryside along the Niger River around the city of Tombouctou (Timbuktu) is one of the poorest regions in Mali and thus one of the poorest places on earth. At the time of a survey in 1987, over a third of the children under age five had had diarrhea in the preceding two weeks. Very few of them were on simple and cheap oral rehydration therapy. None had been vaccinated for diphtheria, pertussis, or typhoid. Forty-one percent of children born do not live to the age of five, three times the mortality rate in the capital of Bamako and one of the highest child mortality rates ever recorded.

As in Tomboctou, there are some regions or peoples at the very bottom of the economic pyramid, despised even by other poor. "In Egypt they were *madfoun*—the buried or buried alive; in Ghana, *ohiabrubro*—the miserably poor, with no work, sick with no one to care for them; in Indonesia, *endek arak tadah*; in Brazil, *miseraveis*—the deprived; in Russia, *bomzhi*—the homeless; in Bangladesh *ghrino gorib*—the despised/hated poor." In Zambia the *balandana sana* or *bapina* were described in these terms: "Lack food, eat once or twice; poor hygiene, flies fall over them, cannot afford school and health costs, lead miserable lives, poor dirty clothing, poor sanitation, access to water, look like made people, live on vegetables and sweet potatoes." In Malawi, the bottom poor were *osaukitsitsa*, "mainly households headed by the aged, the sick, disabled, orphans and widows." Some were described as *onyentchera*, "the stunted poor, with thin bodies, short stature and thin hairs, bodies that did not shine even after bathing, and who experience frequent illnesses and a severe lack of food."

Eating

High mortality in the poorest countries also reflects the continuing problem of hunger. Daily calorie intake is one-third lower in the poorest fifth of countries than in the richest fifth.

A quarter of the poorest countries had famines in the past three decades; none of the richest countries faced a famine. In the poorest nations like Burundi, Madagascar, and Uganda, nearly half of all children under the age of three are abnormally short because of nutritional deficiency.

An Indian family housed in a thatched hut seldom "could have two square meals a day. The lunch would be finished munching some sugarcane. Once in a while they would taste 'sattu' (made of flour), pulses [dried beans], potatoes etc. but for occasions only."

In Malawi, the poorest families "stay without food for 2–3 days or even the whole week . . . and may simply cook vegetables for a meal . . . some households literally eat bitter maize bran (*gaga/deya owawa*) and *gmelina* sawdust mixed with a little maize flour especially during the hunger months of January and February."

Oppression of the Poor

Poor societies sometimes have some form of debt bondage. To take one example, observers of India report "a vicious cycle of indebtedness in which a debtor may work in a moneylender's house as a servant, on his farm as a laborer. . . . The debt may accumulate substantially due to high interest rates, absence due to illness, and expenses incurred for food or accommodations."

Ethnic minorities are particularly prone to oppression. In Pakistan in 1993, the Bengali community of Rehmanabad in Karachi "had been subject to evictions and bulldozing, and on returning to the settlement and constructing temporary housing of reeds and sacks, have faced on-going harassment by land speculators, the police and political movements."

Poor children are particularly vulnerable to oppression. Forty-two percent of children aged ten to fourteen are workers in the poorest countries. Less than 2 percent of children aged ten to fourteen are workers in the richest countries. Although most countries have laws forbidding child labor, the U.S. State Department classifies many countries as not enforcing these laws. Eighty-eight percent of the poorest countries are in this no-enforcement category; none of the richest countries is. For example, we have this story of Pachawak in western Orissa state in India: "Pachawak dropped out of class 3 when one day his teacher caned him severely. Since then he has been working as child labor with a number of rich households. Pachawak's father owns 1.5 acres of land and works as a laborer. His younger brother of 11-years-old also became a bonded laborer when the family had to take a loan for the marriage of the eldest son. The system is closely linked to credit, as many families take loans from landlords, who in lieu of that obligation keep the children as 'kuthia.' Pachawak worked as a cattle grazer from 6 A.M. to 6 P.M. and got paid two to four sacks of paddy a year, two meals a day, and one lungi [wrap-around clothing]."

One particularly unsavory kind of child labor is prostitution. In Benin, for example, "the girls have no choice but to prostitute themselves, starting at 14, even at 12. They do it for 50 francs, or just for dinner."

Another occupation in which children work in poor countries is particularly dangerous: war. As many as 200,000 child soldiers from the ages of six to sixteen fought wars in poor countries like Myanmar, Angola, Somalia, Liberia, Uganda, and Mozambique.

Women are also vulnerable to oppression in poor countries. Over four-fifths of the richest fifth of countries have social and economic equality for women most of the time, according to the *World Human Rights Guide* by Charles Humana. None of the poorest fifth of countries has social and economic equality for women. In Cameroon, "Women in some regions require a husband's, father's, or brother's permission to go out. In addition, a woman's husband or brother has access to her bank accounts, but not vice versa." A 1997 survey in Jamaica found that "in all communities, wife-beating was perceived as a common experience in daily life." In Georgia in the Caucasus, "women confessed that frequent household arguments resulted in being beaten." In Uganda in 1998, when women were asked, "What kind of work do men in your area do?" they laughed and said, "Eat and sleep then wake up and go drinking again."

Growth and Poverty

My World Bank colleagues Martin Ravallion and Shaohua Chen collected data on spells of economic growth and changes in poverty covering the years 1981 to 1999. They get their data from national surveys of household income or expenditure. They require that the methodology of the survey be unchanged over the period that they are examining so as to exclude spurious changes due to changing definitions. They found 154 periods of change in 65 developing countries with data that met this requirement.

Ravallion and Chen defined poverty as an absolute concept within each country: the poor were defined as the part of the population that had incomes below $1 a day at the beginning of each period they were examining. Ravallion and Chen keep this poverty line fixed within each

	Percentage change in average incomes per year	Percent change in poverty rate per year
Strong contraction	−9.8	23.9
Moderate contraction	−1.9	1.5
Moderate expansion	1.6	−0.6
Strong expansion	8.2	−6.1

country during the period they analyze. So the question was, How did aggregate economic growth change the share of people below this poverty line?

The answer was quite clear: fast growth went with fast poverty reduction, and overall economic contraction went with increased poverty. Here I summarize Ravallion and Chen's data by dividing the number of episodes into four equally sized groups from the fastest growing to the fastest declining. I compare the change in poverty in countries with the fastest growth to the poverty change in countries with the fastest decline [see table above].

The increases in poverty were extremely acute in the economies with severe economic declines—most of them in Eastern Europe and Central Asia. These were economies that declined with the death of the old communist system and kept declining while awaiting the birth of a new system. Several of these poverty-increasing declines also occurred in Africa. Poverty shot up during severe recessions in Zambia, Mali, and Côte d'Ivoire, for example.

Countries with positive income growth had a decline in the proportion of people below the poverty line. The fastest average growth was associated with the fastest poverty reductions. Growth was reaching the poor in Indonesia, for example, which had average income growth of 76 percent from 1984 to 1996. The proportion of Indonesians beneath the poverty line in 1993 was one-quarter of what it was in 1984. (A bad re-versal came with Indonesia's crisis over 1997–1999, with average income falling by 12 percent and the poverty rate shooting up 65 percent, again confirming that income and poverty move together.)

All of this in retrospect seems unsurprising. For poverty to get worse with economic growth, the distribution of income would have to get much more unequal as incomes increased. There is no evidence for such disastrous deteriorations in income inequality as income rises. In Ravallion and Chen's data set, for example, measures of inequality show no tendency to get either better or worse with economic growth. If the degree of inequality stays about the same, then income of the poor and the rich must be rising together or falling together.

This is indeed what my World Bank colleagues David Dollar and Aart Kraay have found. A 1 percent increase in average income of the society translates one for one into a 1 percent increase in the incomes of the poorest 20 percent of the population. Again using statistical techniques to isolate direction of causation, they found that an additional one percentage point per capita growth *causes* a 1 percent rise in the poor's incomes.

There are two ways the poor could become better off: income could be redistributed from the rich to the poor, and the income of both the poor and the rich could rise with overall economic growth. Ravallion and Chen's and Dollar and Kraay's findings suggest that on average, growth has been much more of a lifesaver to the poor than redistribution.

To Begin the Quest

The improvement in hunger, mortality, and poverty as GDP per capita rises over time motivates us on our quest for growth. Poverty is not just low GDP; it is dying babies, starving children, and oppression of women and the downtrodden. The well-being of the next generation in poor countries depends on whether our quest to make poor countries rich is successful. I think again back to the woman I saw peering out at me from a house in a village in Pakistan. To that unknown woman I dedicate the elusive quest for growth as we economists, from rich countries and from poor countries, trek the tropics trying to make poor countries rich.

Intermezzo: In Search of a River

In 1710, a fifteen-year-old English boy named Thomas Cresap got off a boat at Havre de Grace, Maryland. Thomas was emigrating to America from Yorkshire in northern England.

Thomas knew what he wanted in America: some land on a river. Riverside land was fertile for growing crops, and the river provided transportation to get the crops to market. He settled on the Susquehanna River that ran through Havre de Grace.

We next hear of Thomas a decade and a half later. In 1727, when he married Hannah Johnson, he had just defaulted on a debt of nine pounds sterling. Thomas struggled to support Hannah and their first child, Daniel, born in 1728. Thomas and Hannah experienced early America's health crisis firsthand as two of their children died in infancy.

Trying to escape his debtors, Thomas decided to move. In his next attempt at getting land on a river, he rented some land from George Washington's father on the Virginia side of the Potomac, not far from what is today Washington, D.C., and began building a log cabin. But he was an outsider, and as he was chopping down trees, a posse of armed neighbors suggested he might want to investigate housing opportunities elsewhere. Thomas turned his ax on his attackers, killed a man in the ensuing battle, then went back home to Maryland to pack up for the move to Virginia and tell Hannah about their new neighbors. "For some reason," the record reports, "she refused to go."

They decided to move to Pennsylvania instead,

settling in March 1730 upriver on the Susquehanna near what is now Wrightsville, Pennsylvania. Thomas thought he had finally found his riverside homeplace. But he once again got into trouble with the neighbors in Pennsylvania. Lord Baltimore, the owner of Maryland, and William Penn, the proprietor of Pennsylvania, were disputing the border between their colonies, and Thomas was loyal to what turned out to be the losing side. He got a grant of two hundred acres of Pennsylvania riverfront land from Lord Baltimore, for which he paid two dollars a year. It appeared to be a good deal, except that the land turned out not to belong to Baltimore, and the Pennsylvanians resolved to drive off these Marylanders.

In October 1730, two Pennsylvanians ambushed Thomas, hit him on the head, and threw him into the Susquehanna. Thomas somehow managed to swim ashore. He appealed for justice to the nearest Pennsylvania judge, who told him that Marylanders were ineligible for justice from Pennsylvania courts.

A couple of hours after dark on January 29, 1733, a mob of twenty Pennsylvanians surrounded Thomas's house and asked him to surrender so they could hang him. Thomas was inside with several other Maryland loyalists, son Daniel, and Hannah, who was eight months pregnant with Thomas Jr. When the mob broke down the door, Thomas opened fire, wounding one Pennsylvanian. The Pennsylvanians wounded one of the children of the Maryland loyalists. Finally, the Pennsylvanians retreated.

The next battle came a year later, in January 1734, when the sheriff of Lancaster County sent an armed posse to arrest Thomas. The posse again broke down the door, and Thomas again opened fire. One of Thomas's men shot one of the attackers, Knoles Daunt. The Pennsylvanians begged Hannah for a candle to attend to Daunt's wound in the leg. The gentle Hannah said she had rather the wound "had been his heart." Knoles Daunt later died of his wounds. The posse again failed to capture Thomas.

Finally in November 1736, a new sheriff of Lancaster Country decided to resolve the Thomas

Cresap problem. At midnight on November 23, the sheriff took a well-armed posse of twenty-four men to serve Thomas with an arrest warrant for the murder of Knoles Daunt. They knocked at the door of the Cresaps'. Inside was the usual assortment of Maryland supporters and the family—Hannah again very pregnant, now with their third child. Thomas asked those peaceable Pennsylvania Quakers what the "Damn'd Quakeing Sons of Bitches" wanted. They wanted to burn down Thomas's house. The Marylanders fled the burning house, and the Pennsylvanians finally captured Thomas.

They put Thomas in irons and marched him off to jail in Philadelphia (a city Thomas called "one of the prettiest towns in Maryland"), where he spent a year in jail. The guards occasionally took him out for fresh air, like the time they exhibited him to a jeering Philadelphia mob as the "Maryland monster."

Finally Thomas's supporters got the Maryland monster released by petitioning the king in London. Having had enough of Pennsylvania, Thomas loaded his family on a wagon and moved back to Maryland, to the western frontier in what is now Oldtown, Maryland, on the banks of the Potomac. They arrived just in time for Hannah to give birth to their fifth, and last, child, Michael.

Thomas kept quarreling with his neighbors, one of whom noted that "Cresap is a person of hot Resentm't and great Acrimony." But this time the quarreling stopped short of battle, and Oldtown finally became his home for the rest of his life. He built his house on a rise overlooking the Potomac river floodplain, which made for good farmland. Unfortunately this particular riverside property lacked transportation because the Potomac was not navigable until Georgetown, 150 miles downstream. The nonnavigable Potomac was fuel to Thomas's continued transportation obsession.

Thomas in the 1740s participated in a group of land and transportation investors, including the Washington family, who explored the idea of building a canal along the unnavigable parts of the Potomac, but the project ran afoul of the threat of war with the French. The canal would eventually be built early in the next century.

Canals and rivers were in hot demand because colonial roads were often choked by mud, and when they were dry, they were deeply rutted. To cope with the suffering, whiskey was passed around frequently to both driver and passengers during the journey. "The horses," said a passenger gratefully, "were sober."

Thwarted by the river, Thomas turned to building his own roads. His road building standards, however, were quite low; his idea of making a road was simply to remove some of the "most difficult obstructions." A son of Thomas's old landlords and investment partners, George Washington, passed through in 1747 on a surveying trip. He described the road leading up to Thomas Cresap's as "ye worst road that ever was trod by Man or Beast."

If Thomas thought he had escaped border wars by moving to the remote frontier, he was wrong. He was now in the midst of the biggest war of his life—the war between the French and the English that lasted from 1754 to 1763.

The war started in part because Thomas (and other English settlers) was not satisfied with his riverside land and looked to the west, where there was much more fertile land along the navigable Ohio River. So Thomas joined the Washingtons and other Virginians in an Ohio River land grab known as the Ohio Company, which gave short shrift to the actual owners of the land, the Shawnees and the Mingoes. And when the Ohio Company tried to build a trading post and fort at the forks of the Ohio (today's Pittsburgh), they ran smack into another enemy, the French from Quebec, who also wanted to steal the Ohio River land. The French chased away the Ohio Company's local military commander, twenty-one-year-old George Washington, after a brief battle in 1754, which started what became known as the French and Indian War. Thomas and his sons Daniel and Thomas, Jr., volunteered to fight against the French as part of the colonial militia, a collection of rural hoodlums known more for their "unruly licentiousness" than for any military skills. Thomas also commanded *one of his African-American slaves, Nemesis, to join the militia. On April 23, 1757, in a battle near what is now Frostburg, Maryland, Thomas, Jr., was killed. A few weeks later, Nemesis was also killed in battle.*

But in the end, with a lot of help from the British, the colonials defeated the French and their Indian allies. That was not the end of Thomas's wartime suffering, however. In 1775, the Revolutionary War broke out. Thomas's youngest son, Michael, was killed early in the war. Thomas and Hannah had lost two of their children to war and two to infant diseases. Thomas's life had been filled with violence, heartbreak, and the struggle to make a living.

Yet in the end, Thomas's quest for a river was successful. Before Michael died, he had staked out land on the Ohio River. Thomas' heirs would farm

fertile lands and later work in manufacturing plants along the Ohio River. The growing American economy, throwing out its tentacles along rivers, canals, and railroads, pulled the Cresaps along out of poverty into prosperity. Life has changed since the days of Thomas, who was my great-great-great-great-great-great-grandfather.

The majority of the world's population have not yet said goodbye to the bad old days before development. The majority of the world's population is not as fortunate as I to be borne along on rivers of prosperity. When those of us from rich countries look at poor countries today, we see our own past poverty. We are all the descendants of poverty. In the long run, we all come from the lower class. We embarked on the quest for growth to try to make poor countries grow out of poverty into riches.

LANT PRITCHETT

DIVERGENCE, BIG TIME

Divergence in relative productivity levels and living standards is the dominant feature of modern economic history. In the last century, incomes in the "less developed" (or euphemistically, the "developing") countries have fallen far behind those in the "developed" countries, both proportionately and absolutely. I estimate that from 1870 to 1990 the ratio of per capita incomes between the richest and the poorest countries increased by roughly a factor of five and that the difference in income between the richest country and all others has increased by an order of magnitude.[1] This divergence is the result of the very different patterns in the long-run economic performance of two sets of countries.

From *Journal of Economic Perspectives* 11, no. 3 (Summer 1997), pp. 3–17.

One set of countries—call them the "developed" or the "advanced capitalist" (Maddison, 1995) or the "high income OECD" (World Bank, 1995)—is easily, if awkwardly, identified as European countries and their offshoots plus Japan. Since 1870, the long-run growth rates of these countries have been rapid (by previous historical standards), their growth rates have been remarkably similar, and the poorer members of the group grew sufficiently faster to produce considerable convergence in absolute income levels. The other set of countries, called the "developing" or "less developed" or "nonindustrialized," can be easily, if still awkwardly, defined only as "the other set of countries," as they have nothing else in common. The growth rates of this set of countries have been, on average, slower than the richer countries, producing divergence in rela-

Table 1. *Average Per Annum Growth Rates of GDP Per Capita in the Presently High-Income Industrialized Countries, 1870–1989*

Country	Level in 1870 (1985 P$)	Per annum growth rates		
		1870–1960	1960–80	1980–94
Average	1757	1.54	3.19	1.51
Std dev. of growth rates		.33	1.1	.51
Australia	3192	.90	2.43	1.22
Great Britain	2740	1.08	2.02	1.31
New Zealand	2615	1.24	1.39	1.28
Belgium	2216	1.05	3.70	1.52
Netherlands	2216	1.25	2.90	1.29
USA	2063	1.70	2.48	1.52
Switzerland	1823	1.94	2.07	.84
Denmark	1618	1.66	2.77	1.99
Germany	1606	1.66	3.03	1.56
Austria	1574	1.40	3.81	1.58
France	1560	1.56	3.53	1.31
Sweden	1397	1.85	2.74	.81
Canada	1360	1.85	3.32	.86
Italy	1231	1.54	4.16	1.62
Norway	1094	1.81	3.78	2.08
Finland	929	1.91	3.77	1.09
Japan	622	1.86	6.28	2.87

Source: Maddison, 1995.
Notes: Data is adjusted from 1990 to 1985 P$ by the U.S. GDP deflator, by a method described later in this article. Per annum growth rates are calculated using endpoints.

tive incomes. But amongst this set of countries there have been strikingly different patterns of growth: both across countries, with some converging rapidly on the leaders while others stagnate; and over time, with a mixed record of takeoffs, stalls and nose dives.

The next section of this paper documents the pattern of income growth and convergence within the set of developed economies. This discussion is greatly aided by the existence of data, whose lack makes the discussion in the next section of the growth rates for the developing countries tricky, but as I argue, not impossible. Finally, I offer some implications for historical growth rates in developing countries and some thoughts on the process of convergence.

Convergence in Growth Rates of Developed Countries

Some aspects of modern historical growth apply principally, if not exclusively, to the "advanced capitalist" countries. By "modern," I mean the period since 1870. To be honest, the date is chosen primarily because there are nearly complete national income accounts data for all of the now-developed economies since 1870. Maddison (1983, 1991, 1995) has assembled estimates from various national and academic sources and has pieced them together into time series that are comparable across countries. An argument can be made that 1870 marks a plausible date for a modern economic period in any case, as it is near an important transition in several countries: for example, the end of the U.S. Civil War in 1865; the Franco-Prussian War in 1870–71, immediately followed by the unification of Germany; and Japan's Meiji Restoration in 1868. Perhaps not coincidentally, Rostow (1990) dates the beginning of the "drive to technological maturity" of the United States, France and Germany to around that date, although he argues that this stage began earlier in Great Britain.[2]

Table 1 displays the historical data for 17 presently high-income industrialized countries, which Maddison (1995) defines as the "advanced capitalist" countries. The first column of Table 1 shows the per capita level of income for each country in 1870, expressed in 1985 dollars. The last three columns of Table 1 show the average per annum growth rate of real per capita income in these countries over three time periods: 1870–1960, 1960–1980 and 1980–1994. These dates are not meant to date any explicit shifts in growth rates, but they do capture the fact that there was a golden period of growth that began some time after World War II and ended sometime before the 1980s.

Three facts jump out from Table 1. First, there is strong convergence in per capita incomes within this set of countries. For example, the poorest six countries in 1870 had five of the six fastest national growth rates for the time period 1870–1960; conversely, the richest five countries in 1870 recorded the five slowest growth rates from 1870 to 1960.[3] As is well known, this convergence has not happened at a uniform rate. There is as much convergence in the 34 years between 1960 and 1994 as in the 90 years from 1870 to 1960. Even within this earlier period, there are periods of stronger convergence pre-1914 and weaker convergence from 1914 to 1950.

Second, even though the poorer countries grew faster than the richer countries did, the narrow range of the growth rates over the 1870–1960 period is striking. The United States, the richest country in 1960, had grown at 1.7 percent per annum since 1870, while the overall average was 1.54. Only one country, Australia, grew either a half a percentage point higher or lower than the average, and the standard deviation of the growth rates was only .33. Evans (1994) formally tests the hypothesis that growth rates among 13 European and offshoot countries (not Japan) were equal, and he is unable to reject it at standard levels of statistical significance.

Third, while the long run hides substantial variations, at least since 1870 there has been no obvious acceleration of overall growth rates over time. As Charles Jones (1995) has pointed out, there is remarkable stability in the growth rates in the United States. For instance, if I predict per capita income in the United States in 1994 based only on a simple time trend regression of (natural log) GDP per capita estimated with data from 1870 to 1929, this prediction made for 65 years ahead is off by only 10 percent.[4] Although this predictive accuracy is not true for every country, it is true that the average growth rate of these 17 countries in the most recent period between 1980 and 1994 is almost exactly the same as that of the 1870–1960 period. However, this long-run stability does mask modest swings in the growth rates over time, as growth was considerably more rapid in the period between 1950 to 1980, especially outside the United States, than either in earlier periods or since 1980.

These three facts are true of the sample of countries that Maddison defines as the "advanced capitalist" countries. However, the discussion of convergence and long-run growth has always been plagued by the fact that the sample of countries for which historical economic data exists (and has been assembled into convenient and comparable format) is severely nonrepresentative. Among a sample of now "advanced capitalist" countries something like convergence (or at least nondivergence) is almost tautological, a point made early on by De Long (1988). Defining the set of countries as those that are the richest *now* almost guarantees the finding of historical convergence, as either countries are rich now and were rich historically, in which case they all have had roughly the same growth rate (like nearly all of Europe) or countries are rich now and were poor historically (like Japan) and hence grew faster and show convergence. However, examples of divergence, like countries that grew much more slowly and went from relative riches to poverty (like Argentina) or countries that were poor and grew so slowly as to become relatively poorer (like India), are not included in the samples of "now developed" countries that tend to find convergence.

Calculating a Lower Bound for Per Capita GDP

This selectivity problem raises a difficult issue in trying to estimate the possible magnitude of convergence or divergence of the incomes since 1870. There is no historical data for many of the less developed economies, and what data does exist has enormous problems with comparability and reliability. One alternative to searching for historical data is simply to place a reasonable lower bound on what GDP per capita could have been in 1870 in any country. Using this lower bound and estimates of recent incomes, one can draw reliable conclusions about the historical growth rates and divergence in cross-national distribution of income levels.

There is little doubt life was nasty, brutish and short in many countries in 1870. But even deprivation has its limit, and some per capita incomes must imply standards of living that are unsustainably and implausibly low. After making conservative use of a wide variety of different methods and approaches, I conclude that $250 (expressed in 1985 purchasing power equivalents) is the lowest GDP per capita could have been in 1870. This figure can be defended on three grounds: first, no one has ever observed consistently lower living standards at any time or place in history; second, this level is well below extreme poverty lines actually set in im-

poverished countries and is inconsistent with plausible levels of nutritional intake; and third, at a lower standard of living the population would be too unhealthy to expand.

Before delving into these comparisons and calculations, it is important to stress that using the purchasing power adjustments for exchange rates has an especially important effect in poor countries. While tradable goods will have generally the same prices across countries because of arbitrage, nontradable goods are typically much cheaper in poorer countries because of their lower income levels. If one applies market exchange rates to convert incomes in these economies to U.S. dollars, one is typically far understating the "true" income level, because nontradable goods can be bought much more cheaply than market exchange rates will imply. There have been several large projects, especially the UN International Comparisons Project and the Penn World Tables, that through the collection of data on the prices of comparable baskets of goods in all countries attempt to express different countries' GDP in terms of a currency that represents an equivalent purchasing power over a basket of goods. Since this adjustment is so large and of such quantitative significance, I will denote figures that have been adjusted in this way by $P\$$. By my own rough estimates, a country with a per capita GDP level of $70 in U.S. dollars, measured in market exchange rates, will have a per capita GDP of $P\$250$.

The first criteria for a reasonable lower bound on GDP per capita is that it be a lower bound on measured GDP per capita, either of the poorest countries in the recent past or of any country in the distant past. The lowest five-year average level of per capita GDP reported for any country in the Penn World Tables (Mark 5) is $P\$275$ for Ethiopia in 1961–65; the next lowest is $P\$278$ for Uganda in 1978–1982. The countries with the lowest level of GDP per capita ever observed, even for a single year, are $P\$260$ for Tanzania in 1961, $P\$299$ for Burundi in 1965 and $P\$220$ for Uganda in 1981 (in the middle of a civil war). Maddison (1991) gives estimates of

GDP per capita of some less developed countries as early as 1820: P$531 for India, P$523 for China and P$614 for Indonesia. His earliest estimates for Africa begin in 1913: P$508 for Egypt and P$648 for Ghana. Maddison also offers increasingly speculative estimates for western European countries going back much further in time; for example, he estimates that per capita GDPs in the Netherlands and the United Kingdom in 1700 were P$1515 and P$992, respectively, and ventures to guess that the average per capita GNP in western Europe was P$400 in 1400. Kuznet's (1971) guess of the trough of the average per capita GDP of European countries in 900 is around P$400.[5] On this score, P$250 is a pretty safe bet.

A complementary set of calculations to justify a lower bound are based on "subsistence" income. While "subsistence" as a concept is out of favor, and rightfully so for many purposes, it is sufficiently robust for the task at hand. There are three related calculations: poverty lines, average caloric intakes and the cost of subsistence. Ravallion, Datt and van de Walle (1991) argue that the lowest defensible poverty line based on achieving minimally adequate consumption expenditures is P$252 per person per year. If we assume that personal consumption expenditures are 75 percent of GDP (the average for countries with GDP per capita less than P$400) and that mean income is 1.3 times the median, then even to achieve median income at the lowest possible poverty line requires a per capita income of $437.[6]

As an alternative way of considering subsistence GDP per capita, begin with the finding that estimated average intake per person per day consistent with working productively is between 2,000 to 2,400 calories.[7] Now, consider two calculations. The first is that, based on a cross-sectional regression using data on incomes from the Penn World Tables and average caloric intake data from the FAO, the predicted caloric consumption at P$250 is around 1,600.[8] The five lowest levels of caloric availability ever recorded in the FAO data for various countries—1,610 calories/person during a famine in Somalia in

1975; 1,550 calories/person during a famine in Ethiopia in 1985; 1,443 calories/person in Chad in 1984; 1,586 calories/person in China in 1961 during the famines and disruption associated with the Cultural Revolution; and 1,584 calories/person in Mozambique in 1987—reveal that nearly all of the episodes of average daily caloric consumption below 1,600 are associated with nasty episodes of natural and/or man-made catastrophe. A second use of caloric requirements is to calculate the subsistence income as the cost of meeting caloric requirements. Bairoch (1993) reports the results of the physiological minimum food intake at $291 (at market exchange rates) in 1985 prices. These calculations based on subsistence intake of food again suggest P$250 is a safe lower bound.

That life expectancy is lower and infant mortality higher in poorer countries is well documented, and this relation can also help establish a lower bound on income (Pritchett and Summers, 1996). According to demographers, an under-five infant mortality rate of less than 600 per 1000 is necessary for a stable population (Hill, 1995). Using a regression based on Maddison's (1991) historical per capita income estimates and infant mortality data from historical sources for 22 countries, I predict that infant mortality in 1870 for a country with income of P$250 would have been 765 per 1000.[9] Although the rate of natural increase of population back in 1870 is subject to great uncertainty, it is typically estimated to be between .25 and 1 percent annually in that period, which is again inconsistent with income levels as low as P$250.[10]

Divergence, Big Time

If you accept: a) the current estimates of relative incomes across nations; b) the estimates of the historical growth rates of the now-rich nations; and c) that even in the poorest economies incomes were not below P$250 at any point—then you cannot escape the conclusion that the last 150 years have seen divergence, big time. The

Figure 1
Simulation of Divergence of Per Capita GDP, 1870–1985
(showing only selected countries)

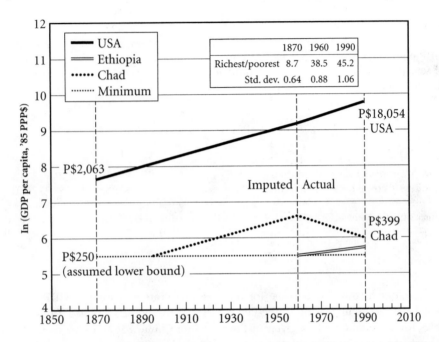

logic is straightforward and is well illustrated by Figure 1. If there had been no divergence, then we could extrapolate backward from present income of the poorer countries to past income assuming they grew at least as fast as the United States. However, this would imply that many poor countries must have had incomes below P$100 in 1870. Since this cannot be true, there must have been divergence. Or equivalently, per capita income in the United States, the world's richest industrial country, grew about four-fold from 1870 to 1960. Thus, any country whose income was not fourfold higher in 1960 than it was in 1870 grew more slowly than the United States. Since 42 of the 125 countries in the Penn World Tables with data for 1960 have levels of per capita incomes below $1,000 (that is, less than four times $250), there must have been substantial divergence between the top and bottom. The figure of P$250 is not meant to be precise or literal and the conclusion of massive divergence

is robust to any plausible assumption about a lower bound.

Consider some illustrative calculations of the divergence in per capita incomes in Table 2. I scale incomes back from 1960 such that the poorest country in 1960 just reaches the lower bound by 1870, the leader in 1960 (the United States) reaches its actual 1870 value, and all relative rankings between the poorest country and the United States are preserved.[11] The first row shows the actual path of the U.S. economy. The second row gives the level of the poorest economy in 1870, which is P$250 by assumption, and then the poorest economies in 1960 and 1990 taken from the Penn World Tables. By division, the third row then shows that the ratio of the top to the bottom income countries has increased from 8.7 in 1870 to 38 by 1960 and to 45 by 1990. If instead one takes the 17 richest countries (those shown in Table 1) and applies the same procedure, their average per capita income

Table 2. Estimates of the Divergence of Per Capita Incomes Since 1870

	1870	1960	1990
USA (P$)	2063	9895	18054
Poorest (P$)	250	257	399
	(assumption)	(Ethiopia)	(Chad)
Ratio of GDP per capita of richest to poorest country	8.7	38.5	45.2
Average of seventeen "advanced capitalist" countries from Maddison (1995)	1757	6689	14845
Average LDCs from PWT5.6 for 1960, 1990 (imputed for 1870)	740	1579	3296
Average "advanced capitalist" to average of all other countries	2.4	4.2	4.5
Standard deviation of natural log of per capita incomes	.51	.88	1.06
Standard deviation of per capita incomes	P$459	P$2112	P$3988
Average absolute income deficit from the leader	P$1286	P$7650	P$12662

Notes: The estimates in the columns for 1870 are based on backcasting GDP per capita for each country using the methods described in the text assuming a minimum of P$250. If instead of that method, incomes in 1870 are backcast with truncation at P$250, the 1870 standard deviation is .64 (as reported in Figure 1).

is shown in the fourth row. The average for all less developed economies appearing in the Penn World Tables for 1960 and 1990 is given in the fifth row; the figure for 1870 is calculated by the "backcasting" imputation process for historical incomes described above. By division, the sixth row shows that the ratio of income of the richest to all other countries has almost doubled from 2.4 in 1870 to 4.6 by 1990.

The magnitude of the change in the absolute gaps in per capita incomes between rich and poor is staggering. From 1870 to 1990, the average absolute gap in incomes of all countries from the leader had grown by an order of magnitude, from $1,286 to $12,662, as shown in the last row of Table 2.[12]

While the growth experience of all countries is equally interesting, some are more equally interesting than others. China and India account for more than a third of the world's population. For the conclusion of divergence presented here, however, a focus on India and China does not change the historical story. One can estimate their growth rates either by assuming that they were at $250 in 1870 and then calculating their

growth rate in per capita GDP to reach the levels given by the Penn World Tables in 1960 (India, $766; China, $567), or by using Maddison's historical estimates, which are shown in Table 3, India's growth rate is a fifth and China's a third of the average for developed economies. Either way, India's and China's incomes diverged significantly relative to the leaders between 1870 and 1960.

The idea that there is some lower bound to GDP per capita and that the lower bound has implications for long-run growth rates (and hence divergence) will not come as news either to economic historians or to recent thinkers in the area of economic growth (Lucas, 1996). Kuznets (1966, 1971) pointed out that since the now-industrialized countries have risen from very low levels of output to their presently high levels, and that their previously very low levels of output were only consistent with a very slow rate of growth historically, growth rates obviously accelerated at some point. Moreover, one suspects that many of the estimates of income into the far distant past cited above rely on exactly this kind of counterfactual logic.

Table 3. Mean Per Annum Growth Rates of GDP Per Capita

	1870–1960	1960–1979	1980–1994
Advanced capitalist countries (17)	1.5	3.2	1.5
	(.33)	(1.1)	(.51)
Less developed countries (28)	1.2	2.5	.34
	(.88)	(1.7)	(3.0)
Individual countries:			
India	.31	1.22	3.07
China	.58	2.58	6.45
Korea (1900)	.71	5.9	7.7
Brazil	1.28	4.13	−.54
Argentina (1900)	1.17	1.99	.11
Egypt (1900)	.56	3.73	2.21

Source: Calculations based on data from Maddison (1995).

Considering Alternate Sources of Historical Data

Although there is not a great deal of historical evidence on GDP estimates in the very long-run for the less developed countries, what there is confirms the finding of massive divergence. Maddison (1995) reports time series data on GDP per capita incomes for 56 countries. These include his 17 "advanced capitalist" countries (presented in Table 1), five "southern" European countries, seven eastern European countries and 28 countries typically classified as "less developed" from Asia (11), Africa (10) and Latin America (7). This data is clearly nonrepresentative of the poorest countries (although it does include India and China), and the data for Africa is very sparse until 1960. Even so, the figures in Table 3 show substantially lower growth for the less developed countries than for the developed countries. If one assumes that the ratio of incomes between the "advanced capitalist" countries and less developed countries was 2.4 in 1870, then the .35 percentage point differential would have produced a rich-poor gap of 3.7 in 1994, similar to the projected increase in the gap to 4.5 in Table 2.

Others have argued that incomes of the developing relative to the developed world were even higher in the past. Hanson (1988, 1991) argues that adjustments of comparisons from official exchange rates to purchasing power equivalents imply that developing countries were considerably richer historically than previously believed. Bairoch (1993) argues that there was almost no gap between the now-developed countries and the developing countries as late as 1800. As a result, his estimate of the growth rate of the "developed" world is 1.5 percent between 1870 and 1960 as opposed to .5 percent for the "developing" world, which implies even larger divergence in per capita incomes than the lower bound assumptions reported above.

Poverty Traps, Takeoffs and Convergence

The data on growth in less developed countries show a variety of experiences, but divergence is not a thing of the past. Some countries are "catching up" with very explosive but sustained bursts of growth, some countries continue to experience slower growth than the richest countries, and others have recently taken nosedives.

Let's set the standard for explosive growth in per capita GDP at a sustained rate of 4.2 percent; this is the fastest a country could have possibly grown from 1870 to 1960, as at this rate a country would have gone from the lower bound in 1870 to the U.S. level in 1960. Of the 108 developing countries for which there are available data in the Penn World Tables, 11 grew faster than 4.2 per annum over the 1960–1990 period. Prominent among these are east Asian economies like Korea (6.9 percent annual growth rate in per capita GDP from 1960–1992), Taiwan (6.3 percent annual growth) and Indonesia (4.4 percent). These countries are growing at an historically unprecedented pace. However, many countries that were poor in 1960 continued to stagnate. Sixteen developing countries had *negative* growth over the 1960–1990 period, including Mozambique (–2.2 percent per annum) and Guyana (–.7 percent per annum). Another 28 nations, more than a quarter of the total number of countries for which the Penn World Tables offers data, had growth rates of per capita GDP less than .5 percent per annum from 1960 to 1990 (for example, Peru with .1 percent); and 40 developing nations, more than a third of the sample, had growth rates less than 1 percent per annum.[13]

Moreover, as Ben-David and Papell (1995) emphasize, many developing countries have seen their economies go into not just a slowdown, but a "meltdown." If we calculate the growth rates in the Penn World Tables and allow the data to dictate one break in the growth rate over the whole 1960–1990 period, then of the 103 developing countries, 81 have seen a deceleration of growth over the period, and the average deceleration is over 3 percentage points. From 1980–1994, growth in per capita GDP averaged 1.5 percent in the advanced countries and .34 percent in the less developed countries. There has been no acceleration of growth in most poor countries, either absolutely or relatively, and there is no obvious reversal in divergence.

These facts about growth in less developed countries highlight its enormous variability and volatility. The range of annual growth rates in per capita GDP across less developed economies

from 1960 to 1990 is from –2.7 percent to positive 6.9 percent.

Taken together, these findings imply that almost nothing that is true about the growth rates of advanced countries is true of the developing countries, either individually or on average. The growth rates for developed economies show convergence, but the growth rates between developed and developing economies show considerable divergence. The growth rates of developed countries are bunched in a narrow group, while the growth rates of less developed countries are all over with some in explosive growth and others in implosive decline.

Conclusion

For modern economists, Gerschenkron (1962) popularized the idea of an "advantage to backwardness," which allows countries behind the technological frontier to experience episodes of rapid growth driven by rapid productivity catch-up.[14] Such rapid gains in productivity are certainly a possibility, and there have been episodes of individual countries with very rapid growth. Moreover, there are examples of convergence in incomes amongst regions. However, the prevalence of absolute divergence implies that while there may be a potential advantage to backwardness, the cases in which backward countries, and especially the most backward of countries, actually gain significantly on the leader are historically rare. In poor countries there are clearly forces that create the potential for explosive growth, such as those witnessed in some countries in east Asia. But there are also strong forces for stagnation: a quarter of the 60 countries with initial per capita GDP of less than $1000 in 1960 have had growth rates less than zero, and a third have had growth rates less than .05 percent. There are also forces for "implosive" decline, such as that witnessed in some countries in which the fabric of civic society appears to have disintegrated altogether, a point often ignored or acknowledged offhand as these countries fail to gather plausible economic statistics and thus drop out of our samples altogether. Backwardness seems to carry severe disadvantages. For economists and social scientists, a coherent model of how to overcome these disadvantages is a pressing challenge.

But this challenge is almost certainly not the same as deriving a single "growth theory." Any theory that seeks to unify the world's experience with economic growth and development must address at least four distinct questions: What accounts for continued per capita growth and technological progress of those leading countries at the frontier? What accounts for the few countries that are able to initiate and sustain periods of rapid growth in which they gain significantly on the leaders? What accounts for why some countries fade and lose the momentum of rapid growth? What accounts for why some countries remain in low growth for very long periods?

Theorizing about economic growth and its relation to policy needs to tackle these four important and distinct questions. While it is conceivable that there is an all-purpose universal theory and set of policies that would be good for promoting economic growth, it seems much more plausible that the appropriate growth policy will differ according to the situation. Are we asking about more rapid growth in a mature and stable economic leader like the United States or Germany or Japan? About a booming rapidly industrializing economy trying to prevent stalling on a plateau, like Korea, Indonesia, or Chile? About a once rapidly growing and at least semi-industrialized country trying to initiate another episode of rapid growth, like Brazil or Mexico or the Philippines? About a country still trying to escape a poverty trap into sustained growth, like Tanzania or Myanmar or Haiti? Discussion of the theory and policy of economic growth seems at times remarkably insensitive to these distinctions.

NOTES

1. To put it another way, the standard deviation of (natural log) GDP per capita across all countries has increased between 60 percent and 100 percent since 1870, in spite of the convergence amongst the richest.
2. For an alternative view, Maddison (1991) argues the period 1820–1870 was similar economically to the 1870–1913 period.
3. The typical measure of income dispersion, the standard deviation of (natural log) incomes, fell from .41 in 1870 to .27 in 1960 to only .11 in 1994.
4. Jones (1995) uses this basic fact of the constancy of growth to good effect in creating a compelling argument that the steadiness of U.S. growth implies that endogenous growth models that make growth a function of non-stationary variables, such as the level of R&D spending or the level of education of the labor force, are likely incorrect as they imply an accelerating growth rate (unless several variables working in opposite directions just happen to offset each other). These issues are also discussed in his paper in this issue.
5. More specifically, Kuznets estimated that the level was about $160, if measured in 1985 U.S. dollars. However, remember from the earlier discussion that a conversion at market exchange rates—which is what Kuznets was using—is far less than an estimate based on purchasing power parity exchange rates. If we use a multiple of 2.5, which is a conservative estimate of the difference between the two, Kuznets's estimate in purchasing power equivalent terms would be equal to a per capita GDP of $400 in 1985 U.S. dollars, converted at the purchasing power equivalent rate.
6. High poverty rates, meaning that many people live below these poverty lines, are not inconsistent with thinking of these poverty lines as not far above our lower bound, because many individuals can be in poverty,

but not very far below the line. For instance, in South Asia in 1990, where 33 percent of the population was living in "extreme absolute poverty," only about 10 percent of the population would be living at less than $172 (my estimates from extrapolations of cumulative distributions reported in Chen, Datt and Ravallion, 1993).

7. The two figures are based on different assumptions about the weight of adult men and women, the mean temperature and the demographic structure. The low figure is about as low as one can go because it is based on a very young population, 39 percent under 15 (the young need fewer calories), a physically small population (men's average weight of only 110 pounds and women of 88), and a temperature of 25° C (FAO, 1957). The baseline figure, although based on demographic structure, usually works out to be closer to 2,400 (FAO, 1974).

8. The regression is a simple log-log of caloric intake and income in 1960 (the log-log is for simplicity even though this might not be the best predictor of the level). The regression is

in (average caloric intake) = 6.37 + .183*ln(GDP per capita),
(59.3) (12.56).

with t-statistics in parentheses, $N = 113$, and R-squared = .554.

9. The regression is estimated with country fixed effects:

ln(IMR) = − .59 In(GDP per capita) _ .013*Trend _ 002*Trend*(1 if.1960)
(23.7)   (32.4)   (14.23)

$N = 1994$ and t-statistics are in parenthesis. The prediction used the average country constant of 9.91.

10. Livi-Basci (1992) reports estimates of population growth in Africa between 1850 and 1900 to be .87 percent, and .93 percent between 1900 and 1950, while growth for Asia is estimated to be .27 1850 to 1900, and .61 1900 to 1950. Clark (1977) estimates the population growth rates between 1850 and

1900 to be .43 percent in Africa and India and lower, .33 percent, in China.

11. The growth rate of the poorest country was imposed to reach $P\$250$ at exactly 1870, and the rate of the United States was used for the growth at the top. Then each country's growth rate was assumed to be a weighted average of those two rates, where the weights depended on the scaled distance from the bottom country in the beginning period of the imputation, 1960. This technique "smushes" the distribution back into the smaller range between the top and bottom while maintaining all cross country rankings. The formula for estimating the log of GDP per capita (GDPPC) in the ith country in 1870 was

$$GDPPC_i^{1870} = GDPPC_i^{1960}*(1/w_i)$$

where the scaling weight w_i was

$w_i = (1 − \alpha_i)*\min (GDPPC^{1960})/P\$250 + \alpha_i*GDPPC_{USA}^{1960}/GDPPC_{USA}^{1970}$,

and where α_i is defined by

$\alpha_i = (GDPPC_i^{1960} − \min (GDPPC^{1960}))/(GDPPC_{USA}^{1960} − \min (GDPPC^{1960}))$.

12. In terms of standard deviations, the method described in the text implies that the standard deviation of the national log of per capita GDP has more than doubled from 1870 to 1990, rising from .51 in 1870 to .88 in 1960 to 1.06 by 1990. In dollar terms, the standard deviation of per capita incomes rose from $459 in 1870 to $2,112 in 1960 in 1960 to $3,988 in 1990 (again, all figures expressed in 1985 dollars, converted at purchasing power equivalent exchange rates).

13. The division into developed and developing is made here by treating all 22 high-income members of the OECD as "developed" and all others as "developing."

14. I say "for modern economists," since according to Rostow (1993), David Hume more than 200 years ago argued that the accumulated technological advances in the leading countries would give the followers an advantage.

REFERENCES

Bairoch, Paul, *Economics and World History: Myths and Paradoxes*. Chicago: University of Chicago Press, 1993.

Barro, Robert, "Economic Growth in a Cross Section of Countries," *Quarterly Journal of Economics*, May 1991, *106*, 407–43.

Barro, Robert, and Xavier Sala-i-Martin, "Convergence," *Journal of Political Economy*, April 1992, *100*, 223–51.

Barro, Robert, and Xavier Sala-i-Martin, *Economic Growth*. New York: McGraw Hill, 1995.

Baumol, William, "Productivity Growth, Convergence and Welfare: What the Long-Run Data Show," *American Economic Review*, December 1986; *76*, 1072–85.

Ben-David, Dan, "Equalizing Exchange: Trade Liberalization and Convergence," *Quarterly Journal of Economics*, 1993, *108*:3, 653–79.

Ben-David, Dan, and David Papell, "Slow-downs and Meltdowns: Post-War Growth Evidence from 74 countries." Centre for Economic Policy Research Discussion Paper Series No. 1111, February 1995.

Canova, Fabio, and Albert Marcet, "The Poor Stay Poor: Non-Convergence Across Countries and Regions." Centre for Economic Policy Research Discussion Paper No. 1265, November 1995.

Caselli, Franseco, Gerardo Esquivel, and Fernando Lefort, "Reopening the Convergence Debate: A New Look at Cross-Country Growth Empirics," mimeo, Harvard University, 1995.

Chen, Shaohua, Gaurav Datt, and Martin Ravallion, "Is Poverty Increasing in the Developing World?" World Bank Policy Research Working Paper No. 1146, June 1993.

Clark, Colin, *Population Growth and Land Use*. London: Macmillan, 1977.

De Long, Bradford, "Productivity Growth, Convergence, and Welfare: Comment," *American Economic Review*, December 1988, *78*, 1138–54.

Dollar, David, and Edward Wolff, *Competitiveness, Convergence, and International Specialization*. Cambridge, Mass.: Massachusetts Institute of Technology Press, 1993.

Easterly, William, Michael Kremer, Lant Pritchett, and Lawrence Summers, "Good Policy or Good Luck? Country Growth Performance and Temporary Shocks," *Journal of Monetary Economics*, December 1993, *32*:3, 459–83.

Evans, Paul, "Evaluating Growth Theories Using Panel Data," mimeo, Ohio State University, 1994.

de la Fuente, Angel, "The Empirics of Growth and Convergence: A Selective Review." Centre for Economic Policy Research No. 1275, November 1995.

FAO, *Calorie Requirements: Report of the Second Committee on Calorie Requirements*. Rome: FAO, 1957.

FAO, *Handbook on Human Nutritional Requirements*. Rome: Food and Agriculture Organization and World Health Organization, 1974.

Gerschenkron, Alexander, *Economic Backwardness in Historical Perspective, a Book of Essays*. Cambridge: Belknap Press, 1962.

Hanson, John R., "Third World Incomes before World War I: Some Comparisons," *Explorations in Economic History*, 1988, *25*, 323–36.

Hanson, John R., "Third World Incomes before World War I: Further Evidence," *Explorations in Economic History*, 1991, *28*, 367–79.

Hill, Kenneth, "The Decline of Childhood Mortality." In Simon, Julian, ed., *The State of Humanity*. Oxford: Blackwell, 1995, pp. 37–50.

International Rice Research Institute, *World Rice Statistics*. Los Banos: International Rice Research Institute, 1987.

Jones, Charles, "R&D Based Models of Economic Growth," *Journal of Political Economy*, August 1995, *103*:4, 759–84.

Kuznets, Simon, *Modern Economic Growth: Rate, Structure and Spread*. New Haven: Yale University Press, 1966.

Kuznets, Simon, *Economic Growth of Nations: Total Output and Production Structure*. Cambridge, Mass.: Belknap Press, 1971.

Livi-Basci, Massimo, *A Concise History of World Population*. Cambridge, Mass: Blackwell, 1992.

Loayza, Norman, "A Test of the International Convergence Hypothesis Using Panel Data." World Bank Policy Research Paper No. 1333, August 1994.

Lucas, Robert, "Ricardian Equilibrium: A Neoclassical Exposition," mimeo, Technion Israel Institute of Technology Economics Workshop Series, June 1996.

Maddison, Angus, "A Comparison of Levels of GDP Per Capita in Developed and Developing Countries, 1700–1980," *Journal of Economic History*, March 1983, *43*, 27–41.

Maddison, Angus, *Dynamic Forces in Capitalistic Development: A Long-Run Comparative View*. New York: Oxford University Press, 1991.

Maddison, Angus, "Explaining the Economic Performance of Nations, 1820–1989." In Baumol, William J., Richard R. Nelson, and Edward N. Wolff, eds., *Convergence of Productivity: Cross-National Studies and Historical Evidence*. New York: Oxford University Press, 1994, pp. 20–61.

Maddison, Angus, *Monitoring the World Economy, 1820–1992*. Paris: Development Centre of the Organisation for Economic Co-operation Development, 1995.

Mankiw, N. Gregory, David Romer, and David Weil, "A Contribution to the Empirics of Economic Growth," *Quarterly Journal of Economics*, May 1992, *107*:2, 407–36.

Nuxoll, Daniel, "Differences in Relative Prices and International Differences in Growth Rates," *American Economic Review*, December 1994, *84*, 1423–36.

Pritchett, Lant, "Where Has All the Education Gone?," mimeo, June 1995a.

Pritchett, Lant, "Population, Factor Accumulation and Productivity." World Bank Policy Research Paper No. 1567, October 1995b.

Pritchett, Lant, and Lawrence H. Summers, "Wealthier is Healthier," *Journal of Human Resources*, 1996, *31*:4, 841–68.

Quah, Danny, "Empirics for Economic Growth and Convergence." Centre for Economic Policy Research Discussion Paper No. 1140, March 1995.

Ravallion, Martin, Gaurav Datt, and Dominique van de Walle, "Quantifying Absolute Poverty in the Developing World," *Review of Income and Wealth*, 1991, *37*:4, 345–61.

Rebelo, Sergio, "Long-Run Policy Analysis and Long-Run Growth," *Journal of Political Economy*, June 1991, 99, 500–21.

Rostow, W. W., *Theorist of Economic Growth from David Hume to the Present: With a Perspective on the Next Century*. New York: Oxford University Press, 1990.

Sachs, Jeffrey, and Andrew Warner, "Economic Convergence and Economic Policies." NBER Working Paper No. 5039, February 1995.

Sala-i-Martin, Xavier, "Regional Cohesion: Evidence and Theories of Regional Growth and Convergence." Centre for Economic Policy Research Discussion Paper No. 1074, November 1994.

Summers, Robert, and Alan Heston, "The Penn World Tables (Mark 5): An Expanded Set of International Comparisons, 1950–88," *Quarterly Journal of Economics*, 1991, *106*:2, 327–68.

World Bank, *World Development Report: Workers in an Integrating Economy*. Washington, D.C.: Oxford University Press for the World Bank, 1995.

THE ECONOMIST

LIBERTY'S GREAT ADVANCE

*   *   *

The past half-century can be seen as a long exploration of the power of liberal trade to raise living standards, not only in the rich world but among the poor too. It has also, more recently, been an exploration of people's preference, when given the choice, for democracy. The process is lamentably patchy and far from complete. Still, it has been an extraordinary success which holds great promise for the future.

The story begins with the growth that took place in western Europe, North America, Austral-asia and Japan once the two great scourges of economic activity—war and trade restrictions—were removed after 1945. These countries were the main signatories of the General Agree-ment on Tariffs and Trade in 1947 (Japan joined in 1955), which began the process of dismantling trade barriers. That group, subsequently known as "the West", increased its income per head fourfold in 1950–2001, a growth rate averaging 2.8% a year. Chart 1 shows how world GDP growth, led by the West, came to be associated with even faster growth in world trade.

The rest of the world—communist, socialist, or just plain poor—also grew, but more slowly: at 2.2% a year on average, or a threefold rise in income per head. Thus the gap between "the West and the rest," as Angus Maddison, an economic historian, described it in an OECD report in 2002 from which these figures are taken, has been widening. It is now especially wide between the richest few countries in the world and the poorest few, which are mainly in Africa; wider, indeed, than ever before. Sceptics about trade use such increases in global inequality as evidence that under liberalism the rich get richer and the poor stay poor. Yet that is wrong.

Such broad figures disguise the underlying trends. These are that countries in Asia have actually been narrowing the gap substantially: there, excluding already-developed Japan, in 1950–2001 income per head increased fivefold. In the early decades, Asian growth could be dismissed as exceptional, given that it was limited mainly to the city states of Hong Kong and Singapore, and two politically anomalous countries, Taiwan and South Korea. But since 1980, not only has growth spread to South-East Asia but it has also accelerated in the world's most populous countries, China and India. Given that Asia as a whole is home to well over half of the world's people, such progress can no longer be dismissed.

1. A Trader's Era
World GDP and trade, 1950–2000

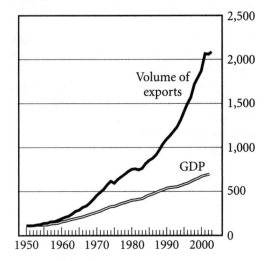

Source: World Trade Organization

From *The Economist* (June 26, 2003).

An Open Secret

The countries that have succeeded in raising living standards rapidly, over long periods, have followed many varieties of economic policy and have lived under many different forms of government. What they have had in common, though, has been a policy of opening their economies to trade and to foreign capital. Not fully, or even nearly so: none, except perhaps tiny Hong Kong, has followed the laisser-faire formula demonised by anti-globalists (which, incidentally, America has not followed either). Nor have they grown by somehow promoting exports and blocking all imports. Rather, they liberalised some markets in order to stimulate competition, internally and from imports; and they ensured that imports of most basic commodities and components faced few barriers, in order to keep prices down for the users of such goods. They adopted liberal trade partially, selectively and mostly gradually. But the important thing was that they adopted it.

2. The Benefits of Integration
Average annual growth of GDP per head 1990–2001, %

Countries that are:

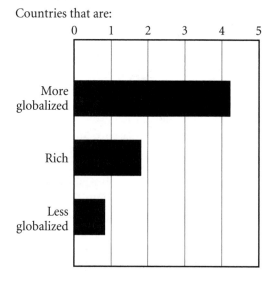

Sources: "Globalization, Growth and Poverty" by David Dollar and Paul Collier, World Bank, 2001; *The Economist*

Chart 2 shows the World Bank's depiction of the effects of such policies since 1990, a period during which the move away from closed, centrally planned economies became a rush, following the fall of the Soviet Union in 1991. Countries that have opened their borders in this way have seen their incomes per head grow rapidly—much more rapidly than either the existing rich countries or those that have not globalised, either by choice or through lack of opportunity. There have been failures, most notably in the former Soviet Union, where Russia and its nearest neighbours, Ukraine and Belarus, suffered economic decline in the 1990s even when they did liberalise some markets; and most recently in Argentina where a fixed exchange rate combined with fiscal profligacy led to disaster. But such failures are heavily outweighed by the successes.

The result is that far from rising, global inequality has actually been falling substantially. Not when measured as the gap between the very richest and the very poorest. Nor when measured, as has until recently been the rather odd norm, as the difference between the average incomes of each country, regardless of population (thus counting Chad and China as if they were of equal size). But if it is measured in the way which is normal within countries, as the distribution of individual incomes, it has narrowed considerably. Given the rapid growth in China over the past 20 years, and the less rapid but still healthy growth in India, that observation makes eminent sense: huge chunks of the world's population have been climbing out of poverty. Even so, it is controversial.

Such things are, admittedly, hard to measure. There is no worldwide census of everyone's individual income, so indirect routes must be used to estimate it. But two different studies, using different methods, have now come up with broadly the same conclusion. One, by Xavier Sala-i-Martin of New York's Columbia University for America's National Bureau of Economic Research, is depicted in chart 3: it shows how rising incomes, especially in Asia, are creating what, in world terms, could be described as a huge middle class. As the bulge moves to the right of the chart, so incomes are becoming more equal.

Another study, by an Indian economist named Surjit Bhalla, in a book for the Institute for International Economics called "Imagine There's No Country", confirmed those findings as well as the consequent drop in world poverty. Measured by the benchmark favoured by the World Bank of income of $2 a day or less, adjusted to cater for differences in purchasing power, the proportion of the world's population in poverty dropped from 56% in 1980 to 23% in 2000, on Mr Bhalla's calculations. Thanks to population growth, the absolute number of people in that category remains large: more than 1.1 billion. But that is still far fewer than in 1990 (1.7 billion) and 1980 (1.9 billion). Before 1980, the absolute numbers were rising. That date roughly coincides with the spread of trade and internal-market liberalisation to many poor countries.

3. Bulging Toward Equality
World distribution of income*, people, m[illions]

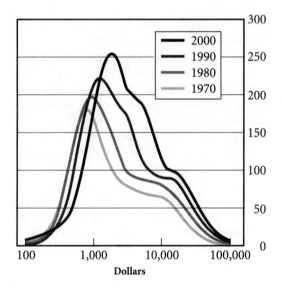

Source: Xavier Sala-i-Martin   *Annual income

The truth about market liberalisation and economic growth is not that it increases inequality, nor that it hurts the poor: just the opposite. Rather, the truth is that some large parts of the poor world are pulling themselves out of poverty while others are not. Those poorer parts include some countries in Asia, including Pakistan and Central Asia, and some in Latin America as well as most of the Middle East, where liberalisation has scarcely been attempted and revenues from oil have lately declined. Most notably, though, they include more or less a whole continent, namely Africa. There, incomes have stagnated or even declined, and life expectancies are falling too, thanks to AIDS and other plagues. Home to 13% of the world's population, the continent accounts for merely 3% of world GDP. The lack of progress in Africa, not the supposed evils of globalisation, is where the most difficult problem of economic development lies.

Democracy Too

Alongside this successful growth in economic liberty, there has also been an impressive expansion of political and civil freedoms. Since 1980, according to the 2002 United Nations Human Development Report (UNHDR), 81 countries have taken "significant" steps towards democracy, with 33 military regimes replaced by civilian governments. Of the world's nearly 200 countries, 140 now hold multi-party elections. That may not make them fully democratic, but 82 of them are, and those are home to 57% of the world's population. Especially pleasing to an independent organ such as *The Economist* is the fact that, according to the UNHDR, 125 countries, with 62% of the world's population, now have a free or partly free press. The spread of daily newspapers in developing countries has risen to 60 copies per 1,000 people, from 29 in 1970–96, and the number of televisions has increased 16-fold.

Recently, it has become fashionable to play down that progress by pointing out that many of the new democracies have not gone beyond elections to build the other, essential, protections for liberty: an independent judiciary, equality before a well-enforced rule of law, and constitutional limits on the abuse of political power. In Zimbabwe, an elected president, Robert Mugabe, has ruined the country, sponsored violence and rigged elections. Constitutions have been violated by elected politicians in Peru and Russia, and judiciaries manipulated. Venezuela's elected president, Hugo Chavez, essentially wrote his own constitution, which he hands out to visitors as a little blue book reminiscent of Mao Zedong's red one.

In sub-Saharan Africa, according to *The Future of Freedom*, a new book by Fareed Zakaria that wrings its hands about "illiberal democracy," 42 out of 48 countries have held multiparty elections since 1990, but most have simply allowed a rotation of plundering governments. A few democracies have even collapsed: Pakistan's elected government was overturned in a coup in 1999 by General (now self-appointed President) Pervez Musharraf.

Such worries are perfectly fair. Much more progress is needed. It would be wrong to celebrate the mere holding of elections if other, arguably even more important, protections for liberty are not present or likely soon to be created. Some democracies, including longstanding ones such as Malaysia and Singapore, essentially have semi-authoritarian regimes. Yet such legitimate concerns should not be allowed to detract from the basic progress that has occurred: in the past 20 years the share of the world's population living in proper democracies has risen from about a third to just over half. Freedom House, a Washington-based think-tank, this year rated 89 countries as being "free societies", up from 75 in 1993, and a further 55 as "partly free". Liberty has had a period of tremendous advance on all fronts.

In the short term, there is cause for optimism that this advance will continue. Despite economic crises in East Asia, Russia and Latin America during the past six years, developing countries still seem to want to liberalise their economies. China has recently joined the World Trade Organisation, bringing the total membership to 146 countries, and Russia is in the queue for membership, along with 25 others. After shrinking slightly in 2001, the volume of world trade started to grow again in 2002, albeit weakly. Efforts have begun to try to implant democracy in Afghanistan and Iraq. Argentina has endured an economic collapse to match the Great Depression of the 1930s, yet has emerged with its democracy intact.

Liberty's Next Retreat?

For all the anti-globalists' cries on their behalf, few of the world's poorer countries show signs of wanting to retreat from liberalism: their question, rather, is whether to extend it rapidly or gradually, and whether they have the domestic governmental institutions to be able to cope with it. Though it does little to promote democracy, China is proving a spur to economic liberalisation in other developing countries: fear that its growth will steal their markets or investment is prompting others to copy its reforms and to adopt international trade rules by joining the WTO. The real doubts are in the pioneers of globalisation, the rich countries.

Business is under attack, even in the homeland of free enterprise, the United States, whether from politicians, single-issue lobby groups or, most dangerously of all, from lawyers. Having made pots of cash from tobacco firms, they are turning their attention to Wall Street and to drug companies. Anti-capitalist demonstrations on May 1st in cities around the world attracted sizeable crowds. Stockmarkets remain weak, despite a quick end to the war in Iraq and a 30% fall in oil prices. So do many economies, especially the biggest and richest ones in western Europe, Japan and the United States.

Plus ça change, once again? Wherever democracy allows a crowd to gather, there will always be some who resent the selfishness inherent in the profit motive, or who stand to lose from the change that economic and technological progress or the evolution of tastes may bring, or who simply like a good march and love to yell abuse at the high and mighty. With the economic, social and even environmental failure of communism and its milder comrade, socialism, still fresh in the memory, there is little chance that any alternative to a capitalist economy could soon garner widespread support. And whenever economies approach the bottom of their inevitable cycles, there is always anxiety that the good times may never return. Yet they always do.

There are, though, some stronger reasons to worry. One, admittedly, is generic to all bad times: the fact that it is when unemployment is rising, or incomes are falling, or prospects seem dim, or threats of war and terrorism spread fear and anger, that politicians come under the greatest pressure—and temptation—to close borders or to slap controls on freedoms of all kinds, whether civil or commercial. They may wish to curry favour with domestic lobbies or merely to look as if they are doing something.

Another reason, however, is peculiar to today and risks greatly amplifying the generic one. It is that the economic and financial-market boom of the 1990s was so extreme that its bust is also producing extreme results: a pile of corporate scandals, resentment at an extraordinary widening of inequalities of income and wealth within the rich countries, a ghastly hole in the retirement funds of millions of ordinary people and, most crucially of all, a gathering disillusion about the ability of democratic institutions to hold culprits accountable for their sins.

A Long Way to Fall

Such results can be seen, in some measure, right across the developed world. But they are at their most noticeable in the United States, for that is where the 1990s boom, along with its extremes of misbehaviour, went the furthest. In the title of a feisty and well-researched book by a commentator and political activist, Arianna Huffington, in America in recent years there were *Pigs at the Trough*, extracting gigantic executive salaries and perks, faking corporate accounts, manipulating equity offerings and granting each other vast piles of share options, among other abuses. More outrageously still, many of those benefiting from this flow of cash managed successfully to lobby Congress and the White House to reject reforms that could have stemmed some of the abuse.

When such excesses have occurred in the past, there has been a political backlash to exploit the popular anger, as under the presidencies of Teddy Roosevelt and Woodrow Wilson in the 1900s. That remains a strong possibility, even though the popularity of the famously pro-business President George Bush is running high, thanks to the wars on terror and Saddam Hussein. The danger is often expressed as one of an over-reaction to the excesses, of an excessive bout of regulation on business. That danger exists; but the worst possibility is that anger at capitalist abuses will tip the balance in domestic politics towards protectionism, as a misguided way to help the weak and vulnerable, and to pander to suspicion of markets and business. If it does, remember to blame those pigs and their love of the trough.

PAUL COLLIER AND JAN WILLEM GUNNING

WHY HAS AFRICA GROWN SLOWLY?

In the 1960s, Africa's future looked bright. On the basis of Maddison's (1995) estimates of per capita GDP for a sample of countries, during the first half of the century Africa had grown considerably more rapidly than Asia; by 1950, the African sample had overtaken the Asian sample. In the 1950s there were uncertainties of political transition, but after 1960 Africa was increasingly free of colonialism, with the potential for governments that would be more responsive to domestic needs. During the period 1960–73, growth in Africa was more rapid than in the first half of the century. Indeed, for this period, African growth and its composition were indistinguishable from the geographically very different circumstances of south Asia (Collins and Bosworth, 1996). Political self-determination in Africa and economic growth seemed to be proceeding hand-in-hand.

However, during the 1970s both political and economic matters in Africa deteriorated. The leadership of many African nations hardened into autocracy and dictatorship. Africa's economies first faltered and then started to decline. While Africa experienced a growth collapse, nations of south Asia modestly improved their economic performance. A good example of this divergence is the comparison of Nigeria and Indonesia. Until around 1970, the economic performance of Nigeria was broadly superior to that of Indonesia, but over the next quarter-century outcomes diverged markedly, despite the common experience for both countries of an oil boom in a predominantly agricultural economy. Since 1980, aggregate per capita GDP in sub-Saharan Africa has declined at almost 1 percent per annum. The decline has been widespread:

32 countries are poorer now than in 1980. Today, sub-Saharan Africa is the lowest-income region in the world. Figure 1 and Table 1, taken together, offer a snapshot of Africa today. Figure 1 is a map of the continent. Table 1 gives some basic information on population, GDP, standard of living, and growth rates for countries of sub-Saharan Africa. We focus on the sub-Saharan countries, setting aside the north African countries of Algeria, Egypt, Libya, Morocco and Tunisia. This is conventional for the studies of this area, since the north African countries are part of a different regional economy—the Middle East—with its own distinctive set of economic issues. It is clear that Africa has suffered a chronic failure of economic growth. The problem for analysis is to determine its causes.

The debate on the causes of slow African growth has offered many different explanations. These can be usefully grouped into a two-by-two matrix, distinguishing on the one hand between policy and exogenous "destiny" and, on the other, between domestic and external factors. Table 2 compares Africa to other developing regions, using this grouping. Until recently it has largely been accepted that the main causes of Africa's slow growth were external, with the debate focusing upon whether external problems were policy-induced or exogenous. Especially during the 1980s, the World Bank, the International Monetary Fund and bilateral donors came to identify exchange rate and trade policies as the primary causes of slow growth in Africa. Table 2 offers some evidence that official exchange rates in sub-Saharan Africa have been more overvalued relative to (often illegal) market rates than is common for other less developed economies of Asia and Latin America. Tariffs and quantitative trade restrictions have also been higher in Africa than elsewhere. The rival

From *Journal of Economic Perspectives* 13, No. 3 (Summer 1999) pp. 3–22.

Figure 1
The Political Geography of Africa

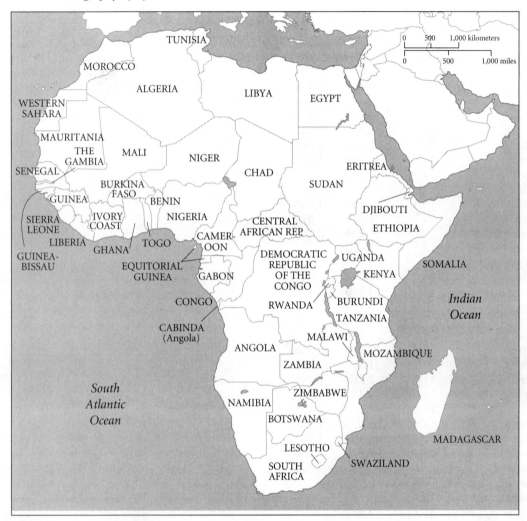

thesis, often favored by African governments, was that the crisis was due to deteriorating and volatile terms of trade, and as Table 2 shows, terms of trade have indeed been more volatile for Africa than for other less developed economies. Jeffrey Sachs and his co-authors have emphasized a further adverse external "destiny" factor: Africa's population is atypically landlocked. As shown in Table 2, a high proportion of the population is remote from the coast or navigable waters.

Recently, attention has shifted to possible domestic causes of slow growth within African nations, but the debate as to the relative importance of policy-induced and exogenous problems has continued. Sachs and his co-authors have attributed slow growth to "the curse of the tropics." Africa's adverse climate causes poor health, and so reduces life expectancy below that in other regions, which puts it at a disadvantage in development. The adverse climate also leads to leached soils and unreliable rainfall, which

Table 1. The Economies of Sub-Saharan Africa

Country	Population (Millions) 1997	GDP US$m at 1990 Prices 1997	GNP per Capita (PPP $) 1997	GNP Average Annual % Growth per Capita 1965–97	Life Expectancy at Birth (years) 1995	% of Population below $1 a Day (early 1990s)	Trade as % of GDP (in PPP) 1997
Angola	11.6	9,886	728	. . .	48	. . .	77
Benin	5.7	2,540	1,240		48	. . .	17
Botswana	1.5	4,458	7,440	7.7	66	33	. . .
Burkina Faso	11.1	3,643	936	0.9	47	. . .	7
Burundi	6.4	939	661	1.1	51	. . .	5
Cameroon	13.9	11,254	1,739	1.4	57	. . .	13
Cape Verde	0.4	393	. . .	. . .	66	. . .	. . .
Central African Republic	3.4	1,420	1,254	−1.2	50	. . .	10
Chad	6.7	1,492	978	0.1	49	. . .	4
Comoros	0.7	251	. . .	. . .	57	. . .	. . .
Congo	2.7	2,433	1,275	1.7	53	. . .	80
Congo, Dem. Rep.	48.0	6,094	698	−3.7	. . .	. . .	7
Côte d'Ivoire	14.3	13,320	1,676	−0.9	50	18	30
Djibouti	0.4	384	. . .	. . .	49	. . .	. . .
Equatorial Guinea	0.4	541	. . .	. . .	49	. . .	. . .
Eritrea	3.4	1,010	990	. . .	52	. . .	. . .
Ethiopia	60.1	11,327	493	−0.5	49	46	7
Gabon	1.1	7,280	6,480	0.4	55	. . .	58
Gambia	1.0	332	1,372	0.5	46	. . .	30
Ghana	18.3	7,892	1,492	−0.9	57	. . .	19
Guinea	7.6	3,699	1,763	. . .	46	26	14
Guinea Bissau	1.1	306	1,041	0.1	45	88	13
Kenya	28.4	9,879	1,150	1.3	55	50	16
Lesotho	2.1	998	2,422	3.2	62	49	. . .
Liberia	2.5	. . .	. . .	. . .	57	. . .	. . .
Madagascar	15.8	3,187	892	−1.9	58	72	11
Malawi	10.1	2,480	688	0.5	45	. . .	21
Mali	11.5	3,132	715	0.5	47	. . .	19
Mauritania	2.4	1,346	1,654	−0.2	53	31	28
Mauritius	1.1	3,755	9,147	3.8	71	. . .	37
Mozambique	18.3	2,144	541	−0.1	47	. . .	15
Namibia	1.6	3,141	4,999	0.7	60	. . .	. . .
Niger	9.8	2,776	824	−2.5	48	62	9
Nigeria	118.4	34,418	854	0.0	51	31	23
Rwanda	5.9	1,979	643	0.1	47	46	9
Sao Tome & Principe	0.1	56	. . .	. . .	. . .	. . .	. . .
Senegal	8.8	6,708	1,670	−0.5	50	54	11
Seychelles	0.1	435	. . .	. . .	. . .	. . .	. . .

Table 1. (continued)

Country	Population (Millions) 1997	GDP US$m at 1990 Prices 1997	GNP per Capita (PPP $) 1997	GNP Average Annual % Growth per Capita 1965–97	Life Expectancy at Birth (years) 1995	% of Population below $1 a Day (early 1990s)	Trade as % of GDP (in PPP) 1997
Sierra Leone	4.4	. . .	401	−1.4	40	. . .	24
Somalia	10.4	. . .	. . .	. . .	48	. . .	. . .
South Africa	43.3	117,089	7,152	0.1	64	24	23
Sudan	27.9	13,119	. . .	−0.2	54	. . .	. . .
Swaziland	0.9	1,031	. . .	. . .	59	. . .	. . .
Tanzania	31.5	4,956	608	. . .	52	11	14
Togo	4.3	1,726	1,408	−0.6	56	. . .	24
Uganda	20.8	6,822	1,131	. . .	44	69	6
Zambia	8.5	3,564	900	−2.0	48	85	26
Zimbabwe	11.7	7,904	2,207	0.5	52	41	21

Sources: *African Development Report* (1998); and *World Development Indicators* (1999).

constrains African agriculture. African nations also appear to have more ethnic diversity than other poor nations of the world, which may make it harder to develop an interconnected economy. In contrast to the domestic destiny argument, Collier and Gunning (1999) have emphasized domestic policy factors such as poor public service delivery. African governments have typically been less democratic and more bureaucratic than their Asian and Latin American counterparts.

Of course, once the conditions for slow growth are established by any combination of these reasons, they can become self-reinforcing in an endogenous process. Weak economic growth helps explain a lower saving rate and a higher proportion of flight capital for Africa compared to the less developed nations of Asia and Africa. Richer countries tend to see their population growth rates drop off, so the poverty of Africa has helped to keep its birth rates high, even as compared to the world's other less developed economies. Similarly, poverty may have increased the incidence of Africa's numerous civil wars, as well as being a consequence of them.

In the discussion that follows, we assess the policy/destiny and domestic/external distinctions in various combinations. During the mid-1990s, African performance started to improve, with a few countries growing quite rapidly. We conclude by assessing these different explanations as guides to whether this improvement is likely to be transient or persistent.

Four Types of Explanation

Domestic-Destiny

Africa has several geographic and demographic characteristics which may predispose it to slow growth. First, much of the continent is tropical and this may handicap the economy, partly due to diseases such as malaria and partly due to hostile conditions for livestock and agriculture. Life expectancy has historically been low, with the population in a high-fertility, high infant-mortality equilibrium. With the advent of basic public health measures, population growth became very high. In particular, Africa has not been through the demographic transition whereby fertility rates decline which occurred in Asia and Latin America over the past 40 years. On one estimate, Africa's low life expectancy and

Table 2. Africa Compared With Other Developing Regions

(figures are unweighted country averages)

	Sub-Saharan Africa	Other LDCs
Domestic-Destiny		
Life expectancy in 1970 (years)	45.2	57.3
Income in 1960 (1985 $ PPP-adjusted)	835.5	1855.2
Ethnic Fractionalization	67.6	32.7
Domestic-Policy		
Political Rights, 1973–90	6.0	4.0
Bureaucracy	1.38	1.72
External-Destiny		
Population <100 km from the sea or river (%)	21.0	52.0
Terms of trade volatility	16.4	12.8
External-Policy		
Parallel market exchange rate premium	40.0	26.0
Average tariffs 1996–98 (%)	21.0	13.0
Quantitative Restrictions, 1988–90 (%)	46.0	21.0
Endogenous		
Growth of GDP per capita, 1965–90	0.5	1.7
Investment rate in 1997 (%)	18.0	25.0
Population growth rate, 1980–97 (%)	2.8	1.8
Capital flight/private wealth, 1990 (%)	39.0	14.0

Sources: Life expectancy, World Development Indicators, 1998. Income and growth: Penn World Tables 5.6. The index of ethno-linguistic diversity is on the scale 0–100 with 0 being homogenous (Mauro, 1995). The Gastil index of political rights is on the range 1–7 with 1 being fully democratic.

The index of bureaucracy is on the scale 0–6 with high score indicating better quality (Knack and Keefer, 1995). Population living less than 100 km from the sea or a navigable river, from Bloom and Sachs (1999), Table 2, (other LDCs is the weighted average for Asia and Latin America). Terms of trade volatility is the standard deviation of annual log changes 1965–92, (Collins and Bosworth, 1996). Parallel exchange rate premium (%), (Easterly and Levine, 1997).

Average tariff: simple average, computed by IMF, we would like to thank Robert Sharer for these numbers. QRs: weighted average incidence of non-tariff measures over product lines; other LDCs is simple average of Latin America and East Asia; from Rodrik (1999, Table 12).

Investment rate and population growth rate, World Development Indicators, 1999 Capital flight/private wealth as of 1990 (Collier and Pattillo, 1999).

high population growth account for almost all of Africa's slow growth (Bloom and Sachs, 1998). The argument is not clear-cut, however. Low life expectancy and high fertility are consequences of low income as well as causes, so the estimates are likely to be biased upwards. The household-level evidence suggests that the effects of poor health on income are small, although these in turn will be biased downwards by the omission of large-scale changes in economic activity which cannot be detected at the household level.

Whether or not Africa's past demographic characteristics have contributed to its slow growth, some African countries seem certain to go through a distinctive and disastrous demographic transition during the next two decades. As a result of AIDS, adult mortality rates will rise dramatically. In Africa, AIDS is a heterosexual disease. During the 1980s in parts of Africa it spread rapidly across the population before the risks became apparent, with up to 20-25 percent of adults now HIV-positive in some countries (World Bank, 1997). This human tragedy will have substantial economic effects during the next decade, especially since infection rates appear to be higher among the more educated, but it does not account for historically slow growth.

A second key characteristic of Africa which may predispose it to slow growth is that soil quality is poor and much of the continent is semi-arid, with rainfall subject to long cycles and unpredictable failure. Soils derive disproportionately from a very old type of rock ("Basement Complex"), which is low in micronutrients and varies considerably between localities. The application of additional macronutrients, which is the fertilizer package associated with the Green Revolution, is generally ineffective with low levels of micronutrients. Africa probably has scope for its own agricultural revolution, but it will depend upon locality-specific packages of micronutrients (Voortman et al., 1999). Since the 1960s, the semi-arid areas of Africa have been in a phase of declining rainfall (Grove, 1991). While there are no estimates of the output consequences of this decline, it may be significant, since agriculture is typically about one-quarter of GDP in this region. Given the lack of irrigation, the unpredictability of rainfall implies high risks in agriculture. With incomplete insurance and a high rate of time preference, households have to use assets for purposes of consumption-smoothing rather than investment. Households can thus become trapped in low-income, high-liquidity equilibria (Dercon, 1997).

A third relevant characteristic of Africa's economies, which can be seen as a result of these semi-arid conditions, is that the continent has very low population density. One by-product is high costs of transport which in turn have added to risk: poor market integration has hampered the use of trade for risk sharing. Another consequence of low population density is that Africa has relatively high natural resource endowments per capita (Wood and Mayer, 1998). High levels of natural resources can cause several problems. High levels of exported natural resources may lead to an appreciation of the exchange rate, which in turn makes manufacturing less competitive. Yet manufacturing may offer larger growth externalities, such as learning, than natural resource extraction. Natural resources may also increase "loot-seeking" activities. Collier and Hoeffler (1998) find that a dependence on natural resources strongly increases the risk of civil war, which has been a widespread phenomenon in Africa.

A further consequence of low population density is that African countries have much higher ethno-linguistic diversity than other regions; when groups come together less, there is less mingling and merging. Easterly and Levine (1997) find that this high level of diversity is the most important single cause of Africa's slow growth. There are various interpretations of this result. A common perception is that Africa's high ethnic diversity accounts for its high incidence of civil war. This turns out to be false: high levels of ethnic and religious diversity actually make societies significantly safer (Collier and Hoeffler, 1999). The effects of ethnic diversity on growth turn out to be contingent upon the political system; diversity has deleterious effects only when it occurs in the context of governments which are undemocratic. Collier (1999) finds that in democratic societies, ethnic diversity has no effect on either growth or the quality of public projects, but that in dictatorships, high levels of diversity reduce growth rates by 3 percentage points and double the rate of project failure relative to homogeneity. Dictatorships tend not to transcend the ethnic group of the dictator, so that the more ethnically fragmented the society, the more narrowly based a dictatorship will be, whereas democratic governments in such societies must be ethnically cross-cutting. In turn, the more narrowly based the government, the greater the payoff to predation relative to the inducement of generalized growth. Africa's problem was thus not its ethnic diversity but its lack of democracy in the context of diversity.

A fourth characteristic of Africa that may hinder its growth prospects is that because of its colonial heritage, Africa has much smaller countries in terms of population than other regions. Sub-Saharan Africa has a population about half that of India, divided into 48 states. These many states, combined with low levels of income, make Africa's national economies radically smaller than those of other regions. Very small states might be economically disadvantaged for several reasons. If government has some fixed costs, either in its administrative role or as a provider of services, then it may be hard for a small state to perform at minimum cost. Moreover, the society may forfeit much more extensive scale economies if it combines small scale with isolation. Some domestic markets will be too small even for the minimum efficient scale of production of a single producer; all domestic markets taken alone will be less competitive than in larger economies. Small economies are also perceived by investors as significantly more risky (Collier and Dollar, 1999a). Finally, they may have a slower rate of technological innovation; Kremer (1993) argues the incidence of discoveries may be broadly proportional to the population, so that if discoveries cannot readily spread between societies, low-population societies will have less innovation. However, in aggregate these effects cannot be large, because growth regressions generally find that state size does not affect a nation's rate of economic growth.

Domestic-Policy

For much of the post-colonial period, most African governments have been undemocratic. The median African government during the 1970s and 1980s was close to autocracy, and far less democratic than the median non-African developing country (as measured by the Gastil scale of political rights shown in Table 2). A typical pattern was that governments were captured by the educated, urban-resident population, with few agricultural or commercial interests. They expanded the public sector while imposing wide-ranging controls on private activity. These choices have been economically costly.

Public employment was expanded, often as

an end in itself. For example, in Ghana by the late 1970s the public sector accounted for three-quarters of formal wage employment (Ghana Central Bureau of Statistics, 1988), and even in a more market-oriented economy like Kenya, the figure was 50 percent as of 1990 (Kenya Central Bureau of Statistics, 1996). Indeed, economic decline may have increased pressure for public sector employment. The large number of public sector employees was reconciled with limited tax revenue by reducing wage rates and non-wage expenditures. The ratio of wage to non-wage expenditures in African governments is double that in Asia, and this has lowered the quality of public services; for example, in education, teaching materials are often lacking. The large, ill-paid public sector became the arena in which ethnic groups struggled for resources. For example, in the Ghanaian public sector, the locally dominant ethnic group received a wage premium of 25 percent over other groups after controlling for worker characteristics, and cognitive skills were completely unrewarded (Collier and Garg, 1999). The combination of low wage levels and payment structures, which rewarded social connections rather than skill, made it difficult for managers to motivate staff, and the difficulties of service delivery were compounded by the low ratio of non-wage to wage expenditures.

Since public sector employment was the main priority, managers were not under severe pressure for actual delivery of services from their political masters. Because of the lack of democracy, neither were they accountable to the broader public. As a result, Africa experienced a paradox of poor public services despite relatively high public expenditure (Pradhan, 1996). Poor service delivery handicapped firms through unreliable transport and power, inadequate telecommunications networks, and unreliable courts. For example, manufacturing firms in Zimbabwe need to hold high levels of inventories, despite high interest rates, due to unreliable delivery of inputs tied to poor transportation infrastructure (Fafchamps et al., 1998). A survey of Ugandan firms found that shortage of electricity was identified as the single most important constraint upon firm growth; indeed, the provision of electricity by firms for their own use was almost as large as the public supply of electricity (Reinikka and Svensson, 1998). A study in Nigeria found that their own generators accounted for three-quarters of the capital equipment of small manufacturers (Lee and Anas, 1991). The poor state of African telecommunications was estimated to reduce African growth rates by 1 percentage point, according to Easterly and Levine (1997). (However, since telecommunications was the main infrastructure variable which they could quantify, and since lack of different kinds of infrastructure is probably highly correlated, their estimate is probably a proxy for a wider range of infrastructural deficiencies.) African commercial courts are more corrupt than those in other regions (Widner, 1999). As a result, firms face greater problems of contract enforcement. Some firms can overcome these by relying upon their social networks to screen potential clients, but it is common to restrict business to long-standing clients (Bigsten et al., 1999). Ethnic minorities, such as Asians in East Africa and Lebanese in West Africa, tend to have more specialized social networks and so are better able than African firms to screen new clients (Biggs et al., 1996). The problem of contract enforcement thus makes markets less competitive and reduces the potential gains from trade, while tending to perpetuate the dominant position of minorities in business.

Poor public service delivery also handicapped households through inefficient education, health and extension services. A survey of primary education expenditures in Uganda found that, of the non-wage money released by the Ministry of Finance, on average, less than 30 percent actually reached the schools (Ablo and Reinikka, 1998). The expansion of the public sector has reduced private initiative. Since major areas of economic activity were reserved for the public sector—often including transport, marketing and banking—and African elites looked to the public sector rather than the private sector for advancement, Africa was slow to develop indigenous entrepreneurs.

African governments built various economic control regimes. A few nations, such as Ethiopia, Angola and Tanzania, had wide-ranging price controls under which private agents had an incentive to reduce production—at least officially marketed production. These governments often attempted to counterbalance these incentives with coercive production targets, but the net effect was usually dramatic declines in economic activity. More commonly, firms were subject to considerable regulation. For example, for many years manufacturing firms wishing to set up in Kenya had to acquire letters of no objection from existing producers, which resulted in a predictably low level of competition. In Uganda, when the government removed the requirement that coffee could only be transported by rail, the market for road haulage expanded sufficiently to induce new entry, which in turn broke an existing cartel, nearly halving haulage rates. Similarly, in Tanzania during the long period when agricultural marketing was heavily regulated, marketing margins for grain were double what they were both before regulation and after deregulation (Bevan et al., 1993). In this period, food prices became much more volatile: between 1964 and 1980 the coefficient of variation (that is, the ratio of the standard deviation to the mean) of maize prices at regional centers doubled, falling again sharply when markets were liberalized.

Government interventions undermined the functioning of product markets in many countries. Private trading, which was often associated with ethnic minorities such as the Indians in East Africa and the Lebanese in West Africa, was sometimes banned. A particularly damaging intervention, practiced even in relatively market-friendly economies such as Kenya, was to ban private inter-district trade in food. Where government marketing monopolies were focused on ensuring the food supply to urban areas, this provision discouraged farmers from specializing in non-food export crops, since they could not rely on being able to buy food locally.

Since the political base of governments was urban, agriculture was heavily taxed and the public agronomic research needed to promote an African green revolution, based on locally-specific packages of micronutrients, was neglected. The main source of agricultural growth has been the gradual adoption of cash crops by smallholders, a process slowed down by government pricing policies (Bevan et al., 1993). While governments favored manufacturing, the basis for industrial growth in this area was also undermined, since trade and exchange rate policies induced industrial firms to produce under uncompetitive conditions and only for small and captive domestic markets.

The same urban bias initially led governments to favor the urban wage labor force. In the immediate post-colonial period, minimum wages rose and unions acquired influence, so that wages increased substantially. However, post-independence inflation has usually eroded minimum wages, so that in most of Africa, wage rigidities in the labor market are not currently a significant impediment to the growth process. The exceptions are South Africa, where the labor market may just be going through such a real wage adjustment now, and the low inflation environments of Ethiopia and the countries in the "franc zone," the 13 former colonies of France in west and central Africa which had currencies pegged to the French franc. While high wage levels are not normally a hindrance to African economies, the job matching process appears to be inefficient, so that job mobility offers unusually high returns (Mengistae, 1998). This is an instance of the high costs of market information; for example, newspapers are expensive and have low circulation.

Financial markets were heavily regulated, with bank lending directed to the government, public enterprises or "strategic" sectors, very limited financial intermediation and virtually no competition between financial institutions. A common proxy for the extent of financial intermediation, known as "financial depth," is the broad money supply, M2, relative to GDP. But although Africa has even less financial depth than other developing areas, currently available evidence suggests that this may have had only a modest impact on its growth. For example, Easterly and Levine (1997) estimate that lack of financial depth reduced the annual growth rate by only 0.3 percentage points. Similarly, microeconomic survey evidence on manufacturing firms indicates that the lack of external finance is not currently the binding constraint on industrial investment (Bigsten et al., 1999).

External-Destiny

Africa is better located than Asia for most developed economy markets. However, most Africans live much further from the coast or navigable rivers than in other regions and so face intrinsically higher transport costs for exports (as shown in Table 2). Further, much of the population lives in countries which are land-locked, so that problems of distance are compounded by political barriers. Even a relatively open border like the one between Canada and the United States appears to be a substantial impediment to trade, in the sense that trade across Canadian provinces or across U.S. states is far greater than trade of equal distance between Canada and the United States (McCallum, 1995). Landlocked countries face national borders on all sides, which may constitute an irreducible barrier to trade even if they have good relations with their neighbors. Typically, growth regressions find that being landlocked reduces a nation's annual growth rate by around half of 1 percent.

A further aspect of external destiny is that Africa's exports are concentrated in a narrow range of commodities, with volatile prices that have declined since the 1960s. The deterioration in the terms of trade for such commodities has undoubtedly contributed to Africa's growth slowdown. However, there is controversy over whether its atypical exposure to terms of trade volatility has been damaging. Deaton and Miller (1996) find little evidence of detrimental effects in the short run. However, case study evidence suggests that shocks have often had longer-run deleterious effects. Investment has been concertinaed into short periods, during which construction booms have raised the unit cost of capital, and government budgets have been destabilized, with spending rising during booms but being difficult to reduce subsequently (Schuknecht, 1999; Collier and Gunning, 1999b).

Africa has attracted much more aid per capita than other regions. Donor allocation rules have typically favored countries which have small populations and low incomes, and were recent colonies—and African countries met all three criteria. There has been a long debate as to whether aid has been detrimental or beneficial for the growth process (for recent overviews, see Gwin and Nelson, 1997; World Bank, 1998). Early critics claimed that aid reduced the incentive for good governance (for example, Bauer, 1982). Since the 1980s, the World Bank and the International Monetary Fund have attempted to make policy improvement a condition for the receipt of aid. Econometric work does not find that aid has had a significant effect on policy: to the extent that aid encourages or discourages policy changes, the two effects apparently offset each other. However, the effect of aid on growth has been shown to be policy-dependent. Where policies are good, aid substantially raises growth rates, where they are poor, diminishing returns rapidly set in so that aid cannot significantly contribute to growth. This result holds whether the measure of policy is objective indicators of the fiscal and exchange rate stance (Burnside and Dollar, 1997), or subjective but standardized ratings of a broader range of policies done by the World Bank (Collier and Dollar, 1999). Until recently, many African policy environments were not good enough for aid to raise growth substantially. Hence, the evidence does not support Bauer's (1982) claim that Africa's large aid receipts were a cause of its slow growth, but does suggest that Africa largely missed the opportunity for enhanced growth which aid provided.

Excluding South Africa and the oil exporters (whose terms of trade have improved), the net aid inflows since 1970 have been around 50 percent greater than the income losses from terms of trade deterioration. The combination was thus somewhat analogous to an increase in export taxation: the terms of trade losses taking money from exporters, while the aid provided money to governments.

External-Policy

In recent decades, African governments adopted exchange rate and trade policies which were atypically anti-export and accumulated large foreign debts. On a range of indicators, Africa has had much higher trade barriers and more misaligned exchange rates than other regions (Dollar, 1992; Sachs and Warner, 1997). Exchange rates were commonly highly overvalued, reflecting the interest of the political elite in cheap imports. Tariffs and export taxes were higher in Africa than in other regions of the world, partly because of the lack of other sources of tax revenue to finance the expansion of the public sector. Exports were sharply reduced as a result of export crop taxation. For example, Dercon (1993) shows that Tanzanian cotton exports would have been 50 percent higher in the absence of taxation. Quantitative restrictions on imports were also used much more extensively, despite yielding no revenue. They often arose because of the difficulties of fine-tuning import demand in a situation where government was attempting to keep exchange rates fixed with few reserves. They probably persisted because they generated large opportunities for corruption, since someone could often be bribed to circumvent the quantitative limits.

The international growth literature has reached a consensus that exchange rate overvaluation and tight trade restrictions are damaging, but controversy continues over the effects of more moderate trade restrictions (Rodrik, 1999).

However, there are reasons why Africa's poor export performance may have been particularly damaging. Since 1980, African export revenue per capita has sharply declined, which in turn has induced severe import compression of both capital goods and intermediate inputs. Moreover, because African economies are so much smaller than other economies, external barriers of a given height have been significantly more damaging (Collier and Gunning, 1999).

By the 1990s, several African economies had accumulated unsustainable international debts, largely from public agencies. Clearly, this is one way in which poor decisions of the past become embedded in the present. There is a good theoretical argument that high indebtedness discourages private investment due to the fear of the future tax liability. There is some supporting evidence for this claim, although since poor policies lower GDP, using high debt/GDP as an explanatory variable may simply be a proxy for poor policies more broadly (Elbadawi et al., 1997).

Policy or Destiny?

The dichotomy between policy and destiny is of course an oversimplification: some apparently exogenous features of Africa have often been induced by policy, and conversely, African policies may reflect exogenous factors.

Consider, first, some of the "exogenous" factors that we have discussed under destiny. For example, the claim by Sachs and Warner (1997) that geography and demography almost fully account for Africa's slow growth rests largely upon the lack of a demographic transition to lower fertility rates in Africa, as has happened in most of Latin America and Asia. However, it is more plausible to regard these continuing high fertility rates as a consequence of slow growth than a cause. The lack of employment opportunities for young women has prevented the opportunity cost of children from rising, and the low returns to education in an environment where many of

the "good" jobs are allocated by political criteria have reduced the incentive for parents to educate their children.

Similarly, the argument that the concentration of Africa's population in the interior is an external force holding down growth can also be seen as an endogenous outcome; specifically, the population has remained in the interior because of the failure of Africa's coastal cities to grow. In turn, this is partly because the failure to industrialize has slowed urbanization, and partly because policy has often been biased against coastal cities; for example, in both Nigeria and Tanzania the capital was relocated from the coast to the interior. Where policy was less biased, as in the Côte d'Ivoire during the 1970s, the coastal population grew so rapidly that it supported massive emigration from the landlocked economy of Burkina Faso: at its peak, around 40 percent of the Ivorien population were immigrants.

Further, being landlocked need not be an economic disadvantage. Developed landlocked economies, such as Switzerland, have atypically low international transport costs because they have oriented their trade towards their neighbors. By contrast, Africa's landlocked economies trade with Europe, so that neighboring countries are an obstacle rather than a market. These patterns of trade are partly a legacy of the colonial economy, but they also reflect the high trade barriers within Africa erected by post-independence governments, and the slow rate of growth. Ultimately, landlocked economies were faced with neighboring markets that were both inaccessible and unattractive, which did not make it desirable to reorient the economy to trade with them. Finally, Africa's continued export concentration in a narrow range of primary commodities, which we discussed earlier as reflecting the destiny of resource endowments, probably also reflects a number of public policy decisions. Other export activities have been handicapped either directly through overvalued exchange rates, or indirectly, through high transactions costs. Poor policy has given Africa a comparative disadvantage in "transaction-intensive" activities such as manufacturing.

Now consider the reverse situation; that is, how some of the dysfunctional policies that we have discussed can also be considered the outcome of exogenous forces. The anti-export policies which we argue hindered growth can be viewed as a consequence of the fact that most of the population lives far from the coast (Gallup and Sachs, 1999). In such societies, it might be argued that the elasticity of growth with respect to openness is lower and so the incentive for openness is reduced. However, at present Africa offers little evidence for this hypothesis. According to the World Bank's standardized ratings of policy (currently confidential), all five of the worst-rated countries on the continent are coastal whereas many of the best-rated countries are landlocked. As another example, it is possible that restrictive import policies are adopted, at least initially, in response to trade shocks like those created by an external dependence on commodity exports (Collier and Gunning, 1999b). The prevalence of natural resources may bring forth a variety of other policy errors, as well. For example, it may worsen policy by turning politics into a contest for rents or, through crowding out manufactured exports, prevent the emergence of potentially the most potent lobby for openness.

Along with being endogenous to fixed effects like geography, policies are also affected by experience. Societies which have experienced high levels of economic risk may place a higher priority on income-sharing arrangements such as expanded opportunities of public employment, rather than focusing on income generation. Societies also learn from past failure. The African nations which have recently implemented the strongest economic reforms, such as Ghana and Uganda, tended to be those which had earlier experienced the worst economic crises. However, African countries facing the challenge of reversing economic failure have lacked significant role models within the continent. In east Asia, Hong Kong, Singapore, Taiwan and Korea provided

early role models, as did Chile since the late 1970s in Latin America. Within-continent models may be important because the information is both closer to hand and more evidently pertinent. Once Africa develops examples of success, the scope for societal learning across the continent will make it unlikely that Africa is "destined" to poor policies by its geography: although its geographic characteristics may have given it some weak tendencies towards poor policies in the initial post-independence period.

Sorting out the policy effects from the destiny effects is a difficult econometric problem. In the ordinary least squares regressions common in the analysis of African growth, the dependent variable is typically the average growth rate over a long period, and a variety of policy and destiny variables enter as the explanatory variables. Depending upon the specification, either policy or destiny can appear important.

An alternative approach is to consider the extent to which African slow growth has been persistent, to take advantage of the insight that policies have varied, whereas destiny-like geographic disadvantages remain constant over time. Along these lines, Diamond (1998) provides a convincing explanation from a historical perspective of why geographic reasons, such as the north-south axis of the continent, caused African agriculture to develop only slowly prior to European colonization, due to a combination of technological isolation and small scale. However, since colonization gradually relaxed some of these constraints (while introducing others), pre-20th century experience is of limited pertinence for explaining patterns of growth in the last few decades.

More recent experience tends to argue that destiny plays less of a role than policy. After all, the economies of Africa did grow relatively quickly through the first half of the 20th century, and up until the early 1970s, which tends to argue that they were not obviously destined for lower growth. The arrival of slow economic growth in the 1970s coincides with a phase in which African economic policy became both statist and biased against exports. Moreover, the main exception to African economic collapse, Botswana, experienced the most rapid growth in the world despite the seeming exogenous disadvantages of being landlocked and having very low population density.

The most sophisticated econometric test of whether something about Africa seems intrinsically connected to slow growth is the study by Hoeffler (1999). She searches for a continental fixed effect using panel regressions of five-year periods over 1965–90. She first estimates a simple growth model in which the explanatory variables are initial income, investment, population growth, and schooling. She then uses the coefficients on these variables to compute the residuals, and regresses the residuals on regional dummies. The Africa dummy is small and insignificant, that is, there is no continental fixed effect to explain. However, she does find that both being landlocked and being tropical significantly reduce growth, and these are indeed locational characteristics of much of Africa. Between them they would reduce the African growth rate by around 0.4 percentage points relative to that of other developing regions.

Whereas in the distant past the economies of Africa may well have been intrinsically disadvantaged by factors like less easy access to water transportation or the geography of the continent, the thesis that this has persisted into recent decades is less plausible. Remember that by 1950 Africa had a higher per capita income than south Asia and its subsequent performance was indistinguishable from that region until the mid-1970s. Coastal Africa is not intrinsically markedly worse-endowed in any geographical sense than much of coastal Asia or Brazil, although its soil types pose distinct challenges for agronomic research.

By contrast, it is easy to point to policies which until very recently have been dysfunctional. Even as of 1998, Africa had the worst policy environment in the world according to the World Bank ratings. Microeconomic evidence shows how these policies damaged the growth of

firms. Poor infrastructure, poor contract enforcement and volatile policies all make the supply of inputs unreliable. Firms have responded to this risky environment partly by reducing risks: they hold large inventories, invest in electricity generators, and restrict their business relations to known enterprises. They have also responded by reducing investment. A striking implication is the conjunction of a high marginal return on capital and a very low rate of investment, even for firms that are not liquidity constrained. In Africa, the elasticity of investment with respect to profits may be as low as 0.07 (Bigsten et al., 1999). Some of the effects of poor policy are highly persistent. Most notably, the colonial governments of Africa provided little education, especially at the secondary level. Although independent governments rapidly changed these priorities, for the past 30 years Africa has had a markedly lower stock of human capital than other continents. The rapid growth in education has, however, gradually narrowed the gap with other regions.

Even if one disagrees with this view that policy is more important in explaining Africa's slow rate of growth and finds the "destiny" explanations more persuasive, this by no means condemns Africa to growing more slowly than other regions. Some of the economic disadvantages of being tropical may be overcome, for example, by the discovery of vaccines or new strains of crops. Moreover, Africa has two potential growth advantages over other regions which should offset against any locational disadvantage. It has lower per capita income and so could benefit from a convergence effect with richer countries, and it has higher aid inflows and so could benefit from aid-induced growth. If public policies were as good as in other regions, aid and convergence should enable even those countries which are land-locked and tropical to grow more rapidly than other developing regions for several decades. Although the growth regressions would imply that in the long term such countries would converge on a lower steady-state income than more favorably located countries, even this is doubtful. If the coastal African nations grew, then being landlocked would cease to be disadvantageous, since the gains from trading with close neighbors would expand.

Domestic or External?

Until recently, there was broad agreement that Africa's problems were predominantly associated with its external relations, although some analysts emphasized the policy-induced lack of openness and markets, while others attributed poor performance to over-dependence on a few commodities, the prices of which were declining and volatile. In our view, the argument that Africa's poor performance originates in its overdependence on commodities has looked weaker in recent years: Africa has lost global market share in its major exports, often spectacularly. The focus of the discussion has consequently shifted to underlying reasons for poor domestic performance, and in turn to domestic factors. The domestic factors, as we have argued, can be divided into those that smack of destiny, like the fact that much of Africa has a tropical climate, and those that are related to policy. Indeed, we believe that domestic policies largely unrelated to trade may now be the main obstacles to growth in much of Africa.

To illustrate our argument, we focus on Africa's failure to industrialize. It might appear that Africa is intrinsically uncompetitive in manufactures because of its high natural resource endowments give it a comparative advantage in that area (Wood and Mayer, 1998). But while Africa may have a comparative advantage in natural resources in the long run, at present African wages are often so low that were African manufacturing to have similar levels of productivity to other regions, it would be competitive. Hence, it is low productivity which needs to be explained.

African manufacturing has been in a low-productivity trap. Because African firms are oriented to small domestic markets, they are not able to exploit economies of scale, nor are they exposed to significant competition, and their technology gap with the rest of the world is unusually wide—yielding large opportunities for learning. This suggests that African manufacturing might have atypically large potential to raise productivity through exporting. However, most African firms fail to step onto this productivity escalator. This is because they face high costs for other reasons. As discussed already, transactions costs are unusually high. With transport unreliable, firms typically need to carry very large stocks of inputs to maintain continuity of production, despite higher interest rates than elsewhere. Telecommunications are much worse than other regions. Malfunctioning of the courts makes contract enforcement unreliable, so that firms are reluctant to enter into deals with new partners, in turn making markets less competitive.

These high transactions costs have a relatively large impact on manufacturing. Compared with natural resource extraction, manufacturing tends to have a high share of intermediate inputs and a low share of value-added to final price. Consequently, transactions costs tend to be much larger relative to value-added. Africa's intrinsic comparative advantage in natural resource exports may thus have been reinforced by public policies which have made manufacturing uncompetitive relative to resource extraction. African policies may have given the region a comparative disadvantage in transactions-intensive activities.

Conclusion: Will Africa Grow?

During the mid-1990s, average African growth accelerated and performance became more dispersed. A few countries such as Uganda, Côte d'Ivoire, Ethiopia and Mozambique started to grow very fast, whereas others such as the Democratic Republic of the Congo and Sierra Leone descended into social disorder. "Africa" became less meaningful as a category. Both the improvement in the average performance and the greater dispersion among countries were consistent with what had happened to policy. During the 1990s many of the most egregious exchange rate, fiscal and trade policies were improved. By 1998, although Africa still ranked as the region with the worst policies on the World Bank ratings, it was also the region with by far the greatest policy dispersion.

However, the faster growth coincided not only with better policies but with improvements in the terms of trade. Further, investment in Africa as a share of GDP is currently only 18 percent. This is much lower than other regions: for example, 23 percent in South Asia and 29 percent on average in lower middle-income countries. Even these figures may understate Africa's true investment shortfall. Capital goods are more expensive in Africa than the international average, so that once the investment share is recalculated at international relative prices it approximately halves. Although it is not possible to disaggregate investment into its public and private components with complete accuracy, estimates suggest that the shortfall in African investment is due to low private investment. Thus, growth may be unsustainable unless there is a substantial increase in private investment.

On an optimistic interpretation of the evidence, Africa's slow growth from the early 1970s into the 1990s has been due to policies which reduced its openness to foreign trade. Since these policies have largely been reversed during the last decade, if this is correct then Africa should be well-placed for continued growth.

The pessimistic interpretation is that Africa's problems are intrinsic, often rooted in geography. This view implies that economic progress in Africa will be dependent upon international efforts to make its environment more favorable, such as research to eradicate tropical diseases, and finance to create transport arteries from the coast to the interior. The thesis that Africa's economic problems are caused by ethnolinguistic fractionalization has similarly intractable implications.

Our own interpretation lies between these extremes. We suggest that while the binding constraint upon Africa's growth may have been externally-oriented policies in the past, those policies have now been softened. Today, the chief problem is those policies which are ostensibly domestically-oriented, notably poor delivery of public services. These problems are much more difficult to correct than exchange rate and trade policies, and so the policy reform effort needs to be intensified. However, even widespread policy reforms in this area might not be sufficient to induce a recovery in private investment, since recent economic reforms are never fully credible. Investment rating services list Africa as the riskiest region in the world. Indeed, there is some evidence that Africa suffers from being perceived by investors as a "bad neighborhood." Analysis of the global risk ratings shows that while they are largely explicable in terms of economic fundamentals, Africa as a whole is rated as significantly more risky than is warranted by these fundamentals (Haque et al., 1999). Similarly, private investment appears to be significantly lower in Africa than is explicable in terms of economic fundamentals (Jaspersen et al., 1999). "Africa" thus seems to be treated as a meaningful category by investors.

The perception of high risk for investing in Africa may partly be corrected by the passage of time, but reforming African governments can also take certain steps to commit themselves to defend economic reforms. Internationally, governments may increasingly make use of rules within the World Trade Organization, and shift their economic relations with the European Union from unreciprocated trade preferences to a wider range of reciprocated commitments. Domestically, there is a trend to freedom of the press, and the creation of independent centers of authority in central banks and revenue authorities, all of which should generally help to reinforce a climate of openness and democracy, which is likely to be supportive of economic reform.

REFERENCES

Ablo, Emanuel and Ritva Reinikka. 1998. "Do Budgets Really Matter? Evidence from Public Spending on Education and Health in Uganda." Policy Research Working Paper No. 1926, World Bank.

African Development Bank. 1998. *African Development Report*. Oxford: Oxford University Press.

Bates, Robert, H. 1983. *Essays in the Political Economy of Rural Africa*. Cambridge: Cambridge University Press.

Bauer, Peter, T. 1982. "The Effects of Aid." *Encounter*. November.

Bevan, David. L., Paul Collier and Jan Willem Gunning. 1993. *Agriculture and the policy environment: Tanzania and Kenya*. Paris: OECD.

Biggs, T., M. Raturi and P. Srivastava. 1996. "Enforcement of Contracts in an African Credit Market: Working Capital Financing in Kenyan Manufacturing." RPED Discussion Paper, Africa Region, World Bank.

Bigsten, Arne, P. Collier, S. Dercon, B. Gauthier, J.W. Gunning, A. Isaksson, A. Oduro, R. Oostendorp, C. Pattillo, M. Soderbom, M. Sylvain, F. Teal and A. Zeufack. 1999, forthcoming. "Investment by Manufacturing Firms in Africa: a Four-Country Panel Data Analysis." *Oxford Bulletin of Economics and Statistics*.

Bloom, John and Jeffrey Sachs. 1998. "Geography, Demography and Economic Growth in Africa." *Brookings Papers in Economic Activity*. 2, 207–95.

Burnside, Craig and David Dollar. 1997. "Aid, Policies and Growth." Policy Research Working Paper No. 1777, World Bank.

Collier, Paul. 1999. "The Political Economy of Ethnicity," in *Proceedings of the Annual Bank Conference on Development Economics*. Pleskovic, Boris and Joseph E. Stiglitz, eds. World Bank, Washington, D.C.

Collier, Paul and David Dollar. 1999. "Aid Allocation and Poverty Reduction." Policy Research Working Paper 2041, World Bank, Washington, DC.

Collier, Paul and David Dollar. 1999a. "Aid, Risk and the Special Concerns of Small States." Mimeo, Policy Research Department, World Bank, Washington, DC.

Collier, Paul and Ashish Garg. 1999, forthcoming. "On Kin Groups and Wages in the Ghanaian Labour Market." *Oxford Bulletin of Economics and Statistics*, 61:2, pp. 131–51.

Collier, P. and J.W. Gunning. 1999. "Explaining African Economic Performance." *Journal of Economic Literature*. March, 37:1, 64–111.

Collier, P. and J.W. Gunning. 1999a, forthcoming. "The IMF's Role in Structural Adjustment." *Economic Journal*. World Bank, Washington, DC.

Collier, P. and J.W. Gunning with associates. 1999b. *Trade Shocks in Developing Countries: Theory and Evidence*. Oxford: Oxford University Press (Clarendon).

Collier, Paul and Anke Hoeffler. 1998. "On the Economic Causes of Civil War." *Oxford Economic Papers*. 50, pp. 563–73.

Collier, Paul and Anke Hoeffler. 1999. "Loot-Seeking and Justice-Seeking in Civil War." Mimeo, Development Research Department, World Bank, Washington DC.

Collier, Paul and Catherine Pattillo, eds. 1999. *Investment and Risk in Africa*. Macmillan: London.

Collins, S. and B.P. Bosworth. 1996. "Economic Growth in East Asia: Accumulation versus Assimilation." *Brookings Papers in Economic Activity*, 2, pp. 135–203.

Deaton, A. and R. Miller. 1996. "International Commodity Prices, Macroeconomic Performance and Politics in Sub-Saharan Africa." *Journal of African Economies*. 5 (Supp.), pp. 99–191.

Dercon, Stefan. 1997. "Wealth, Risk and Activity Choice: Cattle in Western Tanzania." *Journal of Development Economics*. 55:1, pp. 1–42.

Dercon, Stefan. 1993. "Peasant supply response and macroeconomic policies: cotton in Tanzania." *Journal of African Economies*. 2, pp. 157–94.

Diamond, Jared. 1998. *Guns, Germs, and Steel: The Fates of Human Societies*. New York: W.W. Norton & Co.

Dollar, David. 1992. "Outward-Oriented Developing Economies Really do Grow More Rapidly: Evidence from 95 LDCs 1976–85." *Economic Development and Cultural Change*. 40, pp. 523–44.

Easterly, William and Ross Levine. 1997. "Africa's Growth Tragedy: Policies and Ethnic Divisions." *Quarterly Journal of Economics*. CXII, pp. 1203–1250.

Elbadawi, Ibrahim A., Benno J. Ndulu, and Njuguna Ndung'u. 1997. "Debt Overhang and Economic Growth in Sub-Saharan Africa," in *External Finance for Low-Income Countries*. Iqbal, Zubair and Ravi Kanbur, eds. IMF Institute, Washington, DC.

Fafchamps, Marcel, Jan Willem Gunning and Remco Oostendorp. 1998. "Inventories, Liquidity and Contractual Risk in African Manufacturing." Department of Economics, Stanford University, mimeo.

Gallup, John L. and Jeffrey D. Sachs. 1999. "Geography and Economic Growth," in *Proceedings of the Annual World Bank Conference on Development Economics*. Pleskovic, Boris and Joseph E. Stiglitz, eds. World Bank, Washington, DC.

Ghana Central Bureau of Statistics. 1988. *Quarterly Digest of Statistics*. Accra.

Grove, A.T. 1991. "The African Environment," in *Africa 30 Years On*. Rimmer, Douglas, ed. London: James Currey.

Gwin, Catherine and Joan Nelson. 1997. *Perspectives on Aid and Development*. Johns Hopkins for Overseas Development Council, Washington DC.

Haque, Nadeem U., Nelson Mark and Donald J. Mathieson. 1999. "Risk in Africa: its Causes and its Effects on Investment," in *Investment and Risk in Africa*. Collier, Paul and Catherine Pattillo, eds. London: Macmillan.

Hoeffler, Anke A. 1999. "Econometric Studies of Growth, Convergence and Conflicts." D. Phil. Thesis, Oxford University.

Jaspersen, Frederick, Anthony H. Aylward and A. David Cox. 1999. "Risk and Private Investment: Africa Compared with Other Developing Areas," in *Investment and Risk in Africa*. Collier, Paul and Catherine Pattillo, eds. London: Macmillan.

Stephen Knack and Phillip Keefer. 1995. Institutions and Economic Performance: Cross-Country Tests Using Alternative Institutional Measures." *Economics and Politics*. 7:3, pp. 207–28.

Kenya Central Bureau of Statistics. 1996. *Statistical Abstract*. Nairobi.

Kremer, Michael. 1993. "Population Growth and Technological Change: One Million B.C. to 1990." *Quarterly Journal of Economics*. 108:3, pp. 681–716.

Lee, K.S. and A. Anas. 1991. "Manufacturers' Responses to Infrastructure Deficiencies in Nigeria: Private Alternatives and Policy Options," in *Economic Reform in Africa*. Chibber, A. and S. Fischer, eds. World Bank, Washington DC.

Maddison, Angus. 1995. *Monitoring the World Economy*. Paris: OECD.

Mauro, P. 1995. "Corruption and Growth." *Quarterly Journal of Economics*. 110, pp. 681–712.

McCallum, J. 1995. "National Borders Matter: Canada-U.S. Regional Trade Patterns." *American Economic Review*. 85, pp. 615–23.

Mengistae, Taye. 1998. "Ethiopia's Urban Economy: Empirical Essays on Enterprise Development and the Labour Market." D.Phil. Thesis, University of Oxford.

Pradhan, Sanjay. 1996. "Evaluating Public Spending." World Bank Discussion Paper 323, Washington DC.

Reinikka, Ritva and Jakob Svensson. 1998. "Investment Response to Structural Reforms and Remaining Constraints: Firm Survey Evidence from Uganda." Mimeo, Africa Region, World Bank.

Rodrik, Dani. 1999. *Making Openness Work: The New Global Economy and the Developing Countries*. Overseas Development Council, Washington DC.

Sachs, J.D. and Mark Warner. 1997. "Sources of Slow Growth in African Economies." *Journal of African Economies*. 6, pp. 335–76.

Schuknecht, Ludger. 1999. "Tying Governments' Hands in Commodity Taxation." *Journal of African Economies*. 8:2, 152–81.

Voortman, R.L., B.G.J.S. Sonneveld and M.A. Keyzer. 1999. "African Land Ecology: Opportunities and Constraints for Agricultural Development." Mimeo, Centre for World Food Studies, Free University, Amsterdam.

Widner, Jennifer, A. 1999. "The Courts as Restraints," in *Investment and Risk in Africa.* Collier, Paul and Catherine Pattillo, eds. London: Macmillan.

Wood, Adrian and J. Mayer. 1998. "Africa's Export Structure in Comparative Perspective," Study No. 4 of the UNCTAD series *Economic Development and Regional Dynamics in Africa: Lessons from the East Asian Experience.*

World Bank. 1997. *Confronting Aids*, Policy Research Report. Oxford University Press.

World Bank. 1998. *Assessing Aid: What Works, What Doesn't, and Why*, Policy Research Report. Oxford University Press.

World Bank. 1999. *World Development Indicators*. Development Data Center, Washington, D.C.

ROBERT J. BARRO

DEMOCRACY: A RECIPE FOR GROWTH?

It sounds nice to try to install democracy in places like Haiti and Somalia, but does it make any sense? Would an increase in political freedom tend to spur economic growth, the key problem in these poor countries? Is there a reasonable prospect that democratic institutions can be maintained in places with such low standards of living? History provides reasonably clear answers to these questions.

More political freedom does not have an important impact on growth, but improvements in the standard of living tend strongly to precede expansions of political freedoms. In particular,

From *The Wall Street Journal* (December 1, 1994) p. A18.

democracies that arise in poor countries (sometimes because they are imposed from outside) usually do not last.

Theoretically, the effect of more democracy on growth is ambiguous. The negative effects involve the tendency to enact rich-to-poor redistributions of income (including land reforms) under majority voting and the enhanced role of interest groups in systems with representative legislatures. On the other side, democratic institutions provide a check on governmental power and thereby limit the potential of public officials to amass personal wealth and to carry out unpopular (and perhaps unproductive) projects.

Autocracies avoid some of the problems of democracy, but are adverse to growth if the leaders use their power to steal the nation's wealth and to carry out useless investments. In practice, some dictators have favored economic freedom and growth—including the Pinochet government in Chile, the Fujimori administration in Peru and several previous and current regimes in East Asia. Others have restricted economic freedom and deterred development—including many governments in Africa, some in Latin America, the formerly planned economies of Eastern Europe and the Marcos administration in the Philippines.

From an empirical standpoint, the typical effect of democracy on growth can be ascertained from a statistical analysis of data for about 100 countries at various stages of economic development from 1960 to 1990. My study reveals a number of factors that influence the growth rate of real per-capita gross domestic product. The favorable elements include small distortions of market prices, an inclination and ability of the government to maintain the rule of law, high levels of health and education, low government spending on consumption and a low fertility rate.

If these kinds of variables and the current level of per-capita income are held constant, then the overall effect of more democracy on the growth rate is moderately negative. (Democracy is measured by the index of political rights compiled in the serial publication "Freedom in the World.") There is some indication that more democracy raises growth when political freedoms are low but depresses growth once a moderate amount of freedom has been attained.

The data reveal a stronger linkage between economic development and the propensity to experience democracy. Nondemocratic countries that have achieved high standards of living—measured by real per-capita GDP, life expectancy and schooling—tend to become more democratic over time. Examples include Chile, South Korea, Taiwan, Spain and Portugal. Conversely, democratic countries with low standards of living tend to lose political rights over time.

If Prosperity Brings Democracy . . .

These countries will be more democratic . . .	1993	2000	These countries will be less democratic . . .	1993	2000
Iraq	.00	.21	Hungary	1.00	.81
Haiti	.00	.24	Mauritius	1.00	.81
Sudan	.00	.24	Botswana	.83	.66
Syria	.00	.32	Papua New Guinea	.83	.65
Algeria	.00	.33	Nepal	.83	.60
Swaziland	.17	.35	Bolivia	.83	.58
Iran	.17	.41	Bangladesh	.83	.56
Yugoslavia	.17	.41	Gambia	.83	.54
Indonesia	.00	.43	Benin	.83	.50
South Africa	.33	.47	Pakistan	.67	.48
Peru	.33	.51	Mali	.83	.44
Singapore	.33	.61	Congo	.67	.42
Taiwan	.50	.64	Niger	.67	.37
Hong Kong	.33	.67	Central African Republic	.67	.36
Mexico	.50	.72	Zambia	.67	.35

Note: The democracy index uses a scale from 0 to 1, where 0 means no political rights and 1 means virtually full rights. The figures for 1993 and other years are derived from information presented in Raymond Gastil and followers, *Freedom in the World*, various issues. Their subjective classifications follow the basic definition: "Political rights are rights to participate meaningfully in the political process. In a democracy this means the right of all adults to vote and compete for public office, and for elected representatives to have a decisive vote on public policies." The values shown for 2000 are projections based on the author's statistical analysis.

Examples include most of the newly independent African states in the 1970s.

The empirical results can be used to forecast changes in the level of democracy from the last value observed, 1993, into the future. The nearby table displays the cases of especially large projected changes in democracy from 1993 to 2000 (among the 101 countries with the necessary data).

The group with large anticipated increases, on the left side of the table, includes some countries that have virtually no political freedom in 1993. Some of these are among the world's poorest countries, such as Haiti, for which the projected level of democracy in 2000 is also not high. Haiti is expected to raise its democracy (perhaps with the assistance of the U.S.) from zero in 1993 to 0.24 (roughly one-quarter of the way toward a "full representative democracy") in 2000. Some other countries that have essentially no political freedom in 1993 are more well off economically and are therefore forecasted to have greater increases in democracy; for example, the projected value in 2000 is 0.43 for Indonesia, 0.33 for Algeria, and 0.32 for Syria.

Expectations for large increases in democracy also apply to some reasonably prosperous places in which the extent of political freedom lags behind the standard of living. As examples, Singapore is projected to increase its democracy index from 0.33 in 1993 to 0.61 in 2000, Mexico is expected to go from 0.50 to 0.72 (a change that has probably already occurred with the 1994 elections) and Taiwan is forecasted to rise from 0.50 to 0.64.

South Africa is also included on the left side of the table, with a projected increase in the democracy index from 0.33 in 1993 to 0.47 in 2000. However, the political changes in South Africa in 1994 have probably already overshot the mark, and a substantial decline of political freedom is likely after this year.

The examples of large expected decreases in democracy, shown on the right side of the table, consist mainly of relatively poor countries with surprisingly high levels of political freedom in 1993. Many of these are African countries in which the political institutions recently became more democratic: Mali, Benin, Zambia, Central African Republic, Niger and Congo. The model predicts that democracy that gets well ahead of economic development will not last. Three other African countries, The Gambia, Mauritius and Botswana, have maintained democratic institutions for some time, but the analysis still predicts that political freedoms will diminish in these places. (A military coup in July 1994 has already reduced the Gambia's level of political freedom.)

One way to view the findings is that political freedom emerges as a sort of luxury good. Rich places consume more democracy because this good is desirable for its own sake and even though the increased political freedom may have an adverse effect on growth. Basically, rich countries can afford the reduced rate of economic progress.

The analysis has implications for the desirability of exporting democratic institutions from the advanced Western countries to developing nations. Democracy is not the key to economic growth, and political freedoms tend to erode over time if they are out of line with a country's standard of living. Specifically, the U.S. plan to establish democracy in Haiti is a counterproductive policy. It will not improve the standard of living—the main problem in a poor country—and the democracy will almost surely be temporary.

More generally, the advanced Western countries would contribute more to the welfare of poor nations by exporting their economic systems, notably property rights and free markets, rather than their political systems, which typically developed after reasonable standards of living had been attained. If economic freedom were to be established in a poor country, then growth would be encouraged, and the country would tend eventually to become more democratic on its own. Thus, in the long run, the propagation of Western-style economic systems would also be the effective way to expand democracy in the world.

ADAM PRZEWORSKI ET AL.

POLITICAL REGIMES AND ECONOMIC GROWTH

Introduction

With the birth of new nations in Asia and Africa, the fear that democracy would undermine economic growth began to be voiced in the United States. The first statements to that effect were perhaps those by Walter Galenson and by Karl de Schweinitz, who argued, both in 1959, that in poor countries democracy unleashes pressures for immediate consumption, which occurs at the cost of investment, hence of growth. Galenson mentioned both the role of unions and that of governments. He thought that unions "must ordinarily appeal to the worker on an all-out consumptionist platform. No matter how much 'responsibility' the union leader exhibits in his understanding of the limited consumption possibilities existing at the outset of industrialization, he cannot afford to moderate his demands." As for governments, he observed that "the more democratic a government is, . . . the greater the diversion of resources from investment to consumption." According to de Schweinitz (1959: 388), if trade unions and labor parties "are successful in securing a larger share of the national income and limiting the freedom for action of entrepreneurs, they may have the effect of restricting investment surplus so much that the rate of economic growth is inhibited." That argument enjoyed widespread acceptance under the influence of Huntington, who claimed that "the interest of the voters generally leads parties to give the expansion of personal consumption a

From Adam Przeworski, et al. *Democracy and Development: Political Institutions and Well-Being in the World, 1950–1990.* (New York: Cambridge University Press, 2000), pp. 142–74. Some of the authors' notes have been omitted.

higher priority vis-à-vis investment than it would receive in a non-democratic system" (Huntington and Domiguez 1975: 60; Huntington 1968).

Democracy was thus seen as inimical to economic development. Moreover, via a rather dubious inference, proponents of that view concluded that dictatorships were therefore better able to force savings and launch economic growth. To cite a more recent statement: "Economic development is a process for which huge investments in personnel and material are required. Such investment programs imply cuts in current consumption that would be painful at the low levels of living that exist in almost all developing societies. Governments must resort to strong measures and they enforce them with an iron hand in order to marshal the surpluses needed for investment. If such measures were put to a popular vote, they would surely be defeated. No political party can hope to win a democratic election on a platform of current sacrifices for a *bright future*" (Rao 1984: 75).[1]

The reasoning bears reconstruction. First, that argument assumes that poor people have a higher propensity to consume.[2] This is why democracy may be compatible with growth at high but not at low levels of income. Second, the underlying model of growth attributes it to the increase in the stock of physical capital. Finally, democracy is always responsive to pressures for immediate consumption. The chain of reasoning is thus the following: (1) Poor people want to consume immediately. (2) When workers are able to organize, they drive wages up, reduce profits, and reduce investment (by lowering either the rate of return or the volume of profit or both). (3) When people are allowed to vote, governments tend to distribute income away from investment (either they tax and transfer or they undertake less public investment). (4) Lowering investment slows down growth. Note, as well, that this reasoning implies that the impact of mean-preserving inequality on growth is ambivalent: In the Kaldor-Pasinetti models, inequality promotes growth, as it increases the incomes of those who save more, but in the median-voter models it slows down growth to the extent to which the political system responds to demands for redistribution.

Arguments in favor of democracy are not equally sharp, but they all focus in one form or another on allocative efficiency: Democracies can better allocate the available resources to productive uses. One view is that because authoritarian rulers are not accountable to electorates, they have no incentive to maximize total output, but only their own rents. As a result, democracies better protect property rights, thus allowing a longer-term perspective to investors. There is also a vague sense that by permitting a free flow of information, democracies somehow improve the quality of economic decisions.

According to the first view, the state is always ready to prey on the society (North 1990), and only democratic institutions can constrain it to act in a more general interest. Hence, dictatorships, of any stripe, are sources of inefficiency. Barro (1990), Findlay (1990), Olson (1991), and Przeworski (1990) have constructed models that differ in detail but generate the same conclusion. These models assume that some level of government intervention in the economy is optimal for growth. Then they all show that, depending on the details of each model, dictatorships of various stripes can be expected to undersupply or oversupply government activities. One interesting variant of this approach is by Robinson (1995), who thinks that dictators are afraid, at least under some conditions, that development would give rise to political forces that would overturn them, and thus they deliberately abstain from developmentalist policies.

Perhaps the best-known informational argument is based on the Drèze and Sen (1989) observation that no democracy ever experienced a famine, which they attribute to the alarm role of the press and the opposition. Thus, Sen (1994a: 34) observes that "a free press and an active political opposition constitute the best 'early warning system' that a country threatened by famine can possess." He also cites an unlikely source, Mao, reflecting on the great Chinese famine of 1962, to the effect that "without democracy, you have no understanding of what is happening down below." Yet it is not apparent whether this is an argument strictly about avoiding disasters or about average performance.[3]

This summary makes no pretense to being exhaustive. All we want to highlight is that the arguments in favor of dictatorship and those in favor of democracy are not necessarily incompatible. The arguments against democracy claim that it hinders growth by reducing investment; the arguments in its favor maintain that it fosters growth by promoting allocative efficiency. Both may be true: The rate at which productive factors grow may be higher under dictatorship, but the use of resources may be more efficient under democracy. And because these mechanisms work in opposite directions, the net effect may be that there is no difference between the two regimes in the average rates of growth they generate. The patterns of growth may differ, but the average rates of growth may still be the same.

*   *   *

Dictatorships existed predominantly in poor countries: 38.5 percent of annual observations (946 out of 2,481) of dictatorships were in countries with incomes under $1,000, but only 4.5 percent of democracies (75 out of 1,645) were that poor. Democracies flourished in wealthy countries: 46.8 percent of them (769) were observed in countries with incomes above $6,000, whereas only 2.8 percent (68) of dictatorships existed at such income levels. Hence, nearly all our observations of countries with incomes below $1,000, 92.6 percent (946 out of 1,021), are of dictatorships, and nearly all our observations of countries with incomes above

Table 1. Rate of growth of GDP (YG), by per capita income (LEVEL)

LEVEL	Proportion dictatorships	Rate of growth of GDP[a]		
		All	Dictatorships	Democracies
0–1,000	0.9273	3.519	3.464	4.220
1,001–2,000	0.7472	4.636	4.809	4.123
2,001–3,000	0.6207	5.142	5.633	4.335
3,001–4,000	0.5874	4.740	4.915	4.492
4,001–5,000	0.5424	4.552	4.507	4.606
5,001–6,000	0.4308	4.312	4.772	3.963
6,001–	0.0812	3.770	6.054	3.568
Total (N = 4,128)		4.233	4.424	3.945

[a]All cell entries are based on at least 68 observations.

Moving averages of rates of growth by bands of $500

LEVEL	All	Dictatorships	Democracies
250–750	3.071	3.107	2.380
500–1,000	3.689	3.647	4.164
750–1,250	4.140	4.050	4.724
1,000–1,500	4.505	4.682	3.848
1,250–1,750	4.969	5.381	3.932
1,500–2,000	4.827	5.021	4.396
1,750–2,250	4.972	5.092	4.744
2,000–2,500	5.444	5.664	5.055
2,250–2,750	5.793	6.989	3.993
2,500–3,000	4.827	5.599	3.653
2,750–3,250	4.808	4.955	4.613
3,000–3,500	5.130	5.238	4.977
3,250–3,750	4.594	4.183	5.445
3,500–4,000	4.317	4.565	3.965
3,750–4,250	4.382	5.065	3.491
4,000–4,500	4.984	4.908	5.086
4,250–4,750	4.742	4.771	4.714
4,500–5,000	3.965	3.881	4.050
4,750–5,250	4.558	4.580	4.535
5,000–5,500	4.217	4.360	4.088
5,250–5,750	4.116	4.003	4.194
5,500–6,000	4.418	5.350	3.845
5,750–6,250	3.363	4.479	2.878
6,000–	3.770	6.054	3.568

$6,000, 91.9 percent (769 out of 837), are of democracies.

Now, examining the rates of growth in countries classified by intervals of $500 of per capita income (Table 1) shows that very poor countries (under $1,000) grow slowly, at about 3.5 percent. Growth accelerates in wealthier economies, reaching a peak of 5.1 percent between $2,000 and $3,000. Then it slows down again to about 3.8 percent when countries reach incomes above $6,000. Hence, in accordance with Quah (1996), incomes diverge among poor countries, until about $2,500, and they converge among wealthy countries.

If very poor and very rich economies both grow slowly regardless of the regime they have, then this pattern does not present a problem. But if poor countries grow slowly because they are ruled by dictatorships, or rich ones because they are democratic, then we cannot make such an inference, for perhaps if the poor countries had been democratic they would have grown faster. In fact, the 75 democratic years at incomes under $1,000 witnessed growth at the rate of 4.22 percent, but dictatorships grew at the rate of 3.46 percent in equally poor countries. Conversely, if the rich countries had been authoritarian, perhaps they would have grown faster. Again, the 68 authoritarian years at incomes above $6,000 enjoyed growth at the rate of 6.05 percent, whereas democracies had a rate of growth of 3.57 percent at those incomes. Our counterfactual procedure matches the regimes for the conditions under which they existed, specifically for their productive inputs and a variety of other conditions. But to find out how a country observed, say, as a dictatorship would have grown had it been a democracy under the same conditions, we use the information about the way these productive inputs are transformed into outputs under each regime. And this information, about production functions, is derived from the actual observations, which means disproportionately from poor dictatorships and rich democracies. Hence these production functions may be different not because of the impact of regimes but because of the effect of wealth.

Thus, to test whether or not the results depend on the samples, we need to estimate production functions separately for different levels of development, as always measured by per capita income. First we consider only countries with incomes under $3,000, which we shall call "poor." Their production functions are almost identical, and regimes make no difference for the average growth rates. Then we take countries with incomes above $3,000, "wealthy," where the difference between the observed growth rates is particularly high, 4.91 percent for dictatorships, and 3.83 for democracies. The difference between the average values almost vanishes when corrected for selection, but the production functions are quite different. Finally, given that there are very few dictatorships with incomes above $8,000,[4] we need to know if the difference between wealthy dictatorships and wealthy democracies is still due to the composition of the respective samples, so we analyze separately countries within the $3,000–$8,000 income band.

These tests suggest that per capita income of $3,000 is the natural breaking point.[5] The production functions are almost identical in countries with incomes below $3,000, but they differ between regimes in wealthier countries. In particular, the difference between the two regimes becomes visible if we consider only countries within the $3,000–$8,000 income band. Hence, this difference is not due to diminishing returns in wealthy democracies.

Poor Countries

In poor countries, the two regimes are almost identical, with observed rates of growth of 4.34 percent under dictatorship and 4.28 under democracy. The two regimes generate productive inputs at the same rate and use them in identical ways. They invest about 12.5 percent of GDP and increase capital stock at the rate of about 6 percent, and labor force at the rate of about 2.2 percent. An increase of 1 percent in the

Table 2. Per capita income at the beginning and end of the period, by bands of $1,000

Entered	Exited											Total
	0–1	1–2	2–3	3–4	4–5	5–6	6–7	7–8	8–9	9–10	10–	
0–1	30	11	4	1	0	0	1	0	1	0	0	48
1–2	4	12	15	6	2	1	2	1	0	0	2	45
2–3	0	0	1	3	3	1	0	1	0	3	1	13
3–4	0	0	0	2	0	2	0	1	0	0	4	9
4–5	0	0	0	0	2	0	1	0	0	0	5	8
5–	0	0	0	0	0	0	1	1	0	0	10	12
Total	34	23	20	12	7	4	5	4	1	3	22	135

Notes: "Entered" stands for 1950 or the year of independence or the first year data were available, and "Exited" for 1990 or in some cases the last year data were available. Per capita incomes are given in thousands (1985 PPP USD). Cell entries are numbers of countries.

capital stock raises output by about 0.40 percent under both regimes, and an increase in the labor force by 1 percent augments output by about 0.60 percent.[6] Neither regime benefits much from technical progress, about 0.1 percent per annum; both get 2.8 percent in growth from an increase in capital stock, and 1.4 percent from an increase in labor force. With identical supplies of factors and their identical utilization, they grow at the same rate under the two regimes: The selection-corrected average growth rates are the same.

The idea that democracies in poor countries process pressures for immediate consumption, resulting in lower investment and slower growth, seemed persuasive at the time it was advanced, and it was not implausible. There appear to be good reasons to think that people in poor countries want to consume more immediately: They cannot afford to make intertemporal trade-offs if they cannot expect to live to benefit from their short-term sacrifices. It is also plausible that unions, particularly if they are decentralized, and political parties, competing for votes, would push forward demands for immediate consumption. Yet, as likely as that view may seem, it simply is not true. Perhaps this only means that democracy is not very effective at processing what people want; perhaps developmental goals

are not any more attractive to people under dictatorship than under democracy; perhaps poverty is so constraining that even dictators cannot squeeze savings out of indigent people.

The last explanation is most plausible. One piece of evidence is that very few countries that were very poor when we first observed them ever developed. Of the forty-eight countries that entered our purview with incomes below $1,000, only three made it to above $3,000 by 1990. The two miracles were Taiwan, which had an income of $968 in 1950 and $8,067 in 1990, and South Korea, which went from $814 in 1950 to $6,665 in 1990. Thailand had an income of $815 in 1950 and $3,570 in 1990. Four more countries that began under $1,000 made it to more than $2,000, and eleven more to at least $1,000. But at the end of the period, thirty—out of forty-eight—very poor countries remained within the income band in which they had begun. The experiences of countries that were first observed with incomes between $1,000 and $2,000 were more heterogeneous, but, again, of the forty-five first observed at that level, only five experienced sustained growth: Japan, which went from $1,768 in 1950 to $14,317 in 1990, Singapore from $1,845 in 1965 to 11,698 in 1990, Portugal from $1,314 in 1950 to 7,487 in 1990, Greece from $1,480 in 1950 to $6,768 in 1990, and

Malta from $1,377 in 1964 to $6,627 in 1990. Four countries descended to below $1,000, and twelve still had incomes between $1,000 and $2,000 in 1990. In turn, none of the forty-two countries that were first observed with per capita incomes above $2,000 fell below their starting range, and all but seven of them at least doubled their incomes by the end of the period. Because the observation periods were not the same for all countries and typically were shorter for the poorer ones, many of which became independent around 1960, these data are somewhat biased against poor countries. Nevertheless, most countries that we first observed below $2,000 had about thirty years to grow, and yet most remained poor: evidence of a "low-level trap" (Table 2).

Thus, poverty constrains. Whatever the regime, the society is too poor to finance an effective state. Collecting total revenues of $127 per capita, as governments do on the average in countries with incomes under $1,000, can pay for little else than collecting these revenues. Government expenditures add up to $167 per person in these countries, so they run deficits higher than 7 percent of GDP. In countries with incomes between $1,000 and $2,000, governments collect $372 per capita and spend $450, still running deficits over 7 percent. And, like the investment share, government revenue (particularly tax revenue) as a share of GDP increases monotonically in per capita income.[7] Thus already in countries with incomes between $2,000 and $3,000, revenues of the central government add to $668 per capita. Between $3,000 and $4,000 they are $904, and above $6,000 they are $2,608. To put it differently, per capita public expenditures in countries with incomes between $3,000 and $4,000 are larger than total per capita incomes in countries with incomes under $1,000; per capita public expenditures in countries with incomes above $6,000 are about the same as total per capita incomes in countries between $3,000 and $4,000.

Poor countries cannot afford a strong state, and when the state is weak, the kind of regime

matters little for everyday life. In a village located three days' travel away from the capital, often the only presence of the state is a teacher and occasionally roving uniformed bandits.[8] Just calculate: If a mile of road costs about a million dollars, in a country with per capita income under $1,000 it would take the total government expenditures per 600,000 persons to build 100 miles of road. There is little room for regimes to make a difference when the state is that poor.

Note that we are not arguing that a fiscally large or otherwise large state is necessarily good for development, but only that if the state is to be able to make a difference for better conditions, it must have resources. The role of the state in economic development is a notoriously controversial issue. Most of the statistical research on this topic has been mindless: Studies that discover that the state is bad for growth simply stick government-consumption expenditures into the equation for growth and discover that its sign is negative. Needless to say, the same would happen if one did that with private-consumption expenditures: We did it and know it to be so. If one thinks that government-consumption expenditures affect growth, the term introduced into the production-function equation should be the change in government consumption, not the share of government consumption in GDP.[9] But the real test of the impact of government is to consider separately the effects of private and public capital stocks. The idea, due to Barro (1990), is that private capital and public capital play different roles in development and that they are complementary, so that even if the production function exhibits diminishing returns in each stock, the joint returns will be constant or even increasing. Moreover, because the ideal combination of private and public capital stocks is one in which their marginal products are equal (with an appropriate correction if public investment is financed by distortionary taxes), for each level of private capital stock (and investment) there is an optimal level of government capital stock (and investment).[10] The state, as measured by the size of the government capital stock, can thus be too small, just right, or too big.

*   *   *

In sum, poor countries are too poor to afford a strong state, and without an effective state there is little difference any regime can make for economic development. Investment is low in poor democracies, but it is not any higher in poor dictatorships. The labor force grows rapidly in both. Development is factor-extensive: Poor countries benefit almost nothing from technical change. Clearly, this does not imply that all poor countries are the same or even that regimes may not make a difference for other aspects of people's lives; indeed, we show later that they do. But not for economic development in poor countries.

Wealthy Countries

Once countries reach some level of development—somewhere between $2,500 and $3,000, that of Algeria in 1977, Mauritius in 1969, Costa Rica in 1966, South Korea in 1976, Czechoslovakia in 1970, or Portugal in 1966—patterns of economic development under democracy and dictatorship diverge. In countries with incomes above that threshold, regimes do make a difference for how resources are used, for how much people produce and how much they earn.

*   *   *

Conclusion

The main conclusion of this analysis is that there is no trade-off between democracy and development, not even in poor countries. Although not a single study published before 1988 found that democracy promoted growth, and not one published after 1987 concluded in favor of dictatorships (Przeworski and Limongi 1993), there was never solid evidence that democracies were somehow inferior in generating growth—cer-

tainly not enough to justify supporting or even condoning dictatorships. We hope to have put the issue to rest. There is little difference in favor of dictatorships in the observed rates of growth. And even that difference vanishes once the conditions under which dictatorships and democracies existed are taken into account. Albeit in omniscient retrospect, the entire controversy seems to have been much ado about nothing.

Poverty appears to leave no room for politics. In countries with incomes below $3,000, the two regimes have almost identical investment shares, almost identical rates of growth of capital stock and of labor force, the same production function, the same contributions of capital, labor, and factor productivity to growth, the same output per worker, the same labor shares, and the same product wages. Poor countries invest little, get little benefit from total factor productivity, and pay low wages. And though a few countries have escaped this bond of poverty, most poor countries, have remained poor. Democracy is highly fragile in such countries, and thus most of them have dictatorial regimes. But regimes make no difference for growth, quantitatively or qualitatively.

Perhaps surprisingly, affluence differentiates regimes. Wealthier dictatorships invest a somewhat larger share of income, experience higher growth of the labor force, have higher capital and lower labor elasticities, derive more growth from capital input and less from labor input and from total factor productivity, have lower output per worker, have a lower labor share, and pay lower wages. Wealthier dictatorships grow by using a lot of labor and paying it little. Because they repress labor, they can pay it little; perhaps because they can pay it little, they care less how it is used. They pay more for capital—the average relative price of investment goods is higher under dictatorships—and they use it well. But because they rely on force to repress workers, they can pay lower wages and use labor inefficiently.

In the end, total output grows at the same rate under the two regimes, both in poor countries and in wealthier countries. But the reasons are different: In poor countries, regimes simply do not matter. In wealthier countries, their average growth rates are the same, but the patterns of growth are different.

*   *   *

NOTES

1. At least Huntington and his collaborators wrote during a period when many dictatorships, "authoritarian" and "totalitarian," did grow rapidly. But Rao's assertion was made in 1984, after the failure of several Latin American authoritarian regimes and Eastern European communist regimes was already apparent.

2. Pasinetti (1961) claimed that the propensity to consume is higher for workers than for capitalists, and Kaldor (1956) believed that it is higher for wages than for profits, whereas the scholars discussed here seem to assume that in general the marginal propensity to consume declines with income. Barro and Sala-i-Martin (1995: 77–9) show that in the optimal growth model the savings rate decreases as a result of the substitution effect and increases in income as a consequence of the income effect, the net effect being ambivalent.

3. Sah and Stiglitz (1988) compared the quality of the decisions whether or not to undertake a series of economic projects made under different decision rules. Their conclusions are ambivalent: Although majority rule is conducive to good decisions under many conditions, decisions by smaller groups are better when the costs of information are high, whereas decisions by larger groups are superior when the chances of adopting a bad project are high.

4. The wealthiest dictatorship we observed was Singapore, with an income of $11,698, and the wealthiest democracy in our sample, the United States, had an income of $18,095. There were 200 democratic years with incomes above that of Singapore.

5. We have investigated several more income bands, beginning with $0–$3,000 and moving the lower and upper cutoffs by $1,000, until $8,000–$11,000.

6. This is a constrained estimate. Constrained estimates are cited in the rest of this paragraph.

7. Cheibub (1998) shows that selection-corrected tax revenues are the same for the two regimes.

8. The best portrayal of life under a weak state is by Alvaro Mutis (1996).

9. Ram (1986) has shown that the model that introduces the level of government-consumption expenditures into the production-function equation is misspecified. He has developed a specification that allows an assessment of the impact of government on growth without having explicit information about the public capital stock. We (Cheibub and Przeworski 1997) applied Ram's specification to our data set and discovered that the contribution of the state is positive, but for various reasons we have second thoughts about this approach.

10. It is a different matter whether or not a government, even a benevolent one, would implement it. On the time inconsistency of optimal taxation, see Benhabib and Velasco (1996).

REFERENCES

Barro, Robert J. 1990. Government Spending in a Simple Model of Economic Growth. *Journal of Political Economy* 98(5):103–25.

Barro, Robert J., and Xavier Sala-i-Martin. 1995. *Economic Growth.* New York: McGraw-Hill.

Benhabib, Jess, and Andres Velasco. 1996. On the Optimal and Best Sustainable Taxes in an Open Economy. *European Economic Review* 40(1):134–54.

Cheibub, José Antonio. 1998. Political Regimes

and the Extractive Capacity of Governments: Taxation in Democracies and Dictatorships. *World Politics* 50(3): 349–76.

Cheibub, José Antonio, and Adam Przeworski, 1997. Government Spending and Economic Growth under Democracy and Dictatorship. In *Understanding Democracy: Economic and Political Perspectives*, edited by A. Breton, G. Galeotti, P. Salmon, and R. Wintrobe, pp. 107–24. Cambridge University Press.

de Schweinitz, Karl, Jr. 1959. Industrialization, Labor Controls, and Democracy. *Economic Development and Cultural Change* 7(4):385–404.

Drèze, Jean, and Amartya Sen. 1989. *Hunger and Public Action*. Oxford University Press.

Findlay, Ronald. 1990. The New Political Economy: Its Explanatory Power for LDCs. *Economics and Politics* 2(2):193–221.

Galenson, Walter. 1959. *Labor and Economic Development*. New York: Wiley.

Huntington, Samuel P. 1968. *Political Order in Changing Societies*. New Haven, CT: Yale University Press.

Huntington, Samuel P., and Jorge I. Dominguez. 1975. Political Development. In *Macropolitical Theory*, edited by F. I. Greenstein and N. W. Polsby, pp. 1–114. Reading, MA: Addison-Wesley.

Kaldor, Nicolas. 1956. Alternative Theories of Distribution. *Review of Economic Studies* 23:83–100.

Mutis, Alvaro. 1996. *Adventures of Maqroll: Four Novellas*. New York: Harper-Collins.

North, Douglass. 1990. *Institutions, Institutional Change, and Economic Performance*. Cambridge University Press.

Olson, Mancur. 1991. Autocracy, Democracy, and Prosperity. In *Strategy and Choice*, edited by R. J. Zeckhauser, pp. 131–57. Cambridge, MA: MIT Press.

Pasinetti, Luigi. 1961. Rate of Profit and Income Distribution in Relation to the Rate of Economic Growth. *Review of Economic Studies* 29(October):267–79.

Przeworski, Adam. 1990. *The State and the Economy under Capitalism*. Chur, Switzerland: Harwood Academic Publishers.

Quah, Danny T. 1996. Twin Peaks: Growth and Convergence in Models of Distribution Dynamics. *The Economic Journal* 106:1045–55.

Ram, Rati. 1986. Government Size and Economic Growth: A New Framework and Some Evidence from Cross-Section and Time-Series Data. *American Economic Review* 76:191–203.

Rao, Vaman. 1984. Democracy and Economic Development. *Studies in Comparative International Development* 19(4):67–81.

Robinson, James. 1995. Theories of "Bad Policy". *Policy Reform* 1:1–17.

Sah, Raaj K., and Joseph Stiglitz. 1988. Committees, Hierarchies and Polyarchies. *The Economic Journal* 98(June): 451–70.

Sen, Amartya. 1994a. Freedoms and Needs. *The New Republic*, January 10–7, 31–7.

10 GLOBALIZATION

For political scientists, globalization represents the modern intersection between comparative politics (the study of domestic politics across countries) and international relations (the study of foreign relations between countries). As a result, scholars of both international relations and comparative politics have been drawn to this contentious topic. Just as globalization is blurring the lines between the domestic and the international, it is also blurring the lines between comparative politics and international relations.

In 1989, as the Cold War began to draw to a close, Francis Fukuyama published "The End of History?" In this provocative work, Fukuyama argued that all the major challenges to liberal democracy and capitalism had now been vanquished, and that there were no new ideological rivals waiting in the wings. History was essentially coming to a close, since liberalism was the only game in town. Fukuyama's piece set off a furious debate over the future of domestic and international politics, and many have argued that the terrorist attacks of September 11, 2001, conclusively refuted Fukuyama's assertion. However, his argument is still compelling. Nearly two decades after publication of the article, we see that the debates over globalization are in part predicated on his assumption that capitalism would come to penetrate every corner of the globe. Whether this would generate prosperity and go hand in hand with more democracy, as Fukuyama asserted, is still very much contested.

Stanley Hoffman's "Clash of Globalizations" (2002) takes its name from Samuel Huntington's notion of a "Clash of Civilizations," in which he argued, contrary to Fukuyama, that cultural conflict between civilizations would re-place the traditional ideological rivalries between states that marked the twentieth century (see Chapter 3). Hoffman agrees that we are now in a new era but one driven not by cultural divisions that separate civilizations. Rather, all societies now face, in different ways, three distinct forms of globalization—economic, cultural, and political. In each there may be benefits to be gained, but Hoffman is primarily concerned that the negative effects of globalization are likely to outweigh the good, undermining state sovereignty while providing few benefits (or benefits to a few) in return.

James Galbraith's "A Perfect Crime: Inequality in the Age of Globalization" (2002) takes up some of Hoffman's concerns in more detail, focusing specifically on economic globalization and inequality. Drawing on wage data from around the world, Galbraith, a noted critic of liberal economic policies, argues that globalization, promoted by the United States and international institutions like the IMF, has been directly responsible for a dramatic growth of inequality over the past twenty years. Galbraith goes so far as to liken these to a coup d'etat, where states have been "taken over" by the pressures of globalization and the international actors who back them.

Joseph Nye's piece, "Globalization's Democratic Deficit," (2001) ties the discussion more concretely to the realm of citizen politics. His concern is that as traditional areas of domestic policy (such as trade) move into the realm of international affairs, people are finding themselves more and more distant from the policymaking process. But democratic institutions are by nature domestic—they flow from the people's relationship to the state and government. The international system, in contrast, has no state, no government, and thus no citizenry to exercise democratic control. How then, can international relations be subject to public oversight? Nye calls for more open and accountable international institutions, bringing the citizens and politics of all countries directly into the international policymaking process. Similarly, Richard Florida's "The World Is Spiky" (2005) refutes the notion that globalization binds all people equally, mapping a world of highly productive and creative cities and regions, increasingly connected to each other while the peoples around them are left out and left behind.

Finally, we give supporters of globalization a chance to respond. The Economist, a British weekly known for its liberal, pro-market views, rejects many of the critiques of globalization made above. In "Grinding the Poor" (2001), the writer notes that how one calculates inequality (the central point of Galbraith's argument) makes a huge difference in the conclusions one draws. At the core of the argument is the following question: If most societies are experiencing economic growth, albeit at different rates, is there a problem?

FRANCIS FUKUYAMA

THE END OF HISTORY?

In watching the flow of events over the past decade or so, it is hard to avoid the feeling that something very fundamental has happened in world history. The past year has seen a flood of articles commemorating the end of the Cold War, and the fact that "peace" seems to be breaking out in many regions of the world. Most of these analyses lack any larger conceptual framework for distinguishing between what is essential and what is contingent or accidental in world history, and are predictably superficial. If Mr. Gorbachev were ousted from the Kremlin or a new Ayatollah proclaimed the millennium from a desolate Middle Eastern capital, these same commentators would scramble to announce the rebirth of a new era of conflict.

And yet, all of these people sense dimly that there is some larger process at work, a process that gives coherence and order to the daily headlines. The twentieth century saw the developed world descend into a paroxysm of ideological violence, as liberalism contended first with the remnants of absolutism, then bolshevism and fascism, and finally an updated Marxism that threatened to lead to the ultimate apocalypse of nuclear war. But the century that began full of self-confidence in the ultimate triumph of Western liberal democracy seems at its close to be returning full circle to where it started: not to an "end of ideology" or a convergence between capitalism and socialism, as earlier predicted, but to an unabashed victory of economic and political liberalism.

The triumph of the West, of the Western *idea*, is evident first of all in the total exhaustion of viable systematic alternatives to Western liberalism. In the past decade, there have been unmistakable changes in the intellectual climate of the world's two largest communist countries, and the beginnings of significant reform movements in both. But this phenomenon extends beyond high politics and it can be seen also in the ineluctable spread of consumerist Western culture in such diverse contexts as the peasants' markets and color television sets now omnipresent throughout China, the cooperative restaurants and clothing stores opened in the past year in Moscow, the Beethoven piped into Japanese department stores, and the rock music enjoyed alike in Prague, Rangoon, and Tehran.

What we may be witnessing is not just the end of the Cold War, or the passing of a particular period of postwar history, but the end of history as such: that is, the end point of mankind's ideological evolution and the universalization of Western liberal democracy as the final form of human government. This is not to say that there will no longer be events to fill the pages of *Foreign Affairs's* yearly summaries of international relations, for the victory of liberalism has occurred primarily in the realm of ideas or consciousness and is as yet incomplete in the real or material world. But there are powerful reasons for believing that it is the ideal that will govern the material world *in the long run*. To understand how this is so, we must first consider some theoretical issues concerning the nature of historical change.

I

The notion of the end of history is not an original one. Its best known propagator was Karl Marx, who believed that the direction of historical development was a purposeful one deter-

From *The National Interest*, no. 16 (Summer 1989), pp. 3–18. Some of the author's notes have been omitted.

mined by the interplay of material forces, and would come to an end only with the achievement of a communist utopia that would finally resolve all prior contradictions. But the concept of history as a dialectical process with a beginning, a middle, and an end was borrowed by Marx from his great German predecessor, Georg Wilhelm Friedrich Hegel.

For better or worse, much of Hegel's historicism has become part of our contemporary intellectual baggage. The notion that mankind has progressed through a series of primitive stages of consciousness on his path to the present, and that these stages corresponded to concrete forms of social organization, such as tribal, slave-owning, theocratic, and finally democratic-egalitarian societies, has become inseparable from the modern understanding of man. Hegel was the first philosopher to speak the language of modern social science, insofar as man for him was the product of his concrete historical and social environment and not, as earlier natural right theorists would have it, a collection of more or less fixed "natural" attributes. The mastery and transformation of man's natural environment through the application of science and technology was originally not a Marxist concept, but a Hegelian one. Unlike later historicists whose historical relativism degenerated into relativism tout court, however, Hegel believed that history culminated in an absolute moment—a moment in which a final, rational form of society and state became victorious.

It is Hegel's misfortune to be known now primarily as Marx's precursor; and it is our misfortune that few of us are familiar with Hegel's work from direct study, but only as it has been filtered through the distorting lens of Marxism. In France, however, there has been an effort to save Hegel from his Marxist interpreters and to resurrect him as the philosopher who most correctly speaks to our time. Among those modern French interpreters of Hegel, the greatest was certainly Alexandre Kojève, a brilliant Russian émigré who taught a highly influential series of seminars in Paris in the 1930s at the *Ecole Prac-*

tique des Hautes Etudes.[1] While largely unknown in the United States, Kojève had a major impact on the intellectual life of the continent. Among his students ranged such future luminaries as Jean-Paul Sartre on the Left and Raymond Aron on the Right; postwar existentialism borrowed many of its basic categories from Hegel via Kojève.

Kojève sought to resurrect the Hegel of the *Phenomenology of Mind*, the Hegel who proclaimed history to be at an end in 1806. For as early as this Hegel saw in Napoleon's defeat of the Prussian monarchy at the Battle of Jena the victory of the ideals of the French Revolution, and the imminent universalization of the state incorporating the principles of liberty and equality. Kojève, far from rejecting Hegel in light of the turbulent events of the next century and a half, insisted that the latter had been essentially correct. The Battle of Jena marked the end of history because it was at that point that the *vanguard* of humanity (a term quite familiar to Marxists) actualized the principles of the French Revolution. While there was considerable work to be done after 1806—abolishing slavery and the slave trade, extending the franchise to workers, women, blacks, and other racial minorities, etc.—the basic principles of the liberal democratic state could not be improved upon. The two world wars in this century and their attendant revolutions and upheavals simply had the effect of extending those principles spatially, such that the various provinces of human civilization were brought up to the level of its most advanced outposts, and of forcing those societies in Europe and North America at the vanguard of civilization to implement their liberalism more fully.

The state that emerges at the end of history is liberal insofar as it recognizes and protects through a system of law man's universal right to freedom, and democratic insofar as it exists only with the consent of the governed. For Kojève, this so-called "universal homogenous state" found real-life embodiment in the countries of postwar Western Europe—precisely those flabby, prosperous, self-satisfied, inward-looking, weak-willed states whose grandest project was nothing more heroic than the creation of the Common Market.[2] But this was only to be expected. For human history and the conflict that characterized it was based on the existence of "contradictions": primitive man's quest for mutual recognition, the dialectic of the master and slave, the transformation and mastery of nature, the struggle for the universal recognition of rights, and the dichotomy between proletarian and capitalist. But in the universal homogenous state, all prior contradictions are resolved and all human needs are satisfied. There is no struggle or conflict over "large" issues, and consequently no need for generals or statesmen; what remains is primarily economic activity. And indeed, Kojève's life was consistent with his teaching. Believing that there was no more work for philosophers as well, since Hegel (correctly understood) had already achieved absolute knowledge, Kojève left teaching after the war and spent the remainder of his life working as a bureaucrat in the European Economic Community, until his death in 1968.

To his contemporaries at mid-century, Kojève's proclamation of the end of history must have seemed like the typical eccentric solipsism of a French intellectual, coming as it did on the heels of World War II and at the very height of the Cold War. To comprehend how Kojève could have been so audacious as to assert that history has ended, we must first of all understand the meaning of Hegelian idealism.

II

For Hegel, the contradictions that drive history exist first of all in the realm of human consciousness, i.e. on the level of ideas—not the trivial election year proposals of American politicians, but ideas in the sense of large unifying world views that might best be understood under the rubric of ideology. Ideology in this sense is not restricted to the secular and explicit political doctrines we usually associate with the term, but

can include religion, culture, and the complex of moral values underlying any society as well.

Hegel's view of the relationship between the ideal and the real or material worlds was an extremely complicated one, beginning with the fact that for him the distinction between the two was only apparent. He did not believe that the real world conformed or could be made to conform to ideological preconceptions of philosophy professors in any simpleminded way, or that the "material" world could not impinge on the ideal. Indeed, Hegel the professor was temporarily thrown out of work as a result of a very material event, the Battle of Jena. But while Hegel's writing and thinking could be stopped by a bullet from the material world, the hand on the trigger of the gun was motivated in turn by the ideas of liberty and equality that had driven the French Revolution.

For Hegel, all human behavior in the material world, and hence all human history, is rooted in a prior state of consciousness—an idea similar to the one expressed by John Maynard Keynes when he said that the views of men of affairs were usually derived from defunct economists and academic scribblers of earlier generations. This consciousness may not be explicit and self-aware, as are modern political doctrines, but may rather take the form of religion or simple cultural or moral habits. And yet this realm of consciousness in the long run necessarily becomes manifest in the material world, indeed creates the material world in its own image. Consciousness is cause and not effect, and can develop autonomously from the material world; hence the real subtext underlying the apparent jumble of current events is the history of ideology.

Hegel's idealism has fared poorly at the hands of later thinkers. Marx reversed the priority of the real and the ideal completely, relegating the entire realm of consciousness—religion, art, culture, philosophy itself—to a "superstructure" that was determined entirely by the prevailing material mode of production. Yet another unfortunate legacy of Marxism is our tendency to retreat into materialist or utilitarian explanations of political or historical phenomena, and our disinclination to believe in the autonomous power of ideas. A recent example of this is Paul Kennedy's hugely successful *The Rise and Fall of the Great Powers*, which ascribes the decline of great powers to simple economic overextension. Obviously, this is true on some level: an empire whose economy is barely above the level of subsistence cannot bankrupt its treasury indefinitely. But whether a highly productive modern industrial society chooses to spend 3 or 7 percent of its GNP on defense rather than consumption is entirely a matter of that society's political priorities, which are in turn determined in the realm of consciousness.

The materialist bias of modern thought is characteristic not only of people on the Left who may be sympathetic to Marxism, but of many passionate anti-Marxists as well. Indeed, there is on the Right what one might label the Wall Street Journal school of deterministic materialism that discounts the importance of ideology and culture and sees man as essentially a rational, profit-maximizing individual. It is precisely this kind of individual and his pursuit of material incentives that is posited as the basis for economic life as such in economic textbooks. One small example will illustrate the problematic character of such materialist views.

Max Weber begins his famous book, *The Protestant Ethic and the Spirit of Capitalism*, by noting the different economic performance of Protestant and Catholic communities throughout Europe and America, summed up in the proverb that Protestants eat well while Catholics sleep well. Weber notes that according to any economic theory that posited man as a rational profit-maximizer, raising the piece-work rate should increase labor productivity. But in fact, in many traditional peasant communities, raising the piece-work rate actually had the opposite effect of *lowering* labor productivity: at the higher rate, a peasant accustomed to earning two and one-half marks per day found he could earn the same amount by working less, and did

so because he valued leisure more than income. The choices of leisure over income, or of the militaristic life of the Spartan hoplite over the wealth of the Athenian trader, or even the ascetic life of the early capitalist entrepreneur over that of a traditional leisured aristocrat, cannot possibly be explained by the impersonal working of material forces, but come preeminently out of the sphere of consciousness—what we have labeled here broadly as ideology. And indeed, a central theme of Weber's work was to prove that contrary to Marx, the material mode of production, far from being the "base," was itself a "superstructure" with roots in religion and culture, and that to understand the emergence of modern capitalism and the profit motive one had to study their antecedents in the realm of the spirit.

As we look around the contemporary world, the poverty of materialist theories of economic development is all too apparent. The *Wall Street Journal* school of deterministic materialism habitually points to the stunning economic success of Asia in the past few decades as evidence of the viability of free market economics, with the implication that all societies would see similar development were they simply to allow their populations to pursue their material self-interest freely. Surely free markets and stable political systems are a necessary precondition to capitalist economic growth. But just as surely the cultural heritage of those Far Eastern societies, the ethic of work and saving and family, a religious heritage that does not, like Islam, place restrictions on certain forms of economic behavior, and other deeply ingrained moral qualities, are equally important in explaining their economic performance. And yet the intellectual weight of materialism is such that not a single respectable contemporary theory of economic development addresses consciousness and culture seriously as the matrix within which economic behavior is formed.

Failure to understand that the roots of economic behavior lie in the realm of consciousness and culture leads to the common mistake of attributing material causes to phenomena that are essentially ideal in nature. For example, it is commonplace in the West to interpret the reform movements first in China and most recently in the Soviet Union as the victory of the material over the ideal—that is, a recognition that ideological incentives could not replace material ones in stimulating a highly productive modern economy, and that if one wanted to prosper one had to appeal to baser forms of self-interest. But the deep defects of socialist economies were evident thirty or forty years ago to anyone who chose to look. Why was it that these countries moved away from central planning only in the 1980s? The answer must be found in the consciousness of the elites and leaders ruling them, who decided to opt for the "Protestant" life of wealth and risk over the "Catholic" path of poverty and security. That change was in no way made inevitable by the material conditions in which either country found itself on the eve of the reform, but instead came about as the result of the victory of one idea over another.

For Kojève, as for all good Hegelians, understanding the underlying processes of history requires understanding developments in the realm of consciousness or ideas, since consciousness will ultimately remake the material world in its own image. To say that history ended in 1806 meant that mankind's ideological evolution ended in the ideals of the French or American Revolutions: while particular regimes in the real world might not implement these ideals fully, their theoretical truth is absolute and could not be improved upon. Hence it did not matter to Kojève that the consciousness of the postwar generation of Europeans had not been universalized throughout the world; if ideological development had in fact ended, the homogenous state would eventually become victorious throughout the material world.

I have neither the space nor, frankly, the ability to defend in depth Hegel's radical idealist perspective. The issue is not whether Hegel's system was right, but whether his perspective might uncover the problematic nature of many material-

ist explanations we often take for granted. This is not to deny the role of material factors as such. To a literal-minded idealist, human society can be built around any arbitrary set of principles regardless of their relationship to the material world. And in fact men have proven themselves able to endure the most extreme material hardships in the name of ideas that exist in the realm of the spirit alone, be it the divinity of cows or the nature of the Holy Trinity.[3]

But while man's very perception of the material world is shaped by his historical consciousness of it, the material world can clearly affect in return the viability of a particular state of consciousness. In particular, the spectacular abundance of advanced liberal economies and the infinitely diverse consumer culture made possible by them seem to both foster and preserve liberalism in the political sphere. I want to avoid the materialist determinism that says that liberal economics inevitably produces liberal politics, because I believe that both economics and politics presuppose an autonomous prior state of consciousness that makes them possible. But that state of consciousness that permits the growth of liberalism seems to stabilize in the way one would expect at the end of history if it is underwritten by the abundance of a modern free market economy. We might summarize the content of the universal homogenous state as liberal democracy in the political sphere combined with easy access to VCRs and stereos in the economic.

III

Have we in fact reached the end of history? Are there, in other words, any fundamental "contradictions" in human life that cannot be resolved in the context of modern liberalism, that would be resolvable by an alternative political-economic structure? If we accept the idealist premises laid out above, we must seek an answer to this question in the realm of ideology and consciousness. Our task is not to answer exhaustively the challenges to liberalism promoted by every crackpot messiah around the world, but only those that are embodied in important social or political forces and movements, and which are therefore part of world history. For our purposes, it matters very little what strange thoughts occur to people in Albania or Burkina Faso, for we are interested in what one could in some sense call the common ideological heritage of mankind.

In the past century, there have been two major challenges to liberalism, those of fascism and of communism. The former[4] saw the political weakness, materialism, anomie, and lack of community of the West as fundamental contradictions in liberal societies that could only be resolved by a strong state that forged a new "people" on the basis of national exclusiveness. Fascism was destroyed as a living ideology by World War II. This was a defeat, of course, on a very material level, but it amounted to a defeat of the idea as well. What destroyed fascism as an idea was not universal moral revulsion against it, since plenty of people were willing to endorse the idea as long as it seemed the wave of the future, but its lack of success. After the war, it seemed to most people that German fascism as well as its other European and Asian variants were bound to self-destruct. There was no material reason why new fascist movements could not have sprung up again after the war in other locales, but for the fact that expansionist ultranationalism, with its promise of unending conflict leading to disastrous military defeat, had completely lost its appeal. The ruins of the Reich chancellery as well as the atomic bombs dropped on Hiroshima and Nagasaki killed this ideology on the level of consciousness as well as materially, and all of the pro-fascist movements spawned by the German and Japanese examples like the Peronist movement in Argentina or Subhas Chandra Bose's Indian National Army withered after the war.

The ideological challenge mounted by the other great alternative to liberalism, communism, was far more serious. Marx, speaking Hegel's language, asserted that liberal society contained a fundamental contradiction that could not be resolved within its context, that between capital and labor, and this contradiction has constituted the chief accusation against liberalism ever since. But surely, the class issue has actually been successfully resolved in the West. As Kojève (among others) noted, the egalitarianism of modern America represents the essential achievement of the classless society envisioned by Marx. This is not to say that there are not rich people and poor people in the United States, or that the gap between them has not grown in recent years. But the root causes of economic inequality do not have to do with the underlying legal and social structure of our society, which remains fundamentally egalitarian and moderately redistributionist, so much as with the cultural and social characteristics of the groups that make it up, which are in turn the historical legacy of premodern conditions. Thus black poverty in the United States is not the inherent product of liberalism, but is rather the "legacy of slavery and racism" which persisted long after the formal abolition of slavery.

As a result of the receding of the class issue, the appeal of communism in the developed Western world, it is safe to say, is lower today than any time since the end of the First World War. This can he measured in any number of ways: in the declining membership and electoral pull of the major European communist parties, and their overtly revisionist programs; in the corresponding electoral success of conservative parties from Britain and Germany to the United States and Japan, which are unabashedly promarket and anti-statist; and in an intellectual climate whose most "advanced" members no longer believe that bourgeois society is something that ultimately needs to be overcome. This is not to say that the opinions of progressive intellectuals in Western countries are not deeply pathological in any number of ways. But those who believe that the future must inevitably be socialist tend to be very old, or very marginal to the real political discourse of their societies.

One may argue that the socialist alternative was never terribly plausible for the North Atlantic world, and was sustained for the last several decades primarily by its success outside of this region. But it is precisely in the non-European world that one is most struck by the occurrence of major ideological transformations. Surely the most remarkable changes have occurred in Asia. Due to the strength and adaptability of the indigenous cultures there, Asia became a battleground for a variety of imported Western ideologies early in this century. Liberalism in Asia was a very weak reed in the period after World War I; it is easy today to forget how gloomy Asia's political future looked as recently as ten or fifteen years ago. It is easy to forget as well how momentous the outcome of Asian ideological struggles seemed for world political development as a whole.

The first Asian alternative to liberalism to be decisively defeated was the fascist one represented by Imperial Japan. Japanese fascism (like its German version) was defeated by the force of American arms in the Pacific war, and liberal democracy was imposed on Japan by a victorious United States. Western capitalism and political liberalism when transplanted to Japan were adapted and transformed by the Japanese in such a way as to be scarcely recognizable.[5] Many Americans are now aware that Japanese industrial organization is very different from that prevailing in the United States or Europe, and it is questionable what relationship the factional maneuvering that takes place with the governing Liberal Democratic Party bears to democracy. Nonetheless, the very fact that the essential elements of economic and political liberalism have been so successfully grafted onto uniquely Japanese traditions and institutions guarantees their survival in the long run. More important is the contribution that Japan has made in turn to world history by following in the footsteps of the United States to create a truly universal consumer culture that has become both a symbol and an underpinning of the universal homogenous state. V.S. Naipaul traveling in Khomeini's Iran shortly after the revolution noted the omnipresent signs advertising the products of Sony, Hitachi, and JVC, whose appeal remained virtually irresistible and gave the lie to the regime's pretensions of restoring a state based on the rule of the *Shariah*. Desire for access to the consumer culture, created in large measure by Japan, has played a crucial role in fostering the spread of economic liberalism throughout Asia, and hence in promoting political liberalism as well.

The economic success of the other newly industrializing countries (NICs) in Asia following on the example of Japan is by now a familiar story. What is important from a Hegelian standpoint is that political liberalism has been following economic liberalism, more slowly than many had hoped but with seeming inevitability. Here again we see the victory of the idea of the universal homogenous state. South Korea had developed into a modern, urbanized society with an increasingly large and well-educated middle class that could not possibly be isolated from the larger democratic trends around them. Under these circumstances it seemed intolerable to a large part of this population that it should be ruled by an anachronistic military regime while Japan, only a decade or so ahead in economic terms, had parliamentary institutions for over forty years. Even the former socialist regime in Burma, which for so many decades existed in dismal isolation from the larger trends dominating Asia, was buffeted in the past year by pressures to liberalize both its economy and political system. It is said that unhappiness with strongman Ne Win began when a senior Burmese officer went to Singapore for medical treatment and broke down crying when he saw how far socialist Burma had been left behind by its ASEAN neighbors.

But the power of the liberal idea would seem much less impressive if it had not infected the largest and oldest culture in Asia, China. The simple existence of communist China created an alternative pole of ideological attraction, and as such constituted a threat to liberalism. But the past fifteen years have seen an almost total discrediting of Marxism-Leninism as an economic system. Beginning with the famous third plenum of the Tenth Central Committee in 1978, the Chinese Communist party set about decollectivizing agriculture for the 800 million Chinese who still lived in the countryside. The role of the state in agriculture was reduced to that of a tax collector, while production of consumer goods was sharply increased in order to give peasants a taste of the universal homogenous state and thereby an incentive to work. The reform doubled Chinese grain output in only five years, and in the process created for Deng Xiaoping a solid political base from which he was able to extend the reform to other parts of the economy. Economic Statistics do not begin to describe the dynamism, initiative, and openness evident in China since the reform began.

China could not now be described in any way as a liberal democracy. At present, no more than 20 percent of its economy has been marketized, and most importantly it continues to be ruled by a self-appointed Communist party which has given no hint of wanting to devolve power. Deng has made none of Gorbachev's promises regarding democratization of the political system and there is no Chinese equivalent of ghost. The Chinese leadership has in fact been much more circumspect in criticizing Mao and Maoism than Gorbachev with respect to Brezhnev and Stalin, and the regime continues to pay lip service to Marxism-Leninism as its ideological underpinning. But anyone familiar with the outlook and behavior of the new technocratic elite now governing China knows that Marxism and ideological principle have become virtually irrelevant as guides to policy, and that bourgeois consumerism has a real meaning in that country for the first time since the revolution. The various slowdowns in the pace of reform, the campaigns against "spiritual pollution" and crackdowns on political dissent are more properly seen as tactical adjustments made in the process of managing what is an extraordinarily difficult political transition. By ducking the question of political reform while putting the economy on a new footing, Deng has managed to avoid the breakdown of authority that has accompanied Gorbachev's perestroika. Yet the pull of the liberal idea continues to be very strong as economic power devolves and the economy becomes more open to the outside world. There are currently over 20,000 Chinese students studying in the U.S. and other Western countries, almost all of them the children of the Chinese elite. It is hard to believe that when they return home to run the country they will be content for China to be the only country in Asia unaffected by the larger democratizing trend. The student demonstrations in Beijing that broke out first in December 1986 and recurred recently on the occasion of Hu Yao-bang's death were only the beginning of what will inevitably be mounting pressure for change in the political system as well.

What is important about China from the standpoint of world history is not the present state of the reform or even its future prospects. The central issue is the fact that the People's Republic of China can no longer act as a beacon for illiberal forces around the world, whether they be guerrillas in some Asian jungle or middle class students in Paris. Maoism, rather than being the pattern for Asia's future, became an anachronism, and it was the mainland Chinese who in fact were decisively influenced by the prosperity and dynamism of their overseas co-ethnics—the ironic ultimate victory of Taiwan.

Important as these changes in China have been, however, it is developments in the Soviet Union—the original "homeland of the world proletariat"—that have put the final nail in the coffin of the Marxist-Leninist alternative to liberal democracy. It should be clear that in terms of formal institutions, not much has changed in the four years since Gorbachev has come to power: free markets and the cooperative movement represent only a small part of the Soviet economy, which remains centrally planned; the political system is still dominated by the Communist party, which has only begun to democratize internally and to share power with other groups; the regime continues to assert that it is seeking only to modernize socialism and that its ideological basis remains Marxism-Leninism; and, finally, Gorbachev faces a potentially powerful conservative opposition that could undo many of the changes that have taken place to date. Moreover, it is hard to be too sanguine about the chances for success of Gorbachev's proposed reforms, either in the sphere of economics or politics. But my purpose here is not to analyze events in the short-term, or to make predictions for policy purposes, but to look at underlying trends in the sphere of ideology and consciousness. And in that respect, it is clear that an astounding transformation has occurred.

Émigrés from the Soviet Union have been reporting for at least the last generation now that virtually nobody in that country truly believed in Marxism-Leninism any longer, and that this was nowhere more true than in the Soviet elite, which continued to mouth Marxist slogans out of sheer cynicism. The corruption and decadence of the late Brezhnev-era Soviet state seemed to matter little, however, for as long as the state itself refused to throw into question any of the fundamental principles underlying Soviet society, the system was capable of functioning adequately out of sheer inertia and could even muster some dynamism in the realm of foreign and defense policy. Marxism-Leninism was like a magical incantation which, however absurd and devoid of meaning, was the only common basis on which the elite could agree to rule Soviet society.

What has happened in the four years since Gorbachev's coming to power is a revolutionary assault on the most fundamental institutions and principles of Stalinism, and their replacement by other principles which do not amount to liberalism per se but whose only connecting thread is liberalism. This is most evident in the economic sphere, where the reform economists around Gorbachev have become steadily more radical in their support for free markets, to the point where some like Nikolai Shmelev do not mind being compared in public to Milton Friedman. There is a virtual consensus among the currently dominant school of Soviet economists now that central planning and the command system of allocation are the root cause of economic inefficiency, and that if the Soviet system is ever to heal itself, it must permit free and decentralized decision-making with respect to investment, labor, and prices. After a couple of initial years of ideological confusion, these principles have finally been incorporated into policy with the promulgation of new laws on enterprise autonomy, cooperatives, and finally in 1988 on lease arrangements and family farming. There are, of course, a number of fatal flaws in the current implementation of the reform, most notably the absence of a thoroughgoing price reform. But the problem is no longer a conceptual one: Gorbachev and his lieutenants seem to understand the economic logic of marketization well enough, but like the leaders of a Third World country facing the IMF, are afraid of the social consequences of ending consumer subsidies and other forms of dependence on the state sector.

In the political sphere, the proposed changes to the Soviet constitution, legal system, and party rules amount to much less than the establishment of a liberal state. Gorbachev has spoken of democratization primarily in the sphere of internal party affairs, and has shown little intention of ending the Communist party's monopoly of power; indeed, the political reform seeks to legitimize and therefore strengthen the CPSU's rule. Nonetheless, the general principles underlying many of the reforms—that the "people" should be truly responsible for their own affairs, that higher political bodies should be answerable to lower ones, and not vice versa, that the rule of law should prevail over arbitrary police actions, with separation of powers and an independent judiciary, that there should be legal protection for property rights, the need for open discussion of public issues and the right of public dissent, the empowering of the Soviets as a forum in which the whole Soviet people can participate, and of a political culture that is more tolerant and pluralistic—come from a source fundamentally alien to the USSR's Marxist-

Leninist tradition, even if they are incompletely articulated and poorly implemented in practice.

Gorbachev's repeated assertions that he is doing no more than trying to restore the original meaning of Leninism are themselves a kind of Orwellian doublespeak. Gorbachev and his allies have consistently maintained that intraparty democracy was somehow the essence of Leninism, and that the various liberal practices of open debate, secret ballot elections, and rule of law were all part of the Leninist heritage, corrupted only later by Stalin. While almost anyone would look good compared to Stalin, drawing so sharp a line between Lenin and his successor is questionable. The essence of Lenin's democratic centralism was centralism, not democracy; that is, the absolutely rigid, monolithic, and disciplined dictatorship of a hierarchically organized vanguard Communist party, speaking in the name of the demos. All of Lenin's vicious polemics against Karl Kautsky, Rosa Luxemburg, and various other Menshevik and Social Democratic rivals, not to mention his contempt for "bourgeois legality" and freedoms, centered around his profound conviction that a revolution could not be successfully made by a democratically run organization.

Gorbachev's claim that he is seeking to return to the true Lenin is perfectly easy to understand: having fostered a thorough denunciation of Stalinism and Brezhnevism as the root of the USSR's present predicament, he needs some point in Soviet history on which to anchor the legitimacy of the CPSU's continued rule. But Gorbachev's tactical requirements should not blind us to the fact that the democratizing and decentralizing principles which he has enunciated in both the economic and political spheres are highly subversive of some of the most fundamental precepts of both Marxism and Leninism. Indeed, if the bulk of the present economic reform proposals were put into effect, it is hard to know how the Soviet economy would be more socialist than those of other Western countries with large public sectors.

The Soviet Union could in no way be described as a liberal or democratic country now, nor do I think that it is terribly likely that perestroika will succeed such that the label will be thinkable any time in the near future. But at the end of history it is not necessary that all societies become successful liberal societies, merely that they end their ideological pretensions of representing different and higher forms of human society. And in this respect I believe that something very important has happened in the Soviet Union in the past few years: the criticisms of the Soviet system sanctioned by Gorbachev have been so thorough and devastating that there is very little chance of going back to either Stalinism or Brezhnevism in any simple way. Gorbachev has finally permitted people to say what they had privately understood for many years, namely, that the magical incantations of Marxism-Leninism were nonsense, that Soviet socialism was not superior to the West in any respect but was in fact a monumental failure. The conservative opposition in the USSR, consisting both of simple workers afraid of unemployment and inflation and of party officials fearful of losing their jobs and privileges, is outspoken and may be strong enough to force Gorbachev's ouster in the next few years. But what both groups desire is tradition, order, and authority; they manifest no deep commitment to Marxism-Leninism, except insofar as they have invested much of their own lives in it. For authority to be restored in the Soviet Union after Gorbachev's demolition work, it must be on the basis of some new and vigorous ideology which has not yet appeared on the horizon.

If we admit for the moment that the fascist and communist challenges to liberalism are dead, are there any other ideological competitors left? Or put another way, are there contradictions in liberal society beyond that of class that are not resolvable? Two possibilities suggest themselves, those of religion and nationalism.

The rise of religious fundamentalism in recent years within the Christian, Jewish, and

Muslim traditions has been widely noted. One is inclined to say that the revival of religion in some way attests to a broad unhappiness with the impersonality and spiritual vacuity of liberal consumerist societies. Yet while the emptiness at the core of liberalism is most certainly a defect in the ideology—indeed, a flaw that one does not need the perspective of religion to recognize—it is not at all clear that it is remediable through politics. Modern liberalism itself was historically a consequence of the weakness of religiously-based societies which, failing to agree on the nature of the good life, could not provide even the minimal preconditions of peace and stability. In the contemporary world only Islam has offered a theocratic state as a political alternative to both liberalism and communism. But the doctrine has little appeal for non-Muslims, and it is hard to believe that the movement will take on any universal significance. Other less organized religious impulses have been successfully satisfied within the sphere of personal life that is permitted in liberal societies.

The other major "contradiction" potentially unresolvable by liberalism is the one posed by nationalism and other forms of racial and ethnic consciousness. It is certainly true that a very large degree of conflict since the Battle of Jena has had its roots in nationalism. Two cataclysmic world wars in this century have been spawned by the nationalism of the developed world in various guises, and if those passions have been muted to a certain extent in postwar Europe, they are still extremely powerful in the Third World. Nationalism has been a threat to liberalism historically in Germany, and continues to be one in isolated parts of "posthistorical" Europe like Northern Ireland.

But it is not clear that nationalism represents an irreconcilable contradiction in the heart of liberalism. In the first place, nationalism is not one single phenomenon but several, ranging from mild cultural nostalgia to the highly organized and elaborately articulated doctrine of National Socialism. Only systematic nationalisms of the latter sort can qualify as a formal ideology on the level of liberalism or communism. The vast majority of the world's nationalist movements do not have a political program beyond the negative desire of independence from some other group or people, and do not offer anything like a comprehensive agenda for socio-economic organization. As such, they are compatible with doctrines and ideologies that do offer such agendas. While they may constitute a source of conflict for liberal societies, this conflict does not arise from liberalism itself so much as from the fact that the liberalism in question is incomplete. Certainly a great deal of the world's ethnic and nationalist tension can be explained in terms of peoples who are forced to live in unrepresentative political systems that they have not chosen.

While it is impossible to rule out the sudden appearance of new ideologies or previously unrecognized contradictions in liberal societies, then, the present world seems to confirm that the fundamental principles of sociopolitical organization have not advanced terribly far since 1806. Many of the wars and revolutions fought since that time have been undertaken in the name of ideologies which claimed to be more advanced than liberalism, but whose pretensions were ultimately unmasked by history. In the meantime, they have helped to spread the universal homogenous state to the point where it could have a significant effect on the overall character of international relations.

IV

What are the implications of the end of history for international relations? Clearly, the vast bulk of the Third World remains very much mired in history, and will be a terrain of conflict for many years to come. But let us focus for the time being on the larger and more developed states of the world who after all account for the greater part of world politics. Russia and China are not likely to join the developed nations of the West as liberal societies any time in the foreseeable future, but suppose for a moment that Marxism-Leninism ceases to be a factor driving the foreign policies of these states—a prospect which, if not yet here, the last few years have made a real possibility. How will the overall characteristics of a de-ideologized world differ from those of the one with which we are familiar at such a hypothetical juncture?

The most common answer is—not very much. For there is a very widespread belief among many observers of international relations that underneath the skin of ideology is a hard core of great power national interest that guarantees a fairly high level of competition and conflict between nations. Indeed, according to one academically popular school of international relations theory, conflict inheres in the international system as such, and to understand the prospects for conflict one must look at the shape of the system—for example, whether it is bipolar or multipolar—rather than at the specific character of the nations and regimes that constitute it. This school in effect applies a Hobbesian view of politics to international relations, and assumes that aggression and insecurity are universal characteristics of human societies rather than the product of specific historical circumstances.

Believers in this line of thought take the relations that existed between the participants in the classical nineteenth century European balance of power as a model for what a de-ideologized contemporary world would look like. Charles Krauthammer, for example, recently explained that if as a result of Gorbachev's reforms the USSR is shorn of Marxist-Leninist ideology, its behavior will revert to that of nineteenth century imperial Russia.[6] While he finds this more reassuring than the threat posed by a communist Russia, he implies that there will still be a substantial degree of competition and conflict in the international system, just as there was say between Russia and Britain or Wilhelmine Germany in the last century. This is, of course, a convenient point of view for people who want

to admit that something major is changing in the Soviet Union, but do not want to accept responsibility for recommending the radical policy redirection implicit in such a view. But is it true?

In fact, the notion that ideology is a superstructure imposed on a substratum of permanent great power interest is a highly questionable proposition. For the way in which any state defines its national interest is not universal but rests on some kind of prior ideological basis, just as we saw that economic behavior is determined by a prior state of consciousness. In this century, states have adopted highly articulated doctrines with explicit foreign policy agendas legitimizing expansionism, like Marxism-Leninism or National Socialism.

The expansionist and competitive behavior of nineteenth-century European states rested on no less ideal a basis; it just so happened that the ideology driving it was less explicit than the doctrines of the twentieth century. For one thing, most "liberal" European societies were illiberal insofar as they believed in the legitimacy of imperialism, that is, the right of one nation to rule over other nations without regard for the wishes of the ruled. The justifications for imperialism varied from nation to nation, from a crude belief in the legitimacy of force, particularly when applied to non-Europeans, to the White Man's Burden and Europe's Christianizing mission, to the desire to give people of color access to the culture of Rabelais and Moliere. But whatever the particular ideological basis, every "developed" country believed in the acceptability of higher civilizations ruling lower ones—including, incidentally, the United States with regard to the Philippines. This led to a drive for pure territorial aggrandizement in the latter half of the century and played no small role in causing the Great War.

The radical and deformed outgrowth of nineteenth-century imperialism was German fascism, an ideology which justified Germany's right not only to rule over non-European peoples, but over all non-German ones. But in retrospect it seems that Hitler represented a diseased bypath in the general course of European development, and since his fiery defeat, the legitimacy of any kind of territorial aggrandizement has been thoroughly discredited. Since the Second World War, European nationalism has been defanged and shorn of any real relevance to foreign policy, with the consequence that the nineteenth-century model of great power behavior has become a serious anachronism. The most extreme form of nationalism that any Western European state has mustered since 1945 has been Gaullism, whose self-assertion has been confined largely to the realm of nuisance politics and culture. International life for the part of the world that has reached the end of history is far more preoccupied with economics than with politics or strategy.

The developed states of the West do maintain defense establishments and in the postwar period have competed vigorously for influence to meet a worldwide communist threat. This behavior has been driven, however, by an external threat from states that possess overtly expansionist ideologies, and would not exist in their absence. To take the "neorealist" theory seriously, one would have to believe that "natural" competitive behavior would reassert itself among the OECD states were Russia and China to disappear from the face of the earth. That is, West Germany and France would arm themselves against each other as they did in the 1930s, Australia and New Zealand would send military advisers to block each others' advances in Africa, and the U.S.-Canadian border would become fortified. Such a prospect is, of course, ludicrous: minus Marxist-Leninist ideology, we are far more likely to see the "Common Marketization" of world politics than the disintegration of the EEC into nineteenth-century competitiveness. Indeed, as our experiences in dealing with Europe on matters such as terrorism or Libya prove, they are much further gone than we down the road that denies the legitimacy of the use of force in international politics, even in self-defense.

The automatic assumption that Russia shorn

of its expansionist communist ideology should pick up where the czars left off just prior to the Bolshevik Revolution is therefore a curious one. It assumes that the evolution of human consciousness has stood still in the meantime, and that the Soviets, while picking up currently fashionable ideas in the realm of economics, will return to foreign policy views a century out of date in the rest of Europe. This is certainly not what happened to China after it began its reform process. Chinese competitiveness and expansionism on the world scene have virtually disappeared: Beijing no longer sponsors Maoist insurgencies or tries to cultivate influence in distant African countries as it did in the 1960s. This is not to say that there are not troublesome aspects to contemporary Chinese foreign policy, such as the reckless sale of ballistic missile technology in the Middle East; and the PRC continues to manifest traditional great power behavior in its sponsorship of the Khmer Rouge against Vietnam. But the former is explained by commercial motives and the latter is a vestige of earlier ideologically-based rivalries. The new China far more resembles Gaullist France than pre-World War I Germany.

The real question for the future, however, is the degree to which Soviet elites have assimilated the consciousness of the universal homogenous state that is post-Hitler Europe. From their writings and from my own personal contacts with them, there is no question in my mind that the liberal Soviet intelligentsia rallying around Gorbachev have arrived at the end-of-history view in a remarkably short time, due in no small measure to the contacts they have had since the Brezhnev era with the larger European civilization around them. "New political thinking," the general rubric for their views, describes a world dominated by economic concerns, in which there are no ideological grounds for major conflict between nations, and in which, consequently, the use of military force becomes less legitimate. As Foreign Minister Shevardnadze put it in mid-1988:

The struggle between two opposing systems is no longer a determining tendency of the present-day era. At the modern stage, the ability to build up material wealth at an accelerated rate on the basis of front-ranking science and high-level techniques and technology, and to distribute it fairly, and through joint efforts to restore and protect the resources necessary for mankind's survival acquires decisive importance.[7]

The post-historical consciousness represented by "new thinking" is only one possible future for the Soviet Union, however. There has always been a very strong current of great Russian chauvinism in the Soviet Union, which has found freer expression since the advent of glasnost. It may be possible to return to traditional Marxism-Leninism for a while as a simple rallying point for those who want to restore the authority that Gorbachev has dissipated. But as in Poland, Marxism-Leninism is dead as a mobilizing ideology: under its banner people cannot be made to work harder, and its adherents have lost confidence in themselves. Unlike the propagators of traditional Marxism-Leninism, however, ultranationalists in the USSR believe in their Slavophile cause passionately, and one gets the sense that the fascist alternative is not one that has played itself out entirely there.

The Soviet Union, then, is at a fork in the road: it can start down the path that was staked out by Western Europe forty-five years ago, a path that most of Asia has followed, or it can realize its own uniqueness and remain stuck in history. The choice it makes will be highly important for us, given the Soviet Union's size and military strength, for that power will continue to preoccupy us and slow our realization that we have already emerged on the other side of history.

V

The passing of Marxism-Leninism first from China and then from the Soviet Union will mean its death as a living ideology of world historical significance. For while there may be some isolated true believers left in places like Managua, Pyongyang, or Cambridge, Massachusetts, the fact that there is not a single large state in which it is a going concern undermines completely its pretensions to being in the vanguard of human history. And the death of this ideology means the growing "Common Marketization" of international relations, and the diminution of the likelihood of large-scale conflict between states.

This does not by any means imply the end of international conflict per se. For the world at that point would be divided between a part that was historical and a part that was post-historical. Conflict between states still in history, and between those states and those at the end of history, would still be possible. There would still be a high and perhaps rising level of ethnic and nationalist violence, since those are impulses incompletely played out, even in parts of the post-historical world. Palestinians and Kurds, Sikhs and Tamils, Irish Catholics and Walloons, Armenians and Azeris, will continue to have their unresolved grievances. This implies that terrorism and wars of national liberation will continue to be an important item on the international agenda. But large-scale conflict must involve large states still caught in the grip of history, and they are what appear to be passing from the scene.

The end of history will be a very sad time. The struggle for recognition, the willingness to risk one's life for a purely abstract goal, the worldwide ideological struggle that called forth daring, courage, imagination, and idealism, will be replaced by economic calculation, the endless solving of technical problems, environmental concerns, and the satisfaction of sophisticated consumer demands. In the post-historical period there will be neither art nor philosophy, just the perpetual caretaking of the museum of human history. I can feel in myself, and see in others around me, a powerful nostalgia for the time when history existed. Such nostalgia, in fact, will continue to fuel competition and conflict even in the post-historical world for some time to come.

Even though I recognize its inevitability, I have the most ambivalent feelings for the civilization that has been created in Europe since 1945, with its north Atlantic and Asian offshoots. Perhaps this very prospect of centuries of boredom at the end of history will serve to get history started once again.

NOTES

1. Kojève's best known work is his *Introduction à la lecture de Hegel* (Paris: Editions Gallimard, 1947), which is a transcript of the Ecole Practique lectures from the 1930's. This book is available in English entitled *Introduction to the Reading of Hegel* arranged by Raymond Queneau, edited by Allan Bloom, and translated by James Nichols (New York: Basic Books, 1969).

2. Kojève alternatively identified the end of history with the postwar "American way of life," toward which he thought the Soviet Union was moving as well.

3. The internal politics of the Byzantine Empire at the time of Justinian revolved around a conflict between the so-called monophysites and monothelites, who believed that the unity of the Holy Trinity was alternatively one of nature or of will. This conflict corresponded to some extent to one between proponents of different racing teams in the Hippodrome in Byzantium and led to a not insignificant level of political violence. Modern historians would tend to seek the roots of such conflicts in antagonisms between social classes or some other modern economic category, being unwilling to believe that men would kill each other over the nature of the Trinity.

4. I am not using the term "fascism" here in its most precise sense, fully aware of the frequent misuse of this term to denounce anyone to the right of the user. "Fascism" here denotes any organized ultra nationalist movement with universalistic pretensions—not universalistic with regard to its nationalism, of course, since the latter is exclusive by definition, but with regard to the movement's belief in its right to rule other people. Hence Imperial Japan would qualify as fascist while former strongman Stoessner's Paraguay or Pinochet's Chile would not. Obviously fascist ideologies cannot be universalistic in the sense of Marxism or liberalism, but the structure of the doctrine can be transferred from country to country.

5. I use the example of Japan with some caution, since Kojève late in his life came to conclude that Japan, with its culture based on purely formal arts, proved that the universal homogenous state was not victorious and that history had perhaps not ended. See the long note at the end of the second edition of *Introduction à la Lecture de Hegel*, 462-3.

6. See his article, "Beyond the Cold War," *New Republic*, December 19, 1988.

7. Vestnik Ministerstva Inostrannikh Del SSSR no. 15 (August 1988), 27–46.

STANLEY HOFFMANN

CLASH OF GLOBALIZATIONS

A New Paradigm?

What is the state of international relations to-day? In the 1990s, specialists concentrated on the partial disintegration of the global order's traditional foundations: states. During that decade, many countries, often those born of decolonization, revealed themselves to be no more than pseudostates, without solid institutions, internal cohesion, or national consciousness. The end of communist coercion in the former Soviet Union and in the former Yugoslavia also revealed long-hidden ethnic tensions. Minorities that were or considered themselves oppressed demanded independence. In Iraq, Sudan, Afghanistan, and Haiti, rulers waged open warfare against their subjects. These wars increased the importance of humanitarian interventions, which came at the expense of the hallowed principles of national sovereignty and nonintervention. Thus the dominant tension of the decade was the clash between the fragmentation of states (and the state system) and the progress of economic, cultural, and political integration—in other words, globalization.

Everybody has understood the events of September 11 as the beginning of a new era. But what does this break mean? In the conventional approach to international relations, war took place among states. But in September, poorly armed individuals suddenly challenged, surprised, and wounded the world's dominant superpower. The attacks also showed that, for all its accomplishments, globalization makes an awful form of violence easily accessible to hopeless fanatics. Terrorism is the bloody link between

From *Foreign Affairs* 81, no. 4 (July/August 2002), pp. 104–15.

interstate relations and global society. As countless individuals and groups are becoming global actors along with states, insecurity and vulnerability are rising. To assess today's bleak state of affairs, therefore, several questions are necessary. What concepts help explain the new global order? What is the condition of the interstate part of international relations? And what does the emerging global civil society contribute to world order?

Sound and Fury

Two models made a great deal of noise in the 1990s. The first one—Francis Fukuyama's "End of History" thesis—was not vindicated by events. To be sure, his argument predicted the end of ideological conflicts, not history itself, and the triumph of political and economic liberalism. That point is correct in a narrow sense: the "secular religions" that fought each other so bloodily in the last century are now dead. But Fukuyama failed to note that nationalism remains very much alive. Moreover, he ignored the explosive potential of religious wars that has extended to a large part of the Islamic world.

Fukuyama's academic mentor, the political scientist Samuel Huntington, provided a few years later a gloomier account that saw a very different world. Huntington predicted that violence resulting from international anarchy and the absence of common values and institutions would erupt among civilizations rather than among states or ideologies. But Huntington's conception of what constitutes a civilization was hazy. He failed to take into account sufficiently conflicts within each so-called civilization, and he overestimated the importance of religion in the behavior of non-Western elites, who are often secularized and Westernized. Hence he could not clearly define the link between a civilization and the foreign policies of its member states.

Other, less sensational models still have adherents. The "realist" orthodoxy insists that nothing has changed in international relations since Thucydides and Machiavelli: a state's military and economic power determines its fate; interdependence and international institutions are secondary and fragile phenomena; and states' objectives are imposed by the threats to their survival or security. Such is the world described by Henry Kissinger. Unfortunately, this venerable model has trouble integrating change, especially globalization and the rise of nonstate actors. Moreover, it overlooks the need for international cooperation that results from such new threats as the proliferation of weapons of mass destruction (WMD). And it ignores what the scholar Raymond Aron called the "germ of a universal consciousness": the liberal, pro-market norms that developed states have come to hold in common.

Taking Aron's point, many scholars today interpret the world in terms of a triumphant globalization that submerges borders through new means of information and communication. In this universe, a state choosing to stay closed invariably faces decline and growing discontent among its subjects, who are eager for material progress. But if it opens up, it must accept a reduced role that is mainly limited to social protection, physical protection against aggression or civil war, and maintaining national identity. The champion of this epic without heroes is *The New York Times* columnist Thomas Friedman. He contrasts barriers with open vistas, obsolescence with modernity, state control with free markets. He sees in globalization the light of dawn, the "golden straitjacket" that will force contentious publics to understand that the logic of globalization is that of peace (since war would interrupt globalization and therefore progress) and democracy (because new technologies increase individual autonomy and encourage initiative).

Back to Reality

These models come up hard against three realities. First, rivalries among great powers (and the capacity of smaller states to exploit such tensions) have most certainly not disappeared. For a while now, however, the existence of nuclear weapons has produced a certain degree of prudence among the powers that have them. The risk of destruction that these weapons hold has moderated the game and turned nuclear arms into instruments of last resort. But the game could heat up as more states seek other WMD as a way of narrowing the gap between the nuclear club and the other powers. The sale of such weapons thus becomes a hugely contentious issue, and efforts to slow down the spread of all WMD, especially to dangerous "rogue" states, can paradoxically become new causes of violence.

Second, if wars between states are becoming less common, wars within them are on the rise—as seen in the former Yugoslavia, Iraq, much of Africa, and Sri Lanka. Uninvolved states first tend to hesitate to get engaged in these complex conflicts, but they then (sometimes) intervene to prevent these conflicts from turning into regional catastrophes. The interveners, in turn, seek the help of the United Nations or regional organizations to rebuild these states, promote stability, and prevent future fragmentation and misery.

Third, states' foreign policies are shaped not only by realist geo-political factors such as economics and military power but by domestic politics. Even in undemocratic regimes, forces such as xenophobic passions, economic grievances, and transnational ethnic solidarity can make policymaking far more complex and less predictable. Many states—especially the United States—have to grapple with the frequent interplay of competing government branches. And the importance of individual leaders and their personalities is often underestimated in the study of international affairs.

For realists, then, transnational terrorism creates a formidable dilemma. If a state is the victim of private actors such as terrorists, it will try to eliminate these groups by depriving them of sanctuaries and punishing the states that harbor them. The national interest of the attacked state will therefore require either armed interventions against governments supporting terrorists or a course of prudence and discreet pressure on other governments to bring these terrorists to justice. Either option requires a questioning of sovereignty—the holy concept of realist theories. The classical realist universe of Hans Morgenthau and Aron may therefore still be very much alive in a world of states, but it has increasingly hazy contours and offers only difficult choices when it faces the threat of terrorism.

At the same time, the real universe of globalization does not resemble the one that Friedman celebrates. In fact, globalization has three forms, each with its own problems. First is economic globalization, which results from recent revolutions in technology, information, trade, foreign investment, and international business. The main actors are companies, investors, banks, and private services industries, as well as states and international organizations. This present form of capitalism, ironically foreseen by Karl Marx and Friedrich Engels, poses a central dilemma between efficiency and fairness. The specialization and integration of firms make it possible to increase aggregate wealth, but the logic of pure capitalism does not favor social justice. Economic globalization has thus become a formidable cause of inequality among and within states, and the concern for global competitiveness limits the aptitude of states and other actors to address this problem.

Next comes cultural globalization. It stems from the technological revolution and economic globalization, which together foster the flow of cultural goods. Here the key choice is between uniformization (often termed "Americanization") and diversity. The result is both a "disenchantment of the world" (in Max Weber's words) and a reaction against uniformity. The latter takes form in a renaissance of local cultures and languages as well as assaults against Western culture, which is denounced as an arrogant bearer of a secular, revolutionary ideology and a mask for U.S. hegemony.

Finally there is political globalization, a product of the other two. It is characterized by the preponderance of the United States and its political institutions and by a vast array of international and regional organizations and transgovernmental networks (specializing in areas such as policing or migration or justice). It is also marked by private institutions that are neither governmental nor purely national—say, Doctors Without Borders or Amnesty International. But many of these agencies lack democratic accountability and are weak in scope, power, and authority. Furthermore, much uncertainty hangs over the fate of American hegemony, which faces significant resistance abroad and is affected by America's own oscillation between the temptations of domination and isolation.

The benefits of globalization are undeniable. But Friedmanlike optimism rests on very fragile foundations. For one thing, globalization is neither inevitable nor irresistible. Rather, it is largely an American creation, rooted in the period after World War II and based on U.S. economic might. By extension, then, a deep and protracted economic crisis in the United States could have as devastating an effect on globalization as did the Great Depression.

Second, globalization's reach remains limited because it excludes many poor countries, and the states that it does transform react in different ways. This fact stems from the diversity of economic and social conditions at home as well as from partisan politics. The world is far away from a perfect integration of markets, services, and factors of production. Sometimes the simple existence of borders slows down and can even paralyze this integration; at other times it gives integration the flavors and colors of the dominant state (as in the case of the Internet).

Third, international civil society remains embryonic. Many non-governmental organizations reflect only a tiny segment of the populations of their members' states. They largely represent only modernized countries, or those in which the weight of the state is not too heavy. Often, NGOS have little independence from governments.

Fourth, the individual emancipation so dear to Friedman does not quickly succeed in democratizing regimes, as one can see today in China. Nor does emancipation prevent public institutions such as the International Monetary Fund, the World Bank, or the World Trade Organization from remaining opaque in their activities and often arbitrary and unfair in their rulings.

Fifth, the attractive idea of improving the human condition through the abolition of barriers is dubious. Globalization is in fact only a sum of techniques (audio and videocassettes, the Internet, instantaneous communications) that are at the disposal of states or private actors. Self-interest and ideology, not humanitarian reasons, are what drive these actors. Their behavior is quite different from the vision of globalization as an Enlightenment-based utopia that is simultaneously scientific, rational, and universal. For many reasons—misery, injustice, humiliation, attachment to traditions, aspiration to more than just a better standard of living—this "Enlightenment" stereotype of globalization thus provokes revolt and dissatisfaction.

Another contradiction is also at work. On the one hand, international and transnational cooperation is necessary to ensure that globalization will not be undermined by the inequalities resulting from market fluctuations, weak state-sponsored protections, and the incapacity of many states to improve their fates by themselves. On the other hand, cooperation presupposes that many states and rich private players operate altruistically—which is certainly not the essence of international relations—or practice a remarkably generous conception of their long-term interests. But the fact remains that most rich states still refuse to provide sufficient development aid or to intervene in crisis situations such as the genocide in Rwanda. That reluctance compares poorly with the American enthusiasm to pursue the fight against al Qaeda and the Taliban. What is wrong here is not patriotic enthusiasm as such, but the weakness of the humanitarian impulse when the national interest in saying non-American victims is not self-evident.

Imagined Communities

Among the many effects of globalization on international politics, three hold particular importance. The first concerns institutions. Contrary to realist predictions, most states are not perpetually at war with each other. Many regions and countries live in peace; in other cases, violence is internal rather than state-to-state. And since no government can do everything by itself, inter-state organisms have emerged. The result, which can be termed "global society," seeks to reduce the potentially destructive effects of national regulations on the forces of integration. But it also seeks to ensure fairness in the world market and create international regulatory regimes in such areas as trade, communications, human rights, migration, and refugees. The main obstacle to this effort is the reluctance of states to accept global directives that might constrain the market or further reduce their sovereignty. Thus the UN's powers remain limited and sometimes only purely theoretical. International criminal justice is still only a spotty and contested last resort. In the world economy—where the market, not global governance, has been the main beneficiary of the states retreat—the network of global institutions is fragmented and incomplete. Foreign investment remains ruled by bilateral agreements. Environmental protection is badly ensured, and issues such as migration and population growth are largely ignored. Institutional networks are not powerful enough to address unfettered short-term capital movements, the lack of international regulation on bankruptcy and competition, and primitive coordination among rich countries. In turn, the global "governance" that does exist is partial and weak at a time when economic globalization deprives many states of independent monetary and fiscal policies, or it obliges them to make cruel choices between economic competitiveness and the preservation of social safety nets. All the while, the United States displays an increasing impatience toward institutions that weigh on American freedom of action. Movement toward a world state looks increasingly unlikely. The more state sovereignty crumbles under the blows of globalization or such recent developments as humanitarian intervention and the fight against terrorism, the more states cling to what is left to them.

Second, globalization has not profoundly challenged the enduring national nature of citizenship. Economic life takes place on a global scale, but human identity remains national—hence the strong resistance to cultural homogenization. Over the centuries, increasingly centralized states have expanded their functions and tried to forge a sense of common identity for their subjects. But no central power in the world can do the same thing today, even in the European Union. There, a single currency and advanced economic coordination have not yet produced a unified economy or strong central institutions endowed with legal autonomy, nor have they resulted in a sense of postnational citizenship. The march from national identity to one that would be both national and European has only just begun. A world very partially unified by technology still has no collective consciousness or collective solidarity. What states are unwilling to do the world market cannot do all by itself, especially in engendering a sense of world citizenship.

Third, there is the relationship between globalization and violence. The traditional state of war, even if it is limited in scope, still persists. There are high risks of regional explosions in the Middle East and in East Asia, and these could seriously affect relations between the major powers. Because of this threat, and because modern arms are increasingly costly, the "anarchical society" of states lacks the resources to correct some of globalization's most flagrant flaws.

These very costs, combined with the classic distrust among international actors who prefer to try to preserve their security alone or through traditional alliances, prevent a more satisfactory institutionalization of world politics—for example, an increase of the UN's powers. This step could happen if global society were provided with sufficient forces to prevent a conflict or restore peace—but it is not.

Globalization, far from spreading peace, thus seems to foster conflicts and resentments. The lowering of various barriers celebrated by Friedman, especially the spread of global media, makes it possible for the most deprived or oppressed to compare their fate with that of the free and well-off. These dispossessed then ask for help from others with common resentments, ethnic origin, or religious faith. Insofar as globalization enriches some and uproots many, those who are both poor and uprooted may seek revenge and self-esteem in terrorism.

Globalization and Terror

Terrorism is the poisoned fruit of several forces. It can be the weapon of the weak in a classic conflict among states or within a state, as in Kashmir or the Palestinian territories. But it can also be seen as a product of globalization. Transnational terrorism is made possible by the vast array of communication tools. Islamic terrorism, for example, is not only based on support for the Palestinian struggle and opposition to an invasive American presence. It is also fueled by a resistance to "unjust" economic globalization and to a Western culture deemed threatening to local religions and cultures.

If globalization often facilitates terrorist violence, the fight against this war without borders is potentially disastrous for both economic development and globalization. Antiterrorist measures restrict mobility and financial flows, while new terrorist attacks could lead the way for an antiglobalist reaction comparable to the chauvinistic paroxysms of the 1930s. Global terrorism is not the simple extension of war among states to nonstates. It is the subversion of traditional ways of war because it does not care about the sovereignty of either its enemies or the allies who shelter them. It provokes its victims to take measures that, in the name of legitimate defense, violate knowingly the sovereignty of those states accused of encouraging terror. (After all, it was not the Taliban's infamous domestic violations of human rights that led the United States into Afghanistan; it was the Taliban's support of Osama bin Laden.)

But all those trespasses against the sacred principles of sovereignty do not constitute progress toward global society, which has yet to agree on a common definition of terrorism or on a common policy against it. Indeed, the beneficiaries of the antiterrorist "war" have been the illiberal, poorer states that have lost so much of their sovereignty of late. Now the crackdown on terror allows them to tighten their controls on their own people, products, and money. They can give themselves new reasons to violate individual rights in the name of common defense against insecurity—and thus stop the slow, hesitant march toward international criminal justice.

Another main beneficiary will be the United States, the only actor capable of carrying the war against terrorism into all corners of the world. Despite its power, however, America cannot fully protect itself against future terrorist acts, nor can it fully overcome its ambivalence toward forms of interstate cooperation that might restrict U.S. freedom of action. Thus terrorism is a global phenomenon that ultimately reinforces the enemy—the state—at the same time as it tries to destroy it. The states that are its targets have no interest in applying the laws of war to their fight against terrorists; they have every interest in treating terrorists as outlaws and pariahs. The champions of globalization have sometimes glimpsed the "jungle" aspects of economic globalization, but few observers foresaw similar aspects in global terrorist and antiterrorist violence.

Finally, the unique position of the United States raises a serious question over the future of world affairs. In the realm of interstate problems, American behavior will determine whether the non-superpowers and weak states will continue to look at the United States as a friendly power (or at least a tolerable hegemon), or whether they are provoked by Washington's hubris into coalescing against American preponderance. America may be a hegemon, but combining rhetorical overkill and ill-defined designs is full of risks. Washington has yet to understand that nothing is more dangerous for a "hyperpower" than the temptation of unilateralism. It may well believe that the constraints of international agreements and organizations are not necessary, since U.S. values and power are all that is needed for world order. But in reality, those same international constraints provide far better opportunities for leadership than arrogant demonstrations of contempt for others' views, and they offer useful ways of restraining unilateralist behavior in other states. A hegemon concerned with prolonging its rule should be especially interested in using internationalist methods and institutions, for the gain in influence far exceeds the loss in freedom of action.

In the realm of global society, much will depend on whether the United States will overcome its frequent indifference to the costs that globalization imposes on poorer countries. For now, Washington is too reluctant to make resources available for economic development, and it remains hostile to agencies that monitor and regulate the global market. All too often, the right-leaning tendencies of the American political system push U.S. diplomacy toward an excessive reliance on America's greatest asset—military strength—as well as an excessive reliance on market capitalism and a "sovereigntism" that offends and alienates. That the mighty United States is so afraid of the world's imposing its "inferior" values on Americans is often a source of ridicule and indignation abroad.

Odd Man Out

For all these tensions, it is still possible that the American war on terrorism will be contained by prudence, and that other governments will give priority to the many internal problems created by interstate rivalries and the flaws of globalization. But the world risks being squeezed between a new Scylla and Charybdis. The Charybdis is universal intervention, unilaterally decided by American leaders who are convinced that they have found a global mission provided by a colossal threat. Presentable as an epic contest between good and evil, this struggle offers the best way of rallying the population and overcoming domestic divisions. The Scylla is resignation to universal chaos in the form of new attacks by future bin Ladens, fresh humanitarian disasters, or regional wars that risk escalation. Only through wise judgment can the path between them be charted.

We can analyze the present, but we cannot predict the future. We live in a world where a society of uneven and often virtual states overlaps with a global society burdened by weak public institutions and underdeveloped civil society. A single power dominates, but its economy could become unmanageable or disrupted by future terrorist attacks. Thus to predict the future confidently would be highly incautious or naive. To be sure, the world has survived many crises, but it has done so at a very high price, even in times when WMD were not available.

Precisely because the future is neither decipherable nor determined, students of international relations face two missions. They must try to understand what goes on by taking an inventory of current goods and disentangling the threads of present networks. But the fear of confusing the empirical with the normative should not prevent them from writing as political philosophers at a time when many philosophers are extending their conceptions of just society to international relations. How can one make the global house more livable? The answer presupposes a political philosophy that would be both just and acceptable even to those whose values have other foundations. As the late philosopher Judith Shklar did, we can take as a point of departure and as a guiding thread the fate of the victims of violence, oppression, and misery; as a goal, we should seek material and moral emancipation. While taking into account the formidable constraints of the world as it is, it is possible to loosen them.

JAMES K. GALBRAITH

A PERFECT CRIME: INEQUALITY IN THE AGE OF GLOBALIZATION

Most of the world's political leaders have embraced economic globalization on two grounds: that open markets and transnational production networks are unstoppable; and that the benefits will surely flow out to all the world's people, rich and poor. Leading economists and journalists agree, convinced by the logic of laissez-faire, comparative advantage, and technology transfer. Accordingly, they

From *Daedalus* (Winter 2002), pp. 11–25. Some of the author's notes have been omitted.

declare, class conflict and competitive struggle are obsolete.

Yet, outside elite circles, conflict and struggle refuse to disappear. In rich countries, electorates and pressure groups remain protectionist and proregulation, even socialist in parts of Europe; there is wide sympathy for the (nonviolent) protestors of Seattle, Davos, and Genoa. In poor countries, globalization is the new synonym for imperialism and colonialism; generally the word evokes collapse rather than common gain. All in all, if the imposition of deregulation, privatization, free trade, and free capital mobility has in fact raised living standards worldwide, gratitude is devilishly hard to find.

So what are the facts? Has globalization hurt or helped? Oddly, researchers do not know; mostly they do not ask. For the doctrine of globalization as it is understood in elite circles contains the curious assumption that the global market is itself beyond reproach. The formulae for success in that market—from openness and transparency to sound finance to investment in education—remain matters of national responsibility; countries that fail have only their own deficiencies to blame. In line with this view, most research has focused on national conditions and national policies, and not on global conditions or the effects of globalization as such.

Whether such a national focus is appropriate, or whether a global view would be better, is a question of great importance. To resolve it, we would need new efforts to measure economic development and social progress across countries around the world—in effect, we would need to write a global report card. But official initiatives in this vein, notably the World Bank's *Human Development Report*, are caught in contradictions between the cheerful predictions of globalization theory and what the evidence of epidemics, illiteracy, unemployment, and poverty suggests is actually happening—contradictions that have driven several senior figures (most famously, former chief economist Joseph Stiglitz) out of the Bank. Meanwhile, the International Monetary Fund (IMF) and World Trade

Organization (WTO) are today closed societies, sealed off from most forms of serious critical discussion.

So, what can *independent* research contribute to an understanding of the state of the global economy today? Not much, perhaps, beyond the fragmentary evidence of case studies and field reports. Truly independent scholars usually lack the resources to bring together new information on a global scale.

Still, one broader area has attracted attention: economic *inequality* and its relationship to economic growth. In this area, data (collated, as we shall see below, from many independent sources) are already available. A rich (but inexpensive) econometrics can be brought to bear. And much hinges on the findings. For, while inequality and economic growth are hardly the only issues in world development—life, health, literacy, and peace are more important—the perceived relationship between these two economic variables underlies development policy in profound ways.

Long ago, the great economist Simon Kuznets (1901–1985) linked equality to the development process. Kuznets argued that as industrialization began, it might lead to an increasing inequality at first: the rough parity among farmers would give way to an emerging urban-rural divide. But as industrialization deepened, the center of economic gravity would shift to the cities. To live in cities, to work for wages, requires free labor and that every family have some access to cash. The larger the share of basic consumption goods provided through the marketplace, the more equal money incomes must become. Eventually, democracy and social-welfare systems would emerge: progress toward the social democratic frameworks of Western Europe and North America was a pragmatic possibility as well as an ideal.

Kuznets offered an optimistic vision, similar to that of John Maynard Keynes though more austere in style. Properly managed, development could be civilized; it need not lead to the misery and upheaval that Karl Marx had earlier foreseen. But in recent years, as the Marxian threat disappeared, Kuznets's vision also receded. With unions in disorder and welfare states in disrepute, the "Kuznets hypothesis" now serves mainly as a whipping boy of development researchers, to be raised, sometimes at length, but usually to be dismissed as disconfirmed by modern data, generally by economists who see no contradiction between inequality and development.

In a 1993 report entitled the *East Asian Miracle* (hereafter referred to as EAM), economists at the World Bank offered an alternative theory. They argued that early redistributions, especially of land and primary schooling, were preconditions for industrial success in Japan, Korea, Taiwan, China, Singapore, Malaysia, and Thailand. This argument has been widely cited to underpin a case for education as a development tool, to support redistributive policies in the early stages, and especially to argue that development can be market-friendly, provided the "right" pattern of endowments and incentives exists at the outset.

By emphasizing market-friendly preconditions for growth, the EAM team undermined the presumption that development and rising equality normally occur together—even though the Asian evidence did suggest that this was in fact the case in most places. The team also downplayed the policy activism of many Asian states, especially their commitments to planning, industrial policy, financial control, and the development of social welfare—all cornerstones of a normal development process as understood by Keynes and Kuznets in their day.

The EAM's striking hypothesis also called attention, indirectly, to the incompleteness of information about inequality around the world. While there had been many efforts to measure inequalities at the national level, no one had brought those measurements together in a single global data set. As a result, it remained unclear whether one could generalize from the East Asian experience. Were the apparent lessons valid on a wider scale? Was it really true that re-

distributive policies set the stage for growth?

To help answer that question, Klaus Deininger and Lyn Squire of the World Bank decided to mine the economic development literature for surveys of income inequality. Finding thousands of such measures in scores of studies, they evaluated each data point on three criteria. Did the study focus on households, rather than persons? Did it attempt to measure all forms of income, including in-kind incomes? Did it attempt to cover all parts of the society, including rural as well as urban areas? In 1996 they republished the data satisfying these three criteria as a "high-quality" data set on household income inequality since 1950. The Deininger-Squire data set is now a standard reference; a recent version offers nearly 750 country/year observations on which dozens of papers have been based.

The result has been an unintended descent into confusion. As scholars sought systematic relationships between inequality, income, and growth in the World Bank's data, no consistent pattern emerged. Some seemed to confirm the Kuznets hypothesis. Others argued instead that inequality first falls and then rises with rising income: the opposite pattern. The EAM finding of a relationship between low inequality and later growth was first supported, and then questioned, on the ground that the relationship seemed to rest on continent-specific differences between Latin America and Asia.

Meanwhile, pro-equality viewpoints came under challenge, from a quarter associated with older theories and conservative policy views. In Victorian economic thought, inequality was itself the spur of growth. Growth required capital accumulation, and it was the accumulations made possible by concentrating incomes that justified an unequal class structure. The Victorian system worked well enough—so long as, in practice, growth did occur and the working classes enjoyed the benefit of a steadily rising living standard. But, as Keynes particularly well understood, all this had died with World War I.

And then, after sixty years, the very same idea was born again. Let the rich rule—so wrote the supply-side economists who came to power behind Ronald Reagan in America and Margaret Thatcher in Britain. Tax cuts would improve the incentives of the wealthy to "work, save, and invest." High interest rates would reward saving and quash inflation. And a fetish of the entrepreneur spread through political and business culture, a doctrine that implicitly rooted the concept of value in innovation and leadership, rather than in labor or even in the happiness of consumers.

Today, a similar doctrine finds expression in models that emphasize synergies, increasing returns, technological change. Two good educations, in partnership, are more than twice as good as one, so the educated should concentrate into enclaves. Technical development raises the relative productivity of the well trained—therefore, pay the skilled more and the unskilled less. In these cases, inequalities expressed as clusters of privileged opportunity will foster more rapid growth.

Seeking an empirical basis for such claims, Kristin Forbes uses the Deininger and Squire data set to find that increases in inequality are followed by increased growth rates. If valid, these findings would reverse the EAM idea without restoring lost luster to Simon Kuznets.[1]

As matters stand, economists have broached four different possibilities, each with different implications for the strategy of economic development:

The *redistributionist view* holds that egalitarian social policies are a precondition for growth and points to the Asian miracle—before the crash of 1997—as prime evidence. This view emphasizes land reform and education, but tends to resist intervention in market processes once preconditions have been successfully met.

The *neoliberal view* is that policymakers should go for growth, concentrating resources on comparative advantage, exports, and the fostering of technological change. Inequality may well rise, but the success of a growth strategy makes the sacrifice worthwhile.

The *Kuznets and Keynes view* implies that increasing equality is the normal outcome of a process of rising incomes—whether fast or slow—and that social welfare policies are normal outgrowths of the transition to an urban industrial economy. This perspective does not presuppose that redistribution should precede growth; it only implies that inequality will decline as the development process matures. But if Kuznets and Keynes were right, then strategies of planning, industrial diversification, import substitution, financial control, and the welfare state are a legitimate part of the development tool kit; they do not contradict the fundamental project.

The *Scotch verdict*—"not proven"—is that development may be unrelated to social and economic inequalities in any systematic way. This is the fallback position of some who argue for growth as the sole development objective.

Plainly, the world is complex. Many different things could be true. But how many of these four conflicting hypotheses are, actually, correct? At most, one. *Which one?* A great deal rides on the answer.

One reason why the question remains unresolved is that the evidence against which the modern views have been tested—the Deininger-Squire data set—is unreliable.

One cannot but admire the effort of Deininger and Squire to bring some order to the chaotic history of income-inequality measurement. Still, a comparison of coefficient values from their "high-quality" data set quickly reveals fundamental problems.

First, in many parts of the world—in Africa most of all, but also in Latin America, Asia, and even in parts of Europe—measurements are sparse, separated in time by many years or even decades. Second, while some of the rankings seem reasonable—one might expect low inequality readings from Eastern Europe during the communist years—others are, to put it mildly, implausible. Is inequality in India, Pakistan, and Indonesia really in the same general league as in

Norway? Is inequality in Spain really lower than in France? Is inequality in the United States and Australia really comparable to, say, Nigeria or the Sudan? It is doubtful that any Sudanese thinks so.

The thin coverage on which these results are based becomes a more serious problem still when one tries to compute changes in the World Bank's inequality data over some consistent time period. One is rapidly reduced to a data set where half of all observations are from the affluent member countries of the Organization for Economic Cooperation and Development (this is true of the Forbes study, for example). A simple effort to compare changes from the 1980s to the 1990s—the decades for which the Bank reports the *most* observations—shows no data for most of Africa, West Asia, and Latin America. And where observations exist, they are questionable: inequality falls for about half the countries in this exercise, in a decade marked by wide protests against rising inequality! When data and common perception clash so sharply, which is to be believed?

We clearly need more and better data. A new data set should, ideally, approach comprehensive coverage of the global economy on a year-to-year basis, permitting detailed comparison of changes in inequality to changes in GDP. It should be based on data that are reasonably accurate and reasonably consistent across countries.

This turns out to be possible, so long as one is willing to narrow the focus and to return to official sources of information—sources that are very rich, but widely neglected. Inequalities of household income—the focus of Deininger and Squire—are very difficult to measure, and the measurements we do have often come from unofficial surveys.[2]

Levels of pay, on the other hand, may be measured easily and accurately for many countries. Pay is, of course, a large subset of income. Levels of *manufacturing pay*—an important subset of all pay—have been measured with reason-

able accuracy as a matter of official routine in most countries around the world for nearly forty years. The resulting data—payrolls by manufacturing sector—have been placed in a single systematic industrial accounting framework by the United Nations International Development Organization (UNIDO), which makes cross-country comparison both easy and relatively reliable.

In short, if one is willing to look at the growth-inequality relationship through the narrow lens of pay rates and earnings structures, it is possible to get the picture into focus.[3]

The contribution of the University of Texas Inequality Project (UTIP) has been to compute consistent measures of manufacturing pay inequality from this information, using an inequality metric developed in the 1960s by the late econometrician Henri Theil. The application of this technique to UNIDO's industrial data set permits us to generate large numbers of inequality measures that can be compared across countries and through time. The year 2000 release of the UNIDO data set alone contains sufficient information for nearly 3,200 country/year observations between 1963 and 1998 —more than four times the coverage of Deininger and Squire.

A map averaging values of an inequality coefficient computed from these data (see figure 1) graphically displays the key findings. Over the 1963–1998 period, as these data reveal, manufacturing pay inequality was lowest in the social democracies of Scandinavia and in Australia and under the communist regimes of Eastern Europe, China and Cuba (because of the boundary changes, data for Russia here exclude the Soviet years). Southern Europe and North America form a second group of countries with relatively low levels of pay inequality. The wealthier countries of Latin America (such as Argentina, Venezuela, and Colombia) and West Asia (Iran) form a middle group; Russia (after 1991) and South Africa rank slightly higher. The regions of highest inequality are found in a broad equatorial belt, from Peru and Brazil through central Africa and southern Asia, reflecting the largest

Figure 1
Global Inequality
1963–1997

Inequality of manufacturing pay computed by the University of Texas Inequality Project from the UNIDO 2000 edition of Industrial Statistics and averaged over 1963–1997; countries ranked into six quantiles as in Figure 3. Note the high coverage and geographic consistency of inequality patterns in the OECD and across the developing regions. Data for Russia are post-Soviet only; those for China start in 1979. Data for the Czech Republic, Slovakia, and the post-Yugoslav states begin with the formation of those states in the 1990s.

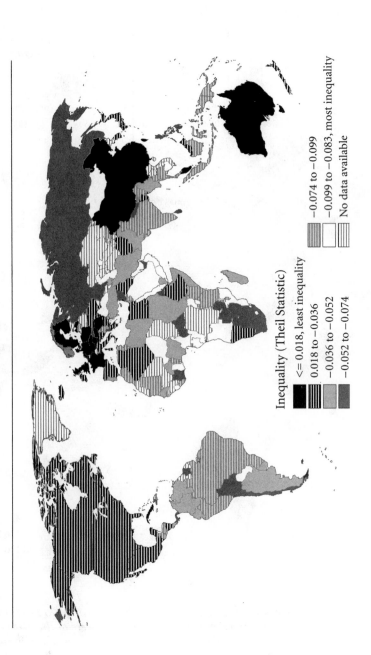

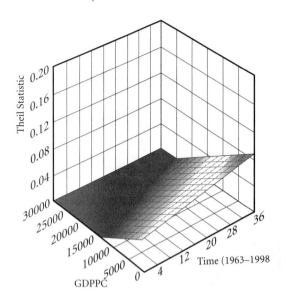

Figure 2
A regression of inequality on income and time, UTIP *data set. The regression reflects a downward sloping Kuznets relation as well as a global drift toward sharply higher inequality over time. (Color scales have a similar gradient but are not matched to previous graphs.)*

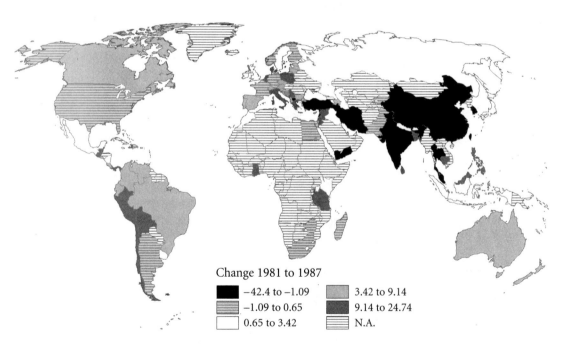

Figure 3
Inequality in the Age of Debt. Changes in inequality from 1981 to 1987. Dark gray indicates the largest increases (notably in Latin America and among oil producers at this time of collapsing oil prices); blue indicates declines; light gray is "neutral." Almost the only cases of declining inequality in this period are in countries insulated from the global financial system (China, India, Iran). Greece and Turkey showed very large increases following their confrontation over Cyprus in the 1970s; declines in the 1980s may be a return to normality, including policy in Greece after the end of military rule.

Figure 4
Patterns of rising inequality in the age of globalization. Changes in inequality from 1988 to 1994. The rise in Russia is extreme. The only significant region of declining inequality is in the boom countries of Southeast Asia—more evidence of the Kuznets effect.

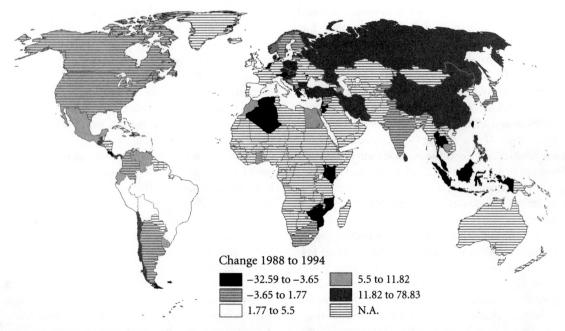

Change 1988 to 1994

■ −32.59 to −3.65	5.5 to 11.82
−3.65 to 1.77	■ 11.82 to 78.83
1.77 to 5.5	N.A.

gaps between city and countryside, between oil and food, and the weakest development of mass manufacturing and the production of capital goods.

These findings are in striking accord with Kuznets's basic hypothesis. Higher incomes and lower pay inequality are strongly associated. Because this is true, there is no reason to expect a systematic relationship between inequality today and growth later, and none can be found. Redistribution in either direction—up or down—is apparently not a precondition for economic growth: instead, successful growth and redistribution tend to go hand in hand.

Although the Kuznets hypothesis relating levels of inequality to levels of pay or income is broadly corroborated by these findings, some doubts about his views do remain. It is debatable, for example, if inequality must increase, as Kuznets supposed, in the earliest stages of industrial development. Yet that question is moot

in most places, so far as modern times and data are concerned: most countries are past the early stages. It may also be that inequality rises slightly in a few of the very richest countries as income grows, due partly to capital gains in technology sectors—a pattern of interest for students of the United States and the United Kingdom, but not broadly relevant to the study of economic development.

On the whole, inequalities of pay within manufacturing tend to be lower in rich countries than in poor. That means that inequality almost surely declines as industrialization deepens and as incomes rise. This finding is consistent over the globe, with limited exceptions, over a thirty-five-year run of annual data, beginning in the early 1960s.

Besides confirming that Kuznets's view of the relationship between growth and inequality remains basically correct, the UTIP data also permit us to detect global patterns in changes of in-equality, to take a fresh look at the New World Order.

This exercise produces a disquieting result. For when the global trend is isolated, we find that in the last two decades, inequality has increased throughout the world in a pattern that cuts across the effect of national income changes. During the decades that happen to co-incide with the rise of neoliberal ideology, with the breakdown of national sovereignties, and with the end of Keynesian policies in the global debt crisis of the early 1980s, inequality rose worldwide. In effect, the Kuznets curve relating inequality to income shifted upward. This find-ing—the upward slope of the plane in figure 2—points to influences on inequality of a global order.

The finding that there is a common global upward trend in inequality provides strong evi-dence for one of two propositions. One possi-bility is that national economic policies have almost universally raised inequality independent of income changes—but for what reason? Alter-natively, it may be that national economic poli-cies alone do not and cannot entirely control national pay structures, that there is a common, and pernicious, global element in the global economy.

In the latter case we have to ask, what is that element? Is there, perhaps, something about the process of global laissez-faire itself that created this outcome? And if so, is it an inherent feature of "globalization?" Or is it only an artifact of the particular policies under which the global mar-ket has been liberalized in recent years?

Figures 3 and 4 illustrate the regional pat-terns of increasing inequality during two key episodes. First, there was the early 1980s, the years of debt crisis and of the oil slump that fol-lowed. During that time, inequality rises most rapidly in the Southern cone of Latin America and in parts of the Middle East. Second, there was the collapse (in part induced, as in Yu-goslavia and Poland, by intractable debts) of the communist world; these countries become the

focus of rising inequalities in the late 1980s. By the mid-1990s, as figure 4 reveals, almost the only countries with declining inequality were the booming countries of Southern Asia (even if the crash after 1997 almost surely took some of them in another direction).

This pattern shows—as clearly as any one in-dicator might hope to do—the serial failure of the global development process as a whole to permit the building of advanced industrial democracies and welfare states on which Kuznets and Keynes rested their hopes fifty years ago. Even so, the figures do not fully cap-ture (though they do reflect) the deepening dis-solution of nation-states, whose extreme cases lead to war, as in Bosnia, Croatia, Kosovo, Macedonia, the eastern Congo, Chechnya, Aceh, southern Colombia, and even Chiapas—all of them among the poorest parts of their parent states. But as inequality deepens, more of this is surely on the way.

Since Kuznets passed out of fashion, economists have generally fallen into two camps: those who believe that redistribution fosters growth, on the one hand, and those who believe on the contrary that rising inequality is a price worth paying for development. These are, however, statements about national conditions. Working with the UTIP data set, it is possible to isolate a different set of factors: those factors that co-evolve in the world economy through time, independently of the movement of national income. The annual pat-tern of these time effects, presented in figure 5, gives us an essential clue so far lacking: the pre-cise turning point at which the global element in inequality ceased declining and started to rise.[4]

As figure 5 shows, the common global element in pay inequalities declines slightly through the late 1970s. It then turns around in 1981–1982, just as Ronald Reagan took office in the United States. At this time, a shift in the global climate of real interest rates brought the latter from near 0 to 5 percent or higher for completely riskless assets—and much higher for most countries with depreciating currencies.

Figure 5
Panel estimates of the worldwide time pattern of rising inequality, controlling for country-specific effects and the effect of changes in per capita real income levels. The method of panel estimates permits calculation of a year-to-year pattern in changing inequality.

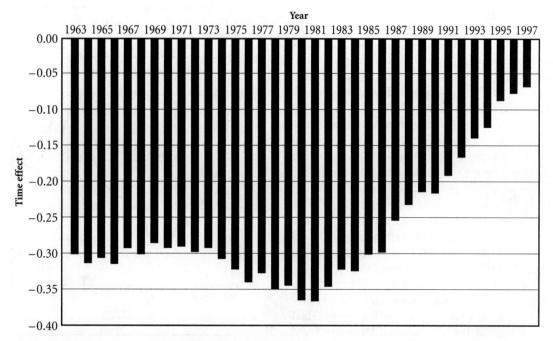

The result was to precipitate a global debt crisis in the course of which many poorer nations were forced first to cut imports and capital spending, and then were pressured to abandon long-standing trade and welfare policies. The years since 1980 have thus seen an empirical test of the second point of view: an extraordinary, systematic increase in inequality. It has not been followed by any increase in the global rate of economic expansion.

For a cause of worldwide rising inequality, one must look to events that characterize the period after 1980, but not before. Growth of trade will not do. Worldwide trade grew very rapidly through the period of "stabilizing development" (the Mexican term) that began in 1945 and ended in the 1970s; it is not a peculiar feature of the environment after 1980.

Nor can accelerating technological change explain the pattern. The story often hinted at for the American case is that the rapid spread of computers after 1980 made "skill-biased technological change" a driving force behind rising pay differentials. But the UTIP (and all other) data clearly show rising inequality in the United States beginning in the 1970s, long before the personal computer revolution. And after 1980, inequality rises more sharply in poorer countries, where of course new technologies spread the least. In a country like Finland, a leader in Internet penetration, inequality hardly rose at all.

What can explain a sequence of events that affects an almost universal spectrum of poorer countries after 1980, excluding only India and China in that decade and a handful of the booming economies of South Asia in the 1990s?

The evidence of timing points toward the effect of rising real interest rates and the debt crisis. For this, the stage was set by the dissolution in 1973 of the Bretton Woods framework of fixed-but-adjustable exchange rates and international supervision of capital flow. As figure 5 shows, the collapse of that framework ended a period of relatively stable growth—and stable pay structures. There then followed a short period of the oil and commodities boom, with *declining* inequality fueled by commercial debt. But this was unsustainable, and it came to a crashing end in the worldwide financial shock that was initiated in 1980–1981 by the United States, as the U.S. Federal Reserve pushed nominal interest rates past 20 percent. The rise in interest rates produced dramatic and continuing cuts in imports, with devastating results for the development prospects of poorer countries. Many of them have never recovered.

Indeed, matters were made worse by the concurrent triumph of neoliberalism in the United States and the United Kingdom in these same years. Following the debt crisis, the rich countries preached the "magic of the marketplace" to the poor. No new financial architecture was created from the wreckage left by the commercial banks. Instead, the International Monetary Fund preached austerity, and then financial deregulation and privatization—sale of state assets at fire-sale prices to foreign investors.

After honing these policies in Latin America, they were applied after 1989 in Russia and Eastern Europe, and then in Asia.

Everywhere, crisis ensued. Only where countries successfully resisted the neo-liberal policy prescriptions—most notably in China, in Northern Europe, and in the United States itself after the mid-1990s—did growth continue and pay inequality remain under reasonable control.

It is not, then, by accident that the effects of neoliberalism at a global level resemble those of a coup d'état at a national level.

In an early analysis using UTIP's data set, George Purcell and I calculated the average effects of twenty-seven coups d'état on our measurements of pay inequality. We found a pattern of striking consistency. After rising four and five years before the coup, inequality would decline

Figure 6
Inequality before, during, and after coups: the case of Chile and the general pattern. The chart on the bottom averages the change of inequality for up to five years before and up to five years after a coup d'état; the average is calculated across twenty-seven historical cases.

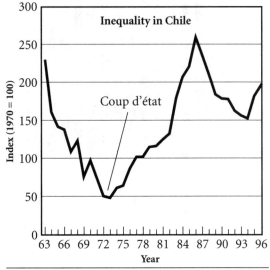

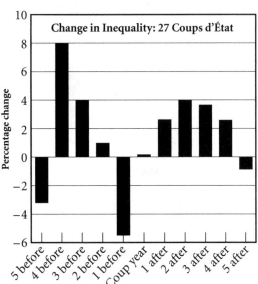

sharply in the two years immediately beforehand. In the year of the coup itself, the decline in inequality would stop. And in the five repressive years that followed (coups, as distinct from revolutions, are almost invariably right-wing), rising inequality would occur systematically in each year, until overall inequality stood far higher than in the period before the coup. Figure 6 presents our data for the canonical case of Chile and the curve that emerges from averaging effects over the twenty-seven cases.

Viewed from a global perspective, the pattern of time effects observed worldwide after 1975 strongly resembles this characteristic curve. Global inequality fell in the late 1970s. In those years, poor countries had the benefit of low interest rates and easy credit, and high commodity prices, especially for oil. Indeed, in the 1970s, the UTIP data shows that it was the lower-income workers in the poorer countries who made the largest gains in pay. But in 1980–1981, the age of low interest rates and high commodity prices ended.

In 1982, the repression took hold—a financial repression, to be sure, but not less real for having taken that form. And while the debt crisis was not accompanied by overt violence—coups are, indeed, often very limited in their *overt* violence—the effects were soon felt worldwide, and with a savage intensity that has continued for two decades.

In sum, it is not increasing trade *as such* that we should fear. Nor is technology the culprit. To focus on "globalization" as such misstates the issue. The problem is a process of integration carried out since at least 1980 under circumstances of unsustainable finance, in which wealth has flowed upwards from the poor countries to the rich, and mainly to the upper financial strata of the richest countries.

In the course of these events, progress toward tolerable levels of inequality and sustainable development virtually stopped. Neocolonial patterns of center-periphery dependence, and of debt peonage, were reestablished, but without the slightest assumption of responsibility by the rich countries for the fate of the poor.

It has been, it would appear, a perfect crime.

And while statistical forensics can play a small role in pointing this out, no mechanism to reverse the policy exists, still less any that might repair the damage. The developed countries have abandoned the pretense of attempting to foster development in the world at large, preferring to substitute the rhetoric of ungoverned markets for the hard work of stabilizing regulation. The prognosis is grim: a descent into apathy, despair, disease, ecological disaster, and wars of separatism and survival in many of the poorest parts of the world.

Unless, of course, the wise spirits of Kuznets and Keynes can be summoned back to life, to deal more constructively with the appalling disorder of the past twenty years.

NOTES

1. See Kristin Forbes, "A Reassessment of the Relationship Between Inequality and Growth," *American Economic Review* 90 (3) (September 2000): 869–887.

2. The only consistent *formal* definition of income we have comes from the income tax, whose code specifies the precise allowable treatment of each type of inflow and outflow. It is tax law that specifies that wages and salaries are income, but that gifts received are not, that reimbursements of business expenses should be deducted, and so on. Since tax laws vary, the concept of income is therefore *nationally specific*, well defined only where precise accounting conventions are codified in the tax laws.

3. The main trade-off is between comprehensiveness and accuracy: we emphasize accurate measurement of a limited domain, manufacturing pay inequality, over implausible measurement of a comprehensive one, income inequality.

4. Our technique here is a two-way fixed effects panel data estimation, which entails creating "dummy" variables for each country and year in the sample. The coefficient estimates

on the country dummies then reveal the pattern of national institutions, while the coefficient estimates of the time dummies reveal the common course of inequality in the global economy over the years, controlling for income changes. The time effects are presented in figure 5.

JOSEPH S. NYE, JR.

GLOBALIZATION'S DEMOCRATIC DEFICIT

Seattle; Washington, D.C.; Prague; Québec City. It is becoming difficult for international economic organizations to meet without attracting crowds of protesters decrying globalization. These protesters are a diverse lot, coming mainly from rich countries, and their coalition has not always been internally consistent. They have included trade unionists worried about losing jobs and students who want to help the underdeveloped world gain them, environmentalists concerned about ecological degradation and anarchists who object to all forms of international regulation. Some protesters claim to represent poor countries but simultaneously defend agricultural protectionism in wealthy countries. Some reject corporate capitalism, whereas others accept the benefits of international markets but worry that globalization is destroying democracy.

Of all their complaints, this last concern is key. Protest organizers such as Lori Wallach attributed half the success of the Seattle coalition to "the notion that the democracy deficit in the global economy is neither necessary nor acceptable." For globalization's supporters, accordingly, finding some way to address its perceived democratic deficit should become a high priority.

From *Foreign Affairs* 80, no. 4 (July/August 2001), pp. 2–6.

It's a Small World

Globalization, defined as networks of interdependence at worldwide distances, is not new. Nor is it just economic. Markets have spread and tied people together, but environmental, military, social, and political interdependence have also increased. If the current political backlash against globalization were to lead to a rash of protectionist policies, it might slow or even reverse the world's economic integration—as has happened at times in the past—even as global warming or the spread of the AIDS virus continued apace. It would be ironic if current protests curtailed the positive aspects of globalization while leaving the negative dimensions untouched.

Markets have unequal effects, and the inequality they produce can have powerful political consequences. But the cliché that markets always make the rich richer and the poor poorer is simply not true. Globalization, for example, has improved the lot of hundreds of millions of poor people around the world. Poverty can be reduced even when inequality increases. And in some cases inequality can even decrease. The economic gap between South Korea and industrialized countries, for example, has diminished in part because of global markets. No poor country, meanwhile, has ever become rich by isolating itself from global markets, although North Korea and Myanmar have impoverished themselves by doing so. Economic globalization, in short, may be a necessary, though not sufficient, condition for combating poverty.

The complexities of globalization have led to calls for a global institutional response. Although a hierarchical world government is neither feasible nor desirable, many forms of global governance and methods of managing common affairs already exist and can be expanded. Hundreds of organizations now regulate the global dimensions of trade, telecommunications, civil aviation, health, the environment, meteorology, and many other issues.

Antiglobalization protesters complain that international institutions are illegitimate because they are undemocratic. But the existing global institutions are quite weak and hardly threatening. Even the much-maligned World Trade Organization (WTO) has only a small budget and staff. Moreover, unlike self-appointed nongovernmental organizations (NGOs), international institutions tend to be highly responsive to national governments and can thus claim some real, if indirect, democratic legitimacy. International economic institutions, moreover, merely facilitate cooperation among member states and derive some authority from their efficacy.

Even so, in a world of transnational politics where democracy has become the touchstone of legitimacy, these arguments probably will not be enough to protect any but the most technical organizations from attack. International institutions may be weak, but their rules and resources can have powerful effects. The protesters, moreover, make some valid points. Not all member states of international organizations are themselves democratic. Long lines of delegation from multiple governments, combined with a lack of transparency, often weaken accountability. And although the organizations may be agents of states, they often represent only certain parts of those states. Thus trade ministers attend WTO meetings, finance ministers attend the meetings of the International Monetary Fund (IMF), and central bankers meet at the Bank for International Settlements in Basel. To outsiders, even within the same government, these institutions can look like closed and secretive clubs. Increasing the perceived legitimacy of international governance is therefore an important objective and requires three things: greater clarity about democracy, a richer understanding of accountability, and a willingness to experiment.

We, the People

Democracy requires government by officials who are accountable and removable by the majority of people in a jurisdiction, together with protections for individual and minority rights. But who are "we the people" in a world where political identity at the global level is so weak? "One state, one vote" is not democratic. By that formula, a citizen of the Maldive Islands would have a thousand times more voting power than would a citizen of China. On the other hand, treating the world as a single global constituency in which the majority ruled would mean that the more than 2 billion Chinese and Indians could usually get their way. (Ironically, such a world would be a nightmare for those antiglobalization NGOs that seek international environmental and labor standards, since such measures draw little support from Indian or Chinese officials.)

In a democratic system, minorities acquiesce to the will of the majority when they feel they are generally full-fledged participants in the larger community. There is little evidence, however, that such a strong sense of community exists at the global level today, or that it could soon be created. In its absence, the extension of domestic voting procedures to the global level makes little practical or normative sense. A stronger European Parliament may reduce the "democratic deficit" within a union of relatively homogeneous European states, but it is doubtful that such an institution makes sense for the world at large. Alfred, Lord Tennyson's "Parliament of man" made for great Victorian poetry, but it does not stand up to contemporary political analysis. Democracy, moreover, exists today only in certain well-ordered nation-states, and that condition is likely to change only slowly.

Still, governments can do several things to respond to the concerns about a global democratic deficit. First, they can try to design international institutions that preserve as much space as possible for domestic political processes to operate. In the WTO, for example, the procedures for settling disputes can intrude on domestic sovereignty, but a country can reject a judgment if it pays carefully limited compensation to the trade partners injured by its actions. And if a country does defect from its WTO trade agreements, the settlement procedure limits the kind of tit-for-tat downward spiral of retaliation that so devastated the world economy in the 1930s. In a sense, the procedure is like having a fuse in the electrical system of a house: better the fuse blow than the house burn down. The danger with the WTO, therefore, is not that it prevents member states from accommodating domestic political choices but rather that members will be tempted to litigate too many disputes instead of resolving them through the more flexible route of political negotiations.

Clearer Connections

Better accountability can and should start at home. If people believe that WTO meetings do not adequately account for environmental standards, they can press their governments to include environment ministers or officials in their WTO delegations. Legislatures can hold hearings before or after meetings, and legislators can themselves become national delegates to various organizations.

Governments should also make clear that democratic accountability can be quite indirect. Accountability is often assured through means other than voting, even in well-functioning democracies. In the United States, for example, the Supreme Court and the Federal Reserve Board respond to elections indirectly through a long chain of delegation, and judges and government

bankers are kept accountable by professional norms and standards, as well. There is no reason that indirect accountability cannot be consistent with democracy, or that international institutions such as the IMF and the World Bank should be held to a higher standard than are domestic institutions.

Increased transparency is also essential. In addition to voting, people in democracies debate issues using a variety of means, from letters to polls to protests. Interest groups and a free press play important roles in creating transparency in domestic democratic politics and can do so at the international level as well. NGOs are self-selected, not democratically elected, but they too can play a positive role in increasing transparency. They deserve a voice, but not a vote. For them to fill this role, they need information from and dialogue with international institutions. In some instances, such as judicial procedures or market interventions, it is unrealistic to provide information in advance, but records and justifications of decisions can later be disclosed for comment and criticism—as the Federal Reserve and the Supreme Court do in domestic politics. The same standards of transparency should be applied to NGOs themselves, perhaps encouraged by other NGOs such as Transparency International.

The private sector can also contribute to accountability. Private associations and codes, such as those established by the international chemical industry in the aftermath of the Bhopal disaster, can prevent a race to the bottom in standards. The practice of "naming and shaming" has helped consumers hold transnational firms accountable in the toy and apparel industries. And although people have unequal votes in markets, the aftermath of the Asian financial crisis may have led to more increases in transparency by corrupt governments than any formal agreements did. Open markets can help diminish the undemocratic power of local monopolies and reduce the power of entrenched and unresponsive government bureaucracies, particularly in countries where parliaments are weak. Moreover, efforts by investors to increase transparency and legal predictability can spill over to political institutions.

New Democrats

Rather than merely rejecting the poorly formulated arguments of the protesters, proponents of international institutions should experiment with ways to improve accountability. Transparency is essential, and international organizations can provide more access to their deliberations, even if after the fact. NGOs could be welcomed as observers (as the World Bank has done) or allowed to file "friend of the court" briefs in WTO dispute-settlement cases. In some cases, such as the Internet Corporation for Assigned Names and Numbers (which is incorporated as a nonprofit institution under the laws of California), experiments with direct voting for board members may prove fruitful, although the danger of their being taken over by well-organized interest groups remains a problem. Hybrid network organizations that combine governmental, intergovernmental, and nongovernmental representatives, such as the World Commission on Dams or U.N. Secretary-General Kofi Annan's Global Compact, are other avenues to explore. Assemblies of parliamentarians can also be associated with some organizations to hold hearings and receive information, even if not to vote.

In the end, there is no single answer to the question of how to reconcile the necessary global institutions with democratic accountability. Highly technical organizations may be able to derive their legitimacy from their efficacy alone. But the more an institution deals with broad values, the more its democratic legitimacy becomes relevant. People concerned about democracy will need to think harder about norms and procedures for the governance of globalization. Neither denying the problem nor yielding to demagogues in the streets will do.

RICHARD FLORIDA

THE WORLD IS SPIKY

*Globalization Has Changed the
Economic Playing Field, but
Hasn't Leveled It*

**A
Population**

*Urban areas house half of all the
world's people, and continue to
grow in both rich and poor
countries.*[1]

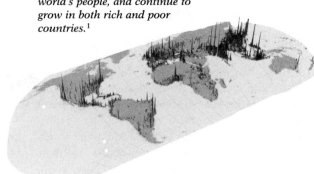

T he world, according to the title of the *New York Times* columnist Thomas Friedman's book, is flat. Thanks to advances in technology, the global playing field has been leveled, the prizes are there for the taking, and everyone's a player—no matter where on the surface of the earth he or she may reside. "In a flat world," Friedman writes, "you can innovate without having to emigrate."

Friedman is not alone in this belief: for the better part of the past century economists have been writing about the leveling effects of technology. From the invention of the telephone, the automobile, and the airplane to the rise of the personal computer and the Internet, technological progress has steadily eroded the economic importance of geographic place—or so the argument goes.

But in partnership with colleagues at George Mason University and the geographer Tim Culden, of the Center for International and Security Studies, at the University of Maryland, I've begun to chart a very different economic topography. By almost any measure the international economic landscape is not at all flat. On the contrary, our world is amazingly "spiky." In terms of both sheer economic horsepower and cutting-edge innovation, surprisingly few regions truly matter in today's global economy. What's more,

From *The Atlantic Monthly* (October 2005), pp. 48–51.

Peaks, Hills, and Valleys

When looked at through the lens of economic production, many cities with large populations are diminished and some nearly vanish. Three sorts of places make up the modern economic landscape. First are the cities that generate innovations. These are the tallest peaks; they have the capacity to attract global talent and create new products and industries. They are few in number, and difficult to topple. Second are the economic "hills" —places that manufacture the world's established goods, take its calls, and support its innovation engines. These hills can rise and fall quickly; they are prosperous but insecure. Some, like Dublin and Seoul, are growing into innovative, wealthy peaks; others are declining, eroded by high labor costs and a lack of enduring competitive advantage. Finally there are the vast valleys—places with little connection to the global economy and few immediate prospects.

the tallest peaks—the cities and regions that drive the world economy—are growing ever higher, while the valleys mostly languish.

The most obvious challenge to the flat-world hypothesis is the explosive growth of cities worldwide. More and more people are clustering in urban areas—the world's demographic mountain ranges, so to speak. The share of the world's population living in urban areas, just three

B
Light Emissions
Economic activity — roughly estimated here using light-emissions data — is remarkably concentrated. Many cities, despite their large population barely register.[2]

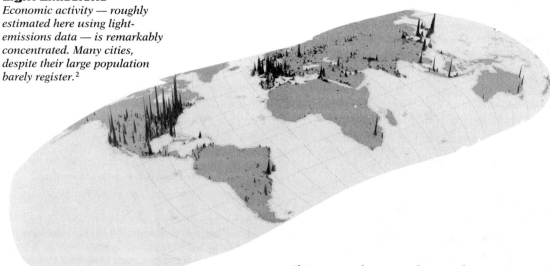

percent in 1800, was nearly 30 percent by 1950. Today it stands at about 50 percent; in advanced countries three out of four people live in urban areas. Map A shows the uneven distribution of the world's population. Five megacities currently have more than 20 million inhabitants each. Twenty-four cities have more than 10 million inhabitants, sixty more than 5 million, and 150 more than 2.5 million. Population density is of course a crude indicator of human and economic activity. But in does suggest that at least some of the tectonic forces of economics are concentrating people and resources, and pushing up some places more than others.

Still, differences in population density vastly understate the spikiness of the global economy; the continuing dominance of the world's most productive urban areas is astounding. When it comes to actual economic output, the ten largest U.S. metropolitan areas combined are behind only the United States as a whole and Japan. New York's economy alone is about the size of Russia's or Brazil's, and Chicago's is on a par with Sweden's. Together New York, Los Angeles,

Chicago, and Boston have a bigger economy than all of China. If U.S. metropolitan areas were countries, they'd make up forty-seven of the biggest 100 economies in the world.

Unfortunately, no single, comprehensive information source exists for the economic production of all the world's cities. A rough proxy is available, though. Map B shows a variation on the widely circulated view of the world at night, with higher concentrations of light—indicating higher energy use and, presumably, stronger economic production—appearing in greater relief. U.S. regions appear almost Himalayan on this map. From their summits one might look out on a smaller mountain range stretching across Europe, some isolated peaks in Asia, and a few scattered hills throughout the rest of the world.

Population and economic activity are both spiky, but it's innovation—the engine of economic growth—that is most concentrated. The World Intellectual Property Organization recorded about 300,000 patents from resident inventors in more than a hundred nations in 2002 (the most recent year for which statistics are available). Nearly two thirds of them went to American and Japanese inventors. Eighty-five percent went to the residents of just five coun-

C

Patents

Just a few places produce most of the world's innovations. Innovation remains difficult without a critical mass of financiers, entrepreneurs, and scientists, often nourished by world-class universities and flexible corporations.

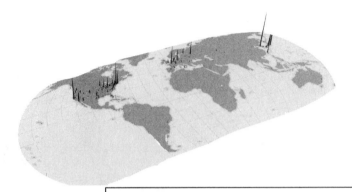

The Geography of Innovation

Commercial innovation and scientific advance are both highly concentrated—but not always in the same places. Several cities in East Asia—particularly in Japan—are home to prolific business innovation but still depend disproportionately on scientific breakthroughs made elsewhere. Likewise, some cities excel in scientific research but not in commercial adaptation. The few places that do both well are very strongly positioned in the global economy. These regions have little to fear, and much to gain, from continuing globalization.

tries (Japan, the United States, South Korea, Germany, and Russia).

Worldwide patent statistics can be somewhat misleading, since different countries follow different standards for granting patents. But patents granted in the United States—which receives patent applications for nearly all major innovations worldwide, and holds them to the same strict standards—tell a similar story. Nearly 90,000 of the 170,000 patents granted in the United States in 2002 went to Americans. Some 35,000 went to Japanese inventors, and 11,000 to Germans. The next ten most innovative countries—including the usual suspects in Europe plus Taiwan, South Korea, Israel, and Canada—produced roughly 25,000 more. The rest of the broad, flat world accounted for just five percent of all innovations patented in the United States. In 2003 India generated 341 U.S. patents and China 297. The University of California alone generated more than either country. IBM accounted for five times as many as the two combined.

This is not to say that Indians and Chinese are not innovative. On the contrary, AnnaLee Saxenian, of the University of California at Berkeley, has shown that Indian and Chinese entrepreneurs founded or co-founded roughly 30 percent of all Silicon Valley startups in the late 1990s. But these fundamentally creative people had to travel to Silicon Valley and be absorbed into its innovative ecosystem before their

ideas became economically viable. Such ecosystems matter, and there aren't many of them.

Map C—which makes use of data from both the World Intellectual Property Organizations and the U.S. Patent and Trademark Office—shows a world composed of innovation peaks and valleys. Tokyo, Seoul, New York, and San Francisco remain the front-runners in the patenting competition. Boston, Seattle, Austin, Toronto, Vancouver, Berlin, Stockholm, Helsinki, London, Osaka, Taipei, and Sydney also stand out.

Map D shows the residence of the 1,200 most heavily cited scientists in leading fields. Scientific advance is even more concentrated than patent production. Most occurs not just in a handful of countries but in a handful of cities—primarily in the United States and Europe. Chinese and Indian cities do not even register. As far as global innovation is concerned, perhaps a few dozen places worldwide really compete at the cutting edge.

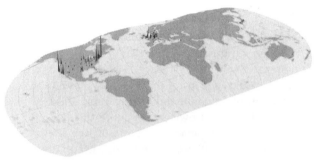

D

Scientific Citations

The world's most prolific and influential scientific researchers overwhelmingly reside in U.S. and European cities.[4]

Concentrations of creative and talented people are particularly important for innovation, according to the Nobel Prize–winning economist Robert Lucas. Ideas flow more freely, are honed more sharply, and can be put into practice more quickly when large numbers of innovators, implementers, and financial backers are in constant contact with one another, both in and out of the office. Creative people cluster not simply because they like to be around one another or they prefer cosmopolitan centers with lots of amenities, though both those things count. They and their companies also cluster because of the powerful productivity advantages, economies of scale, and knowledge spillovers such density brings.

So although one might not *have* to emigrate to innovate, it certainly appears that innovation, economic growth, and prosperity occur in those places that attract a critical mass of top creative talent. Because globalization has increased the returns to innovation, by allowing innovative products and services to quickly reach consumers worldwide, it has strengthened the lure that innovation centers hold for our planet's best and brightest, reinforcing the spikiness of wealth and economic production.

The main difference between now and even a couple of decades ago is not that the world has become flatter but that the world's peaks have become slightly more dispersed—and that the world's hills, the industrial and service centers that produce mature products and support innovation centers, have proliferated and shifted. For the better part of the twentieth century the United States claimed the lion's share of the global economy's innovation peaks, leaving a few outposts in Europe and Japan. But America has since lost some of those peaks, as such industrial-age powerhouses as Pittsburgh, St. Louis, and Cleveland have eroded. At the same time, a number of regions in Europe, Scandinavia, Canada, and the Pacific Rim have moved up.

The world today looks flat to some because the economic and social distances between peaks worldwide have gotten smaller. Connection between peaks has been strengthened by the easy mobility of the global creative class—about 150 million people worldwide. They participate in a global technology system and a global labor market that allow them to migrate freely among the world's leading cities. In a Brookings Institution study the demographer Robert Lang and the world-cities expert Peter Taylor identify a relatively small group of leading city-regions—London, New York, Paris, Tokyo, Hong Kong, Singapore, Chicago, Los Angeles, and San Francisco among them—that are strongly connected to one another.

But Lang and Taylor also identify a much larger group of city-regions that are far more locally oriented. People in spiky places are often more connected to one another, even from half a world away, than they are to people and places in their veritable back yards.

———

The flat-world theory is not completely misguided. It is a welcome supplement to the widely accepted view (illustrated by the Live 8 concerts and Bono's forays into Africa, by the writings of Jeffrey Sachs and the UN Millennium project) that the growing divide between rich and poor countries is the fundamental feature of the world economy. Friedman's theory more accurately depicts a developing world with capabilities that translate into economic development. In his view, for example, the emerging economies of India and China combine cost advantages, high-tech skills, and entrepreneurial energy, enabling those countries to compete effectively for industries and jobs. The tensions set in motion as the playing field is leveled affect mainly the advanced countries, which see not only manufacturing work but also higher-end jobs, in fields such as software development and financial services, increasingly threatened by off-shoring.

But the flat-world theory blinds us to far more insidious tensions among the world's growing peaks, sinking valleys, and shifting hills. The innovative, talent-attracting "have" regions seem increasingly remote from the talent-exporting "have-not" regions. Second-tier cities, from Detroit and Wolfsburg to Nagoya and Mexico City, are entering an escalating and potentially devastating competition for jobs, talent, and investment. And inequality is growing across the world and within countries.

This is far more barrowing than the flat world Friedman describes, and a good deal more treacherous than the old rich-poor divide. We see its effects in the political backlash against globalization in the advanced world. The recent rejection of the EU constitution by the French, for example, resulted in large part from high rates of "no" votes in suburban and rural quarters, which understandably fear globalization and integration.

But spiky globalization also wreaks havoc on poorer places. China is seeing enormous concentrations of talent and innovation in centers such as Shanghai, Shenzhen, and Beijing, all of which are a world apart from its vast, impoverished rural areas. According to detailed polling by Richard Burkholder, of Callup, average household incomes in urban China are now triple those in rural regions, and they've grown more than three times as fast since 1999; perhaps as a result, urban and rural Chinese now have very different, often conflicting political and lifestyle values. India is growing even more divided, as Bangalore, Hyderabad, and parts of New Delhi and Bombay pull away from the rest of that enormous country, creating destabilizing political tensions. Economic and demographic forces are sorting people around the world into geographically clustered "tribes" so different (and often mutually antagonistic) as to create a somewhat Hobbesian vision.

We are thus confronted with a difficult predicament. Economic progress requires that the peaks grow stronger and taller. But such growth will exacerbate economic and social disparities, fomenting political reactions that could threaten further innovation and economic progress. Managing the disparities between peaks and valleys worldwide—raising the valleys without shearing off the peaks—will be among the top political challenges of the coming decades.

NOTES

1. Map data source: Center for International Earth Science Information Network, Columbia University, and Centro Internacional de Agricultura Tropical.
2. Map data source: U.S. Defense Meteorological Satellite Program.
3. Map data source: World Intellectual Property Organization; U.S. Patent and Trademark Office.
4. Map data source: Michael Batty, Centre for Advanced Spatial Analysis, University College London (www.casa.ucl.ac.uk).

THE ECONOMIST

GRINDING THE POOR

Sceptics Charge that Globalisation Especially Hurts Poor Workers in the Developing Countries. It Does Not.

For the most part, it seems, workers in rich countries have little to fear from globalisation, and a lot to gain. But is the same thing true for workers in poor countries? The answer is that they are even more likely than their rich-country counterparts to benefit, because they have less to lose and more to gain.

Orthodox economics takes an optimistic line on integration and the developing countries. Openness to foreign trade and investment should encourage capital to flow to poor economies. In the developing world, capital is scarce, so the returns on investment there should be higher than in the industrialised countries, where the best opportunities to make money by adding capital to labour have already been used up. If poor countries lower their barriers to trade and investment, the theory goes, rich foreigners will want to send over some of their capital.

If this inflow of resources arrives in the form of loans or portfolio investment, it will supplement domestic savings and loosen the financial constraint on additional investment by local companies. If it arrives in the form of new foreign-controlled operations, FDI, so much the better: this kind of capital brings technology and skills from abroad packaged along with it, with less financial risk as well. In either case, the addition to investment ought to push incomes up, partly by raising the demand for labour and partly by making labour more productive.

From *The Economist* (September 27, 2001).

This is why workers in FDI-receiving countries should be in an even better position to profit from integration than workers in FDI-sending countries. Also, with or without inflows of foreign capital, the same static and dynamic gains from trade should apply in developing countries as in rich ones. This gains-from-trade logic often arouses suspicion, because the benefits seem to come from nowhere. Surely one side or the other must lose. Not so. The benefits that a rich country gets through trade do not come at the expense of its poor-country trading partners, or vice versa. Recall that according to the theory, trade is a positive-sum game. In all these transactions, both sides—exporters and importers, borrowers and lenders, shareholders and workers—can gain.

What, if anything, might spoil the simple theory and make things go awry? Plenty, say the sceptics.

First, they argue, telling developing countries to grow through trade, rather than through building industries to serve domestic markets, involves a fallacy of composition. If all poor countries tried to do this simultaneously, the price of their exports would be driven down on world markets. The success of the East Asian tigers, the argument continues, owed much to the fact that so many other developing countries chose to discourage trade rather than promote it. This theory of "export pessimism" was influential with many developing-country governments up until the 1980s, and seems to lie behind the thinking of many sceptics today.

A second objection to the openness-is-good orthodoxy concerns not trade but FDI. The standard thinking assumes that foreign capital pays for investment that makes economic sense—the kind that will foster development. Experience shows that this is often not so. For one reason or another, the inflow of capital may produce little or nothing of value, sometimes less than nothing. The money may be wasted or stolen. If it was borrowed, all there will be to show for it is an insupportable debt to foreigners. Far from merely failing to advance development, this kind of financial integration sets it back.

Third, the sceptics point out, workers in developing countries lack the rights, legal protections and union representation enjoyed by their counterparts in rich countries. This is why, in the eyes of the multinationals, hiring them makes such good sense. Lacking in bargaining power, workers do not benefit as they should from an increase in the demand for labour. Their wages do not go up. They may have no choice but to work in sweatshops, suffering unhealthy or dangerous conditions, excessive hours or even physical abuse. In the worst cases, children as well as adults are the victims.

Is Trade Good for Growth?

All this seems very complicated. Can the doubters be answered simply by measuring the overall effect of openness on economic growth? Some economists think so, and have produced a variety of much-quoted econometric studies apparently confirming that trade promotes development. Studies by Jeffrey Sachs and Andrew Warner at Harvard, by David Dollar and Aart Kraay of the World Bank, and by Jeffrey Frankel of Harvard and David Romer of Berkeley, are among the most frequently cited. Studies such as these are enough to convince most economists that trade does indeed promote growth. But they cannot be said to settle the matter. If the application of econometrics to other big, complicated questions in economics is any guide, they probably never will: the precise economic linkages that underlie the correlations may always be too difficult to uncover.

This is why a good number of economists, including some of the most distinguished advocates of liberal trade, are unpersuaded by this

kind of work. For every regression "proving" that trade promotes growth, it is too easy to tweak a choice of variable here and a period of analysis there to "prove" that it does not. Among the sceptics, Dani Rodrik has led the assault on the pro-trade regression studies. But economists such as Jagdish Bhagwati and T.N. Srinivasan, both celebrated advocates of trade liberalisation, are also pretty scathing about the regression evidence.

Look elsewhere, though, and there is no lack of additional evidence, albeit of a more variegated and less easily summarised sort, that trade promotes development. Of the three criticisms just stated of the orthodox preference for liberal trade, the first and most influential down the years has been the "export pessimism" argument—the idea that liberalising trade will be self-defeating if too many developing countries try to do it simultaneously. What does the evidence say about that?

Pessimism Confounded

It does not say that the claim is nonsense. History shows that the prediction of persistently falling export prices has proved correct for some commodity exporters: demand for some commodities has failed to keep pace with growth in global incomes. And nobody will ever know what would have happened over the past few decades if all the developing countries had promoted trade more vigorously, because they didn't. But there are good practical reasons to regard the pessimism argument, as applied to poor-country exports in general, as wrong.

The developing countries as a group may be enormous in terms of geography and population, but in economic terms they are small. Taken together, the exports of all the world's poor and middle-income countries (including comparative giants such as China, India, Brazil and Mexico, big oil exporters such as Saudi Arabia, and large-scale manufacturers such as South Korea, Taiwan and Malaysia) represent only about 5% of global output. This is an amount roughly equivalent to the GDP of Britain. Even if growth in the global demand for imports were somehow capped, a concerted export drive by those parts of the developing world not already engaged in the effort would put no great strain on the global trading system.

In any event, though, the demand for imports is not capped. In effect, export pessimism involves a fallacy of its own—a "lump-of-trade" fallacy, akin to the idea of a "lump of labour" (whereby a growing population is taken to imply an ever-rising rate of unemployment, there being only so many jobs to go round). The overall growth of trade, and the kinds of product that any particular country may buy or sell, are not pre-ordained. As Mr. Bhagwati and Mr. Srinivasan argued in a recent review of the connections between trade and development, forecasts of the poor countries' potential to expand their exports have usually been too low, partly because forecasters concentrate on existing exports and neglect new ones, some of which may be completely unforeseen. Unexpected shifts in the pattern of output have often proved very important.

Pessimists also make too little of the scope for intra-industry specialisation in trade, which gives developing countries a further set of new opportunities. The same goes for new trade among developing countries, as opposed to trade with the rich world. Often, as developing countries grow, they move away from labour-intensive manufactures to more sophisticated kinds of production: this makes room in the markets they previously served for goods from countries that are not yet so advanced. For example, in the 1970s, Japan withdrew from labour-intensive manufacturing, making way for exports from the East Asian tigers. In the 1980s and 1990s, the tigers did the same, as China began moving into those markets. And as developing countries grow by exporting, their own demand for imports rises.

It is one thing to argue that relying on trade is likely to be self-defeating, as the export pes-

simists claim; it is another to say that trade actually succeeds in promoting growth. The most persuasive evidence that it does lies in the contrasting experiences from the 1950s onwards of the East Asian tigers, on one side, and the countries that chose to discourage trade and pursue "import-substituting industrialisation" (ISI) on the other, such as India, much of Latin America and much of Africa.

Years ago, in an overlapping series of research projects, great effort went into examining the developing countries' experience with trade policy during the 1950s, 60s and early 70s. This period saw lasting surges of growth without precedent in history. At the outset, South Korea, for instance, was a poor country, with an income per head in 1955 of around $400 (in today's prices), and such poor economic prospects that American officials predicted abject and indefinite dependence on aid. Within a single generation it became a mighty exporter and world-ranking industrial power.

Examining the record up to the 1970s, and the experience of development elsewhere in East Asia and other poor regions of the world, economists at the OECD, the World Bank and America's National Bureau of Economic Research came to see the crucial importance of "outward orientation"—that is, of the link between trade and growth. The finding held across a range of countries, regardless of differences in particular policies, institutions and political conditions, all of which varied widely. An unusually impressive body of evidence and analysis discredited the ISI orthodoxy and replaced it with a new one, emphasising trade.

The Trouble with ISI

What was wrong with ISI, according to these researchers? In principle, nothing much; the problems arose over how it worked in practice. The whole idea of ISI was to drive a wedge between world prices and domestic prices, so as to create a bias in favour of producing for the home market and therefore a bias against producing for the export market. In principle, this bias could be modest and uniform; in practice, ISI often produced an anti-export bias both severe and wildly variable between industries. Managing the price-rigging apparatus proved too much for the governments that were attempting it: the policy produced inadvertently large and complex distortions in the pattern of production that often became self-perpetuating and even self-reinforcing. Once investment had been sunk in activities that were profitable only because of tariffs and quotas, any attempt to remove those restrictions was strongly resisted.

ISI also often had an even more pernicious consequence: corruption. The more protected the economy, the greater the gains to be had from illicit activity such as smuggling. The bigger the economic distortions, the bigger the incentive to bribe the government to tweak the rules and tilt the corresponding pattern of surpluses and shortages. Corruption and controls go hand in hand. ISI is not the only instance of this rule in the developing countries, but it has proved especially susceptible to shady practices.

Today, developing-country governments are constantly, and rightly, urged to battle corruption and establish the rule of law. This has become a cliché that all sides in the development debate can agree on. But defeating corruption in an economy with pervasive market-suppressing controls, where the rewards to illegality are so high, is extraordinarily hard. This is a connection that people who favour closed or restricted markets prefer to ignore. Limited government, to be sure, is not necessarily clean; but unlimited government, history suggests, never is.

Remember, Remember

On the whole, ISI failed; almost everywhere, trade has been good for growth. The trouble is, this verdict was handed down too long ago. Economists are notoriously ignorant of even recent economic history. The lessons about what

world markets did for the tigers in the space of few decades, and the missed opportunities of, say, India (which was well placed to achieve as much), have already been forgotten by many. The East Asian financial crisis of 1997–98 also helped to erase whatever lessons had been learned. And yet the prosperity of East Asia today, crisis and continuing difficulties notwithstanding, bears no comparison with the economic position of India, or Pakistan, or any of the other countries that separated themselves for so much longer from the international economy.

By and large, though, the governments of many developing countries continue to be guided by the open-market orthodoxy that has prevailed since the 1980s. Many want to promote trade in particular and engagement with the world economy in general. Even some sceptics might agree that trade is good for growth —but they would add that growth is not necessarily good for poor workers. In fact, it is likely to be bad for the poor, they argue, if the growth in question has been promoted by trade or foreign capital.

Capital inflows, they say, make economies less stable, exposing workers to the risk of financial crisis and to the attentions of western banks and the International Monetary Fund. Also, they argue, growth that is driven by trade or by FDI gives western multinationals a leading role in third-world development. That is bad, because western multinationals are not interested in development at all, only in making bigger profits by ensuring that the poor stay poor. The proof of this, say sceptics, lies in the evidence that economic inequality increases even as developing countries (and rich countries, for that matter) increase their national income, and in the multinationals' direct or indirect use of third-world sweatshops. So if workers' welfare is your main concern, the fact that trade promotes growth, even if true, is beside the point.

Yet there is solid evidence that growth helps the poor. Developing countries that have achieved sustained and rapid growth, as in East Asia, have made remarkable progress in reduc-

Figure 1
Growth is Good to the Poor.
Change in per capita income, %.

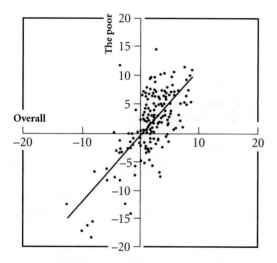

Note: Each point represents one country. Horizontal axis shows change overall in per capita income; vertical axis shows change in per capita income of the poor.
Source: World Bank

ing poverty. And the countries where widespread poverty persists, or is worsening, are those where growth is weakest, notably in Africa. Although economic policy can make a big difference to the extent of poverty, in the long run growth is much more important.

It is sometimes claimed that growth is less effective in raising the incomes of the poor in developing countries than in rich countries. This is a fallacy. A recent study confirms that, in 80 countries across the world over the past 40 years, the incomes of the poor have risen one for one with overall growth (see figure 1).

If all this is true, why does global income inequality seem to be widening? First, the evidence is not at all clear-cut. Much depends on how you make your comparisons. An overall comparison of country aggregates—comparing rich countries with poor countries—is generally more encouraging than a comparison of the richest 10% of people in the world with the poorest 10%. In 1975, America's income per head was 19 times

bigger than China's ($16,000 against $850); by 1995, the ratio had fallen to six ($23,000 against $3,700). On the other hand it is true that Africa's income per head is rising more slowly than America's: as a result, their income-gap ratio has increased, from 12 in 1975 to 19 in 1995. But it would be odd to blame globalisation for holding Africa back. Africa has been left out of the global economy, partly because its governments used to prefer it that way. China has embraced the global economy with a vengeance—and see how well it has done.

Better Than Nothing

Statistical difficulties aside, suppose it were true that global inequality is increasing. Would that be a terrible indictment of globalisation, as sceptics seem to suppose? Perhaps not. It would be disturbing, and extremely surprising, if poor countries engaged in globalisation were failing to catch up—but they aren't, as China and many other avid globalisers show. It would also be disturbing if inequality across the world as a whole were rising because the incomes of the poorest were falling in absolute terms, rather than merely in relative terms—but this is extremely rare. Even in Africa, which is doing so badly in relative terms, incomes have been rising and broader measures of development have been getting better. It may be too little, but it is not nothing, merely because other countries have been doing better.

The sceptics are right to be disturbed by sweatshops, child labour, bonded labour and the other gross abuses that go on in many poor countries (and in the darkest corners of rich ones, too). But what makes people vulnerable to these practices is poverty. It is essential to ask if remedial measures proposed will reduce poverty: otherwise, in attacking the symptoms of the problem, you may be strengthening their underlying cause. It is one thing for the sceptics to insist, for instance, that child labour be prohibited; it is quite another to ensure that the children concerned go to school instead, rather than being driven to scrape a living in even crueller conditions.

The barriers to trade that many sceptics call for seem calculated to make these problems worse. Some sceptics want, in effect, to punish every export worker in India for the persistence of child labour in parts of the Indian economy. This seems morally indefensible as well as counter-productive in economic terms. The same goes for the campaign to hobble the multinationals. The more thoroughly these companies penetrate the markets of the third world, the faster they introduce their capital and working practices, the sooner poverty will retreat and the harder it will be for such abuses to persist.

This is not to deny that the multinationals are in it for the money—and will strive to hire labour as cheaply as they can. But this does not appear to be a problem for the workers who compete to take those jobs. People who go to work for a foreign-owned company do so because they prefer it to the alternative, whatever that may be. In their own judgment, the new jobs make them better off.

But suppose for the moment that the sceptics are right, and that these workers, notwithstanding their own preferences, are victims of exploitation. One possibility would be to encourage foreign firms to pay higher wages in the third world. Another course, favoured by many sceptics, is to discourage multinationals from operating in the third world at all. But if the aim is to help the developing-country workers, this second strategy is surely wrong. If multinationals stopped hiring in the third world, the workers concerned would, on their own estimation, become worse off.

Compared with demands that the multinationals stay out of the third world altogether, the idea of merely shaming them into paying their workers higher wages seems a model of logic and compassion. Still, even this apparently harmless plan needs to be handled cautiously.

The question is, how much more is enough? At one extreme, you could argue that if a multi-national company hires workers in developing countries for less than it pays their rich-country counterparts, it is guilty of exploitation. But to insist on parity would be tantamount to putting a stop to direct investment in the third world. By and large, workers in developing countries are paid less than workers in rich countries because they are less productive: those workers are attractive to rich-country firms, despite their lower productivity, because they are cheap. If you were to eliminate that offsetting advantage, you would make them unemployable.

Of course you could argue that decency merely requires multinationals to pay wages that are "fair," even if not on a par with wages in the industrial countries. Any mandatory increase in wages runs the risk of reducing the number of jobs created, but you could reply that the improvement in welfare for those who get the higher pay, so long as the mandated increase was moderate and feasible, would outweigh that drawback. Even then, however, two difficult questions would still need to be answered. What is a "fair" wage, and who is to decide?

What Fairness Requires

A "fair" wage can be deduced, you might argue, from economic principles: if workers are paid a wage that is less than their marginal productivity, you could say they are being exploited. Some sceptics regard it as obvious that third-world workers are being paid less than this. Their reasoning is that such workers are about as productive as their rich-country counterparts, and yet are paid only a small fraction of what rich-country workers receive. Yet there is clear evidence that third-world workers are not as productive as rich-country workers. Often they are working with less advanced machinery; and their productivity also depends on the surrounding economic infrastructure. More tellingly, though, if poor-country workers were being paid less than their marginal productivity, firms could raise their profits by hiring more of them in or-

Table 1. The Lure of Multinationals

Average wage paid by foreign affiliates and average domestic manufacturing wage by host-country income, 1994

	All countries	High-income	Middle-income	Low-income
Average wage paid by affiliates, $'000	15.1	32.4	9.5	3.4
Average domestic manufacturing wage, $'000	9.9	22.5	5.4	1.7
Ratio	1.5	1.4	1.8	2.0

Source: Edward M. Graham, Institute for International Economics

der to increase output. Sceptics should not need reminding that companies always prefer more profit to less.

Productivity aside, should "good practice" require, at least, that multinationals pay their poor-country employees more than other local workers? Not necessarily. To hire the workers they need, they may not have to offer a premium over local wages if they can provide other advantages. In any case, lack of a premium need not imply that they are failing to raise living standards. By entering the local labour market and adding to the total demand for labour, the multinationals would most likely be raising wages for all workers, not just those they hire.

In fact, though, the evidence suggests that multinationals do pay a wage premium—a reflection, presumably, of efforts to recruit relatively skilled workers. Table 1 shows that the wages paid by foreign affiliates to poor-country workers are about double the local manufacturing wage; wages paid by affiliates to workers in middle-income countries are about 1.8 times the local

manufacturing wage (both calculations exclude wages paid to the firms' expatriate employees). The numbers come from calculations by Edward Graham at the Institute for International Economics. Mr. Graham cites other research which shows that wages in Mexico are highest near the border with the United States, where the operations of American-controlled firms are concentrated. Separate studies on Mexico, Venezuela, China and Indonesia have all found that foreign investors pay their local workers significantly better than other local employers.

Despite all this, you might still claim that the workers are not being paid a "fair" wage. But in the end, who is to make this judgment? The sceptics distrust governments, politicians, international bureaucrats and markets alike. So they end up appointing themselves as judges, overruling not just governments and markets but also the voluntary preferences of the workers most directly concerned. That seems a great deal to take on.

11 POLITICAL VIOLENCE

In this chapter we look at violence against states and peoples that is not carried out by states themselves. Recall from Chapter 2 that the state is commonly defined as the monopoly of violence over a territory. States use this force at the domestic level to generate stability through such institutions as the law and police. At the international level, armies and diplomacy help generate peace. But, at times, the monopoly of force may escape state control, as in the case of revolutions and terrorism.

In some circumstances, the public may seek to overthrow the current regime through revolution. Theda Skocpol transformed political science with her piece, "France, Russia, China: A Structural Analysis of Social Revolutions" (1976). Expanded in her 1979 book States and Social Revolutions, Skocpol's thinking on revolution contributed to political science by returning our attention to the state, and States and Social Revolutions went on to become one of the most cited works in the field. Why do revolutions, sweeping transformations in existing regime and state institutions, occur? In each case, Skocpol believes that a particular set of conditions in the state and society is necessary to set such revolutions in motion. Her analysis, influenced by Marx, is "structural." That is to say, institutions are central (if not decisive) in shaping the likelihood for dramatic political change.

While Skocpol emphasizes the importance of institutions in bringing about revolution, Martha Crenshaw's 1981 piece, "The Causes of Terrorism," focuses more on the individual motivations that lead people to resort to terrorist acts. Crenshaw notes that certain structural preconditions can foster terrorism, but this is not enough. Central is the role of a minority or elite group, their grievances and perceived lack of alternatives, and the internal culture they foster. Where Skocpol portrays revolutions as events in which people (even leaders) play a relatively small role, empowered by larger institutional conditions, Crenshaw emphasizes the role of individual and group motivation in carrying out terrorist acts. Overall, it is worth asking oneself how well Crenshaw's work, written twenty years before the attacks of September 11, remains useful in helping us understand current terrorist threats.

If Skocpol helps us to understand the structural sources of political violence, and Crenshaw the individual factors, then Buruma and Margalit's "Occidentalism" (2002) helps us to understand the role of ideas and ideology in these conflicts. Their notion of "Occidentalism" is a hatred of modernity and the West for its emphasis on materialism, individualism, and the mediocrity that mass-democratic life inevitably produces. These anti-Western views are not new, nor did they originate in the Middle East or Islam. Rather, they emerged from within the West itself in reaction to modernization, and they can be found at the core of earlier fascist and communist ideologies. The current struggle against terrorism can thus be seen as simply a new variant of an ongoing struggle against modernity (and not the end of history, as Fukuyama asserted in Chapter 10).

Our last piece applies the work of these scholars to Al Qaeda. Jack Goldstone's "States, Terrorists, and the Clash of Civilizations" (2002) categorizes terrorism into a limited number of forms, similar to those of Crenshaw. However, he also emphasizes the notion of a hybrid system, in which movements for national revolution merge with groups that hold international revolutionary goals. This is consistent with the discussion in Chapter 10 of how globalization blurs the line between domestic and international politics. Goldstone does not believe that the resolution of specific domestic conflicts or structural problems will bring an end to this recent form of terrorism. If anything, Goldstone sees that solutions will be found in part in the establishment of authority where states have failed (see Chapter 2). Al Qaeda's terrorism utilizes state weaknesses and a globalized world to become an agent seeking revolutionary change. Whether states are able to maintain their capacity and autonomy, and whether they can and will share this power to achieve a common counterterrorist goal, will be critical in their ability to defeat Al Qaeda.

THEDA SKOCPOL

FRANCE, RUSSIA, CHINA: A STRUCTURAL ANALYSIS OF SOCIAL REVOLUTIONS

A revolution," writes Samuel P. Huntington in *Political Order in Changing Societies*, "is a rapid, fundamental, and violent domestic

From *Comparative Studies in Society and History* 18, no. 2 (April 1976) pp. 175–203. Some of the author's notes have been omitted.

change in the dominant values and myths of a society, in its political institutions, social structure, leadership, and government activities and policies."[1] In *The Two Tactics of Social Democracy in the Democratic Revolution*, Lenin provides a different, but complementary perspective: "Revolutions," he says, "are the festivals of the oppressed and the exploited. At no other time are the masses of the people in a position to come forward so actively as creators of a new social order."[2]

Together these two quotes delineate the distinctive features of *social revolutions*. As Huntington points out, social revolutions are rapid, basic transformations of socio-economic and political institutions, and—as Lenin so vividly reminds us—social revolutions are accompanied and in part effectuated through class upheavals from below. It is this combination of thoroughgoing structural transformation and massive class upheavals that sets social revolutions apart from coups, rebellions, and even political revolutions and national independence movements.

If one adopts such a specific definition, then clearly only a handful of successful social revolutions have ever occurred. France, 1789, Russia, 1917, and China, 1911–49, are the most dramatic and clear-cut instances. Yet these momentous upheavals have helped shape the fate of the majority of mankind, and their causes, consequences, and potentials have preoccupied many thoughtful people since the late eighteenth century.

Nevertheless, recently, social scientists have evidenced little interest in the study of social revolutions as such. They have submerged revolutions within more general categories—such as "political violence," "collective behavior," "internal war," or "deviance"—shorn of historical specificity and concern with large-scale social change.[3] The focus has been mostly on styles of behavior common to wide ranges of collective incidents (ranging from riots to coups to revolutions, from panics to hostile outbursts to "value-oriented movements," and from ideological sects to revolutionary parties), any of which might occur in any type of society at any time or place. Revolutions tend increasingly to be viewed not as "locomotives of history," but as extreme forms of one or another sort of behavior that social scientists, along with established authorities everywhere, find problematic and perturbing.

Why this avoidance by social science of the specific problem of social revolution? Ideological bias might be invoked as an explanation, but even if it were involved, it would not suffice. An earlier generation of American social scientists, certainly no more politically radical than the present generation, employed the "natural history" approach to analyze handfuls of cases of great revolutions.[4] In large part, present preoccupation with broader categories can be understood as a reaction against this natural history approach, deemed by its critics too "historical" and "a-theoretical."

In the "Introduction" to a 1964 book entitled *Internal War*, Harry Eckstein defines "a theoretical subject" as a "set of phenomena about which one can develop informative, testable generalizations that hold for all instances of the subject, and some of which apply to those instances alone."[5] He goes on to assert that while "a statement about two or three cases is certainly a generalization in the dictionary sense, a generalization in the methodological sense must usually be based on more; it ought to cover a number of cases large enough for certain rigorous testing procedures like statistical analysis to be used."[6] Even many social scientists who are not statistically oriented would agree with the spirit of this statement: theory in social science should concern itself only with general phenomena; the "unique" should be relegated to "narrative historians."

Apparently it directly follows that no theory specific to social revolution is possible, that the *explanandum* of any theory which sheds light on social revolutions must be something more general than social revolution itself. Hence the efforts to conceptualize revolution as an extreme instance of patterns of belief or behavior which are also present in other situations or events.

This approach, however, allows considerations of technique to define away substantive problems. Revolutions are not just extreme forms of individual or collective behavior. They are distinctive conjunctures of socio-historical structures and processes. One must comprehend them as complex wholes—however few the cases—or not at all.

Fortunately social science is not devoid of a way of confronting this kind of problem. Social revolutions *can* be treated as a "theoretical subject." To test hypotheses about them, one may employ the comparative method, with national historical trajectories as the units of comparison. As many students of society have noted, the comparative method is nothing but that mode of multivariate analysis to which sociologists necessarily resort when experimental manipulations are not possible and when there are "too many variables and not enough cases"—that is, not enough cases for statistical testing of hypotheses.[7] According to this method, one looks for concomitant variations, contrasting cases where the phenomena in which one is interested are present with cases where they are absent, controlling in the process for as many sources of variation as one can, by contrasting positive and negative instances which otherwise are as similar as possible.

Thus, in my inquiry into the conditions for the occurrence and short-term outcomes of the great historical social revolutions in France, Russia and China, I have employed the comparative historical method, specifically contrasting the positive cases with (a) instances of non-social revolutionary modernization, such as occurred in Japan, Germany and Russia (up to 1904), and with (b) instances of abortive social revolutions, in particular Russia in 1905 and Prussia/Germany in 1848. These comparisons have helped me to understand those aspects of events and of structures and processes which distinctively rendered the French, Chinese and Russian Revolutions successful social revolutions. In turn, the absence of conditions identified as positively crucial in France, Russia and China constitutes equally well an explanation of why social revolutions have not occurred, or have failed, in other societies. In this way, hypotheses developed, refined, and tested in the comparative historical analysis of a handful of cases achieve a potentially general significance.

Explaining the Historical Cases: Revolution in Modernizing Agrarian Bureaucracies

Social revolutions in France, Russia and China occurred, during the earlier world-historical phases of modernization, in agrarian bureaucratic societies situated within, or newly incorporated into, international fields dominated by more economically modern nations abroad. In each case, social revolution was a conjuncture of three developments: (1) the collapse or incapacitation of central administrative and military machineries; (2) widespread peasant rebellions; and (3) marginal elite political movements. What each social revolution minimally "accomplished" was the extreme rationalization and centralization of state institutions, the removal of a traditional landed upper class from intermediate (regional and local) quasi-political supervision of the peasantry, and the elimination or diminution of the economic power of a landed upper class.

In the pages that follow, I shall attempt to explain the three great historical social revolutions, first, by discussing the institutional characteristics of agrarian states, and their special vulnerabilities and potentialities during the earlier world-historical phases of modernization, and second, by pointing to the peculiar characteristics of old regimes in France, Russia and China, which made them uniquely vulnerable among the earlier modernizing agrarian states to social-revolutionary transformations. Finally, I shall suggest reasons for similarities and differences in the outcomes of the great historical social revolutions.

An agrarian bureaucracy is an agricultural society in which social control rests on a division of labor and a coordination of effort between a semi-bureaucratic state and a landed upper class.[8] The landed upper class typically retains, as an adjunct to its landed property, considerable (though varying in different cases) undifferentiated local and regional authority over the peasant majority of the population. The partially

bureaucratic central state extracts taxes and labor from peasants either indirectly through
landlord intermediaries or else directly, but with
(at least minimal) reliance upon cooperation
from individuals of the landed upper class. In
turn, the landed upper class relies upon the
backing of a coercive state to extract rents
and/or dues from the peasantry. At the political
center, autocrat, bureaucracy, and army monopolize decisions, yet (in varying degrees and
modes) accommodate the regional and local
power of the landed upper class and (again, to
varying degrees) recruit individual members
of this class into leading positions in the state
system.

Agrarian bureaucracies are inherently vulnerable to peasant rebellions. Subject to claims
on their surpluses, and perhaps their labor, by
landlords and state agents, peasants chronically
resent both. To the extent that the agrarian economy is commercialized, merchants are also
targets of peasant hostility. In all agrarian bureaucracies at all times, and in France, Russia
and China in non-revolutionary times, peasants
have had grievances enough to warrant, and recurrently spur, rebellions. Economic crises
(which are endemic in semi-commercial agrarian economies anyway) and/or increased demands from above for rents or taxes might
substantially enhance the likelihood of rebellions
at particular times. But such events ought to be
treated as short-term precipitants of peasant unrest, not fundamental underlying causes.

Modernization is best conceived not only
as an *intra*societal process of economic development accompanied by lagging or leading
changes in non-economic institutional spheres,
but also as a world-historic *inter*societal phenomenon. Thus,

> a necessary condition of a society's modernization
> is its incorporation into the historically unique
> network of societies that arose first in Western Eu-
> rope in early modern times and today encom-
> passes enough of the globe's population for the
> world to be viewed for some purposes as if it con-
> sisted of a single network of societies.[9]

Of course, societies have always interacted.
What was special about the modernizing intersocietal network that arose in early modern Europe was, first, that it was based upon trade
in commodities and manufactures, as well as
upon strategic politico-military competition between independent states,[10] and, second, that it
incubated the "first (self-propelling) industrialization" of England after she had gained
commercial hegemony within the Western
European-centered world market.[11]

In the wake of that first commercial-
industrial breakthrough, modernizing pressures
have reverberated throughout the world. In the
first phase of world modernization, England's
thoroughgoing commercialization, capture of
world market hegemony, and expansion of manufactures (both before and after the technological Industrial Revolution which began in the
1780s), transformed means and stakes in the traditional rivalries of European states and put immediate pressure for reforms, if only to facilitate
the financing of competitive armies and navies,
upon the other European states and especially
upon the ones with less efficient fiscal machineries.[12] In the second phase, as Europe modernized and further expanded its influence around
the globe, similar militarily compelling pressures
were brought to bear on those non-European societies which escaped immediate colonization,
usually the ones with pre-existing differentiated
and centralized state institutions.

During these phases of global modernization,
independent responses to the dilemmas posed by
incorporation into a modernizing world were
possible and (in some sense) necessary for governmental elites in agrarian bureaucracies. Demands for more and more efficiently collected
taxes; for better and more generously and continuously financed militaries; and for "guided"
national economic development, imitating the
available foreign models, were voiced within
these societies especially by bureaucrats and the
educated middle strata. The demands were made
compelling by international military competition
and threats. At the same time, governmental

leaders did have administrative machineries, however rudimentary, at their disposal for the implementation of whatever modernizing reforms seemed necessary and feasible (at given moments in world history). And their countries had not been incorporated into dependent economic and political positions in a world stratification system dominated by a few fully industrialized giants.

But agrarian bureaucracies faced enormous difficulties in meeting the crises of modernization. Governmental leaders' realm of autonomous action tended to be severely limited, because few fiscal or economic reforms could be undertaken which did not encroach upon the advantages of the traditional landed upper classes which constituted the major social base of support for the authority and functions of the state in agrarian bureaucracies. Only so much revenue could be squeezed out of the peasantry, and yet landed upper classes could often raise formidable obstacles to rationalization of tax systems. Economic development might mean more tax revenues and enhanced military prowess, yet it channelled wealth and manpower away from the agrarian sector. Finally, the mobilization of mass popular support for war tended to undermine the traditional, local authority of landlords or landed bureaucrats upon which agrarian bureaucratic societies partly relied for the social control of the peasantry.

Agrarian bureaucracies could not indefinitely "ignore" the very specific crises, in particular fiscal and martial, that grew out of involvement with a modernizing world, yet they could not adapt without undergoing fundamental structural changes. Social revolution helped accomplish "necessary" changes in some but was averted by reform or "revolution from above" in others. Relative stagnation, accompanied by subincorporation into international power spheres, was still another possibility (e.g., Portugal, Spain?). Social revolution was never deliberately "chosen." Societies only "backed into" social revolutions.

All modernizing agrarian bureaucracies have peasants with grievances and face the unavoidable challenges posed by modernization abroad. So, in some sense, potential for social revolution has been built into all modernizing agrarian bureaucracies. Yet, only a handful have succumbed. Why? A major part of the answer, I believe, lies in the insight that "not oppression, but weakness, breeds revolution."[13] It is the breakdown of a societal mode of social control which allows and prompts social revolution to unfold. In the historical cases of France, Russia and China, the unfolding of social revolution depended upon the emergence of revolutionary crises occasioned by the incapacitation of administrative and military organizations. That incapacitation, in turn, is best explained not as a function of mass discontent and mobilization, but as a function of a combination of pressures on state institutions from more modernized countries abroad, and (in two cases out of three) built-in structural incapacities to mobilize increased resources in response to those pressures. France, Russia and China were also special among all agrarian bureaucracies in that their agrarian institutions afforded peasants not only the usual grievances against landlords and state agents but also "structural space" for autonomous collective insurrection. Finally, once administrative/military breakdown occurred in agrarian bureaucracies with such especially insurrection-prone peasantries, then, and only then, could organized revolutionary leaderships have great impact upon their societies' development—though not necessarily in the ways they originally envisaged.

Breakdown of Societal Controls: Foreign Pressures and Administrative/Military Collapse

If a fundamental cause and the crucial trigger for the historical social revolutions was the incapacitation of administrative and military machineries in modernizing agrarian bureaucracies, then how and why did this occur in France, Russia and China? What differentiated these agrarian bureaucracies which succumbed to social revolution from others which managed to respond to modernizing pressures with reforms from above? Many writers attribute differences in response to qualities of will or ability in governmental leaders. From a sociological point of view, a more satisfying approach might focus on the interaction between (a) the magnitude of foreign pressures brought to bear on a modernizing agrarian bureaucracy, and (b) the particular structural characteristics of such societies that underlay contrasting performances by leaders responding to foreign pressures and internal unrest.

Overwhelming foreign pressures on an agrarian bureaucracy could cut short even a generally successful government program of reforms and industrialization "from above." Russia is the obvious case in point. From at least the 1890s onward, the Czarist regime was committed to rapid industrialization, initially government-financed out of resources squeezed from the peasantry, as the only means of rendering Russia militarily competitive with Western nations. Alexander Gerschenkron argues that initial government programs to promote heavy industry had succeeded in the 1890s to such an extent that, when the government was forced to reduce its direct financial and administrative role after 1904, Russia's industrial sector was nevertheless capable of autonomously generating further growth (with the aid of foreign capital investments.)[14] Decisive steps to modernize agriculture and free peasant labor for permanent urban migration were taken after the unsuccessful Revolution of 1905.[15] Had she been able to sit out World War I, Russia might have recapitulated the German experience of industrialization facilitated by bureaucratic guidance.

But participation in World War I forced Russia to fully mobilize her population including her restive peasantry. Army officers and men were subjected to years of costly fighting, and civilians to mounting economic privations—all for nought. For, given Russia's "industrial backwardness . . . enhanced by the fact that Russia was very largely blockaded . . . ," plus the "inferiority of the Russian military machine to the German in everything but sheer numbers . . . , military defeat, with all of its inevitable consequences for the internal condition of the country, was very nearly a foregone conclusion."[16] The result was administrative demoralization and paralysis, and the disintegration of the army. Urban insurrections which brought first middle-strata moderates and then the Bolsheviks to power could not be suppressed, owing to the newly-recruited character and war weariness of the urban garrisons.[17] Peasant grievances were enhanced, young peasant men were politicized through military experiences, and, in consequence, spreading peasant insurrections from the spring of 1917 on could not be controlled.

It is instructive to compare 1917 to the Revolution of 1905. Trotsky called 1905 a "dress rehearsal" for 1917, and, indeed, many of the same social forces with the same grievances and similar political programs took part in each revolutionary drama. *What accounts for the failure of the Revolution of 1905 was the Czarist regime's ultimate ability to rely upon the army to repress popular disturbances.* Skillful tactics were involved: the regime bought time to organize repression and assure military loyalty with well-timed liberal concessions embodied in the October Manifesto of 1905 (and later largely retracted). Yet, it was of crucial importance that the futile 1904–05 war with Japan was, in comparison with the World War I morass, circumscribed, geographically peripheral, less demanding of resources and manpower, and quickly concluded once defeat was apparent.[18] The peace treaty was signed by late 1905, leaving the Czarist government free to bring military reinforcements back from the Far East into European Russia.

The Russian Revolution occurred in 1917 because Russia was too inextricably entangled with foreign powers, friend and foe, economically and militarily more powerful than she. Foreign entanglement must be considered not only to explain the administrative and military incapacitation of 1917, but also entry into World War I. That involvement cannot be considered "accidental." Nor was it "voluntary" in the same sense as Russia's entry into the 1904 war with Japan.[19] Whatever leadership "blunders" were involved, the fact remains that in 1914 both the Russian state and the Russian economy depended heavily on Western loans and capital. Moreover, Russia was an established part of the European state system and could not remain neutral in a conflict that engulfed the whole of that system.[20]

Foreign pressures and involvements so inescapable and overwhelming as those that faced Russia in 1917 constitute an extreme case for the earlier modernizing agrarian bureaucracies we are considering here. For France and China the pressures were surely no more compelling than those faced by agrarian bureaucracies such as Japan, Germany and Russia (1858–1914) which successfully adapted through reforms from above that facilitated the extraordinary mobilization of resources for economic and military development. Why were the Bourbon and Manchu regimes unable to adapt? Were there structural blocks to effective response? First, let me discuss some general characteristics of all agrarian states, and then point to a peculiar structural characteristic shared by Bourbon France and Manchu China which I believe explains these regimes' inability to meet snow-balling crises of modernization until at last their feeble attempts triggered administrative and military disintegration, hence revolutionary crises.

Weber's ideal type of bureaucracy may be taken as an imaginary model of what might logically be the most effective means of purposively organizing social power. According to the ideal type, fully developed bureaucracy involves the existence of an hierarchically arrayed officialdom, where officials are oriented to superior authority in a disciplined manner because they are dependent for jobs, livelihood, status and career-advancement on resources and decisions channeled through that superior authority. But in preindustrial states, monarchs found it difficult to channel sufficient resources through the "center" to pay simultaneously for wars, culture and court life on the one hand, and a fully bureaucratic officialdom on the other. Consequently, they often had to make do with "officials" recruited from wealthy backgrounds, frequently, in practice, landlords. In addition, central state jurisdiction rarely touched local peasants or communities directly; governmental functions were often delegated to landlords in their "private" capacities, or else to non-bureaucratic authoritative organizations run by local landlords.

Inherent in all agrarian bureaucratic regimes were tensions between, on the one hand, state elites interested in preserving, using, and extending the powers of armies and administrative organizations and, on the other hand, landed upper classes interested in defending locally and regionally based social networks, influence over peasants, and powers and privileges associated with the control of land and agrarian surpluses. Such tensions were likely to be exacerbated once the agrarian bureaucracy was forced to adapt to modernization abroad because foreign military pressures gave cause, while foreign economic development offered incentives and models, for state elites to attempt reforms which went counter to the class interests of traditional, landed upper strata. Yet there were important variations in the ability of semi-bureaucratic agrarian states to respond to modernizing pressures with reforms which sharply and quickly increased resources at the disposal of central authorities. What can account for the differences in response?

*   *   *

The Manchu Dynasty proved unable to mobilize resources sufficient to meet credibly the challenges posed by involvement in the modernizing world. "[T]he problem was not merely the very real one of the inadequate resources of the Chinese economy as a whole. In large measure the financial straits in which the Peking government found itself were due to . . . [inability to] command such financial capacity as there was in its empire."[21] Part of the explanation for this inability lay in a characteristic which the Chinese state shared with other agrarian states: lower and middle level officials were recruited from the landed gentry, paid insufficient salaries, and allowed to engage in a certain amount of "normal" corruption, withholding revenues collected as taxes from higher authorities.[22] Yet, if the Manchu Dynasty had encountered the forces of modernization at the height of its powers (say in the early eighteenth century) rather than during its declining phase, it might have controlled or been able to mobilize sufficient resources to finance modern industries and equip a centrally controlled modern army. In that case, officials would never have been allowed to serve in their home provinces, and thus local and regional groups of gentry would have lacked institutional support for concerted opposition against central initiatives. But, as it happened, the Manchu Dynasty was forced to try to cope with wave after wave of imperialist intrusions, engineered by foreign industrial or industrializing nations anxious to tap Chinese markets and finances, immediately after a series of massive mid-nineteenth-century peasant rebellions. The Dynasty had been unable to put down the Taiping Rebellion on its own, and the task had fallen instead to local, gentry-led, self-defense associations and to regional armies led by complexly interrelated gentry who had access to village resources and recruits. In consequence of the gentry's role in putting down rebellion, governmental powers formerly accruing to central authorities or their bureaucratic agents, including, crucially, rights to collect and allocate various taxes, devolved upon local, gentry-dominated, sub-district governing associations and upon provincial armies and officials increasingly aligned with the provincial gentry against the center.[23]

Unable to force resources from local and regional authorities, it was all Peking could do simply to meet foreign indebtedness, and after 1895 even that proved impossible.

Throughout the period from 1874 to 1894, the ministry [of Revenue in Peking] was engaged in a series of largely unsuccessful efforts to raise funds in order to meet a continuing series of crises—the dispute over Ili with Russia, the Sino-French War [1885], floods and famines, the Sino-Japanese War [1895]. . . . After 1895 the triple pressure of indemnity payments, servicing foreign loans, and military expenditures totally wrecked the rough balance between income and outlay which Peking had maintained [with the aid of foreign loans] until that time.[24]

The Boxer Rebellion of 1900, and subsequent foreign military intervention, only further exacerbated an already desperate situation.

Attempts by dynastic authorities to remedy matters through a series of "reforms" implemented after 1900—abolishing the Confucian educational system and encouraging modern schools;[25] organizing the so-called "New Armies" (which actually formed around the nuclei of the old provincial armies);[26] transferring local governmental functions to provincial bureaus;[27] and creating a series of local and provincial gentry-dominated representative assemblies[28]—only exacerbated the sorry situation, right up to the 1911 breaking point. "Reform destroyed the reforming government."[29] With each reform, dynastic elites thought to create powers to counterbalance entrenched obstructive forces, but new officials and functions were repeatedly absorbed into pre-existing local and (especially) regional cliques of gentry.[30] The last series of reforms, those that created representative assemblies, ironically provided cliques of gentry with legitimate representative organs from which to launch the liberal, decentralizing "Constitutionalist movement" against the Manchus.

What ultimately precipitated the "revolution of 1911" was a final attempt at reform by the central government, one that directly threatened the financial interests of the gentry power groups for the purpose of strengthening central government finances and control over national economic development:

The specific incident that precipitated the Revolution of 1911 was the central government's decision to buy up a [railroad] line in Szechwan in which the local gentry had invested heavily. . . . The Szechwan uprising, led by the moderate constitutionalists of the Railway Protection League, sparked widespread disturbances that often had no connection with the railway issue. . . .[31]

Conspiratorial groups affiliated with Sun Yat Sen's T'eng Meng Hui, and mainly composed of Western-educated students and middle-rank New Army officers, joined the fray to produce a series of military uprisings. Finally,

> . . . the lead in declaring the independence of one province after another was taken by two principal elements: the military governors who commanded the New Army forces and the gentry-official-merchant leaders of the provincial assemblies. These elements had more power and were more conservative than the youthful revolutionarists of the T'eng Meng Hui.[32]

The Chinese "Revolution of 1911" irremediably destroyed the integument of civilian elite ties—traditionally maintained by the operation of Confucian educational institutions and the central bureaucracy's policies for recruiting and deploying educated officials so as to strengthen "cosmopolitan" orientations at the expense of local loyalties—which had until that time provided at least the semblance of unified governance for China. "Warlord" rivalries ensued as gentry interests attached themselves to regional military machines, and this condition of intra-elite disunity and rivalry (only imperfectly and temporarily overcome by Chiang Kai-Shek's regime between 1927 and 1937)[33] condemned China to incessant turmoils and provided openings (as well as cause) for lower-class, especially peasant, rebellions and for Communist attempts to organize and channel popular unrest.

Peasant Insurrections

If administrative and military breakdown in a modernizing agrarian bureaucracy were to inaugurate social revolutionary transformations, rather than merely an interregnum of intra-elite squabbling, then widespread popular revolts had to coincide with and take advantage of the hiatus of governmental supervision and sanctions. Urban insurrections provided indispensable support during revolutionary interregnums to radical political elites vying against other elites for state power: witness the Parisian *sans culottes'* support for the Jacobins;[34] the Chinese workers' support for the Communists (between 1920 and 1927);[35] and the Russian industrial workers' support for the Bolsheviks. But fundamentally more important in determining final outcomes were the peasant insurrections which in France, Russia and China constituted irreversible attacks on the powers and privileges of the traditional landed upper classes.

Agrarian bureaucracy has been the only historical variety of complex society with differentiated, centralized government that has, in certain instances, incubated a lower-class stratum that was *simultaneously strategic* in the society's economy and polity (as surplus producer, payer of rents and taxes, and as provider of corvée and military manpower), and yet *organizationally autonomous* enough to allow the "will" and "tactical space" for collective insurrection against basic structural arrangements.

How have certain agrarian bureaucracies exemplified such special propensity to peasant rebellion? As Eric Wolf has pointed out, "ultimately, the decisive factor in making a peasant rebellion possible lies in the relation of the peasantry to the field of power which surrounds it. A rebellion cannot start from a situation of complete impotence. . . ."[36] If they are to act upon, rather than silently suffer, their omnipresent grievances, peasants must have "internal leverage" or "tactical mobility." They have this to varying degrees according to their position in the total agrarian social structure. Institutional patterns which relate peasants to landlords and peasants to each other seem to be the co-determinants of degrees of peasant "tactical mobility." Sheer amounts of property held by peasants gain significance only within institutional contexts. If peasants are to be capable of self-initiated rebellion against landlords and state officials, they must have (a) some institutionally based collective solidarity, and (b) autonomy from direct, day-to-day supervision and control by landlords in their work and leisure activities. Agricultural regimes featuring large estates worked by serfs or laborers tend to be inimical to peasant rebellion—witness the East Elbian Junker regime[37]—but the reason is not that serfs and landless laborers are economically poor, rather that they are subject to close and constant supervision and discipline by landlords or their agents. If large-estate agriculture is lacking, an agrarian bureaucracy may still be relatively immune to widespread peasant rebellion if landlords control sanctioning machineries,[38] such as militias and poor relief agencies, at local levels. On the other hand, landlords as a class, and the "system" as a whole, will be relatively vulnerable to peasant rebellion if: (a) sanctioning machineries are centralized; (b) agricultural work and peasant social life are controlled by peasant families and communities themselves. These conditions prevailed in France and Russia and meant that, with the incapacitation of central administrative and military bureaucracies, these societies became susceptible to the spread and intensification of peasant revolts which in more normal circumstances could have been contained and repressed.

It is worth emphasizing that peasant actions in revolutions are not intrinsically different from peasant actions in "mere" rebellions or riots. When peasants "rose" during historical social revolutionary crises, they did so in highly traditional rebellious patterns: bread riots, "defense" of communal lands or customary rights, riots against "hoarding" merchants or landlords, "social banditry." Peasants initially drew upon traditional cultural themes to justify rebellion. Far from becoming revolutionaries through adoption of a radical vision of a desired new society, "revolutionary" peasants have typically been "backward-looking" rebels incorporated by circumstances beyond their control into political

processes occurring independently of them, at the societal "center."[39]

* * *

Historians agree that the Russian Emancipation of the serfs in 1861, intended by the Czar as a measure to stabilize the agrarian situation, actually enhanced the rebellious potential of the ex-serfs. Heavy redemption payments and inadequate land allotments fuelled peasant discontent. More important, legal reinforcement of the *obshchina*'s (peasant commune's) authority over families and individuals fettered ever-increasing numbers of peasants to the inadequate lands, reinforced collective solidarity, retarded the internal class differentiation of the peasantry, and left communes largely free to run their own affairs subject only to the collective fulfillment of financial obligations to the state.[40] Estate owners were deprived of most direct authority over peasant communities.[41]

Not surprisingly, given this agrarian situation, widespread peasant rebellions erupted in Russia in 1905, when the Czarist regime simultaneously confronted defeat abroad and an anti-autocratic movement of the middle classes, the liberal gentry, and the working classes at home. "Economic hardship created a need for change; peasant tradition, as well as revolutionary propaganda, suggested the remedy [i.e., attacks on landlords and land seizures]; official preoccupation and indecisiveness invited the storm; and soon the greatest disturbance since the days of Pugachev was under way."[42]

In the wake of the unsuccessful Revolution of 1905, the Czarist regime abandoned its policy of shoring up the peasant commune. It undertook the break-up of repartitional lands into private holdings and implemented measures to facilitate land sales by poorer peasants and purchases by richer ones.[43] Between 1905 and 1917, these measures, in tandem with general economic developments, did something to alleviate agrarian stagnation, promote permanent rural migration to urban industrial areas, and increase class differentiation and individualism in the countryside.[44] However, by 1917, little enough had been accomplished—only one-tenth of all peasant families had been resettled on individual holdings[45]—that peasant communities engaged in solidary actions against both landlords and any rich peasant "separators" who did not join their struggle.

"Any shrewd observer of Russian conditions who weighed the lessons of the agrarian disorders of 1905 could have foreseen that a breakdown of central power and authority was almost certain to bring an even greater upheaval in its train."[46] And, indeed, between the spring and the autumn of 1917, "side by side with the mutiny of the Russian army marched a second great social revolutionary movement: the seizure of the landed estates by the peasantry."[47]

> The peasant movement of 1917 was primarily a drive of the peasantry against the *pomyeschik* class. Among the cases of agrarian disturbance, violent and peaceful, 4,954, overwhelming the largest number, were directed against landlords, as against 324 against the more well-to-do peasants, 235 against the Government and 211 against the clergy.[48]

> The broad general result of the wholesale peasant land seizure of 1917 was a sweeping levelling in Russian agriculture. The big latifundia, even the small estate, ceased to exist. On the other hand landless or nearly landless peasants obtained larger allotments.[49]

For the peasants simply applied traditional communal repartitional procedures to lands seized from the landlords. Their revolt, together with the Bolsheviks' victory, ". . . sealed forever the doom of the old landed aristocracy."[50]

The Chinese case presents decisive contrasts with France and Russia but nevertheless confirms our general insight about the importance of structurally conditioned "tactical space" for peasant insurrection as a crucial factor in the translation of administrative/military breakdown into social revolution.

Except in infertile and marginal highland areas, Chinese peasants, though mostly family smallholders or tenants,[51] did not live in their own village communities clearly apart from landlords.

> The Chinese peasant . . . was a member of two communities: his village and the marketing system to which his village belonged ["typically including fifteen to twenty-five villages . . ." dependent on one of 45,000 market towns]. An important feature of the larger marketing community was its elaborate system of stratification. . . . Those who provided *de facto* leadership within the marketing community *qua* political system and those who gave it collective representation at its interface with larger polities were gentrymen—landed, leisured, and literate. . . . It was artisans, merchants, and other full-time economic specialists, not peasants, who sustained the heartbeat of periodic marketing that kept the community alive. It was priests backed by gentry temple managers . . . who gave religious meaning to peasants' local world.[52]

Voluntary associations, and clans where they flourished, were likewise contained within marketing communities, headed and economically sustained by gentry. Thus kinship, associational and clientage ties cut across class distinctions between peasants and landlords in traditional China. Gentry controlled at local levels a variety of sanctioning machineries, including militias and other organizations which functioned *de facto* as channels of poor relief.[53]

Not surprisingly, therefore, settled Chinese peasant agriculturalists did not initiate class-based revolts against landlords, either in premodern or in revolutionary (1911–49) times. Instead, peasant rebellion manifested itself in the form of accelerating rural, violence and social banditry, spreading outward from the mountainous "border areas" at the edges of the empire or at the intersections of provincial boundaries. Social banditry invariably blossomed during periods of central administrative weakness or collapse and economic deflation and catastrophe. Precisely because normal traditional Chinese agrarian-class relations were significantly commercialized, local prosperity depended upon overall administrative stability, and peasants were not cushioned against economic dislocations by kin or village communal ties. During periods of dynastic decline, local (marketing) communities "closed in" upon themselves normatively, economically, and coercively,[54] and poorer peasants, especially in communities without well-to-do local landed elites, lost property and livelihood, and were forced to migrate. Such impoverished migrants often congregated as bandits or smugglers operating out of "border area" bases and raiding settled communities. Ultimately they might provide (individual or group) recruits for rebel armies led by marginal elites vying for imperial power.[55]

The nineteenth and the first half of the twentieth centuries constituted a period of dynastic decline and interregnum in China, complicated in quite novel ways by Western and Japanese economic and military intrusions. Peasant impoverishment, local community closure, spreading social banditry and military conflicts among local militias, bandit groups, and warlord and/or "ideological" armies, characterized the entire time span, and peaked during the mid-nineteenth and mid-twentieth centuries.

The Communist movement originated as a political tendency among a tiny fraction of China's nationalist and pro-modern intellectual stratum and created its first mass base among Chinese industrial workers concentrated in the treaty ports and to a lesser degree among students and southeast Chinese peasants. But after 1927, the Chinese Communists were forced out of China's cities and wealthier agrarian regions by Kuomintang military and police repression. Would-be imitators of the Bolsheviks were thus forced to come to terms with the Chinese agrarian situation. This they did initially (between 1927 and 1942) by recapitulating the experiences and tactics of traditional rebel elite contenders for imperial power in China. Scattered, disorganized and disoriented Communist leaders, along with military units (which had split off from KMT or warlord armies) of varying degrees of loyalty, retreated to mountainous border areas, there often to ally with already existing bandit groups.[56] Gradually the fruits of raiding expeditions, plus the division and weakness of opposing armies, allowed the "Communist" base areas to expand into administrative regions.

Only after a secure and stable administrative region had finally been established in Northwest China (after 1937) could the Communists finally turn to the intra-market-area and intra-village political organizing that ultimately bypassed and then eliminated the gentry, and so made their drive for power unique in China's history. Before roughly 1940, ideological appeals, whether "Communist" or "Nationalist" played little role in mediating Communist elites' relations to peasants, and spontaneous class struggle, fuelled from below, played virtually no role in achieving whatever (minimal) changes in agrarian class *relations* were accomplished in Communist base areas.[57] To be sure, ideology was important in integrating the Party, an elite organization, and in mediating its relationship with the Red Army. But until Party and Army established relatively secure and stable military and administrative control over a region, Communist cadres were not in a position to penetrate local communities in order to provide organization, leadership, and encouragement for peasants themselves to expropriate land. This finally occurred in even given administrative/military collapse. In premodern times, France, North China in the 1940s.[58] Once provided with military and organizational protection from landlord sanctions and influence, peasants often reacted against landlords with a fury that exceeded even what Party policy desired. Perhaps Communist ideological appeals were partially responsible for peasant insurrection. More likely, even at this stage, the Communist organizations' important input to local situations was not a sense of grievances, or their ideological articulation, but rather simply *protection* from traditional social controls: William Hinton's classic *Fanshen: A Documentary of Revolution in a Chinese Village* vividly supports such an interpretation.[59]

Even to gain the military strength they needed to defeat the Kuomintang, the Chinese Communists had to shove aside—or encourage and allow peasants to shove aside—the traditional landed upper class and establish a more direct link to the Chinese peasantry than had ever before been established between an extra-local Chinese rebel movement and local communities.[60] The Chinese Communists also established more direct links to peasants than did radical elites in Russia or France. The Chinese Revolution, at least in its closing stages, thus has more of the aspect of an elite/mass movement than the other great historical social revolutions. Yet the reasons for this peasant mass-mobilizing aspect have little to do with revolutionary ideology (except in retrospect) and everything to do with the "peculiarities" (from a European perspective) of the Chinese agrarian social structure. That structure did not afford settled Chinese peasants institutional autonomy and solidarity against landlords, yet it did, in periods of political-economic crisis, generate marginal poor-peasant outcasts whose activities exacerbated the crises and whose existence provided potential bases of support for oppositional elite-led rebellions or, in the twentieth-century world context, a revolutionary movement. Thus Chinese Communist activities after 1927 and ultimate triumph in 1949 depended directly upon *both* the insurrectionary potentials and the blocks to peasant insurrection built into the traditional Chinese social structure.

Radical Political Movements and Centralizing Outcomes

Although peasant insurrections played a decisive role in each of the great historical social revolutions, nevertheless an exclusive focus on peasants—or on the peasant situation in agrarian bureaucracies—cannot provide a complete explanation for the occurrence of social revolutions, Russia and China were recurrently rocked by massive peasant rebellions,[61] yet peasant uprisings did not fuel structural transformations until the late eighteenth century and after. Obviously agrarian bureaucracies were exposed to additional and unique strains and possibilities once English and then European commercialization-industrialization became a factor in world history and development. The stage was set for the entry of marginal elites animated by radical nationalist goals.

Who were these marginal elites? What sectors of society provided the social bases for nationalist radicalisms? *Not* the bourgeoisie proper: merchants, financiers and industrialists. These groups have had surprisingly little *direct* effect upon the politics of modernization in any developing nation, from England to the countries of the Third World today. Instead, their activities, commerce and manufacturing, have created and continuously transformed, indeed revolutionized, the national and international *contexts* within which bureaucrats, professionals, politicians, landlords, peasants, and proletarians have engaged in the decisive political struggles. To be sure, in certain times and places, the "bourgeois" commercial or industrial context has been pervasive enough virtually to determine political outcomes, even without the overt political participation of bourgeois actors. But such was not the case in the earlier modernizing agrarian bureaucracies, including France, Russia and China.

Instead, nationalist radicals tended to "precipitate out" of the ranks of those who possessed specialized skills and were oriented to state activities or employments, but either lacked traditionally prestigious attributes such as nobility, landed wealth, or general humanist education, or else found themselves in situations where such attributes were no longer personally or nationally functional. Their situations in political and social life were such as to make them, especially in times of political crises, willing to call for such radical reforms as equalization of mobility opportunities, political democracy, and (anyway, before the revolution) extension of civil liberties. Yet the primary orientation of these marginal elites was toward a broad goal that they shared with all those, including traditionally prestigious bureaucrats, whose careers, livelihoods, and identities were intertwined with state activities: the goal of extension and rationalization of state powers in the name of national welfare and prestige.

*   *   *

In Russia, by 1917, the revolutionary sects, such as the Bolsheviks and the Left Social Revolutionaries, constituted the surviving politically organized representatives of what had earlier been an out-look much more widespread among university-educated Russians: extreme alienation, disgust at Russia's backwardness, preoccupation with public events and yet refusal to become involved in the round of civil life.[62] As Russia underwent rapid industrialization after 1890, opportunities for university education were extended beyond the nobility—a circumstance which helped to ensure that universities would be hotbeds of political radicalism—yet, before long, opportunities for professional and other highly skilled employments also expanded. Especially in the wake of the abortive 1905 Revolution, Russia's university-educated moved toward professional employments and liberal politics.[63] Yet when events overtook Russia in 1917, organized radical leadership was still to be found among the alienated intelligentsia.

In China, as in Russia, radical nationalist modernizers came from the early student generations of university-educated Chinese.[64] Especially at first, most were the children of traditionally wealthy and prestigious families, but urban and "rich peasant" backgrounds, respectively, came to be overrepresented in the (pre-1927) Kuomintang and the Communist elites.[65] With the abolition of the Confucian educational system in 1904, and the collapse of the imperial government in 1911, even traditionally prestigious attributes and connections lost their meaning and usefulness. At the same time, neither warlord regimes, nor the Nationalist government after 1927 offered much scope for modern skills

or credentials; advancement in these regimes went only to those with independent wealth or personal ties to military commanders. Gradually, the bulk of China's modern-educated, and especially the young, came to support the Communist movement, some through active commitment in Yenan, others through passive political support in the cities.[66]

Two considerations help to account for the fact that radical leadership in social revolutions came specifically from the ranks of skilled and/or university-educated marginal elites oriented to state employments and activities. First, agrarian bureaucracies are "statist" societies. Even before the era of modernization official employments in these societies constituted both an important route for social mobility and a means for validating traditional status and supplementing landed fortunes. Second, with the advent of economic modernization in the world, state activities acquired greater-than-ever objective import in the agrarian bureaucratic societies which were forced to adapt to modernization abroad. For the concrete effects of modernization abroad first impinged upon the state's sphere, in the form of sharply and suddenly stepped up military competition or threats from more developed nations abroad. And the cultural effects of modernization abroad first impinged upon the relatively highly educated in agrarian bureaucracies, that is upon those who were mostly either employed by the state or else connected or oriented to its activities.

*   *   *

The earlier modernizing agrarian bureaucracies that (to varying degrees) successfully adapted to challenges from abroad did so either through revolution, or basic reforms "from above" or social revolution "from below." Either traditional bureaucrats successfully promoted requisite reforms or else their attempts precipitated splits within the upper class which could, if the peasantry were structurally insurrection-prone, open the door to social revolution. In the context of administrative/military disorganization and spreading peasant rebellions, tiny, organized radical elites that never could have created revolutionary crises on their own gained their moments in history. As peasant insurrections undermined the traditional landed upper classes, and the old regime officials and structures tied to them, radical elites occupied center stage, competing among themselves to see who could seize and build upon the foundations of central state power.

"A complete revolution," writes Samuel Huntington, ". . . involves . . . the creation and institutionalization of a new political order."[67] A social revolution was consummated when one political elite succeeded in creating or capturing political organizations—a revolutionary army, or a revolutionary party controlling an army—capable of restoring minimal order and incorporating the revolutionary masses, especially the peasantry, into national life. No political elite not able or willing to accept the peasants' revolutionary economic gains could hope to emerge victorious from the intra-elite or inter-party conflicts that marked revolutionary interregnums. Elites with close social or politico-military ties to traditional forms of landed upper-class institutional power (i.e., the privileged rentier bourgeoisie of France, the Kerensky regime in Russia, the [post-1927] Kuomintang in China) invariably lost out.

The historical social revolutions did not culminate in more liberal political arrangements. At opening stages of the French, Russian (1905) and Chinese revolutions, landed upper-class/middle-strata political coalitions espoused "parliamentary liberal" programs.[68] But events pushed these groups and programs aside, for the organized elites who provided the ultimately successful leadership in all social revolutions ended up responding to popular turmoil—counterrevolutionary threats at home and abroad, peasant anarchist tendencies, and the international crises faced by their societies—by creating *more* highly centralized, bureaucratized and rationalized state institutions than those that existed prior to the revolutions. This response,

moreover, was entirely in character for elites adhering to world views which gave consistent primacy to organized political action in human affairs.[69]

*   *   *

Let me sum up what this essay has attempted to do. To explain the great historical social revolutions, I have, first, conceptualized a certain type of society, the agrarian bureaucracy, in which social control of the lower strata (mainly peasants) rests with institutions locally and regionally controlled by landed upper classes, together with administrative and military machineries centrally controlled; and second, I have discussed differences between agrarian bureaucracies which did and those which did not experience social revolutions in terms of (a) institutional structures which mediate landed upper-class relations to state apparatuses and peasant relations to landed upper classes and (b) types and amounts of international political and economic pressures (especially originating with more developed nations) impinging upon agrarian bureaucracies newly incorporated into the modernizing world. According to my analysis, social revolutions occurred in those modernizing agrarian bureaucracies—France, Russia and China—which *both* incubated peasantries structurally prone to autonomous insurrection *and* experienced severe administrative and military disorganization due to the direct or indirect effects of military competition or threats from more modern nations abroad.

In the process of elucidating this basic argument, I have at one point or another alluded to evidence concerning Prussia (Germany), Japan (and Turkey), and Russia in 1905. Obviously the coverage of these and other "negative" cases has been far from complete. Yet partial explanations have been offered for the avoidance of social revolution by Prussia/Germany, Japan and Russia through 1916. Japan and Russia escaped administrative/military collapse in the face of moderate challenges from abroad because their traditional governmental elites were significantly differentiated from landed upper classes. Prussia lacked a structurally autonomous, insurrection-prone peasantry, and therefore when, in 1848, the King hesitated for a year to use his armies to repress popular disturbances, the Junker-led army, manned by peasants from the estates east of the Elbe, remained loyal and intact until it was finally used to crush the German Revolutions during 1849–50.

This comparative historical analysis has been meant to render plausible a theoretical approach to explaining revolutions which breaks with certain long-established sociological proclivities. While existing theories of revolution focus on discontent, and its articulation by oppositional programs or ideologies, as the fundamental cause of revolutions, I have emphasized mechanisms and dynamics of societal social control through political and class domination. Moreover, while other theories view the impact of modernization (as a cause of revolution) in terms of the effects of processes of economic development on class structures, "system equilibrium," or societal members' levels of satisfaction, my approach focuses on the effects of modernization—viewed also as an intersocietal politico-strategic process—upon adaptive capacities of the agrarian bureaucratic states and upon the opportunities open to political elites who triumph in revolutions.

Obviously, thorough testing of these ideas will require more precise delineation of concepts and the extension of hypotheses derived from this analysis to new cases. But I have made a start. And I hope that especially those who disagree with my conclusions will themselves turn to historical evidence to argue their cases. Social science can best grow through the interplay of theory and historical investigation, and comparative historical analysis represents one indispensable tool for achieving this.

NOTES

1. Samuel P. Huntington, *Political Order in Changing Societies* (New Haven: Yale University Press, 1968), p. 264.

2. Stephan T. Possony, ed., *The Lenin Reader* (Chicago: Henry Regnery Company, 1966), p. 349.

3. For important examples see: Ted Robert Gurr, *Why Men Rebel* (Princeton, New Jersey: Princeton University Press, 1970); Neil J. Smelser, *Theory of Collective Behavior* (New York: The Free Press of Glencoe, 1963), and Harry Eckstein, "On the Etiology of Internal Wars," *History and Theory* 4(2) (1965).

4. Crane Brinton, *The Anatomy of Revolution* (New York: Vintage Books, 1965; original edition, 1938); Lyford P. Edwards, *The Natural History of Revolution* (Chicago: University of Chicago Press, 1971; originally published in 1927); George Sawyer Petee, *The Process of Revolution* (New York: Harper and Brothers, 1938); and Rex D. Hopper, "The Revolutionary Process," *Social Forces* 28 (March, 1950): 270–9.

5. Harry Eckstein, ed., *Internal War* (New York: The Free Press, 1964), p. 8.

6. *Ibid.*, p. 10.

7. See: Ernest Nagel, ed., *John Stuart Mill's Philosophy of Scientific Method* (New York: Hafner Publishing Co., 1950); Marc Bloch, "Toward a Comparative History of European Societies," in Frederic C. Lane and Jelle C. Riemersma, eds., *Enterprise and Secular Change* (Homewood, Illinois: The Dorsey Press, 1953), pp. 494–521; William H. Sewell, Jr., "Marc Bloch and the Logic of Comparative History," *History and Theory* 6(2) (1967): 208–18; Neil J. Smelser, "The Methodology of Comparative Analysis," (unpublished draft); and S. M. Lipset, *Revolution and Counterrevolution* (New York: Anchor Books, 1970), part I.

8. In formulating the "agrarian bureaucracy" societal type concept, I have drawn especially upon the work and ideas of S. N. Eisenstadt in *The Political Systems of Empires* (New York: The Free Press, 1963); Barrington Moore, Jr., in *Social Origins of Dictatorship and Democracy* (Boston: Beacon

Press, 1967); and Morton H. Fried, "On the Evolution of Social Stratification and the State," pp. 713–31 in Stanley Diamond, ed., *Culture in History* (New York: Columbia University Press, 1960). The label "agrarian bureaucracy" is pilfered from Moore. Clear-cut instances of agrarian bureaucratic societies were: China, Russia, France, Prussia, Austria, Spain, Japan, Turkey.

9. Terence K. Hopkins and Immanuel Wallerstein, "The Comparative Study of National Societies," *Social Science Information* 6 (1967), 39.

10. See Immanuel Wallerstein, *The Modern World System: Capitalist Agriculture and the Origins of the European World-Economy in the Sixteenth Century* (New York and London: Academic Press, 1974).

11. E. J. Hobsbawm, *Industry and Empire* (Baltimore, Md.: Penguin Books, 1969).

12. See Walter L. Dorn, *Competition for Empire, 1740–1763* (New York: Harper and Row, 1963; originally, 1940).

13. Christopher Lasch, *The New Radicalism in America* (New York: Vintage Books, 1967), p. 141.

14. Alexander Gerschenkron, "Problems and Patterns of Russian Economic Development," pp. 42–72 in Cyril E. Black, ed., *The Transformation of Russian Society* (Cambridge, Mass.: Harvard University Press, 1960).

15. Geroid Tanquary Robinson, *Rural Russia Under the Old Regime* (Berkeley and Los Angeles: University of California Press, 1969; originally published in 1932), Chap. 11.

16. William Henry Chamberlin, *The Russian Revolution*, Volume I (New York: Grosset and Dunlap, 1963; originally published in 1935), pp. 64–65.

17. Katharine Chorley, *Armies and the Art of Revolution* (London: Faber and Faber, 1943), Chap. 6.

18. *Ibid.*, pp. 118–9.

19. In 1904, "[t]he Minister of Interior, von Plehve, saw a desirable outlet from the [tur-bulent domestic] situation in a 'little victorious war' " (Chamberlin, *op. cit.*, p. 47).

20. See: Leon Trotsky, *The Russian Revolution* (selected and edited by F. W. Dupee) (New York: Anchor Books, 1959; originally published in 1932), Volume I, Chap. 2; and Roderick E. McGrew, "Some Imperatives of Russian Foreign Policy," pp. 202–29 in Theofanis George Stavrou, ed., *Russia Under the Last Tsar* (Minneapolis: University of Minnesota Press, 1969).

21. Albert Feuerwerker, *China's Early Industrialization* (New York: Atheneum, 1970; originally published in 1958), p. 41.

22. Chung-li Chang, *The Chinese Gentry* (Seattle: University of Washington Press, 1955); Ping-ti Ho, *The Ladder of Success in Imperial China* (New York: Columbia University, Press, 1962); and Franz Michael, "State and Society in Nineteenth Century China," *World Politics* 7 (April, 1955): 419–33.

23. Philip Kuhn, *Rebellion and Its Enemies in Late Imperial China* (Cambridge, Mass.: Harvard University Press, 1970).

24. Feuerwerker, *op. cit.*, pp. 40–41.

25. Mary C. Wright, ed., *China in Revolution: The First Phase, 1900–1913* (New Haven: Yale University Press, 1968), pp. 24–26.

26. Yoshiro Hatano, "The New Armies," pp. 365–82 in Wright, ed., *op. cit.*; and John Gittings, "The Chinese Army," pp. 187–224 in Jack Gray, ed., *Modern China's Search for a Political Form* (London: Oxford University Press, 1969).

27. John Fincher, "Political Provincialism and the National Revolution," in Wright, ed., *op. cit.*, p. 202.

28. Fincher, *op. cit.*; and P'eng-yuan Chang, "The Constitutionalists," in Wright, ed., *op. cit.*

29. Wright, ed., *op. cit.*, p. 50.

30. Fincher, *op. cit.*

31. Wright, ed., *loc. cit.*

32. John King Fairbank, *The United States and China* (Third Edition) (Cambridge, Mass.: Harvard University Press, 1971), p. 132.

33. Martin C. Wilbur, "Military Separatism and the Process of Reunification Under the Nationalist Regime, 1922–1937," pp. 203–63 in Ping-ti Ho and Tang Tsou, eds., *China in Crisis*, Volume I, Book I (Chicago: University of Chicago Press, 1968).

34. Albert Soboul, *The Sans Culottes* (New York: Anchor Books, 1972; originally published in French in 1968); and George Rudé, *The Crowd in the French Revolution* (London: Oxford University Press, 1959).

35. Jean Chesneaux, *The Chinese Labor Movement, 1919–1927* (Stanford: Stanford University Press, 1968).

36. Eric R. Wolf, *Peasant Wars of the Twentieth Century* (New York: Harper and Row, 1969), p. 290.

37. In 1848 the East Elbian region of "Germany" escaped general peasant insurrection, and the Prussian armies that crushed the German Revolutions of 1848 were recruited from the East Elbian estates, officers and rank-and-file alike. See: Theodore Hamerow, *Restoration, Revolution, Recreation* (Princeton, N.J.: Princeton University Press, 1958); and Hajo Holborn, *A History of Modern Germany, 1648–1840* (New York: Alfred A. Knopf, 1963).

38. "Sanctioning machineries" are organizations which control forceful or remunerative sanctions. "Social control" also involves normative pressures, but to be truly binding, especially in hierarchical situations, these must typically be "backed up" by application or credible threat of application of force or manipulation of needed remuneration.

39. See Wolf, *op. cit.*, "Conclusion"; and Moore, *op. cit.*, Chap. 9 and "Epilogue."

40. Terence Emmons, "The Peasant and the Emancipation," and Francis M. Watters, "The Peasant and the Village Commune," both in Wayne S. Vucinich, ed., *The Peasant in Nineteenth-Century Russia* (Stanford: Stanford University Press, 1968); and Robinson, *op. cit.*

41. Jerome Blum, *Lord and Peasant in Russia* (Princeton, N.J.: Princeton University Press, 1961), pp. 598–9; and Robinson, *op. cit.*, pp. 78–79.

42. Robinson, *op. cit.*, p. 155.

43. *Ibid.*, pp. 188–207.

44. Gerschenkron, *op. cit.*, pp. 42–72.

45. Robinson, *op. cit.*, pp. 225–6.

46. Chamberlin, *op. cit.*, p. 257.

47. *Ibid.*, p. 242.

48. *Ibid.*, p. 252.

49. *Ibid.*, p. 256.

50. *Ibid.*, p. 256.

51. R. H. Tawney, *Land and Labour in China* (Boston: Beacon Press, 1966; originally published in 1932), Chap. 2.

52. G. William Skinner, "Chinese Peasants and the Closed Community: An Open and Shut Case," *Comparative Studies in Society and History* 13(3) (July, 1971), pp. 272–3.

53. Kuhn, *op. cit.*, *passim*.

54. Skinner, *op. cit.*, 278ff.

55. See: Skinner, *op. cit.*, Kuhn, *op. cit.*; and George E. Taylor, "The Taiping Rebellion: Its Economic Background and Social Theory," *Chinese Social and Political Science Review* 16 (1933): 545–614.

56. See: Mark Selden, *The Yenan Way in Revolutionary China* (Cambridge, Mass.: Harvard University Press, 1971), Chaps. 1–2; Dick Wilson, *The Long March 1935* (New York: Avon Books, 1971); and Agnes Smedly, *The Great Road: The Life and Times of Chu Teh* (New York: Monthly Review Press, 1956).

57. Selden, *op. cit.*; Franz Schurmann, *Ideology and Organization in Communist China* (second edition) (Berkeley and Los Angeles: University of California Press, 1968), pp. 412–37; Ilpyong J. Kim, "Mass Mobilization Policies and Techniques Developed in the Period of the Chinese Soviet Republic," pp. 78–98 in A. Doak Barnett, ed., *Chinese Communist Politics in Action* (Seattle: University of Washington Press, 1969).

58. Selden, *op. cit.*; and Schurmann, *op. cit.*

59. William Hinton, *Fanshen: A Documentary of Revolution in a Chinese Village* (New York:

Vintage Books, 1968; first published in 1966).

60. Schurmann, *op. cit.*, pp. 425–31.

61. See, for example, Roland Mousnier, *Peasant Uprisings in the Seventeenth Century: France, Russia and China* (New York: Harper and Row, 1972; originally published in French, 1967).

62. George Fischer, "The Intelligentsia and Russia," pp. 253–73 in Black, ed., *op. cit.*

63. George Fischer, "The Russian Intelligentsia and Liberalism," pp. 317–36 in Hugh McLean, Martin Malia and George Fischer, eds., *Russian Thought and Politics—Harvard Slavic Studies, Volume IV* (Cambridge, Mass.: Harvard University Press, 1957); and Donald W. Treadgold, "Russian Radical Thought, 1894–1917," pp. 69–86 in Stavrou, ed., *op. cit.*

64. John Israel, "Reflections on the Modern Chinese Student Movement," *Daedalus* (Winter, 1968): 229–53; and Robert C. North and Ithiel de Sola Pool, "Kuomintang and Chinese Communist Elites," pp. 319–455 in Harold D. Lasswell and Daniel Lerner, eds., *World Revolutionary Elites* (Cambridge, Mass.: The M.I.T. Press, 1966).

65. North and Pool, *op. cit.*

66. John Israel, *Student Nationalism in China: 1927–1937* (Stanford: Hoover Institute Publications, 1966).

67. Huntington, *op. cit.*, p. 266.

68. See: Hampson, *A Social History* . . . , Chap. 2; Sidney Harcave, *The Russian Revolution of 1905* (London: Collier Books, 1970; first published in 1964); and P'eng-yuan Chang, "The Constitutionalists," pp. 143–83 in Wright, ed., *op. cit.*

69. On the Bolsheviks, see Robert V. Daniels, "Lenin and the Russian Revolutionary Tradition," pp. 339–54 in McLean, Malia and Fischer, eds., *op. cit.* Daniels argues that "the more autocratic societies like prerevolutionary Russia . . . prompted historical theories which put a premium on individual will, power and ideas . . . ," p. 352.

MARTHA CRENSHAW

THE CAUSES OF TERRORISM

Terrorism occurs both in the context of violent resistance to the state as well as in the service of state interests. If we focus on terrorism directed against governments for purposes of political change, we are considering the premeditated use or threat of symbolic, low-level violence by conspiratorial organizations. Terrorist violence communicates a political message; its ends go beyond damaging an enemy's material resources.[1] The victims or objects of terrorist attack have little intrinsic value to the terrorist group but represent a larger human audience whose reaction the terrorists seek. Violence characterized by spontaneity, mass participation, or a primary intent of physical destruction can therefore be excluded from our investigation.

The study of terrorism can be organized around three questions: why terrorism occurs, how the process of terrorism works, and what its social and political effects are. Here the objective is to outline an approach to the analysis of the causes of terrorism, based on comparison of different cases of terrorism, in order to distinguish

From *Comparative Politics* 13, no. 4 (July 1981) pp. 379–99.

a common pattern of causation from the historically unique.

The subject of terrorism has inspired a voluminous literature in recent years. However, nowhere among the highly varied treatments does one find a general theoretical analysis of the causes of terrorism. This may be because terrorism has often been approached from historical perspectives, which, if we take Laqueur's work as an example, dismiss explanations that try to take into account more than a single case as "exceedingly vague or altogether wrong."[2] Certainly existing general accounts are often based on assumptions that are neither explicit nor factually demonstrable. We find judgments centering on social factors such as the permissiveness and affluence in which Western youth are raised or the imitation of dramatic models encouraged by television. Alternatively, we encounter political explanations that blame revolutionary ideologies, Marxism-Leninism or nationalism, governmental weakness in giving in to terrorist demands, or conversely government oppression, and the weakness of the regime's opponents. Individual psychopathology is often cited as a culprit.

Even the most persuasive of statements about terrorism are not cast in the form of testable propositions, nor are they broadly comparative in origin or intent. Many are partial analyses, limited in scope to revolutionary terrorism from the Left, not terrorism that is a form of protest or a reaction to political or social change. A narrow historical or geographical focus is also common; the majority of explanations concern modern phenomena. Some focus usefully on terrorism against the Western democracies.[3] In general, propositions about terrorism lack logical comparability, specification of the relationship of variables to each other, and a rank-ordering of variables in terms of explanatory power.

We would not wish to claim that a general explanation of the sources of terrorism is a simple task, but it is possible to make a useful beginning by establishing a theoretical order for different types and levels of causes. We approach terrorism as a form of political behavior resulting from the deliberate choice of a basically rational actor, the terrorist organization. A comprehensive explanation, however, must also take into account the environment in which terrorism occurs and address the question of whether broad political, social, and economic conditions make terrorism more likely in some contexts than in others. What sort of circumstances lead to the formation of a terrorist group? On the other hand, only a few of the people who experience a given situation practice terrorism. Not even all individuals who share the goals of a terrorist organization agree that terrorism is the best means. It is essential to consider the psychological variables that may encourage or inhibit individual participation in terrorist actions. The analysis of these three levels of causation will center first on situational variables, then on the strategy of the terrorist organization, and last on the problem of individual participation.

This paper represents only a preliminary set of ideas about the problem of causation; historical cases of terrorism are used as illustrations, not as demonstrations of hypotheses. The historical examples referred to here are significant terrorist campaigns since the French Revolution of 1789; terrorism is considered as a facet of secular modern politics, principally associated with the rise of nationalism, anarchism, and revolutionary socialism.[4] The term *terrorism* was coined to describe the systematic inducement of fear and anxiety to control and direct a civilian population, and the phenomenon of terrorism as a challenge to the authority of the state grew from the difficulties revolutionaries experienced in trying to recreate the mass uprisings of the French Revolution. Most references provided here are drawn from the best-known and most-documented examples: Narodnaya Volya and the Combat Organization of the Socialist-Revolutionary party in Russia, from 1878 to 1913; anarchist terrorism of the 1890s in Europe, primarily France; the Irish Republican Army (IRA) and its predecessors and successors from 1919 to the present; the Irgun Zwai Leumi in Mandate Palestine from 1937 to 1947; the Front de Libération Nationale (FLN) in Algeria from 1954 to 1962; the Popular Front for the Liberation of Palestine from 1968 to the present; the Rote Armee Fraktion (RAF) and the 2nd June Movement in West Germany since 1968; and the Tupamaros of Uruguay, 1968–1974.

The Setting for Terrorism

An initial obstacle to identification of propitious circumstances for terrorism is the absence of significant empirical studies of relevant cross-national factors. There are a number of quantitative analyses of collective violence, assassination, civil strife, and crime,[5] but none of these phenomena is identical to a campaign of terrorism. Little internal agreement exists among such studies, and the consensus one finds is not particularly useful for the study of terrorism.[6] For example, Ted Robert Gurr found that "modern" states are less violent than developing countries and that legitimacy of the regime inhibits violence. Yet, Western Europe experiences high levels of terrorism. Surprisingly, in the 1961–1970 period, out of 87 countries, the United States was ranked as having the highest number of terrorist campaigns.[7] Although it is impractical to borrow entire theoretical structures from the literature on political and criminal violence, some propositions can be adapted to the analysis of terrorism.

To develop a framework for the analysis of likely settings for terrorism, we must establish conceptual distinctions among different types of factors. First, a significant difference exists between *preconditions*, factors that set the stage for terrorism over the long run, and *precipitants*, specific events that immediately precede the occurrence of terrorism. Second, a further classification divides preconditions into enabling or permissive factors, which provide opportunities for terrorism to happen, and situations that directly inspire and motivate terrorist campaigns.

Precipitants are similar to the direct causes of terrorism.[8] Furthermore, no factor is neatly compartmentalized in a single nation-state; each has a transnational dimension that complicates the analysis.

First, modernization produces an interrelated set of factors that is a significant permissive cause of terrorism, as increased complexity on all levels of society and economy creates opportunities and vulnerabilities. Sophisticated networks of transportation and communication offer mobility and the means of publicity for terrorists. The terrorists of Narodnaya Volya would have been unable to operate without Russia's newly established rail system, and the Popular Front for the Liberation of Palestine could not indulge in hijacking without the jet aircraft. In Algeria, the FLN only adopted a strategy of urban bombings when they were able to acquire plastic explosives. In 1907, the Combat Organization of the Socialist-Revolutionary party paid 20,000 rubles to an inventor who was working on an aircraft in the futile hope of bombing the Russian imperial palaces from the air.[9] Today we fear that terrorists will exploit the potential of nuclear power, but it was in 1867 that Nobel's invention of dynamite made bombings a convenient terrorist tactic.

Urbanization is part of the modern trend toward aggregation and complexity, which increases the number and accessibility of targets and methods. The popular concept of terrorism as "urban guerilla warfare" grew out of the Latin American experience of the late 1960s.[10] Yet, as Hobsbawn has pointed out, cities became the arena for terrorism after the urban renewal projects of the late nineteenth century, such as the boulevards constructed by Baron Haussman in Paris, made them unsuitable for a strategy based on riots and the defense of barricades.[11] In preventing popular insurrections, governments have exposed themselves to terrorism. P.N. Grabosky has recently argued that cities are a significant cause of terrorism in that they provide an opportunity (a multitude of targets, mobility, communications, anonymity, and audiences) and a recruiting ground among the politicized and volatile inhabitants.[12]

Social "facilitation," which Gurr found to be extremely powerful in bringing about civil strife in general, is also an important permissive factor. This concept refers to social habits and historical traditions that sanction the use of violence against the government, making it morally and politically justifiable, and even dictating an appropriate form, such as demonstrations, coups, or terrorism. Social myths, traditions, and habits permit the development of terrorism as an established political custom. An excellent example of such a tradition is the case of Ireland, where the tradition of physical force dates from the eighteenth century, and the legend of Michael Collins in 1919–21 still inspires and partially excuses the much less discriminate and less effective terrorism of the contemporary Provisional IRA in Northern Ireland.

Moreover, broad attitudes and beliefs that condone terrorism are communicated transnationally. Revolutionary ideologies have always crossed borders with ease. In the nineteenth and early twentieth centuries, such ideas were primarily a European preserve, stemming from the French and Bolshevik Revolutions. Since the Second World War, Third World War revolutions—China, Cuba, Algeria—and intellectuals such as Frantz Fanon and Carlos Marighela[13] have significantly influenced terrorist movements in the developed West by promoting the development of terrorism as routine behavior.

The most salient political factor in the category of permissive causes is a government's inability or unwillingness to prevent terrorism. The absence of adequate prevention by police and intelligence services permits the spread of conspiracy. However, since terrorist organizatons are small and clandestine, the majority of states can be placed in the permissive category. Inefficiency or leniency can be found in a broad range of all but the most brutally efficient dictatorships, including incompetent authoritarian states such as tsarist Russia on the eve of the emergence of Narodnaya Volya as well as modern liberal democratic states whose desire to protect civil liberties constrains security measures. The absence of effective security measures is a necessary cause, since our limited information on the subject indicates that terrorism does not occur in the communist dictatorships; and certainly repressive military regimes in Uruguay, Brazil, and Argentina have crushed terrorist organizations. For many governments, however, the cost of disallowing terrorism is too high.

Turning now to a consideration of the direct causes of terrorism, we focus on background conditions that positively encourage resistance to the state. These instigating circumstances go beyond merely creating an environment in which terrorism is possible; they provide motivation and direction for the terrorist movement. We are dealing here with reasons rather than opportunities.

The first condition that can be considered a direct cause of terrorism is the existence of concrete grievances among an identifiable subgroup of a larger population, such as an ethnic minority discriminated against by the majority. A social movement develops in order to redress these grievances and to gain either equal rights or a separate state; terrorism is then the resort of an extremist faction of this broader movement. In practice, terrorism has frequently arisen in such situations: in modern states, separatist nationalism among Basques, Bretons, and Québeçois has motivated terrorism. In the colonial era, nationalist movements commonly turned to terrorism.

This is not to say, however, that the existence of a dissatisfied minority or majority is a necessary or a sufficient cause of terrorism. Not all those who are discriminated against turn to terrorism, nor does terrorism always reflect objective social or economic deprivation. In West Germany, Japan, and Italy, for example, terrorism has been the chosen method of the privileged, not the downtrodden. Some theoretical studies have suggested that the essential ingredient that must be added to real deprivation is the perception on the part of the deprived that this condition is not what they deserve or expect, in short, that discrimination is unjust. An attitude study, for example, found that "the idea of justice or fairness may be more centrally related to attitudes toward violence than are feelings of deprivation. It is the perceived injustice underlying the deprivation that gives rise to anger or frustration."[14] The intervening variables, as we have argued, lie in the terrorists' perceptions. Moreover, it seems likely that for terrorism to occur the government must be singled out to blame for popular suffering.

The second condition that creates motivations for terrorism is the lack of opportunity for political participation. Regimes that deny access to power and persecute dissenters create dissatisfaction. In this case, grievances are primarily political, without social or economic overtones. Discrimination is not directed against any ethnic, religious, or racial subgroup of the population. The terrorist organization is not necessarily part of a broader social movement; indeed, the population may be largely apathetic. In situations where paths to the legal expression of opposition are blocked, but where the regime's repression is inefficient, revolutionary terrorism is doubly likely, as permissive and direct causes coincide. An example of this situation is tsarist Russia in the 1870s.

Context is especially significant as a direct cause of terrorism when it affects an elite, not the mass population. Terrorism is essentially the result of elite disaffection; it represents the strategy of a minority, who may act on behalf of a wider popular constituency who have not been consulted about, and do not necessarily approve of, the terrorists' aims or methods. There is remarkable relevance in E. J. Hobsbawm's comments on the political conspirators of post-Napoleonic Europe: "All revolutionaries regarded themselves, with some justification, as small elites of the emancipated and progressive operating among, and for the eventual benefit of, a vast and inert mass of the ignorant and misled common people, which would no doubt welcome liberation when it came, but could not be expected to take much part in preparing it."[15]

Many terrorists today are young, well-educated, and middle class in background. Such students or young professionals, with prior political experience, are disillusioned with the prospects of changing society and see little chance of access to the system despite their privileged status. Much terrorism has grown out of student unrest; this was the case in nineteenth century Russia as well as post–World War II West Germany, Italy, the United States, Japan, and Uruguay.

Perhaps terrorism is most likely to occur precisely where mass passivity and elite dissatisfaction coincide. Discontent is not generalized or severe enough to provoke the majority of the populace to action against the regime, yet a small minority, without access to the bases of power that would permit overthrow of the government through coup d'état or subversion, seeks radical change. Terrorism may thus be a sign of a stable society rather than a symptom of fragility and impending collapse. Terrorism is the resort of an elite when conditions are not revolutionary. Luigi Bonanate has blamed terrorism on a "blocked society" that is strong enough to preserve itself (presumably through popular inertia) yet resistant to innovation. Such self-perpetuating "immobilisme" invites terrorism.[16]

The last category of situational factors involves the concept of a precipitating event that immediately precedes outbreaks of terrorism. Although it is generally thought that precipitants are the most unpredictable of causes, there does seem to be a common pattern of government actions that act as catalysts for terrorism. Government use of unexpected and unusual force in response to protest or reform attempts often compels terrorist retaliation. The development of such an action-reaction syndrome then establishes the structure of the conflict between the regime and its challengers. There are numerous historical examples of a campaign of terrorism precipitated by a government's reliance on excessive force to quell protest or squash dissent. The tsarist regime's severity in dealing with the populist movement was a factor in the development of Narodaya Volya as a terrorist organization in 1879. The French government's persecution of anarchists was a factor in subsequent anarchist terrorism in the 1890s. The British government's execution of the heros of the Easter Rising set the stage for Michael Collins and the IRA. The Protestant violence that met the Catholic civil rights movement in Northern Ireland in 1969 pushed the Provisional IRA to retaliate. In West Germany, the death of Beno Ohnesorg at the hands of the police in a demonstration against the Shah of Iran in 1968 contributed to the emergence of the RAF.

This analysis of the background conditions for terrorism indicates that we must look at the terrorist organization's perception and interpretation of the situation. Terrorists view the context as permissive, making terrorism a viable option. In a material sense, the means are placed at their disposal by the environment. Circumstances also provide the terrorists with compelling reasons for seeking political change. Finally, an event occurs that snaps the terrorists' patience with the regime. Government action is now seen as intolerably unjust, and terrorism becomes not only a possible decision but a morally acceptable one. The regime has forfeited its status as the standard of legitimacy. For the terrorist, the end may now excuse the means.

The Reasons for Terrorism

Significant campaigns of terrorism depend on rational political choice. As purposeful activity, terrorism is the result of an organization's decision that it is a politically useful means to oppose a government. The argument that terrorist behavior should be analyzed as "rational" is based on the assumption that terrorist organizations possess internally consistent sets of values, beliefs, and images of the environment. Terrorism is seen collectively as a logical means to advance desired ends. The terrorist organization engages in decision-making calculations that an analyst can approximate. In short, the terror-

ist group's reasons for resorting to terrorism constitute an important factor in the process of causation.[17]

Terrorism serves a variety of goals, both revolutionary and subrevolutionary. Terrorists may be revolutionaries (such as the Combat Organization of the Socialist-Revolutionary Party in the nineteenth century or the Tupamaros of the twentieth); nationalists fighting against foreign occupiers (the Algerian FLN, the IRA of 1919–21, or the Irgun); minority separatists combatting indigenous regimes (such as the Corsican, Breton, and Basque movements, and the Provisional IRA); reformists (the bombing of nuclear construction sites, for example, is meant to halt nuclear power, not to overthrow governments); anarchists or millenarians (such as the original anarchist movement of the nineteenth century and modern millenarian groups such as the Red Army faction in West Germany, the Italian Red Brigades, and the Japanese Red Army); or reactionaries acting to prevent change from the top (such as the Secret Army Organization during the Algerian war or the contemporary Ulster Defence Association in Northern Ireland).[18]

Saying that extremist groups resort to terrorism in order to acquire political influence does not mean that all groups have equally precise objectives or that the relationship between means and ends is perfectly clear to an outside observer. Some groups are less realistic about the logic of means and ends than others. The leaders of Narodnaya Volya, for example, lacked a detailed conception of how the assassination of the tsar would force his successor to permit the liberalization they sought. Other terrorist groups are more pragmatic: the IRA of 1919–21 and the Irgun, for instance, shrewdly foresaw the utility of a war of attrition against the British. Menachem Begin, in particular, planned his campaign to take advantage of the "glass house" that Britain operated in.[19] The degree of skill in relating means to ends seems to have little to do with the overall sophistication of the terrorist ideology. The French anarchists of the 1890s, for example, acted in light of a well-developed philosophical doctrine but were much less certain of how violence against the bourgeoisie would bring about freedom. It is possible that anarchist or millenarian terrorists are so preoccupied with the splendor of the future that they lose sight of the present. Less theoretical nationalists who concentrate on the short run have simpler aims but sharper plans.

However diverse the long-run goals of terrorist groups, there is a common pattern of proximate or short-run objectives of a terrorist strategy. Proximate objectives are defined in terms of the reactions that terrorists want to achieve in their different audiences.[20] The most basic reason for terrorism is to gain recognition or attention—what Thornton called advertisement of the cause. Violence and bloodshed always excite human curiosity, and the theatricality, suspense, and threat of danger inherent in terrorism enhance its attention-getting qualities. In fact, publicity may be the highest goal of some groups. For example, terrorists who are fundamentally protesters might be satisfied with airing their grievances before the world. Today, in an interdependent world, the need for international recognition encourages transnational terrorist activities, with escalation to ever more destructive and spectacular violence. As the audience grows larger, more diverse, and more accustomed to terrorism, terrorists must go to extreme lengths to shock.

Terrorism is also often designed to disrupt and discredit the processes of government, by weakening it administratively and impairing normal operations. Terrorism as a direct attack on the regime aims at the insecurity and demoralization of government officials, independent of any impact on public opinion. An excellent example of this strategy is Michael Collins's campaign against the British intelligence system in Ireland in 1919–21. This form of terrorism often accompanies rural guerrilla warfare, as the insurgents try to weaken the government's control over its territory.

Terrorism also affects public attitudes in both a positive and a negative sense, aiming at creating either sympathy in a potential constituency or fear and hostility in an audience identified as the "enemy." These two functions are interrelated, since intimidating the "enemy" impresses both sympathizers and the uncommitted. At the same time, terrorism may be used to enforce obedience in an audience from whom the terrorists demand allegiance. The FLN in Algeria, for example, claimed more Algerian than French victims. Fear and respect were not incompatible with solidarity against the French.[21] When terrorism is part of a struggle between incumbents and challengers, polarization of public opinion undermines the government's legitimacy.

Terrorism may also be intended to provoke a counterreaction from the government, to increase publicity for the terrorists' cause and to demonstrate to the people that their charges against the regime are well founded. The terrorists mean to force the state to show its true repressive face, thereby driving the people into the arms of the challengers. For example, Carlos Marighela argued that the way to win popular support was to provoke the regime to measures of greater repression and persecution.[22] Provocative terrorism is designed to bring about revolutionary conditions rather than to exploit them. The FLN against the French, the Palestinians against Israel, and the RAF against the Federal Republic all appear to have used terrorism as provocation.

In addition, terrorism may serve internal organizational functions of control, discipline, and morale building within the terrorist group and even become an instrument of rivalry among factions in a resistance movement. For example, factional terrorism has frequently characterized the Palestinian resistance movement. Rival groups have competed in a vicious game where the victims are Israeli civilians or anonymous airline passengers, but where the immediate goal is influence within the resistance movement rather than the intimidation of the Israeli public or international recognition of the Palestinian cause.

Terrorism is a logical choice when oppositions have such goals and when the power ratio of government to challenger is high. The observation that terrorism is a weapon of the weak is hackneyed but apt. At least when initially adopted, terrorism is the strategy of a minority that by its own judgment lacks other means. When the group perceives its options as limited, terrorism is attractive because it is a relatively inexpensive and simple alternative, and because its potential reward is high.

Weakness and consequent restriction of choice can stem from different sources. On the one hand, weakness may result from the regime's suppression of opposition. Resistance organizations who lack the means of mounting more extensive violence may then turn to terrorism because legitimate expression of dissent is denied. Lack of popular support at the outset of a conflict does not mean that the terrorists' aims lack general appeal. Even though they cannot immediately mobilize widespread and active support, over the course of the conflict they may acquire the allegiance of the population. For example, the Algerian FLN used terrorism as a significant means of mobilizing mass support.[23]

On the other hand, it is wrong to assume that where there is terrorism there is oppression. Weakness may mean that an extremist organization deliberately rejects nonviolent methods of opposition open to them in a liberal state. Challengers then adopt terrorism because they are impatient with time-consuming legal methods of eliciting support or advertising their cause, because they distrust the regime, or because they are not capable of, or interested in, mobilizing majority support. Most terrorist groups operating in Western Europe and Japan in the past decade illustrate this phenomenon. The new millenarians lack a readily identifiable constituency and espouse causes devoid of mass appeal. Similarly, separatist movements represent at best only a minority of the total population of the state.

Thus, some groups are weak because weakness is imposed on them by the political system they operate in, others because of unpopularity. We are therefore making value judgments about the potential legitimacy of terrorist organizations. In some cases resistance groups are genuinely desperate, in others they have alternatives to violence. Nor do we want to forget that nonviolent resistance has been chosen in other circumstances, for example, by Gandhi and by Martin Luther King. Terrorists may argue that they had no choice, but their perceptions may be flawed.[24]

In addition to weakness, an important rationale in the decision to adopt a strategy of terrorism is impatience. Action becomes imperative. For a variety of reasons, the challenge to the state cannot be left to the future. Given a perception of limited means, the group often sees the choice as between action as survival and inaction as the death of resistance.

One reason for haste is external: the historical moment seems to present a unique chance. For example, the resistance group facing a colonial power recently weakened by a foreign war exploits a temporary vulnerability: the IRA against Britain after World War I, the Irgun against Britain after World War II, and the FLN against France after the Indochina war. We might even suggest that the stalemate between the United States and North Vietnam stimulated the post-1968 wave of anti-imperialist terrorism, especially in Latin America. There may be other pressures or catalysts provided by the regime, such as the violent precipitants discussed earlier or the British decision to introduce conscription in Ireland during World War I.

A sense of urgency may also develop when similar resistance groups have apparently succeeded with terrorism and created a momentum. The contagion effect of terrorism is partially based on an image of success that recommends terrorism to groups who identify with the innovator. The Algerian FLN, for example, was pressured to keep up with nationalists in Tunisia and Morocco, whose violent agitation brought about independence in 1956. Terrorism spread rapidly through Latin America in the post-1968 period as revolutionary groups worked in terms of a continental solidarity.

Dramatic failure of alternative means of obtaining one's ends may also fuel a drive toward terrorism. The Arab defeat in the 1967 war with Israel led Palestinians to realize that they could no longer depend on the Arab states to further their goals. In retrospect, their extreme weakness and the historical tradition of violence in the Middle East made it likely that militant nationalists should turn to terrorism. Since international recognition of the Palestinian cause was a primary aim (given the influence of outside powers in the region) and since attacks on Israeli territory were difficult, terrorism developed into a transnational phenomenon.

These external pressures to act are often intensified by internal politics. Leaders of resistance groups act under constraints imposed by their followers. They are forced to justify the organization's existence, to quell restlessness among the cadres, to satisfy demands for revenge, to prevent splintering of the movement, and to maintain control. Pressures may also come from the terrorists' constituency.

In conclusion, we see that terrorism is an attractive strategy to groups of different ideological persuasions who challenge the state's authority. Groups who want to dramatize a cause, to demoralize the government, to gain popular support, to provoke regime violence, to inspire followers, or to dominate a wider resistance movement, who are weak vis-à-vis the regime, and who are impatient to act, often find terrorism a reasonable choice. This is especially so when conditions are favorable, providing opportunities and making terrorism a simple and rapid option, with immediate and visible payoff.

Individual Motivation and Participation

Terrorism is neither an automatic reaction to conditions nor a purely calculated strategy. What psychological factors motivate the terrorist and influence his or her perceptions and interpretations of reality? Terrorists are only a small minority of people with similar personal backgrounds, experiencing the same conditions, who might thus be expected to reach identical conclusions based on logical reasoning about the utility of terrorism as a technique of political influence.

The relationship between personality and politics is complex and imperfectly understood.[25] Why individuals engage in political violence is a complicated problem, and the question why they engage in terrorism is still more difficult.[26] As most simply and frequently posed, the question of a psychological explanation of terrorism is whether or not there is a "terrorist personality," similar to the authoritarian personality, whose emotional traits we can specify with some exactitude.[27] An identifiable pattern of attitudes and behavior in the terrorism-prone individual would result from a combination of ego-defensive needs, cognitive processes, and socialization, in interaction with a specific situation. In pursuing this line of inquiry, it is important to avoid stereotyping the terrorist or oversimplifying the sources of terrorist actions. No single motivation or personality can be valid for all circumstances.

What limited data we have on individual terrorists (and knowledge must be gleaned from disparate sources that usually neither focus on psychology nor use a comparative approach) suggest that the outstanding common characteristic of terrorists is their normality. Terrorism often seems to be the connecting link among widely varying personalities. Franco Venturi, concentrating on the terrorists of a single small group, observed that "the policy of terrorism united many very different characters and mentalities" and that agreement on using terrorism was the cement that bound the members of Narodnaya Volya together.[28] The West German psychiatrist who conducted a pretrial examination of four members of the RAF concluded that they were "intelligent," even "humorous," and showed no symptoms of psychosis or neurosis and "no particular personality type."[29] Psychoanalysis might penetrate beneath superficial normality to expose some unifying or pathological trait, but this is scarcely a workable research method, even if the likelihood of the existence of such a characteristic could be demonstrated.

Peter Merkl, in his study of the pre-1933 Nazi movement—a study based on much more data than we have on terrorists—abandoned any attempt to classify personality types and instead focused on factors like the level of political understanding.[30] An unbiased examination of conscious attitudes might be more revealing than a study of subconscious predispositions or personalities. For example, if terrorists perceive the state as unjust, morally corrupt, and violent, then terrorism may seem legitimate and justified. For example, Blumenthal and her coauthors found that "the stronger the perception of an act as violence, the more violence is thought to be an appropriate response."[31] The evidence also indicates that many terrorists are activists with prior political experience in nonviolent opposition to the state. How do these experiences in participation influence later attitudes? Furthermore, how do terrorists view their victims? Do we find extreme devaluation, depersonalization, or stereotyping? Is there "us versus them" polarization or ethnic or religious prejudice that might sanction or prompt violence toward an out-group? How do terrorists justify and rationalize violence? Is remorse a theme?

The questions of attitudes toward victims and justifications for terrorism are especially important because different forms of terrorism involve various degrees of selectivity in the choice of victims. Some acts of terrorism are extremely discriminate, while others are broadly indiscriminate. Also, some terrorist acts require more intimate contact between terrorist and victim than others. Thus, the form of terrorism practiced —how selective it is and how much personal domination of the victim it involves—would determine the relevance of different questions.

Analyzing these issues involves serious methodological problems. As the Blumenthal study emphasizes, there are two ways of analyzing the relationship between attitudes and political behavior.[32] If our interest is in identifying potential terrorists by predicting behavior from the existence of certain consciously held attitudes and beliefs, then the best method would be to survey a young age group in a society determined to be susceptible. If terrorism subsequently occurred, we could then see which types of individuals became terrorists. (A problem is that the preconditions would change over time and that precipitants are unpredictable.) The more common and easier way of investigating the attitudes-behavior connection is to select people who have engaged in a particular behavior and ask them questions about their opinions. Yet attitudes may be adopted subsequent, rather than prior, to behavior, and they may serve as rationalizations for behavior engaged in for different reasons, not as genuine motivations. These problems would seem to be particularly acute when the individuals concerned have engaged in illegal forms of political behavior.

Another problem facing the researcher interested in predispositions or attitudes is that terrorists are recruited in different ways. Assuming that people who are in some way personally attracted to terrorism actually engage in such behavior supposes that potential terrorists are presented with an appropriate opportunity, which is a factor over which they have little control.[33] Moreover, terrorist groups often discourage or reject potential recruits who are openly seeking excitement or danger for personal motives. For instance, William Mackey Lomasney, a member of the Clan na Gael or American Fenians in the nineteenth century (who was killed in 1884 in an attempt to blow up London Bridge) condemned the "disgraceful" activities of the hotheaded and impulsive Jeremiah O'Donovan Rossa:

> Were it not that O'Donovan Rossa has openly and unblushingly boasted that he is responsible for those ridiculous and futile efforts . . . we might hesitate to even suspect that any sane man, least of all one professedly friendly to the cause, would for any consideration or desire for notoriety take upon himself such a fearful responsibility, and, that hav-

ing done so, he could engage men so utterly incapable of carrying out his insane designs.[34]

Lomasney complained that the would-be terrorists were:

> such stupid blundering fools that they make our
> cause appear imbecile and farcical. When the fact
> becomes known that those half-idiotic attempts
> have been made by men professing to be patriotic
> Irishmen what will the world think but that Irish
> revolutionists are a lot of fools and ignoramuses,
> men who do not understand the first principles of
> the art of war, the elements of chemistry or even
> the amount of explosive material necessary to re-
> move or destroy an ordinary brick or stone wall.
> Think of the utter madness of men who have no
> idea of accumulative and destructive forces under-
> taking with common blasting powder to scare and
> shatter the Empire.[35]

Not only do serious terrorists scorn the inepti-
tude of the more excitable, but they find them a
serious security risk. Rossa, for example, could
not be trusted not to give away the Clan na
Gael's plans for terrorism in his New York newspaper articles. In a similar vein, Boris Savinkov, head of the Combat Organization of the
Socialist-Revolutionary party in Russia, tried to
discourage an aspirant whom he suspected of
being drawn to the adventure of terrorism:

> I explained to him that terrorist activity did not
> consist only of throwing bombs; that it was much
> more minute, difficult and tedious than might be
> imagined; that a terrorist is called upon to live a
> rather dull existence for months at a time, eschew-
> ing meeting his own comrades and doing most
> difficult and unpleasant work—the work of sys-
> tematic observation.[36]

Similar problems in analyzing the connection between attitudes and behavior are due to
the fact that there are role differentiations between leaders and followers. The degree of formal organization varies from the paramilitary
hierarchies of the Irgun or the IRA to the semi-
autonomous coexistence of small groups in contemporary West Germany or Italy or even to the
rejection of central direction in the nineteenth
century anarchist movement in France. Yet even

Narodnaya Volya, a self-consciously democratic
group, observed distinctions based on authority.
There are thus likely to be psychological or background differences between leaders and cadres.
For example, a survey of contemporary terrorist
movements found that leaders are usually older
than their followers, which is not historically unusual.[37] In general, data are scant on individual
terrorist leaders, their exercise of authority, the
basis for it, and their interactions with their followers.[38] Furthermore, if there is a predisposition to terrorism, the terrorism-prone individual
who obtains psychic gratification from the experience is likely to be a follower, not a leader who
commands but does not perform the act.

An alternative approach to analyzing the
psychology of terrorism is to use a deductive
method based on what we know about terrorism
as an activity, rather than an inductive method
yielding general propositions from statements of
the particular. What sort of characteristics
would make an individual suited for terrorism?
What are the role requirements of the terrorist?

One of the most salient attributes of terrorist
activity is that it involves significant personal
danger.[39] Furthermore, since terrorism involves
premeditated, not impulsive, violence, the terrorist's awareness of the risks is maximized. Thus,
although terrorists may simply be people who enjoy or disregard risk,[40] it is more likely that they
are people who tolerate high risk because of intense commitment to a cause. Their commitment
is strong enough to make the risk of personal
harm acceptable and perhaps to outweigh the
cost of society's rejection, although defiance of
the majority may be a reward in itself. In either
case, the violent activity is not gratifying per se.

It is perhaps even more significant that terrorism is a group activity, involving intimate relationships among a small number of people.
Interactions among members of the group may
be more important in determining behavior than
the psychological predispositions of individual
members. Terrorists live and make decisions under conditions of extreme stress. As a clandestine minority, the members of a terrorist

group are isolated from society, even if they live in what Menachem Begin called the "open underground."[41]

Terrorists can confide in and trust only each other. The nature of their commitment cuts them off from society; they inhabit a closed community that is forsaken only at great cost. Isolation and the perception of a hostile environment intensify shared belief and commitment and make faith in the cause imperative. A pattern of mutual reassurance, solidarity, and comradeship develops, in which the members of the group reinforce each other's self-righteousness, image of a hostile world, and sense of mission. Because of the real danger terrorists confront, the strain they live under, and the moral conflicts they undergo, they value solidarity highly.[42] Terrorists are not necessarily people who seek "belonging" or personal integration through ideological commitment, but once embarked on the path of terrorism, they desperately need the group and the cause. Isolation and internal consensus explain how the beliefs and values of a terrorist group can be so drastically at odds with those of society at large. An example of such a divorce from social and political reality is the idea of the RAF that terrorism would lead to a resurgence of Nazism in West Germany that would in turn spark a workers' revolt.[43]

In their intense commitment, separation from the outside world, and intolerance of internal dissent, terrorist groups resemble religious sects or cults. Michael Barkun has explained the continued commitment of members of millenarian movements, a conviction frequently expressed in proselytizing in order to validate beliefs, in terms of the reinforcement and reassurance of rightness that the individual receives from other members of the organization. He also notes the frequent practice of initiation rites that involve violations of taboos, or "bridge-burning acts," that create guilt and prevent the convert's return to society. Thus the millenarian, like the terrorist group, constitutes "a community of common guilt."[44] J. Bowyer Bell has commented on the religious qualities of dedication and

moral fervor characterizing the IRA: "In the Republican Movement, the two seemingly opposing traditions, one of the revolution and physical force, and the other of pious and puritanical service, combine into a secular vocation."[45]

If there is a single common emotion that drives the individual to become a terrorist, it is vengeance on behalf of comrades or even the constituency the terrorist aspires to represent. (At the same time, the demand for retribution serves as public justification or excuse.) A regime thus encourages terrorism when it creates martyrs to be avenged. Anger at what is perceived as unjust persecution inspires demands for revenge, and as the regime responds to terrorism with greater force, violence escalates out of control.

There are numerous historical demonstrations of the central role vengeance plays as motivation for terrorism. It is seen as one of the principal causes of anarchist terrorism in France in the 1890s. The infamous Ravachol acted to avenge the "martyrs of Clichy," two possibly innocent anarchists who were beaten by the police and sentenced to prison. Subsequent bombings and assassinations, for instance that of President Carnot, were intended to avenge Ravachol's execution.[46] The cruelty of the sentences imposed for minor offenses at the "Trial of the 193," the hanging of eleven southern revolutionaries after Soloviev's unsuccessful attack on the tsar in 1879, and the "Trial of the 16" in 1880 deeply affected the members of Narodnaya Volya. Kravchinski (Stepniak) explained that personal resentment felt after the Trial of the 193 led to killing police spies; it then seemed unreasonable to spare their employers, who were actually responsible for the repression. Thus, intellectually the logic first inspired by resentment compelled them to escalate terrorism by degrees.[47] During the Algerian war, the French execution of FLN prisoners; in Northern Ireland, British troops firing on civil rights demonstrators; in West Germany, the death of a demonstrator at the hands of the police—all served to precipitate terrorism as militants sought to avenge their comrades.

The terrorists' willingness to accept high risks may also be related to the belief that one's death will be avenged. The prospect of retribution gives the act of terrorism and the death of the terrorist meaning and continuity, even fame and immortality. Vengeance may be not only a function of anger but of a desire for transcendence.

Shared guilt is surely a strong force in binding members of the terrorist group together. Almost all terrorists seem compelled to justify their behavior, and this anxiety cannot be explained solely by reference to their desire to create a public image of virtuous sincerity. Terrorists usually show acute concern for morality, especially for sexual purity, and believe that they act in terms of a higher good. Justifications usually focus on past suffering, on the glorious future to be created, and on the regime's illegitimacy and violence, to which terrorism is the only available response. Shared guilt and anxiety increase the group's interdependence and mutual commitment and may also make followers more dependent on leaders and on the common ideology as sources of moral authority.

Guilt may also lead terrorists to seek punishment and danger rather than avoid it. The motive of self-sacrifice notably influenced many Russian terrorists of the nineteenth century. Kaliayev, for example, felt that only his death could atone for the murder he committed. Even to Camus, the risk of death for the terrorist is a form of personal absolution.[48] In other cases of terrorism, individuals much more pragmatic than Kaliayev, admittedly a religious mystic, seemed to welcome capture because it brought release from the strains of underground existence and a sense of content and fulfillment. For example, Meridor, a member of the Irgun High Command, felt "high spirits" and "satisfaction" when arrested by the British because he now shared the suffering that all fighters had to experience. He almost welcomed the opportunity to prove that he was prepared to sacrifice himself for the cause. In fact, until his arrest he had felt "morally uncomfortable," whereas afterwards he

felt "exalted."[49] Menachem Begin expressed similar feelings. Once, waiting as the British searched the hotel where he was staying, he admitted anxiety and fear, but when he knew there was "no way out," his "anxious thoughts evaporated." He "felt a peculiar serenity mixed with incomprehensible happiness" and waited "composedly," but the police passed him by.[50]

Vera Figner, a leader of the Narodnaya Volya, insisted on physically assisting in acts of terrorism, even though her comrades accused her of seeking personal satisfaction instead of allowing the organization to make the best use of her talents. She found it intolerable to bear a moral responsibility for acts that endangered her comrades. She could not encourage others to commit acts she would not herself commit; anything less than full acceptance of the consequences of her decisions would be cowardice.[51]

It is possible that the willingness to face risk is related to what Robert J. Lifton has termed "survivor-guilt" as well as to feelings of group solidarity or of guilt at harming victims.[52] Sometimes individuals who survive disaster or escape punishment when others have suffered feel guilty and may seek relief by courting a similar fate. This guilt may also explain why terrorists often take enormous risks to rescue imprisoned comrades, as well as why they accept danger or arrest with equanimity or even satisfaction.

It is clear that once a terrorist group embarks on a strategy of terrorism, whatever its purpose and whatever its successes or failures, psychological factors make it very difficult to halt. Terrorism as a process gathers its own momentum, independent of external events.

Conclusions

Terrorism per se is not usually a reflection of mass discontent or deep cleavages in society. More often it represents the disaffection of a fragment of the elite, who may take it upon themselves to act on the behalf of a majority unaware of its plight, unwilling to take action to remedy grievances, or unable to express dissent. This discontent, however subjective in origin or minor in scope, is blamed on the government and its supporters. Since the sources of terrorism are manifold, any society or polity that permits opportunities for terrorism is vulnerable. Government reactions that are inconsistent, wavering between tolerance and repression, seem most likely to encourage terrorism.

Given some source of disaffection—and in the centralized modern state with its faceless bureaucracies, lack of responsiveness to demands is ubiquitous—terrorism is an attractive strategy for small organizations of diverse ideological persuasions who want to attract attention for their cause, provoke the government, intimidate opponents, appeal for sympathy, impress an audience, or promote the adherence of the faithful. Terrorists perceive an absence of choice. Whether unable or unwilling to perceive a choice between terrorist and nonterrorist action, whether unpopular or prohibited by the government, the terrorist group reasons that there is no alternative. The ease, simplicity, and rapidity with which terrorism can be implemented and the prominence of models of terrorism strengthen its appeal, especially since terrorist groups are impatient to act. Long-standing social traditions that sanction terrorism against the state, as in Ireland, further enhance its attractiveness.

There are two fundamental questions about the psychological basis of terrorism. The first is why the individual takes the first step and chooses to engage in terrorism: why join? Does the terrorist possess specific psychological predispositions, identifiable in advance, that suit him or her for terrorism? That terrorists are people capable of intense commitment tells us little, and the motivations for terrorism vary immensely. Many individuals are potential terrorists, but few actually make that commitment. To explain why terrorism happens, another question is more appropriate: Why does involvement

continue? What are the psychological mechanisms of group interaction? We are not dealing with a situation in which certain types of personalities suddenly turn to terrorism in answer to some inner call. Terrorism is the result of a gradual growth of commitment and opposition, a group development that furthermore depends on government action. The psychological relationships within the terrorist group—the interplay of commitment, risk, solidarity, loyalty, guilt, revenge, and isolation—discourage terrorists from changing the direction they have taken. This may explain why—even if objective circumstances change when, for example, grievances are satisfied, or if the logic of the situation changes when, for example, the terrorists are offered other alternatives for the expression of opposition—terrorism may endure until the terrorist group is physically destroyed.

NOTES

1. For discussions of the meaning of the concept of terrorism, see Thomas P. Thornton, "Terror as a Weapon of Political Agitation," in Harry Eckstein, ed. *Internal War* (New York, 1964), pp. 71–99; Martha Crenshaw Hutchinson, "The Concept of Revolutionary Terrorism," *Revolutionary Terrorism: The FLN in Algeria, 1954–1962* (Stanford: The Hoover Institution Press, 1978) chap. 2; and E. Victor Walter, *Terror and Resistance* (New York, 1969).

2. Walter Laqueur, "Interpretations of Terrorism—Fact, Fiction and Political Science," *Journal of Contemporary History*, 12 (January 1977), 1–42. See also his major work *Terrorism* (London: Weidenfeld and Nicolson, 1977).

3. See, for example, Paul Wilkinson, *Terrorism and the Liberal State* (London: Macmillan, 1977), or J. Bowyer Bell, *A Time of Terror: How Democratic Societies Respond to Revolutionary Violence* (New York, 1978).

4. This is not to deny that some modern terrorist groups, such as those in West Germany, resemble premodern millenarian movements. See specifically Conor Cruise O'Brien, "Liberty and Terrorism," *International Security*, 2 (1977), 56–67. In general, see Norman Cohn, *The Pursuit of the Millenium* (London: Secker and Warburg, 1957), and E.J. Hobsbawm, *Primitive Rebels: Studies in Archaic Forms of Social Movement in the 19th and 20th Centuries* (Manchester: Manchester University Press, 1971).

5. A sampling would include Douglas Hibbs, Jr., *Mass Political Violence: A Cross-National Causal Analysis* (New York, 1973); William J. Crotty, ed. *Assassinations and the Political Order* (New York, 1971); Ted Robert Gurr, *Why Men Rebel* (Princeton, 1971), and Gurr, Peter N. Grabosky, and Richard C. Hula, *The Politics of Crime and Conflict* (Beverly Hills, 1977).

6. For a summary of these findings, see Gurr, "The Calculus of Civil Conflict," *Journal of Social Issues*, 28 (1972), 27–47.

7. Gurr, "Some Characteristics of Political Terrorism in the 1960s," in Michael Stohl, ed. *The Politics of Terrorism* (New York, 1979), pp. 23–50 and 46–47.

8. A distinction between preconditions and precipitants is found in Eckstein, "On the Etiology of Internal Wars," *History and Theory*, 4 (1965), 133–62. Kenneth Waltz also differentiates between the framework for action as a permissive or underlying cause and special reasons as immediate or efficient causes. In some cases we can say of terrorism, as he says of war, that it occurs because there is nothing to prevent it. See *Man, the State and War* (New York, 1959), p. 232.

9. Boris Savinkov, *Memoirs of a Terrorist*, trans. Joseph Shaplen (New York: A. & C. Boni, 1931), pp. 286–87.

10. The major theoreticians of the transition from the rural to the urban guerrilla are Carlos Marighela, *For the Liberation of Brazil* (Harmondsworth: Penguin Books, 1971), and Abraham Guillen, *Philosophy of the Urban Guerrilla: The Revolutionary Writings of Abraham Guillen*, trans. and edited by Donald C. Hodges (New York, 1973).

11. Hobsbawm, *Revolutionaries: Contemporary Essays* (New York, 1973), pp. 226–27.

12. Grabosky, "The Urban Context of Political Terrorism," in Michael Stohl, ed., pp. 51–76.

13. See Amy Sands Redlick, "The Transnational Flow of Information as a Cause of Terrorism," in Yonah Alexander, David Carlton, and Wilkinson, eds. *Terrorism: Theory and Practice* (Boulder, 1979), pp. 73–95. See also Manus I. Midlarsky, Martha Crenshaw, and Fumihiko Yoshida, "Why Violence Spreads: The Contagion of International Terrorism," *International Studies Quarterly*, 24 (June 1980), 262–98.

14. Monica D. Blumenthal, et al., *More About Justifying Violence: Methodological Studies of Attitudes and Behavior* (Ann Arbor: Survey Research Center, Institute for Social Research, University of Michigan, 1975), p. 108. Similarly, Peter Lupsha, "Explanation of Political Violence: Some Psychological Theories Versus Indignation," *Politics and Society*, 2 (1971), 89–104, contrasts the concept of "indignation" with Gurr's theory of relative deprivation, which holds that expectations exceed rewards (see *Why Men Rebel*, esp. pp. 24–30).

15. Hobsbawm, *Revolutionaries*, p. 143.

16. Luigi Bonanate, "Some Unanticipated Consequences of Terrorism," *Journal of Peace Research*, 16 (1979), 197–211. If this theory is valid, we then need to identify such blocked societies.

17. See Barbara Salert's critique of the rational choice model of revolutionary participation in *Revolutions and Revolutionaries* (New York, 1976). In addition, Abraham Kaplan discusses the distinction between reasons and causes in "The Psychodynamics of Terrorism," *Terrorism—An International Journal*, 1, 3 and 4 (1978), 237–54.

18. For a typology of terrorist organizations, see Wilkinson, *Political Terrorism* (New York, 1975). These classes are not mutually exclusive, and they depend on an outside assessment of goals. For example, the Basque ETA would consider itself revolutionary as well as separatist. The RAF considered itself a classic national liberation movement, and the Provisional IRA insists that it is combatting a foreign oppressor, not an indigenous regime.

19. Bell presents a succinct analysis of Irgun strategy in "The Palestinian Archetype: Irgun and the Strategy of Leverage," in *On Revolt: Strategies of National Liberation* (Cambridge [Ma.], 1976), chap. 3.

20. See Thornton's analysis of proximate goals in "Terror as a Weapon of Political Agitation," in Eckstein, ed. pp. 82–88.

21. Walter's discussion of the concept of "forced choice" explains how direct audiences, from whom the victims are drawn, may accept terrorism as legitimate; see *Terror and Resistance*, pp. 285–89.

22. See Marighela, *For the Liberation of Brazil*, pp. 94–95. The West German RAF apparently adopted the idea of provocation as part of a general national liberation strategy borrowed from the Third World.

23. See Hutchinson, *Revolutionary Terrorism*, chap. 3, pp. 40–60.

24. See Michael Walzer's analysis of the morality of terrorism in *Just and Unjust Wars* (New York, 1977), pp. 197–206. See also Bernard Avishai, "In Cold Blood," *The New York Review of Books*, March 8, 1979, pp. 41–44, for a critical appraisal of the failure of recent works on terrorism to discuss moral issues. The question of the availability of alternatives to terrorism is related to the problem of discrimination in the selection of victims. Where victims are clearly responsible for a regime's denial of opportunity, terrorism is more justifiable than where they are not.

25. See Fred I. Greenstein, *Personality and Politics: Problems of Evidence, Inference, and Conceptualization* (Chicago, 1969).

26. See Jeffrey Goldstein, *Aggression and Crimes of Violence* (New York, 1975).

27. A study of the West German New Left, for example, concludes that social psychological models of authoritarianism do help explain the dynamics of radicalism and even the transformation from protest to terrorism. See S. Robert Lichter, "A Psychopolitical Study of West German Male Radical Students," *Comparative Politics*, 12 (October 1979), pp. 27–48.

28. Franco Venturi, *Roots of Revolution: A History of the Populist and Socialist Movements in Nineteenth Century Russia* (London: Weidenfeld and Nicolson, 1960), p. 647.

29. Quoted in *Science*, 203, 5 January 1979, p. 34, as part of an account of the proceedings of the International Scientific Conference on Terrorism held in Berlin, December, 1978. Advocates of the "terrorist personality" theory, however, argued that terrorists suffer from faulty vestibular functions in the middle ear or from inconsistent mothering resulting in dysphoria. For another description see John Wykert, "Psychiatry and Terrorism," *Psychiatric News*, 14 (February 2, 1979), 1 and 12–14. A psychologist's study of a single group, the Front de Libération du Québec, is Gustav Morf, *Terror in Quebec: Case Studies of the FLQ* (Toronto: Clarke, Irvin, and Co., 1970).

30. Peter Merkl, *Political Violence Under the Swastika: 581 Early Nazis* (Princeton, 1974), 33–34.

31. Blumenthal, et al., p. 182.

32. Ibid., p. 12. Lichter also recognizes this problem.

33. Ibid., pp. 12–13.

34. William O'Brien and Desmond Ryan, eds. *Devoy's Post Bag*, vol. II (Dublin: C.J. Fallon, Ltd., 1953), p. 51.

35. Ibid., p. 52.

36. Savinkov, *Memoirs*, p. 147.

37. Charles A. Russell and Bowman H. Miller,

"Profile of a Terrorist," *Terrorism—An International Journal*, 1 (1977), reprinted in John D. Elliott and Leslie K. Gibson, eds. *Contemporary Terrorism: Selected Readings* (Gaithersburg, Md.: International Association of Chiefs of Police, 1978), pp. 81–95.

38. See Philip Pomper's analysis of the influence of Nechaev over his band of followers: "The People's Revenge," *Sergei Nechaev* (New Brunswick [N.J.], 1979), chap. 4.

39. A Rand Corporation study of kidnappings and barricade-and-hostage incidents concluded that such tactics are not necessarily perilous, while admitting that drawing statistical inferences from a small number of cases in a limited time period (August, 1968 to June, 1975) is hazardous. See Brian Jenkins, Janera Johnson, and David Ronfeldt, *Numbered Lives: Some Statistical Observations from 77 International Hostage Episodes*, Rand Paper P-5905 (Santa Monica: The Rand Corporation, 1977).

40. Psychiatrist Frederick Hacker, for example, argues that terrorists are by nature indifferent to risk; see *Crusaders, Criminals and Crazies* (New York, 1976), p. 13.

41. Menachem Begin, *The Revolt* (London: W.H. Allen, 1951).

42. J. Glenn Gray, "The Enduring Appeals of Battle," *The Warriors: Reflections on Men in Battle* (New York, 1970), chap. 2, describes similar experiences among soldiers in combat.

43. Statements of the beliefs of the leaders of the RAF can be found in *Textes des prisonniers de la Fraction armée rouge et dernières lettres d'Ulrike Meinhof* (Paris: Maspéro, 1977).

44. Michael Barkun, *Disaster and the Millennium* (New Haven, 1974), pp. 14–16. See also Leon Festinger, et al., *When Prophecy Fails* (New York, 1964).

45. Bell, *The Secret Army* (London: Anthony Blond, 1970), p. 379.

46. Jean Maitron, *Histoire du mouvement anarchiste en France (1880–1914)* (Paris: Societé universitaire d'éditions et de librairie, 1955), pp. 242–43.

47. S. Stepniak (pseudonym for Kravchimski), *Underground Russia: Revolutionary Profiles and Sketches from Life* (London: Smith, Elder, and Co., 1882), pp. 36–37; see also Venturi, pp. 639 and 707–08.

48. See "Les meurtriers délicats" in *L'Homme Révolté* (Paris: Gallimard, 1965), pp. 571–79.

49. Ya'acov Meridor, *Long is the Road to Freedom* (Tujunga [Ca.]: Barak Publications, 1961), pp. 6 and 9.

50. Begin, p. 111.

51. Vera Figner, *Mémoires d'une révolutionnaire*, trans. Victor Serge (Paris: Gallimard, 1930), pp. 131 and 257–62.

52. Such an argument is applied to Japanese Red Army terrorist Kozo Okamoto by Patricia Steinhof in "Portrait of a Terrorist," *Asian Survey*, 16 (1976), 830–45.

AVISHAI MARGALIT AND IAN BURUMA

OCCIDENTALISM

1.

In 1942, not long after the attack on Pearl Harbor, a group of Japanese philosophers got together in Kyoto to discuss Japan's role in the world. The project of this ultra-nationalist gathering was, as they put it, to find a way to "overcome modern civilization." Since modern civilization was another term for Western civilization, the conference might just as well have been entitled "Overcoming the West." In a complete reversal of the late-nineteenth-century goal of "leaving Asia and joining the West," Japan was now fighting a "holy war" to liberate Asia from the West and purify Asian minds of Western ideas. Part of the holy war was, as it were, an exercise in philosophical cleansing.

The cleansing agent was a mystical mishmash of German-inspired ethnic nationalism and Zen- and Shinto-based nativism. The Japanese were a "world-historical race" descended from the gods, whose divine task it was to lead all Asians into a new age of Great Harmony, and so on. But what was "the West" which had to be purged? What needed to be "overcome"? The question has gained currency, since the chief characteristics of this Western enemy would have sounded familiar to Osama bin Laden, and other Islamic extremists. They are, not in any particular order, materialism, liberalism, capitalism, individualism, humanism, rationalism, socialism, decadence, and moral laxity. These ills would be overcome by a show of Japanese force, not just military force, but force of will, of spirit, of soul. The key characteristics of the Japanese or "Asian" spirit were self-sacrifice, discipline, austerity, individual submission to the collective good, worship of divine leadership, and a deep faith in the superiority of instinct over reason.

There was of course more at stake in Japan's war with the West, but these were the philosophical underpinnings of Japanese wartime propaganda. The central document of Japan's claim to national divinity was entitled *Cardinal Principles of the National Polity (Kokutai no Hongi)*. Issued in 1937 by the ministry of education, this document claimed that the Japanese were "intrinsically quite different from so-called citizens of Western nations," because the divine imperial bloodlines had remained unbroken, and "we always seek in the emperor the source of our lives and activities." The Japanese spirit was "pure" and "unclouded," whereas the influence of Western culture led to mental confusion and spiritual corruption.

Western, especially German, ideas inspired some of this. A famous right-wing professor, Dr. Uesugi Shinkichi, began his spiritual life as a Christian, studied statecraft in Wilhelminian Germany, and returned home to write (in 1919): "Subjects have no mind apart from the will of the Emperor. Their individual selves are merged with the Emperor. If they act according to the mind of the Emperor, they can realize their true nature and attain the moral ideal."[1] Of such stuff are holy warriors made.

Similar language—though without the neo-Shintoist associations—was used by German National Socialists and other European fascists. They, too, fought against that list of "soulless" characteristics commonly associated with liberal societies. One of the early critical books about Nazi thinking, by Aurel Kolnai, a Hungarian refugee, was actually entitled *The War Against the West*.[2] Nazi ideologues and Japanese militarist propagandists were fighting the same

From *The New York Review of Books* (January 17, 2002).

Western ideas. The West they loathed was a multinational, multicultural place, but the main symbols of hate were republican France, capitalist America, liberal England, and, in Germany more than Japan, the rootless cosmopolitan Jews. Japanese propaganda focused on the "Anglo-American beasts," represented in cartoons of Roosevelt and Churchill wearing plutocratic top hats. To the Nazis "the eternal Jew" represented everything that was hateful about liberalism.

War against the West is partly a war against a particular concept of citizenship and community. Decades before the coming of Hitler, the spiritual godfather of Nazism, Houston Stewart Chamberlain, described France, Britain, and America as hopelessly "Jewified" countries. Citizenship in these places had degenerated into a "purely political concept."[3] In England, he said, "every Basuto nigger" could get a passport. Later he complained that the country had "fallen utterly into the hands of Jews and Americans."[4] Germany in his view, and that of his friend Kaiser Wilhelm II, was the only nation with enough national spirit and racial solidarity to save the West from going under in a sea of decadence and corruption. His "West" was not based on citizenship but on blood and soil.

Oswald Spengler warned in 1933 (of all years) that the main threats to the Occident came from "colored peoples" (*Farbigen*).[5] He prophesied, not entirely without reason, huge uprisings of enraged peoples in the European colonies. He also claimed that after 1918 the Russians had become "Asiatic" again, and that the Japanese Yellow Peril was about to engulf the civilized world. More interesting, however, was Spengler's view that the ruling white races (*Herrenvölker*) were losing their position in Europe. Soon, he said, true Frenchmen would no longer rule France, which was already awash with black soldiers, Polish businessmen, and Spanish farmers. The West, he concluded, would go under because white people had become soft, decadent, addicted to safety and comfort. As he put it: "Jazz music and nigger dances

are the death march of a great civilization."

If criticism of the West was influenced by half-baked ideas from Germany, more positive views of the West were also influenced by German ideas. The Slavophiles and the Westernizers, who offered opposing views of the West in nineteenth-century Russia, were both equally inspired by German intellectual currents. Ideas for or against the West are in fact to be found everywhere. The East does not begin at the river Elbe, as Konrad Adenauer believed, nor does the West start in Prague, as Milan Kundera once suggested. East and West are not necessarily geographical territories. Rather, Occidentalism, which played such a large part in the attacks of September 11, is a cluster of images and ideas of the West in the minds of its haters. Four features of Occidentalism can be seen in most versions of it; we can call them the City, the Bourgeois, Reason, and Feminism. Each contains a set of attributes, such as arrogance, feebleness, greed, depravity, and decadence, which are invoked as typically Western, or even American, characteristics.

The things Occidentalists hate about the West are not always the ones that inspire hatred of the US. The two issues should not be conflated. A friend once asked in astonishment: "Why does he hate me? I didn't even help him." Some people hate the US because they were helped by the US, and some because they were not. Some resent the way the US helped their own hateful governments gain or stay in power. Some feel humiliated by the very existence of the US, and some by US foreign policy. With some on the left, hatred of the US is all that remains of their leftism; anti-Americanism is part of their identity. The same goes for right-wing cultural Gaullists. Anti-Americanism is an important political issue, related to Occidentalism but not quite the same thing.

2.

Anti-liberal revolts almost invariably contain a deep hatred of the City, that is to say, everything represented by urban civilization: commerce, mixed populations, artistic freedom, sexual license, scientific pursuits, leisure, personal safety, wealth, and its usual concomitant, power. Mao Zedong, Pol Pot, Hitler, Japanese agrarian fascists, and of course Islamists all extolled the simple life of the pious peasant, pure at heart, uncorrupted by city pleasures, used to hard work and self-denial, tied to the soil, and obedient to authority. Behind the idyll of rural simplicity lies the desire to control masses of people, but also an old religious rage, which goes back at least as far as the ancient superpower Babylon.

The "holy men" of the three monotheistic religions—Christianity, Judaism, and Islam—denounced Babylon as the sinful city-state whose politics, military might, and very urban civilization posed an arrogant challenge to God. The fabled tower of Babylon was a symbol of hubris and idolatry: "Let us build a city and a tower, whose top may reach unto heaven; and let us make us a name" (Genesis 11:4). Indeed, God took it as a challenge to Himself: "And now nothing will be restrained from them, which they imagined to do" (Genesis 11:6). That is, the citizens of this urban superpower will act out their fantasies to become God.

"He loveth not the arrogant," the Koran (16:23) tells us, and goes on to say: "Allah took their structures from their foundation, and the roof fell down on them from above; and the Wrath seized them from directions they did not perceive" (16:26). The prophet Isaiah already prophesied that Babylon, "the glory of all kingdoms," would end up as "Sodom and Gomorrah" (Isaiah 13:19), and that the arrogant would be overthrown so that even an "Arabian pitch tent" would not inhabit the place (13:20). The Book of Revelation goes on to say about Babylon the great, "the mother of harlots and of the abominations of the earth" (17:5), that it "is fallen, is fallen" (18:2).

There is a recurring theme in movies from poor countries in which a young person from a remote village goes to the big city, forced by circumstances or eager to seek a new life in a wider, more affluent world. Things quickly go wrong. The young man or woman is lonely, adrift, and falls into poverty, crime, or prostitution. Usually, the story ends in a gesture of terrible violence, a vengeful attempt to bring down the pillars of the arrogant, indifferent, alien city. There are echoes of this story in Hitler's life in Vienna, Pol Pot's in Paris, Mao's in Beijing, or indeed of many a Muslim youth in Cairo, Haifa, Manchester, or Hamburg.

In our world you don't even have to move to the city to feel its constant presence, through advertising, television, pop music, and videos. The modern city, representing all that shimmers just out of our reach, all the glittering arrogance and harlotry of the West, has found its icon in the Manhattan skyline, reproduced in millions of posters, photographs, and images, plastered all over the world. You cannot escape it. You find it on dusty jukeboxes in Burma, in discothèques in Urumqi, in student dorms in Addis Ababa. It excites longing, envy, and sometimes blinding rage. The Taliban, like the Nazi provincials horrified by "nigger dancing," like Pol Pot, like Mao, have tried to create a world of purity where visions of Babylon can no longer disturb them.

The Taliban, to be sure, have very little idea what the fleshpots of the West are really like. For them even Kabul sparkled with Occidental sinfulness, exemplified by girls in school and women with uncovered faces populating and defiling the public domain. But the Taliban, like other purists, are much concerned with the private domain too. In big, anonymous cities, separation between the private and the public makes hypocrisy possible. Indeed, in Occidentalist eyes, the image of the West, populated by city-dwellers, is marked by artificiality and hypocrisy, in contrast to the honesty and purity of a Bedouin shepherd's life. Riyadh, and its grandiose Arabian palaces, is the epitome of hypocrisy. Its typical denizens behave like puritanical Wahhabites in public and greedy Westerners at home. To an Islamic radical, then, urban hypocrisy is like keeping the West inside one like a worm rotting the apple from within.

Most great cities are also great marketplaces. Voltaire saw much of what he admired about England in the Royal Exchange, "where the Jew, the Mahometan, and the Christian transact together as tho' they all profess'd the same religion, and give the name of Infidel to none but bankrupts."[6] Those who hate what Voltaire respected, who see the marketplace as the source of greed, selfishness, and foreign corruption, also hate those who are thought to benefit from it most: immigrants and minorities who can only better their fortunes by trade. When purity must be restored, and foreign blood removed from the native soil, it is these people who must be purged: the Chinese from Pol Pot's Phnom Penh, the Indians from Rangoon or Kampala, and the Jews from everywhere.

Sometimes such impurities can extend to nations, or even great powers. In their professed aim to bring back true Asian values to the East, Japanese wartime leaders promised to kick out the white imperialists as one way to "overcome unrestrained market competition."[7] Whatever Israel does, it will remain the alien grit in the eyes of Muslim purists. And the US will always be intolerable to its enemies. In bin Laden's terms, "the crusader-Jewish alliance, led by the US and Israel," cannot do right. The hatred is unconditional. As he observed in a 1998 interview for al-Jazeera TV: "Every grown-up Muslim hates Americans, Jews, and Christians. It is our belief and religion. Since I was a boy I have been at war with and harboring hatred towards the Americans." The September angels of vengeance picked their target carefully. Since the Manhattan skyline is seen as a provocation, its Babylonian towers had to come down.

3.

What did Hitler mean by "Jewish science"? For that matter, what explains the deep loathing of Darwin among Christian fundamentalists? Nazi propagandists argued that scientific truth could not be established by such "Jewish" methods as empirical inquiry or subjecting hypotheses to the experimental test; natural science had to be "spiritual," rooted in the natural spirit of the *Volk*. Jews, it was proposed, approached the natural world through reason, but true Germans reached a higher understanding through creative instinct and a love of nature.

Chairman Mao coined the slogan "Science is simply acting daringly." He purged trained scientists in the 1950s and encouraged Party zealots to embark on crazy experiments, inspired by the equally zany theories of Stalin's pseudoscientist T.D. Lysenko. "There is nothing special," Mao said, "about making nuclear reactors, cyclotrons or rockets. . . . You need to have spirit to feel superior to everyone, as if there was no one beside you."[8] All the sense of envious inferiority that Mao and his fellow Party provincials felt toward people of higher education is contained in these words. Instinct, spirit, daring . . . In 1942, a Japanese professor at Tokyo University argued that a Japanese victory over Anglo-American materialism was assured because the former embodied the "spiritual culture" of the East.

Like those towers of Babel in New York, the "Jewish" idea that "science is international" and human reason, regardless of bloodlines, is the best instrument for scientific inquiry is regarded by enemies of liberal, urban civilization as a form of hubris. Science, like everything else, must be infused with a higher ideal: the German *Volk*, God, Allah, or whatnot. But there may also be something else, something even more primitive, behind this. Worshipers of tribal gods, or even of allegedly universal ones, including Christians, Muslims, and Orthodox Jews, sometimes have a tendency to believe that infidels either have corrupt souls or have no souls at all. It is not for nothing that Christian missionaries speak of saving souls. In extreme cases, this can furnish enough justification to kill unbelievers with impunity.

Soul is a recurring theme of Occidentalism. The nineteenth-century Slavophiles pitted the "big" Russian soul against the mechanical, soulless West. They claimed to stand for deep feelings and profound understanding of suffering. Westerners, on the other hand, were deemed to be mechanically efficient, and to have nothing but an uncanny sense for calculating what is useful. The skeptical intellect, to promoters of soul, is always viewed with suspicion. Occidentalists extol soul or spirit but despise intellectuals and intellectual life. They regard the intellectual life as fragmented, indeed as a higher form of idiocy, with no sense of "totality," the "absolute," and what is truly important in life.

It is a fairly common belief among all peoples that "others" don't have the same feelings that we do. The notion that life is cheap in the Orient, or that coolies feel no pain, is a variation of this, but so is the idea we have heard expressed many times in China, India, Japan, and Egypt that Westerners are dry, rational, cold, and lacking in warm human feelings. It is a mark of parochial ignorance, of course, but it also reflects a way of ordering society. The post-Enlightenment Anglo-Franco-Judeo-American West sees itself as governed by secular political institutions and the behavior of all citizens as bound by secular laws. Religious belief and other matters of the spirit are private. Our politics are not totally divorced from shared values or moral assumptions, and some of our current leaders would like to see more religion brought into our public life; but still the West is not governed by spiritual leaders who seek to mediate between us and the divine world above. Our laws do not come from divine revelation, but are drawn up by jurists.

Societies in which Caesars are also high priests, or act as idols of worship, whether they be Stalinist, monarchical, or Islamist, use a different political language. Again, an example from World War II might be useful. Whereas the Allies, led by the US, fought the Japanese in the name of freedom, the Japanese holy war in Asia was fought in the name of divine justice and peace. "The basic aim of Japan's national policy lies in the firm establishment of world peace in

accordance with the lofty spirit of All the World Under One Roof, in which the country was founded." Thus spoke Prime Minister Konoe in 1940. Islamists, too, aim to unite the world under one peaceful roof, once the infidels and their towers have been destroyed.

When politics and religion merge, collective aims, often promoted in the name of love and justice, tend to encompass the whole world, or at least large chunks of it. The state is a secular construct. The Brotherhood of Islam, the Church of Rome, All the World Under One Japanese Roof, world communism, all in their different ways have had religious or millenarian goals. Such goals are not unknown in the supposedly secular states of the West either. Especially in the US, right-wing Christian organizations and other religious pressure groups have sought to inject their religious values and agendas into national politics in ways that would have shocked the Founding Fathers. That Reverend Jerry Falwell described the terrorist attacks on New York and Washington as a kind of punishment for our worldly sins showed that his thinking was not so far removed from that of the Islamists.

But ideally, the US and other Western democracies are examples of what Ferdinand Toennies termed a *Gesellschaft*, whose members are bound by a social contract. The other kind of community, the *Gemeinschaft*, is based on a common faith, or racial kinship, or on deep feelings of one kind or another. Typically, one German thinker, Edgar Jung, described World War I as a clash between the Intellect (the West) and the Soul (Germany).

4.

Enemies of the West usually aspire to be heroes. As Mussolini exhorted his new Romans: "Never cease to be daring!" Islamism, Nazism, fascism, communism are all heroic creeds. Mao's ideal of permanent revolution was a blueprint for continually stirring things up, for a society invigorated by constant heroic violence. The common enemy of revolutionary heroes is the settled bourgeois, the city dweller, the petty clerk, the plump stockbroker, going about his business, the kind of person, in short, who might have been working in an office in the World Trade Center. It is a peculiar trait of the bourgeoisie, perhaps the most successful class in history, at least so far, according to Karl Marx, to be hated so intensely by some of its most formidable sons and daughters, including Marx himself. Lack of heroism in the bourgeois ethos, of committing great deeds, has a great deal to do with this peculiarity. The hero courts death. The bourgeois is addicted to personal safety. The hero counts death tolls, the bourgeois counts money. Bin Laden was asked by his interviewer in 1998 whether he ever feared betrayal from within his own entourage. He replied: "These men left worldly affairs, and came here for jihad."

Intellectuals, themselves only rarely heroic, have often displayed a hatred of the bourgeois and an infatuation with heroism—heroic leaders, heroic creeds. Artists in Mussolini's Italy celebrated speed, youth, energy, instinct, and death-defying derring-do. German social scientists before World War II were fascinated by the juxtaposition of the hero and the bourgeois: Werner Sombart's *Händler und Helden (Merchants and Heroes)* and Bogislav von Selchow's *Der bürgerliche und der heldische Mensch (The Civil and the Heroic Man)* are but two examples of the genre. Von Selchow was one, among many others, by no means all German, who argued that bourgeois liberal society had become cold, fragmented, decadent, mediocre, lifeless. The bourgeois, he wrote, is forever hiding himself in a life without peril. The bourgeois, he said, is anxious to eliminate "fighting against Life, as he lacks the strength necessary to master it in its very nakedness and hardness in a manly fashion."[9]

To the likes of von Selchow or Ernst Jünger, World War I showed a different, more heroic side of man. That is why the Battle of Langemarck, a particularly horrific episode in 1914, in which Jünger himself took part, became such a

subject for hero worship. Some 145,000 men died in a sequence of utterly futile attacks. But the young heroes, many of them from elite universities like the Japanese kamikaze pilots thirty years later, were supposed to have rushed to their early graves singing the *Deutschlandied*. The famous words of Theodor Körner, written a century before, were often evoked in remembrance: "Happiness lies only in sacrificial death." In the first week of the current war in Afghanistan, a young Afghan warrior was quoted in a British newspaper. "The Americans," he said, "love Pepsi Cola, but we love death." The sentiments of the Langemarck cult exactly.

Even those who sympathize with the democratic West, such as Alexis de Tocqueville, have pointed out the lack of grandeur, the intellectual conformity, and the cultural mediocrity that is supposed to be inherent in our systems of government. Democracy, Tocqueville warned, could easily become the tyranny of the majority. He noted that there were no great writers in America, or indeed anything that might be described as great. It is a common but somewhat questionable complaint. For it is not at all clear that art and culture in New York is any more mediocre than it is in Damascus or Beijing.

Much in our affluent, market-driven societies is indeed mediocre, and there is nothing admirable about luxury per se, but when contempt for bourgeois creature comforts becomes contempt for life you know the West is under attack. This contempt can come from many sources, but it appeals to those who feel impotent, marginalized, excluded, or denigrated: the intellectual who feels unrecognized, the talentless art student in a city filled with brilliance, the time-serving everyman who disappears into any crowd, the young man from a third-world country who feels mocked by the indifference of a superior West; the list of possible recruits to a cult of death is potentially endless.

Liberalism, wrote an early Nazi theorist, A. Moeller v.d. Bruck, is the "liberty for everybody to be a mediocre man." The way out of mediocrity, say the sirens of the death cult, is to submerge one's petty ego into a mass movement, whose awesome energies will be unleashed to create greatness in the name of the Führer, the Emperor, God, or Allah. The Leader personifies all one's yearnings for grandeur. What is the mere life of one, two, or a thousand men, if higher things are at stake? This is a license for great violence against others: Jews, infidels, bourgeois liberals, Sikhs, Muslims, or whoever must be purged to make way for a greater, grander world. An American chaplain named Francis P. Scott tried to explain to the Tokyo War Crimes Tribunal the extraordinary brutality of Japanese soldiers during the war. After many interviews with former combatants, he concluded that "they had a belief that any enemy of the emperor could not be right, so the more brutally they treated their prisoners, the more loyal to the emperor they were being."[10]

The truest holy warrior, however, is not the torturer but the kamikaze pilot. Self-sacrifice is the highest honor in the war against the West. It is the absolute opposite of the bourgeois fear for his life. And youth is the most capable of sacrificial acts. Most kamikazes were barely out of high school. As bin Laden has said, "The sector between fifteen and twenty-five is the one with ability for jihad and sacrifice."

5.

Aurel Kolnai argued in 1938 in his *War Against the West* that "the trend towards the emancipation of women [is] keenly distinctive of the West." This somewhat sweeping claim seems to be born out by the sentiments of Kolnai's enemies. Here is Alfred Rosenberg, the Nazi propagandist: "Emancipation of woman from the women's emancipation movement is the first demand of a generation of women which would like to save the Volk and the race, the Eternal-Unconscious, the foundation of all culture, from decline and fall."[11] Leaving aside what this woolly-headed thinker could have meant by the Eternal-Unconscious, the meaning is clear

enough. Female emancipation leads to bourgeois decadence. The proper role for women is to be breeders of heroic men. One reason the Germans imported such huge numbers of workers from Poland and other countries under Nazi occupation was the dogmatic insistence that German women should stay at home.

Bin Laden is equally obsessed with manliness and women. It is indeed one of his most cherished Occidentalist creeds. "The rulers of that region [the Gulf States] have been deprived of their manhood," he said in 1998. "And they think the people are women. By God, Muslim women refuse to be defended by these American and Jewish prostitutes." The West, in his account, is determined "to deprive us of our manhood. We believe we are men."

Few modern societies were as dominated by males as wartime Japan, and the brutal policy of forcing Korean, Chinese, and Filipina, as well as Japanese, girls to serve in military brothels was a sign of the low status of women in the Japanese empire. And yet, the war itself had the peculiar effect of emancipating Japanese women to a degree that cannot possibly have been intended. Because most able-bodied men were needed on the battlefronts, women had to take care of their families, trade in the black markets, and work in the factories. Unlike the men, who experienced defeat as a deep humiliation, many Japanese women regarded the Allied victory as a step toward their liberation. One of the most important changes in postwar Japan was that women got the right to vote. They did so in large numbers as early as 1946. A new constitution was drawn up mostly by American jurists, but the articles concerning women's rights were largely the work of a remarkable person called Beate Sirota, who represented most things enemies of the West would have loathed. She was European, educated, a woman, and a Jew.

To all those who see military discipline, self-sacrifice, austerity, and worship of the Leader as the highest social ideals, the power of female sexuality will be seen as a dire threat. From ancient times women are the givers and the guardians of life. Women's freedom is incompatible with a death cult. Indeed, open displays of female sexuality are a provocation, not only to holy men, but to all repressed people whose only way to exaltation is death for a higher cause. Pictures of partly naked Western women advertising Hollywood movies, or soft drinks, or whatever, by suggesting sexual acts, are as ubiquitous in the world as those images of the Manhattan skyline. They are just as frustrating, confusing, and sometimes enraging. For again they promise a sinful, libidinous world of infinite pleasure beyond most people's reach.

6.

There is no clash of civilizations. Most religions, especially monotheistic ones, have the capacity to harbor the anti-Western poison. And varieties of secular fascism can occur in all cultures. The current conflict, therefore, is not between East and West, Anglo-America and the rest, or Judeo-Christianity and Islam. The death cult is a deadly virus which now thrives, for all manner of historical and political reasons, in extreme forms of Islam.

Occidentalism is the creed of Islamist revolutionaries. Their aim is to create one Islamic world guided by the *sharia* (Islamic law), as interpreted by trusted scholars who have proved themselves in jihad (read "revolution"). This is a call to purify the Islamic world of the idolatrous West, exemplified by America. The aim is to strike at American heathen shrines, and show, in the most spectacular fashion, that the US is vulnerable, a "paper tiger" in revolutionary jargon. Through such "propaganda by action" against the arrogant US, the forces of jihad will unite and then impose their revolution on the Islamic world.

Ayatollah Khomeini was a "Stalinist" in the sense that he wanted to stage a revolution in one significant country, Iran, before worrying about exporting it. Bin Laden, by contrast, is a "Trotskyite," who views Afghanistan as a base from which to export revolution right away. There is a tension between the "Stalinists" and the "Trotskyites" within the Islamist movement. September 11 gave the "Trotskyites" an advantage.

Al-Qaeda is making a serious bid to stage an Islamist revolution that would bring down governments from Indonesia to Tunisia. It has not succeeded yet. We can expect more "propaganda by action" against the US and US installations, accompanied by crude Occidentalist propaganda. The West, and not just the geographical West, should counter this intelligently with the full force of calculating bourgeois anti-heroism. Accountants mulling over shady bank accounts and undercover agents bribing their way will be more useful in the long-term struggle than special macho units blasting their way into the caves of Afghanistan. But if one thing is clear in this murky war, it is that we should not counter Occidentalism with a nasty form of Orientalism. Once we fall for that temptation, the virus has infected us too.

NOTES

1. D.C. Holtom, *Modern Japan and Shinto Nationalism* (University of Chicago, 1943), p. 10.
2. Viking, 1938.
3. *Briefe 1882–1924* (Munich: Bruckmann, 1928).
4. *England und Deutschland* (Munich: Bruckmann, 1915).
5. *Jahr der Entscheidung* (Munich: C.H. Beck, 1933).
6. *Letters Concerning the English Nation* (Oxford University Press, 1994), p. 30.
7. Akira Iriye, *Power and Culture: The Japanese-American War 1941–1945* (Harvard University Press, 1981).
8. Jasper Becker, *Hungry Ghosts: Mao's Secret Famine* (Free Press, 1996), p. 62.
9. Quoted in Kolnai, *The War Against the West*, p. 215.

10. Arnold C. Brackman, *The Other Nuremberg: The Untold Story of the Tokyo War Crimes Tribunals* (Morrow, 1987), p. 251.

11. Quoted in George L. Mosse, *Nazi Culture: Intellectual, Cultural and Social Life in the Third Reich* (Grosset and Dunlap, 1966), p. 40.

JACK A. GOLDSTONE

STATES, TERRORISTS, AND THE CLASH OF CIVILIZATIONS

On September 11, 2001 the United States was attacked by a foreign adversary on its own mainland for the first time in almost two hundred years; no such attack had taken place since the War of 1812. Yet in the twenty-first century, that adversary was not another state. It was a terrorist "NGO," or non-governmental organization, the terrorist group al-Qaeda. This attack has raised new questions about the nature of terrorism, and about the role of states and non-state groups in sponsoring and fighting international violence. It has led the United States to develop a foreign policy based on a "war on terrorism." Yet if that war is to be successful, rather than just a moralistic stance, we need to clearly understand our adversary—who they are, why they are fighting, how they operate, and how they might be halted.

Understanding Terrorism—Three Types of Terrorist Movements

Terrorism—the deliberate attack on civilians through the assassination of leaders or creating mass casualties and/or destruction of property, in order to demonstrate the power of the attacker and to intimidate a population—has been

From Craig Calhoun, Paul Price, and Ashley Timmer, eds., *Understanding September 11* (New York: The New Press, for the Social Science Research Council, 2002), pp. 139–58. Some of the author's notes have been omitted.

a tactic of war at least since the Huns attacked the Roman Empire. It has been used by both governments and non-government organizations, regular militaries and irregular guerillas. The goal of "ridding the world of terrorism" thus boils down, in essence, to ridding the world of war and civil conflict; as long as the latter occurs, terrorist tactics will likely be used by one side or the other in pursuit of their goals.

However, the terrorist act of September 11 represents something new and distinct from the terrorism that has accompanied conflicts throughout history. It represents an attempt to lift a religious war to a global scale, by striking a highly visible and destructive blow that would herald the "clash of civilizations."[1]

In order to understand the unique threat posed by the group responsible for this action, it is necessary to show how their operations are distinct from other terrorist activity. We can begin by dividing the many and varied terrorist groups operating in the world into roughly three distinct types, according to their composition and their goals:

I. National or regional liberation or other extremist or ethnic movements that use terrorist tactics aimed at regimes deemed to be illegitimate occupiers of territory. These are widespread and numerous, and have included the Sendero Luminoso in Peru, the FARC in Colombia, the Tamil Tigers in Sri Lanka, the ETA in Spain, the IRA in Britain; many of the rebel armies operating in West and East Africa.

This category also includes extremists in the US such as the radical anti-government groups who inspired Timothy McVeigh's attack on the Oklahoma Federal Building. Some of these groups operate exclusively locally, on the territory in which they reside. Others operate internationally, either obtaining weapons, sanctuary, or other assistance from other countries, or striking across international borders.

However, what is common to all of these groups is that their goal is or was to liberate a particular territory. It is thus conceivable to either negotiate or achieve some settlement relevant to their goals that will not involve the overthrow of many different nations' regimes, nor a wholesale change in international cultural and political norms.

II. International movements aimed at overthrowing widespread systems of social and political organization, and whose goals would necessarily involve the destruction of many nations' regimes. The most familiar of these movements to Europeans and Americans of the twentieth century were facism and communism. Nazism used terror in its rise to power (against Jews to be sure, but the brownshirts used terror against any adversaries who stood in their way). In addition, international terrorist movements seeking to destroy capitalist regimes ranged from guerrilla fighters in Latin America to such groups as the Red Brigade in Europe and the Red Army Faction in Japan. With such groups, no negotiation over autonomy or governance in a particular nation was more than just a temporary truce. What such movements sought was nothing less than the international overthrow of liberal capitalism and the remaking of governance and authority in their own mold (whether fascist or communist).

In fact, many of these movements had both national liberation and international change as their goals. In some cases, the movements focused on the liberation and reshaping of particular nations (fascism in Italy, communism in Russia) as their primary goal. However, international change always remained a key element in their program, and thus international expansion and power projection were an inevitable accompaniment to their control of specific territories or nations.

While fascism and communism now seem to us to represent "evil" forces, there have also been international movements aimed at overthrowing systems of social and political organization that used terrorist tactics for what now seem to be more noble ends. Anti-colonial movements assisted each other throughout Asia and Africa in attacking colonial regimes. While both freedom fighters and colonial regimes might claim to aim strictly to attack the military forces of their opponents, in practice attacks on civilians were often unavoidable and even deliberate elements of these bitter struggles. Today, a variety of national and international NGO's aimed at protecting animal rights and natural ecosystems have conducted terrorist raids on the property of producers of genetically modified crops, energy companies, and laboratories that carry out animal research.

III. Hybrid movements, in which national liberation movements with local territorial aims join forces with international movements with global aims. In this partnership, the local national liberation movement gains military and financial support for its forces; in return it gives its support to the ideology and operations of the global movements. The global movement thus gains new bases for operations and expansion, and new areas to recruit supporters for its international operations.

The United States has, on some occasions, been deeply concerned with terrorist groups of type I, when they took place on territories deemed critical to U.S. interests. Thus for example the United States fought against terrorist guerrilla movements in the Philippines after both the Spanish-American War and World War II. The United States also fought against terrorist guerrilla movements in Latin America when they threatened U.S. interests (as in Nicaragua in the 1920s). Yet in general, the U.S. has treated most of these movements (including the ETA, the IRA, the Tamil Tigers, and for most of its existence the South African ANC) as local problems that are not central to U.S. foreign policy. These movements only became critical when they became *hybrids* of type III, most especially when local national liberation movements allied with international communism. Indeed, much of the cold war was concerned precisely with identifying and countering type III movements allied with communism throughout the developing world, from Cuba to Vietnam to central America to Africa.

After the collapse of the Soviet Union in 1989–1991, most local national liberation movements lost any identification with an international movement aiming at the widespread destruction of other nations' regimes and sociopolitical systems. There was thus a widespread belief that U.S. foreign policy would no longer be troubled by hybrid terrorist organizations of type III, and that most terrorism would remain linked to local national liberation struggles and thus to groups of type I.

But this is not what has happened. Instead, in the course of the very struggle against communism, indeed in one of the key actions that led to its fall—the support of the liberation of Afghanistan from communist and Soviet control—the United States and other allies fostered a new international terrorist movement aimed at the destruction of western liberal regimes. Almost without their realizing it, this new international terrorist movement has grown and linked up with a variety of national liberation movements to form new hybrid movements of type III. This new type II movement I shall label *International Islamic Terrorism*, or IIT.

The New World of International Islamic Terrorism

International Islamic Terrorism aims to reestablish a unified Muslim ascendancy in the world against the current dominance of secular and Western powers. It perceives a wide range of governments as illegitimate occupying powers, including not only the United States, which has armed forces stationed throughout the Muslim world, and Israel, but also those governments of Muslim countries that are avowedly secular or allied with Western powers. This includes the majority of governments in countries with large Muslim populations, including Saudi Arabia, Egypt, Turkey, Indonesia, Pakistan, and the Philippines, among others. This broad opposition to both non-Islamic regimes *and* secularized regimes within the Islamic world is something relatively new.

From the 1940s through the 1970s, the Islamic world had many followers of anticolonialist and Arab-nationalist ideologies.[2] However, these ideologies were avowedly secular. The regimes in power in such countries as Egypt, Iraq, and Syria today stem from the Arab nationalist tide of that era. The regimes of the Shah in Iran, of Suharto in Indonesia, and of various military and democratic leaders in Pakistan endorsed variants of Islam as national religions, but they did not subscribe to any internationalist creed for the expansion of Islam beyond their borders or the reshaping of other governments. The Palestine Liberation Organization—drawing on Palestinians of all religions including Christians, Muslims, and varied sects—was a secular movement for the creation of a free Palestinian state.

These regimes promised to restore the power of Arab and Muslim nations by liberating them from Western colonial control and building powerful, autonomous states. Yet these promises went largely unfulfilled. Even with the enormous development of oil exports to provide a source of wealth and leverage over the West, the Muslim nations stretching from Morocco to Indonesia remained far poorer than their former colonial masters, and dependent on foreign investment and assistance. At the same time, modernization went far enough to create tens of thousands of college-educated youth, acutely aware of the subordinate positions of their countries and their cultures in global affairs.

Although many of these youths were educated as engineers or other professionals, and had parents who had embraced the secular creeds of post–World War II Arab and Muslim liberation, the new generation growing up in the 1960s and 1970s remained frustrated at the position of Muslim countries in the world, and turned to the study of Islam to seek alternative orientations. Teaming up with Muslim clerics who also—for their own reasons—were aggrieved at the secular regimes in their countries, and the incursions of Western morals and manners into Muslim lands, these youths energized a movement for a radical Islamicization of Muslim nations.

In this, there is something similar to the phenomenon of the 1960s in the United States and Europe. There, many college-educated youths from affluent backgrounds came to question the moral basis for their own society, and challenged the legitimacy of their government's positions on issues ranging from family structures to civil and women's rights to involvement in Vietnam. The openness of U.S. society allowed the "New Left" to spread its views; some were generally adopted and influenced policy. Yet more extreme attacks on capitalist enterprise and private property were not tolerated, and groups like the Yippies became the target of FBI control. In response, some New Left groups became even more extreme, turning in some cases into flat-out terrorist bombers, such as the Weather Underground or the Symbionese Liberation Army.

In most Muslim countries, the openness of American society was absent, for even the anti-colonial and secular Arab nationalist movements had given rise to closed and authoritarian, not democratic, regimes. The destruction of those regimes, and their replacement with Islamicized governments, thus became an avowed goal of the Islamicist movements in those countries. As a result, these Islamicist movements were harshly repressed by regimes who saw them as a threat. Just as with the Weather Underground in the U.S., but only after much larger-scale conflicts, repressive campaigns against Islamic terrorist groups in Egypt, in Syria, in Iran, and elsewhere in the Muslim world from the 1970s through the 1990s managed to break up these movements and suppress their activity.

That might have been the end of terrorist Islamist groups, except for three otherwise unconnected developments. First and most important was a series of coups and revolutions in the Kingdom of Afghanistan. Second was a profound shift in the struggle for the liberation of Palestine against Israel. Third was the collapse of the Shah's regime and the rise of an Islamicized regime in Iran. Let us consider each of these in turn.

Afghanistan and the Mujahedeen[3]

In 1973, after pursuing a decade-long program of modest liberalization and modernization, the regime of King Zahir Shah of Afghanistan was overthrown in a coup d'etat by a former prime Minister, Mohammed Daud. Daud sought to create a more firmly centralized and modernized regime. However, Daud had to deal with two competing organized factions among the Afghan elite: The communists, who wanted to agressively modernize the country under government control on the model of the Soviet Union; and the Islamists who wanted to halt those aspects of modernization that most impinged on family organization, local tribal autonomy, and clerical authority. After five years of trying to manage these competing interests while increasing his own personal control, Daud was overthrown in 1978 by leftists in the military who brought the communists to power.

Once in power, the communists sought to bring about a revolutionary reorganization of Afghan society by imposing radical land reform, modernizing and secularizing family law, and purging the bureaucracy and military of Islamicist and anti-communist elements. Yet the narrow elite of the communist party had little or no popular support for these actions, and the communists' policies aroused a growing national opposition to their rule. Within a little over a year, armed rebellion had broken out in over half the provinces of Afghanistan. In 1979, the Afghan communists invited the Soviet Army into the country to help them maintain their grip on power. The Soviet "invasion," as it was viewed by most Afghans, turned the domestic struggle against the Afghan communist regime into a national liberation movement with international ramifications.

Two distinct groups came to aid the Afghans in their struggle against the Soviets. From within the Muslim world, especially from Egypt, Saudi Arabia, Iran, and Pakistan, came many youths from the Islamicist movements that had been developing and struggling throughout the Muslim world (including one Osama bin Laden). These individuals, whose departure from their own country was often supported by their own regimes as a way of exporting trouble-makers, found a battlefield in which they were now strongly encouraged to fight for Islam against a godless and foreign power. The Muslim freedom fighters, or "Mujahedeen," were also given generous assistance by the governments of Iran, Pakistan, and Saudi Arabia. In each case, these regimes could burnish their Islamic credentials by supporting a clearly Islamic struggle. In addition, for Iran and Pakistan, who shared long borders with Afghanistan, support for the Muslim opposition also meant influence in any future liberated Afghan nation.

The second group of supporters were Western powers, chiefly the U.S., who supported the Mujahedeen as a way to attack the Soviet Union and turn back international communism. Western powers gave the Mujahedeen advanced tactical and weapons training, and sophisticated arms including mines and anti-tank and anti-aircraft weapons, making it possible for them to stand up to the massive and well-equipped Soviet armies.

Yet instead of using their influence to moderate the Islamicist current in the anti-Soviet opposition, and instill a pro-western and democratic ideology in the Afghan freedom fighters, Western nations—including the U.S.—chose to keep a low profile by funnelling their aid through Pakistan. This was in large part because since the 1979 revolution in Iran, discussed below, Iran had become an active enemy of the U.S. In seeking to secure influence in a post–Soviet-occupation Afghanistan, it thus seemed to make sense to work through Pakistan, who was seeking to secure its influence by its support of anti-Soviet groups. Thus Iran supported the Shi'a Islamic groups fighting in Afghanistan, mainly drawn from the Hezara ethnic group of western and central Afghanistan, while Pakistan supported the majority group of Sunni Muslims, drawn from the Pashtun, Uzbeck, and Tajik groups in the South, North, and East of the country. The net result was to stamp an Islamic cast ever more firmly on the Afghan resistance.

Drawing on nearly unlimited flows of weapons from Saudi Arabian and U.S. funds, and nearly unlimited flows of military recruits from sanctuaries for Afghan refugees in Iran and Pakistan, the Mujahedeen were able to wear down the Soviet occupation forces. In 1989, the Soviet Union withdrew its military, leaving a battleground of ethnically and religiously divided Islamic militias contending for control of the country.

From 1989 to 1994, regional commanders switched alliances with bewildering speed, and local populations were repeatedly prey to warlord struggles for territory. However in 1994, in the southern city of Kandahar, a religious leader named Muhammed Omar rallied a group of local Mujahedeen and religous students to seize power from the local warlords. Drawing support from the majority Pashtun ethnic group and their tribal forces, from the idealist foreign Mujahedeen fighters who came to support what they saw as the most truly Islamicized movement in Afghanistan, and above all from Pakistan who believed it could control this movement, and thus indirectly control Afghanistan, Mohammed Omar's movement—the Taliban—quickly spread out from its base in Kandahar and by 1998 controlled 90% of the country.

This result of the way the liberation of Afghanistan played out was wholly unforseen. Instead of a national liberation movement of type I, which might have aimed terror operations only at Soviet and Soviet-allied forces within the country, there developed in Afghanistan a type III hybrid terrorist movement, in which the national liberation forces were joined—and indeed largely funded and inspired by—an internationally recruited and organized network of "Islamic fighters" whose goal was to create Islamicized societies and turn back all secular and westernized forces that threatened Muslim peoples and Muslim lands. Under the Taliban, Afghanistan thus became not merely a new national state, but a home to an international movement aiming to restore Muslim power by overturning secular governments and Western influence throughout the world. Furthermore, this new international Islamic movement had been trained and equipped by the U.S. and its allies, over the course of its struggle against the Soviet military, with the latest armory of lethal weaponry and tactics of stealth and guerrilla attack against its foes. Once the Taliban had established control, Afghanistan thus became the site of sophisticated training operations and communications for a network of Islamic warriors with international aims and ambitions.

Palestine and the Intifada[4]

Since 1948, the Palestine Liberation Organization (PLO) had aimed to return the lands composing the State of Israel to Palestinian settlement and control. After several Arab-Israel Wars from 1948 to 1967, however, Israeli-occupied territories had expanded, and the PLO was reduced to conducting terrorist actions from various external bases, including Lebanon and Tunisia. Dissatisfaction with the efforts of the foreign-based PLO, and again, frustration among a new generation of often college-educated Palestinians with their seemingly permanent second-class status in an occupied

Palestine (university education in Palestine increased greatly under Israeli occupation), led to an indigenous struggle against Israeli authority and settlements, known as the "Intifada."

Beginning in 1987, the Intifada relied on a new generation of Palestinian elites, based in the occupied territories. Many of these elites as well as their followers drew inspiration from the international Islamicist movement, and gained their funding and ideological support from many of the same Iranian, Egyptian and Saudi organizations—including the Muslim Brethren and Islamic Jihad—that had contributed to the struggle to liberate Afghanistan. There thus grew up a wholly new, Islamicized branch of Palestinian resistance to Israel, the "Islamic Resistance Movement," popularly known as Hamas. This new movement displaced the older generation of more secular PLO fighters.

However, after the Oslo accords of 1993 and the Gaza Jericho agreement of 1994, the PLO returned to Palestine, as the leader of a new territorial entity, the Palestinian Authority (PA). At first, the PA under Yassir Arafat sought to secure its own control of its territory in Gaza and the West Bank and to reduce that of the new Islamic organizations. Yet from 1994 to 2000, no further progress was made in extending the territory or power of the Palestinian authority. The prestige and authority of the PA among the Palestinians was diminished, while that of the Islamic movements grew.

By late 2000, a confrontation at the al-Asqa mosque in Jerusalem led to the resumption of an active military and terror campaign between Israel and the Palestinian resistance groups. In this new round of struggle, both the secular and Islamic wings of resistance were actively involved, yet the Islamicist movement represented by Hamas, Hezbollah (nurtured by Iran, as noted below), and Islamic Jihad continuously threatened to take control of the resistance away from the more secular PA. As a result, like the Afghan liberation movement, the Palestine liberation movement also became a type III hybrid, in which an international Islamic movement has joined and even taken the leadership of what had previously been a more secular movement with strictly local nationalist goals. The campaign for Palestine liberation, in the eyes of these groups, thus becomes just one more battleground in the global competition between the West and Islam.

The Iranian Revolution

In 1979, just a few years after the overthrow of Zahir Shah in Afghanistan, the regime of Shah Reza Pahlevi of Iran also collapsed. Yet while Zahir Shah fell to a coup, the Shah of Iran's regime was replaced by a fundamentalist Islamic movement that immediately aimed to create a base for international challenges to Western influence. The Shah of Iran had been a major recipient of Western aid, and like Zahir Shah of Afghanistan, sought to build a more modern and liberalized nation, but to retain his personal authority. Yet these goals proved incompatible. Modernized elites agitated for more democratic institutions, and railed against the corruption of the Shah's regime. At the same time, the Shah of Iran had embarked on a series of land reforms, and curtailments of clerical authority, that antagonized the traditional elites. When in the 1970s excessive debt and oil-financed spending drove up inflation and undermined the position of the urban middle class, while past agricultural reforms had led to huge movements of unemployed rural families to the cities, the foundations were set for a massive cross-class coalition uniting the opponents of the Shah. In the late 1970s, human-rights pressures from the Carter regime in the U.S. encouraged the opposition, and an anti-inflation campaign of imprisonment and harassment by the Shah against traditional business elites (intended to deflect blame for inflation away from the Shah's government) drove a critical ally over to the opposition. Inspired by militant clerics, led by modernized professionals, funded by traditional merchants and business leaders, and supported by underemployed urban masses, the opposition to the Shah took to

the strees in 1978–1979 and brought down his government.

There then ensued a struggle for control of the revolution between its clerical visionary leaders and its modernizing professional organizers, won by the former with the aid of the new Islamic Guard, drawn from urban youth, who terrorized Iranians who sought a more secularized or Western-leaning regime. The outcome was the first instance of a large, populous, and powerful Islamic country that overthrew a modernizing secular government and replaced it with a clergy-led Islamicist regime.

The new Iranian regime was a model for promoters of Islam throughout the Muslim world. Yet its influence was limited for two reasons. First, the brand of Islamic fundamentalism in Iran was that of the Shi'a branch of the faith, which had followers primarily in Iran and contiguous regions. Outside of Iran, the Shi'a were a minority in all other large and populous Muslim states, where Sunnis were generally the dominant branch of Islam. Second, Iran soon became embroiled in a decade-long war with the secular Arab state of Iraq, which fully occupied Iran's energies in regard to international affairs.

However, since the end of the Iraq-Iran war, Iran has again sought to project its support for Islamicized rebellion against Western and non-Muslim forces across international borders. As we noted above, Iran was an important supporter of Mujahedeen forces in Afghanistan, although its influence was confined to the Shi'a groups within that country. Iran has also sponsored anti-Israel terrorist groups, mainly Hezbollah. Iran's actions too have thus fostered the transformation of national liberation movements of type I into hybrid movements of type III, and provided a territorial base of operations for international Islamic terrorist movements.

To sum up, developments in Afghanistan, Palestine, and Iran gave renewed life to Islamicist movements that had been unable to overcome authorities and establish themselves in such secular Muslim states as Egypt, Saudi Arabia, Syria, or Pakistan. The Afghanistan revolution drew Islamicist supporters together, gave them a mission, combat experience, and sophisticated weapons and training; and under the Taliban, they gained a territorial base. The development of an indigenous *intifada* and the growing role of Hamas in Palestine gave the international Islamicist movement another territorial bridgehead and campaign front against Westernized powers. In addition, the existence of a fundamentalist regime in Iran gives the international Islamicist movement a territorial and funding base controlled by a soveriegn nation whose leadership shares their goals. Together, these events from the late 1970s through the 1990s created a formidable basis for an international Islamic movement that is prepared to use terror to advance its goals.

Let us now look more closely at the goals and activity of that movement, to see how these led up to the events of September 11, 2001.

Al-Qaeda and September 11: Who, How, and Why

Al-Qaeda was founded during the winding down of the Afghan conflict, in 1988 or 1989, to serve as a clearing-house providing a variety of support, training, and guidance services to those individuals seeking to further the international strengthening of Islam through direct action against the West. Led by Osama bin Laden of Saudi Arabia and Muhammed Atef of Egypt, al-Qaeda became a leading branch of the international Islamic terrorist movement (IIT). The IIT is not a single structure, but rather my label for a loosely linked network of groups with common aims, including in addition to al-Qaeda such groups as Islamic Jihad, Hezbollah, Hamas, Abu Sayef, the National Islamic Front, and many other, smaller groups. What the various groups that compose the IIT have in common is a desire to destroy the dominance of Western power and culture in the world, and particularly to drive

out all Western forces and allied secular regimes in the Muslim world. Their targets thus include not only Israel, but also the governments of Egypt, Saudi Arabia, and Pakistan, and also the governments and populations of the United States, Britain, Russia, and other European and pro-Western regimes.

The IIT is a new and especially troubling threat to the United States and its allies precisely because its aims are *not* limited to the liberation of a particular region or territories. Rather, it aims at the liberation of a broad swathe of territories from Morocco to the Philippines, and believes that such liberation requires attacks to undermine the power and prestige of Western powers around the world. Thus wherever Western forces are to be found—whether on Western countries' territories, or in embassies in Africa, military installations in Saudi Arabia or Lebanon or Somalia, or aviation or any other presence around the world—they are legitimate targets for attack. This is a wholly different mode of terrorist activity and goals than existed with prior anti-colonialist or Arab nationalist movements in Islamic countries.

However, while generously distributing support to Islamicist causes in many countries, bin Laden also took al-Qaeda in a direction no other Islamicist group had dared go: planning sophisticated assaults directly targeting U.S. facilities, armed forces, and even U.S. territory.

Al-Qaeda is suspected of playing a role in almost all the major terrorist assaults on U.S. personnel and facilities carried out by Islamicist groups since 1989. These include the assault on U.S. forces in Somalia in 1993, the attempted bombing of the World Trade Center in 1993, the bombings of U.S. military posts in Saudi Arabia in 1996, bombings of the U.S. embassies in Dar es Salaam and Nairobi in 1998, the attack on the U.S. destroyer the U.S.S. Cole in Yemen in 2000, and the Sept. 11 attacks. Each of these attacks displays a willingness to make U.S. forces or territory a primary target, and meticulous planning for complex operations, often simultaneously against multiple targets. So far, I believe these characteristics distinguish al-Qaeda from any other IIT groups, most of which remain hybrids of type II, aiming to combine their Islamicist goals 'with liberation of specific territories. It thus makes excellent sense, while understanding the broader context of IIT in which al-Qaeda developed, to focus on al-Qaeda and its leadership as the most critical threat to U.S. personnel, facilities, and territory.

Al-Qaeda is a truly international organization. Its recruits include thousands of former fighters in the Afghan war, plus other individuals drawn to al-Qaeda through their involvement with other Islamicist organizations, whether those are other terrorist groups such as Egyptian Jihad, or simply mosques or religious schools (*madrasas*) in any number of countries who promote hatred of the West and the goal of restoring the global dominance of Islam. Many of its leaders are recruited from college educated individuals from affluent backgrounds, who have been radicalized by experiencing the relative power and wealth of the West, the relative poverty of many of their Islamic compatriots, and the often exclusionary and corrupt nature of government in their home countries.

For such educated elites, the goal of restoring the glory of Islam on a global basis is not illusory, but a reasonable extrapolation of past history. From the seventh to the tenth century, Islamic forces swept all enemies—both Christian Western and Asian—before them, creating the vast Islamic empire of the Caliphate. Islamic forces conquered all of Spain, all of North Africa, and all of the Middle East. However, in the 11th and 12th centuries, the West struck back. In the Crusades, Christians retook the Holy Lands of the Eastern Mediterranean, and embarked on the reconquest of Spain in the Western Mediterranean. Furthermore, in the 13th and 14th centuries Russia expanded to the north, and Spanish kingdoms expanded in the West. Yet at the same time, the Ottoman Turks were building their empire in Turkey. By the 17th century, the Ottomans had re-established an Islamic empire that stretched from Morocco to Iran, and which had pushed the West out of Turkey, Greece, Romania, parts of Hungary, and the Balkans (including the still-Muslim territories of Albania and Bosnia). Then the West reasserted itself again, and by the early 20th century, the Ottoman Empire had been dismembered by the European powers. Thus, for Islam to reassert itself and expand at the expense of the West in the 21st century would be simply the normal pattern of history. It should be appreciated that however unrealistic this aspiration seems to modern Western peoples, it is not a wholly irrational or unfounded aspiration among Muslims. Moreover, in many regions of the world, the Muslim religion is today the fastest growing religion—by the peaceful means of conversion and natural population growth.

What is uniquely dangerous about al-Qaeda is that in addition to their goal of achieving Muslim dominance on a global scale, they draw on apocalyptic texts that argue for embracing death and inflicting death upon one's enemies as the favored path to their goal. Whereas mainstream Islam is a peaceful religion that has, through most of its history, advocated peaceful coexistence with other faiths, al-Qaeda draws on and propagates strategies of death and destruction, shaping not only its own operations but the hybrid terrorist/national liberation movements that it has come to influence.

In addition to its elite leaders, al-Qaeda draws followers from throughout the Muslim world, wherever lack of opportunity makes a career as an international terrorist more attractive than menial labor and poverty. In this, al-Qaeda is like gangs in U.S. inner cities or social protest movements throughout the world. It is not poverty *per se* that gives birth to terrorists (or gangs or protest). Rather, poverty provides a situation in which there is fairly low competition by other occupations when leaders who seek to mobilize supporters against perceived injustices, and who offer attractive short-term rewards, come to recruit. Al-Qaeda can draw on veterans of the Afghan liberation and other liberation struggles (Bosnia, Kosovo), as well as the graduates of Islamicist religious schools that preach the evils of Western influence, as recruits for their activities; both of these groups have little opportunity to become anchored in conventional occupations.

It is this combination of educated elites and large numbers of potential recruits with few other opportunities or anchors to "normal" life that allows al-Qaeda to conduct a large number of sophisticated operations. For example, in order to plan and carry out the 9/11 attacks, leaders for each of several groups had to be recruited who would pilot the planes and act as the information conduits to the overall leadership. Then followers had to be placed who would provide the "muscle" to overpower the airplane crews and passengers. All of these individuals had to be financed and monitored, and then activated when the time for action came.

It deserves to be noted that despite the horrifying success of the 9/11 attacks, the outcome could have been much more severe. It is astounding that the World Trade Center collapse killed under 3,000 people, out of more than 10 times that many who were in the immediate area at the time of the attack. It is a stroke of luck that the attack on the Pentagon hit the one area of the building that had been recently reinforced by reconstruction to withstand attack. It is a blessing that the last plane, apparently also bound for Washington, D.C., was held on the ground for an unscheduled delay long enough for information to reach the passengers about the ongoing attacks, allowing them to act to prevent that plane from reaching its intended target. There may have been yet one more team of hijackers that was also on a plane that was held on the ground, but who got away only to be subsequently arrested on a train with credit cards showing several hundred thousand dollars in charges and box-cutters identical to those used in the 9/11 assaults. In short, the potential for catastrophe was even greater than what actually transpired.

The creativity of al-Qaeda in developing methods of conventional massive destruction suggests considerable ingenuity. However, having tried car bombs and now airplanes as guided missiles, it seems likely that al-Qaeda will try to escalate its attacks still further. Its pattern has been to shift targets and methods of destruction in order to keep its adversaries off-balance. It is not unreasonable to suppose that al-Qaeda will try to obtain, and use, non-conventional weapons of mass destruction, including nuclear, biological, chemical, or radiological armaments.

In other words, al-Qaeda represents an exceptional and new threat to U.S. and Western interests. It is the most aggressive and sophisticated anti-U.S. spearhead of a broad international Islamic terrorist network, that not only conducts direct attacks on U.S. targets but also reshapes various national liberation movements to join its cause. Instead of the world of terrorism that we anticipated after the collapse of the Soviet Union, with almost exclusively type I terrorist groups, we instead face a world with highly active type II and type III groups, with multiple territorial bases and broad international operations.

Responding to International Islamic Terrorism

It is a futile goal to seek to rid the world of terrorism. Type I terrorist groups will continue to operate as long as there are civil and international conflicts. Yet these become direct threats to Western civilization more broadly, and to the U.S. in particular, when they are supplanted by terrorist organizations of type II and type III. The reasonable, and necessary, goal of U.S. policy regarding terrorism should therefore be to undermine and disable terrorist groups of type II, and to return the hybrids of type III to more localized goals of type I groups.

However, that is not an easy task. At this point, after allowing the IIT to build up over several decades from the 1970s to the present, an entire generation has grown up in the Islamic world strongly influenced by IIT groups. As with the threat from communism, it may take a decade or more of concerted effort to end this threat. Let us examine possible responses. We should consider both those responses that, although frequently mentioned in the media, would *not* be effective in curtailing ITT—specifically, imposing a settlement on Israel/Palestine and alleviating poverty in the Islamic world—and other responses which promise to be more effective.

Will settling the Israeli-Palestinian conflict end the threat from International Islamic Terror? No. For al-Qaeda and its followers, the goal is nothing less than the removal of Western influence from as many lands as possible, and the spread of a "purified" Islam into all those lands occupied by the faithful. Although for the nationalist Palestinian Liberation groups, a minimal goal would be the establishment of a secure Palestinian state controlling key holy sites and with the economic and political capacity to preserve its autonomy while coexisting with Israel, for the IIT groups, coexistence with Israel—even if agreed to by Palestinians—is not a satisfactory outcome. The hybridization of Palestinian liberation movements with international Islamicist movements has produced a mix in which "For the Islamists, Palestine had been lost in large measure as God's punishment for turning away from Islam. They believed that Palestine was part of a larger God-given Islamic endowment; thus no human had the right to cede control of any part of such lands to non-Muslims. While the PLO . . . focused on gaining control of the lands occupied in 1967, a policy recognized formally in the Oslo Accords, the [Islamists] rejected any Israeli presence in the Middle East. [Hamas therefore] undertook an ideological campaign devoted to the idea that not one inch of Palestine can be ceded to Israel."[5] In this view, no negotiation of land for peace, or for anything else, is possible.

Moreover, even the destruction of Israel would not suffice to satisfy the IIT goals. That would simply be a victory in one battle, on one battlefront. A liberated Palestine would then be a base for the IIT groups to seek to expand "purified" Islam throughout the Muslim lands of the near East and North Africa. The most recent historical manifestation of the Islamic Caliphate, or world empire, was the Ottoman Empire, which included Turkey, much of the Balkans (including the still-Muslim lands of Bosnia and Albania), and North Africa across Egypt, Algeria, Libya, Tunisia, and Morocco, as well as the Middle East. The struggle to restore the Caliphate would thus extend from Palestine to seek to undermine all Western-allied Muslim regimes.

In short, no conceivable outcome of the Israeli-Palestinian conflict would reduce the enmity or activity of IIT. Quite the contrary—the only hope for a peaceful resolution of the Israeli-Palestinian conflict is to reduce or remove the influence of the IIT within the Palestinian liberation movement, so that a resolution to the conflict can be negotiated that focuses strictly on satisfying the interests of Palestinians and Israelis with regard to the lands they inhabit.

Will reducing poverty stem the rise of IIT? It is well known to social scientists who analyze revolution, rebellion, and political violence that while poorer countries have more of all of these types of conflict, there is no simple relationship between poverty and political violence.[6] India is far poorer than most Western nations, and most Mexicans are far poorer than most Americans. But these countries have never provided a direct threat to the U.S. Saudi Arabia and many Near Eastern states, such as Iran, are richer than many African states; yet the former have provided more anti-U.S. terrorists than the latter.

It is true that poverty and a lack of opportunity for careers and livelihoods that anchor people in everyday life increase the number of potential recruits for rebellious and terrorist movements. However, those potential recruits are only activated by the organization, money, weapons, and ideology provided by the leaders of the IIT. Those leaders do not come from poverty. Although much of their resentment is fueled by the relative wealth of the West (and often of their own government leaders) compared to their ordinary co-religionists, there is no reason to believe that raising income levels in poor countries around the world will immediately end the resentment felt by radical Islamists toward the West.

If poor people blame themselves for their condition, they work to overcome it. If they blame a corrupt or evil government for their condition, they may rebel against it. If they blame a foreign power or foreign culture for undermining their society and causing their condition, they may mobilize against that foreign power. It is not poverty as such, but perceptions of *injustice* that motivate political violence. And how those perceptions of justice are shaped is crucial in determining the spread of IIT. If humanitarian assistance is delivered in such a way as to demonstrate the concern of Western powers for Muslim peoples, it may somewhat offset the perception that poverty is an unjust imposition by the West. Or it may simply appear as one more handout from the conquerer to a beaten-down people. The *fact of the relative poverty of many Muslim peoples relative to the West, and indeed the absolute poverty of many peoples in the Muslim world, is not going to be changed in the near future.* However, the consequences of that poverty for international terrorism depends on the perceptions that are created and spread regarding the causes of that poverty. If Muslim peoples are persuaded that the corruption of Western morals and the injustice of Western capitalism have imposed their conditions on them from outside, then enmity toward Western civilization will multiply. However, if Muslim peoples are persuaded that they can improve their situation with sound government and hard work, and that Western powers will assist and not hinder that process, then the poverty that exists will not be an extensive breeding ground for terror.

Much of that perception depends on education.

Education in the Islamic World

Education is something of a two-edged sword. The Islamic world, like the West, has seen an enormous expansion in university education. Islamic elites have recognized that they cannot run modern military establishments, oil refineries, and financial systems—all foundations of their regimes' power—without university-trained elites. Yet as with other great expansions of university enrollments, as in western Europe in the 19th century, in Russia in the early 20th century, and in many countries after World War II (including the United States), a certain fraction of university graduates have been drawn to idealism, reform, and rebellion. This has been all the more so in Muslim countries in the late 20th century for three reasons. First, the narrow oil-based economies of many Muslim countries do not provide the economic opportunities found in more diversified economies for an educated managerial and technical elite. Second, the closed and authoritarian regimes of many Muslim countries do not allow for either reform, or a broad array of roles in politics. Third, in order to satisfy the demands of clerics, many universities remain partially or fully staffed by Islamic clergy in order to provide an Islamic education and train a new generation of clergy. The result is a combination of relatively high unemployment and economic frustration among university graduates, relatively high political frustration with the closed and unresponsive nature of the political regime, and an infusion of Islamism absorbed from the study of (often radical) Islamic texts.

At the same time, elementary and secondary education has grown more slowly. In many countries, the public school system is underfinanced. Clergy-run schools (as in many inner-cities in this country) provide the most compelling alternative for education. In many cases, religious schools are attached to charitable foundations that not only pay for the schools but also provide living stipends for students. In the last two decades, there has been a proliferation of Islamic religious schools (*madrasas*), often funded by Saudi and other overseas charitable foundations seeking to show their support for a renewal of Islam. However, many of these schools have taken into their curriculum a particularly venemous anti-Western bias, drawn not from the Koran but from more recent writings of Islamicist writers seeking to exalt Islam and condemn Western powers for the current condition of Muslims and Muslim nations.

The net outcome of these trends in education has been the production of both radicalized elites and willing conscripts to the IIT cause. Although there are moderate Islamic scholars and teachers, they have been increasingly shouted down and displaced by more radical Islamist institutions and leaders. This has been true on the West Bank and in Gaza, in Afghanistan, in Iran, and in parts of Pakistan, Egypt, and Saudi Arabia, even in Indonesia.

To alter these trends in education, there is much the West can do. Free gifts of textbooks in local languages, which adopt neither a Eurocentric nor Islamist anti-Western view, but teach global history as a process of peaceful competition and integration, punctuated by dismal and deplorable episodes of violence, would be useful. Publication of weekly newspapers—or financial support for newpapers, radio and TV stations—that portray a more balanced viewpoint for consumption in the Islamic world would also help.

During the struggle against communism, Western powers took it for granted that anti-Western media and propaganda needed to be vigorously countered by media presenting Western viewpoints. Yet in the struggle against Islamic terrorism, the West has been tardy and niggling in its efforts to counter a similar barrage of anti-Western portrayals. IIT is, like communism, a revolutionary movement with global aims and operations. It can only be countered by similar measures.

However, delivering a better balanced education requires an adequately funded and staffed public education system with secular leadership. This requires competent and capable states.

State-Building

One of the first policy declarations of the Bush administration regarding the struggle with the Taliban, since sensibly retracted, is that the United States would not be drawn into "state-building." We also initially resisted the idea of being drawn into state-building in Bosnia. Yet we should ask ourselves why this is so. In the struggle against communism, the chief approach to countering its international spread was precisely efforts at state-building, whether in Western Germany and western Europe more generally; in South Korea; in Taiwan; and less successfully in many other nations. Strong states—if not also anti-Western—are a critical element in the struggle against IIT. Such states can suppress terrorist training and activity in their territories; deliver educational services and provide employment for educated elites; and maintain legitimate banking and financial systems. Weak or failed states are unable to fulfil these functions and thus provide a vacuum in which IIT can flourish.

It is important to recognize that IIT is a nongovernmental organization, or NGO (or more accurately, a loosely linked network of allied NGO's). NGO's may operate beyond state boundaries, but they need physical locations in which to operate, train, hold and disburse funds, have leaders meet and plan operations. Destroying one state refuge or territory of operations will not destroy IIT, however much it may diminish their operations in the short term, as long as IIT can find other territories in which to operate. Strong states that control their territories can curtail or terminate the activity of NGO's on their territory. But it requires an alliance of states cooperating to effectively end the operations of an international NGO.

States also compete with IIT for the loyalty, energy, and support of their peoples. Where IIT groups are more successful than states in providing such basic services as protection, education, and welfare, they are naturally more influential over the local population than states. Strong and successful states who provide these services thus reduce the scope for IIT to gain support by taking up roles that states fail to fulfil.

It is not a novelty for states to compete against NGO's—the international anti-slavery movement and the European democratic/constitutional movement of the 19th century targeted states, as did the communist international of the 20th century. Clearly, in some cases the NGO's outlasted their state opponents; in other cases not. However, in recent years the proliferation of NGO's with international financial and other operations make it all too easy for IIT to shelter itself by blending in with the host of international Islamic charitable and religious NGO's. It thus makes heavy demands on intelligence and state cooperation to locate and target the supporting operations of IIT activity.

Toward a Conclusion

It is important in this struggle, as in all such struggles, to know our adversary. It is not the Muslim world, or Arab nations, or Islamic peoples. Most Muslims are *not* fundamentalists or aiming at global domination by Islam. Not all Islamic fundamentalists, much less many Muslims, believe that terror, suicidal sacrifice, and violence are the best way to secure the future of Islam or combat Western influence. Most Muslims, like most people everywhere, are interested in taking care of their families, in surviving each day and living in peace. Yet it is the goal of international Islamic terrorists to turn all Muslims against the West and against Westernized governments and elites in Muslim countries, and to convince as many Muslims as possible to take up arms against Western powers and Western influence.

The key to defeating the threat of IIT is thus to demonstrate to Muslims that support of IIT goes *against* their own best interests. This can best be achieved by showing the world that IIT is *not effective* against the West, and is *illegitimate* as a force for Islam.

The first goal is largely a military and police task. It involves military action against nations that support and harbor IIT groups and hybrids; it involves police action to track down IIT cells wherever they are operating and to neutralize them; and it involves homeland security measures to prevent effective operations by IIT in the future. As the al-Qaeda network has been the most effective and dangerous IIT group, it is reasonable to make elimination of that organization's leaders and operatives a chief priority. On this goal, once galvanized by the events of September 11, the United States and its allies appear to be making good progress.

The second goal, however, is equally if not more important. Unless the injustice and illegitimacy of IIT is made manifest, unless their propaganda that Western powers and Western culture are responsible for the suffering of all Muslims anywhere in the Islamic world is refuted, the destruction of particular al-Qaeda leaders and operatives will only result in others taking their place. A sustained and systemic effort to support Muslim leaders, clerics, and lay elites who call for co-existence with the West, who emphasize self-strengthening of Islamic peoples, and who decry the wasteful suicide and violence by Muslims is needed.

The war against international Islamic terrorism is not a war against Islam. Nor is it a war against all terrorism. It is a war against a specific and recently developed international movement that threatens U.S. and Western populations and interests on a global scale. It is not a war that can be won by military means alone. It is not a war that can be ended by sacrificing Israel. It is not a war that can be ended without the cooperation of Muslim countries and their governments. But it is a war that can be won by the cooperation of Western and Muslim peoples and nations who treasure peace, against a common enemy.

Notes

1. Samuel Huntington, *The Clash of Civilizations and the Remaking of World Order*. New York: Simon and Schuster, 1996.
2. Mark Katz, *Revolutions and Revolutionary Waves*. New York: St. Martin's Press, 1997.
3. This section is based largely on Anwar al-Huq Ahady, "The Afghanistan Revolutionary Wars," in *Revolutions, Theoretical, Comparative, and Historical Studies*, 3rd edition, edited by Jack A. Goldstone. Fort Worth, TX: Harcourt College Publishers, 2003.
4. This section is based largely on Glenn E. Robinson, *Building a Palestinian State: The Incomplete Revolution*. Bloomington: Indiana University Press, 1997.
5. Robinson, p. 124.
6. Jack A. Goldstone, *Revolutions: Theoretical, Comparative, and Historical Studies*.

CREDITS

Chapter 1: What is Comparative Politics?

2: Lichbach, Mark Irving and Alan S. Zuckerman, "Research Traditions and Theory in Comparative Politics: An Introduction," from *Comparative Politics: Rationality, Culture, and Structure*. Copyright © by Mark Irving Lichbach and Alan S. Zuckerman 1997. Reprinted with the permission of Cambridge University Press.

7: Lave, Charles A. and James G. March, "Observation, Speculation, and Modeling," from *Introduction to Models in the Social Sciences*, 1st Edition, © 1975. Reprinted by permission of Pearson Education, Inc., Upper Saddle River, NJ.

Chapter 2: The State

37: Juergensmeyer, Mark, "The New Religious State," first appeared in *Comparative Politics*, Volume 27, Number 4, July 1995. © 1995 by Mark Juergensmeyer. Reprinted with the permission of the author and of *Comparative Politics*.

46: Herbst, Jeffrey, "War and the State in Africa," *International Security*, 14:4 (Spring 1990). Copyright © 1990 by the President and Fellows of Harvard College and the Massachusetts Institute of Technology. Reprinted with the permission of MIT Press Journals.

61: Rotberg, Robert I., "The New Nature of Nation-State Failure," *The Washington Quarterly*, 25:3 (Summer 2002). Copyright © 2002 by the Center for Strategic and International Studies (CSIS) and the Massachusetts Institute of Technology. Reprinted with the permission of MIT Press Journals.

Chapter 3: Nations and Society

70: Hobsbawm, Eric, "Nationalism," from *The Age of Revolution*. Copyright © 1962 by E. J. Hobsbawm. Reprinted with permission of Weidenfeld & Nicolson, an imprint of The Orion Publishing Group.

79: "The Global Menace of Local Strife," *The Economist* (May 22, 2003). Copyright © 2003 *The Economist Newspaper Ltd*. All rights reserved. Reprinted with permission. Further reproduction prohibited. www.economist.com.

Chapter 4: Political Economy

Chapter 5: Authoritarianism and Totalitarianism

Chapter 6: Democracy

Chapter 7: Advanced Democracies

Chapter 8: Communism and Post-Communism

Chapter 9: Less-Developed and Newly Industrializing Countries

Chapter 10: Globalization

Chapter 11: Political Violence